Chile
& Easter Island
a travel survival kit

Wayne Bernhardson

Chile & Easter Island – a travel survival kit

3rd edition

Published by

Lonely Planet Publications

Head Office: PO Box 617, Hawthorn, Vic 3122, Australia
Branches: 155 Filbert St, Suite 251, Oakland, CA 94607, USA
10 Barley Mow Passage, Chiswick, London W4 4PH, UK
71 bis rue du Cardinal Lemoine, 75005 Paris, France

Printed by

Colorcraft Ltd, Hong Kong

Photographs by

Wayne Bernhardson (WB)
Gerry Leitner (GL)
Alan Samagalski (AS)
Front cover: Girl with Alpaca (Juan Pablo-Lira, The Image Bank)
Back cover: Cactus Flower (WB)

First Published

July 1987

This Edition

June 1993

Although the authors and publisher have tried to make the information as accurate as possible, they accept no responsibility for any loss, injury or inconvenience sustained by any person using this book.

National Library of Australia Cataloguing in Publication Data

Bernhardson, Wayne.
Chile & Easter Island : a travel survival kit.

3rd ed.
Includes index.
ISBN 0 86442 181 8.

1. Chile – Guidebooks. 2. Easter Island – Guidebooks. I. Title. (Series : Lonely Planet travel survival kit).

918.30465

Wayne Bernhardson

Wayne Bernhardson was born in North Dakota, grew up in Tacoma, Washington, and spent most of the 1980s shuttling between North and South America en route to a PhD in geography from the University of California, Berkeley. With his wife María Massolo, he is co-author of LP's *Argentina, Uruguay & Paraguay: a travel survival kit.* He has travelled widely in Central and South America, and has lived for extended periods in Chile, Argentina, and the Falkland (Malvinas) Islands. Wayne lives with María and their daughter Clío in Oakland, California.

From the Author

Special thanks to Rodolfo and Mary Massolo of Olavarría, Buenos Aires province, who provided the vehicle for touring Chile, and to Carlos Massolo and Laura Alvarez of Villa Regina, Río Negro, Argentina, for their invaluable assistance in updating the material on the Chilean Lake District. Many others in Chile were exceptionally helpful and hospitable in the process of pulling this all together, especially the motivated personnel of Sernatur, including Macarena Velasco of Santiago (a particularly valuable contribution), Gina Rubio of Valdivia, Patricio Yañez Strange (for his great patience) and Santiago Moreira of Puerto Montt, and Enzo Hernández B of Coyhaique. Others in Chile who deserve mention include Hernán Torres Santibañez, Martín Montalva Paredes, Jorge Hidalgo Lehuedé, Maximiliano Grez Reyes, Francisco Javier Araya and Lourdes López Illa of Santiago, Horacio Larraín of Antofagasta, Eduardo Nuñez of Arica, and Adrian Turner and Catherine Caulfield-Giles of Traucomontt Tours in Puerto Montt.

In Australia, Tony Wheeler showed great faith in my ability to undertake and complete the project. Special mention also goes to Eric Ketunen of Lonely Planet's Oakland office, whose faxes to Australia expedited many matters, not the least of which was payment.

Probably the most indispensable people in finishing the project were the street mechanics of Chile, without whom 'Lola' would never have arrived in Santiago nor left the capital for Arica, let alone returned to Argentina.

From the Publisher

This book was edited by James Lyon, with additional copy editing and proofreading from Simone Calderwood, Diana Saad, Frith Pike and Sharan Kaur. Sally Woodward was responsible for the mapping, illustrations, design and cover, with additional illustrations from Ann Jeffree. Thanks also to Sharon Wertheim for the index.

This Book

The first two editions of *Chile & Easter Island – a travel survival kit* were written by Alan Samalgalski. This, the third edition, was reseached again from scratch, rewritten and considerably expanded by Wayne Bernhardson.

Many independent travellers and others contributed to an improved book with their correspondence. These include:

Stuart Anderson (UK), Raquel Arriagada (Chi), J Azevedo, Jose L Balcazar (Sp), Kevin Bell (Aus), Bruno Beulens (B), Brigitte Beller (F), Roger Billingsley (UK), Erwin Bittner, S F Boalch (UK), Ulrika Bohman (Sw), Paola Branas (CH), Andy & Cheryl Briggs (USA), Anna Brownfield (Aus), K A W Brunton (SA), Barbara Bucklin (USA), Paul Carter (NZ), Courtney Chamberlin (USA), Thomas C Clough (UK), Kevin Conlan (USA), Van Aert Constant (B), R M Davidson (UK), Arjen Daverveld &

Roel Wiche (NL), Samuel Davies (UK), Lief de Jonghe & Peter Dhollander (B), Jacqueline Dineen (C), Eliana Dockendorff (Chi), William Donaldson (C), Robert Dunn (USA), Barbara Egli (CH), Joachim Eitel (D), Simon Elms (NZ), Tony England (USA), Mary Eschbach (USA), Naomi Feinstein (UK), Andrew & Hilary Fenemor (NZ), Christal Flueter (USA), Umberto Francione (I), Patrick Frew (UK), Agneta Freyschss (Sw), Paul W Garber (Chi), John Gerritson (NZ), Jim Hart (UK), Michael Hawley (USA), Jacques Herivault (C), Ben Herman (USA), Patricia Maya Herrera (Chi), Elisabeth Heueisen, W D Holladay (UK), Anette Jacobsen (Dk), Vagn Aage Jacobsen (Dk), Alan Jamison (Aus), Stuart Jenner (UK), Pierre Kenyon (USA), T J Kerr (USA), Howard Kessler (USA), Anke Kessler (Chi), Riaz Khan (UK), Quentin King (Aus), Lothar M Kirsch (D), Jim & Karen Kitchen (USA), Jim Kraft (USA), Ralf J Krenzin (D), Cathy Kristiansen (USA), Sheila Krysz (Aus), Gary Kuehn (USA), Joachim Lange (D), Joan Lapinski (USA), Pete Larrett (USA), Augusta Lazzati (I), Jean Leutz (C), Jean Levasseur (C), Joyce Renee Lewis (USA), Dario Lorenzetti (I), Susan Lupton (UK), Jenny Major (F), German Martinez (Chi), Mike McDonald (Arg), Heather McNeil (C), Adelaide H Metcalf (USA), Fernke Meyer (Nl), Peter Mitchell (NZ), Vivienne Mitchell (UK), Earl Moen (USA), Janet Moore (UK), Toni Muller (CH), Maureen Munro (USA), Sharon Murray (USA), Anthony Newlove (B), Ryszard Niedzielslki (P), Rosi Nüesch & Andy Kündig (CH), Denise O'Hara, Thomas Osthoff (D), Timothy Page (UK), Leonardo Pagliarin (I), Tony Perkins (UK), Michael Phillips, Donald E Phipps (USA), Judy Price (USA), Knick & Lyn Pyles (USA), Harriet Quint (C), Patricia Redman (C), Andrew Robinson (UK), Alex Rossi (UK), Fernando Rusowsky (Chi), M M Sale (NZ), James Savage (UK), Rexy Schusster (F), Mark Seltzer (C), Sharon Shula (USA), Mark E Smith (USA), Pernille & Ole Sonne (Dk), Finn Sorensen (Dk), Alison Steen (USA), Douglas Stevens (C), Orville Stone (USA), Dennis Strellman (USA), Melissa Swan (USA), Marie Swarthing (Sw), Vesa Taiveaho (Fin), Chris & Emma Tatton (UK), Peter & Donna Thomas (USA), Ken Timewell (C), David Trads (Dk), Ian Turland (Aus), Adrian Turner (UK), Jan Ulin (Sw), Francisco Valle (Chi), Michael Walensky (USA), Simon Watson-Taylor (Chi), Ken Wilbert (USA), Russell Willis (Aus), Diarmuid Wilson (UK), Joseph Yallowitz (USA), Mark Yates (UK)

Aus – Australia, B – Belgium, C – Canada, CH – Switzerland, Chi – Chile, D – Germany, Dk – Denmark, F – France, Fin – Finland, I – Italy, NL – Netherlands, NZ – New Zealand, P – Poland, SA – South Africa, Sw – Sweden, UK – United Kingdom, USA – United States of America

Warning & Request

Things change – prices go up, schedules change, good places go bad and bad places go bankrupt – nothing stays the same. So if you find things better or worse, recently opened or long since closed, please write and tell us and help make the next edition better.

Your letters will be used to help update future editions and, where possible, important changes will also be included in a Stop Press section in reprints.

We greatly appreciate all information that is sent to us by travellers. Back at Lonely Planet we employ a hard-working readers' letters team to sort through the many letters we receive. The best ones will be rewarded with a free copy of the next edition or another Lonely Planet guide if you prefer. We give away lots of books, but, unfortunately, not every letter/postcard receives one.

Contents

Map Legend

BOUNDARIES

International Boundary
Internal Boundary
National Park or Reserve
The Equator
The Tropics

SYMBOLS

NATIONAL — National Capital
PROVINCIAL — Provincial or State Capital
Major — Major Town
Minor — Minor Town
Places to Stay
Places to Eat
Post Office
Airport
Tourist Information
Bus Station or Terminal
66 — Highway Route Number
Mosque, Church, Cathedral
Temple or Ruin
Hospital
Lookout
Camping Area
Picnic Area
Hut or Chalet
Mountain or Hill
Railway Station
Road Bridge
Railway Bridge
Road Tunnel
Railway Tunnel
Escarpment or Cliff
Pass
Ancient or Historic Wall

ROUTES

Major Road or Highway
Unsealed Major Road
Sealed Road
Unsealed Road or Track
City Street
Railway
Subway
Walking Track
Ferry Route
Cable Car or Chair Lift

HYDROGRAPHIC FEATURES

River or Creek
Intermittent Stream
Lake, Intermittent Lake
Coast Line
Spring
Waterfall
Swamp
Salt Lake or Reef
Glacier

OTHER FEATURES

Park, Garden or National Park
Built Up Area
Market or Pedestrian Mall
Plaza or Town Square
Cemetery

Note: not all symbols displayed above appear in this book

Introduction

On the Pacific coast of South America, Chile is a stringbean country rarely wider than 180 km, but it stretches from the tropics nearly to the Antarctic. For nearly all of its length, the imposing Andes mountains isolate it from Bolivia and Argentina, but it also shares a short border with Peru in the Atacama desert. Along its 4300 km coastline, Chile offers a great variety of environments – the nearly waterless Atacama, the Mediterranean central valley, a mountainous but temperate lake district, and the spectacular alpine glaciers and fjords of Patagonia, with some of South America's finest national parks, where trekking and fishing are among the world's best. Always within sight is the massive Andean crest where, just a few hours from Santiago, there is world-class skiing, while scores of beach resorts appeal to travellers of all categories.

Until recently, for many travellers, Chile has been an international pariah because of the bloody 1973 coup which resulted in the death of the constitutional president, socialist Salvador Allende, and his replacement by military dictator General Augusto Pinochet. Since General Pinochet's rejection by Chilean voters in a referendum, and Chile's return to democratic government in 1989, the country has once again become a popular destination. General Pinochet's regime was a remarkably durable anomaly in Chilean history, where military intervention has been the exception rather than the rule since the country's independence from Spain in the early 19th century.

Chile's people are mostly of European extraction, but the indigenous American tradition is strong and visible in several parts of the country. The desert north, once part of the Inca Empire, preserves important archaeological remains, while Aymara Indians still farm the valleys and terraces of the Andean foothills and tend their flocks of llamas and alpacas on the high plains of the altiplano. At a time when political and economic difficulties have prevented many travellers from visiting Peru, Chile still offers an alternative for those interested in Andean cultures.

South of the Chilean heartland, hundreds of thousands of Mapuche Indians inhabit communities whose symbolic importance in Chilean life greatly exceeds their political and economic significance. Until the end of the 19th century, the Mapuche maintained an effective and heroic resistance to the southward advance of Chilean rule, earning a grudging respect from the expansionist Chilean state. Cities like Temuco and Osorno are proud of their indigenous heritage.

For visitors with a taste for the exotic or romantic, Chile has two unique insular possessions. Distant Easter Island (Rapa Nui), with its giant stylised statues, has long

attracted explorers, adventurers, anthropologists and archaeologists, but tourist access is better than ever, with its Polynesian hospitality an unexpected bonus. Nearer the mainland, the Juan Fernández Islands were the refuge of marooned Scotsman Alexander Selkirk, whose solitary experiences inspired Daniel Defoe's novel *Robinson Crusoe*. It is also a national park, as its many endemic plant species have made it an international biosphere reserve.

Chile's people are remarkably friendly and hospitable to foreigners. No longer a place to avoid because of its unfortunate recent history, the country has begun to attract travellers whose itineraries once included only Peru and Bolivia. Its tremendous geographic diversity, and surprising cultural variety, have made it an important destination in its own right.

Facts about the Country

HISTORY

Indigenous Cultures

When Europeans first arrived in present-day Chile in the 16th century, they encountered a variety of native peoples whose customs and economies differed greatly. While politically subject to the Incas of Cuzco, most native cultures in the region predated the Incas by centuries or even millennia. In the canyons of the desert north, sedentary Aymara farmers cultivated maize in transverse valleys irrigated by the rivers which descended from the Andes; at higher elevations, they grew potatoes and tended flocks of llamas and alpacas. To the south, beyond the Río Loa, Atacameño peoples practised a similar livelihood, while Chango fisherfolk occupied coastal areas from Arica almost to the Río Choapa, south of present-day La Serena. Diaguita Indians inhabited the interior of this latter region, which comprises the drainages of the Copiapó, Huasco and Elqui rivers.

Inca rule barely touched the present-day

Araucanian Indians

Central Valley and southern forests of Chile, where the Araucanian (Picunche and Mapuche) Indians fiercely resisted incursions from the north. The Picunche lived in permanent agricultural settlements, while the Mapuche, who practised shifting cultivation, were more mobile and much more difficult for the Incas, and later the Spaniards, to subdue. Several groups closely related to the Mapuche – Pehuenches, Huilliches, and Puelches – lived in the southern lake district, while Cunco Indians fished and farmed on the island of Chiloé and along the shores of the gulfs of Reloncaví and Ancud. Not until the late 19th century did the descendants of Europeans establish a permanent presence beyond the Río Biobío.

South of the Chilean mainland, numerous small populations of Indians subsisted on hunting and fishing – the Chonos, Qawashqar (Alacalufes), Tehuelches, Yamaná (Yahgans), and Onas (Selknam). These isolated archipelagic peoples long avoided contact with Europeans, but are now extinct or nearly so.

The Spanish Invasion

In 1494, the papal Treaty of Tordesillas ratified the Spanish-Portuguese division of the Americas, granting all territory west of Brazil to Spain, which rapidly consolidated its formal authority and, by the mid-16th century, controlled most of an area extending from Florida and Mexico to central Chile. In the same period, they founded most of South America's important cities, including Lima, Santiago, Asunción and La Paz.

Spain's successful invasion of the Americas was accomplished by groups of adventurers, lowlifes and soldiers-of-fortune against whom the colonists of Botany Bay look like exemplary citizens – Diego de Almagro, one of the early explorers of Chile and northern Argentina, originally arrived in Panama after fleeing a Spanish murder charge. Few in number (Francisco

Pizarro took Peru with only 180 men), the conquerors were determined and ruthless, exploiting factionalism among Indian groups and frightening native peoples with their horses, vicious dogs and firearms, but their greatest ally was infectious disease to which native American peoples lacked immunity.

Pedro de Valdivia

Before Pizarro's assassination in 1541, he assigned the task of conquering Chile to Pedro de Valdivia. After some difficulty in recruitment (Almagro's earlier expedition had suffered terribly, especially in its winter crossing from Argentina of the bitterly cold and nearly waterless Puna de Atacama), Valdivia's expedition left Peru in 1540, crossed the desert and reached Chile's fertile Mapocho Valley in 1541, subduing local Indians and founding the city of Santiago on February 12. Only six months later, the Indians counterattacked, destroyed the city, and nearly wiped out the settlers' supplies. The Spaniards held out and, six years later, their numbers had grown to nearly 500 with assistance and reinforcements from Peru. Meanwhile they founded the cities of La Serena and Valparaíso. Valdivia also worked southward, founding Concepción, Valdivia, and Villarrica. Despite his death at the battle of Tucapel in 1553, at the hands of Mapuche forces led by the famous *caciques* (chiefs) Caupolicán and Lautaro, Valdivia had laid the groundwork for a new society.

Colonial Society in Chile

Ironically, throughout the Americas, the structure of Indian societies more strongly influenced the economic and political structure of early colonial society than the directives of peninsular authorities. The primary goal of the Spanish conquistadores was the acquisition of gold and silver, and they ruthlessly appropriated precious metals through outright robbery when possible, and by other no less brutal means when necessary. El Dorado, the legendary city of gold, proved elusive, but the Spaniards soon realised that the true wealth of the Indies consisted of the surprisingly large Indian populations of Mexico, Peru, and other lands.

Disdaining physical labour themselves, the Spaniards exploited the indigenous populations of the New World through mechanisms such as the *encomienda*, best translated as 'entrustment', by which the Crown granted rights to Indian labour and tribute in a particular village or area to an individual Spaniard (*encomendero*). Institutions such as the Catholic Church also held encomiendas. In theory, Spanish legislation required the holder of the encomienda to reciprocate with instruction in the Spanish language and the Catholic religion, but in practice imperial administration was inadequate to ensure compliance and avoid the worst abuses. Spanish overseers worked Indians mercilessly in the mines and extracted the maximum in agricultural produce.

In the most densely populated parts of the Americas, some encomenderos became extraordinarily wealthy, but the encomienda itself failed when Indian populations declined rapidly, not so much from overwork and physical punishment as because the Indians, isolated for at least 10,000 years from Old World diseases, could not withstand the onslaught of smallpox, influenza, typhus and other such killers. In some parts of the New World, these diseases reduced the native population by more than 95%.

In Chile, the encomienda was most important in the irrigated valleys of the desert north (then part of Peru), where the population was large and sedentary – the most highly organised Indian peoples were the easiest to subdue and control, since they were accustomed to similar forms of exploitation. In hierarchical states like the Inca Empire, the Spaniards quickly and easily occupied positions of authority.

In central Chile, the Spaniards quickly established dominance, but the semi-sedentary and nomadic peoples of the south mounted vigorous resistance, and even into the late-19th century the area was unsafe for White settlers. Crossing the Andes, the Mapuche had tamed feral horses which had multiplied rapidly on the fine pastures of the Argentine Pampas; they soon became expert riders, aiding their mobility and ability to strike.

Even where Spanish supremacy went unchallenged, Indians outnumbered Spaniards. Since few women accompanied the early settlers, Spanish men, especially of the lower classes, had both formal and informal relationships with Indian women; the resulting children, of mixed Spanish and Indian parentage, were known as *mestizos* and soon outnumbered the Indian population as many natives died through epidemics, forced labour abuses, and warfare. As the Indian population declined, encomiendas became nearly worthless, and Spaniards sought new alternatives for their livelihood.

Rise of the Latifundio

In Chile, unlike many other parts of Spanish America, the encomienda became highly correlated with land ownership; despite the Crown's disapproval, Chile was too remote for adequate imperial oversight. Valdivia had rewarded his followers with enormous grants, some valleys stretching from the Andes to the Pacific. More than anywhere else in the Americas, the system of control resembled the great feudal estates of Valdivia's homeland of Extremadura in Spain. Such estates *(latifundios)*, many intact as late as the 1960s, became an enduring feature of Chilean agriculture and the dominant force in Chilean society.

As the Indian population declined and the encomienda's importance diminished, Chile's neo-aristocracy had to look elsewhere for its labour force. The country's growing mestizo population, systematically excluded from land ownership, provided the solution. Landless and 'vagrant', these ostensible 'Spaniards' soon attached themselves as *inquilinos* (tenant farmers) to the large rural estates, which evolved from livestock *estancias* into agricultural *haciendas* or, as they became more commonly known in Chile, *fundos*.

As inquilinos, labourers and their families became personally dependent on the *hacendado* (master) in exchange for certain rights. Paying little or no rent, they could occupy a shack on the estate, graze livestock on its more remote sections, and cultivate a patch of land for household use. In return, they provided labour during annual *rodeos* (roundups of cattle) and watched out for their master's interests. American geographer George McC McBride found this relationship of 'man and master' endured well into the 20th century and permeated all aspects of Chilean society:

> There was a landholding aristocracy, well educated, far-travelled, highly cultured, in full control of the national life; and, quite apart from them, a lower class, often spoken of with mixed disdain and affection as the *rotos* (ragged ones), constituting the fixed tenantry of the rural estates. This distinction, clearly an agrarian one in its origin, was carried into the social structure of the entire people. It gave its cast to the nation.

Other groups gave their cast to the nation as well. Even though the large estates remained intact, they did not always remain in the same hands. Later immigrants, especially Basques, became a major influence from the late 17th century to the end of the colonial era. Surnames such as Eyzaguirre, Urrutia and Larraín became prominent in Chilean commerce and those families purchased many landed estates, as well as those confiscated from the expelled Jesuits and offered at public auction. Adopting the pseudo-aristocratic values of the early landed gentry, Basque families have remained important in Chilean politics, society and business.

In the colonial era, mining and business brought greater wealth than land per se. Only after political independence, having broken the mercantile links with imperial Spain, did Chile's agricultural economy begin to flourish.

The Independence Movements

Within a few decades of Columbus' Caribbean landing, Spain possessed an empire twice the size of Europe, stretching from California to Cape Horn. Yet the empire disintegrated rapidly in the early 19th century; in less than two decades; by the late 1820s, only Puerto Rico and Cuba remained in Spanish hands.

Many factors contributed to the rise of Latin American independence movements. One was the emergence of a class of *criollos* (creoles), American-born Spaniards, who soon distinguished themselves from the Iberians. In every Latin American country, the development of a definable American identity increased the desire for self-government.

Equally importantly, the influential criollo merchants resented Spain's rigid mercantile trade system. To facilitate tax collection, all trade to the mother country had to pass overland through Panama to the Caribbean and Havana, rather than directly by ship from the port of Valparaíso. This extraordinarily cumbersome system hampered the commerce of Chile and other Latin American countries and eventually cost Spain its American empire.

Spain's own stagnant economy could not provide the manufactured goods which the American colonies demanded. Spain also had to contend with interloping European countries, as Britain, Holland and France all acquired minor bases in the Caribbean and elsewhere in the New World. By the late 18th century the British had obtained trade concessions from Spain and were surreptitiously encouraging criollo political aspirations.

Several other factors contributed, directly and indirectly, to the independence drive which began between 1808 and 1810: the successful North American rebellion against England, the overthrow of the French monarchy, Napoleon's invasion of Spain (which disrupted communications between Spain and America and allowed the colonies a period of temporary autonomy), and European intellectual trends. The fact that colonial armies consisted mainly of criollos and mestizos, rather than peninsular troops, made it much easier to challenge Spain.

The Revolutionary Wars

During the colonial period, the formal jurisdiction of the Audiencia of Chile stretched roughly from present-day Chañaral in the north to Puerto Aisén in the south, and also encompassed the trans-Andean Cuyo region of modern Argentina, comprising the provinces of Mendoza, San Juan and San Luis. The audiencia was an administrative subdivision of the much larger Viceroyalty of Peru whose capital, Lima, was South America's most important city. But Chile was distant from Lima, and developed in near isolation from Peru, with a very distinct identity from its northern neighbour.

Independence movements throughout South America united to expel Spain from

Bernardo O'Higgins

the continent by the 1820s. From Venezuela, a criollo army under Simón Bolívar fought its way across the Andes to the Pacific and then south towards Peru. José de San Martín's Ejército de los Andes (Army of the Andes) – nearly a third of them liberated slaves – marched over the cordillera from Argentina into Chile, occupied Santiago and sailed north to Lima.

San Martín's army also included numerous Chileans who had fled the reimposition of Spanish colonial rule after the Napoleonic Wars. The Argentine general appointed Bernardo O'Higgins second-in-command of his forces. O'Higgins, son of an Irish immigrant who had served as Viceroy of Peru under Spanish rule, became Supreme Director of the new Chilean republic. San Martín helped drive Spain from Peru, transporting his army in ships either seized from the Spaniards or purchased from Britons or North Americans. British and North American merchants also financed the purchase of arms and ammunition, knowing that expulsion of the Spaniards would create new commercial opportunities. Scotsman Thomas Cochrane, a colourful former Royal Navy officer, founded and commanded the Chilean Navy.

The Early Republic

Spanish administrative divisions provided the framework for the political geography of the new South American republics. At independence, Chile was but a fraction of its present size, consisting of the *intendencias* (administrative units of the Spanish Empire) of Santiago and Concepción, with ambiguous boundaries with Bolivia in the north, Argentina to the east, and the hostile Mapuche Indians south of the Río Biobío. It lost the important trans-Andean province of Cuyo to the Provincias Unidas del Río de la Plata (United Provinces of the River Plate), forerunner of modern Argentina.

Although other Latin American countries emerged from the wars in severe economic difficulties, Chile quickly achieved a degree of political stability which permitted rapid development of agriculture, mining, industry and commerce. Regional quarrels were far less serious and violent than they were, for example, in Argentina. Despite social and economic cleavages, the population was relatively homogeneous and less afflicted by racial problems than most other Latin American states. The country was well situated to take advantage of international economic trends, as the port of Valparaíso became an important outlet for Chilean wheat which satisfied the unprecedented demand of the California gold rush.

O'Higgins dominated Chilean politics for the first five years after formal independence in 1818, enacting political, social, religious and educational reforms, but the landowning elite which at first supported him soon objected to increased taxes, abolition of titles and limitations on the inheritance of landed estates. Pressured by military forces allied with the aristocracy, he resigned in 1823 and went into exile in Peru. He died there in 1842, never having returned to his homeland.

Apart from deposing the Spaniards, political independence did not alter the structure of Chilean society, which was dominated by large landowners. The embodiment of landowning interests was Diego Portales, a businessman who, as Minister of the Interior, was the country's de facto dictator until his execution after an uprising in 1837. His custom-drawn constitution centralised power in Santiago, and established Roman Catholicism as the state religion. It also limited suffrage to literate and propertied adult males, and established indirect elections for the presidency and the national Senate; only the lower Chamber of Deputies was chosen directly by voters. Portales' constitution lasted, with some changes, until 1925.

Territorial Expansion

At independence, Chile was a small, compact country whose northern limit was the southern border of the present-day region of Antofagasta, and whose southern limit was the Río Biobío. From the mid-19th century, railroad construction began to revolutionise internal transport. Military triumphs over Peru and Bolivia in the War of the Pacific (1879-1883) and treaties with the Mapuche Indians (from 1881) incorporated the nitrate-rich Atacama desert and temperate southern territories under Chilean authority. At the same time, however, Chile had to abandon its claims to most of enormous, sparsely populated Patagonia to Argentina.

Santiago's intervention in the Atacama, ostensibly to protect the interests of Chilean nationals labouring in the nitrate fields, proved to be a bonanza. Just as guano financed Peruvian independence, so nitrates brought prosperity to Chile, or at least to certain sectors of Chilean society. British, North American and German investors supplied most of the capital.

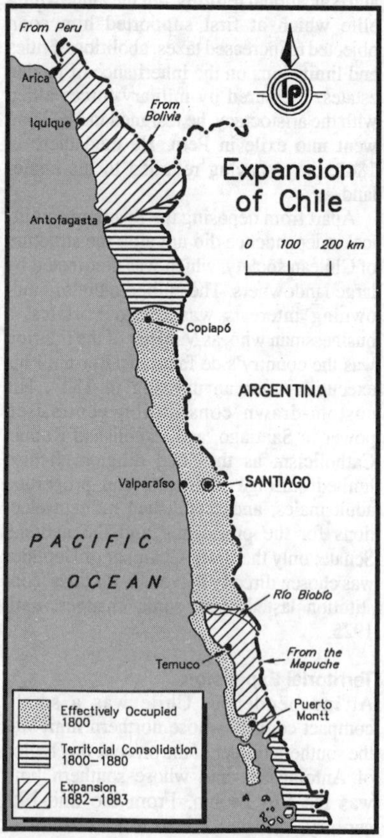

On the route from Europe and North America via Cape Horn, Valparaíso had been the first Pacific port of call since the California gold rush. Soon the nitrate ports of Antofagasta and Iquique also became important in international commerce, until the opening of the Panama Canal nearly eliminated traffic around the Horn, and the development of petroleum-based fertilisers made mineral nitrates obsolete.

Chile also sought a broader Pacific presence, as Chilean vessels sailed to Australia, Asia and Polynesia. Extremists even advocated annexation of the Philippines, still under Spanish control at the time. Chile's only imperial possession, however, was tiny, remote Easter Island (Isla de Pascua or Rapa Nui), annexed in 1888.

Reforms under Balmaceda

Chile emerged from the War of the Pacific considerably enriched by the nitrates and, later, the copper of the Atacama – nitrates were Chile's major source of foreign exchange for nearly half a century. Expansion of mining created a new working class, as well as a class of nouveaux riches, both of whom challenged the political power of the landowning oligarchy.

The first political figure to tackle the dilemma of Chile's maldistributed wealth and power was President José Manuel Balmaceda, elected in 1886. Balmaceda's administration undertook major public works projects, expanding the rail network and building new roads, bridges and docks, hospitals and schools, extending telegraph lines and postal services, and improving hospitals and schools.

Balmaceda's policies met resistance from a conservative Congress, which in 1890 rejected his budget, voted to depose him, and appointed naval Commander Jorge Montt to head a provisional government. More than 10,000 Chileans died in the ensuing civil war, in which Montt's naval forces controlled the country's ports and eventually defeated the government despite the army's support for Balmaceda. After several months' asylum in the Argentine embassy, Balmaceda shot himself to death.

Although weakening the presidential system, Balmaceda's immediate successors continued many of his public works projects and also opened Congress to popular rather than indirect elections. Major reform, though, did not occur until after WW II.

The 20th Century

Despite economic hardship due to a declining nitrate industry, the election of President Arturo Alessandri Palma was a hopeful sign for the Chilean working class. To reduce the power of the landed oligarchy, he proposed greater political autonomy for the provinces, and land and income taxes to finance social benefits to alleviate working conditions and improve health, education and welfare. Congressional conservatives obstructed these reforms, though, and army opposition forced Alessandri's resignation in 1924.

For several years, Carlos Ibáñez del Campo, a dictatorial army officer, occupied the presidency and other positions of power, but misguided or miscarried economic policies (exacerbated by global depression) led to widespread opposition which forced him into Argentine exile in 1931.

After Ibáñez' ouster, Chilean political parties realigned. Several leftist groups briefly imposed a 'Socialist Republic' and merged to form the Socialist Party, to which future President Salvador Allende belonged. Splits between Stalinists and Trotskyites divided the Communist Party, while splinter groups from existing radical and reformist parties created a bewildering mix of new political organisations.

For most of the 1930s and 1940s the democratic left dominated Chilean politics, and government intervention in the economy through CORFO, the state development corporation, became increasingly important.

Meanwhile, the US role in the Chilean economy also grew steadily, since German investment had declined after WW I and the invention of synthetic nitrates undercut British economic influence.

In the first two decades of the 20th century, North American companies had gained control of the copper mines, which had become the cornerstone of the Chilean economy. WW II augmented the demand for Chilean copper, and it promoted economic growth while Chile remained neutral in the conflict.

Rural Developments

In the 1920s as much as 75% of Chile's rural population still depended on haciendas which controlled 80% of the country's prime agricultural land. Inquilinos remained at the mercy of landowners for access to land, housing and subsistence. Their votes belonged to the landowners, who used them to influence Congress and maintain the existing system of land tenure.

To some degree, the Alessandri government avoided antagonising the landed elite, partly because urban leftists pressed for lower food prices and restrictions on exports of agricultural produce. These controls kept food prices artificially low to the detriment of the producer. This pleased urban consumers, but also satisfied landowners who could maintain control over their land and their workers.

As protected industry expanded and government promoted public works, employment increased and the lot of urban workers improved. That of rural workers, however, deteriorated rapidly; real wages fell, forcing day labourers to the cities in search of work. Inquilinos suffered reduced land allotments, supplies of seed, fertiliser and other assistance, as well as rights to graze animals, and had to supply the landowner more labour. Given abundant labour, haciendas had little incentive to modernise and production stagnated, a situation that changed little until the 1960s.

Elections: 1952 to 1961

In 1952, former dictator General Carlos Ibáñez del Campo won the presidency as an authoritarian but 'apolitical' candidate, largely because of widespread disenchantment with predecessor Gabriel González Videla and political parties in general. For the first time, physician and former health minister Salvador Allende stood as the Socialist candidate, with covert support from the Communists, receiving barely 5% of the vote in a last-place finish.

Surprisingly, Ibáñez tried to curtail the political power of landowners by reducing their control over the votes of their tenants and labourers; he also revoked an earlier law banning the Communist Party, but his government faltered in the face of high inflation and partisan politicking. In 1958 a new coalition of leftists, FRAP (Frente de Acción Popular, Popular Action Front), contested the presidential elections, with Allende as their candidate, while Jorge Alessandri, son of Arturo Alessandri, represented a coalition between the Conservative and Liberal parties, and Eduardo Frei represented the recently formed Christian Democrats, a reformist party whose goals resembled FRAP's but whose philosophical basis was Catholic humanism.

Personally popular, Alessandri won the election with less than 32% of the vote, while Allende managed 29% and Frei 21%, easily the best showing ever by a Christian Democrat. In the 1961 congressional races, this translated into control of Congress by FRAP and the Christian Democrats, both strongly committed to land reform. The following year, Alessandri accepted a modest land reform, beginning a decade's battle with the haciendas. Though Alessandri's term saw little concrete progress in this matter, the new laws provided a legal basis for expropriation of land from large estates and its transfer to farm workers.

The Christian Democratic Period

In the 1964 presidential election, a two-way battle pitted Allende, the candidate of FRAP, against Frei, supported by the Christian Democrats and conservative groups who detested the leftist physician. During the campaign, both the Christian Democrats and FRAP promised agrarian reform, supported rural unionisation and promised an end to the hacienda system. Frei won the election with 56% as Allende, undermined by leftist factionalism, polled only 39%.

Genuinely committed to social transformation, the Christian Democrats attempted to control inflation, improve the balance of payments, implement agrarian reform, and improve public health, education and social services. Their policies, however, threatened both the traditional elite's privileges and the radical left's working class support. Fearful of losing their influence, the FRAP parties urged faster and more radical action. According to Chilean analyst César Caviedes, the 1964 election marked a shift from personalism to ideology in Chilean politics.

The Christian Democrats had other difficulties. In the last years of Jorge Alessandri's presidency, the economy had declined and limited opportunities in the countryside drove the dispossessed to the cities, where they built spontaneous squatter settlements, or *callampas* ('mushrooms', since they seemed to spring up overnight). As the Christian Democrats inherited these problems, one common response was to attack the visible export sector, dominated by US interests; Frei advocated 'Chileanisation' of the copper industry, while Allende and his backers supported 'nationalisation'.

The Christian Democrats also faced challenges from violent groups like the MIR (Movimiento de Izquierda Revolucionario, Leftist Revolutionary Movement), which had begun among upper middle class students in Concepción, a southern university town and important industrial centre; among its leaders was Andrés Pascal Allende, a nephew of Salvador Allende. MIR's activism appealed to coal miners, textile workers and other urban labourers who formed the allied Frente de Trabajadores Revolucionarios (Revolutionary Workers Front); it also agitated among peasants who longed for land reform. Other leftist groups also supported strikes and land seizures by Mapuche Indians and rural labourers.

Too slow to appease leftists, Frei's reforms were too rapid for the National party (formed by the merger of the Conservatives and Liberals in 1965), which obstructed his efforts in Congress – there was even dissension within his own party over the pace and objectives of rural reform. Despite improved living conditions for many rural workers and impressive gains in education and public health, increasing inflation, dependence on foreign markets and capital, and inequitable distribution of wealth continued to plague the country. The Christian Democrats could not satisfy rising expectations in an increasingly militant and polarised society.

Allende Comes to Power

As the 1970 presidential election approached, the leftist coalition, now known as Unidad Popular (Popular Unity), once again chose Salvador Allende as its candidate. Unidad Popular offered a radical programme, including nationalisation of mines, banks, insurance companies, and other key elements in the economy, plus expropriation and redistribution of large landholdings.

The other major candidates were Christian Democrat Radomiro Tomic (too left-wing for conservatives) and the aged Jorge Alessandri, standing for the National Party. Alessandri appealed to the old elite and middle classes with the prospect of restored law and order, perceived to have eroded under the Christian Democrats. In one of Chile's closest elections ever, Allende won a plurality of 36%, while Alessandri drew 35% and Tomic 28%. Both losers made serious strategic errors, Alessandri by not even trying in rural areas of Unidad Popular and Christian Democratic strength, Tomic by taking the Christian Democratic left for granted.

Under the constitution, if no candidate obtained an absolute majority, Congress had to confirm the result and could in theory choose the runner-up, although by custom it had never done so. Since no party had a congressional majority, the Christian Democrats pressured Allende for constitutional guarantees to preserve the democratic process, in return for their support. After agreeing to these guarantees, Allende assumed the presidency in October 1970.

The First Years of Allende

Allende headed a multi-party coalition of Socialists, Communists and Radicals which disagreed on the objectives of the new government. Lacking any real electoral mandate, he faced an opposition Congress and the suspicion of the US government, under President Nixon and Secretary of State Henry Kissinger. Right-wing extremists advocated Allende's overthrow by violent means. One ugly omen was the assassination of General René Schneider, commander-in-chief of the army, who had steadfastly proclaimed the military's apolitical respect for the constitution.

Allende's economic programme, accomplished by evading rather than confronting Congress, included state takeover of many private enterprises and massive income redistribution. By increasing government spending, the new president expected to stimulate demand and encourage private enterprise to increase production and reduce unemployment, to bring the country out of recession. This worked briefly, but apprehensive businessmen and landowners, worried over expropriation and nationalisation, sold off stock and disposed of farm machinery and livestock. Industrial production nosedived, leading to shortages, rising prices (inflation exceeded 500% in 1973), and black marketeering. Agricultural production also faltered and the government had to use scarce foreign currency to import food, as workers' real incomes fell below the levels under the Christian Democrats. To deal with urban shortages, the government organised public companies to compete with private wholesalers and distributors, but this alienated Chilean retailers.

Chilean politics grew increasingly polarised and confrontational, as many of Allende's supporters resented his indirect approach to transformation of the state and its economy. MIR intensified its guerrilla activities, while stories circulated about the creation of armed communist organisations in Santiago's factories. Peasants, frustrated with an agrarian reform which favoured collectives of inquilinos over sharecroppers and *afuerinos* (outside labourers), seized land and agricultural production fell.

Expropriation of US-controlled copper mines and other enterprises, plus conspicuously friendly relations with Cuba (Allende publicly accepted the personal gift of a submachine gun from Fidel Castro), provoked hostility from the USA. Later hearings in the US Congress indicated that President Nixon and Henry Kissinger played an active role in bringing down Allende by cutting off credit from international finance organisations, while providing both financial and moral support to his opponents. Until the late 1980s, except during the Carter administration, the US maintained friendly relations with the Chilean military.

Faced with such difficulties, the government tried to forestall conflict by proposing clearly defined limits on nationalisation. Unfortunately, neither extreme leftists, who believed that only force could achieve socialism, nor their rightist counterparts who believed only force could prevent it, allowed any room for compromise.

The Rightist Backlash

In October 1972, Allende's government confronted a widespread strike by an alliance of shopkeepers, professionals, bank clerks, right-wing students, and even some urban and rural labourers. Its leaders were the independent truckers' association, which demanded that the government abandon plans for a state-owned trucking enterprise. Supported by both the Christian Democrats and the National Party, the strike threatened the government's viability.

As the government's authority crumbled, the military assumed responsibility for law and order and for censoring opposition media under a state of emergency. Allende invited General Carlos Prats, commander of the army, to occupy the critical post of Interior Minister, and also included an admiral and an air force general in his cabinet. By November, the truckers' strike was settled, as the government promised not to nationalise transport or wholesale trading, and to return private businesses occupied by workers to their owners.

Despite the economic crisis, Unidad Popular's 44% of the vote in the March 1973 congressional elections demonstrated that Allende's support had actually increased since 1970 – but the unified opposition's strengthened control of Congress underscored the polarisation of Chilean politics. Credible reports that the Nixon administration had conspired against Allende prevented the opposition from carrying out plans for impeachment, but in June 1973 there was an unsuccessful military coup.

The next month truckers and other rightists once again struck, supported by the entire opposition. Having lost support of the military, General Prats resigned, to be replaced by the relatively obscure General Augusto Pinochet Ugarte, whom both Prats and Allende thought loyal to constitutional government. This was a major miscalculation, as events revealed that the officer from Valparaíso had silently harboured a grudge against leftists for decades.

Golpe de Estado

On 11 September 1973, General Pinochet led a brutal *golpe de estado* (coup) which overthrew the Unidad Popular government and resulted in Allende's death (an apparent suicide) and the death of thousands of his supporters. Air force jets bombed La Moneda, the presidential palace, while the army attacked and bombed other parts of Santiago, including factories and working class neighbourhoods.

Police and the military apprehended thousands of leftists, suspected leftists and sympathisers. Many were herded into the National Stadium, in Santiago's middle-class Ñuñoa neighbourhood, where they suffered beatings, torture and even execution. Security forces built bonfires of 'subversive' literature and government publications, imposed a curfew, and shot or jailed those who defied it. Estimates of deaths range from as few as 2500 to as many as 80,000. Hundreds of thousands went into exile.

The military argued that force was necessary to remove Allende because his government had fomented political and economic chaos and he was himself planning to overthrow the constitutional order by force. Certainly inept policies brought about this 'economic chaos', but reactionary sectors, encouraged and abetted from abroad, exacerbated scarcities of commodities and food, producing a black market which further undercut the government. Allende's record of persistently standing for election and his pledge to the opposition implied commitment to the democratic process, but his inability or unwillingness to control other groups to his left terrified the middle classes as well as the oligarchy. His last words, part of a radio address just before the attacks on the Moneda, expressed his ideals but underlined his failure:

> My words are not spoken in bitterness, but in disappointment. They will be a moral judgement on those who have betrayed the oath they took as soldiers of Chile...They have the might and they can enslave us, but they cannot halt the world's social processes, not with crimes, nor with guns... May you go forward in the knowledge that, sooner rather than later, the great avenues will open once again, along which free citizens will march in order to build a better society. Long live Chile! Long live the people! Long live the workers! These are my last words, and I am sure that this sacrifice will constitute a moral lesson which will punish cowardice, perfidy and treason.

The Military Dictatorship

Many opposition leaders, some of whom had encouraged the coup, expected a quick return to civilian government, but General Pinochet had other ideas.

From 1973 to 1989, he headed a durable junta which dissolved Congress, banned leftist parties and suspended all others, prohibited nearly all political activity, and ruled by decree. Assuming the presidency in 1974, Pinochet sought to remake completely the country's political and economic culture; many have seen parallels between Pinochet and Spanish dictator Francisco Franco, who also considered himself his country's saviour from chaos.

Under Pinochet's command, the armed forces and police sought to eradicate leftist influence by repression, torture and murder. Detainees came from all sectors of society, from peasants to professionals. Although both the Carabineros (national police) and Investigaciones (plainclothes police) practised torture, the CNI (Centro Nacional de Informaciones, National Information Centre) and its predecessor DINA were most notorious for torturing political prisoners.

International assassinations were not unusual – General Prats was murdered in Buenos Aires a year after the coup, while Christian Democratic leader Bernardo Leighton barely survived a bomb attack in Rome in 1975. Perhaps the most notorious case was the murder of Orlando Letelier, Allende's foreign minister, by a car bomb in Washington DC in 1976. Retired army general Manuel Contreras has taken desperate legal measures to avoid extradition to the USA for his alleged responsibility in the Letelier case.

By 1977 even air force General Gustavo Leigh, a member of the junta, thought the campaign against 'subversion' so successful that he proposed a return to civilian rule, but Pinochet forced Leigh's resignation, ensuring the army's dominance and perpetuating himself in power. In 1980, Pinochet felt confident enough to submit a new, customised constitution to the electorate and wager his own political future on it. In a plebiscite with very narrow options, about two-thirds of the voters approved the constitution and ratified Pinochet's presidency until 1989. Many voters abstained in protest but, with relative prosperity and political stability, even some opposition figures did not dispute the results despite their limited access to TV, radio and the press.

Political parties began to function openly again in 1987. In October 1988, Pinochet held another plebiscite, as stipulated by the 1980 constitution, in which he asked the country to extend his presidency until 1997. This time, though, voters rejected him. In multi-party elections which took place in 1989, Christian Democrat Patricio Aylwin, compromise candidate of a coalition of opposition parties known as the Concertación para la Democracia, defeated Pinochet protégé Hernán Büchi, a conservative economist and candidate of Renovación Nacional. Aylwin's four-year term expires in 1994, and new elections are scheduled for late 1993.

GEOGRAPHY & CLIMATE

Few countries of Chile's size, slightly larger than Texas at about 800,000 sq km, can boast such a formidable variety of landscapes – rocky Andean peaks, snow-capped volcanos, broad river valleys and deep canyons, waterless deserts, icy fjords, deep blue glaciers, turquoise lakes, sandy beaches and precipitous headlands. It owes this diversity – a 'crazy geography' or 'geographical extravaganza' in the words of Chilean writer Benjamín Subercaseaux – to extremes of latitude and altitude: not counting Antarctica, Chilean territory extends some 4300 km north to south between the Andes and the Pacific Ocean, equivalent to the distance from Havana to Hudson Bay; on average less than 200 km wide from east to west, it rises from sea level to more than 6000 metres. Describing these geographical contrasts, British diplomat James Bryce observed that 'the difference is as great as that between the verdure of Ireland and the sterility of the Sahara'.

Chile's present boundaries are the result of conquest and expansion, first by Spain and later by the republic itself. Only at the end of the 19th century did Chile reach its present extent, from the city of Arica in the northern Atacama desert to the islands of Tierra del Fuego in the south. Chile also possesses the Pacific islands of Easter Island (Isla de Pascua, or Rapa Nui in the local Polynesian language) and Juan Fernández. It also claims a large sector of Antarctica, which overlaps with British and Argentine claims.

Administrative Regions

For administrative purposes, the country is divided into thirteen regions. Except for the Metropolitan Region of Santiago, they are numbered ordinally from north to south, but normally written as a Roman numeral. The longer names are often abbreviated, so it's usually just O'Higgins, Aisén, Magallanes etc.

Administrative Regions

Number		*Name*	*Capital*
I	(primera)	Región de Tarapacá	Iquique
II	(segunda)	Región de Antofagasta	Antofagasta
III	(tercera)	Región de Atacama	Copiapó
IV	(cuarta)	Región de Coquimbo	La Serena
V	(quinta)	Región de Valparaíso	Valparaíso
		Región Metropolitana Santiago	
VI	(sexta)	Región del Libertador General Bernardo O'Higgins	Rancagua
VII	(septima)	Región de Maule	Talca
VIII	(octava)	Región del Biobío	Concepción
IX	(novena)	Región de la Araucanía	Temuco
X	(décima)	Región de Los Lagos	Puerto Montt
XI	(undécima)	Región de Aisén del General Carlos Ibáñez del Campo	Coihaique
XII	(duadécima)	Región de Magallanes y Antártica Chilena	Punta Arenas

Geographical Regions

Chile's customary, rather than formal, regional divisions reflect ecological zonation and human economy rather than arbitrary political boundaries. Generally, the structure of this book is based on geographical regions.

Norte Grande The regions of Tarapacá and Antofagasta together comprise the *Norte Grande* (Great North), running from the Peruvian border to the province of Chañaral and dominated by the Atacama desert. Transverse river valleys, subterranean water sources and springs, and diversions of distant streams sustain cities such as Arica, Iquique and Antofagasta, which occupy narrow coastal plains. These sources also irrigate the limited but productive farmland even though, in the entire Norte Grande, only the Río Loa regularly reaches the sea, and some weather stations have *never* recorded rainfall. Since the colonial era, mining of silver, nitrates and copper has been the principal economic activity, although irrigated agriculture and native livestock herding are locally significant.

Despite its aridity and tropical latitude, the Atacama is a remarkably temperate desert, moderated by the cool, north-flowing Peru (Humboldt) Current which parallels the coast. High humidity produces an extensive cloud cover and even thick fogs known as *camanchaca*, which condense on the steep escarpment of the coastal range. Toward the Bolivian border, the canyons of the *precordillera* (foothills) lead to the *altiplano* or high steppe, where Indian herders graze their llamas and alpacas, and high mountain passes.

Norte Chico South of Chañaral, the regions of Atacama and Coquimbo form the transitional *Norte Chico* (Little North), whose approximate southern boundary is the Río Aconcagua. The desert relents to support scrub and occasional forest, which becomes denser as rainfall increases to the south. Like the Norte Grande, the Norte Chico is rich in minerals, but there is also considerable irrigated agriculture in the major river valleys, especially the Elqui. In those rare years of substantial rainfall, the landscape erupts with wildflowers.

Middle Chile South of the Río Aconcagua begins the fertile heartland of Middle Chile. The intermontane *Valle Central* (central valley) extends through most of this area, which contains the capital, Santiago (with at least a third of the country's population), the major port of Valparaíso, and the bulk of its industry and employment, plus important copper mines. Middle Chile is also the country's chief agricultural zone and, in total, holds perhaps 70% of the country's population.

The heartland enjoys a Mediterranean climate, with maximum temperatures averaging 28°C in January and 10°C in July; the rainy season is from May to August. Evenings and nights can be cool, even during summer. At the highest elevations, however, snow lasts into early summer, permitting excellent skiing for much of the year.

South of the city of Concepción, the Río Biobío marks Chile's 19th-century frontier, homeland of the Mapuche Indians and now an area of cereal and pastoral production, extensive native forests and plantations of introduced conifers. Although the rural population is fairly dense, most of the population lives in towns and cities, of which Concepción, its port of Talcahuano, and Temuco are the most important.

Lake District Beyond the Río Toltén, south of Temuco, lies the magnificent Lake District, one of the country's greatest tourist attractions. Comprising the provinces of Cautín, Valdivia, Osorno and Llanquihue, its numerous foothill lakes are framed by more than a score of snow-capped volcanos, many of them still active. Fishing, agriculture and timber are also major industries. Climatically, the area resembles the Pacific Northwest of the USA, with pleasant but changeable summer weather and cool, damp winters. Winter brings snow to the Andes, occasionally blocking the passes between Chile and Argentina.

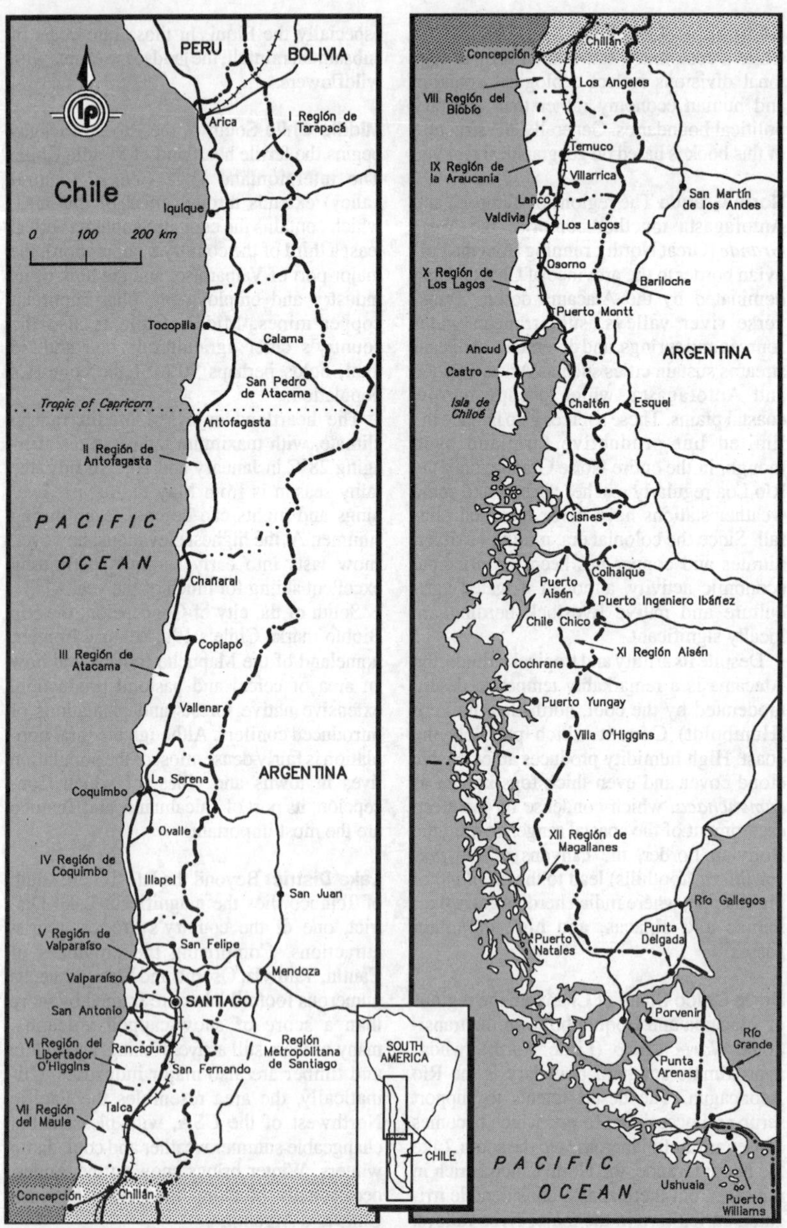
PERU
BOLIVIA
Chile
0 100 200 km
Arica
I Región de Tarapacá
Iquique
Tocopilla
Calama
San Pedro de Atacama
Tropic of Capricorn
Antofagasta
II Región de Antofagasta
PACIFIC OCEAN
Chañaral
Copiapó
III Región de Atacama
Vallenar
ARGENTINA
Coquimbo
La Serena
Ovalle
IV Región de Coquimbo
Illapel
San Juan
V Región de Valparaíso
San Felipe
Valparaíso
Mendoza
SANTIAGO
San Antonio
Región Metropolitana de Santiago
VI Región del Libertador O'Higgins
Rancagua
San Fernando
Talca
VII Región del Maule
Concepción
Chillán
SOUTH AMERICA
CHILE
Concepción
Chillán
VIII Región del Biobío
Los Angeles
Temuco
IX Región de la Araucanía
Villarrica
San Martín de los Andes
Lanco
Valdivia
Los Lagos
Osorno
X Región de Los Lagos
Bariloche
Puerto Montt
Ancud
ARGENTINA
Castro
Isla de Chiloé
Chaitén
Esquel
Cisnes
Puerto Aisén
Coihaique
Puerto Ingeniero Ibáñez
Chile Chico
XI Región Aisén
Cochrane
Puerto Yungay
Villa O'Higgins
XII Región de Magallanes
Río Gallegos
Puerto Natales
Punta Delgada
Porvenir
Río Grande
Punta Arenas
PACIFIC OCEAN
Ushuaia
Puerto Williams

Chiloé South of Puerto Montt, Chiloé is the country's largest island, with a lengthy coastline, dense forests and many small farms. Renowned for inclement weather, it has fewer than 60 days of sunshine per year and up to 150 days of storms, but in summer it can be magnificent.

Chilean Patagonia South of the Lake District, Chilean Patagonia comprises the regions of Aisén and Magallanes, about 30% of the country's territory. It is a rugged, mountainous area, battered by westerly winds and storms which drop enormous amounts of snow and rain on the seaward slopes of the Andes, although the area around Lago Carrera has a balmy microclimate like that of Middle Chile. The Campo de Hielo Sur, the southern continental icefield, separates the two regions; Magallanes and its capital of Punta Arenas, on the Straits of Magellan, are more easily accessible from Argentine Patagonia than from the Chilean mainland. Before the opening of the Panama Canal in 1914, Punta Arenas was a major port of call for international shipping, but its prosperity now depends on oil, gas, fishing and wool.

In Magallanes and Tierra del Fuego, temperatures drop to a summer average of just 11°C, and to a winter average of about 4°C. Dampness and wind chill can make the temperature feel even lower. The weather is highly changeable, even though the nearly incessant winds moderate in the winter. The best time to visit is the southern summer (December to February), when very long days permit outdoor activities despite the unpredictable weather.

Across the straits lies Tierra del Fuego, divided between Chile and Argentina, where oil extraction and wool are the main industries. Chile's settled southern extreme is Navarino Island, separated from Tierra del Fuego by the Beagle Channel, although there are many smaller land masses to the south, including the Wollaston islands, with their famous Cape Horn, and the Diego Ramírez islands. Chile also maintains a presence, which pretends to be a permanent settlement, in Antarctica.

The Andes

Like the Pacific Ocean, the Andes mountains run the length of the country. In the far north, near the Bolivian border, they include a number of symmetrical volcanos more than 6000 metres high, while east of Santiago they present an imposing wall of sedimentary and volcanic peaks. Between Copiapó and the Biobío, the range comprises nearly half the country's width, with some of South America's highest peaks. Despite numerous passes, transport and communications are difficult, and have isolated Chile from the rest of South America for most of its history. South of the Biobío, lower in altitude, the Andes are a less formidable barrier except where seasonal snowfields and permanent glaciers obstruct passage between east and west.

Despite their scenic grandeur, the seismically unstable Andes are a major hazard throughout Chile. Many of the country's major cities (including Santiago, La Serena and Valdivia) have suffered earthquake damage or destruction, and volcanic eruptions are a potential menace in other areas.

FLORA & FAUNA

Chile's northern deserts and high-altitude steppes, soaring mountains, alpine and sub-Antarctic forests and extensive coastline all support distinctive flora and fauna which will be unfamiliar to most visitors, or at least those from the northern hemisphere. To protect these environments, Chile's Corporación Nacional Forestal (CONAF) administers an extensive system of national parks, the more accessible of which are briefly described below. More detailed descriptions can be found in individual chapters. A handful of reserves are not part of the CONAF system; these are mentioned in the appropriate chapter.

National Parks

For many visitors, Chile's national parks are a major reason for visiting the country. One of Latin America's first national park systems, it dates from the mid-1920s, with the establishment of Parque Nacional Vicente Pérez Rosales in the Lake District. Since then, the state has created many other parks and reserves, administered by CONAF, mostly but not exclusively in the Andean region.

Before visiting the parks, you can go to the CONAF office at Avenida Bulnes 285, Departamento 303 in Santiago (☎ 696-6749) for maps and brochures which are often in short supply in the parks themselves. There may be a charge for some of these. Regional CONAF offices will sometimes assist in transportation to more isolated areas.

Chilean protected areas are of three main types: *parques nacionales* (national parks), *reservas nacionales* (national reserves), and *monumentos naturales* (natural monuments). National parks are generally extensive areas with a variety of natural ecosystems, while national reserves are areas open to economic exploitation on a sustainable basis, and may include some relatively pristine areas. Natural monuments are smaller but more strictly protected, usually with a single outstanding natural feature.

Along with Sernatur, the national tourist service, CONAF publishes the very useful and inexpensive paperback *Juventud, Turismo y Naturaleza: Guía Práctica para el Visitante de Areas Silvestres Protegidas*, which includes a great deal of up-to-date information on Chilean parks, including access by public transport. Another worthwhile book is the beautifully illustrated but expensive *Chile: Sus Parques Nacionales y Otras Areas Protegidas* (Incafo, Madrid 1982). For English speakers, William C Leitch's eloquent survey of *South America's National Parks* (The Mountaineers, Seattle, 1990) contains a valuable chapter on the history and natural history of half a dozen of Chile's most popular parks. Birders should acquire *Guía de Campo de las Aves de Chile* (Editorial Universitaria, Santiago, 1986) by Braulio Araya M and Guillermo Millie H.

Parque Nacional Lauca In the northern region of Tarapacá, east of the city of Arica, this 138,000-hectare park offers extraordinary natural attractions, including active and dormant volcanos, clear blue lakes with abundant bird life, and extensive steppes which support flourishing populations of the endangered vicuña, a wild relative of the llama and alpaca. Living in tiny villages with picturesque colonial churches, Aymara Indian shepherds graze their animals on the same pastures.

Adjacent to the park are two other protected areas which are less accessible, the Reserva Nacional Las Vicuñas and Monumento Natural Salar de Surire. The latter features huge nesting colonies of flamingos.

Parque Nacional Pan de Azúcar Set in the coastal desert of the regions of Antofagasta and Atacama, near the city of Chañaral, this 43,000-hectare park features a stark but beautiful shoreline, and unique flora which draws moisture from the coastal fog. Among the fauna are pelicans, penguins, otters and sea lions.

Parque Nacional Fray Jorge In the region of Coquimbo, 75 km from the city of Ovalle, 10,000-hectare Fray Jorge is an ecological island of humid forest usually found several hundred km to the south. Like Pan de Azúcar, its vegetation depends on coastal fog.

Reserva Nacional Río Clarillo Only 45 km from Santiago and suitable for a day trip, this 10,000-hectare reserve offers a variety of Andean ecosystems.

Parque Nacional El Morado This 3000-

hectare mountain park featuring the Morales Glacier, source of the Río Morado, is only 93 km from Santiago.

Parque Nacional La Campana Easily accessible both from Santiago and Valparaíso/Viña del Mar, this 8000-hectare park is a good choice at any time of year for a short trek through tranquil forests of native oaks and palms.

Parque Nacional Juan Fernández Consisting of three islands several hundred km west of Valparaíso, this 9300-hectare unit is one of Chile's hidden ecological treasures, with spectacular scenery and a great variety of endemic plant species. It is best known as the site of exile for Scottish mariner Alexander Selkirk, immortalised as Robinson Crusoe in Daniel Defoe's novel.

Parque Nacional Rapa Nui Rapa Nui is the Polynesian name for Easter Island, with its huge, enigmatic stone statues, 3700 km west of Valparaíso. Despite its distance and isolation, it is a popular if expensive tourist destination.

Parque Nacional Laguna del Laja In the Andean foothills of the Biobío region, this 12,000-hectare park offers waterfalls, lakes, volcanos and bird life, with numerous trails suitable for hiking.

Parque Nacional Nahuelbuta In the high coastal range of the Araucanía region, Nahuelbuta's 7000 hectares preserve the largest remaining Araucaria (monkey-puzzle tree) forests in the area.

Parque Nacional Conguillío In the Andean portion of the Araucanía, 80 km from Temuco, 60,000-hectare Conguillío features mixed forests of Araucaria, cypress and southern beech surrounding the active, snow-capped Volcán Llaima.

Parque Nacional Huerquehue Small but scenic, 12,500-hectare Huerquehue has excellent hiking trails with outstanding views of nearby Parque Nacional Villarrica (see below). It is 120 km from Temuco.

Parque Nacional Villarrica One of the gems of the Lake District, Villarrica's smoking, symmetrical cone overlooks the lake and town of the same name. Its 61,000 hectares make a popular destination for trekkers and climbers.

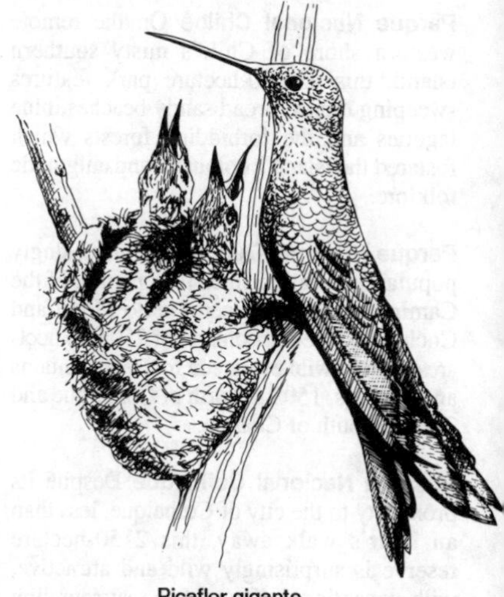
Picaflor gigante

Parque Nacional Puyehue One of Chile's most visited parks, 107,000-hectare Puyehue is only 80 km from the city of Osorno, but still offers scenery and solitude to dedicated visitors. There is outstanding hiking and hidden hot springs near Volcán Puyehue, which erupted in 1960 to form a striking volcanic desert as yet colonised by only a few hardy plants.

Parque Nacional Vicente Pérez Rosales Founded in 1926, Vicente Pérez Rosales is Chile's oldest national park, named for a famous Chilean explorer, politician and writer who helped found the city of Puerto Montt. Its 251,000 hectares include the spectacular Lago Todos Los Santos, which provides a scenic alternative route to Bariloche, Argentina, via Argentina's Parque Nacional Nahuel Huapi.

Parque Nacional Alerce Andino Just 50 km from Puerto Montt, this 40,000-hectare park preserves large tracts of the last remaining alerce trees, which resemble the giant redwoods of California.

Parque Nacional Chiloé On the remote western shore of Chile's misty southern island, this 43,000-hectare park features sweeping dunes, broad sandy beaches, blue lagoons and the forbidding forests which fostered the island's colourful and enigmatic folklore.

Parque Nacional Queulat An increasingly popular destination since the opening of the Camino Austral between Puerto Montt and Cochrane, Queulat consists of 150,000 hectares of truly wild evergreen forest, mountains and glaciers, 150 km north of Coihaique and 200 km south of Chaitén.

Reserva Nacional Coihaique Despite its proximity to the city of Coihaique, less than an hour's walk away, this 2150-hectare reserve is surprisingly wild and attractive, with exceptional views of the surrounding area and good opportunities for camping and hiking.

Reserva Nacional Río Simpson Though downgraded from national park status, this 41,000-hectare reserve, which straddles the highway between Coihaique and Puerto Aisén, is a pleasant and accessible destination with verdant forests, waterfalls and a spectacular canyon.

Parque Nacional Laguna San Rafael Glaciers reach the sea at one of Chile's most impressive parks, part of the Campo de Hielo Norte (northern Patagonian icefield) and accessible only by air or sea, 200 km south of Puerto Chacabuco. Its nearly 1.8 million hectares deserve a visit, but it is either expensive or time-consuming to do so.

Parque Nacional Torres del Paine Of all Chile's parks, Torres del Paine is the showpiece, a world biosphere reserve with all the diverse scenery of Alaska in only 180,000 hectares, and a wealth of wildlife, including the Patagonian guanaco, a wild relative of the Andean llama. It is 150 km from Puerto Natales and 400 km from Punta Arenas, in the region of Magallanes.

Guanaco

Monumento Natural Cueva del Milodón Only 16 km from Punta Arenas, this area (150 hectares) contains the cave where pioneers found remains of the milodon, a huge Pleistocene ground sloth.

Reserva Nacional Magallanes Just seven km west of Punta Arenas, this hilly forest reserve consists of 13,500 hectares of southern beech and Magellanic steppe.

GOVERNMENT

Chile's constitution, ratified by the electorate in a controversial plebiscite in 1980, is a custom document which was largely the work of Pinochet supporter Jaime Guzmán, then a conservative law professor and later a senator, assassinated by leftists in 1990. It provides for a popularly elected president and a bicameral congress, with a 46-member senate and a 120-member chamber of deputies; eight senators are 'institutional', appointed by General Pinochet and not subject to popular vote. Although the President continues to reside in Santiago and work at the Palacio de la Moneda there, the Congress now meets in Valparaíso.

Administratively, the country consists of a Metropolitan Region, including the capital of Santiago and its surroundings, plus a dozen more distinct regions, one of which includes the Chilean Antarctic (where territorial claims are on hold by international agreement). The regions, in turn, are subdivided into provinces, which are further subdivided into *comunas*, which are the units of local government. Traditionally, Chilean politics are highly centralised, with nearly all decisions of importance made in Santiago.

Political Parties

Since new legislation in 1987, conventional political parties have operated legally, but armed clandestine groups like MIR still operate against the civilian government of President Aylwin, as they did against Pinochet. The opposition press is more vigorous than at any time in recent memory, with both newspapers and magazines clamouring for judgement of the military. Many prominent exiles have returned to Chile, including Allende's widow Hortensia Bussi. The Roman Catholic Church and the trade union movement are also major outlets for dissent.

Ironically, some political parties supported the coup against Allende in the expectation that the military would return power to civilians as soon as the 'subversives' were eliminated. The left wing of the Christian Democratic party opposed the coup, while the right wing supported it, but soon turned against Pinochet when it became clear he had no intention of relinquishing power. The National Party largely supported the coup, though a number of National Party leaders eventually spoke out against the general. After the coup the Communist Party, once a relatively moderate group which favoured alliance with the Christian Democrats, began to advocate armed resistance.

The range and variation of Chilean political parties and their incessant transformations make it very difficult for any but the most experienced observer to follow Chilean electoral politics. In the 1989 elections, 17 parties with little in common except their opposition to Pinochet formed an unlikely coalition known as the Concertación para la Democracia, choosing Christian Democrat Patricio Aylwin as a compromise candidate for the presidency. Aylwin easily defeated Pinochet's reluctant protegé Hernán Büchi, who stood for Renovación Nacional (a direct descendant of the National Party), and independent businessman Francisco Errázuriz, a right-wing populist known by his nickname 'Fra-Fra'. Despite Büchi's widely acknowledged economic expertise and the Concertación's inability to identify him directly with military repression (he was barely out of university at the time of the coup), Chileans were clearly ready for a change. Factionalism within the right also contributed to Büchi's defeat, as the Unión Demócratica Independiente (UDI) had major disagreements with Renovación.

Whether the Concertación will hold together for 1993's presidential elections is unclear, but the June 1992 municipal elections, the first in 21 years, were a major success as coalition candidates outpolled conservative parties by 53% to 31%, with the remainder of the vote going to minor outsiders, including the Communists. No serious factionalism is apparent, but the defection of even a few of the allied parties could open the gates for a return to conservative rule. Socialist Ricardo Lagos is a possible Concertación candidate for president.

Trade unions, once a bastion of political support and activity for leftist candidates, suffered greatly under the dictatorship's repression and legislation. Many older, more experienced leaders died or disappeared, were imprisoned, or forced into exile. Many unions are nearly bankrupt, and have neither paid, full-time organisers nor offices from which to operate. High unemployment and low wages have discouraged membership, while strikes become illegal after 60 days. Picketing by strikers or soliciting money to help strikers' families is illegal, while employers may use non-union labour to break strikes.

The Military

Despite the return to civilian rule, the military retain considerable power and the constitution institutionalises this, at least in the short term – Pinochet's Senate appointees, with help from elected conservatives, can block reform, and he himself will take a senate seat upon retirement from the army in 1997. All the armed forces enjoy great autonomy, as the civilian president lacks authority to discipline their chiefs or even junior officers. President Aylwin has proposed a constitutional amendment to redress this deficiency, but cannot do so without the unlikely compliance of the Senate. Even if approved, this amendment would not apply to the present commanders.

Barring death or incapacitation, Pinochet (born 1915) will remain a significant force in Chilean politics. Defiantly resistant to change, he cultivated a reputation for stubbornness, illuminated by a popular joke during the dictatorship:

One day, General César Mendoza, then director of the Carabineros, is dozing in his office when the portrait of Liberator Bernardo O'Higgins whispers to him: 'Mendoza, this country's in bad shape! I want out! Bring me a horse!' Mendoza, not known for his smarts, runs to Pinochet and stutters 'G-G-General, O'Higgins spoke to me!' Pinochet brushes him off, but the persistent Mendoza finally drags him to his office. When they arrive, a disappointed O'Higgins admonishes the country's top policeman: 'Ay, Mendoza! I said a horse, not a mule!'

In his later years in power, Pinochet cultivated a grandfatherly image as a figure on whose continued influence political and economic stability depended. Like Suharto of Indonesia, he portrayed himself as the 'father of development' – embarking on lengthy tours of the country and dedicating new buildings, ports and other public works. The Camino Austral (southern highway) in the Aisén region, for example, officially bears his name, at least for the moment.

Pinochet's continuing power depends on his command of the army. The total strength of the armed forces is about 100,000, more than half of them in the army; nearly half the army personnel consists of officers and non-commissioned officers. Like the other services, the army is highly disciplined, cohesive and far more loyal to its commanders than to the civilian head of state. Civilians, however, have sometimes exploited inter-service rivalries, especially between the older army and navy and the newer air force. Still, Chile has a larger military budget than any of its neighbours, and the services are insulated from budgetary responsibility in part by a legal provision which entitles them to 10% of the profits from state copper sales, about US$300 million annually.

Prussian officer Emilio Körner, contracted to reform the Chilean officer training academy in the late 19th century, is responsible for the army's organisation. As head of its general staff from 1891 to 1910, he introduced German instructors, uniforms, discipline and modern equipment. Even today, Chilean soldiers in parade dress bear a disconcerting resemblance to jackbooted German troops of the 1930s and 1940s.

Although the Pinochet regime is often seen as an aberration and the army as apolitical, Chile has suffered four civil wars, 10 successful coups, and many uprisings and mutinies since independence from Spain. Military service is obligatory for males, but there is growing sentiment for eliminating conscription.

Geopolitics

One of the mainstays of military ideology and influence is the idea of geopolitics, a 19th-century European doctrine first elaborated by German geographer Friedrich

Ratzel and later exaggerated in National Socialist ideology in the 1930s. According to this world view, the state resembles a biological organism which must grow (expand) or die. This means that the state must effectively occupy the territories which it claims, in which process it comes into conflict with other states. Historically, this has been the justification for Chilean expansion into Tarapacá and the Pacific islands, as well as Antarctica.

Other South American countries, particularly Argentina and Brazil, share this perspective. General Pinochet has even written a textbook entitled *Geopolítica*, while his Argentine and Brazilian counterparts expound on topics such as the 'Fifth Column' of Chilean immigrants in Patagonia (largely humble and illiterate sheep shearers from the economically depressed island of Chiloé) or the justification of territorial claims in the Antarctic in accordance with each country's longitudinal 'frontage' on the icebound continent. Chile has gone so far as to establish a 'permanent' settlement of families in Antarctica, with formal state services such as banking and housing. The tenets of geopolitics are most popular among, but not restricted to, the military.

ECONOMY

One Latin American economist has referred to Chile as a 'fruit fly' because every economic experiment happens so much faster there than anywhere else (fruit flies are used in genetic experiments because they breed very rapidly). When Pinochet's junta seized power, it had no strategy beyond a vague wish to eradicate leftist influence and stabilise the economy. Its pledge to reduce inflation, return confiscated property appealed to conservatives and professionals opposed to Allende, but it soon adopted a more radical economic programme.

Pinochet appointed civilian economists, trained at or associated with the economics department at the University of Chicago, to direct government policy. These so-called 'Chicago Boys' favoured monetarist policies which severely reduced the government's role, reducing expenditures to a minimum and eliminating regulatory functions in order to promote commerce. They eliminated price controls, reduced tariffs in the interests of free trade, and sold off most state-owned industries to private entrepreneurs, while new financial codes encouraged foreign investment. Codelco (the Corporación del Cobre, the national copper company) remained under state ownership, but the government compensated North American mining companies for their losses. State-owned banks froze interest rates for savings, but private banks raised them, causing a flow of personal savings into private institutions.

For some years, inflation remained high despite shrinking domestic demand and declining imports. Industrial production also declined and some inefficient industries disappeared, although growth of 'non-traditional' exports, such as off-season temperate fruits to Europe and North America, helped compensate for falling copper prices. Despite falling wages unemployment reached nearly 20% by early 1976, and Chile's already ramshackle social security system broke down as bankrupt firms defaulted on insurance payments and the government refused to pay unemployment benefits to redundant workers.

In some callampas, where unemployment reached 80% or more, only church-organised soup kitchens prevented starvation. The government's response was the PEM (Programa de Empleo Minimo, Minimum Employment Program), which paid a token monthly salary to individuals who swept streets or performed other minor public works duties.

As private owners acquired former state banks, interest rates escaped government controls and subsequently soared. Firms borrowing money to avoid bankruptcy fell into debt to private banks and finance companies. Not surprisingly financiers – some of them Chicago Boys using foreign loan money – obtained failed enterprises at little cost and developed their own personal business empires.

When inflation finally fell, real wages and salaries rose only slowly, increasing consumer demand for goods and services. Since local industry could not satisfy this demand, imported manufactures filled the vacuum. Duty-free zones in the northern city of Iquique and the southern city of Punta Arenas fuelled the import boom.

Foreign investment failed to appear in the amounts and form that economists had expected. Although wages were low, the local market was too small to interest foreign companies which, in any event, could export goods to Chile's unprotected markets from better situated countries with equally low wages. Chile continued to rely on the export of primary products such as minerals, timber, fruit and seafood in order to earn foreign exchange.

Private firms borrowed large sums of foreign capital to finance expansion, but this was sustainable only so long as exports increased (as they did in the late 1970s) and the money was invested productively. Problems developed after 1979 when government linked the peso to the appreciating US dollar as an anti-inflation measure. An orgy of cheap imports, combined with the increasing price of Chilean exports, created a growing deficit in Chile's balance of trade.

In the early 1980s, global recession reduced the price of copper and other mineral exports, but Chile's international debt (almost all of it created by foreign loans to private banks and firms) increased. By the end of 1981, loan repayments were consuming 75% of export earnings. Interest rates climbed, bankruptcies increased and unemployment soared.

In 1982 the government sought to promote exports by devaluing the peso and further reducing wages, but inflation soon wiped out any benefits for Chilean exporters. Rising local and global interest rates exacerbated the banks' debt problems. Allowed to float, the peso plummeted by 40% against the US dollar and, with the Chicago Boys' policies in shambles, the junta backtracked and bailed out key private banks and finance houses in early 1983.

Maintaining its monetarist orientation, in order to gain quick windfalls to reduce its debt, the Chilean government has continued to privatise its assets. One of its more controversial moves was the sale of half the Chilean telephone system to Australian businessman Alan Bond in 1988.

In recent years, the Chilean economy has improved greatly on a macro scale, but elite sectors have benefited more from economic growth than the poor. Chile has been able to repay some of its external debt, and inflation is very low in comparison with most other Latin American countries, at about 15% annually. But unemployment and underemployment remain very high – countless city dwellers earn a precarious subsistence as street vendors of cheap ice cream, candy, cigarettes or other cheap goods such as audio cassettes. Wages remain low; teachers for example, rarely earn more than US$200 per month, and others make much less.

While the Aylwin government has taken a more sympathetic approach toward the problems of the poor and dispossessed, it has largely continued the junta's macro-economic policies. At the same time, the export economy is more diverse and less vulnerable to fluctuations in international markets; the mining sector, for instance, no longer relies exclusively on copper, but also produces less traditional commodities like lithium. In 1991, the gross domestic product grew by 6%.

Fresh fruit exports have also increased and diversified, after a brief glitch in 1989 – a handful of Chilean table grapes in Philadelphia were found to be poisoned with cyanide, leading to a suspension of US fruit imports from Chile. This angered all sectors of Chilean society, but the industry has since recovered, and expected to export US$1.1 billion worth of fruit in 1992.

Since 1987, Chile has enjoyed a trade surplus which has progressively increased. How the de facto revaluation of the peso in early 1992 will affect this situation is not yet clear. Chile's most important trading partners are the USA, Japan, Germany, Brazil and Argentina.

Top : Pelicans, Iquique (WB)
Bottom Left : Street scene, Valdivia, Lake District (AS)
Bottom Right : Produce market, Valdivia, Lake District (WB)

Top : Aymara boy, Chucuyo (WB)
Bottom : Fishing village, Isla Chiloé (AS)

POPULATION & PEOPLE

Chile's population of about 13.5 million is unevenly distributed. More than a third reside in Gran Santiago, which includes the capital and its immediate suburbs; no other city is larger than about 250,000. Moreover, about 75% live in the Chilean heartland (including the cities of Valparaíso and Viña del Mar), which comprises only 20% of the country's total land area. More than 80% of Chileans live in cities or towns, but south of the Río Biobío, there is still a dense rural population.

In the desert north, nearly everyone lives in the large coastal cities of Arica, Iquique, Antofagasta, La Serena and Coquimbo, although the mining centres of Calama/Chuquicamata, El Salvador and Copiapó are relatively large as well. South of Santiago, the most important cities are Rancagua, the Concepción-Talcahuano conurbation, Valdivia, Osorno and Puerto Montt. Beyond Puerto Montt, where the fractured landscape complicates communications, the only notable towns are Coihaique, in the Aisén region, and Punta Arenas in Magallanes.

Most Chileans are mestizos, although many can still claim purely European descent. In much of the country, social class is still a greater issue than race – working-class people and others resentfully call the country's elite *momios* (mummies) because, to paraphrase the words of film director Miguel Littín, they are so resistant to change that they might as well be embalmed. In the southern region of La Araucanía, there is a large, visible and increasingly militant Mapuche Indian population, mostly in and around the city of Temuco. Above the once densely peopled transverse river valleys of the desert north, Aymara and Atacameño peoples farm the terraces of the precordillera and pasture their llamas and alpacas in the altiplano.

Chile did not experience the massive 19th and 20th-century European immigration which neighbouring Argentina did – at the end of the 19th century, only a small percentage of Chileans were foreign-born. After the

European upheavals of 1848, many Germans settled near present-day Valdivia, Osorno and Puerto Montt in southern Chile, where use of the German language is still vigorous, if not widespread. Other immigrant groups included the French, Italians, Yugoslavs (particularly in Magallanes and Tierra del Fuego), European Jews, and Palestinians.

European immigration did not alter the structure of Chilean society, but added non-Spanish elements to the middle and upper classes. The established aristocracy (the original landed gentry), of mostly Spanish Basque origin, welcomed wealthy immigrants with British, French or German surnames like Edwards, Subercaseaux and Gildemeister. Despite their small numbers, European immigrants became economically powerful, controlling rural estates and commercial, financial, and industrial institutions.

EDUCATION

Chile's 94% literacy rate is one of Latin America's highest. From the age of five to 12, education is free and compulsory, although attendance is low in some rural areas.

Universities are traditionally free and open, but after the coup of 1973 the military government installed its own rectors throughout the country; its sweeping university reform of the 1980s reduced state funding, raised student fees, and downgraded or eliminated ostensibly 'subversive' careers such as sociology and psychology; the Universidad de Chile was a particular target. Like other Latin American countries, Chile suffers from a glut of lawyers and other professionals, and a shortage of trained people in engineering and other more practical fields. The military reform of higher education made it easy to open private 'universities', but most of these are glorified business schools with part-time faculty and dubious standards.

ARTS

Although derivative of European precedents in many ways, Chilean art, literature and music have been influential beyond the country's borders. Chilean literature has pro-

---

The Paths of Mistral & Neruda

Gabriela Mistral and Pablo Neruda have opened a window on Chile and Latin America through their poetry, but their biographies are no less revealing. In some ways, no two individuals could be more different than these two Nobel Prize winners, but the parallels and divergences in their lives disclose both unifying and contrasting aspects of Chilean life and culture.

They were contemporaries, but of different generations; Mistral was born in 1889, Neruda in 1904. Both belonged to the provinces: Mistral to the remote Elqui valley of the Norte Chico, Neruda to the southern city of Temuco, though his birthplace was Parral, in the heartland province of Maule, and he lived in Santiago, Valparaíso and in a small beach community at Isla Negra. Both poets used pseudonyms: Gabriela Mistral's given name was Lucila Godoy Alcayaga, while Pablo Neruda's was Neftalí Ricardo Reyes Basoalto. Both adopted their aliases out of timidity: the young rural schoolmistress Lucila Godoy sat in the audience at Santiago's Teatro Municipal while a surrogate received a prize for her 'Sonnets on Death', in memory of a young suitor who had committed suicide; Neftalí Reyes feared the ridicule of his working-class family.

Both enjoyed literary success at a young age. The government rewarded each with diplomatic posts which subsidised their creative writing; in consequence, both travelled extensively and became celebrities outside their own country and the South American continent, which produced no Nobel Prize winner in literature until Mistral's award in 1945. In 1971, Neruda became the third Latin American writer to receive the prize (Guatemalan novelist Miguel Angel Asturias was the second, in 1967).

Despite these similarities, they were very different in other respects. After the death of her beloved, Mistral never married and devoted her life to children and their education at schools from La Serena to Punta Arenas – when she taught in Temuco, the young Neruda and his friends worshipped her. She even travelled abroad to reform the Mexican system of public instruction. She lived austerely, though her stern features masked the sensitivity of a woman whose poetry was compassionate and mystical. Though friends with political figures, most notably President Pedro Aguirre Cerda, her politics were not a matter of public controversy.

Gabriela Mistral

Neruda, by contrast, became a flamboyant figure whose private life was public knowledge, who built eccentric houses and filled them with outlandish objects, and whose politics more than once landed him in trouble. Unlike the sombre Mistral, his face was usually smiling, often pensive, but never grim. While consul in Java in the 1930s, he married a Dutch woman, left her for Delia del Carril (a decade older than himself) a few years later, and after nearly 20 years left Delia for the much younger Matilde Urrutia, for whom he built and named La Chascona, his Santiago house at the foot of Cerro San Cristóbal.

Neruda's houses, including his beachfront favourite at Isla

duced writers of international stature, including Nobel Prize-winning poets Gabriela Mistral and Pablo Neruda, the latter also an important political activist. Much of their work is readily available in English translation. For suggested readings of these and other authors, see the Facts for the Visitor chapter.

Many Chilean intellectuals have been educated in European capitals, particularly Paris. In the 19th and early 20th centuries Santiago self-consciously emulated European, especially French, cultural trends in art, music and architecture. There are many important art museums and galleries. Even in the provinces, live theatre is an important medium of expression.

Until the military coup of 1973, Chilean cinema was among the most experimental in Latin America. Director Alejandro Jodorowsky's surrealistic *El Topo* (The Mole), an underground success overseas, included a performance by the legendary San Francisco area band Country Joe and the Fish. Exiled director Miguel Littín's *Alsino & the Condor*, nominated for an Academy

---

Negra, and La Sebastiana in Valparaíso, were material expressions of his personality, improvised with an eclectic assortment of objects amassed on his travels and at his diplomatic posts – entire rooms are filled with shells, bowsprit figureheads, ships-in-bottles, and of course books, all of which delighted him and his guests and now draw thousands of visitors. The houses themselves break all the rules of standard architecture and, for that reason, intrigue the visitor as much as they pleased the owner. In his autobiography, he wrote that 'I have...built my house like a toy house and I play in it from morning till night'.

For all his wealth, Neruda never forgot his modest origins nor abandoned his political convictions, and did not consider his privileged lifestyle incompatible with his leftist beliefs – lacking heirs, he left everything to the Chilean people through a foundation. After Franco's rebels defeated the Spanish Republic, the Chilean diplomat devoted his energies to helping refugees escape the dictator's revenge. In Spain he had made a personal commitment to the Communist party, although he did not enrol officially until his return to Chile, where he was elected Senator for Tarapacá and Antofagasta, the mining provinces of the Norte Grande. After managing Gabriel González Videla's successful presidential campaign of 1946, he fell afoul of the president's caprice and went into hiding and then exile in Argentina, escaping by foot and horseback across the southern Andes to Argentina.

After González Videla left office, Neruda returned to Chile and continued his political activities without reducing his prolific output of poetry. In 1969 he was the Communist candidate for the presidency, but resigned in support of Salvador Allende's candidacy and later became Allende's ambassador to France. He received the Nobel Prize during his tenure in France but died less than a fortnight after the military coup of 1973.

Mistral's reflective and mystical verse was uncontroversial, but Neruda's poetry could be committed and combative and, although no government could suppress literature which could be found in almost every household, the military regime of General Pinochet did its best to erase his memory. After his death, his houses were vandalised with police and military complicity, but his widow Matilde and dedicated volunteers persisted, to establish the Fundación Neruda in spite of legal and extra-legal obstacles. It now administers the estate and has successfully restored all three houses which are now open to the public. Both Chileans and foreigners flock to them and, with a few extreme exceptions, even those who disagreed with his politics enjoy and respect his work.

Gabriela Mistral, meanwhile, remains a modest but reassuring presence in Chilean life and literature. Every day, thousands of Santiago's citizens pass the mural of Gabriela and her 'children' on the Alameda, at the base of Cerro Santa Lucía, while many more pay her homage at the museum which bears her name in the village of Vicuña, in her native Elqui valley. Though she died in New York, she is buried near her birthplace, the hamlet of Montegrande. ■

Pablo Neruda

Award as Best Foreign Film in 1983, is readily available on video.

Probably the best-known manifestation of Chilean popular culture is the *La Nueva Canción Chilena* (New Chilean Song Movement), whose practitioners wedded the country's folkloric heritage to the political passions of the late 1960s and early 1970s. Its most legendary figure is Violeta Parra, best known for her enduring theme *Gracias a la Vida* (Thanks to Life), but her children Isabel and Angel, also performers, established the first of many *peñas* (musical and cultural centres) in Santiago in the mid-1960s. Individual performers such as Victor Jara, brutally executed during the 1973 coup, and groups like Quilapayún and Inti-Illimani acquired international reputations for both their music and their political commitment.

Many Chilean folk musicians, exiled during the Pinochet dictatorship, performed regularly in Europe, North America, and Australia, and their recordings are available both in Chile and overseas.

CULTURE

English-speaking visitors will find Chile, like Argentina, more accessible than other Latin American countries because of its superficial resemblance to their own societies. Foreign travellers are less conspicuous than in countries like Peru and Bolivia, which have large indigenous populations, and can more easily integrate themselves into everyday life. Chileans are exceptionally hospitable and frequently invite foreigners to visit their homes and participate in daily activities.

Sport is extremely important to Chileans, although few Chilean athletes are known outside their country. Soccer is the national pastime; the most popular team is Colo Colo, named for the Mapuche cacique, but tennis, cycling and other individual sports are also popular.

RELIGION

About 90% of Chileans are Roman Catholic, but evangelical Protestantism has recently gained importance. There are also Lutherans, Jews, Presbyterians, Mormons and Pentecostals. The proselytising Mormons have caused great controversy, and their churches have been the target of numerous bombings by leftist groups.

Catholicism has provided Chile some of its most compelling cultural monuments – the colonial adobe churches of the Norte Grande, the San Francisco Church and the imposing Cathedral of Santiago, and the modest but dignified shingled chapels of Chiloé. Countless roadside shrines, some of which are extraordinary manifestations of folk art, also testify to the pervasiveness of religion in Chilean society.

Like Chilean political parties, the Church has many factions, but its Vicaria de la Solidaridad compiled an outstanding human rights record during the Pinochet dictatorship. At great risk to themselves, Chilean

Cathedral

priests frequently worked in the shantytowns of Santiago and other large cities. Such activism has continued in today's more permissive political climate.

LANGUAGE

Spanish is Chile's official language and is almost universally understood, but there is also a handful of native languages, some spoken by a very few individuals. In the desert north, more than 20,000 speak Aymara, although most are bilingual in Spanish; in the south, there are perhaps half a million Mapuche speakers. Perhaps the most intriguing linguistic minority are the 2000-plus speakers of Rapa Nui, the Polynesian language of most of Easter Island's population.

Every visitor to Chile should attempt to learn some Spanish, whose basic elements are easily acquired. If possible, take a short course before you go. Even if you can't do so, Chileans are gracious hosts and will encourage your Spanish, so there is no need to feel self-conscious about vocabulary or pronunciation. There are many common cognates, so if you're stuck try Hispanicising an English word – it is unlikely you'll make a truly embarrassing error. Do not, however, admit to being *embarazada* (literally 'embarrassed') unless you are in fact pregnant!

Note that in American Spanish, the plural of the familiar 'tu' is *ustedes* rather than *vosotros*, as in Spain. Chileans and other Latin Americans readily understand European Spanish, but may find it quaint or pretentious.

Chilean Spanish

Chilean speakers relax terminal and even some internal consonants almost to the point of disappearance, so that it can be difficult to distinguish plural from singular. For example, *las islas* (the islands) may sound more like 'la ila' to an English speaker. Chileans speak rather more rapidly than other South Americans, and rather less clearly – the conventional *¿quieres?* (do you want?) sounds more like 'querí' on the tongue of a Chilean.

Vocabulary There are many differences in vocabulary between European and American Spanish, and among Spanish-speaking countries in the Americas. There are also considerable regional differences within these countries not attributable to accent alone – Chilean speech, for instances, contains many words adopted from Mapuche, while the residents of Santiago sometimes use *coa*, a slang generally attributed to the lower classes. Check the glossary for some of these terms.

Chileans and other South Americans normally refer to the Spanish language as *castellano* rather than *español*.

Phrasebooks & Dictionaries

Lonely Planet's *Latin American Spanish* phrasebook, by Anna Cody, is a worthwhile addition to your backpack. Another exceptionally useful resource is the *University of Chicago Spanish-English, English-Spanish Dictionary*, whose small size, light weight and thorough entries make it perfect for overseas travel.

Pronunciation

Spanish pronunciation is, in general, consistently phonetic. Once you are aware of the basic rules, they should cause little difficulty. Speak slowly to avoid getting tongue-tied until you become confident of your ability.

Pronunciation of the letters f, k, l, n, p, q, s and t is virtually identical with English, and y is identical when used as a consonant; ll is a separate letter, pronounced as a y and coming after l in the alphabet. Ch and ñ are also separate letters; in the alphabet they come after c and n respectively.

Vowels Spanish vowels are very consistent and have easy English equivalents:

a is like 'a' in 'father'
e is like the 'e' in 'met'; at the end of a word it's like the 'ey' in 'hey'
i is like 'ee' in 'feet'

o is like 'o' in 'for'
u is like 'oo' in 'boot'; after consonants other than 'q', it is more like English 'w'
y is a consonant except when it stands alone or appears at the end of a word, in which case its pronunciation is identical to Spanish 'i'

Consonants Spanish consonants generally resemble their English equivalents, but there are some major exceptions:

b resembles its English equivalent, but is undistinguished from 'v'; for clarification, refer to the former as 'b larga', the latter as 'b corta' (the word for the letter itself is pronounced like English 'bay')
c is like the 's' in 'see' before 'e' and i, otherwise like English 'k'
d closely resembles 'th' in 'feather'
g before 'e' and 'i' like a guttural English 'h'; otherwise like 'g' in 'go'
h is invariably silent; if your name begins with this letter, listen carefully when immigration officials summon you to pick up your passport
j most closely resembles English 'h', but is slightly more guttural
ñ is like 'ni' in 'onion'
r is nearly identical to English except at the beginning of a word, when it is often rolled
rr is very strongly rolled
v resembles English, but see 'b', above
x is like 'x' in 'taxi' except for very few words for which it follows Spanish or Mexican usage as 'j'
z is like 's' in 'sun'

Diphthongs Diphthongs are combinations of two vowels which form a single syllable. In Spanish, the formation of a diphthong depends on combinations of 'weak' vowels (i and u) or strong ones (a, e, and o). Two weak vowels or a strong and a weak vowel make a diphthong, but two strong ones are separate syllables.

A good example of two weak vowels forming a diphthong is the word *diurno* (during the day). The final syllable of *obligatorio* (obligatory) is a combination of weak and strong vowels.

Stress Stress, often indicated by visible accents, is very important, since it can change the meaning of words. In general, words ending in vowels or the letters n or s have stress on the next-to-last syllable, while those with other endings have stress on the last syllable. Thus *vaca* (cow) and *caballos* (horses) both have accents on their next-to-last syllables.

Visible accents, which can occur anywhere in a word, dictate stress over these general rules. Thus *sótano* (basement), *América* and *porción* (portion) all have the stress on the syllable with the accented vowel. When words are written all in capitals, the accent is often not shown, but it still affects the pronunciation.

Basic Grammar

Nouns in Spanish are masculine or feminine. The definite article ('the' in English) agrees with the noun in gender and number; for example, the Spanish word for 'train' is masculine, so 'the train' is *el tren*, and the plural is *los trenes*. The word for 'house' is feminine, so 'the house' is *la casa*, and the plural is *las casas*. The indefinite articles (a, an, some) work in the same way: *un libro* (a book) is masculine singular, while *una carta* (a letter) is feminine singular. Most nouns ending in 'o' are masculine and those ending in 'a' are generally feminine. Normally, nouns ending in a vowel add 's' to form the plural, while those ending in a consonant add 'es': *unos libros* (some book), *unas cartas* (some letters). Gender also affects demonstrative pronouns: *este* is the masculine form of 'this', while *esta* is the feminine form and *esto* the neuter; 'these', 'that' and 'those' are formed by adding 's'.

Adjectives also agree with the noun in gender and number, and usually come after the noun. Possessive adjectives *mi* (my), *tu* (your) *su* (his/her) etc agree with the thing possessed, not with the possessor. For example 'his suitcase' is *su maleta*, while 'his suitcases' is *sus maletas*. A simple way to indicate possession is to use the preposition *de* (of). 'Juan's room', for instance, would be *la habitación de Juan* (literally, 'the room of Juan').

Personal pronouns are usually not used with verbs. There are three main categories of verbs: those which end in 'ar' such as *hablar* (to speak), those which end in 'er' such as *comer* (to eat), and those which end in 'ir' such as *reir* (to laugh); there are many irregular verbs, such as *ir* (to go) and *venir* (to come).

To form a comparative, add *más* (more) or *menos* (less) before the adjective. For example, *alto* is 'high', *más alto* 'higher' and *lo más alto* 'the highest'.

Greetings & Civilities

In their public behaviour, Chileans are exceptionally polite and expect others to reciprocate. Never, for example, approach a stranger for information without extending a greeting like *buenos días* or *buenas tardes*. Most young people use the informal 'tu' and its associated verb forms among themselves, but if in doubt you should use the more formal 'usted' and its forms.

hello	*hola*
good morning	*buenos días*
good afternoon	*buenas tardes*
good evening	*buenas noches*
good night	*buenas noches*
goodbye	*adiós, chau*
please	*por favor*
thank you	*gracias*
you're welcome	*de nada*

Useful Words & Phrases

yes	*sí*
no	*no*
and	*y*
to/at	*a*
for	*por, para*
of/from	*de, desde*
in	*en*
with	*con*
without	*sin*
before	*antes*
after	*después*
soon	*pronto*
already	*ya*
now	*ahora*
right away	*en seguida, al tiro*
here	*aquí*
there	*allí*
I understand	*entiendo*
I don't understand	*no entiendo*

I don't speak much Spanish.
No hablo mucho castellano.

Where?	*¿Dónde?*
Where is ...?	*¿Dónde está ...?*
Where are ...?	*¿Dónde están ...?*
When?	*¿Cuando?*
How?	*¿Cómo?*
I would like ...	*Me gustaría ...*
coffee	*café*
tea	*té*
beer	*cerveza*
How much?	*¿Cuanto?*
How many?	*¿Cuantos?*

Getting Around

plane	*avión*
train	*tren*
bus	*ómnibus*, or just *bus*
small bus	*colectivo, micro*
ship	*barco, buque*
car	*auto*
taxi	*taxi*
truck	*camión*
pickup	*camioneta*
bicycle	*bicicleta*
motorcycle	*motocicleta*
hitchhike	*hacer dedo*
airport	*aeropuerto*
train station	*estación de ferrocarril*
bus terminal	*terminal de buses*

I would like a ticket to ...
Quiero un boleto/pasaje a ...

What's the fare to ...?
¿Cuanto cuesta a ...?

When does the next plane/train/bus leave for ...?
¿Cuando sale el próximo avión/tren/ómnibus para ....?

student/university discount
descuento estudiantil/universitario

first/last/next	*primero/último/próximo*
first/second class	*primera/segunda clase*
single/return	*ida/ida y vuelta*
left luggage	*guardería, equipaje*
tourist office	*oficina de turismo*

Accommodation

hotel
hotel, pensión, residencial
Is there ...? Are there ...?
¿Hay ...?
single room
habitación single
double room
habitación doble
What does it cost?
¿Cuanto cuesta?
per night
por noche
full board
pensión completa
shared bath
baño compartido
private bath
baño privado
too expensive
demasiado caro
cheaper
mas económico
May I see it?
¿Puedo verlo?
I don't like it
No me gusta.
the bill
la cuenta

Toilets

The most common word for 'toilet' is *baño*, but *servicios sanitarios*, or just *servicios* (services) is a frequent alternative. Men's toilets will usually bear a descriptive term such as *hombres*, *caballeros* or *varones*. Women's toilets will say *señoras* or *damas*.

Post & Telecommunications

post office	*correo*
letter	*carta*
parcel	*paquete*
postcard	*postal*
airmail	*correo aéreo*
registered mail	*certificado*
stamps	*estampillas*
person to person	*persona a persona*
collect call	*cobro revertido*

Geographical Expressions

The expressions below are among the most common you will encounter in this book and in Spanish language maps and guides.

bay	*bahía*
bridge	*puente*
farm	*fundo*
glacier	*glaciar, ventisquero*
highway	*carretera, camino, ruta*
hill	*cerro*
lake	*lago*
marsh	*estero*
mount	*cerro*
mountain range	*cordillera*
national park	*parque nacional*
pass	*paso*
ranch	*estancia*
river	*río*
waterfall	*cascada, salto*

Countries

The list below includes only countries whose spelling differs in English and Spanish.

Canada	*Canadá*
Denmark	*Dinamarca*
England	*Inglaterra*
France	*Francia*
Germany	*Alemania*
Great Britain	*Gran Bretaña*
Ireland	*Irlanda*
Italy	*Italia*
Japan	*Japón*
Netherlands	*Holanda*
New Zealand	*Nueva Zelandia*
Peru	*Perú*
Scotland	*Escocia*
Spain	*España*
Sweden	*Suecia*
Switzerland	*Suiza*
United States	*Estados Unidos*
Wales	*Gales*

Numbers

1	*uno*
2	*dos*
3	*tres*
4	*cuatro*
5	*cinco*
6	*seis*
7	*siete*
8	*ocho*
9	*nueve*
10	*diez*
11	*once*
12	*doce*
13	*trece*
14	*catorce*
15	*quince*
16	*dieciseis*
17	*diecisiete*
18	*dieciocho*
19	*diecinueve*
20	*veinte*
21	*veintiuno*
22	*veintidós*
23	*veintitrés*
24	*veinticuatro*
30	*treinta*
31	*treinta y uno*
32	*treinta y dos*
33	*treinta y tres*
40	*cuarenta*
41	*cuarenta y uno*
42	*cuarenta y dos*
50	*cincuenta*
60	*sesenta*
70	*setenta*
80	*ochenta*
90	*noventa*
100	*cien*
101	*ciento uno*
102	*ciento dos*
110	*ciento diez*
120	*ciento veinte*
130	*ciento treinta*
200	*doscientos*
300	*trescientos*
400	*cuatrocientos*
500	*quinientos*
600	*seiscientos*
700	*setecientos*
800	*ochocientos*
900	*novecientos*
1000	*mil*
1100	*mil cien*
1200	*mil doscientos*
2000	*dos mil*
5000	*cinco mil*
10,000	*diez mil*
50,000	*cincuenta mil*
100,000	*cien mil*
1,000,000	*un millón*

Ordinal Numbers

1st	*primero/a*
2nd	*segundo/a*
3rd	*tercero/a*
4th	*cuarto/a*
5th	*quinto/a*
6th	*sexto/a*
7th	*septimo/a*
8th	*octavo/a*
9th	*noveno/a*
10th	*décimo/a*
11th	*undécimo/a*
12th	*duadécimo/a*

Days of the Week

Monday	*lunes*
Tuesday	*martes*
Wednesday	*miércoles*
Thursday	*jueves*
Friday	*viernes*
Saturday	*sábado*
Sunday	*domingo*

Time

Eight o'clock is *las ocho*, while 8.30 is *las ocho y treinta* (literally, 'eight and thirty') or *las ocho y media* (eight and a half). However, 7.45 is *las ocho menos quince* (literally, 'eight minus fifteen') or *las ocho menos cuarto* (eight minus one quarter).

Times are modified by morning *(de la manaña)* or afternoon *(de la tarde)* instead of am or pm. It is also common to use the 24-hour clock, especially with transportation schedules.

Facts for the Visitor

VISAS & EMBASSIES

Except for nationals of neighbouring countries, passports are obligatory. Citizens of Canada, the UK, the USA, Australia and most Western European countries do not need a visa. New Zealanders, and citizens of a few other countries, do need to obtain a visa in advance, and should not arrive at the border without one or they may be sent back to the nearest Chilean consulate. On arrival, visitors receive a tourist card and entry stamp which allow a stay of up to 90 days, renewable for an additional 90. For this extension, visit the Departamento de Extranjería (☎ 672-5320), Moneda 1342 in Santiago, between 9 am and 1.30 pm; it costs about US$7.50. Do not lose your tourist card, which Chilean border authorities take very seriously; for a replacement, visit the Policía Internacional (☎ 371292) at General Borgoño 1052 in Santiago, from 8.30 am to 12.30 pm or 3 to 7 pm.

You do not need an International Health Certificate, but it is advisable to have a medical checkup before your trip.

Motorists should note that, although personal visas may be extended for beyond the initial 90 days, vehicle permission may not be, and it will be necessary to leave the country and return.

Chilean Embassies & Consulates

Chile has diplomatic representation in most parts of the world; those listed are the ones most likely to be useful to intending visitors. In some places there is a tourist information section with a separate address.

Argentina
  San Martín 439, Buenos Aires (☎ 394-6582)

Australia
  10 Culgoa Circuit, O'Malley ACT 2606 (☎ 286-2430)

Bolivia
  Avenida H Siles 5843, Barrio Obrajes, La Paz (☎ 785275)

Brazil
  Praia do Flamengo 382, No 401, Flamengo, Rio de Janeiro (☎ 552-5349)
  Avenida Paulista 1009, 10th floor, São Paulo (☎ 284-2044)

Canada
  151 Slater St, Suite 605, Ottawa, Ontario (☎ 235-4402)
  Tourist Information: 56 Sparks St, Suite 801, Ottawa, Ontario (☎ 235-4402)
  Consulates:
  330 Bay Street, Suite 1003, Toronto, Ontario (☎ 366-9570)
  1010 St Catherine West, Suite 731, Montréal, Québec (☎ 861-8006)

New Zealand
  7th floor, Robert Jones House, 1-3 Welleston St, Wellington (☎ 725180)

Paraguay
  Guido Spano 1687, Asunción (☎ 600671)

Peru
  Javier Prado Oeste 790, San Isidro, Lima (☎ 407965)

UK
  12 Devonshire St, London (☎ 580-6393)

Uruguay
  Andes 1365, 1st floor, Montevideo (☎ 98-2223)

USA
  1736 Massachusetts Ave NW, Washington DC (☎ 785-3159)
  Tourist Information: 1732 Massachusetts Ave NW, Washington, DC (☎ 785- 1746)
  Consulates:
  866 United Nations Plaza, Room 302, New York, NY (☎ 980-3366)
  79 Milk Street, Boston, Massachusetts (☎ 426-1678)
  Public Ledger Building, Suite 444, Chestnut & Sixth St, Philadelphia, Pennsylvania (☎ 829-9520)
  1110 Brickell Ave, Suit 616, Miami, Florida (☎ 373-8623)
  1360 Post Oak Blvd, Suite 2330, Houston, Texas (☎ 621-5853)
  510 West Sixth St, Suite 1204, Los Angeles, California (☎ 624-6357)
  870 Market St, Suite 1062, San Francisco, California (☎ 982-7662)

Visa Extensions

If staying longer than six months, it's probably simplest to make a brief visit to Argentina, Peru or Bolivia, then return and start your six months all over again. There is no formal obstacle to doing so, although border officials sometimes question returnees from Mendoza (Argentina) to determine whether they are working illegally in Chile.

Foreign Embassies in Chile

All major European and South American countries, and many others as well, have embassies in Santiago. The neighbouring countries of Argentina, Bolivia and Peru have consulates in a number of other cities, and their addresses are listed in the entries on those places.

Argentina
  Vicuña Mackenna 41 (☎ 222-8977)
Australia
  Gertrudis Echeñique 420 (☎ 228-5065)
Austria
  Barros Errázuriz 1968, 3rd floor (☎ 223-4774)
Belgium
  Providencia 2653, 11th floor (☎ 232-1071)
Bolivia
  Avenida Santa María 2796 (☎ 232-8180)
Brazil
  Alfonso Ovalle 1665 (☎ 698-2347)
Canada
  Ahumada 11, 10th floor (☎ 696-2256)
Denmark
  Avenida Santa María 0182, 2nd floor (☎ 376056)
Finland
  Monseñor Sótero Sanz de Villalba 55, Oficina 71 (☎ 232-4573)
France
  Condell 65 (☎ 225-1030)
Germany
  Agustinas 785, 7th floor (☎ 335031)
Israel
  San Sebastián 2812, 5th floor (☎ 246-1570)
Italy
  Clemente Fabres 1050 (☎ 223-2467)
Japan
  Providencia 2653, 19th floor (☎ 232-1807)
Mexico
  San Sebastián 2839, 6th floor (☎ 246-7835)
Netherlands
  Las Violetas 2368 (☎ 223-6825)
New Zealand
  Isidora Goyenechea 3516 (☎ 231-4204)
Norway
  Américo Vespucio Norte 548 (☎ 228-1024)
Paraguay
  Huérfanos 886, Depto 514 (☎ 394640)
Perú
  Providencia 2653 (☎ 232-6275)
Spain
  Avenida Andrés Bello 1895 (☎ 235-2755)
Sweden
  Avenida 11 de Septiembre 2353, 16th floor (☎ 231-2733)
Switzerland
  Providencia 2653, Oficina 1602 (☎ 232-2693)
UK
  Avenida El Bosque Norte 0125, 3rd floor (☎ 231-3737)
USA
  Embassy: Agustinas 1343
  Consulate (visas): Merced 230 (☎ 671-0133)
Uruguay
  Pedro de Valdivia 711 (☎ 274-4066)

VISITING ARGENTINA

Even if you don't plan to spend a lot of time in Argentina, you may want to make some short visits, either making one of the crossings through the Lake District, or to reach the far south of Chile which has no road connections except through Argentine Patagonia. For full details, see Lonely Planet's *Argentina, Uruguay & Paraguay – a travel survival kit*.

Visas

Nationals of the United States, Canada and most Western European countries do not require visas, but Australians and New Zealanders, who do need them, must submit their passports with a payment of US$15. The Argentine consulate in Santiago is particularly efficient, and ordinarily the visa will be ready the following day.

Customs

On entering Argentina, the customs officers will probably only check your bags for fresh fruit. Officials generally defer to foreign visitors, but if you cross the border frequently and carry electronic equipment such as cameras or a laptop computer, it is helpful to have a typed list with serial numbers stamped by authorities.

Money

A new currency, known as the peso, replaced the wildly inflated austral in early 1992. One new peso, on a par with the US dollar, equals 10,000 australs. Outside large cities, changing travellers' cheques in may be difficult or impossible without paying a very high commission, so carry a supply of cash dollars. Since the 'dollarisation' of the Argentine economy, many merchants readily accept US dollars in lieu of Argentine pesos, thus avoiding many currency dilemmas – but expect to receive your change in pesos.

Health

Argentina requires no vaccinations for visitors entering from any country and, in general, the country presents few serious health hazards, especially in Patagonia.

Getting Around

In Argentine Patagonia, distances are immense, roads can be very bad, and some travellers find the desert monotonous, so the occasional flight is sometimes a welcome relief. Argentina's three major airlines, Líneas Aéreas del Estado (LADE), Austral and Aerolíneas Argentinas, have extensive networks in southern Patagonia and Tierra del Fuego. LADE fares are very cheap, in some cases less than the bus fare for the same route, but demand is high, especially in summer; try the airport if LADE staff insist that flights are completely booked.

Argentine buses, resembling those in Chile, are modern, comfortable and fast. Most large towns have a central bus terminal, though some companies operate from their own private offices. In some more remote and less populated areas, buses are few or even non-existent, so be patient.

Northern Argentina has an extensive rail network although services have deteriorated in recent years. There are no passenger railways in southern Patagonia, where the main forms of transport are buses and planes.

Hitching is relatively easy in Argentina, but traffic in Patagonia and Tierra del Fuego is sparse and there may be long waits between lifts.

DOCUMENTS

It is advisable to carry your passport – though the military are keeping a low public profile under the present civilian government, the Carabineros (national police) can still demand identification at any moment. In general, Chileans are very document oriented and your passport is essential for cashing travellers' cheques, checking into a hotel, and many other routine activities.

Motorists need an International Driving Permit to complement their national or state licences, but highway checkpoints are no longer the danger or nuisance they were under the military regime. Carabineros at checkpoints or on the highways are generally firm but polite and fair, with a much higher reputation for personal integrity than most Latin American police. *Never* attempt to bribe them.

CUSTOMS

There are no restrictions on import and export of local and foreign currency. Duty-free allowances include 400 cigarettes or 50 cigars or 500 grams of tobacco, 2½ litres of alcoholic beverages, and perfume for personal use. Though Chilean officials generally defer to foreign visitors, if you cross the border frequently and carry equipment such as cameras or a laptop computer, it is helpful to have a typed list of the items, with serial numbers, stamped by authorities.

Inspections are usually routine, although some travellers have had to undergo more thorough examinations because of recent drug smuggling from Peru and Bolivia. Travellers from the First Region of Tarapacá and the Twelfth Region of Magallanes, both of which enjoy *zona franca* (free zone) status, are subject to internal customs inspections when leaving those regions.

Officials of the SAG (Servicio Agrícola-Ganadero – Agriculture and Livestock Service) rigorously check luggage for fruit, the entry of which is strictly controlled to prevent the spread of diseases and pests which might threaten Chile's booming fruit exports. It's also illegal to transport fresh fruit from northern Chile to the central heartland; there are several checkpoints along north-south routes in the Atacama desert.

MONEY

Currency

The unit of currency is the peso (Ch$). Notes come in denominations of 500, 1000, 5000 and 10,000 pesos. Coin values are 1, 5, 10, 50 and 100 pesos, although one-peso coins are now rare. Copper-coloured coins recently replaced the lightweight aluminium coins, which are no longer legal tender. In small villages, it can be difficult to change bills larger than Ch$1000.

There is no restriction on the export or import of local currency, but demand for pesos is minimal outside Chile, except in a few border towns and capitals.

US dollars are by far the preferred foreign currency, although Argentine pesos can be readily exchanged in Santiago, at border crossings and in tourist centres such as Viña del Mar and the southern Lake District; if arriving from Argentina, it is probably better to change surplus Argentine currency directly into Chilean pesos rather than into dollars. Generally, only Santiago will have a ready market for European currencies, although the German mark may find purchasers in the Lake District.

Exchange Rates

A$1	=	Ch$258
Arg$1	=	Ch$372
Bol$1	=	Ch$94
Can$1	=	Ch$298
DM1	=	Ch$225
FFr1	=	Ch$66
It£1000	=	Ch$235
NZ$1	=	Ch$195
UK£1	=	Ch$529
US$1	=	Ch$373

These are official rates as at March 1993. Exchange rates have been fairly stable; during the period of research the 'parallel rate' for the peso actually increased from Ch$370 to Ch$350 against the US dollar. This parallel rate is that offered by *casas de cambio* (exchange houses); banks generally pay about 5% less. For the most up-to-date information, see *Estrategia* (Chile's equivalent of the *Wall Street Journal* or *Financial Times*) or the financial pages of *El Mercurio*.

Cash dollars may be exchanged at banks, cambios, hotels and some travel agencies, and often in shops or on the street. At present, cash dollars earn a slightly better rate of exchange than travellers' cheques and avoid commissions which, however, are usually less odious than in Argentina.

Travellers' cheques are unquestionably safer than cash but in a few cities, such as Calama, it can be difficult to find a bank which will change them. Consequently, you should bring at least some cash dollars. Some travellers have reported that lost Thomas Cook cheques will not be replaced unless you notify the Santiago office of the loss within 24 hours. Contact the local representative Turismo Tajamar (☎ 231-5112), Orrego Luco 23, or phone collect to the office in the USA (☎ (609) 987-7300).

If you have travellers' cheques in US dollars, it may be better to convert them to cash and then change the cash for pesos. This is more problematic than it once was, but the American Express office and a few other places in Santiago will still do it. It may be difficult to change Visa travellers' cheques.

To receive money from abroad, have your home bank send a draft. Money transferred by cable should arrive in a few days; Chilean banks will give you your money in US dollars on request. It is possible, and easier, to get a cash advance on Visa or MasterCard.

Costs

Revaluation of the Chilean peso and tourist industry inflation have increased costs considerably in the past two years, so that Chile is no longer a travel bargain. It is still possible to travel on a budget, since modest lodging, food and transport are still much cheaper than in Europe, North America, and even Argentina. Allow a minimum of US$15 per day for basic expenses, but if you purchase food at markets or eat at modest restaurants you may get by more cheaply.

Tipping

In restaurants, it is customary to tip about

10% of the bill. In general, waiters and waitresses are poorly paid, and if you can afford to eat out you can probably afford to tip. Even a small *propina* will be appreciated. Taxi drivers do not require tips, although you may round off the fare for convenience.

Bargaining

Usually only purchases from handicrafts markets will be subject to bargaining. Hotel prices are generally fixed and prominently displayed, but in the off-season or a slow summer, haggling may be possible; for long-term stays it is definitely possible. At top-end hotels, an offer to pay in US dollars may avoid IVA *(impuesto de valor agregado*, the value added tax).

On occasion, long-distance bus or *taxi colectivo* (shared taxi) fares are open to negotiation, especially those between Santiago and Mendoza, Argentina.

Credit Cards

Credit cards, particularly those which allow cash advances or travellers' cheque purchases (American Express, Visa and MasterCard), can be very useful. Fincard offices in many Chilean cities will provide cash advances against Visa or MasterCard. Usually, though, credit-card purchases and cash advances will be charged at the less advantageous bank rate of exchange, and revaluation of local currency can make your bill even higher, so be aware of fluctuations in the rate. Credit cards are, however, very useful if you must show 'sufficient funds' before entering another South American country, or in an emergency.

WHEN TO GO

For residents of the northern hemisphere, Chile offers the inviting possibility of two summers in the same year, but the country's geographical variety can make a visit rewarding in any season. Santiago and Middle Chile are best in the verdant spring or during the fall harvest, while popular natural attractions such as Parque Nacional Torres del Paine in Magallanes and the Lake District are best in summer. Conversely, Chilean ski resorts draw many foreigners during the northern summer. The Atacama desert is temperate and attractive at any time of year, although nights can be very cold at higher altitudes. In the northern altiplano, the rainy season is the summer months of December, January and February, but this usually means only a brief afternoon thunderstorm.

Easter Island is cooler, slightly cheaper and much less crowded outside the summer months of December, January and February. The same is true of the Juan Fernández Islands, which can be inaccessible if winter rains erode the dirt airstrip; March is an excellent time for a visit.

WHAT TO BRING

Chile is a mostly temperate, mid-latitude country and seasonally appropriate clothing for North America or Europe will be equally suitable here. In the desert north you will want lightweight cottons, but at the higher elevations of the Andes and in Patagonia you should carry warm clothing even in summer. From Temuco south, rain is possible at any time of the year, and a small light umbrella is useful in the city (but not in the gales of Magallanes, where heavier raingear is desirable). In winter, budget hotels in the south may not provide sufficient blankets, so a warm sleeping bag is a good idea even if you're not camping.

There is no prejudice against backpackers and, during the summer, many young Chileans visit remote parts of the country on a shoestring themselves. Outdoor equipment is generally inferior to that made in North America or Europe, so bring camping gear from home. Higher quality products will be very expensive, except at the free zones of Iquique and Punta Arenas, where the selection will not be so great as in Europe or North America.

Personal preference largely determines the best way to carry your baggage. A large zip-up bag or duffel with a wide shoulder strap is convenient for buses, trains and planes, but awkward to carry for long distances, while a backpack is most convenient if you expect to do a lot of walking. Internal frame packs, with a cover which protects the straps from getting snagged in storage on buses or planes, can be a good compromise.

Don't overlook small essentials like a Swiss Army knife, needle and cotton, a small pair of scissors, contraceptives, sunglasses, and swimming gear. Basic supplies like toothbrushes and toothpaste, shaving cream, shampoo and tampons are readily available, except in very small, remote places.

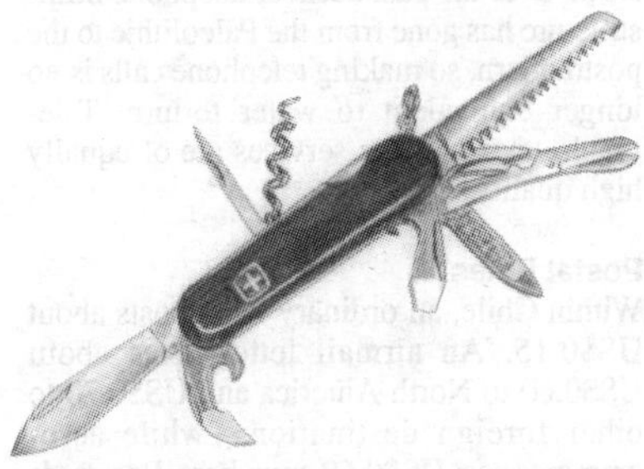

TOURIST OFFICES

Local Offices

Every regional capital and some other cities have a local representative of Sernatur, the national tourist service, while many municipalities have their own tourist office, usually on the main plaza or at the bus terminal. In lesser destinations, these offices may be open during the summer only.

Overseas Representatives

Chilean embassies and consulates in major cities usually have a tourist representative in their delegation (see above, under Visas & Embassies). Try also representatives of LAN-Chile or Ladeco, Chile's two major international airlines, for tourist information.

USEFUL ORGANISATIONS

Chile has a small network of youth hostels, which generally open in January and February only and do not usually require a membership card. For information contact the Asociación Chilena de Albergues Turísticos Juveniles (☎ 233-3220), Avenida Providencia 2594, Oficina 420, Santiago. Since hostel sites change from year to year, it is very useful to have the most current listing.

CONAF, the national forest service, administers Chile's many national parks. Its main offices (☎ 696-6749) are at Avenida Bulnes 285, Departamento 303, in Santiago, but its offices in regional capitals are also very helpful; these are listed in the appropriate city entries. Travellers with environmental interests may wish to contact CODEFF (Comité Pro Defensa de la Fauna y Flora, ☎ 377290, 277-0393), Santa Filomena 185, Santiago.

Climbers should call the Federación de Andinismo (☎ 222-0888) at Almirante Simpson 77, Santiago. Another important organisation is the Sociedad Lonko Kilápan, Balmaceda 1533, Oficina 8, in Temuco, which promotes environmentally sustainable development among Chile's native peoples. It is presently assisting the Pehuenche of Quepula-Ralco, in the upper Biobío, with respect to development issues in the face of the Chilean government's hydroelectric plans for the river basin.

Chile's automobile club, the Automóvil Club Chileno or ACCHI, has offices in most major Chilean cities, provides useful information, sells maps, and rents cars. It readily offers member services and grants discounts to members of its foreign counterparts, such as the American Automobile Association (AAA) in the USA or the Automobile Association (AA) in the UK. Its central office (☎ 212-5702) is at Avenida Vitacura 8620, Santiago, while its tourist information service (☎ 274-9078) is at Fidel Oteíza 1964. Membership costs about US$30 for three months, a potentially good investment since it includes towing and other road-side services within 25 km of an Automóvil Club office.

BUSINESS HOURS & HOLIDAYS

Traditionally, business hours in Chile commence by 8 am, but shops close at midday for three or even four hours, during which people return home for lunch and a brief siesta. After the siesta, shops reopen until 8 or 9 pm. In Santiago, government offices and many businesses have adopted a more conventional 9 am to 6 pm schedule. Banks and government offices are often open to the public only in the mornings.

There are numerous national holidays, on which government offices and businesses are closed.

1 January
: *Año Nuevo* (New Year)

March/April
: *Semana Santa* (Holy Week, the week before Easter)

1 May
: *Día del Trabajo* (Labour Day)

21 May
: *Glorias Navales* (commemorating the naval Battle of Iquique)

30 May
: *Corpus Christi*

29 June
: *Día de San Pedro y San Pablo* (St Peter & St Paul's Day)

15 August
: *Asunción de la Virgen* (Assumption)

11 September
: *Pronunciamiento Militar de 1973* (Military Coup of 1973)

18 September
: *Día de la Independencia Nacional* (National Independence Day)

19 September
: *Día del Ejército* (Armed Forces Day)

12 October
: *Día de la Raza* (Columbus Day)

1 November
: *Todo los Santos* (All Saints' Day)

8 December
: *Inmaculada Concepción* (Immaculate Conception)

25 December
: *Navidad* (Christmas Day)

CULTURAL EVENTS

Throughout the year, but especially in summer, Chileans from Arica to Punta Arenas celebrate a variety of local and national cultural festivals. Other than religious holidays such as Easter and Christmas, the most significant are the Fiestas Patrias of mid-September (see Business Hours & Holidays, above), but many localities have their own favourites. For listings, see individual city entries.

In summer, many communities throughout the country hold rodeos at which Chilean *huasos* (cowboys) show their stuff. For the latest information, contact the Federación de Rodeos (☎ 384639) in Santiago.

POST & TELECOMMUNICATIONS

Correos de Chile's postal services are reasonably dependable, but sometimes rather slow. Over the past decade, telephone infrastructure has gone from the Paleolithic to the postmodern, so making telephone calls is no longer equivalent to water torture. Telegraph, telex and fax services are of equally high quality.

Postal Rates

Within Chile, an ordinary letter costs about US$0.15. An airmail letter costs about US$0.60 to North America and US$0.70 to other foreign destinations, while aerogrammes cost US$0.60 anywhere. Postcards are slightly cheaper.

Sending Mail

Chilean post offices are open weekdays from 9 am to 6 pm and Saturdays from 9 am to noon. Send essential overseas mail *certificado* (registered) to ensure its arrival. Mail may be opened if it appears to contain money.

Sending parcels is straightforward, although a customs official may want to inspect your package before a postal clerk will accept it. Vendors in or near the post office will wrap parcels upon request.

Receiving Mail

You can receive mail via *lista de correos* or poste restante (equivalent to general delivery) at any Chilean post office. Santiago's American Express office offers mail services to its clients, while some embassies will also hold correspondence for their citizens. To collect mail from a post office (or from Amex or an embassy), you need your passport as proof of identity. Instruct your correspondents to address letters clearly and to indicate a date until which the post office should hold them; otherwise they may be returned or destroyed.

If expected correspondence does not arrive, ask the clerk to check under every possible combination of your initials, even 'M' (for Mr, Ms etc). There may be particular confusion if correspondents use your middle name, since Chileans use both paternal and maternal surnames for identification, with the former listed first. Thus a letter to 'Augusto Pinochet Ugarte' will be found under the listing for 'P' rather than 'U', while a letter to North American 'Ronald Wilson Reagan' may be found under 'W' even though 'Reagan' is the proper surname.

Telephone

ENTEL, the former state telephone monopoly, and the private Compañía de Teléfonos de Chile (CTC) offer domestic and international long-distance services throughout most of the country. ENTEL services are slightly cheaper and, in a few areas, the only alternative for international collect calls. From the Tenth Region south, Telefónica del Sur provides long-distance service.

Approximate charges for domestic calls from Santiago are: to Valparaíso, US$0.40 for the first three minutes and US$0.10 for each additional minute; to more distant places, about US$0.70 for the first three minutes. Approximate international charges are: to the USA and Canada, US$9 for the first three minutes and US$3 for each additional minute; to Europe and Australia, US$10.50 for the first three minutes and US$3.50 for each additional minute; to other Latin American countries, US$8 for the first three minutes and US$2.70 for each additional minute. There are late evening discounts, but most ENTEL and CTC offices close by 10 pm.

Local calls from public telephone boxes cost Ch$50 (about US$0.15) for five minutes, but also take Ch$100 coins. A liquid-crystal readout indicates the remaining credit on your call; when it reaches zero, insert another coin unless you plan to finish soon. Phone boxes do not provide change, but if there is at least Ch$50 credit remaining you may make another call by pressing a button rather than inserting another coin.

Long-distance domestic and international calls are possible from CTC phone boxes; some of these accept coins, but others take only *fichas* (tokens), which are usually more convenient. *Cobro revertido* (reverse charge or collect) calls overseas are simple from these phones, but credit card calls appear to be possible in theory only. There is a handful of phones with direct optic-fibre connections to operators in North America and Europe. Otherwise, dial 182 for an overseas operator.

When calling or answering the telephone, the proper salutation is *aló* or *hola* (hello). Exchange pleasantries before getting to the point of your conversation.

Fax, Telex & Telegraph

ENTEL, Telex-Chile, and VTR offer telex, telegraph and fax services.

Telexes to Australia are US$5.60 per minute; to the USA and Europe US$4.20 per minute. Telegrams to Australia are US$1.70 per word, to the USA and Europe US$0.80 per word.

ADDRESSES

In Chilean cities and towns, the names of streets, plazas and other features are often very long and elaborate, eg Calle Cardenal José Maria Caro; or Avenida Libertador

General Bernardo O'Higgins. Long names are often shortened on maps, in writing or in speech, so the first example might appear on a map as J M Caro, or just Caro. The second example might appear as Av Gral O'Higgins or Av B O'Higgins, or just O'Higgins. The word *'calle'* (street) is usually omitted on maps.

Some addresses include the expression *'local'* followed by a number, eg Calle San Cochrane 56, Local 5. 'Local' means it's one of several offices at the same street number.

Some street numbers start with a zero, eg Avenida San Martín 084. This usually happens when an old street is extended in the direction of the smaller numbers, beyond the original number 1. If, for example, the street numbers are increasing from south to north, San Martín 084 will be south of San Martín 84, which will be south of San Martín 184.

The abbreviation 's/n' following a street address stands for *sin numero* (without number), and indicates that the address does not have a street number.

TIME

For most of the year, Chile is four hours behind GMT, but from mid-December to mid-March the country observes daylight savings time (summer time); because of its great latitudinal range, this means that summer sunrise in the desert tropics of Arica, where day and night are roughly equal throughout the year, occurs after 8 am. Easter Island (Rapa Nui) is two hours behind the mainland.

ELECTRICITY

Electric current operates on 220 volts, 50 cycles. In Santiago, numerous electrical supply stores on Calle San Pablo, west of the Puente pedestrian mall, sell transformers for appliances.

LAUNDRY

In recent years, self-service laundromats have become more common in both Santiago and other cities, but it is only slightly more expensive to leave your clothes and pick them up later. Most inexpensive hotels will have a place where you can wash your own clothes and hang them to dry. In some places maid service will be reasonable, but agree on charges in advance.

WEIGHTS & MEASURES

The metric system is used throughout the country, but for weight the traditional *quintal* of 46 kilos is still common.

BOOKS

Chilean Literature & Fiction

Pablo Neruda and Gabriela Mistral, both Nobel Prize-winning poets, are major figures in Chilean, Latin American and world literature. Much of their work is available in English translation, such as Neruda's *The Heights of Macchu Picchu* (Jonathan Cape, London, 1966), *Canto General* (University of California Press, 1991), *Passions and Impressions* (Farrar, Strauss & Giroux, New York, 1983), and his rambling, selective but still readable *Memoirs* (Farrar, Strauss & Giroux, New York, 1977). For an interestingly conceived view of Neruda and his work, see Luis Poirot's *Pablo Neruda, Absence and Presence* (Norton, New York, 1990), a collection of outstanding B&W photos with accompanying text from Neruda, friends and admirers (both Chilean and foreign). Especially poignant are the photos of Neruda's houses in Santiago, Valparaíso and Isla Negra after their vandalisation by the military.

US poet Langston Hughes translated some of Gabriela Mistral's work in *Selected Poems of Gabriela Mistral* (Indiana University Press, 1957), while a different book with the same title was published by the Library of Congress and Johns Hopkins Press in 1971. For an interpretation of her work, try Margot Arce de Vásquez's *Gabriela Mistral, the Poet and Her Work* (New York University Press, 1964).

With novels in the 'magical realism' tradition of Latin American fiction, Isabel Allende (niece of the late Salvador Allende) has become a popular writer overseas as well as in Chile. Among her works are *House of the Spirits*, *Of Love and Shadows* and *Eva Luna*, all available in Bantam paperbacks.

José Donoso's novel *Curfew* (Weidenfield & Nicholson, New York, 1988), offers a portrait of life under the dictatorship through the eyes of a returned exile. Antonio Skármeta's *I Dreamt the Snow was Burning* (Reader's International, London, 1985) is a novel of the early post-coup years.

Geography

Several readable texts integrate Latin American history with geography. Try Arthur Morris's *South America* (Hodder & Stoughton, 1979), the detailed chapter on Chile in Harold Blakemore and Clifford Smith's collection *Latin America* (Methuen, 1983), and *The Cambridge Encyclopedia of Latin America* (1985), which is rather broader in conception.

History

For an account of early European exploration of Chile and other parts of South America, see J H Parry's *The Discovery of South America* (Paul Elek, London, 1979). Another good source is Edward J Goodman's *The Explorers of South America* (University of Oklahoma Press, 1992).

Although it does not focus specifically on Chile, James Lockhart and Stuart Schwartz's *Early Latin America* (Cambridge, 1983) makes an original but persuasive argument that the structures of native societies like the Mapuche were more important than Spanish domination in the cultural transitions of the colonial period. Uruguayan historian Eduardo Galeano presents a bitter indictment of European invasion and its consequences in *The Open Veins of Latin America, Five Centuries of the Pillage of a Continent* (Monthly Review Press, New York, 1973). Do not miss Alfred Crosby's fascinating account of the South American ecological transformations in comparison with other mid-latitude lands settled by Europeans in *Ecological Imperialism: the Biological Expansion of Europe, 900-1900* (Cambridge, 1986).

On the South American wars of independence, the standard work is John Lynch's *The Spanish-American Revolutions 1808-1826* (W W Norton, New York, 1973). Richard W Slatta's comparison of Argentine gauchos and Chilean huasos with stockmen of other countries in the beautifully illustrated *Cowboys of the Americas* (Yale University Press, 1990) is well worth a look.

General

One widely available book on Chile from the Spanish conquest to the late 1970s is Brian Loveman's rather glib *Chile: The Legacy of Hispanic Capitalism* (Oxford University Press, 1979) which, despite its polemical and condescending tone, is fairly accurate. Far superior, if less fashionable, is Arnold Bauer's *Chilean Rural Society from the Spanish Conquest to 1930* (Cambridge, 1975), an account of the Chilean countryside and its historical importance based on painstaking archival research. Though dated in many ways, George McCutcheon McBride's *Chile: Land and Society* (American Geographical Society, New York, 1936), is a vivid portrait of life on the latifundio, which changed little until the late 1960s.

Chile's turn-of-the-century development, based on the nitrate boom, is the subject of many books. Two of the best in English are Thomas F O'Brien's *The Nitrate Industry and Chile's Crucial Transition* (New York University Press, 1982) and Michael Monteón's *Chile in the Nitrate Era* (University of Wisconsin Press, 1982). German writer Theodor Plivier's *Revolt on the Pampas* (Michael Joseph, London, 1937) is a hard-to-find fictional account of uprisings in the nitrate enterprises.

Allende & the Unidad Popular

Publishing on the Allende years is a minor industry in its own right and, as in the 1970s, it's still hard to find a middle ground. Try *Allende's Chile* (International Publishers, New York, 1977) by Edward Boorstein, a US economist who worked for the UP government. A more recent and wide-ranging attempt to explain the UP's failure is Edy Kaufman's *Crisis in Allende's Chile: New*

Perspectives (Praeger, New York & London, 1988).

For a first-hand account of the countryside during these years, read Kyle Steenland's *Agrarian Reform under Allende: Peasant Revolt in the South* (University of New Mexico Press, Albuquerque, 1977), based on research in Cautín Province from 1972 to 1973.

For background on US involvement in the campaign against Allende, try *The United States & Chile: Imperialism & the Overthrow of the Allende Government* (Monthly Review Press, New York, 1975) by James Petras & Morris Morley. For a more thorough historical perspective, see Robert J Alexander's *The Tragedy of Chile* (Greenwood Press, Westport, Connecticut, 1978). Nathaniel Davis, former US ambassador to Chile, relates his side of the story in *The Last Two Years of Salvador Allende* (Cornell University Press, 1985).

For a more conservative view, tempered by its critical account of extremism among right-wing elements, see Alistair Horne's *A Small Earthquake in Chile* (Papermac, London, 1990; first published 1972). Sergio Bitar, a member of Allende's cabinet, provides systematic analysis of the achievements and failures of the UP in *Chile, Experiment in Democracy* (Institute for the Study of Human Issues, Philadelphia, 1986).

Joan Jara, the English wife of murdered folk singer Victor Jara, has written a personal account of life during the 1960s and 1970s in *Victor: An Unfinished Song* (Jonathan Cape, London, 1983). The death of a politically involved US citizen in the 1973 coup was the subject of Thomas Hauser's *The Execution of Charles Horman: An American Sacrifice* (Harcourt Brace Jovanovich, New York, 1978), which implicated US officials and was the basis of the film *Missing*.

The assassination of Orlando Letelier, a career diplomat and defence minister under President Allende, has been the subject of several books, including John Dinges and Saul Landau's *Assassination on Embassy Row* (Pantheon, New York, 1980), and Taylor Branch's and Eugene Popper's *Labyrinth* (Penguin, 1983).

The Military Dictatorship

Chile: The Pinochet Decade, by Phil O'Brien and Jackie Roddick (Latin America Bureau, London, 1983) covers the junta's early years, concentrating on the economic measures of the 'Chicago Boys'. From the same organisation and written by a number of contributors is *The Poverty Brokers: The IMF & Latin America*, which includes a discussion on Chile. Pinochet himself has offered the autobiographical *Camino Recorrido: Memorias de Un Soldado* in two volumes (Instituto Geográfico Militar, Santiago, 1990). As a counterpoint, consult Genaro Arriagada's *Pinochet: the Politics of Power* (Unwin Hyman, Boston, 1988), a critical account by a Christian Democratic intellectual who details the evolution of the military regime from a collegial junta to a personalistic, but institutionalised dictatorship.

A riveting account of an exile's secret return is the famous Colombian writer Gabriel García Márquez's *Clandestine in Chile* (Henry Holt, New York, 1987), the story of filmmaker Miguel Littín's secret working visit to Chile in 1985. Argentine writer Jacobo Timerman, famous for criticism of his country's military dictatorship of the late 1970s, has also written *Chile: Death in the South* (Knopf, New York, 1987).

Contemporary Chilean Politics

An outstanding and non-polemical explanation of the complexities of 20th-century Chilean politics is *The Politics of Chile: a Sociogeographical Assessment* by César Caviedes (Westview Press, Boulder, Colorado, 1979). For an account of the Pinochet years and their aftermath which eschews partisan rhetoric and focuses on the complexities of political events over the past two decades, see Pamela Constable's and Arturo Valenzuela's *A Nation of Enemies* (WW Norton, New York, 1991).

The Military, Politics & Geopolitics

One standard overview of the military in Latin America is John J Johnson's *The Military & Society in Latin America* (Stanford, 1964). For analysis of geopolitics in Chile, see Philip Kelly and Jack Child's edited volume, *Geopolitics of the Southern Cone & Antarctica* (Lynne Rienner, London, 1988). A more general account, dealing with Argentina, Brazil and Paraguay as well, is Caviedes' *The Southern Cone: Realities of the Authoritarian State* (Rowman & Allenheld, Totowa, New Jersey, 1984).

Travel Literature

Chile has inspired some excellent travel writing. Although Bruce Chatwin's *In Patagonia* (Summit Books, New York, 1977) deals more with Argentina, it is one of the most informed syntheses of life and landscape about any part of South America. His collection *What Am I Doing Here?* (Penguin, 1989) contains a beautiful essay on Chiloé Island.

Don't overlook works of greater antiquity. Charles Darwin's *Voyage of the Beagle*, available in many editions, is as fresh as yesterday. His accounts of Chiloé and other parts of the Chilean landscape are truly memorable, and a lightweight paperback copy would be a perfect companion for any trip to Chile.

Easter Island (Rapa Nui)

There is a voluminous literature on Rapa Nui, spanning the 250 years since Europeans first landed on the island. See the Easter Island chapter for more details.

Travel Guides

Other guidebooks can supplement or complement this one, especially if you are visiting countries other than Chile. As well as this book, Lonely Planet's *Travel Survival Kit* series includes books on Argentina, Uruguay & Paraguay, Bolivia, Peru, Ecuador & the Galápagos Islands, Colombia, and Brazil. If you're interested in trekking in the region, LP's *Trekking in Patagonia* has detailed descriptions and maps of some 28 walks in the Andes, mostly in national parks and reserves in Chile, but some across the border into Argentina. LP's *Latin American Spanish Phrasebook* would be useful for those without a good grasp of the language, while budget travellers covering a large part of the continent should look for Lonely Planet's *South America on a shoestring*.

Hilary Bradt's and John Pilkington's *Backpacking in Chile and Argentina* (Bradt Enterprises, 1980) has information about hiking and camping in the Southern Cone countries.

Since the 1920s *The South American Handbook* (Trade & Travel Publications, Bath), now edited by Ben Box, has been the standard guide to the continent. Its encyclopedic comprehensiveness and observant humour make it great armchair reading even though you can never visit every obscure destination it details. It appeals to travellers of every kind, but unfortunately and unavoidably, the area covered is so large that many sections are quickly outdated. Though it is produced in annual editions, it retains some phrases that were written more than half a century ago.

Illustrated with exceptional photographs, the *APA Insight Guides* volume on Chile is excellent, if selective, in cultural and historical analysis, but weak on the nuts-and-bolts of everyday travel. Typographical errors are maddeningly common.

For Chile's national parks, do not miss William Leitch's beautifully written but also selective *South America's National Parks* (The Mountaineers, Seattle, 1990), which is superb on environment and natural history but much weaker on practical aspects of South American travel. Rae Natalie Prosser de Goodall's bilingual guidebook *Tierra del Fuego*, published in Argentina, was due for a new edition in late 1991.

One of the most useful sources of information is the *Turistel* guide series, published by the Compañía de Teléfonos de Chile, annually updated, reasonably priced, and now available in English translation. The Spanish version has separate volumes on the north, centre and south of the country, plus an additional one on camping and campgrounds which has more detailed maps of some important areas. The English version combines all three main guides in a single volume.

Although oriented toward motorists, Turistel guides provide excellent maps (beautifully drawn, despite frequent minor errors) and thorough background information. However, they are selective, rarely covering budget accommodation and not, for instance, identifying offices of ENTEL, whose long-distance rates are cheaper than CTC's. Their biggest drawback, though, is the flimsy paper binding which makes them unusable after one season – handle with care.

Bookshops

Chile is not a major Latin American publishing centre, but Santiago does have a number of bookshops which can reward motivated browsers or explorers. For details, see the chapter on Santiago.

MAPS

Besides the Turistel series (see above), two good maps of Chile are available at kiosks and street vendors in the main towns and cities: the *Gran Mapa Caminero de Chile* published by Informaciones Unidas Para América Latina, and the *Atlas Caminero de Chile* published by Silva & Silva Ltda. Still, the Turistel guides are a better bargain, containing superb maps of Chilean cities and towns. Esso's inexpensive *Planos* has detailed, indexed street maps of Santiago, Antofagasta, Valparaíso, Viña del Mar, Concepción and Talcahuano; it's available at most Esso stations.

For more detailed maps, visit the retail outlets of the Instituto Geográfico Militar at Alameda 240 (near the Holiday Inn Crowne Plaza) or at Dieciocho 369 in Santiago. Its *Plano Guía del Gran Santiago* (1989) is the local equivalent of *London A-Z*, while its *Guía Caminera* (1991) is an up-to-date highway map. Their 1:50,000 topographic series is valuable for trekkers, although maps of some sensitive border areas (where most of the national parks are) may not be available. Individual maps cost about US$8 each in Santiago. Traucomontt Tours, Egaña 82 in Puerto Montt, carries a good selection of IGM maps, including the detailed map of the Camino Austral.

You may find some of these maps at specialist bookshops like Stanford's in London, or in the map rooms of major university libraries. In most major cities, the Automóvil Club de Chile (ACCHI) has an office which sells maps, although not all of them are equally well stocked. If you belong to an auto club at home, ask for a discount.

For members of the American Automobile Association (AAA) and its affiliates, there is a South American road map which is adequate for initial planning.

Australian cartographer Kevin Healey's vivid two-sheet *Contemporary Reference Map of South America* (1:5,000,000) is packed with information but not really suitable for a trip. Even more detailed are his 1:4,000,000 maps which cover the continent in three sheets. His latest is an excellent 1:30,000 map of Easter Island. All these maps are distributed in North America by ITM, Box 2290, Vancouver, BC V6B 3W5, Canada, and in the UK by Bradt Publications, 41 Nortoft Road, Chalfont St Peter, Bucks SL90LA.

MEDIA

Chile is a very literate country, but the press is still recovering from the repression of the Pinochet years and quality journalism is very limited. In recent years, the end of government monopoly in the electronic media has opened up the airwaves to a greater variety of programming than in the past. Chilean cinema is experiencing a minor renaissance.

Newspapers & Magazines

El Mercurio, Santiago's oldest and most prestigious daily, tends to follow a very conservative editorial policy. *La Epoca*, born during the 'No' campaign against Pinochet's continuance in office, is a serious Christian Democratic tabloid which is probably the most complete alternative source of news, while *La Nación* is the official government daily. There are many sleazy tabloids, such as *La Segunda* and *Ultimas Noticias*, which sensationalise crime and radical political dissent (which they seem to consider synonymous).

Estrategia is the daily voice of Chile's financial community and the best source to consult for trends in the exchange rate. Since late 1991, the *News Review* has appeared as a weekly newspaper for the English-speaking population of Chile. Its German language equivalent is *El Cóndor*, now in its 56th year.

Radio & TV

Broadcasting is far less regulated than before and there are many stations on both AM and FM bands. TV stations include the government-owned Televisión Nacional (TVN) and the Universidad Católica's Channel 13, plus several private stations. International cable service is widely available, and common in many top-end hotels.

Cinema

Despite the limited funds for directors, Chilean cinema has achieved some international reputation, both before and after the military dictatorship. Alejandro Jodorowsky's *El Topo* (The Mole) is a 1960s cult classic, while Miguel Littín's *Alsino & the Condor* was nominated for an Academy Award as Best Foreign Film in 1983.

There are also a number of foreign films about Chile. The documentary *Chile: Hasta Cuándo?*, by Australian film-maker David Bradbury, is an indictment of the military regime's brutality. Costa-Gavras' 1982 film *Missing*, available on video, is based on Thomas Hauser's book *The Execution of Charles Horman: An American Sacrifice*.

FILM & PHOTOGRAPHY

The latest in consumer electronics is available in Chile at much lower prices than in neighbouring countries, especially at the free zones in Iquique (First Region) and Punta Arenas (Twelfth Region), which are good places to replace a lost or stolen camera. Colour slide film can also be purchased cheaply at Iquique or Punta Arenas, but everything is rather more expensive in the rest of the country. Developing colour prints is fairly inexpensive, but slides are much more costly, especially with frames.

HEALTH

In general, Chile presents few serious health hazards, though there were localised outbreaks of cholera after the major 1991 epidemic in Peru. The Ministry of Health prohibited restaurants from serving *raw* vegetables that grow in the ground (such as lettuce, cabbage, celery, cauliflower, beets and carrots) and raw seafood in the form of *ceviche*, which is also suspect (ceviche must now be made with seafood which is cooked and then cooled). Santiago's drinking water is adequately treated and the author has drunk tap water in most other parts of the country without problems, but if you have any doubts, stay with bottled mineral waters.

Residents of the USA can call the Center for Disease Control's International Traveler's Hotline (☎ (404) 332-4559) where, by punching in the country's phone code ('56' for Chile), you can get recorded information on vaccinations, food and water, and current health problems. For latest details on the cholera situation, contact your country's consulate in Santiago upon arrival.

If you wear glasses, bring an extra pair and your prescription. Losing your glasses can be a real nuisance, although in many places you can get new spectacles made up quickly, cheaply and competently.

If you require a particular medication, take an adequate supply and a copy of the prescription, with the generic rather than the brand name.

Ordinary toilet paper does not readily disintegrate in Chilean sewers, so most bathrooms have a basket where you discard what you have used. Cheaper accommodation and public toilets rarely provide toilet paper, so carry your own wherever you go.

Health Care Books

For basic health information when travelling, a good source is Dr Richard Dawood's *Travellers' Health: How to Stay Healthy Abroad* (Oxford, 1989). Bradt & Pilkington's *Backpacking in Chile and Argentina* (Bradt Enterprises, 1980) has a good section on hazards of hiking and camping in the region. Other possibilities include *The Traveller's Health Guide* by Dr Anthony Turner (Roger Lascelles, London, 1979), *Staying Healthy in Asia, Africa & Latin America* (Moon Publications, Chico, California, USA) and *Where There is No Doctor* by David Werner (Hesperian Foundation).

For children's health problems, see Maureen Wheeler's *Travel with Children*, published by Lonely Planet.

Predeparture Preparations

Vaccinations Chile requires no vaccinations for entry from any country, but visitors to nearby tropical countries should consider prophylaxis against typhoid, malaria and other diseases. Typhoid, polio, tetanus, and hepatitis immunisation are recommended. All vaccinations should be recorded on an International Health Certificate, which is available from your physician or health department.

Typhoid protection lasts three years and is useful if you travel in rural areas. You may get side effects such as pain at the point of injection site, fever, headache and general discomfort.

A complete series of oral polio vaccines is essential if you haven't had them before. Tetanus and diphtheria boosters are necessary every 10 years, and highly recommended.

Gamma globulin injections provide some protection against infectious hepatitis. Gamma globulin is not a vaccine but a ready-made antibody.

Malaria does not exist in Chile, but if you are coming from a malarial zone, you should continue to take anti-malarial drugs for a further six weeks.

Health Insurance Relatively small costs can pay great benefits if you get sick. Look for a policy which will pay your return costs and reimburse you for lost air tickets and other fixed expenses; such policies often cover losses from theft as well. The international travel policies handled by STA or other budget travel organisations are usually good value.

Medical Kit All standard medications are available in well stocked pharmacies. Many common prescription drugs can be purchased legally over-the-counter in Chile. Possible medical supplies include:

1. Aspirin or Panadol – for pain or fever.
2. Antihistamine (such as Benadryl) – useful as a decongestant for colds, allergies, to ease the itch from insect bites or stings or to help prevent motion sickness.
3. Antibiotics – useful if you're travelling well off the beaten track, but they must be prescribed and you should carry the prescription with you.
4. Kaolin preparation (Pepto-Bismol), Imodium or Lomotil – for stomach upsets.
5. Rehydration mixture – for treatment of severe diarrhoea; this is particularly important if travelling with children.
6. Antiseptic, mercurochrome and antibiotic powder or similar 'dry' spray – for cuts and grazes.
7. Calamine lotion – to ease irritation from bites or stings.
8. Bandages and band-aids – for minor injuries.
9. Scissors, tweezers and a thermometer – mercury thermometers are prohibited by airlines.
10. Insect repellent, sunblock, suntan lotion, chapstick and water purification tablets.

Food & Water

Most North Americans, Europeans and Australians will find Chilean food is generally easy on the stomach, but the great variety of shellfish may take some adaptation. Because of the cholera scare, raw shellfish, salad greens and other fresh unpeeled vegetables are not safe to eat. The water supply of Santiago and most other cities is safe, with little danger of dysentery or similar ailments, but take precautions in rural areas, where latrines may be close to wells and untreated water may be taken from rivers or irrigation ditches. Water in the Atacama desert and its cities has a strong mineral content. Easter Island's water has a similar reputation, but the author found it both safe and tasty.

Geographical & Climatic Considerations

Altitude Sickness From the passes between Chile and the Argentine city of Mendoza, northwards to the Bolivian border, altitude sickness *(apunamiento* or *soroche)* represents a potential health hazard. In the thinner atmosphere above 3000 metres or even lower in some cases, lack of oxygen causes many individuals to suffer headaches, nausea, shortness of breath, physical weakness and other symptoms which can lead to very serious consequences, especially if combined with heat exhaustion, sunburn or hypothermia. Most people recover within a few hours or days as their body produces more red blood cells to absorb oxygen, but if the symptoms persist it is imperative to descend to lower elevations. For mild cases, everyday painkillers such as aspirin or *chachacoma*, a tea made from the leaves of a common Andean shrub, will relieve symptoms until your body adapts. In the northern Chilean Andes, coca leaves are a common remedy, but authorities frown upon their usage even by native peoples, who consume them surreptitiously. Avoid smoking, drinking alcohol, eating heavily or exercising strenuously.

Heat Exhaustion & Sunburn Although Chile is mostly a temperate country, its northern zones lie within the Tropic of Capricorn and the sun's nearly direct rays can be devastating, especially at high altitude. In the desert, summer temperatures are usually not oppressive, but dehydration can still be a very serious problem. Drink plenty of liquids and keep your body well covered with light cotton clothing. Wear a hat which shades your head and neck. Damage to the ozone layer has increased the level of ultraviolet radiation in southern South America, so protection from the sun is especially important – use an effective sun screen on exposed parts of your body and good quality sunglasses. Sweating can also lead to a loss of salt, so adding some salt to your food can be a good idea. Salt tablets should only be taken to treat heat exhaustion caused by salt deficiency.

Hypothermia Hypothermia occurs when the body loses heat faster than it can produce it and the core temperature of the body falls. At high altitudes and in Patagonia, changeable weather can leave you vulnerable to exposure: after dark, temperatures can drop from balmy to below freezing, while a sudden soaking and high winds can lower your body temperature so rapidly that you may not survive. Disorientation, dizziness, slurred speech, stumbling, shivering, numb skin and physical exhaustion are all symptoms of hypothermia, and indications that you should seek warmth, shelter and food. Avoid travelling alone; partners are less likely to fall victim to hypothermia.

You should always be prepared for cold, wet or windy conditions, even if you're just out walking or hitching. Wear woollen clothing, or synthetics which retain warmth when wet. Carry high-energy, easily digestible snacks such as chocolate or dried fruit, both of which are readily available in Chile. If bad weather is approaching, seek shelter before you are caught out.

Diarrhoea & Dysentery

Although public health standards are reasonably high in Chile, stomach problems can arise from dietary changes – they don't necessarily mean you've caught something. Introduce yourself gradually to exotic and/or highly spiced foods.

Avoid rushing to the pharmacy and gulping antibiotics at the first signs. The best thing to do is to rest, avoid eating solids, and drink plenty of liquids (tea or herbal solutions, without sugar or milk). Many cafés in Chile serve excellent camomile tea *(agua de manzanilla)*; otherwise, try mineral water *(agua mineral)*. As you recover, keep to simple foods like yoghurt, lemon juice and boiled vegetables.

Ordinary 'traveller's diarrhoea' rarely lasts more than a few days, so if it lasts more than a week you must get treatment, move on to antibiotics, or see a doctor. Lomotil or Imodium can relieve the symptoms, but not actually cure the cause of the problem. For children, Imodium is preferable, but do not use such drugs if you have a high fever or are severely dehydrated.

After a severe bout of diarrhoea or dysentery, you will probably be dehydrated, with painful cramps. Relieve these with fruit juices or tea, with a tiny bit of dissolved salt. Antibiotics can help treat severe diarrhoea, especially if accompanied by nausea, vomiting, stomach cramps or mild fever.

Sexually Transmitted Diseases

Sexual contact with an infected partner spreads these diseases and, while abstinence is the only certain preventative, condoms are also effective. Gonorrhoea and syphilis are the most common of these diseases; sores, blisters or rashes around the genitals, and discharge or pain when urinating are common symptoms. Symptoms may be less obvious or even absent in women. The symptoms of syphilis eventually disappear completely, but the disease can cause severe problems in later years. Both gonorrhoea and syphilis can be treated effectively with antibiotics. There is no cure for herpes.

AIDS is far more serious, and is most commonly transmitted by unsafe sexual activity. Avoiding unsafe sexual practices and using condoms and are the most effective preventatives. Currently, the port city of Valparaíso has the highest rate of AIDS infection in Chile.

AIDS can also be spread by intravenous drug abuse, through infected blood transfusions or by using dirty needles – vaccinations, acupuncture and tattooing are potentially as dangerous as intravenous drug use if the equipment is not clean. If you need an injection or a blood test (obligatory if you are involved in an auto accident), purchase a new syringe from a pharmacy and ask the doctor or nurse to use it.

Women's Health

Gynaecological Problems Poor diet, lowered resistance due to the use of antibiotics for stomach upsets and even contraceptive pills can lead to vaginal infections when travelling in hot climates. Keeping the genital area clean, wearing cotton underwear and skirts or loose-fitting trousers will help prevent infections.

Yeast infections, characterised by rash, itch and discharge can be treated with a vinegar or even lemon juice douche or with yoghurt. Nystatin suppositories are the usual medical prescription. Trichomonas is a more serious infection with a discharge and a burning sensation when urinating. Male sexual partners must also be treated; if a vinegar-water douche is not effective, seek medical attention. Flagyl is the prescribed drug.

Pregnancy Most miscarriages occur during the first three months of pregnancy, so this is the riskiest time to travel. The last three months should also be spent within reasonable distance of good medical care. Pregnant women should avoid all unnecessary medication, but vaccinations and malarial prophylactics should still be taken where possible. Take additional care to prevent illness and pay particular attention to diet and nutrition.

WOMEN TRAVELLERS

For women travelling alone, Chile is probably safer than most other Latin American countries, although you should not be complacent. Unwelcome physical contact, particularly on crowded buses or trains, is not unusual, but if you're physically confident, a slap or a well aimed elbow should discourage any further incident. If not, try a scream – also very effective.

Other nuisances include vulgar language, generally in the presence of other males, which usually emphasises feminine physical attributes. If you respond aggressively ('Are you talking to me?'), you will probably put your aggressor to shame.

Single women checking in at low-budget hotels, both in Santiago and elsewhere, may find themselves objects of curiosity or suspicion, since prostitutes often frequent such places. If you otherwise like the place, ignore this and it should disappear. Outside the larger cities, women travelling alone are objects of curiosity, since Chilean women generally do not travel alone. You should interpret questions as to whether you are running away from parents or husband as expressions of concern.

If you hitchhike, exercise caution and avoid getting into a vehicle with more than one man. Chilean men are very *machista* (chauvinist), but rarely violent in public behaviour towards women.

DANGERS & ANNOYANCES

Chile is much less hazardous than most other Latin American countries, but certain precautions will reduce risks and make your trip more enjoyable.

Personal Security & Theft

Although street crime appears to be increasing, personal security problems are minor compared with many other South American countries. Truly violent crime is rare in Santiago; both men or women can travel in most parts of the city at any time of day or night without excessive apprehension. The port city of Valparaíso has an unfortunate reputation for robberies in some of its southern neighbourhoods. Summer is the crime season in beach resorts like Viña del Mar, Reñaca and La Serena, though these are by no means violent places – be alert for pickpockets and avoid leaving valuables on the beach while you go for a swim.

Take precautions against petty theft, such as purse snatching. Be especially wary of calculated distractions, such as someone tapping you on the shoulder or spilling something on you, since these 'accidents' are often part of a team effort to relieve you of backpack or other valuables. Grip your bag or purse firmly, carry your wallet in a front pocket, and avoid conspicuous displays of expensive jewellery. Valuables such as passports and air tickets can be conveniently carried in a light jacket or vest with one or two zip-up or button-up pockets. Money belts and neck pouches are common alternatives, though some travellers find them uncomfortable; an elastic leg pouch may be less cumbersome.

Baggage insurance is a good idea. Do not leave valuables such as cash or cameras in your hotel room. Many budget hotels have only token locks or none at all, although they usually have secure left luggage areas.

Despite the return to democratic government, armed opposition groups such as MIR and the Frente Patriótico Manuel Rodríguez continue to operate in Santiago and, to a much lesser degree, in the provinces. It is not unknown for them to commandeer taxis or private vehicles and for the police to follow in pursuit, but the chances of being caught in the crossfire are very small.

Unauthorised political demonstrations still take place and can be very contentious; the police will sometimes use tear gas or truck-mounted water cannon – known as *guanacos* after the spitting wild New World camels – to break them up. US institutions, such as banks and churches, are often the targets of protest. All travellers, but Mormons in particular, should be aware that 53 Mormon chapels in Chile were bombed in 1990, usually when unoccupied.

The Police & Military

Chilean police, much less known for corruption than their counterparts in other South American countries, behave professionally and politely in ordinary circumstances. They can demand identification at any time, so you should carry your passport. The military take themselves very seriously, even under civilian government, so avoid photographing military installations. In the event of a military coup or other emergency, state-of-siege regulations may suspend all civil rights, so make sure someone knows your whereabouts, and contact your embassy or consulate for advice.

Natural Hazards

The Pacific coast of South America is part of the 'ring of fire' which stretches from Asia to Alaska to Tierra del Fuego. Volcanic eruptions are not unusual; in 1991, for example, the explosion of Volcán Hudson in the Aisén Region buried Chile Chico and Los Antíguos (Argentina) knee-deep in ash. Earthquakes are common.

Volcanic activity is unlikely to pose any immediate threat to travellers, since volcanos usually give some notice before a big eruption. A few popular resorts are especially vulnerable, particularly the town of Pucón at the base of Volcán Villarrica.

Earthquakes are another matter, since they can be very serious and occur without warning. Construction often does not meet seismic safety standards – adobe buildings are especially vulnerable. Travellers in budget accommodation should make contingency plans for safety, including evacuation, before going to sleep at night.

Recreational Hazards

Many of Chile's finest beach areas have dangerous offshore rip currents, so ask before entering the water and be sure someone on shore knows your whereabouts.

In wilderness areas such as Parque Nacional Torres del Paine, accidents have become common enough that authorities no longer permit solo trekking.

WORK

It is not unusual for visiting travellers to work as English-language instructors in Santiago, but wages are much lower than they would be in the USA or Europe, and full-time employment is hard to come by. It is fairly easy to obtain residence and work permits but many do not bother to do so. The most reputable employers will insist on the proper visa. If you need one, go to the Departamento de Extranjería (☎ 672-5320), Moneda 1342, Santiago. Business hours are from 9 am to 1.30 pm.

ACTIVITIES

Chileans are very fond of a variety of sports, both as participants and spectators, but the most popular is soccer. In the callampas, children will clear a vacant lot, mark the goal with stones, and make a ball of old rags and socks to pursue their pastime. Even in exclusive country clubs the sport is popular.

In the summer, the beach is the most popular vacation spot. Paddle-ball, a game like tennis, has gained major popularity – courts have sprung up around the country, and many people play on the beach.

Other popular sports include tennis, basketball, volleyball and cycling. Other outdoor activities such as canoeing, climbing, kayaking, trekking, windsurfing and hang-gliding are gaining popularity. Rivers like the Maipo, Claro and Biobío are increasingly popular for whitewater rafting, although hydroelectric development seriously threatens the Biobío.

Skiing, although expensive, can be world-class. Skiers may wish to consult Chris Lizza's *South America Ski Guide* (1992), published by Bradt Publications in the UK and by Hunter Publications in the USA.

HIGHLIGHTS

For most visitors, Chile's principal attraction will be natural attractions like the soaring volcanos of the Andes and the Lake District, the wild alpine scenery of Parque Nacional Torres del Paine and Laguna San Rafael, and the stark deserts of the Norte Grande, with their unique wildlife and the Tatio geysers. Chile's extensive coastline offers both spectacular scenery and conventional tourist activities.

There are many appealing cultural features: the Indian peoples, archaeological remains, and colonial Andean churches of the Norte Grande; the enigmatic monuments of Easter Island; the vineyards of Middle Chile and the urban delights of Santiago; and the striking vernacular architecture of the island of Chiloé.

ACCOMMODATION

The spectrum of accommodation in Chile ranges from youth hostels and campgrounds to five-star luxury hotels. Where you stay will depend on your budget and your standards, where you are, and how hard you look, but you should be able to find something reasonable. You may also find yourself invited into Chilean homes, and generally you should not hesitate to accept. The remainder of this section details alternatives from cheapest to dearest.

Youth Hostels

Chilean youth hostels *(albergues juveniles)* cater mainly to school children and students on holiday, and occupy temporary sites at sports stadiums, campgrounds, schools or churches. Usually open in January and February only, they charge only a couple of dollars per night for a dormitory bed, making them just about the cheapest accommodation in Chile. A few insist on a youth hostel card. For up-to-date information, contact the Asociación Chilena de Albergues Turísticos Juveniles, Avenida Providencia 2594, Oficina 420, Santiago (☎ 233-3220). Since hostel sites often change from year to year, it is very useful to have the most current listing. A hostel card, valid worldwide, costs about US$15.

Camping & Refugios

Sernatur's Santiago headquarters has a free pamphlet called *Camping* which lists campgrounds throughout Chile and gives details of their facilities. The sites are usually in wooded areas and have excellent facilities – hot showers, toilets and laundry, firepits for cooking, restaurants or snack bars, grocery stores. Some even have swimming pools or lake access. The Compañía de Teléfonos de Chile publishes an annually updated Turistel camping guide with very detailed information and excellent maps – for some tourist areas, the maps are better than those in the regular Turistel guide. For an excellent practical guide to visiting and camping in Chilean parks, obtain the paperback guidebook *Juventud, Turismo y Naturaleza* from Sernatur or CONAF.

Chilean campgrounds are not the bargain they once were, since most sites charge a five-person minimum; this means that for singles or couples they can be more expensive than basic *hospedajes* or *residenciales* (see below). This is true both at private campgrounds, and in national parks where concessionaires control the franchise. In some remote parts of Chile there is free camping, but drinkable water and sanitary facilities are often lacking.

For comfort, invest in a good, dome-style tent with rainfly before coming to South America, where camping equipment will be costly and inferior. A three-season sleeping bag should be adequate for almost any weather conditions you are likely to encounter. A campstove which can burn a variety of fuels is a good idea, since white gas *(bencina blanca)* is expensive and available only at chemical supply shops or hardware stores. Firewood is a limited and often expensive resource which, in any event, smudges your pots and pans. Bring or buy mosquito repellent, since many campsites are near rivers or lakes.

There are also *refugios*, which are rustic – sometimes *very* rustic – shelters for hikers and trekkers in the national parks. Some of them are free.

Casas de Familia

In summer, especially in the Lake District, families often rent rooms to visitors. A *casa de familia* can be an excellent bargain, with access to cooking and laundry facilities, hot showers, and Chilean hospitality. Tourist offices often maintain lists of such accommodation.

Hospedajes, Pensiones & Residenciales

These offer the cheapest accommodation but the differences among them are sometimes ill-defined – all may be called hotels. An *hospedaje* is usually a large family home which has a few extra bedrooms for guests (the bath is shared). Some are not permanent businesses but temporary expedients in times of economic distress.

Similarly, a *pensión* offers short-term accommodation in a family home, but may also have permanent lodgers. Meals are sometimes available. *Residenciales*, which are permanent businesses but sometimes only seasonal, more commonly figure in tourist office lists. In general, they occupy buildings designed for short-stay accommodation, although some cater to clients who intend only *very* short stays – say two hours or so. Prostitutes occasionally frequent them, but so do young couples with no other indoor alternative for their passion. Except for a little noise, such activities should not deter you, even if you have children. Room and furnishings are modest, usually including beds with clean sheets and blankets. A few have private baths, but more commonly you will share toilet and shower facilities with other guests. Never hesitate to ask to see a room.

Hotels
Hotels vary from one-star austerity to five-star luxury, but correlation between these categories and their standards is less than perfect – many one-star places are better value than three and four-star hotels. In general, hotels will provide a room with attached private bath, often a telephone, and sometimes *música funcional* (elevator Muzak) or a TV. Normally they will have a restaurant; breakfast may be included in the price. In the top categories you will have room service and laundry service, swimming pools, bars, shopping galleries and other luxuries; these are most common in the major cities and resorts.

Rentals
If you're staying in a place for an extended period, house and apartment rentals can save money. In Santiago, check listings in Sunday's *El Mercurio*. In resorts like Viña del Mar, La Serena, or Villarrica, you can lodge several people for the price of one by renting an apartment and cooking your own meals. In towns like Valdivia and La Serena, people line the highway approaches in summer to offer houses and apartments. You can also check the tourist office or local papers.

FOOD
From the tropics to the pole, Chile's varied cuisine features seafood, beef, fresh fruit and vegetables. The waters of the Pacific Ocean's cool Humboldt Current are a cornucopia of fish and shellfish for Chilean kitchens, while the fields, orchards and pastures of Middle Chile fill the table with excellent produce.

Places to Eat
Chilean restaurants range from hole-in-the-wall snack bars to sumptuous international venues. Most Chilean cities feature a central market with many small, cheap restaurants of surprisingly high quality.

There are several categories of eating establishments. Bars serve snacks and both alcoholic and non-alcoholic drinks, while *fuentes de soda* are similar but do serve alcohol. Snack bars sell fast food. *Cafeterías* serve modest meals; *hosterías* are more elaborate and usually located outside the main cities. A *salón de té* is not quite literally a teahouse, but a bit more upscale than a cafetería. Fully fledged *restaurantes* are distinguished by quality and service. Distinctions are less than exact, and the term 'restaurante' can be applied to every category of establishment. Almost all serve alcoholic and non-alcoholic drinks.

Except in strictly family establishments it is customary – and expected – to leave a 10% tip. The menu is *la carta*; the bill is *la cuenta*.

Breakfast
Breakfast *(desayuno)* usually comprises toast *(pan tostado)* with butter *(mantequilla)* or jam *(mermelada)* and tea *(té)*; eggs or sandwiches are also common. *Huevos fritos* are fried eggs, usually served in a *paila* (small frying pan). *Huevos revueltos* are scrambled, *huevos pasados* are boiled, and *huevos a la copa* are poached. *Bien cocidos* means well cooked and *duros* are hard-boiled.

Snacks
One of the world's finest snacks is the *empanada*, a tasty turnover with vegetables, hard-boiled egg, olive, beef, chicken, ham and cheese or other filling. These are cheap and available almost everywhere – travellers coming from Argentina will find the Chilean empanada much larger than its Argentine

counterpart, so don't order a dozen for lunch or your bus trip. Empanadas *al horno* (baked) are lighter than empanadas *fritas* (fried).

Humitas are corn tamales, frequently wrapped in corn husks and steamed; when served in this manner they are *humitas en chala* – a very popular and tasty snack. There are numerous breads, including *chapalele*, made with potatoes and flour and boiled; *milcao*, another type of potato bread; and *sopaipa*, recognisable by its dark brown exterior, which is made from wheat flour and fruit, but not baked.

Sandwiches are popular snacks throughout the day. Among sandwich fillings, *churrasco* (steak), *jamón* (ham) and *queso* (cheese) are most widely available. Cold ham and cheese make an *aliado*, while a sandwich with ham and melted cheese constitutes a *Barros Jarpa*, after a Chilean painter known for consuming them in large quantities. A steak sandwich with melted cheese is a *Barros Luco*, the favourite of former President Ramón Barros Luco (1910-1915). Beefsteak with tomato and other vegetables is a *chacarero*.

Chile's cheapest fast food is a *completo*, a hot dog with absolutely everything.

Lunch & Dinner

Many places offer a cheap set meal *(comida corrida* or *almuerzo del día)* for lunch *(almuerzo* or *colación)* and, less often, for dinner *(cena)*. Some of the most common dishes are listed below, but there are many other possibilities. Do not hesitate to ask waiters for an explanation of any dish.

Lunch can be the biggest meal of the day. Set menus tend to be almost identical at cheaper restaurants, generally consisting of *cazuela*, a stew of potato or maize with a piece of beef or chicken, a main course of rice with chicken or meat, and a simple dessert. Soup is *caldo* or *sopa*. *Porotos* (beans) are a common budget entree. One of Chile's most delicious and filling traditional dishes is *pastel de choclo*, a maize casserole filled with vegetables, chicken and beef.

The biggest standard meal in Chile is *lomo a lo pobre*, an enormous slab of beef topped with two fried eggs and buried in chips. This is not a low-cal snack, and you may wish to monitor your cholesterol level before and after eating.

Beef, in a variety of cuts and styles of preparation, is the most popular main course at *parrillas* – restaurants which grill everything from steak to sausages over charcoal. The *parrillada* proper is an assortment of steak and other cuts which will appall vegetarians and heart specialists. A traditional parrillada will include offal such as *chunchules* (small intestines), *tripa gorda* (large intestine), *ubre* (udder), *riñones* (kidneys), and *morcilla* (blood sausage). Salad *(ensalada)* will usually accompany the meal.

Many restaurants of all kinds offer *pollo con papas fritas* (chicken with chips), and *pollo con arroz* (chicken with rice).

Seafood

Chilean seafood, with its extraordinary variety, is among the world's best. One of the finest dishes is *curanto*, a hearty stew of fish, shellfish, chicken, pork, lamb, beef and potato. A speciality of Chiloé and southern Chile, curanto is eaten with chapalele or milcao bread.

Popular seafood soups are the delicious *sopa de mariscos*, or *cazuela de mariscos*, which is more of a stew. Fish soup is *sopa de pescado*. Try *chupe de cóngrio* (conger eel stew) or, if available, *chupe de locos* (abalone stew), both cooked in a thick sauce of butter, bread crumbs, cheese and spices. Locos may be in *veda* (quarantine) because of over-exploitation. *Paila marina* is a fish chowder.

Do not miss the market restaurants in cities like Iquique, Concepción, Temuco and Puerto Montt. Some dishes, like sea urchins, are acquired tastes, but they will rarely upset your stomach. Do insist on all shellfish being thoroughly cooked, which is obligatory since the cholera scare of 1991-92; even the traditional *ceviche* (marinated raw fish or shellfish) must now be cooked, although it is still served cold.

A few seafood terms worth knowing are:

fish	*pescado*
shrimp	*camarones*
prawns	*camarones grandes*
cra	*cangrejo* or *jaiva*
king crab	*centolla*
mussels	*cholgas*
oysters	*ostras*
scallops	*ostiones*
shellfish	*mariscos*
clams	*almejas*
sea urchins	*erizos*
squid	*calamares*
octopus	*pulpo*

Desserts

Dessert *(postre)* is commonly fresh fruit or *helado* (ice cream). The latter has improved greatly over the past several years, at least at those ice creameries featuring *elaboración artesanal* (family rather than factory production). Also try *arroz con leche* (rice pudding), *flan* (egg custard), and *tortas* (cakes). In the Lake District, Chileans of German descent bake exquisite *kuchen* (pastries) filled with local fruit – raspberries are a regional speciality.

Ethnic Food

Santiago has a large selection of 'ethnic' restaurants, with eight pages of restaurants and bars in the Santiago yellow pages. French, Italian, Spanish, German and Chinese are the most common, but Brazilian, Arab, Mexican and other national cuisines are also available. Another good place to look for restaurants is the Santiago entry in the Turistel Centro guide book.

In the coastal cities of northern Chile, such as Arica and Iquique, there are many Chinese restaurants. These *chifas* are generally cheap, good value, and a pleasant change.

Vegetarian Dishes

While most Chileans are carnivores, vegetarianism is no longer the mark of an eccentric. Santiago has some excellent vegetarian fare but, other than in strictly vegetarian restaurants, you may have to make a special request. If presented with meat that you don't want, it may help to claim allergy *(alergia)*.

Every town has a market with a wide variety of fruit and vegetables – produce from the Chilean heartland reaches the limits of the republic and overseas. Remember that agricultural regulations forbid carrying fruit from the Norte Grande to Middle Chile, or to import it from foreign countries.

Fast Food

Santiago's fast-food restaurants are mostly inferior clones of Kentucky Fried Chicken or McDonalds. Except at the best Italian restaurants, pizzas are generally small, greasy and inferior. The Dino's chain in the Lake District offers passable standard dishes.

DRINKS

Non-Alcoholic Drinks

Soft Drinks Chileans guzzle prodigious amounts of soft drink, from the ubiquitous Coca Cola to Seven-Up, Sprite and sugary local brands such as Bilz. Mineral water, both carbonated *(con gas)* and plain *(sin gas)*, is widely available, but tap water is potable almost everywhere. The most popular mineral waters are Cachantún and Chusmiza, but others are equally good.

Fruit Juices & Licuados *Jugos* (juices) are varied and excellent. Besides the common *naranja* (orange), *toronja* (grapefruit), *limón* (lemon) and *piña* (pineapple), *mora* (blackberry), *maracuyá* (passion fruit), and *sandía* (watermelon) are also available. *Mote con huesillo*, sold by countless street vendors but closely monitored for hygiene, is a peach nectar with barley kernels.

Licuados are milk-blended fruit drinks, but on request can be made with water. Common flavours are *banana*, *durazno* (peach), and *pera* (pear). Unless you like your drinks *very* sweet, ask them to hold the sugar ('sin azúcar, por favor').

Coffee & Tea Chilean coffee will dismay most caffeine aficionados. Except in the more exclusive neighbourhoods of Santiago and Viña del Mar, semi-soluble Nescafé is

Top : Pallachata volcanos, Parque Nacional Lauca (WB)
Bottom Left : Puerto Natales (WB)
Bottom Right : View down the Caracoles, Portillo (GL)

Top : Indian bullock cart, Chol Chol, Lake District (AS)
Bottom : Alpaca kid, Parque Nacional Lauca (WB)

the norm. *Café con leche* is literally milk with coffee – a teaspoon of coffee is scooped into your cup, which is then filled with hot milk. *Café negro* is coffee with hot water alone.

Likewise, *té con leche* is a teabag submerged in warm milk. Normally your tea will be served black, probably with lemon and at least three packets of sugar. If you prefer just a touch of milk, it is easier to ask for *un poquito de leche* later rather than try to explain your eccentric habits in advance.

Yerba mate, or 'Paraguayan tea', is consumed much more widely in the River Plate countries than in Chile, but you can find it in Chilean supermarkets. Chileans consume herbal teas *(aguas)* such as *manzanilla* (camomile) and *boldo* in considerable quantities.

Alcohol

Wines & Wine Regions Chilean wines are South America's best and rate among the finest in the world; reds *(tintos)* and whites *(blancos)* can be excellent. The country's wine-growing districts stretch from the Copiapó valley of the Norte Chico's Third Region (Atacama) to the drainage of the Río Biobío, in the Eighth Region.

From north to south, rainfall increases and irrigation decreases. In the Copiapó area, known as the *zona pisquera*, exclusively irrigated vineyards produce grapes with high sugar content which is made into pisco. From the drainage of the Río Aconcagua to the Río Maule, there is a middle zone with a Mediterranean climate in which irrigation is still crucial. Reduced irrigation takes place in the more humid conditions south of the Maule. The Biobío drainage receives sufficient rainfall to make irrigation unnecessary, but that same weather makes the harvest unsuitable for finer wines.

The variety of conditions, made even more complex by Chile's abrupt topography, produces a considerable variety of wines. While Atacama wineries specialise in *pisco* (grape brandy), they also produce small quantities of white and sparkling wines. Middle Chile's *zona de regadío* produces the country's best-known wines, mostly Cabernet Sauvignon and other reds planted under French tutelage in the 19th century. Acreages planted to whites such as Chardonnay and Riesling are increasing. Many major wineries in this zone lack sufficient acreage to produce the quantity they require, and buy quality grapes on contract. The major labels include Concha y Toro, Undurraga, Cousiño Macul, Errázuriz Panquehue, Ochagavía, Santa Rita, Canepa, Manquehue, Tarapacá and Carmen. Several of these wineries are open to the public.

To the south, in the transitional zone of the Maule, reds give way to whites like Sauvignon Blanc and Sémillon. Curicó and Talca are the centres of production for brands like Miguel Torres and Viña San Pedro, whose wineries also welcome visitors. Like the zone around Copiapó, the Biobío drainage is a peripheral, pioneer zone for wine grapes, with relatively small yields of common reds and whites which are mostly blended and used for jug wines. Further south, in the Araucanía, there are scattered vineyards, but commercial production is precarious indeed.

Wine aficionados who plan a trip to South America should look at Harm de Blij's *Wine Regions of the Southern Hemisphere* (Rowman & Allenheld, Totora, New Jersey, 1985), which contains excellent chapters on the Chilean, Argentine and Brazilian wine industries.

Other Alcoholic Drinks Chile's table wines should satisfy most visitors' alcoholic thirst, but don't refrain from trying the powerful grape brandy pisco, often served in the form of a pisco sour, with lemon juice, egg white and powdered sugar. It may also be served with ginger ale *(chilcano)* or vermouth *(capitán)*.

Escudo is the best of the Chilean bottled beers, but Becker has recently gained popularity. Bars and restaurants commonly sell draught beer (known as *chopp* and pronounced 'shop'), which is cheaper than bottled beer *(cerveza)* and often better.

Gol is a translucent alcoholic mixture of butter, sugar and milk, left to ferment for a fortnight. It's drunk in the south, but you probably won't find it in restaurants. *Guinda* is a cherry-like fruit which is the basis of *guindado*, a fermented alcoholic drink with brandy, cinnamon, and clove. A popular holiday drink is *cola de mono* ('tail of the monkey'), which consists of aguardiente, coffee, clove and vanilla.

ENTERTAINMENT

Cinemas

Traditionally Chileans flock to the cinema, although outside Santiago the video revolution has brought about the closure of many theatres, which were often the only show in town. Still, in the capital and larger cities like Valparaíso and Viña del Mar, major theatres offer the latest films from Europe, the USA, and Latin America. Repertory houses, cultural centres and universities provide a chance to see classics or less commercial films you may have missed. Films are usually shown in the original language, with Spanish sub-titles.

In Santiago, the main cinema district is along Paseo Huérfanos and adjacent streets like Estado. Prices have risen in recent years, but are still significantly lower than in North America; many cinemas offer substantial mid-week discounts.

Theatre

Both in Santiago and the provinces, live theatre is well attended and high quality, from the classics and serious drama to burlesque. In the southern Lake District, many towns offer summer theatre presentations in their annual cultural festivals.

Peñas

Peñas are nightclubs whose performers offer unapologetically political material based on folk themes. The famous New Chilean Song Movement had its origins in the peñas of the 1960s, and many Chilean performers exiled after the military coup of 1973 kept the flame alive in similar venues in their adopted countries.

Nightclubs

In cities like Santiago and Viña, Chilean nightclubs tend to be tacky affairs, where traditional music and dances are sanitised and presented in glitzy but costly settings for foreign visitors. In ports like Valparaíso and Iquique, they can be disreputable *boites*, frequented by prostitutes and sailors.

Spectator Sports

By far the most popular spectator sport is soccer, whose British origins are apparent from the names of teams like Santiago Morning and Everton. Other popular spectator sports include tennis, boxing and, increasingly, basketball.

THINGS TO BUY

In artisans' *ferias*, found throughout the country, it is often difficult to choose among a variety of quality handicrafts. There are especially good choices in Santiago's Bellavista neighbourhood, Viña del Mar, Valdivia, the Puerto Montt suburb of Angelmó, and the village of Dalcahue, near Castro on the island of Chiloé. Copper and leather goods are excellent choices, while woollens from the Andean north resemble those from Peru or Bolivia.

In the southern Lake District, Mapuche Indian artisans produce a wide variety of quality ceramics, basketry, silverwork, weavings (some will note parallels with the Navajo of Arizona and New Mexico), and carvings. These are widely available in popular tourist destinations like Temuco, Villarrica and Pucón.

Getting There & Away

Chile has air connections from North America, the UK, Europe and Australia/New Zealand. The trans-Pacific route from Australia via Tahiti, though expensive, permits a stopover on Easter Island (Rapa Nui).

Another possibility is to fly to a neighbouring country such as Argentina, Bolivia or Peru, and continue to Chile by air or land. One-way international tickets within South America are usually very expensive but a few, such as the Arica-La Paz route, are fairly reasonable in comparison with slow and difficult overland travel.

International flights within South America tend to be costly, unless purchased as part of inter-continental travel.

AIR

Most long-distance flights to Chile arrive in Santiago, landing at the Aeropuerto Internacional Arturo Merino Benítez in the suburb of Pudahuel. There are some flights to Arica, in northern Chile, which might be convenient for travellers who want to see the north of the country and then go southwards by land to central Chile. There are also flights from neighbouring countries to regional centres including Arica, Puerto Montt and Punta Arenas.

Recently privatised LAN-Chile is the national carrier, but upstart Ladeco has earned an excellent reputation.

South America is a relatively expensive destination from almost everywhere, but discount fares can reduce the bite considerably. If possible, take advantage of seasonal discounts and try to avoid travelling at peak times such as Christmas or New Year. Advance purchase for a given period of time, usually less than six months, will usually provide the best and most flexible deal.

Advance Purchase Excursion tickets must be bought well before departure, but can be a good deal if you know exactly where you will be going and how long you will be staying. Such tickets have minimum and maximum stay requirements, rarely allow stopovers, and are difficult or impossible to modify without monetary penalties.

Economy class ('Y' tickets), valid for 12 months, offer the greatest flexibility. However, if you try to extend beyond a year you'll have to pay the difference of any price increase in the interim period.

A Miscellaneous Charges Order (MCO) is a voucher for a fixed dollar amount, convertible to a ticket on any IATA airline. In countries such as Panama or Colombia that require an onward ticket as a condition for entry, this will usually satisfy immigration authorities; in a pinch, you can exchange it for cash at the local offices of the issuing airline.

For travel to widely separated areas in Europe, the Americas, and Asia, Round-the-World (RTW) tickets can be a great bargain. Generally valid for a year, these permit numerous stopovers so long as you continue in the same direction; but once chosen, the itinerary is fixed. RTW fares with South American stopovers are available from Australia, Europe and the USA. A 'Circle Pacific' fare including Tahiti may permit a cheap stopover in Easter Island.

Air-fare discounting is unusual in South America. Standby can be a cheap alternative from Europe to the US, but not to Chile or other parts of South America. Foreigners in Chile may pay air fares in local currency and take advantage of the parallel exchange rate, but the difference with the official rate is relatively small at present.

Air Travellers with Special Needs

If you have special needs of any sort – you've broken a leg, you're vegetarian, travelling in a wheelchair, taking the baby, terrified of flying – you should let the airline know as soon as possible so that they can make arrangements accordingly. You should remind them when you reconfirm your booking (at least 72 hours before departure) and again when you check in at the airport. It may also be worth ringing round the airlines before you make your booking to find out how they can handle your particular needs.

Airports and airlines can be surprisingly helpful, but need advance warning. Most international airports will provide escorts from check-in desk to plane where needed, and there should be ramps, lifts, accessible toilets and reachable phones. Aircraft toilets, on the other hand, are likely to present a problem; travellers should discuss this with the airline at an early stage and, if necessary, with their doctor.

Guide dogs for the blind will often have to travel in a specially pressurised baggage compartment with other animals, away from their owner; though smaller guide dogs may be admitted to the cabin. All guide dogs will be subject to the same quarantine laws (six months in isolation etc) as any other animal when entering or returning to countries currently free of rabies such as the UK or Australia.

Deaf travellers can ask for airport and in-flight announcements to be written down for them.

Children under two travel for 10% of the standard fare (free on some airlines) as long as they don't occupy a seat, although they get no baggage allowance. 'Skycots' should be provided by the airline if requested in advance; these will take a child weighing up to about 10 kg. Children between two and 12 can usually occupy a seat for half to two-thirds of the full fare, and they do get get a baggage allowance. Push chairs can often be taken as hand luggage.

To/From the USA

From the USA, the principal gateways to South America are Miami, New York and Los Angeles. Airlines which serve Santiago from the USA include LAN-Chile, Ladeco, American, Avianca, Varig Brazilian, Lloyd Aéreo Boliviano and United (which acquired Pan American's South American routes). LAP (Líneas Aéreas Paraguayas) has discount fares via Miami and Asunción for stays up to three months; US domestic carriers make the connection to Miami. Advertised return fares range from about US$750 to US$1000, not including tax, with some conditions applying. For example, an LAP return ticket from San Francisco to Santiago cost US$899. They also have a discount fare of about US$1100 which includes an air pass to several South American capital cities.

One alternative to landing in Santiago is to fly to Lima (Peru), or to Arica (in northern Chile) – Lloyd Aéreo Boliviano and Ladeco both fly from Miami to Arica. For visitors to the Atacama Desert, this would save a long trip north from Santiago. The quoted fare is US$975 without discounts, departing Mondays only.

Most major airlines have ticket 'consolidators' which offer substantial discounts on fares to Latin America, but things change so rapidly that even newspaper listings can be quickly out of date. Among the best sources of information are the Sunday travel pages of major North American dailies such as the *New York Times*, the *Los Angeles Times* or the *San Francisco Examiner*. If you're in a university town, look for bargains in the campus newspaper, such as the *Daily Californian* in Berkeley. There will usually be a listing for the local affiliate of American Student Council Travel, whose main offices are:

New York
    205 E 42nd St (☎ 661-1450)
    356 W 34th St (☎ 239-4257)
Los Angeles
    1093 Broxton Ave (☎ 208-3551)
San Diego
    4429 Cass St (☎ 270-6401)
La Jolla
    UCSD Student Center, B-023 (☎ 452-0630)
San Francisco
    312 Sutter St (☎ 421-3473)
Berkeley
    2511 Channing Way (☎ 848-8604)

Boston
729 Boylston St, Suite 201 (☎ 266-1926)
Seattle
1314 NE 43rd St (☎ 632-2448)

Student Travel Network may also offer good deals. Check their offices at:

Los Angeles
2500 Wilshire Blvd, Suite 507 (☎ 380-2184)
San Francisco
166 Geary St, Suite 702 (☎ 391-8407)
San Diego
6447 El Cajon Blvd (☎ 286-1322)
Honolulu
1831 S King St, Suite 202 (☎ 942-7455)
Dallas
6609 Hillcrest Ave (☎ 360-0097)

The magazine *Travel Unlimited* (PO Box 1058, Allston, Mass 02134) publishes details of the cheapest air fares and courier possibilities for destinations all over the world from the USA.

To/From Canada

LAN-Chile no longer has direct service to Canada, but there are good connections via New York, Miami and Los Angeles. Aerolíneas Argentinas does fly from Toronto and Montreal to Buenos Aires, with connections to Santiago.

Travel CUTS, the Canadian student travel service, has offices in all major cities. The *Toronto Globe & Mail* and the *Vancouver Sun* carry travel agents' ads. The magazine *Great Expeditions* (PO Box 8000-411, Abbotsford BC V2S 6H1) is also useful.

To/From the UK & Europe

It is generally cheaper to fly to New York or Miami than to go directly to South America from Europe, but LAN-Chile and other airlines have direct flights between Santiago and major European cities including Madrid, Paris, Rome, Zurich, London, Frankfurt and Amsterdam.

So-called 'bucket shops' in London offer some of the best deals. Try Trailfinders (☎ (71) 938-3366) at 46 Earls Court Rd, London W8 6EJ, or STA Travel at 74 Old Brompton Rd, London SW7 (☎ (71) 937-9962) or 117 Euston Rd, London NW1. Journey Latin America (☎ (81) 747-8315) at 16 Devonshire Rd, Chiswick, London W4 2HD, specialises in travel to South America. Look in the listings magazines *Time Out* and *City Limits*, plus the Sunday papers and *Exchange & Mart* for ads. Also look out for the free magazines widely available in London – start by looking outside the main railway stations. Advertised fares from London to Santiago start around £370 one way, £630 return.

Most British travel agents are registered with ABTA (Association of British Travel Agents). If you have paid for your flight to an ABTA-registered agent who then goes out of business, ABTA will guarantee a refund or an alternative. Unregistered bucket shops are riskier but also sometimes cheaper.

The Globetrotters Club (BCM Roving, London WC1N 3XX) publishes a newsletter called *Globe* which covers obscure destinations and can help in finding travelling companions.

Similar fares to those from London are available from other European cities; Paris, Amsterdam, Brussels and Antwerp are all good places for cheap fares – try NBBS in Amsterdam. The newsletter *Farang* (La Rue 8 à 4261 Braives, Belgique) deals with exotic destinations; so does the magazine *Aventure du Bout du Monde* (116 rue de Javel, 75015 Paris).

Since Chile has re-established diplomatic relations with Russia and Cuba, another possible route is via Cuba with Aeroflot or Cubana, but the obligatory stopovers in Cuba are not cheap.

To/From Australia & New Zealand

Several travel agencies offer cheap air tickets from Australia. STA Travel, which does not require its clients to prove student status, has offices in all capital cities:

Melbourne
220 Faraday St, Carlton (☎ 347-6911)
Hobart
Union Building, University of Tasmania (☎ 233825)

Sydney
 1A Lee St, Railway Square (☎ 212-1255)
Adelaide
 Level 4, The Arcade, Union House, Adelaide University (☎ 223-6620)
Perth
 Hackett Hall, University of West Australia (☎ 380-2302)
Canberra
 Arts Centre, Australian National University (☎ 470800)
Brisbane
 Northern Security Building, 40 Creek St (☎ 221-9629)

Another company is Flight Centres International, with offices in Sydney, Melbourne and Adelaide. Also check out advertisements in Saturday editions of newspapers like *The Age* or the *Sydney Morning Herald*.

South America is one of the most expensive places to fly to from Australia. It can be cheaper to get a return flight to Los Angeles or Miami, and buy a return ticket to South America from there. However, it will take a few extra days of flying time, and a few more days in the USA which will consume any savings on the air fare – it's only worth it if you want to visit the USA anyway.

There are two more direct routes to Chile from Australia or New Zealand. The first is via Tahiti with Qantas or UTA, connecting with a LAN-Chile flight to Santiago with a possible stopover in Easter Island. A ticket for this route from Sydney or Melbourne, good for up to six months, will cost around A$2549 return, and not much less one way. The other possibility is to fly Qantas or Air New Zealand to Auckland, connecting with the Aerolíneas Argentinas trans-Antarctica flight to Buenos Aires and then a shorter flight to Santiago. The flight from Sydney to Buenos Aires costs from around A$2455 return, including an onward connection to another South American city.

A Round-the-World ticket from Australia, offered by Aerolíneas Argentinas and Qantas, allows stopovers in Auckland, Buenos Aires, London, Paris, Bahrain, Singapore and other cities, but details must be arranged in advance, and it does not permit stopovers in North America. Including a return flight from Buenos Aires to Santiago, the ticket costs about A$3200 and is great value if you want to combine Latin America with Europe. A similar RTW fare is offered by Aerolíneas Argentinas and KLM, for around A$2850.

To/From Peru

Aero Perú has flights from Lima to Santiago four days a week for US$262 one way. They have daily flights from Lima to Tacna, which is in Peru but only 50 km from the northern Chilean city of Arica, for US$79 one way.

To/From Bolivia

Lloyd Aéreo Boliviano (LAB) has twice-weekly flights between Santiago and La Paz for US$215 one way. LAN-Chile also flies this route. LAB also connects La Paz with Arica for US$92 one way.

To/From Argentina

Many airlines fly between Santiago and Buenos Aires for about US$240 one way, but there are also Ladeco and Aerolíneas Argentinas flights from Santiago to Mendoza (US$88) and to Córdoba. TAN, the regional carrier of Argentina's Neuquén province, connects Bariloche with Puerto Montt for US$56. There are projected Aerolíneas flights between Iquique (Chile) and Jujuy (Argentina) in summer only; past flights have connected Salta and Antofagasta.

LAND

Chile has a handful of border crossings with Peru and Bolivia, and many with Argentina, not all of which are served by public transportation.

To/From Peru

Tacna to Arica is the only overland crossing between Peru and Chile. There is a choice of bus, taxi or train. For details, see the Arica entry in the Norte Grande chapter.

To/From Bolivia

Road and rail connections exist between Bolivia and Chile, but neither is fast or especially comfortable. There is a twice-weekly passenger train, *El Dorado de los Andes*, between La Paz and Arica, as well as a weekly *ferrobus*, a sort of bus on rails. Buses, via Visviri or Tambo Quemado, are more frequent and cheaper; for details, see the Arica entry in the Norte Grande chapter. There are also buses from Iquique to the border post of Colchane.

A weekly rail service, as well as the occasional bus, links Calama to Ollagüe, with connections to Oruro and La Paz; from Calama there are easy bus connections to the coastal city of Antofagasta, the former Chilean rail terminus. For details, see the Calama entry in the Norte Grande chapter.

It is possible to travel from Bolivia to San Pedro de Atacama via the Portezuelo del Cajón, near the juncture of the Chilean, Bolivian and Argentine borders, but no regular public transport exists in this area.

To/From Argentina

Except in Patagonia, every land crossing to Argentina involves crossing the Andes. Some passes are closed in winter.

Calama to Salta The 4069-metre Lago Sico pass has superseded the higher Huaytiquina pass, but is usually open only from December to March. Atahualpa and Buses Géminis make weekly crossings in summer, with connections from Arica, Iquique and Antofagasta, but bookings are heavy. Automobile traffic is almost nil, so forget about hitching.

There is sometimes an Argentine passenger train from Salta to the border at Socompa, but only freight service beyond, although the very uncomfortable Chilean train will sometimes carry passengers to the abandoned station of Augusta Victoria (where it is possible to hitch to Antofagasta), or to Baquedano, on the Ruta Panamericana.

Copiapó to Tucumán via Catamarca There is no public transport over the 4726-metre Paso de San Francisco, and it is probably suitable for 4WD vehicles only.

La Serena to San Juan Dynamited by the Argentine military during the Beagle Channel dispute of 1978-79, the 4779-metre Agua Negra pass is now open for automobile traffic and bus service may commence soon. Check in La Serena or San Juan.

Santiago to Mendoza & Buenos Aires Many bus companies service this most popular of crossing points between the two countries. From either of Santiago's major bus terminals, try Tas Choapa, Chile Bus, Igi Llaima, Fénix Pullman Norte or TAC. Taxi colectivos are faster, more comfortable and only slightly more expensive. Winter snow sometimes closes the route, but never for long.

Talca to Malargüe & San Rafael The 2553-metre Paso Pehuenche, south-east of Talca, was due to open in late 1992, though there is no indication yet of public transport on the route. A route may open from Curicó over the 2938-metre Paso del Planchón, also to San Rafael.

Lake District Routes There are a number of scenic crossings in the southern lake district, several of which involve bus-boat shuttles. These are very popular in summer, so make bookings in advance whenever possible.

Temuco to Zapala & Neuquén
: The most northerly of Lake District routes crosses the Andes over the 1884-metre Pino Hachado pass, directly east of Temuco via Curacautín and Lonquimay, along the upper Río Biobío. An alternative route, slightly to the south, uses the 1298-metre Icaima pass. Both have occasional bus traffic in summer.

Temuco to San Martín de los Andes
: The most popular route from Temuco passes Lago Villarrica, Pucón and Currarehue en route to the Mamuil Malal pass (known to Argentines as Paso Tromen). On the Argentine side, the road skirts the northern slopes of Volcán Lanín. There is regular summer bus service, but the pass is closed in winter.

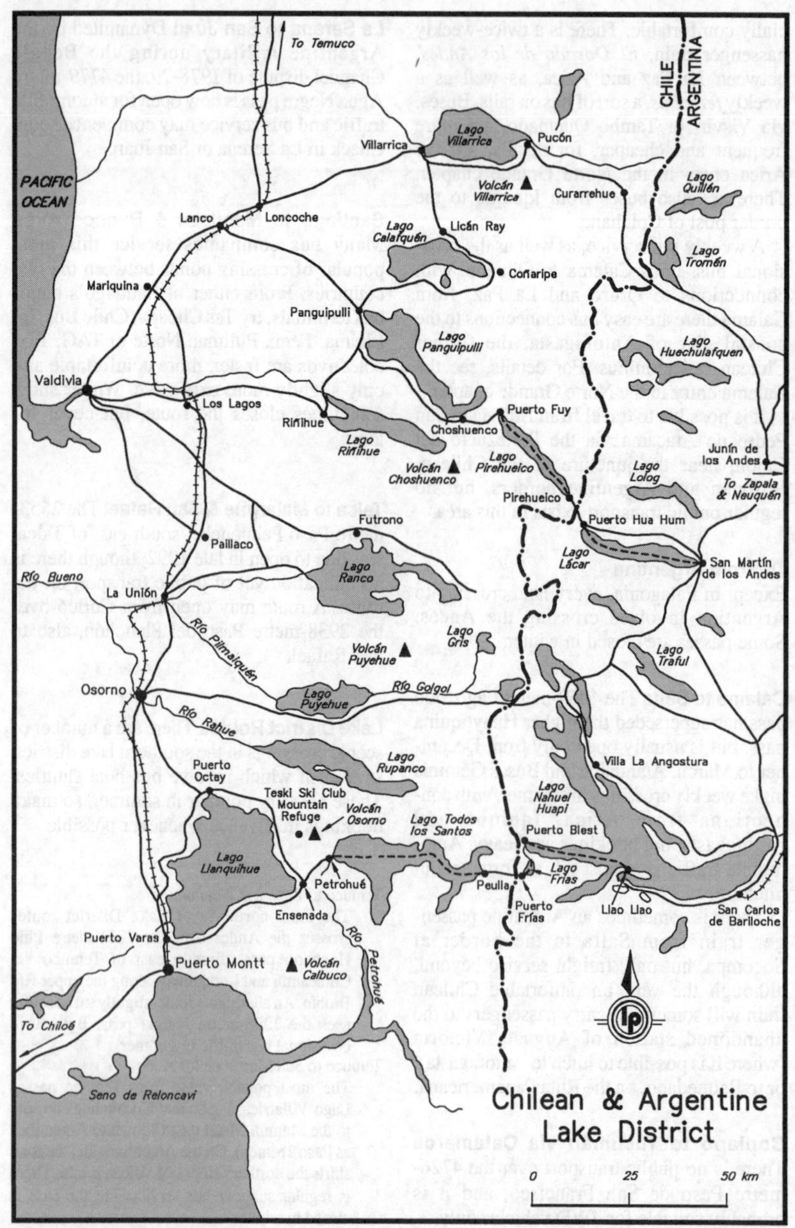
To Temuco
CHILE
ARGENTINA
PACIFIC OCEAN
Villarrica
Lago Villarrica
Pucón
Volcán Villarrica
Curarrehue
Lago Quillén
Lanco
Loncoche
Lago Calafquén
Licán Ray
Coñaripe
Lago Tromen
Mariquina
Panguipulli
Lago Panguipulli
Lago Huechulafquen
Valdivia
Los Lagos
Riñihue
Puerto Fuy
Choshuenco
Lago Riñihue
Volcán Choshuenco
Lago Pirehueico
Lago Lolog
Junín de los Andes
To Zapala & Neuquén
Pirehueico
Puerto Hua Hum
Futrono
Paillaco
Lago Lácar
San Martín de los Andes
Río Bueno
Lago Ranco
La Unión
Río Pilmaiquén
Lago Gris
Volcán Puyehue
Lago Traful
Osorno
Río Golgol
Lago Puyehue
Río Rahue
Lago Rupanco
Villa La Angostura
Puerto Octay
Teski Ski Club Mountain Refuge
Volcán Osorno
Lago Todos los Santos
Lago Nahuel Huapi
Puerto Blest
Lago Llanquihue
Petrohué
Peulla
Lago Frías
Llao Llao
Ensenada
Puerto Frías
San Carlos de Bariloche
Puerto Varas
Río Petrohué
Puerto Montt
Volcán Calbuco
To Chiloé
Seno de Reloncaví
Chilean & Argentine Lake District
0
25
50 km

Valdivia to San Martín de los Andes
This route starts with a bus from Valdivia to Panguipulli, Choshuenco and Puerto Fuy, followed by a ferry across Lago Pirehueico to the village of Pirehueico. From Pirehueico a local bus goes to Argentine customs at Paso Hua Hum, where there is a bus or ferry to San Martín.

Osorno to Bariloche via Paso Puyehue
This crossing is the quickest land route in the Lake District, passing through Parque Nacional Puyehue on the Chilean side and Parque Nacional Nahuel Huapi on the Argentine side.

Puerto Montt to Bariloche
This bus-ferry combination via Parque Nacional Vicente Pérez Rosales, very popular in summer, starts in Puerto Montt or Puerto Varas and goes from Petrohué, at the west end of Lago Todos los Santos, by ferry to Peulla, where a bus crosses the Pérez Rosales pass to Argentine immigration at Puerto Frías. After crossing Lago Frías by launch, there is a short bus hop to Puerto Blest on Lago Nahuel Huapi and another ferry to Puerto Pañuelo (Llao Llao). From Llao Llao, there is a frequent bus service to Bariloche.

Southern Patagonian Routes Since the opening of the Camino Austral (Southern Highway) south of Puerto Montt, it has become more common to cross between Chile and Argentina south in this region. There are also several crossing points in extreme southern Patagonia and Tierra del Fuego.

Puerto Ramírez to Esquel
There are two options here. From the Chilean village of Villa Santa Lucía, on the Camino Austral, there is a side road which forks at Puerto Ramírez, at the east end of Lago Yelcho. The north fork goes to Futaleufú, where a new bridge crosses the river to the Argentine side and colectivos to Esquel. The south fork goes to Palena and Argentine customs at Carrenleufú, where there is bus service to Corcovado, Trevelin and Esquel.

Puerto Cisnes to José de San Martín
A side road off the Camino Austral climbs the valley of the Río Cisnes to the 939-metre Appeleg pass and the Argentine province of Chubut, but there is no public transport.

Coihaique to Comodoro Rivadavia
There are three buses per week, often heavily booked, from Coihaique to Comodoro Rivadavia via Río Mayo. For private vehicles, there is an alternative route via Balmaceda to Perito Moreno via the 502-metre Paso Huemules.

Puerto Ingeniero Ibáñez to Perito Moreno
This route follows the north of Lago General Carrera (Lago Buenos Aires on the Argentine side). There is no public transport, but as all vehicles must pass through the Carabineros post on the lakefront in Puerto Ibáñez, some patient waiting may yield a lift.

Chile Chico to Los Antíguos
From Puerto Ibáñez, take the ferry to Chile Chico on the southern shore of Lago Carrera and a bus to Los Antíguos, which has connections to the Patagonian coastal town of Caleta Olivia. There is now also a road to Chile Chico from Cruce El Maitén, at the western end of Lago Carrera.

Cochrane to Bajo Caracoles
Probably the most desolate of the crossings in the Aisén region, the 647-metre Paso Roballos links the hamlet of Cochrane with a flyspeck outpost in Argentina's Santa Cruz province.

Puerto Natales to Río Turbio & Calafate
Frequent buses connect Puerto Natales to the Argentine coal mining town of Río Turbio, where many Chileans work; from Río Turbio there are further connections to Río Gallegos and Calafate. Twice weekly or more in summer there are buses from Chile's Parque Nacional Torres del Paine and Puerto Natales to Calafate, the gateway to Argentina's Parque Nacional Los Glaciares, via Paso Cancha de Carreras. By the time this is published, a new and shorter route may have opened from Torres del Paine to Los Glaciares, bypassing Calafate over the Sierra de Baguales.

Punta Arenas to Río Gallegos
There are many buses daily between Punta Arenas and Río Gallegos, a six-hour trip on a surprisingly rough highway.

Punta Arenas to Tierra del Fuego
From Punta Arenas, a three-hour ferry trip or a ten-minute flight takes you to Porvenir, on Chilean Tierra del Fuego, where there are two buses weekly to the Argentine city of Río Grande, which has connections to Ushuaia.

Puerto Williams to Ushuaia
Every Saturday, if demand is sufficient, there is a ferry from Puerto Williams on Navarino Island (reached by plane or boat from Punta Arenas) to Ushuaia. This service is frequently interrupted.

LEAVING CHILE

Departure Tax Chilean departure tax for international flights is US$12.50 or its equivalent in national currency. For domestic flights, there is a modest departure tax of about US$5.

Getting Around

Travel within Chile is easy. There are fast, punctual and comfortable buses on the main highways, and they are generally preferable to railways, which have been neglected since the early 1970s. Flights are reasonably priced, with occasional bargain discounts, and there are several interesting passenger ferries.

AIR

Because of Chile's latitudinal extension, you may want to avoid tiresome and time-consuming backtracking by taking an occasional flight. For instance, you can travel overland through Chilean and Argentine Patagonia to Tierra del Fuego, then fly from Punta Arenas to Puerto Montt or Santiago. The return flight should be no more expensive than a combination of bus fares and accommodation.

Two major airlines, LAN-Chile and Ladeco, offer domestic and international services, although a cut-rate competitor, Pacific Air, has recently commenced country-wide operations. Both Ladeco and LAN-Chile prohibit smoking on all domestic flights, except those to Easter Island (Rapa Nui) on which there is a choice of smoking or non-smoking.

Minor regional airlines include DAP, which connects Punta Arenas with Tierra del Fuego, the Falkland Islands, and Antarctica. Lassa and Líneas Aéreas Robinson Crusoe, both operate air taxis to the Juan Fernández Islands. Several air taxi companies connect isolated settlements in the Aisén region, south of Puerto Montt.

The accompanying chart indicates both domestic fares and those to neighbouring countries. On most flights, a certain number of half-price seats are available and, if your travel schedule is flexible, you may be able to take advantage of these.

Air Passes

For US$300, LAN-Chile offers a 21-day pass known as the 'Visit Chile Pass' which allows flights to and from selected airports north or south of Santiago. Destinations include Arica, Iquique, Calama, Antofagasta, Copiapó, Concepción, Puerto Montt and Punta Arenas. For US$780 extra, the air pass can include Easter Island – a minor saving as the usual fare to Easter Island from Santiago is US$812 return.

Passes, which must be purchased outside Chile, are available only to foreigners and nonresidents of Chile. They are valid for a maximum of 21 days, but there is no minimum restriction. Intermediate stops can be omitted.

Ladeco has a similar pass, also for about US$300. It does not include Easter Island, but it is more flexible with respect to mainland airports. This pass allows stopovers at Balmaceda/Coihaique, an area of considerable interest to travellers, and several other cities and towns.

To/From Easter Island (Rapa Nui)

LAN-Chile has two or three flights per week between Santiago and Tahiti, which stop at Easter Island; Santiago-Easter Island costs US$812 return. Flights from Australia, New Zealand or the Pacific via Tahiti can include Easter Island (see the Getting There & Away chapter). LAN-Chile's Visit Chile Pass can include Easter Island (see above). For more details, see the Easter Island chapter.

Reservations & Timetables

Both Ladeco and LAN-Chile have computerised booking services, so you can book domestic and international flights from their offices anywhere in the country or overseas. Both also publish detailed timetables to which they adhere very closely. You will find central airline offices in the Santiago chapter, and regional offices in each city entry. Telephone reservations are also simple.

Airport Departure Tax

The airport tax for domestic flights is about

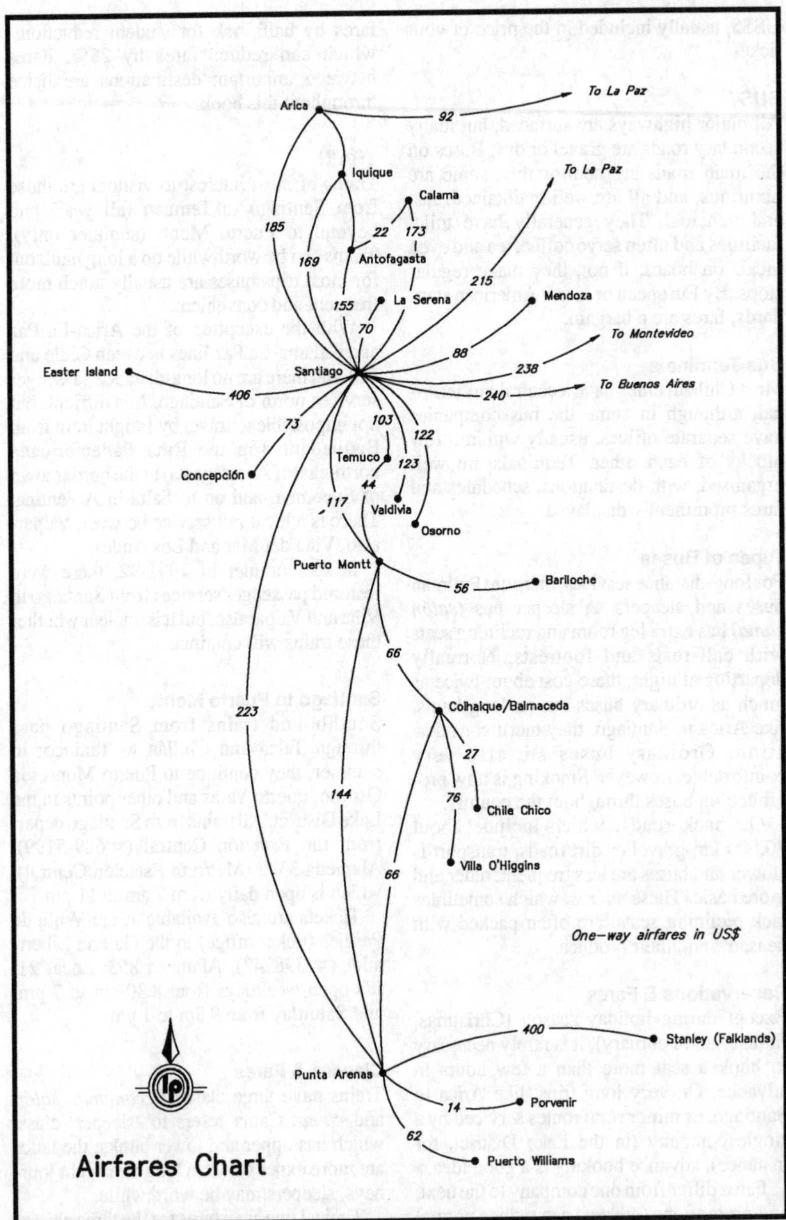
To La Paz
Arica
92
Iquique
To La Paz
Calama
185
22
173
169
Antofagasta
215
155
La Serena
Mendoza
70
To Montevideo
88
Easter Island
Santiago
238
406
240
To Buenos Aires
73
103
122
Temuco
123
Concepción
44
Valdivia
117
Osorno
Puerto Montt
56
Bariloche
66
223
Coihaique/Balmaceda
27
144
76
Chile Chico
Villa O'Higgins
66
One-way airfares in US$
400
Stanley (Falklands)
Punta Arenas
Porvenir
14
62
Puerto Williams
Airfares Chart

US$5, usually included in the price of your ticket.

BUS

All major highways are surfaced, but many secondary roads are gravel or dirt. Buses on the main roads are comfortable, some are luxurious, and all are well maintained, fast and punctual. They generally have toilet facilities and often serve coffee, tea and even meals on board; if not, they make regular stops. By European or North American standards, fares are a bargain.

Bus Terminals

Most Chilean cities have a central bus terminal, although in some the bus companies have separate offices, usually within a few blocks of each other. Terminals are well organised, with destinations, schedules and fares prominently displayed.

Types of Buses

For long-distance services, there are Pullman buses and sleepers. A sleeper bus *(salón cama)* has extra leg room and reclining seats with calf-rests and footrests. Normally departing at night, these cost about twice as much as ordinary buses but on long hauls, like Arica to Santiago, they merit consideration. Ordinary buses are also very comfortable, however. Smoking is now prohibited on buses throughout the country.

On back roads, which include about 70,000 km gravel or dirt roads, transport is slower and buses are less frequent, older and more basic. These *micros*, which sometimes lack reclining seats, are often packed with peasants and their produce.

Reservations & Fares

Except during holiday season (Christmas, January and February), it is rarely necessary to book a seat more than a few hours in advance. On very long trips, like Arica to Santiago, or minor rural routes serviced by a single company (in the Lake District, for instance), advance booking is a good idea.

Fares differ from one company to the next, and promotions *(ofertas)* can reduce normal fares by half. Ask for student reductions, which can reduce fares by 25%. Fares between important destinations are listed throughout this book.

TRAIN

Trains of most interest to visitors are those from Santiago to Temuco (all year) and beyond to Puerto Montt (summer only). Trains can be worthwhile on a long haul, but for most trips buses are usually much more frequent and convenient.

With the exception of the Arica-La Paz and Calama-La Paz lines between Chile and Bolivia, there are no long-distance passenger services north of Santiago. It is difficult but not impossible to travel by freight train from Baquedano (on the Ruta Panamericana north-east of Antofagasta) to the border town of Socompa, and on to Salta in Argentina. There is a local rail service between Valparaíso, Viña del Mar and Los Andes.

In the summer of 1991-92, there were restored passenger services from Santiago to Viña and Valparaíso, but it is unclear whether these trains will continue.

Santiago to Puerto Montt

Southbound trains from Santiago pass through Talca and Chillán to Temuco; in summer, they continue to Puerto Montt via Osorno, Puerto Varas and other points in the Lake District. All trains from Santiago depart from the Estación Central (☎ 689-5199), Alameda 3322 (Metro to Estación Central), which is open daily from 7 am to 11 pm.

Tickets are also available at the Venta de Pasajes (ticket office) in the Galería Libertador (☎ 398247), Alameda 853, Local 21. It's open weekdays from 8.30 am to 7 pm, and Saturday from 9 am to 1 pm.

Classes & Fares

Trains have three classes: *economía*, *salón* and *cama*. Cama refers to 'sleeper' class, which has upper and lower bunks; the latter are more expensive. On long overnight journeys, sleepers may be worthwhile.

Typical one-way fares for the three classes

are listed below, in US dollars; a round-trip fare is slightly cheaper than two singles.

Destination	*Economía*	*Salón*	*Cama upper*	*Cama lower*
Concepción	$10	$13	$19	$27
Temuco	$13	$17	$24	$35
Valdivia	$16	$20	$26	$36
Osorno	$17	$21	$28	$38
Puerto Montt	$19	$24	$29	$40

Timetables

Departures from Santiago may change, so check an official timetable. A number of trains go only as far as Chillán or Linares, and not all trains stop at every station. Train timetables are roughly as follows:

Train	*Destination*	*Departure*
Salón	Concepción	daily, 8.30 am
Expreso	Concepción	daily, 9 am
Salón	Concepción	daily, 1.30 pm
Expreso	Chillán	daily, 4 pm
Salón	Concepción	daily, 5.30 pm
Rápido	Puerto Montt	daily, 6.30 pm
Expreso	Puerto Montt	daily, 9.15 pm
Rápido	Concepción	daily, 10.30 pm

Approximate journey times from Santiago are:

Concepción	9 hours
Temuco	13 hours
Osorno	18½ hours
Puerto Montt	20-22 hours

CAR

Even though the public transport system is very extensive, many of the most interesting parts of Chile are easily accessible only by motor vehicle. Off the main highways, where buses may be few or nonexistent, you cannot easily stop where you want and then continue by public transport.

Operating a car in Chile is much cheaper than in Europe but rather dearer than in the USA. The price of *bencina* (petrol) is about US$0.45 per litre, that of *gas-oil* (diesel fuel) somewhat cheaper. There is a minimal price difference between 93-octane *super* and 81-octane *común*.

Advantages of driving include freedom from timetables, the ability to stay wherever you like (particularly if you have camping equipment), the opportunity to get off the beaten track, and the flexibility to stop whenever you see something interesting. In some places – like the Atacama Desert or on Easter Island – a car is definitely the best way to get around. Security problems are minor, but you should always lock your vehicle and leave any valuables out of sight.

Motorists should be aware that foreign vehicles may be imported for 90 days only; unlike tourist visas, permits may not be extended and the vehicle must leave the country.

Road Rules

While Chileans sometimes drive carelessly or a bit too fast (especially in the cities), if you have come from Argentina you will think them saints. Most Chilean drivers are courteous to pedestrians, and will rarely do anything wilfully dangerous. Driving after dark is not advisable, especially in rural areas in southern Chile, where pedestrians, domestic animals and wooden carts are difficult to see on or near the highways.

Formally, Chile requires an International or Inter-American Driving Permit to supplement your national or state driving licence. In practice, the Carabineros (national police, who patrol the highways) pay more attention to the international licence. They will not harass you for minor equipment violations.

You should *never* attempt to bribe the Carabineros. If you are involved in any automobile accident, your licence will be confiscated until the case is resolved, although local officials will usually issue a temporary driving permit within a few days. A blood alcohol test is obligatory; purchase a sterile syringe at the hospital or clinic pharmacy when the Carabineros take you there. After this you will be taken to the police station to make a statement and then, under most circumstances, released. Ordinarily you cannot leave Chile until the matter is

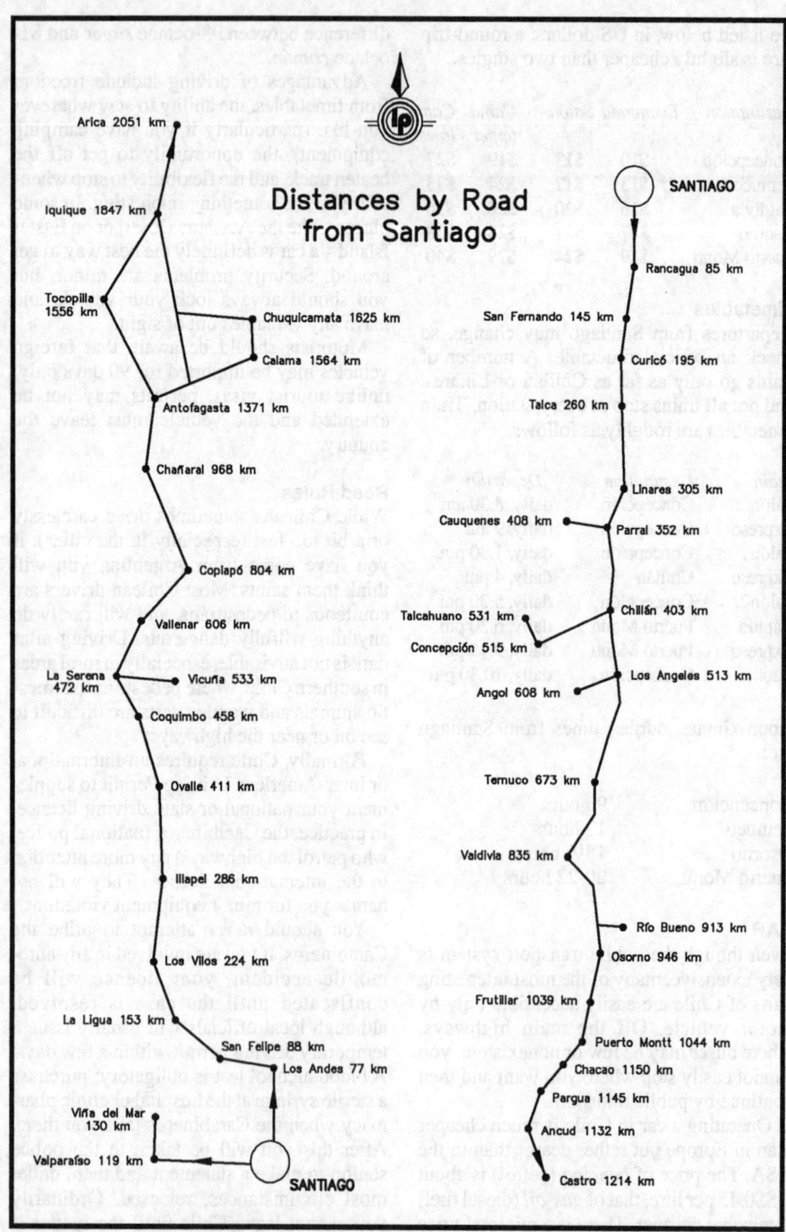
Distances by Road
from Santiago
Arica 2051 km
Iquique 1847 km
Tocopilla
1556 km
Chuquicamata 1625 km
Calama 1564 km
Antofagasta 1371 km
Chañaral 968 km
Copiapó 804 km
Vallenar 606 km
La Serena
472 km
Vicuña 533 km
Coquimbo 458 km
Ovalle 411 km
Illapel 286 km
Los Vilos 224 km
La Ligua 153 km
San Felipe 88 km
Los Andes 77 km
Viña del Mar
130 km
Valparaíso 119 km
SANTIAGO
SANTIAGO
Rancagua 85 km
San Fernando 145 km
Curicó 195 km
Talca 260 km
Linares 305 km
Cauquenes 408 km
Parral 352 km
Talcahuano 531 km
Chillán 403 km
Concepción 515 km
Los Angeles 513 km
Angol 608 km
Temuco 673 km
Valdivia 835 km
Río Bueno 913 km
Osorno 946 km
Frutillar 1039 km
Puerto Montt 1044 km
Chacao 1150 km
Pargua 1145 km
Ancud 1132 km
Castro 1214 km

resolved; consult your consulate, insurance carrier and a lawyer.

The Automóvil Club de Chile (ACCHI) offers its members, and members of associated overseas motoring organisations (such as the AAA in the USA), low-cost road service and towing in and around major cities. Your membership may bring discounts on accommodation, camping, rental cars, tours and other services. Contact ACCHI at Avenida Vitacura 8620, Santiago (☎ 212-5702), or its tourist information service at Fidel Oteíza 1964 (☎ 274-9078).

Rental

Major international rental agencies such as Hertz, Avis and Budget have offices in Santiago and in major cities and other tourist areas throughout Chile. The Automóvil Club also rents cars at some of its offices. To rent a car, you must have a valid driver's licence, be at least 25 years of age, and present either a credit card such as MasterCard or Visa, or a large cash deposit.

Even at smaller agencies, basic rental charges are now very high, the cheapest and smallest vehicles going for about US$20 per day plus US$0.20 per km. Adding the cost of insurance, petrol and IVA *(impuesto de valor agregado*, the value added tax or VAT), it becomes very pricey indeed to operate a rental vehicle without several others to share expenses. Weekend or weekly rates, with unlimited mileage, are a much better bargain. Small vehicles with unlimited mileage cost about US$100 for a weekend or US$250 per week.

One-way rentals are difficult or impossible. If you want to rent a car in Arica and drive it to Punta Arenas and leave it there, you will also have to pay for its return to Arica. Some offices will arrange this, but it is really not very practical.

Purchase

If you are spending several months in Chile, purchasing a car merits consideration, but it has both advantages and disadvantages. On the one hand, it is more flexible than public transport and likely to be cheaper than multiple rentals; reselling it at the end of your stay can make it even more economical. On the other hand, any used car can be a risk, especially on rugged back roads. Fortunately, there seems to be a competent and resourceful street mechanic in even the smallest hamlet.

Chile no longer has a domestic automobile industry, but good imported vehicles are available at prices higher than Europe or the USA, but much more reasonable than in Argentina. Japanese and Korean vehicles like Toyota and Hyundai are especially popular, but Argentine Peugeots are also common. Parts are readily available, except for some older models. You should not expect to find a dependable used car for less than about US$2000, much more for recent models.

If you purchase a car you must change the title within 30 days; failure to do so can result in a fine of several hundred dollars.

BICYCLE

Bicycling is an interesting and inexpensive alternative for travelling around Chile – although camping is not a bargain for the solo cyclist, and it will probably be cheaper to stay at residenciales. Racing bicycles are suitable for most paved routes, but on the gravelled roads of the Atacama or Patagonia a *todo terreno* (mountain bike) is a better choice.

Cycling is an increasingly popular recreational activity and there are many good routes, but the weather can be a drawback. From Temuco south, it is changeable and you must be prepared for rain; from Santiago north, especially in the Atacama, sources of water are infrequent. In some areas, the wind can slow your progress to a crawl; north to south is generally easier than south to north. Chilean motorists are usually courteous, but on narrow, two-lane highways without shoulders, they can be a real hazard to cyclists.

HITCHING

Along with Argentina, Chile is probably the best country for hitching in all of South

America. The major drawback is that Chilean vehicles are often packed with families with children, but truck drivers will often help backpackers. At the *servicentros* on the outskirts of Chilean cities on the Ruta Panamericana, where truckers gas up their vehicles, it is often worth soliciting a ride.

Women can and do hitchhike alone, but should exercise caution and especially avoid getting into a car with more than one man. In Patagonia, where distances are great and vehicles few, hitchers should expect long waits and carry warm, wind-proof clothing. Carry some snack food and a water bottle, especially in the desert north.

Along the Panamericana, from Arica to Puerto Montt, hitching is fairly reliable, but competition may be great in the summer months, when Chilean students hit the highway with their backpacks. In the Atacama you may wait for some time, but almost every ride will be a long one. Along the Camino Austral, in the Eleventh Region (Aisén), vehicles of any kind are few except between Coihaique and Puerto Aisén, and hitching requires great patience.

BOAT

Though there are bus services along the new Camino Austral Longitudinal (Southern Longitudinal Highway) between Puerto Montt and Coihaique, if you're going to Chaitén or Puerto Chacabuco it is easier to take a ferry from either Puerto Montt or the island of Chiloé. Navimag (Naviera Magallanes) and Transmarchilay operate several important ferry routes in the region.

Puerto Montt to Puerto Chacabuco

Navimag and Transmarchilay operate services from Puerto Montt or nearby Pargua to Puerto Chacabuco, with connecting buses to Coihaique. For details of schedules and fares, see the Puerto Montt entry in the Lake District chapter. Transmarchilay also runs a tourist ship, the *Skorpios*, to the Laguna San Rafael glacier.

Puerto Montt to Puerto Natales

Navimag operates ferries from Puerto Montt to Puerto Natales. These ships depart about three times monthly, taking about three days to Puerto Natales. For details of schedules and fares, see the Puerto Montt entry in the Lake District chapter.

Chiloé Island to the Mainland

There are three connections between Chiloé and the mainland. The most frequent is with Transmarchilay or Cruz del Sur ferries between Chacao, at the northern tip of the island, and Pargua, on the mainland. For details of fares and schedules, see the Chiloé chapter.

The other connections are by Transmarchilay ferries between the ports of Chonchi or Quellón on Chiloé, and Chaitén or Puerto Chacabuco on the mainland. For details of fares and schedules, see the Lake District, Chiloé and Aisén chapters.

Patagonia & Tierra del Fuego There is a frequent ferry link between Punta Arenas and Porvenir, the only town in Chilean Tierra del Fuego. For details of fares and schedules, see the Punta Arenas entry in the Magallanes chapter.

LOCAL TRANSPORT

To/From the Airport

LAN-Chile and Ladeco often provide a bus between the town centre and the airport – either their own or one run by a local company. Cost of this bus is sometimes included in your air ticket, sometimes not. Top-end hotels sometimes provide transportation for their clients, but in a few places you must use public transport or a taxi to get to the airport.

Bus

Even small Chilean towns have extensive bus systems which can seem chaotic to the novice rider. Buses, however, are clearly numbered and usually carry a placard indicating their final destination. Since many identically numbered buses serve slightly different routes, pay attention to these placards. On boarding, tell the driver your final destination and he will tell you the fare and give you a ticket. Do not lose this ticket, which may be checked en route.

Train

Both Santiago and Valparaíso have commuter rail networks. The former runs from Rancagua, capital of the Sixth Region of the same name, to Estación Central on the Alameda in Santiago, while the latter runs from Los Andes and San Felipe to Viña del Mar and the port. For details, see the respective city sections.

Underground

Santiago is the only Chilean city with a subway, the Metro, which is fast, efficient, clean and cheap. For details, see the chapter on Santiago.

Taxi

Most Chilean cabs are metered, but fares vary. In Santiago, it costs Ch$150 (about US$0.40) to *bajar la bandera* ('lower the flag'), plus either Ch$20, Ch$21 or Ch$30 per 100 metres. Each cab carries a placard indicating its authorised fare. This irregular fare system may be standardised by the time this book appears.

In some towns, such as Viña del Mar, cabs may cost twice as much. In others, such as Coquimbo, meters are less common, so it is wise to agree upon a fare in advance if possible. Drivers are generally polite and honest, but there are exceptions. Tipping is not necessary, but you may tell the driver to keep small change.

Santiago

Since the 1970s, Santiago has grown both out and up. It continues to sprawl, but there are ever more skyscrapers, both downtown and in the nearby suburb of Providencia, which has been usurping the role of the downtown area as the city's commercial and financial centre.

HISTORY

Gazing west from the rocky overlook of Cerro Santa Lucía to the skyscrapers and apartment blocks of metropolitan Santiago, it's hard to imagine that just six months after Pedro de Valdivia's founding of Santiago in 1541, Mapuche Indians nearly obliterated the embryonic city. Spanish troops regrouped on the fortified summit of Cerro Santa Lucía and Valdivia made immediate plans to rebuild the precarious settlement.

Valdivia had laid out a regular grid from the present-day Plaza de Armas, but for two years 'Santiago del Nuevo Extremo' was little more than a besieged hillside camp. Its tile-roofed adobe houses resisted fire, but colonists nearly starved under pressure from the Indians. Two years passed before assistance arrived from Peru; after returning to Peru himself for new troops and supplies, Valdivia pushed southwards, founding Concepción in 1550 and Valdivia in 1552.

All these early settlements were merely fortified villages. In Santiago, most houses were built around central patios, enhanced with gardens and grape arbors, but open sewers ran down the middle of the streets. As the settlements became more secure, soldiers formed households with Indian women. Tradespeople like shoemakers, blacksmiths, armourers and tanners provided services for the colonists. In the beginning, the towns were administrative centres for the new colony and bases for sorties into Mapuche territory, but most of the population lived in the countryside.

By the late-16th century, Santiago was a settlement of just 200 houses, inhabited by not more than 700 Spaniards and mestizos and several thousand Indian labourers and servants. Occasionally flooded by the Río Mapocho, it nevertheless lacked a safe water supply, and communications between town and countryside were difficult. Despite their precarious position, wealthy encomenderos and other elite elements sought to emulate European nobility, with platoons of servants and imported products from Europe and China. Expelled by the Mapuche from the area south of the Biobío, Spaniards lacked ammunition, weapons and horses, but in wealthy houses there were velvet, silk and other luxuries.

Subject to the Viceroyalty of Peru, Chile remained a backwater of imperial Spain for nearly three centuries, yielding little exportable wealth. As colonial rule ended in the early 19th century, Chile's population – including the 100,000 sovereign Mapuches south of the Biobío – was perhaps half a million, 90% of whom lived in the countryside. Santiago had barely 30,000 residents, city streets were still unpaved, and the country roads were still potholed tracks. There were few schools and libraries and, although the University of San Felipe (founded in 1758 as a law school) provided intellectual spark, cultural life was bleak.

Not until the late-18th century did Santiago acquire the substance of a city proper, as new *tajamares* (dikes) restrained the Mapocho, improved roads handled increased commerce between the capital and Valparaíso, and authorities began various beautification projects to please the landowning aristocracy. By the 19th century, the capital had more than 100,000 inhabitants, and a railway and telegraph line linked it with Valparaíso, a bustling port and commercial centre of 60,000 people.

The landed aristocracy built sumptuous houses, adorned them with imported luxuries, founded prestigious social clubs, and visited their fundos during the holidays.

Social life revolved around clubs, the track, the opera and outings to the exclusive Parque Cousiño. Those of the governing class fashioned themselves as ladies and gentlemen who valued civilised customs, tradition and breeding, sending their children to be educated in Europe. For the elite at least it is still true that, as British diplomat James Bryce remarked at the turn of the century:

> The leading landowners spend the summers in their country houses and the winter and spring in Santiago, which has thus a pleasant society, with plenty of talent and talk among the men, a society more enlightened and abreast of the modern world than are those of the more northern republics, and with a more stimulating atmosphere.

From its inauspicious beginning, Santiago has become one of South America's largest cities – the Metropolitan Region contains well over four million inhabitants. The Museo de Santiago, in the colonial Casa Colorada off the Plaza de Armas, documents the city's phenomenal growth, in large part a function of oppression in the countryside. Poverty, lack of opportunity, and paternalistic fundos drove farm labourers and tenants north to the nitrate mines, and also into the cities – between 1865 and 1875, Santiago's population increased from 115,000 to more than 150,000, mainly due to domestic migration. This trend continued in the 20th century and, by the 1970s, more than 70% of all Chileans lived in cities, mostly in the heartland.

After WW II, rapid industrialisation created urban jobs, but never enough to satisfy demand. In the 1960s, continued rural turmoil fostered urban migration, resulting in squatter settlements known as *callampas* (mushrooms, so called because they sprang up virtually overnight) around the outskirts of Santiago and other major cities. Planned decentralisation has eased some of the pressure on Santiago, and regularisation, including the granting of land titles, has transformed many callampas. They still contrast, however, with the affluent eastern suburbs like El Golf, Vitacura, La Reina, Las Condes and Lo Curro.

ORIENTATION

Although Santiago is immense, its central core is a relatively small, roughly triangular area bounded by the Río Mapocho on the north, the Vía Norte Sur in the west, and the Avenida del Libertador General Bernardo O'Higgins (more commonly and manageably known as the Alameda, a shorthand for the earlier 'Alameda de las Delicias') in the south. The apex of the triangle is the Plaza Baquedano, where the Alameda intersects two other main thoroughfares, Avenida Providencia and Avenida Vicuña Mackenna.

In the centre of this triangle is the Plaza de Armas, with the city's most important public buildings, including the *municipalidad* (city hall), the cathedral, and the main post office. The Paseo Ahumada, a pedestrian mall, leads south to the Alameda. A block south of the Plaza de Armas, the Paseo Ahumada intersects with the Paseo Huérfanos, another pedestrian mall. The presidential palace, La Moneda, is on the Calle Moneda facing the Plaza de la Constitución. Near the Plaza de Armas is the former congress building, now home to the foreign ministry.

One of Santiago's most attractive parks, Cerro Santa Lucía, overlooks the Alameda near the Plaza Baquedano. The other main park is the enormous Cerro San Cristóbal, which rises dramatically from the plain to the north of Avenida Providencia. Between the park and the Mapocho, on either side of Avenida Pío Nono, is the Bellavista neighbourhood, Santiago's lively 'Paris quarter'. The riverside Parque Forestal is a verdant buffer between downtown and residential areas.

Within the centre, the street plan corresponds to the standard grid which the Spaniards imposed on all their American possessions, but most streets are too narrow for the heavy rush-hour traffic and a blanket of smog frequently hangs over the city, as the phalanx of the Andes blocks the dispersal of pollutants. However, there are many beautifully landscaped parks in which to take refuge from the pollution.

Travellers who plan an extended stay in Santiago should acquire Carlos Ossandón Guzmán's *Guía de Santiago* (Editorial Universitaria, 1988), which has gone through eight editions. It has good maps and illustrations, is especially strong on architectural history, and also contains a valuable summary in English.

INFORMATION

Tourist Office

Sernatur (☎ 698-2151), the national tourist service, has moved to Avenida Providencia 1550, midway between the Manuel Montt and Pedro de Valdivia Metro stations. The staff are friendly and capable, offering maps and other information, including lists of accommodation, restaurants and bars, museums and art galleries, transport out of Santiago, and leaflets on other parts of the country. It's open weekdays from 9 am to 5 pm and Saturday from 9 am to 1 pm.

There is also a Sernatur representative (☎ 601-9320) inside the international terminal at Pudahuel Airport, open weekdays from 9 am to 9 pm and weekends from 9 am to 5.30 pm. English is spoken at both offices.

The Municipalidad de Santiago maintains

a tourist kiosk at the intersection of Paseo Ahumada and Paseo Huérfanos, the pedestrian malls, a block from the Plaza de Armas. It is also very helpful but less well stocked with written information, though it distributes the monthly English-language publication *Santiago Tour* (US$1.50). It's open daily from 9 am to 9 pm. Another useful monthly publication, usually available free of charge despite a cover price of about US$2, is the bilingual *Guiamérica*, with encyclopedic listings of upscale hotels and travel agencies, but also very interesting articles on many out-of-the-way places and unusual topics.

All these offices distribute, free of charge, the pocket-size *Plano del Centro de Santiago*; this handy map details downtown, Providencia and other inner suburbs of the capital, and includes a useful diagram of the Metro system.

Money

There are numerous exchange houses on Agustinas, between Bandera and Ahumada, which will change travellers' cheques and foreign cash. At Pudahuel airport, the Banco de Chile operates exchange facilities near the customs offices. Rates are a bit lower at banks and at the airport, so change minimal amounts unless you're arriving on a weekend.

The easiest way to locate money changers is to stroll down Paseo Ahumada where, if you remotely resemble a gringo, aggressive touts will direct you to nearby exchange facilities (most of these men are trustworthy, but one traveller reported an unpleasant experience in a disreputable-looking office reached by a back alley). Cambios pay slightly less for travellers' cheques than for US cash, but do not usually charge a commission. The man who leads you there will expect a small tip. On Saturdays, when most downtown cambios are closed, try Lacov Tour at Ahumada 131, Local 13.

American Express (☎ 672-2156), Agustinas 1360, will exchange travellers' cheques for US cash, which can be useful in more remote destinations. Citibank will also change its own travellers' cheques for US cash. Thomas Cook, Agustinas 1058, deals only with replacing lost or stolen cheques, but Cambio Andes, Agustinas 1036, changes Thomas Cook cheques for US cash. Readers have also recommended Cambios Afex, Moneda 1169, to change cheques for cash.

Besides American Express, other credit card agencies in Santiago include Visa (☎ 672-8518) and MasterCard (☎ 695-2023), both at Morandé 315.

Post & Telecommunications

The Correo Central (main post office), which handles poste restante services and also has a philatelic desk, is on the north side of the Plaza de Armas. It's open weekdays from 8 am to 10 pm, Saturday from 8 am to 6 pm, and Sunday from 9 am to 1 pm. For a small fee, they will wrap parcels. There is another large downtown post office at Moneda 1155.

For long-distance overseas calls, go to ENTEL at Paseo Huérfanos 1133, open weekdays from 8.30 am to 10 pm, weekends from 9 am to 2 pm. CTC has many long-distance offices, the most convenient of which is at Moneda 1151, but there are others at Monjitas 760, San Diego 685, Santo Domingo 974, the Estación Central, Avenida 11 de Septiembre 2155, Local 166, in Providencia, and at Metro stations at Moneda, Universidad de Chile, Manuel Montt, Pedro de Valdivia, Tobalaba, and Escuela Militar.

For telegrams and telexes, go to Telex-Chile at Morandé 147, opposite the Plaza de la Constitución. It's open weekdays from 8.30 am to 8.30 pm, Saturday from 9 am to 2 pm, and Sunday from 9.30 am to 1.30 pm. Try also VTR Telecomunicaciones at Bandera 168.

Foreign Embassies

For the addresses of diplomatic representatives of overseas and neighbouring countries, see the Facts for the Visitor chapter.

Cultural Centres

The restored Estación Mapocho, where pas-

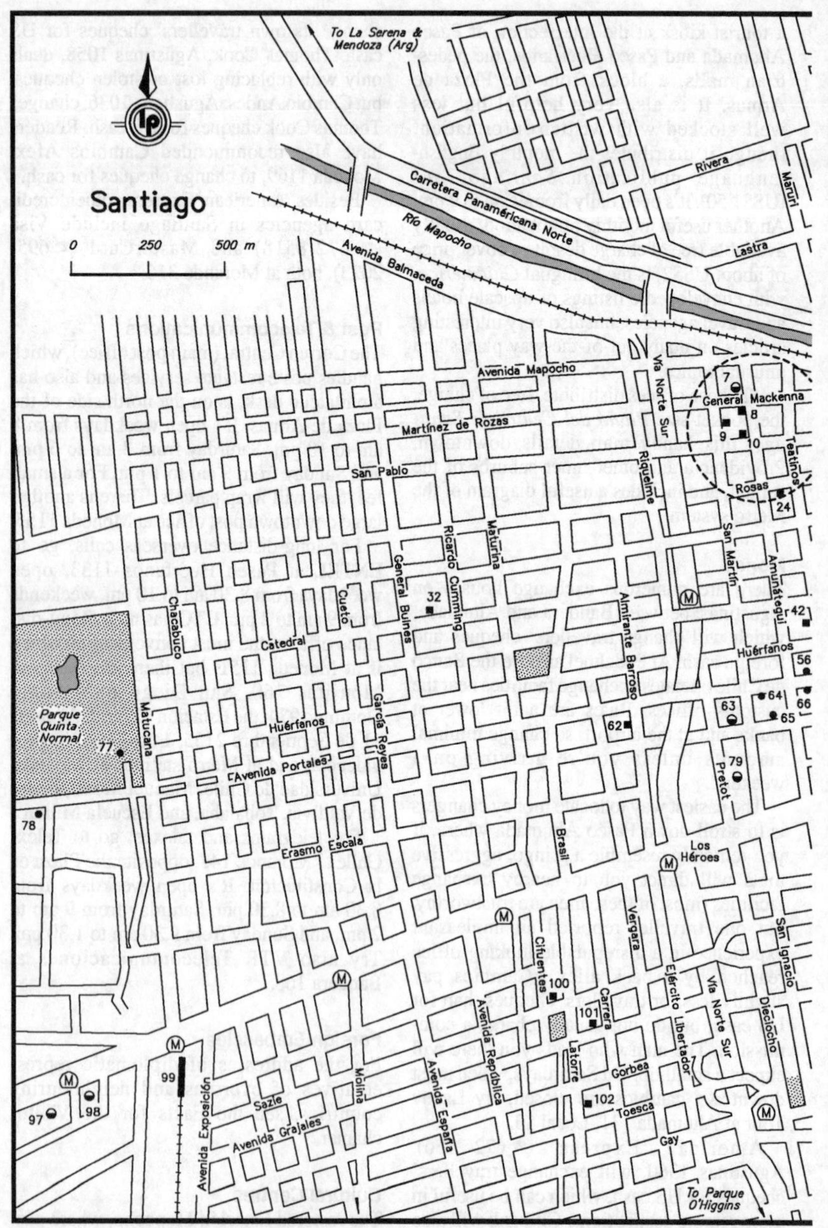
Santiago
0 250 500 m
To La Serena & Mendoza (Arg)
Rivera
Maruri
Carretera Panaméricana Norte
Río Mapocho
Avenida Balmaceda
Lastra
Avenida Mapocho
Martínez de Rozas
San Pablo
Vía Norte Sur
Riquelme
General Mackenna
Teatinos
Rosas
San Martín
Amunátegui
Ricardo Cumming
Maturina
General Bulnes
Cueto
Catedral
Chacabuco
Almirante Barroso
Huérfanos
Parque Quinta Normal
Matucana
García Reyes
Avenida Portales
Erasmo Escala
Brasil
Pretot
Los Héroes
Vergara
Ejército Libertador
San Ignacio
Cifuentes
Carrera
Avenida República
Dieciocho
Latorre
Gorbea
Avenida España
Toesca
Gay
Sazle
Molina
Avenida Grajales
Avenida Exposición
To Parque O'Higgins
7
8
9
10
24
32
42
56
62
63
64
65
66
77
78
79
97
98
99
100
101
102

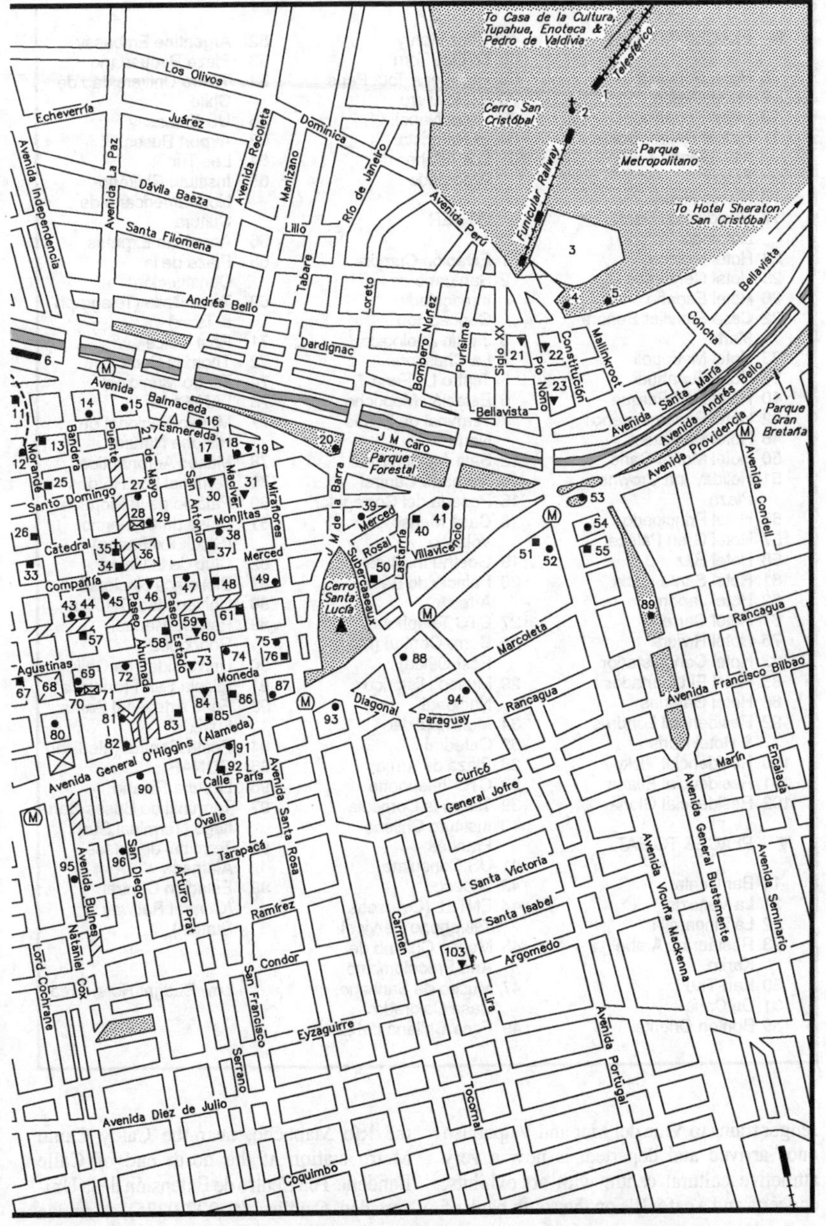
To Casa de la Cultura, Tupahue, Enoteca & Pedro de Valdivia
Teleférico
Cerro San Cristóbal
Parque Metropolitano
Funicular Railway
To Hotel Sheraton San Cristóbal
Bellavista
Concha
Mallinkroot
Constitución
Pío Nono
Siglo XX
Purísima
Bombero Núñez
Loreto
Avenida Perú
Río de Janeiro
Dominica
Manizano
Avenida Recoleta
Lillo
Tabare
Los Olivos
Juárez
Echeverría
Dávila Baeza
Santa Filomena
Avenida La Paz
Avenida Independencia
Andrés Bello
Dardignac
Avenida Balmaceda
Esmerelda
Bellavista
J M Caro
Parque Forestal
Avenida Santa María
Avenida Andrés Bello
Avenida Providencia
Parque Gran Bretaña
Avenida Condell
Bandera
Puente
21 de Mayo
San Antonio
MacIver
Miraflores
Morandé
Santo Domingo
Monjitas
Merced
Catedral
Compañía
Paseo
Paseo Estado
Ahumada
Agustinas
Moneda
J M de la Barra
Merced
Rosal
Lastarria
Villavicencio
Subercaseaux
Cerro Santa Lucía
Marcoleta
Rancagua
Avenida Francisco Bilbao
Diagonal Paraguay
Avenida General O'Higgins (Alameda)
Calle París
Avenida Santa Rosa
Curicó
General Jofre
Ovalle
Tarapacá
San Diego
Arturo Prat
Avenida Bulnes
Natániel Cox
Lord Cochrane
Santa Victoria
Santa Isabel
Ramírez
Condor
Argomedo
Carmen
Lira
San Francisco
Eyzaguirre
Serrano
Avenida Diez de Julio
Coquimbo
Tocornal
Avenida Portugal
Avenida Vicuña Mackenna
Avenida General Bustamente
Marín
Encalada
Avenida Seminario

■ PLACES TO STAY

8 Hotel Souvenir
9 Hotel Caribe
10 Hotel Pudahuel
11 Hotels Retiro, Colonial, Florida & San Felipe
13 Nuevo Hotel
17 Residencial Santo Domingo
24 Hotel Indiana
25 Hotel Cervantes
26 Hotel España
32 Casa Familiar Señora Marta
33 Hotel Metropoli
37 Hotel Tupahue
40 Hostal del Parque
42 Hotel Panamericano
48 Hotel So Paulo
50 Hotel Monte Carlo
51 Holiday Inn Crowne Plaza
55 Hotel Principado
57 Hotel Gran Palace
58 Hotel Ritz
61 Hotel Santa Lucía
62 Hotel Japón
67 Hotel Carrera
76 Hotel Riviera
83 Hotel Conquistador
85 Hotel El Libertador
86 Hotel Galerías
92 Residencial Londres & Hotel Paris
100 Residencial Vicky
101 Residencial Eliana
102 Residencial Gloria

▼ PLACES TO EAT

14 Bar Central
21 La Venezia
22 La Zingarella
23 Restaurant Arabe Karim
30 Kan-Thu
31 Da Carla
39 Bontón Oriental
46 Chez Henry
59 Le Due Torri
60 Pastelería Tout Paris
70 El Novillero
73 Pizza Napoli
84 El Naturista
103 Los Adobes de Argomedo

OTHER

1 Estación Cumbre
2 Santuario de la Inmaculada Concepción
3 Jardín Zoológico
4 La Chascona
5 Teatro La Feria
6 Estación Mapocho
7 Terminal de Buses Norte
12 Sala Agustín Sire
15 Mercado Central
16 Posada del Corregidor
18 Casa Manso de Velasco
19 Goethe Institute
20 Palacio de Bellas Artes
27 CTC Telephone
28 Cerro Central (Main Post Office)
29 Museo Historico Nacional
34 Municipalidad
35 Catedral
36 Plaza de Armas
38 CTC Telephone
39 Teatro la Comedia
40 Instituto Chileno-Francés
41 US Consulate
43 Ladeco
44 ENTEL (Overseas Telephone Service)
45 Museo Chileno de Arte Precolombino
47 Museo de Santiago; Casa Colorada
49 Feria Chilena del Libro
52 Argentine Embassy
53 Plaza Baquedano
54 Teatro Universidad de Chile
56 US Embassy
63 Airport Buses
64 Lee Tur
65 Instituto Chilteno-Norteamericano de Cultura
66 American Express
68 Plaza de la Constitución
69 Telex Chile (Telegraph & Telex)
71 Post Office
72 Thomas Cook
74 Teatro Municipal
75 LAN-Chile
77 Museo Nacional de Historia Natural
78 Museo Aeronautico
79 Terminal Los Héroes
80 Palacio de la Moneda
81 Bolsa de Comercio (Stock Exchange)
82 Club de la Unión
87 Biblioteca Nacional
88 Universidad Católica
89 Parque Manuel Rodríguez
90 Universidad de Chile
91 Iglesia San Francisco
93 Feria Artesanal Santa Lucía
94 Posta Central (Medical)
95 CONAF
96 Librería Rivano
97 Terminal de Buses Santiago (Terminal Sur)
98 Terminal de Buses Alameda
99 Estación Central (Central Railway Station)

Low Budget Hotel Area

senger trains to Viña del Mar and Valparaíso once arrived and departed, is now a very attractive cultural centre with art exhibits, concerts and a café. It's on the south bank of the Río Mapocho, near the Cal y Canto Metro station at the north end of Calle Bandera. The Centro de Extensión de la Universidad Católica (☎ 222-0275), Alameda

390, regularly presents artistic and photographic exhibits

The Instituto Chileno-Norteamericano de Cultura (☎ 698-6099), Moneda 1467, likewise has frequent photographic and artistic exhibits on various topics in various media. There is also a decent English-language library, which carries North American newspapers and magazines, and free films (usually in video format). Other comparable cultural centres include the Instituto Chileno Británico at Santa Lucía 124 (with current British newspapers and periodicals), the Goethe Institute (☎ 383815) at Esmeralda 650, and the Instituto Chileno Francés (☎ 398433) at Merced 298.

Several Santiago suburbs have their own cultural institutes, including the Instituto de Cultural de Las Condes (☎ 220-4849) at Avenida Apoquindo 6570 (open daily except Monday from 10.30 am to 1.30 pm and 3.30 to 7 pm) and the Casa de la Cultura de la Municipalidad de Ñuñoa (☎ 225-3919) at Avenida Irarrázaval 4055 (open daily from 10 am to 8 pm). Both change programmes frequently.

Travel Agencies

Downtown Santiago seems to have travel agencies on nearly every corner, on streets like Agustinas, Teatinos and Huérfanos, and in the affluent suburb of Providencia. For good prices on air tickets, see Miguel Gallegos at Lee Tur (☎ 672-7918, 696-7881), Agustinas 1476, Oficina 602.

Several agencies operate adventure or eco-tourism excursions. Probably the most comprehensive is Southern Summits (☎ 393712, fax 337784), Merced 102/106, which covers the country from the altiplano of the Norte Grande to pinnacles of Torres del Paine in tours of varying difficulty, including several in the neighbourhood of Santiago. Another similar agency is Kipaventur (☎ 235-1874), Manuel Montt 243-A in Providencia, which will arrange climbing and riding trips in the Cajón del Maipo east of Santiago, the nearby Andes, and to wildlife sites on the Pacific coast.

Other agencies with similar orientation include Altué Expediciones (☎ 232-1103), Encomenderos 83, and Grado Diez (☎ 251-2804), Las Urbinas 56, both in Providencia.

Bookshops & Newsstands

Santiago's largest and most well stocked bookstore is the Feria Chilena del Libro, Huérfanos 623 at Miraflores. With an excellent selection of books in both Spanish and English, it's a fine place to browse. Try also the branch at Providencia 2124. Editorial Universitaria, Agustinas 1138, is also a very good and serious store. Librería Albers, Merced 820, carries books and magazines in Spanish, German and English, including Lonely Planet guides.

Calle San Diego, south of the Alameda, contains Santiago's largest concentration of used bookshops, although quality varies. One of the best, Librería Rivano at San Diego 119, Local 7, has a fine collection on Chilean history, not all of which is displayed to the public.

Possibly the city's best is Librería Chile Ilustrado, Avenida Providencia 1652, Local 6 (☎ 460683), with a superb selection of books on Chilean history, archaeology, anthropology and folklore. Specialising in rare materials, but with much general interest stock, it's open weekdays from 9.30 am to 1.30 pm and from 4 to 7.30 pm, Saturday from 10 am to 1.30 pm. In the same complex is a smaller shop, known simply as Books, with a good selection of used paperbacks in English. Next door is the feminist bookshop Lila, which appears to be staffed exclusively by men.

For other books in English, try Librería Inglesa at Huérfanos 669, Local 11, or at Pedro de Valdivia 47 in Providencia. Newspapers and magazines in English and many other European languages, as well from other Latin American countries, are available at two kiosks at the intersections of Paseos Ahumada and Huérfanos. If a newspaper appears to have been around more than a few days, you can often haggle over the price.

Medical Services

For medical emergencies, contact the Posta

Central (☎ 341650) at Avenida Portugal 125 (Metro: Universidad Católica).

Dangers & Annoyances
Santiago has a growing reputation for petty street crime, especially downtown and in areas like Cerro Santa Lucía. The US Embassy recommends that visitors take cabs everywhere after dark, and avoid buses which are said to crawl with pickpockets, but adds that Americans can expect to visit Chile without incident. My own opinion is that travellers should be alert, but not obsessed with matters of personal security.

National Parks
For trekking and mountaineering information, go to the main offices of the Corporación Nacional Forestal (☎ 696-6749), known by its acronym CONAF, at Avenida Bulnes 285, Departamento 303. There is a regional office (☎ 832-3221) at Eliodoro Yañez 1810 in Providencia.

Camping Equipment
For camping supplies, try Southern Summits (☎ 393712) at Merced 102/104 or Distribuidora Nielsen (☎ 556-1155), both close to the Baquedano Metro station.

Camera Repair
For prompt and efficient, but not cheap, camera repair service, contact Harry Müller Thierfelder (☎ 698-3596), Ahumada 312, Oficina 312.

WALKING TOUR
The central tourist circuit starts at the **Estación Mapocho**, on the corner of Bandera and Balmaceda on the south-west bank of the Río Mapocho, which was the station for the rail link with Valparaíso and Viña del Mar from 1912 until the mid-1980s. It is now a cultural centre. On Balmaceda, between 21 de Mayo and Puente, the 1872 wrought-iron **Mercado Central**, designed by architect Fermín Vivaceta, is one of Santiago's most colourful attractions and a fine place for lunch or an early dinner.

Two blocks south-east is the **Posada del Corregidor** at Esmeralda 732. It's a white-washed, two-storey adobe structure with an attractive wooden balcony, built in 1780 and open to the public. Go down Enrique MacIver to the corner of Santo Domingo, where the early-18th century **Casa Manso de Velasco** resembles the Posada del Corregidor. Head north-west to Santo Domingo 961 and the **Templo de Santo Domingo**, a massive stone church dating from 1808.

Walk north-west of Santo Domingo for two blocks, then south-west for one block, to the **Plaza de Armas**, the city's historical centre, flanked by the **Correo Central** (main post office), the **Museo Histórico Nacional** and the historic colonial **Catedral**. The **Museo Catedral**, reached via a passageway from the Plaza de Armas, houses collections of colonial religious ornaments and relics.

Two blocks north-west of the plaza, at Morandé 441, stands the former **Congreso Nacional**, which has become the Ministry of Foreign Relations since the transfer of the Congress to Valparaíso. Nearby but now used for government offices, the **Palacio Edwards**, Catedral 1187 at Morandé, belonged to one of Chile's elite families. Immediately behind the ex-Congreso, are the **Tribunales de Justicia** (Law Courts), at Morandé 345. At Compañía 1340, the 1862 Moorish-style **Palacio de la Alhambra** is now an art gallery. A short distance away, at Bandera 361, is the **Museo Chileno de Arte Precolombino**, once the colonial customs house.

Running south-west from the Plaza de Armas is the **Paseo Ahumada**, the main pedestrian mall of Santiago where dozens of hawkers, one step ahead of the Carabineros, peddle everything from shampoo to seat belts. Buskers, of diverse style and quality, congregate in the evening – but the shrill Protestant evangelicals often drown out the rest. A few blocks south-west, another pedestrian mall, **Paseo Huérfanos**, intersects with Paseo Ahumada.

South-west of Huérfanos, between Teatinos and Morandé, is the **Plaza de la Constitución**, with the late-colonial **Palacio de La Moneda**, occupying an entire block between it and the **Plaza de La Libertad**. Formerly the presidential residence, it was badly damaged by air force attacks during the 1973 coup but restored in recent years. Other nearby buildings of note are the **Bolsa de Comercio** (stock exchange) at La Bolsa 64, and the **Club de La Unión** at Alameda 1091, where Santiago's stockbrokers hold their power lunches.

A short walk across the Alameda (it is safer, if not faster, to take the Metro underpass) is the **Universidad de Chile**, with the striking **Iglesia de San Francisco** at Alameda 834, a few blocks south-east. It's one of Santiago's oldest buildings, and it houses the **Museo de Arte Colonial**, an important collection of colonial art. Exhibits include a wall-size painting, attributed to an 18th-century artist, detailing the genealogy of the Franciscan order and its patrons. The several rooms depicting the life of St Francis of Assisi will exhaust all but the most earnestly devout. The museum is open daily, except Monday, from 10 am to 1 pm and 3 to 6 pm.

Continue along the Alameda, and cross to the other side and you'll see the monolithic **Biblioteca Nacional**, at the corner with MacIver. Two blocks north, another building of interest is the impressive **Teatro Municipal**, at Agustinas 794 on the corner of San Antonio.

THINGS TO SEE

Palacio de La Moneda

Under the direction of Italian-born architect Joaquín Toesca, construction of a mint started in 1788 near the modern Mercado Central on the Río Mapocho. The flood-prone site proved inadequate and the project soon moved to its present location, a former Jesuit farm, where it was finally completed in 1805. Toesca also contributed his talents to Santiago's cathedral, on the Plaza de Armas.

In the mid-19th century, La Moneda became the residence of Chilean presidents, but the last to actually live there was Carlos Ibáñez del Campo, from 1952 to 1958. After the military coup of 1973, General Pinochet governed from the Edificio Diego Portales, on the Alameda near Cerro Santa Lucía, but since the Moneda's restoration in 1981 both Pinochet and elected President Patricio Aylwin have had offices here.

By special arrangement, with 20 days' advance notice, it is possible to take a guided tour of the interior. Contact the Dirección Administrativa del Palacio de La Moneda (☎ 671-4103); the building itself is on Calle Moneda, between Morandé and Teatinos.

Museums

For a complete listing of Santiago museums, pick up Sernatur's leaflet *Galerías de Arte y Museos*, available from the tourist office, which also gives opening hours and transport details. Most museums are closed Monday.

Museo Chileno de Arte Precolombino In the late-colonial (1805) Palacio de la Real Aduana (royal customs house) at Bandera 361, this beautifully arranged museum of Precolombian art chronicles 4500 years of pre-Columbian civilisation. There are separate displays for Mesoamerica (Mexico, Guatemala and Central America), the central Andes (Peru and Bolivia), the northern Andean area (Colombia and Ecuador), and the southern Andean region (modern Chile and Argentina plus, rather anomalously, parts of Brazil). Most of the items, in a remarkable state of preservation, come from the personal collections of the noted Larraín family, but there are also special exhibits from time to time.

The museum is open Tuesday to Saturday from 10 am to 6 pm, Sunday from 10 am to 1 pm. Admission is about US$0.85, but it's free on Sundays.

Museo de Santiago In the colonial Casa Colorada, half a block from the Plaza de Armas, this museum documents the capital's growth from its modest nucleus to the present sprawl. Exhibits include maps, paintings, dioramas and colonial dress. Particularly intriguing are the diorama of the 1647 earthquake (when 10% of the population died), a model of the Iglesia de La Compañía after the fire of 1863, and the diorama of the departure of troops for the north in the War of the Pacific. There is also a life-size re-creation of a *sarao*, a parlour gathering of Santiago's late-colonial elite.

At Merced 860, the museum is open Tuesday to Saturday from 10 am to 4 pm, Sundays and holidays from 10 am to 3 pm. Admission costs US$0.85.

Palacio de Bellas Artes Santiago's turn-of-the-century fine arts museum, modelled on the Petit Palais in Paris, fronts an entire block in the Parque Forestal, on José M de La Barra near Avenida José Maria Caro. It has permanent collections of French, Italian, Dutch and Chilean paintings, plus occasional and sometimes very spectacular special exhibitions (such as the early 1992 collections from China).

Admission is US$0.65, but children pay half. Opening hours are Tuesday to Saturday from 11 am to 8 pm, Sundays and holidays from 11 am to 2 pm.

Mercado Central

Santiago's central market is a distinctive wrought-iron structure, occupying the entire block bounded by San Pablo, Puente, 21 de Mayo and Avenida Balmaceda, across from the Río Mapocho. Besides an appealing selection of fresh fruit, vegetables and fish, there are a number of eating places ranging from the modest to the finest.

Cerro Santa Lucía

Honeycombed with gardens, footpaths and fountains, Cerro Santa Lucía (known to the Mapuche as Huelén) has been a handy hilltop sanctuary from the congestion and bustle of downtown Santiago since 1875. At its base, on the Alameda, sits a large stone engraved with the text of a letter in which

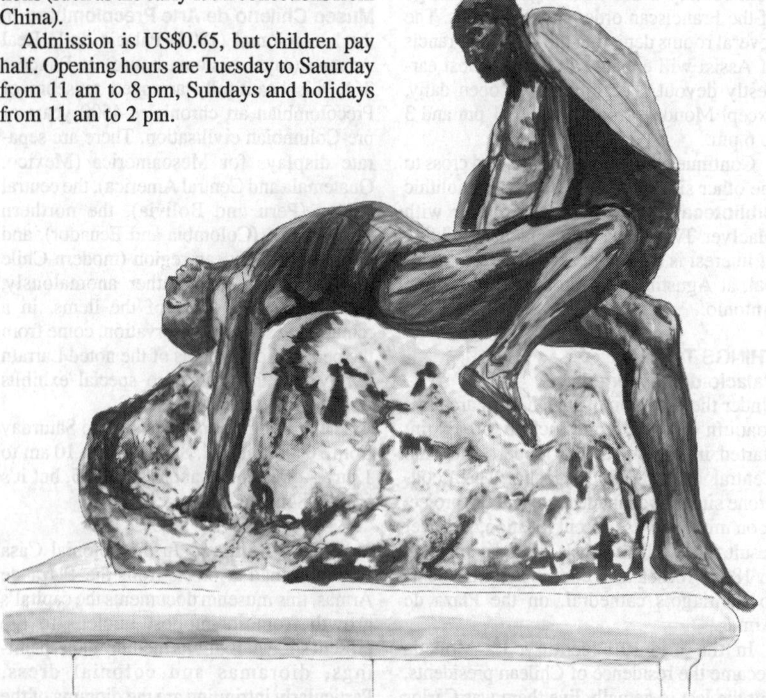

Statue in front of the Fine Arts Museum

Pedro de Valdivia extolled the beauty of the newly conquered territories to King Carlos V of Spain. A short distance to the north is a striking mural of Nobel Prize winning poet Gabriela Mistral. Also fronting the Alameda is a very attractive fountain, around which staircases climb to the summit. Santa Lucía's landscaping is a modern development – Bryce noted in 1914 that 'The buildings which had defaced it having been nearly all removed, it is now laid out as a pleasure ground, and planted with trees'.

Cerro Santa Lucía is an easy walk from downtown, or a short ride on the Metro to Santa Lucía station. It has acquired an unfortunate reputation for night-time muggings and is much safer during the day, although one woman reported a mid-afternoon attack.

Bellavista

Across the Río Mapocho, on both sides of shady Calle Pío Nono and many side streets, Bellavista is one of Santiago's liveliest neighbourhoods, with countless ethnic restaurants and a very active crafts fair on Friday and Saturday evenings.

La Chascona (Museo Neruda) The Fundación Neruda (☎ 777-8741) conducts tours of Pablo Neruda's eclectic Bellavista house, nicknamed after the poet's widow Matilde Urrutia, on a shady cul-de-sac at Márques de La Plata 0195, a short distance off Pío Nono

Tour schedules are rather complex: Tuesday and Wednesday at 10.30 and 11.30 am and 12.30, 3 and 4.30 pm; Thursday there is an additional tour at 6 pm and Friday yet another at 7 pm. Saturday tours begin at 10 and 11 am and noon, and at 3, 4 and 5 pm. Reservations are normally essential, so call ahead, but if you're in the neighbourhood you can try dropping by. Admission costs US$2; tours last an hour and are very thorough. The Fundación also arranges one-day bus tours (lunch included) which take in the poet's three houses; here, at Isla Negra and in Valparaíso (see the Middle Chile chapter for these two).

Cerro San Cristóbal

Crowned by a 36-metre white statue of the Virgin Mary, 860-metre Cerro San Cristóbal towers above downtown Santiago from the north side of the Río Mapocho. Reached by funicular railway, telesférico (cable car), bus, or on foot, it is part of the Parque Metropolitano, the largest open space in central Santiago and a major recreational resource for residents of the capital. There are several restaurants, snack bars and coffee shops.

The easiest way to reach the summit of San Cristóbal is to take the funicular which climbs 485 metres from the Plaza Caupolicán at the north end of Pío Nono. It operates daily from about 10 am to 8.30 pm, with slightly longer hours on weekends and holidays. There is an intermediate stop at the **Jardín Zoológico** (zoo), which has a modest collection of exotic animals.

The funicular, built in 1925, runs to the **Terraza Bellavista** from where, on a rare clear day, there are extraordinary views of the city and its surroundings. At the summit is the **Santuario Inmaculada Concepción**, where Pope John Paul II said mass during his visit to Santiago in 1984.

A short walk from the Terraza is the Estación Cumbre, the start of the 2000-metre long **telesférico** which goes from Cerro San Cristóbal, via Tupahue, to a station near the north end of Avenida Pedro de Valdivia Norte (about 1200 metres from the Pedro de Valdivia Metro station); hours are the same as for the funicular.

At the Tupahue telesférico station is the **Piscina Tupahue**, with large swimming pools. A short walk east from Tupahue are the **Casa de la Cultura** (an art museum), Santiago's famous **Enoteca**, (a restaurant and wine museum), and the **Jardín Botánico Mapulemu** (the botanical garden). Further east, there are also large swimming pools at **Piscina Antilén**, which can be reached only by bus or on foot.

From either direction, the funicular-telesférico combination (about US$4), plus the Metro, is a good way to orient yourself to Santiago's complex geography. Winter hours may be limited to Friday afternoons and weekends.

Buses Tortuga Tour also link the Plaza Caupolicán with Avenida Pedro de Valdivia Norte via Tupahue, on a winding, roundabout road.

Parque Quinta Normal

One of Santiago's largest open spaces is the 40-hectare Parque Quinta Normal, west of downtown, with several commendable museums. Formerly an area of prestigious mansions, the Quinta Normal is now much less exclusive but of great historical interest. Take the Metro to Estación Central and then walk or catch a bus up Matucana.

On the park's southern edge, at Avenida Portales 3530, is the **Museo Aeronáutico** (Aeronautical Museum), housed in an offbeat structure designed for the Paris Exhibition of 1889 and dismantled and installed opposite the Quinta Normal after the turn of the century. Near the park entrance is the **Parque Museo Ferroviario**, a tribute to pioneers of the Chilean railroads.

Within the park proper is the **Museo Nacional de Historia Natural**. The exhibits include the mummified body of a 12-year-old child, sacrificed at least 500 years ago and discovered in 1954 by a team from the Universidad de Chile on the icy summit of El Plomo, a 5000-metre peak near Santiago. (There are reports that this mummy is a credible replica of the original, which is kept under wraps.) Bone fragments of the giant Pleistocene ground sloth known as the 'milodon', from the famous cave near Puerto Natales in southern Chile (see the Magallanes chapter), are also on display. Beyond the lagoon, visit the **Museo de Ciencia y Tecnología**, a recent addition.

Parque O'Higgins

In a previous incarnation as Parque Cousiño, 80-hectare Parque O'Higgins was the preserve of Santiago's elite, but it is now a more egalitarian place. **Fantasilandia** is an amusement park for children, open daily except Monday in summer but Sundays only the rest of the year. The section known as **El Pueblito**, featuring full-size replicas of rural constructions, also contains the **Museo del Huaso**, honouring Chile's counterpart to the Argentine gaucho. To get there, take the Centro line of the Metro to Parque O'Higgins station.

Parque de Las Esculturas

At the other end of Santiago, in the affluent suburb of Providencia, this open-air sculpture garden is a pleasant hangout on the banks of the Río Mapocho. There is also an indoor exhibition hall at Avenida Santa María 2201, a short walk across the river from the Pedro de Valdivia Metro station.

LANGUAGE COURSES

For intensive (but not inexpensive) language courses, try the Instituto de Idiomas Bellavista (☎ 777-5933), Dominica 25 near the Cerro San Cristóbal.

ORGANISED TOURS

If time is limited, consider a tour of Santiago and its surroundings.

Turismo Latino (☎ 341463), Turquesa 334, runs day and night tours of the capital (around US$20 each), excursions to Viña del Mar and Valparaíso (around US$40), visits to the Cousiño Macul and Concha y Toro wineries, and ski trips to Farellones, Valle del Nevado, and Portillo (see below under Ski Resorts). Chilean Travel Services (☎ 696-7820), Agustinas 1291, 5th floor, Oficina F, has also been recommended for city tours. It may be slightly cheaper to sign up on the spot rather than to make advance reservations.

A Santiago city tour includes sights like the Iglesia de San Francisco, Cerro Santa Lucía and Cerro San Cristóbal. There are also half-day tours to Santiago's major museums, including the Museo Chileno de Arte Precolombino, the Museo de Arte Colonial at the Iglesia de San Francisco, and the Museo de Historia Natural in the Quinta Normal. Day tours to Valparaíso and Viña del Mar take in the waterfront, the Academia Naval, the Universidad de Santa María, the Museo Baburizza de Pintura and the Viña del Mar casino.

PLACES TO STAY

Places to Stay – bottom end

Santiago has abundant budget accommodation, but travellers should be selective – lodgings in this category differ much more in quality than in price.

Youth Hostels During the summer months, Santiago has three hostels where accommodation costs about US$5 per person. All fairly central and south of the Alameda, these are the 'small and homey' *Residencial Eliana* (☎ 672-6100) at Grajales 2013 near Los Héroes Metro station, *Residencial Gloria* (☎ 698-8315) at Almirante Latorre 449, and *Residencial Vicky* (☎ 672-2269) at Sazie 2107.

Hotels, Hospedajes & Residenciales Santiago's main budget hotel zone is a seedy but not really dangerous neighbourhood near the Terminal de Buses Norte, on the corner of General Mackenna and Amunátegui, where accommodation ranges from acceptable to truly squalid. Most of the cheap places are on General Mackenna, Amunátegui, San Pablo and San Martín. Single women may feel uncomfortable here late at night, especially on General Mackenna, where many of Santiago's prostitutes hang out.

Best in the area is the labyrinthine *Hotel Caribe* (☎ 696-6681), San Martín 851, which I have patronised for over a decade and which is still good value at US$5 per person with shared bath and hot showers. Although popular with travellers, it's large enough to ensure that there's usually a room, though singles may be at a premium. Rooms are spartan but some are very large, and the manager and staff are very friendly. Ask for a room at the back or upstairs, since foot traffic on the squeaky-clean floors makes the lobby and passageway a bit noisy. There are flimsy hasps and padlocks on the doors, but you can leave valuables in the safe; they will happily and securely store your personal belongings at no charge if you go trekking or take some other excursion. Meals, snacks and drinks are available at reasonable prices.

Now rivalling the Caribe among budget travellers is the recently remodelled, more central, and very slightly cheaper *Nuevo Hotel* (☎ 671-5698), with entrances at both San Pablo 1182 and Morandé 791. Another recommendation is *Hotel Pudahuel*, San Pablo 1417-19 at Amunátegui, which one reader describes as an 'old, beautiful, European-style building', with large and bright rooms.

Besides these, hotels in the area are dubious, but try *Hotel Indiana* at Rosas 1334, a dilapidated mansion with dependable hot water, or *Hotel Souvenir* at Amunátegui 856, which has primordial plumbing, dim lighting, sagging staircases and murky corridors, but clean sheets and hot water. Others offer little more than cubicles, such as *Hotel Retiro*, General Mackenna 1266, which may do in a pinch. Comparable places include *Hotel Colonial* (☎ 556-9685), Mackenna 1262, and *Hotel Florida* (☎ 671-3794), Mackenna 1250. Best of a bad bunch is probably *Hotel San Felipe*, Mackenna 1248, but avoid the front rooms of all these hotels – Mackenna is a busy, noisy street with heavy bus and auto traffic.

Another good neighbourhood for inexpensive accommodation is the Barrio París Londres, south of the Alameda near the Iglesia San Francisco. One very popular place is *Residencial Londres* (☎ 382215) at Londres 54, a great value at US$5/10 with hot water, clean and secure rooms, and a pleasant and helpful staff. Arrive early, since it's very popular and fills up quickly – singles are almost impossible to get. If nothing's available, try *Hotel París*, around the corner at Calle París 813, where doubles cost US$15. Other have recommended the nearby *Hotel Opera*, 'a little shabby but the rooms are spacious', with friendly management, about US$7 a single with shared bath.

Costlier than the Londres or París, but very central, is the *Residencial Santo Domingo*, Santo Domingo 735. Well west of the Plaza de Armas is *Residencial del Norte* (☎ 695-1876), Catedral 2207, which charges US$10 per person in a family atmosphere. More conveniently located is *Hotel España*

(☎ 698-5245) at Morandé 510, with clean but stark rooms at US$15/25 for singles/doubles.

Some of the best bargains in this category are private houses or apartments – see the tourist kiosk at Ahumada and Huérfanos for a list. One very central alternative is *Casa Familiar Señora Marta* (☎ 672-6090), Catedral 1029, Departamento 401.

Places to Stay – middle

Santiago's mid-range accommodation is generally better value than its budget selection. Many of these hotels have agreeable little rooms with private bath and toilet; for a few bucks more there is often telephone, TV and refrigerator. Sernatur's free pamphlet, *Alojamiento – Región Metropolitana*, lists the capital's mid-range and upscale accommodation.

Hotel Cervantes (☎ 696-5318), Morandé 631 near Santo Domingo, is very central, with rooms with private bath at US$27/35. There are slightly cheaper doubles with shared bath and hot water, plus a decent restaurant. Some rooms are a bit cramped but others are spacious and bright. *Hotel Japón* (☎ 698-4500), Almirante Barroso 160 near Agustinas, is good value at US$29/34, with pleasant gardens and an English-speaking owner who will exchange books.

Another reasonable hotel in the centre is *Hotel São Paulo* (☎ 398031), San Antonio 357 between Compañía and Huérfanos, with prices from US$32/37 for singles/doubles. One highly recommended place is *Hotel Metropoli* (☎ 672-3987), at Sótero del Río 465, a small street off Catedral between Teatinos and Morandé, just a few blocks from the Plaza de Armas. For US$37/41, you get a clean, comfortable room with private bath in a central location. *Hotel Ritz* (☎ 393401), Paseo Estado 248, is comfortable and central for US$39/49, but the traffic noise is considerable. Try also the pleasant *Hotel Riviera* (☎ 331176), Miraflores 106, with smallish rooms at US$41/46.

One of the best in this range is *Hotel Monte Carlo* (☎ 381176), Subercaseaux 209, opposite Cerro Santa Lucía. Rooms are small but cheery, all have private bathrooms and the staff are friendly. Beware, however, of noise from the busy street. Rather quieter is the *Hotel Principado* (☎ 222-8142) at Arturo Buhrle 015. Just off Vicuña Mackenna and near the Baquedano Metro station, it charges US$44/53. *Hotel Santa Lucía* (☎ 398201), Huérfanos 779, 4th floor, is also good value at about US$50/60. Rooms are attractive with TV, telephone, refrigerator and private bath – one correspondent thought it much better value than the far more prestigious Hotel Carrera (see below), but rooms facing the street can be very noisy.

There are a number of other decent hotels in the US$30/50 range. These include *Hotel El Libertador* (☎ 394212) at Alameda 853 for US$33/40; *Hotel Gran Palace* (☎ 671-2551) at Huérfanos 1178 for US$37/46; *Hotel Panamericano* (☎ 672-3060) at Teatinos 320 (US$40/46); and *City Hotel* (☎ 695-4526) at Compañía 1063 for US$45/51.

Places to Stay – top end

Santiago has many first-rate hotels, including most of the well known chains. Most have restaurants, cafés, bars and money exchange services for their clients, and are very expensive.

Hotel Tupahue (☎ 383810), San Antonio 477 near Monjitas, has singles/doubles for US$85/95, including continental breakfast, but the air-conditioning is suspect and it's not really good value. *Hotel Conquistador* (☎ 696-5599) is at Miguel Cruchaga 920, a small street off Estado near the Alameda. Rates, with breakfast, start at US$92/108. One correspondent has praised the new *Hotel Aloha* (☎ 233-2230), Francisco Noguera 146 in Providencia, which has doubles for US$90 (Metro Pedro de Valdivia).

The *Hostal del Parque* (☎ 392694) is at Merced 294 near Lastarría, opposite the Sociedad de Arte Precolombino Nacional. Prices are US$88/104.

The glittering *Hotel Galerías*, (☎ 384011) a block from the Alameda at San Antonio 65,

Top : Cerro Santa Lucía, Santiago (GL)
Bottom Left : Old building, Santiago (AS)
Bottom Right : Paseo Puente, Santiago (WB)

Top : Downtown Santiago & Providencia (WB)
Bottom : Port of Valparaíso (WB)

has rooms for US$118/130, and features a swimming pool. At the *Holiday Inn Crowne Plaza* (☎ 381042) Alameda 136 near Vicuña Mackenna, rates start at US$171/195. The hotel has offices, shops, car rentals and a post office. A new *Hyatt* (☎ 218-1234) has opened on Avenida President Kennedy in Las Condes, with rooms starting at US$150.

At the venerable *Hotel Carrera* (☎ 698-2011), overlooking the Palacio de La Moneda and the Plaza de la Constitución at Teatinos 180, rates start at US$189/201. One correspondent complained that its hot water supply was erratic. (Affluent activists might relish the room from which, in 1985, deadly serious opponents of the dictatorship aimed a time-delay bazooka at General Pinochet's office – the recoil was too strong for a photo tripod and the explosion destroyed the room's interior instead.) The *Sheraton San Cristóbal* (☎ 233-5000) at Santa María 1742 at Calle El Cerro, at the base of Cerro San Cristóbal, has rooms starting at US$230/254.

PLACES TO EAT

Santiago has an abundance of restaurants from the basic to the elegant, especially around the bus terminals, the Huérfanos and Ahumada pedestrian malls, the Plaza de Armas and the Alameda. You can find Italian pasta, Indian curry, Middle Eastern stuffed grape leaves and Chilean parrilla. Sernatur's free publications will give you some idea of this formidable range, but the *Centro* volume of CTC's Turistel guide series has the most comprehensive and systematic listing.

Avoid greasy McDonalds clones like *Burger Inn* or *Max Beef*. For cheap snacks, pastries and drinks there's a string of stand-up places in the arcade on the south side of the Plaza de Armas – try *Pollo Montserrat* for cheap fried chicken with chips. In the same arcade, highly regarded *Chez Henry* is no longer cheap, but neither is it outrageous – for about US$3.50 their famous pastel de choclo is the only meal you'll need all day (other dishes are dearer, but selective diners can still eat well at moderate prices). Portions are huge, but the ready-made items from the takeaway deli are cheaper and no less appealing. Their ice cream is among Santiago's best.

For breakfast, don't miss the delicious croissants, pastries and coffee at *Pastelería Tout Paris*, Agustinas 847. Another good place for pastries is *Bontón Oriental*, Merced 345 near Cerro Santa Lucía – its modest appearance camouflages unexpected delicacies such as a very fine apple strudel. For good, inexpensive coffee and cocoa, go to any of the several stand-up bars, such as *Café Haití* at Ahumada 140, *Café Caribe* almost next door at Ahumada 120, and *Café Cousiño* at Matías Cousiño 107, all of which have many other branches around town.

Many travellers have recommended *Bar Central*, San Pablo 1063, which serves generous portions of excellent seafood and is also popular with Santiaguinos. *Queijo e Mel*, Huérfanos 749, offers modest and moderately priced Brazilian food. Carnivores should try *El Novillero*, Moneda 1145.

Vegetarians can munch at *El Naturista*, Moneda 846, and *El Vegetariano*, Huérfanos 872, both of which are moderately priced. There are excellent lunch specials at *Silvestre*, Huérfanos 965, with ravioli, rice, mixed vegetables, omelettes, desserts, drinks and much more. One reader enthusi-

Ice-cream seller

astically recommended *Kan-Thu*, at Santo Domingo 769.

For lunch, one of Santiago's best and cheapest eating places is the *Mercado Central* (Central Market) on San Pablo, a few blocks north of the Plaza via Puente, with a wealth of tremendous seafood dishes – be adventurous. Its lively atmosphere makes the historic building worth visiting in its own right, while the varied food at the numerous stalls and restaurants is often a bargain. The most appealing places to dine are the the tables among the central fruit and vegetable stands, but those restaurants are not dramatically better than the smaller, cheaper places on the periphery.

North of the Mapocho, Santiago's Bellavista neighbourhood, at the foot of Cerro San Cristóbal along Pío Nono and its side streets, is a great dining area, especially lively on the weekends. Restaurants in this area, where poet Pablo Neruda once lived, include the pizzería *La Zingarella*, Pío Nono 185, *La Venezia* at Pío Nono 200, and the *Restaurant Arabe Karim*, with cheapish kebabs and other Arabic dishes. South of the Mapocho, try *Pérgola de la Plaza* a bar-restaurant at José V Lastarria 305-321 behind the Hostal del Parque, which is very popular for wine and pastries. Renovated and used as artists' studios, the surrounding buildings house a cluster of arts and crafts shops.

Santiago has a good selection of ethnic restaurants. For pasta dishes there is *Da Carla* at MacIver 577. Another recommended Italian restaurant is *San Marco* at Huérfanos 618, while more than one LP reader found *Le Due Torri*, San Antonio 258 at Huérfanos, one of the best restaurants in town and good value to boot. For Italian fast food, try *Pizza Napoli* at Estado 149 or Avenida 11 de Septiembre 1935.

German food is the fare at *Der Münchner*, Diego de Velásquez 2105, while French cuisine is the rule at *Les Assassins*, Merced 297. *Los Adobes de Argomedo* (☎ 222-2104), Argomedo 411 at Lira, is a gaudy pseudo-folkloric restaurant-nightclub with stereotypical entertainment, to which some Santiaguinos feel obliged to take foreign visitors, but the Chilean food is good and varied. Expect to pay around US$20 per person, with wine. Although it is very large, reservations are a good idea.

Providencia is an increasingly popular place for restaurants. For exceptionally good ice cream, go to *Sebastián*, Andrés de Fuenzalida 26 (Metro Pedro de Valdivia or Los Leones) or *Coppelic* on Avenida Providencia, which unfortunately closes early. For good pizza, try *La Pizza Vera*, Providencia 2630, which has a good variety but is a bit on the pricey side. For drinks, snacks and top-40 music in an Anglophile environment, try the *Red Pub* at Suecia 29.

ENTERTAINMENT

Theatre & Music

Santiago has a vigorous theatre tradition and many attractive venues for both drama and music. Most prestigious is the Teatro Municipal de Santiago (☎ 332804), Agustinas 749, with offerings from classical to popular. The Teatro Universidad de Chile (☎ 345295) is at Baquedano 043, while Teatro El Conventillo (☎ 777-4164) is across the Mapocho at Bellavista 173. Nearby is Teatro La Feria (☎ 377371), at Crucero Exéter 0250.

The Teatro La Comedia (☎ 391523) offers dramatic presentations at Merced 349, near Cerro Santa Lucía. The Sala Agustín Sire, operated by the Universidad de Chile's theatre department, is downtown at Morandé 750. Also downtown is the Teatro Opera, Huérfanos 837. Teatro Esmeralda (☎ 777-4189), across the Alameda at San Diego 1035, held a Shakespeare festival in January and February1992. Also during summer, there is an inexpensive open-air theatre programme in the Parque Manuel Rodríguez (formerly Parque Bustamante), south of Plaza Baquedano.

Cinema

Santiago's commercial cinema district is along Paseo Huérfanos and nearby side streets. Many cinemas have half-price discounts on Wednesdays.

The Universidad Católica's Centro de Extensión (☎ 222-0275), Alameda 390, has low-price international 'cine arte' (art film) cycles on a regular basis, as does Cine Arte Normandie (☎ 696-1634) at Tarapacá 1181.

Nightclubs

One correspondent enjoyed the live entertainment ('a mix of vaudeville and 1950s nightclubs') and dancing at La Cucaracha, Bombero Nuñez 159 in Bellavista, which also had good food but was rather expensive.

THINGS TO BUY

Chile's artisanal products include lapis lazuli, black pottery, and copperware, plus attractively carved wooden moai from Easter Island. The Feria Artesanal La Merced, Merced at MacIver, is a good place for an overview, but there are two well stocked shops, El Rincón Chileno and Chile Típico, in the gallery at Moneda 1025. Try also Huimpalay, at Huérfanos 1162, or Claustro del 900, Portugal 351, which is located in an old convent.

Farther out of the centre, several people have recommended the market at Los Graneros del Alba, Avenida Apoquindo 8600, which also has music and dancing on weekends. Take the Metro to the end of the line at Escuela Militar and catch a bus out Avenida Apoquindo. Mornings are the best time to go.

GETTING THERE & AWAY

Given Chile's 'crazy geography', Santiago is an unavoidable reality – nearly every visitor either arrives at the capital or passes through here at one time or another.

Air

International Most major international airlines have offices or representatives in Santiago. The following list includes the most important ones.

Aeroflot
  Agustinas 640, 23rd floor (☎ 632-4092)
Aerolíneas Argentinas
  Moneda 756 (☎ 394121)
Aero Perú
  Fidel Oteíza 1953, 5th floor (☎ 274-3434)
Air France
  Agustinas 1136 (☎ 698-2421)
Alitalia
  O'Higgins (Alameda) 949, 10th floor (☎ 698-3336)
American
  Huérfanos 1199 (☎ 671-6266)
Avianca
  Moneda 1118 (☎ 695-4105)
British Airways
  Huérfanos 669, 5th floor (☎ 338366)
Canadian Pacific
  Huérfanos 669, Local 9 (☎ 393058)
Ecuatoriana
  O'Higgins (Alameda) 949 , 25th floor (☎ 696-4251)
Iberia
  Agustinas 1115 (☎ 698-1716)
KLM
  San Sebastián 2839, 2nd floor (☎ 233-0991)
Ladeco
  Huérfanos 1157 (☎ 698-2778)
  Pedro de Valdivia 0210, Providencia (☎ 251-7204)
LAN-Chile
  Agustinas 640 (☎ 632-3442)
  Pedro de Valdivia 0139, Providencia (☎ 232-8712)
LASSA
  Avenida Larraín 7941, La Reina (☎ 273-4354)
Líneas Aéreas Paraguayas (LAP)
  Agustinas 1141, 2nd floor (☎ 671-4404)
Lufthansa
  Moneda 970, 17th floor (☎ 696-1072)
Lloyd Aéreo Boliviano (LAB)
  Moneda 1170 (☎ 671-2334)
Pluna
  Agustinas 1046 (☎ 696-8400)
SAS
  Miraflores 178, 15th floor (☎ 391105)
Swissair
  Estado 10, 15th floor (☎ 337014)
Transportes Aéreos Robinson Crusoe
  Monumento 2570, Maipú (☎ 531-3772)
Varig
  Miraflores 156 (☎ 395261)
Viasa
  Agustinas 1141, 6th floor (☎ 698-2401)

Domestic Ladeco and LAN-Chile are the main domestic carriers. Ladeco has daily flights from Santiago to Antofagasta, Calama, Iquique, Arica, Puerto Montt and Punta Arenas. They also have less frequent flights to Temuco, Valdivia and Osorno.

LAN-Chile has daily flights from Santiago to Antofagasta, Iquique, Arica, Puerto

Montt and Punta Arenas. They have flights about six days a week to Calama, and two or three days a week to Easter Island.

Bus

International From Santiago, there are direct buses to every South American country except the Guianas and, apparently, Bolivia, although only masochists are likely to attempt the 4½ to 10-day marathons to destinations like Quito, Guayaquil, Bogotá and Caracas. Tepsa (☎ 779-2563) and Ormeño (☎ 776-4116) cover these routes, with stops in Lima. Most international buses now depart from the Terminal Sur, stopping at the Terminal Norte to take on passengers.

Argentina, of course, is the most frequent destination. Lines which cross the Andes to Mendoza (seven hours) include Chile Bus, Fénix (☎ 776-3253), Nueva O'Higgins San Martín (☎ 380410), Pluma (☎ 671-5223), and Tas Choapa (☎ 779-4925). Tas Choapa and Bus Norte (☎ 779-5333) both have a direct service to Bariloche (21 hours). Igi Llaima and Buses Jac (☎ 695-5925) go to Junín de Los Andes, San Martín de Los Andes and Neuquén via Temuco (summer only). To Córdoba, try Chevalier (☎ 671-5223) or TAC (☎ 779-6920). TAC has the only direct service from Santiago to Mar del Plata (36 hours). For Buenos Aires (23 hours), consult Chi-Ar (☎ 695-1508), CATA (☎ 696-5845), Chevalier, Fénix, Nueva O'Higgins San Martín, Pluma, TAC and Tas Choapa.

Typical fares from Santiago to Argentina include Mendoza for US$20, Bariloche US$35, Córdoba US$57 and Buenos Aires US$64. It is generally cheaper, and not much less convenient to take a bus to Mendoza and make your connection elsewhere in Argentina from there. Argentine trains, if not crippled by strikes, are notably cheaper than buses. There is a very frequent service from Mendoza to Buenos Aires.

Coitram and other agencies have taxi colectivos to Mendoza, which are only slightly more expensive and much quicker than buses – and drivers may stop on request for photo opportunities on the spectacular Andean crossing. They leave from the Terminal Sur and cost about US$28, although you may be able to haggle outside peak season, especially if the taxi is about to leave and has one or more vacant seats. Tickets may also be purchased at the Terminal Norte.

Chile Bus has buses to Río de Janeiro via Mendoza, Rosario, Santa Fe, Paraná, Paso de Los Libres, Uruguaiana, Porto Alegre, Florianópolis, Curitiba and São Paulo. There are several departures weekly for the 72-hour endurance test. Chevalier and Pluma run similar routes; the latter goes to Asunción and Montevideo as well.

Other approximate international fares from Santiago include Lima (Peru) US$66, Montevideo (Uruguay) US$70, Quito (Ecuador) US$104, Bogotá (Colombia) US$150, and Caracas (Venezuela) US$190.

Domestic Santiago has four main bus terminals – the Terminal de Buses Norte for northbound travellers; the Terminal de Buses Santiago (also known as Terminal Sur) for southbound travellers; the adjacent Terminal Libertador Bernardo O'Higgins (also called the Terminal de Buses Alamaeda) also for southbound travellers; and the newer Terminal Los Héroes, on Pretot near the Alameda, where some long-distance buses from the Terminal Sur make an additional stop for passengers. Some companies which operate buses in both directions sell tickets at more than one terminal, but you will still have to catch northbound buses from the Terminal Norte and southbound ones from the Terminal Sur or the Terminal Los Héroes.

The Terminal de Buses Norte (☎ 671-2141), at Amunátegui 920 on the corner of General Mackenna, is three blocks west of the Cal y Canto Metro station. Some buses to Mendoza (Argentina) also leave from here. Companies which serve northern destinations include:

Andes Mar (☎ 699-2053)
to Los Vilos, Ovalle, La Serena and Copiapó

Buses Evans (☎ 698-5953)
to Arica and intermediate points along the Panamericana

Buses Ligua (☎ 698-7339)
to La Ligua
Buses Lit (☎ 699-2263)
to Los Vilos, Coquimbo and La Serena
Buses Tal (☎ 672-4415)
to the Norte Chico
Carmelita (☎ 698-6615)
to Coquimbo, La Serena, Antofagasta, Iquique and Arica
Combarbalá Rima (696-0313)
to various parts of the Norte Chico
Expreso Norte (☎ 698-3089)
to the Norte Chico
Fénix Pullman Norte (☎ 695-2010)
to Arica and intermediate points
Fichtur (☎ 698-5559)
with luxury services to Arica and intermediate points
Flecha Norte (☎ 698-1437)
to Los Vilos, Arica and intermediate points
Flota Barrios (☎ 698-1494)
to Valparaíso/Viña del Mar and north to Arica and intermediate points
Geminis (☎ 696-4426)
to Arica and intermediate points
Inca Bus (☎ 672-1817)
to the Norte Chico
Kenny Bus (☎ 697-0632)
to Los Vilos and La Serena
Libac (☎ 696-4486)
to Coquimbo, La Serena, Vallenar and Calama
Los Corsarios (☎ 696-3912)
to Los Vilos and La Serena
Los Diamantes de Elqui (☎ 672-4415)
to Los Vilos, La Serena and Copiapó
Nueva Transmar (☎ 699-1566)
to beach resorts from Valparaíso north
Palacios
to Coquimbo, La Serena and Vicuña
Pullman Bus (☎ 698-5559)
to Arica and intermediate points
Ramos Cholele (☎ 672-6378)
to Iquique and Arica
Tas Choapa (☎ 695-4692)
to Los Vilos, Copiapó and intermediate points
Tramaca (☎ 672-6840)
to Antofagasta, Calama, Arica and intermediate points
Vía Choapa (☎ 698-0922)
to the Norte Chico

The Terminal de Buses Sur (☎ 779-1385), Alameda 3800 between Los Muermos and Ruiz Tagle, is one block west of the Universidad de Santiago Metro station. Companies with southern destinations include:

Bus Norte (☎ 779-5433)
to the southern Lake District and Punta Arenas
Buses Dar (☎ 779-1351)
to Los Angeles and the northern Lake District
Buses Vásquez (☎ 779-5915)
to Los Angeles and Angol
Cruz del Sur (☎ 779-3852)
to the Lake District and Chiloé Island
Fénix Pullman (☎ 779-4648)
to Los Angeles, Angol, Valdivia and intermediate points
Inter Sur (☎ 779-6312)
to many destinations in the Lake District
Longitudinal Sur (☎ 779-5856)
to Temuco and Valdivia
Pullman Lit (☎ 521-7198)
to the southern mainland and nearly all the coastal resorts
Tas Choapa (☎ 779-4694)
to Chillán, Concepción/Talcahuano, Temuco, Puerto Montt and intermediate stops on the Panamericana
Transbus (☎ 779-8649)
to Rancagua, Talca, Chillán and Concepción
Turibus (☎ 779-1377)
to the southern Lake District and Punta Arenas
Vía Tur (☎ 779-3839)
to Chillán and mainland points south
Varmontt (☎ 231-3505)
to the southern Lake District

The smaller Alameda terminal is at the corner of Alameda and Jotabeche, at the southern exit from the Metro station. It handles only two companies, including Tur Bus (☎ 776-3133) which has frequent buses to Valparaíso and Viña del Mar, and also serves Lake District destinations such as Temuco, Valdivia, Osorno, Villarrica and Puerto Montt.

Fares can vary dramatically among companies, so explore several possibilities. Discounts are common, and bargaining is even possible at times – for instance, on the route from Santiago to Mendoza. Sample fares and journey times from Santiago are:

Antofagasta	US$27	18 hours
Arica	US$40	28 hours
Chillán	US$8	6 hours
Concepción	US$9	8 hours
Copiapó	US$17	11 hours
Iquique	US$37	26 hours
La Serena	US$12	7 hours

Osorno	US$17	14 hours
Puerto Montt	US$19	16 hours
Puerto Varas	US$18	15 hours
Punta Arenas	US$51	60 hours
Temuco	US$11	11 hours
Valdivia	US$13	13 hours
Valparaíso	US$2.50	2 hours
Villarrica	US$12	13 hours
Viña del Mar	US$2.50	2 hours

For long journeys, especially to the north, consider a *salón cama* bus, which has reclining sleeperette seats with footrests, calf-rests and extra legroom. A salón cama ticket from Santiago to Arica costs around US$52.

Some buses, for destinations close to Santiago, leave from the smaller Terminal de Buses Borja, near the Terminal de Buses Alameda, at Alameda 3250.

Train

To/From the South Trains to Concepción, Temuco, Valdivia, Osorno and Puerto Montt leave from the Estación Central (☎ 689-5199), Alameda 3322 (Metro: Estación Central). Only in summer is there a service south of Temuco. Station hours are daily from 7 am to 11 pm.

If the Estación Central is inconvenient, book your passage at the Venta de Pasajes (ticket office; ☎ 398247) in the Galería Libertador, Alameda 853, Local 21. It's open weekdays from 8.30 am to 7 pm, and Saturday from 9 am to 1 pm. There is another office (☎ 228-2983) at the Galería Comercial Sur, at the Escuela Militar Metro station, which keeps the same hours. For details of fares and timetables on the southern line, see the Getting Around chapter.

To/From Valparaíso The rail service to Valparaíso has been recently restored, but perhaps only for the summer of 1992 and not permanently. The train leaves from Estación Central, costs about US$1.40 and takes three hours or more – half the price of the bus, but taking nearly twice as long. There is only a single train on weekdays, but four or five on weekends and holidays.

GETTING AROUND

To/From Airports

Aeropuerto Internacional Arturo Merino Benítez The international airport (☎ 601-9001) is at Pudahuel, 26 km west of central Santiago. Get there by bus from the Tour Express downtown terminal (☎ 671-7380), Moneda 1523 near San Martín. There are about 30 round trips daily from between 6.30 am and 9.15 pm. At other times, they meet incoming flights on arrival. This very efficient and dependable service costs about US$1.50 and takes about 30 minutes. Buses from Pudahuel leave from the front of the airport terminal, and will drop you at the city terminal or just about anywhere along the route. Taxi fares are open to negotiation; a cab to or from downtown can cost anywhere from about US$10 (if your Spanish is good) to US$25, but may be shared.

From Los Héroes Metro station, Metropuerto provides a similar and slightly cheaper service. Minibuses belonging to Shuttle (☎ 635-3030) will transport passengers door-to-door between the airport and any part of Santiago for US$7 – call the day before your flight if possible.

Aeropuerto Nacional Cerrillos This small airport (☎ 557-2640) handles a limited number of domestic flights, including those to the Juan Fernández Islands. It is in the suburb of Cerrillos, easily reached by bus or taxi colectivo from the Alameda.

Aeródromo Eulogio Sánchez Known colloquially as 'Tobalaba' after the eastern suburb in which it is located, this rarely has commercial flights.

Metro

Santiago has an excellent Metro system with two lines in operation and others in early stages of construction. It's the most convenient system of public transport and far simpler than city buses, although it does not yet serve some important areas, such as the middle-class inner suburb of Ñuñoa. The Terminal Sur, the Estación Central, and

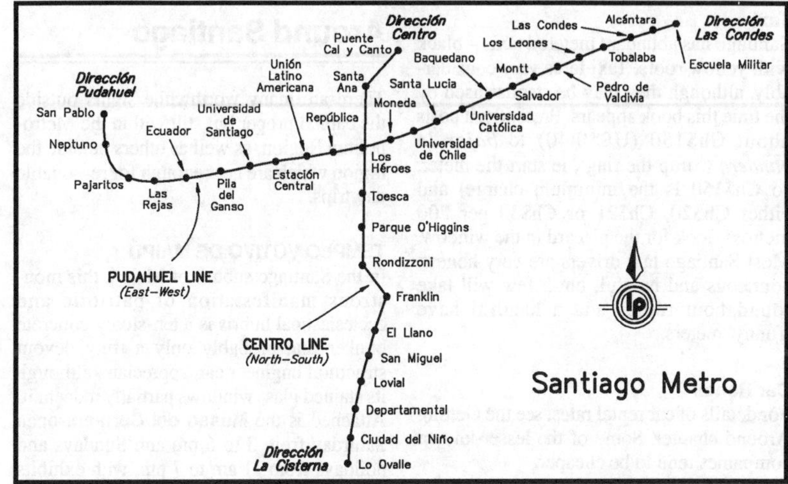

many foreign embassies (most of which are in Providencia or Las Condes) are easily reached by Metro. It operates Monday to Saturday from 6.30 am to 10.30 pm and Sundays and public holidays from 8 am to 10.30 pm. Trains are quiet, comfortable and very frequent.

Signs on station platforms indicate the direction in which the trains are heading. On the older east-west (Pudahuel) line, Dirección Las Condes heads toward Escuela Militar station in the wealthy eastern suburbs, while Dirección Pudahuel goes to San Pablo station (it does *not* reach the international airport). On the newer north-south (Centro) line, Dirección Centro reaches the Puente Cal y Canto station a few blocks north of the Plaza de Armas, while Dirección La Cisterna heads towards the southern suburb of Lo Ovalle. Los Héroes, beneath the Alameda, is the only transfer station between the two lines.

Fares on the Centro line are a flat US$0.15; fares on the Pudahuel line are a flat US$0.30. Tickets can be purchased from agents at each station. Carnets (booklets of ten tickets) are also available at a slight discount. While the cash saving is minimal, it saves time to buy a booklet of tickets beforehand.

Tickets have a magnetic strip on the back. After slipping your ticket into a slot in the turnstile, pass through onto the platform; your ticket is not returned. At your stop, you simply walk through the exit.

Bus

Santiago's buses go everywhere cheaply, but it takes a while to learn the system – check the destination signs in their windows or ask other passengers waiting at the stop. Fares are usually a flat rate of around US$0.25 per trip; hang on to your ticket, since inspectors may ask for it.

Taxi Colectivo

Taxi colectivos are, in effect, five-passenger buses on fixed routes. They are quicker and more comfortable than most buses and not much more expensive – about US$0.70 within Santiago city limits, although some to outlying suburbs like Puente Alto are a bit dearer. Taxi colectivos look like ordinary taxis but have an illuminated roof sign and a placard in the window which states the fixed fare.

Taxi
Santiago has abundant metered taxis – black with yellow roofs. Taxi fares vary considerably, although they may be standardised by the time this book appears. Presently, it costs about Ch$150 (US$0.40) to *bajar la bandera* ('drop the flag', ie start the meter, so Ch$150 is the minimum charge) and either Ch$20, Ch$21 or Ch$30 per 200 metres – look for the placard in the window. Most Santiago taxi drivers are very honest, courteous and helpful, but a few will take roundabout routes and a handful have 'funny' meters.

Car Rental
For details of car rental rates, see the Getting Around chapter. Some of the lesser-known companies tend to be cheaper.

Budget, Hertz, Western, National, Avis, Galerías and American all have offices outside the airport terminal building at Pudahuel. City offices are:

American
  Las Condes 9225 (☎ 220-2354)
Atal
  Avenida Costanera 1051, Torres de Tajamar (☎ 225-7727)
Automóvil Club de Chile (ACCHI)
  Marchant Pereira 122, Providencia (☎ 274-4167)
Avis
  La Concepción 334 (☎ 495757)
  Hotel Sheraton, Santa María 1742 (☎ 274-7621)
Bert
  Francisco Bilbao 2032 (☎ 43736)
Bond
  Vitacura 2737 (☎ 233-6195)
Budget
  Bilbao 3028 (☎ 204-9091)
Chilean
  Bellavista 0195 (☎ 376902)
Dollar
  Avenida Vitacura 5454, Las Condes (☎ 486840)
First
  Andrés Bello 1429 (☎ 499019)
Hertz
  Costanera 1469 (☎ 225-9328)
Galerías
  San Antonio 65, in the Hotel Galerías (☎ 384011)
National
  La Concepción 212, Providencia (☎ 251-7552)
Travirentacar
  General Holley 114 (232-2607)

Around Santiago

There are many worthwhile sights outside the capital proper but still within the Metropolitan Region, as well as others outside the region which are near enough for reasonable day trips.

TEMPLO VOTIVO DE MAIPÚ

In the Santiago suburb of Maipú, this monstrous manifestation of patriotic and ecclesiastical hubris is a ten-storey concrete bunker that probably only a truly devout structural engineer can appreciate, although its stained glass windows partially redeem it. Attached is the **Museo del Carmen**, open Saturday from 3 to 6 pm and Sundays and holidays from 11 am to 7 pm, with exhibits on religious history and customs. On the grounds, there are also late colonial ruins which are fenced off because of earthquake damage.

From the Alameda in Santiago, take any bus that says Templo. Taxi colectivos leave from Calle Amunátegui.

WINERIES

Viña Santa Carolina

There are several wineries within Santiago proper, but the most accessible is the Viña Santa Carolina (☎ 238-2855), Rodrigo de Araya 1341, near the Estadio Nacional in Ñuñoa. Although the sprawling capital has displaced the vineyards themselves, the historical *casco* (main house) of the Julio Pereira estate and the *bodegas* (warehouses) are still here, and open to the public for weekend tours. Taxi colectivos out Avenida Vicuña Mackenna will leave you within easy walking distance.

Viña Cousiño Macul

This winery is also within Santiago's city limits, but the grounds themselves are not open to the public. Tours of the bodegas take place daily at 11 am; take a bus or taxi colectivo out Américo Vespucio Sur to Avenida Quilín.

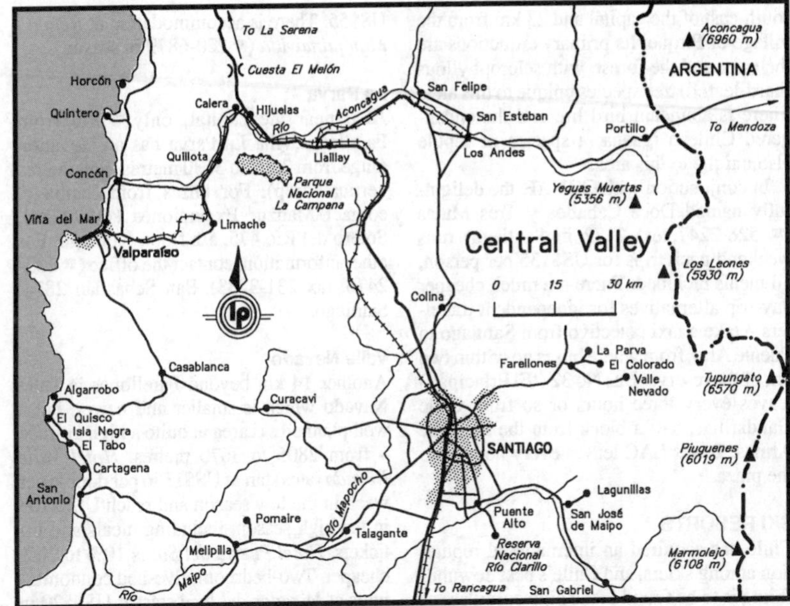

Viña Concha y Toro
At Lozcano 1220 in the village of Pirque, near Puente Alto, in the Cajón del Maipo (the canyon of the Río Maipo) south-east of Santiago, Viña Concha y Toro (☎ 850-3123, 850-1407), is the largest winery in Chile. Tours of the grounds and vats take place daily at 10.30 am and 1, 3 and 5.30 pm, but call ahead to be sure of a spot. At the end of the tour you can taste three different wines for about US$1. From Santiago's Plaza Italia, at the corner of Tarapacá and San Francisco, taxi colectivos to Puente Alto and Pirque cost about US$1.

Viña Undurraga
This is another major winery (☎ 817-2308), 34 km south-west of the capital on the old highway to Melipilla, with its grounds and buildings open to the public weekdays from 9.30 am to noon and 2 to 4 pm. Buses Peñaflor (☎ 776-1025) covers this route from the Terminal de Buses Borja, near the Alameda terminal at Alameda 3250, Santiago.

POMAIRE
In this small, dusty village near Melipilla, south-west of Santiago, skilled potters spend their days at their wheels to produce unique and remarkably inexpensive ceramics – a punchbowl with half a dozen cups, for instance, costs only about US$6. Unfortunately, most of these items are too large and fragile for most travellers to take home, but it's still worth a day trip from the capital for a tour and a small souvenir. From Santiago, take Buses Melipilla (☎ 776-2060) from the Terminal de Buses Borja, Alameda 3250.

RESERVA NACIONAL RÍO CLARILLO
One of Santiago's closest nature reserves, 10,000-hectare Río Clarillo is a scenic tributary canyon of the Cajón del Maipo,

south-east of the capital and 23 km from the village of Pirque. Its primary attractions are the river and the forest, with sclerophyllous (hard-leafed) tree species unique to this area. There is abundant bird life and the endangered Chilean iguana, a species of reptile also unique to this area.

In conjunction with CONAF, the delightfully named Doce Caballos y Tres Mulas (☎ 528-2247, ext 2172 in Santiago) runs weekend pack trips for US$135 per person, all meals included. There are much cheaper day-trip alternatives for independent travellers – take a taxi colectivo from Santiago to Puente Alto, from where buses go within two km of the reserve. Bus No 32 ('El Principal') leaves every three hours or so from Calle Gandarillas, half a block from the Plaza de Armas. Buses LAC leaves every hour from the plaza.

SKI RESORTS

Chile has acquired an international reputation among skiers, and Chile's best downhill skiing is to be found in the high cordillera of Middle Chile. Most of the ski areas here extend to over 3300 metres, and so have longer runs, a longer season, and generally deep, dry snow. Portillo in particular has a reputation for dry powder snow. The season generally runs from June to early October. Most resorts vary their rates from low season (mid-June to early July and mid-September to early October), to mid-season (mid-August to mid-September), to high season, the most expensive (early July to mid-August).

Farellones-Colorado

This is one of the closest sites to Santiago, only 45 km east of the capital. The ski area has over a dozen lifts running up to 3333 metres above sea level, and a vertical drop of 903 metres.

Centro de Ski El Colorado Farellones (☎ 246-3344, fax 220-7738), Avenida Apoquindo 4900, Local 47/48 in the Santiago suburb of Las Condes, offers day excursions including round-trip transportation, rental equipment and lift tickets for US$55. There is accommodation at *Refugio Manquimávida* (☎ 220-6879 in season).

La Parva

Also near the capital, only 4 km from Farellones, Villa La Parva has an elevation range from 2662 to 3630 metres (968 metres vertical drop). For buses from Santiago, contact Manzur Excursiones (☎ 774284), Sótero del Río 475, 5th floor, Santiago. For other information, contact the office (☎ 233-2476, fax 231-3233), San Sebastián 2874, Santiago.

Valle Nevado

Another 14 km beyond Farellones is Valle Nevado which is smaller and newer, but a well planned ski area at quite a high altitude – from 2805 to 3670 metres. *Hotel Valle Nevado* rates start at US$1186 per double per week in the low season and reach US$2103 in the high season, including meals and lift tickets. *Hotel Puerta del Sol* is 10% to 20% cheaper. Two-bedroom, five-bed condominiums at *Mirador del Inca* start at US$520 in the low season and climb to US$1180 in the high season, without meals. All accommodation includes transportation to and from Pudahuel airport. For bookings contact the office (☎ 212-8730, fax 211-5255), Avenida Las Condes 7730, Santiago.

Lagunillas

This small resort, 84 km south-east of Santiago via San José de Maipo, has a ski field which ranges from 2250 to 2580 metres above sea level. Accommodation is available at the refugio of the Club Andino de Chile, which can be contacted at Sierra Bella 1231, Santiago. At Lo Valdés, farther up the Cajón del Maipo, there is lodging at the *Refugio Alemán* (☎ 850-1773), which has excellent food in a spectacular setting. Manzur Expediciones (see under La Parva) also provides bus transportation.

Portillo

This famous resort is 152 km from Santiago, on the trans-Andean highway to Mendoza (Argentina). Just a short distance from the

Chilean customs post, it has been the site of several downhill speed records. Altitudes range from 2590 to 3330 metres.

Accommodation at *Hotel Portillo* is not cheap, with singles/doubles starting at US$970/1550 for a week's stay in low season, although this includes all meals, eight days of lift tickets, and taxes. There are lower priced alternatives which involve camp beds and shared bath, but even those run $475 per person per week including lift tickets. For more information contact the Centro de Ski Portillo (☎ 231-3411, fax 231-7164), Roger de Flor 2911, Santiago.

PARQUE NACIONAL LA CAMPANA

After Darwin scaled the 1840-metre peak of Cerro La Campana, which he called 'Bell Mountain', he fondly recalled one of his finest experiences in South America:

> The evening was fine, and the atmosphere so clear, that the masts of the vessels at anchor in the bay of Valparaíso, although no less than twenty-six geographical miles distant, could be distinguished clearly as little black streaks. A ship doubling the point under sail, appeared as a bright white speck...
>
> The setting of the sun was glorious; the valleys being black, whilst the snowy peaks of the Andes yet retained a ruby tint. When it was dark, we made a fire beneath a little arbour of bamboos, fried our *charqui* (dried strips of beef), took our *mate*, and were quite comfortable. There is an inexpressible charm in thus living in the open air...
>
> We spent the day on the summit, and I never enjoyed one more thoroughly. Chile, bounded by the Andes and the Pacific, was seen as in a map. The pleasure from the scenery, in itself beautiful, was heightened by the many reflections which arose from the mere view of the Campana range with its lesser parallel ones, and of the broad valley of Quillota directly intersecting them...

Created in 1967 by private donation, Parque Nacional La Campana occupies 8000 hectares in a nearly roadless segment of the coastal range which once belonged to the Jesuit hacienda of San Isidro. The park is administered by CONAF, and is divided into a number *sectors* for administrative purposes. In geological structure and vegetation, its jagged scrubland resembles the mountains of Southern California and protects remaining stands of the Roble de Santiago *(Nothofagus obliqua)*, the northernmost species of the common South American genus, and the Chilean palm *(Jubaea chilensis)*.

The Chilean palm, also known as the Palma de Coquitos for its tasty fruits (one Chilean writer called them miniature coconuts), grows up to 25 metres in height and measures up to 1½ metres in diameter. In more accessible areas, it declined greatly in the 19th century because it was exploited for its sugary sap, obtained by toppling the tree and stripping it of its foliage. According to Darwin, each palm yielded up to 90 gallons of sap, which cutters concentrated into treacle by boiling it. In some parts of the park there are ruined ovens which were used for this purpose, as well as kilns for producing charcoal.

Geography & Climate

In the province of Quillota in the Fifth Region (Valparaíso), La Campana is about 40 km east of Viña del Mar and 110 km north-west of Santiago, via the Ruta Panamericana. Altitudes range from 400 metres above sea level to 2222 metres on the summit of Cerro Roble. The park has a Mediterranean climate strongly influenced by the ocean. Annual maximum temperatures average 19°C and minimum temperatures 9°C, but these statistics obscure dramatic variation – summer can be very hot and dry, while there is occasional snow at higher elevations in winter. Mean annual rainfall, about 800 mm, falls almost entirely between May and September. Profuse wildflowers and a more dependable water supply make spring the best time for a visit, but the park is open all year.

Palmas de Ocoa

Reached by a sometimes rough gravel road from the village of Hijuelas, on the Ruta Panamericana, Palmas de Ocoa is the northern entrance to La Campana.

At Casino, two km beyond the park entrance, a good walking trail connects the

Palmas de Ocoa sector (Sector Ocoa) with Granizo (see below), 14 km to the north. To reach the high saddle of the Portezuelo de Granizo takes about two hours of steady hiking through the palm-studded canyon of the Estero Rabuco. On clear days, which are becoming rarer, the Portezuelo offers some of the views which so impressed Darwin.

About halfway up the canyon is a good flat campsite where wild blackberries are abundant and the fruit from abandoned grapevines ripens in late summer. Water is very limited. Farther up the canyon, just below the Portezuelo, there is a conspicuous and dependable spring, but elsewhere livestock have fouled the water, so carry a water bottle. At the Portezuelo, the trail forks: the lower branch plunges into Cajón Grande, while the other follows the contour westward before dropping into Granizo.

The hike from Palmas de Ocoa to Granizo, or vice-versa, is an ideal weekend excursion across the coastal range, allowing the hiker to continue to either Santiago or Viña, depending on the starting point. It is probably better to start from Granizo, where public transport is better – at Palmas de Ocoa, CONAF rangers will help you get a lift back to the Panamericana, where it is easy to flag a bus back to Santiago.

Also in the Palmas de Ocoa sector, another hiking trail leads six km to Salto de La Cortadera, an attractive waterfall which is best during the spring runoff. Ask the rangers for directions to the trailhead.

Cerro La Campana & Cerro Roble

Darwin needed no permission to climb these peaks, but you do. Before attempting the summits, consult CONAF rangers.

Places to Stay

Camping is the only alternative in the park proper – CONAF has five formal camping areas at Sector Granizo, three at Sector Cajón Grande, and one at Sector Ocoa. It is possible to make day trips from Viña del Mar and even from Santiago, though a trip from Santiago can be rather time-consuming because there is no regularly scheduled public transportation between Hijuelas and Sector Ocoa.

CONAF permits backcountry camping, but inform the rangers before attempting the routes between Palmas de Ocoa and Granizo or Cajón Grande. This is steep, rugged country, and fire is a very serious hazard, especially in summer and autumn.

Getting There & Away

La Campana enjoys good access from both Santiago and Viña del Mar. The Granizo and Cajón Grande sectors can be reached by Línea Ciferal from Valparaíso and Viña del Mar, every 30 minutes in season. Local transport (AGDABUS) leaves every 20 minutes from Limache and Olmué. Both involve about a one-km walk to the park entrance.

Direct access to Sector Ocoa is more problematic. Most any northbound bus from Santiago will drop you at Hijuelas (there is a sharp and poorly marked turnoff to the park just before the bridge across the Río Aconcagua), but from there you will have to hitch or walk 12 km to the park entrance, or else hire a taxi.

Middle Chile

Middle Chile, the country's heartland, comprises the Metropolitan Region of Santiago, plus the Fifth Region of Valparaíso, the Sixth Region of O'Higgins the Seventh Region of Maule and the Eighth Region of Biobío. Its most significant feature is the fertile central valley which is, at its widest, just 70 km between the Andean foothills and the coastal range. Only at the southern edge does the valley floor extend to the Pacific. Endowed with rich alluvial soils, a pleasant Mediterranean climate, and Andean meltwater for irrigation, this is Chile's chief farming region, ideal for cereal farming, fruit, and vineyards.

Since the arrival of Europeans, large estates have dominated Chile's regional economy and society, but landowners rarely developed their properties efficiently, provoking a contentious agrarian reform in the 1960s and early 1970s. After the 1973 coup, the dictatorship returned many large farms to their former owners and dissolved co-operatives in favour of individual family farms.

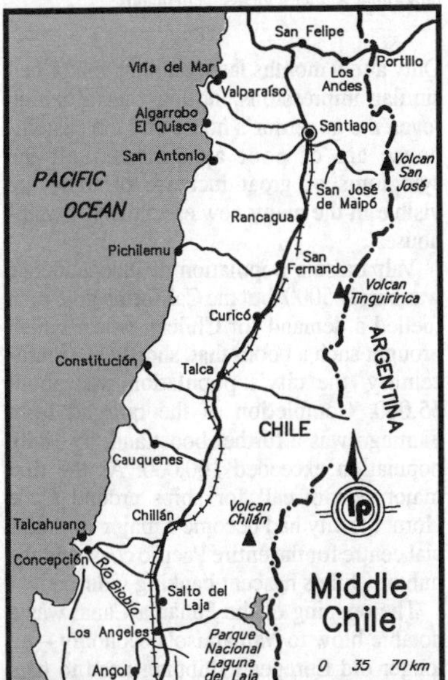

Middle Chile contains about 70% of the country's population and most of its industry. Nearly a third live in the sprawling capital of Santiago, but the region also includes the major port of Valparaíso and Chile's most famous resort, the 'garden city' of Viña del Mar. Copper mines dot the sierras of the Metropolitan Santiago, Valparaíso and O'Higgins regions. North of the Río Biobío, Concepción and its port of Talcahuano play an important role in the national economy. Throughout the region, the imposing crest of the Andes is never far out of sight, but the Libertadores Pass north-west of Santiago is the only all-season crossing to Argentina.

Valparaíso & the Coast

North-west of Santiago, Valparaíso (population over 300,000) and its nearby coastline play a dual role in Chile. Valparaíso is a vital port and one of South America's most distinctive urban areas, while Viña del Mar, a resort of international stature, and other coastal towns to the north are a favourite summer playground.

VALPARAÍSO

Often called *La Perla del Pacífico* (Pearl of the Pacific), or Valpo for short, Valparaíso is Chile's principal port and second largest city. It has a commercial centre which occupies a narrow strip of land between the waterfront and the hills, with distinctive, sinuous, cobbled streets, irregular intersections and architectural landmarks. This is overlooked by precipitous cliffs, and hills covered by suburbs and shantytowns which are linked to

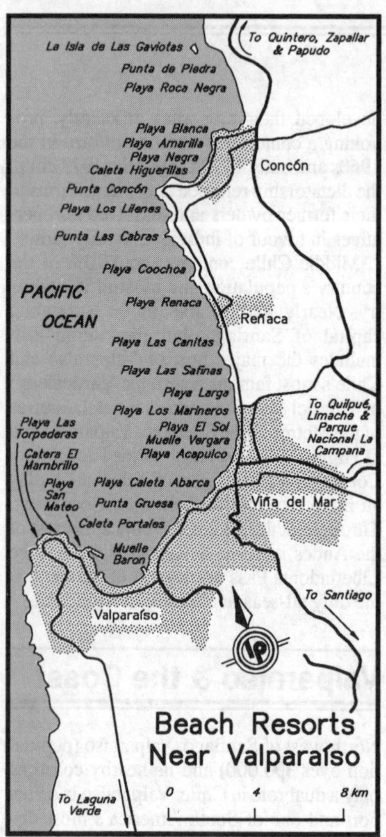

the city centre by meandering roads, footpaths which resemble staircases, and *ascensores* (funicular railways which climb the steep slopes).

History

Historians credit Juan de Saavedra, a lieutenant from Diego de Almagro's expedition whose troops met a supply ship from Peru in what is now the Bahía de Valparaíso in 1536, as the founder of the city. Despite Pedro de Valdivia's designation of the bay as the port of Santiago and the building of some churches, more than two and a half centuries passed before the Spanish crown established a *cabildo* (town council) in 1791. Not until 1802 did Valparaíso legally become a city.

Spanish mercantilism retarded Valparaíso's growth in the colonial era, but after independence foreign merchants quickly established their presence. One visitor in 1822 remarked that Englishmen and North Americans so dominated the city that 'but for the mean and dirty appearance of the place, a stranger might almost fancy himself arrived at a British settlement'. Its commerce was disorderly but vigorous:

> The whole space between the beach and Customhouse was filled with goods and merchandize of various kinds – timber, boxes, iron-bars, barrels, bales, etc. – all exposed without any method or arrangement in the open street. Interspersed among them were a number of mules, some standing with loaded, others with unloaded panniers; while the drivers, called peons, dressed in the characteristic garb of the country, made the place ring with their noisy shouts. Here and there porters were busied in carrying away packages; boatmen stood ready to importune you with incessant demands....

Only a few months later, another visitor had similar impressions, noting that although 'even the governor's house and the customhouse are of poor appearance....all the symptoms of great increase of trade are visible in the many new erections for warehouses'.

Valparaíso's population at independence was barely 5000, but the California gold rush fuelled a demand for Chilean wheat which brought such a boom that, shortly after midcentury, the city's population was about 55,000. Completion of the railroad from Santiago was a further boost and, by 1880, population exceeded 100,000. As the first major port-of-call for ships around Cape Horn, the city had become a major commercial centre for the entire Pacific coast and the hub of Chile's nascent banking industry.

The opening of the Panama Canal was a notable blow to Valparaíso's economy – no longer did European shipping need to take the much longer and more arduous Cape Horn route. Furthermore, Chilean exports of mineral nitrates declined as Europeans found synthetic substitutes, indirectly affecting Valparaíso by further reducing maritime commerce in the region. The Great Depression was a calamity, as demand for Chile's other mineral exports declined. Not until after WW II was there a significant recovery, as the country began to industrialise.

As the capital of the Fifth Region, Valparaíso is an important administrative centre. Its major industries are food processing, and exporting the products of the mining and fruit-growing sectors. The conspicuous presence of the Chilean navy is also an important factor in the city's economy. Valparaíso is less dependent on tourism than neighbouring Viña del Mar, but many Chilean vacationers make brief excursions from nearby beach resorts.

Orientation

The city of Valparaíso, 120 km north-west of Santiago at the south end of the Bahía de Valparaíso, has an extraordinarily complicated layout which probably only a lifetime resident can completely fathom. In the congested commercial centre, pinched between the port and the almost sheer hills, nearly all the major streets parallel the shoreline, which curves north as it approaches the exclusive resort suburb of Viña del Mar. Avenida Errázuriz runs the length of the waterfront, alongside the railway, before intersecting Avenida España, the main road to Viña del Mar.

Behind and above the commercial centre, Valparaíso's many hills are a rabbit's warren of steep footpaths, zigzag roads and blind alleys where even the best map sometimes fails the visitor. The best available map, and an excellent investment at about US$1, is Esso's *Planos*, available at Esso petrol stations, which also contains city maps of Antofagasta, Viña del Mar, Santiago, Concepción and Talcahuano. It has not been updated since 1983, but it is easily the most accurate and complete. Turistel's *Centro* volume covers only small sectors of the port in detail.

Information

Tourist Information The office at Valparaíso's Municipalidad, Condell 1490, is open weekdays from 8.30 am to 2 pm and 3 to 5 pm. The municipal tourist kiosk on Muelle Prat (the pier) has friendly and well informed personnel but a limited amount of printed material, including barely adequate maps of Valparaíso and Viña del Mar. It's open Friday from 4 to 8 pm, Saturday and Sunday from 10.30 am to 2.30 pm and 4 to 8 pm. There is also an office (☎ 213246) in the Terminal Rodoviario (the bus station) open from October to March. For information about places to eat, pick up *Guía Gastronómica*, the free, locally published guide to dining in Valparaíso, Viña and Concón.

Better tourist information is available in Viña del Mar.

Money Valparaíso has three exchange houses, Cambios Gema at Esmeralda 940, Local 3, Inter Cambio on Plaza Sotomayor, and Exprinter at Prat 895.

Post & Telecommunications The post office is on Prat at its junction with Plaza Sotomayor. CTC has long-distance telephone services at Esmeralda 1054, Pedro Montt 2023, and at the Terminal Rodoviario.

Consulates Foreign consuls may prefer to live in Viña del Mar, but they have to work in Valparaíso. The Argentine Consulate (☎ 213691) is at Blanco 1215, Oficina 1102; the Peruvian Consulate (☎ 253403) is one floor up at Oficina 1202. The British Consulate (☎ 256117) is at Blanco 725, Oficina 26.

Cultural Centres The Centro Cultural Valparaíso is at Esmeralda 1083. There is a branch of the Instituto Chileno-Norteamericano de Cultura (☎ 256897) nearby at Esmeralda 1061.

Medical Services Hospital Carlos van Buren (☎ 254074) is at Avenida Colón 2454, corner of San Ignacio.

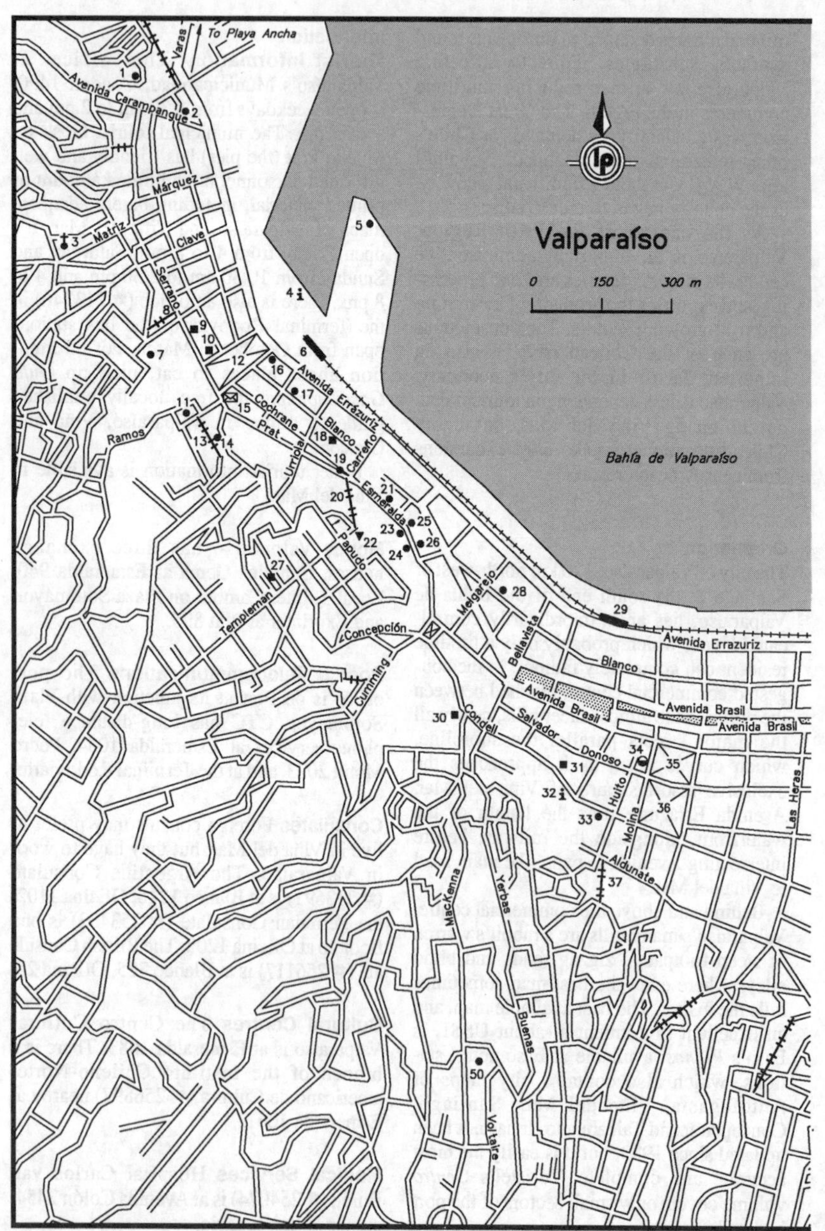
Valparaíso
0
150
300 m
Bahía de Valparaíso
To Playa Ancha
Varas
Avenida Carampangue
Márquez
Matriz
Clave
Serrano
Ramos
Cochrane
Prat
Blanco
Urriola
Avenida Errázuriz
Carreño
Esmeralda
Papudo
Templeman
Concepción
Cumming
Melgarejo
Bellavista
Avenida Errazuriz
Blanco
Avenida Brasil
Avenida Brasil
Avenida Brasil
Salvador
Donoso
Condell
MacKenna
Huito
Molina
Las Heras
Aldunate
Yerbas
Buenas
Voltaire
1
2
3
4
5
6
7
8
9
10
11
12
13
14
15
16
17
18
19
20
21
22
23
24
25
26
27
28
29
30
31
32
33
34
35
36
37
50

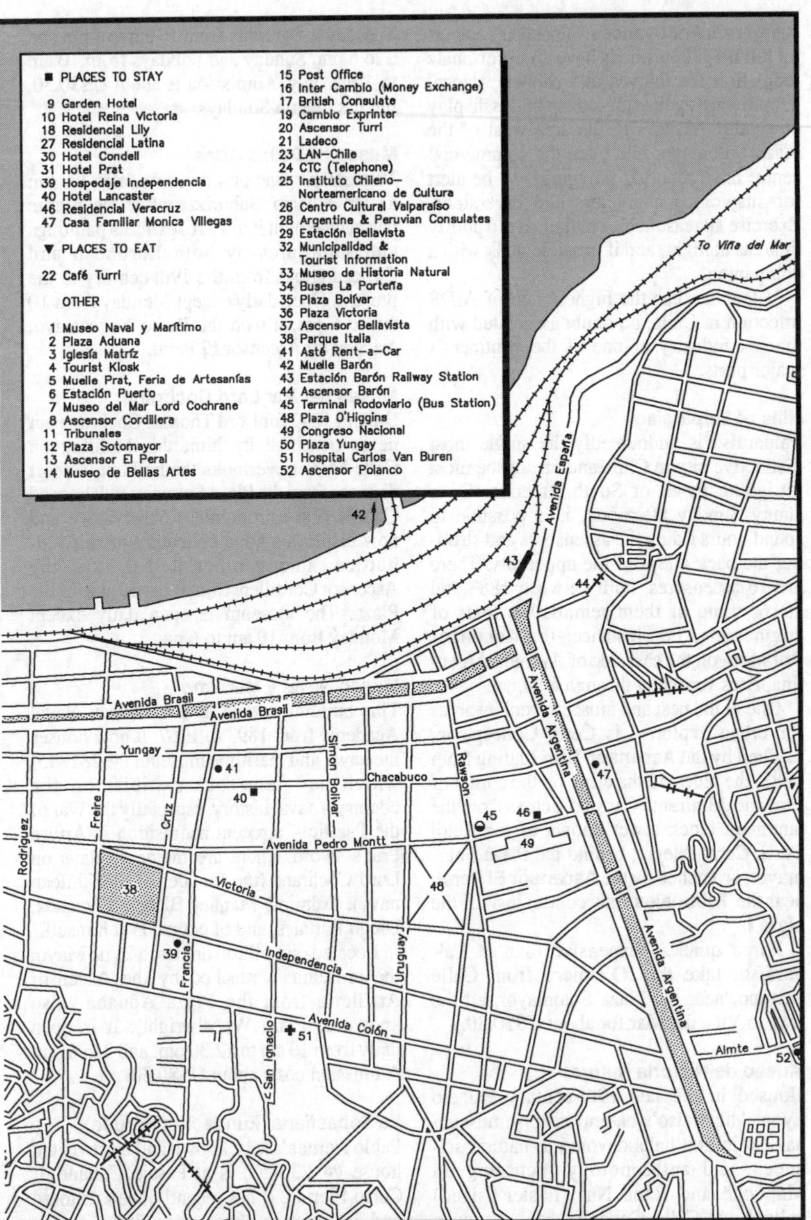
■ PLACES TO STAY
9 Garden Hotel
10 Hotel Reina Victoria
18 Residencial Lily
27 Residencial Latina
30 Hotel Condell
31 Hotel Prat
39 Hospedaje Independencia
40 Hotel Lancaster
46 Residencial Veracruz
47 Casa Familiar Monica Villegas
▼ PLACES TO EAT
22 Café Turri
OTHER
1 Museo Naval y Marítimo
2 Plaza Aduana
3 Iglesia Matríz
4 Tourist Kiosk
5 Muelle Prat, Feria de Artesanías
6 Estación Puerto
7 Museo del Mar Lord Cochrane
8 Ascensor Cordillera
11 Tribunales
12 Plaza Sotomayor
13 Ascensor El Peral
14 Museo de Bellas Artes
15 Post Office
16 Inter Cambio (Money Exchange)
17 British Consulate
19 Cambio Exprinter
20 Ascensor Turri
21 Ladeco
23 LAN–Chile
24 CTC (Telephone)
25 Instituto Chileno–Norteamericano de Cultura
26 Centro Cultural Valparaíso
28 Argentine & Peruvian Consulates
29 Estación Bellavista
32 Municipalidad & Tourist Information
33 Museo de Historia Natural
34 Buses La Porteña
35 Plaza Bolívar
36 Plaza Victoria
37 Ascensor Bellavista
38 Parque Italia
41 Asté Rent–a–Car
42 Muelle Barón
43 Estación Barón Railway Station
44 Ascensor Barón
45 Terminal Rodoviario (Bus Station)
48 Plaza O'Higgins
49 Congreso Nacional
50 Plaza Yungay
51 Hospital Carlos Van Buren
52 Ascensor Polanco
To Viña del Mar
Avenida España
Avenida Brasil
Avenida Brasil
Yungay
Chacabuco
Avenida Argentina
Avenida Argentina
Rawson
Simon Bolívar
Cruz
Freire
Rodríguez
Avenida Pedro Montt
Victoria
Independencia
Francia
Uruguay
San Ignacio
Avenida Colón
Almte

Dangers & Annoyances Valparaíso's colourful hill neighbourhoods have an unfortunate reputation for thieves and robbers – local people warn against any conspicuous display of wealth. Visitors to the area west of the Plaza Sotomayor and even the commercial centre have reported muggings, so be alert for suspicious characters and diversions. Exercise all reasonable caution, avoid poorly lit areas at night, and if possible walk with a companion.

Valparaíso has the highest rate of AIDS infection in Chile, no doubt associated with the sex industry of one of the continent's major ports.

Hills of Valparaíso

Valparaíso is undoubtedly the single most distinctive city in Chile and one of the most intriguing in all of South America. On a sunny Sunday afternoon, it is possible to spend hours riding the ascensores and strolling the back alleys of the upper city. There are 16 ascensores, built between 1883 and 1916, some of them remarkable feats of engineering. For instance, the **Ascensor Polanco**, on the east side of Avenida Argentina, rises vertically through a tunnel.

One of the best and most convenient areas for urban explorers is Cerro Concepción, reached by the **Ascensor Turri** (dating from 1883, the oldest in the city), on the corner of Prat and Almirante Carreño, across from the landmark clock tower known as the Reloj Turri. Cerro Alegre, behind the Plaza Sotomayor, is reached by the **Ascensor El Peral**, near the **Tribunales** (law courts) just off the plaza.

For a quick, inexpensive tour of Valparaíso, take the 'O' micro from Calle Serrano, near the Plaza Sotomayor, all the way to Viña del Mar for about US$0.30.

Museo de Historia Natural

Housed in the late 19th-century Palacio Lyon, Valparaíso's natural history museum has exhibition halls devoted to natural sciences, and anthropology focussing on Mapuche and Rapa Nui (Easter Island) culture. At Calle Condell 1546, it's open Tuesday to Saturday from 10 am to 1 pm and 2 to 6 pm, Sunday and holidays from 10 am to 1 pm only. Admission is about US$0.30, but it's free on Sundays.

Museo de Bellas Artes

Valparaíso's fine arts museum, also known as the Palacio Baburizza after the nitrate baron who built it in 1916, exhibits paintings and sculptures by both European and Chilean artists from the 19th century to the present. Open daily except Monday from 10 am to 6 pm, it's on the Paseo Yugoeslavo, reached by Ascensor El Peral.

Museo del Mar Lord Cochrane

Built in 1842 for Lord Thomas Cochrane but never occupied by him, this building on Calle Merlet overlooks the harbour, a short distance from the Plaza Sotomayor. It housed Chile's first astronomical observatory and now displays a good collection of ships-in-bottles, among other items. Take the Ascensor Cordillera from the west side of the Plaza. The museum is open daily except Monday from 10 am to 6 pm.

Museo Naval y Marítimo

This building served as the Chilean Naval Academy from 1893 to 1967. It now houses the naval and maritime museum (☎ 281845) which has numerous exhibits on the country's naval history, especially the War of the Pacific – a recent acquisition is Arturo Prat's sword. There are major displays on Lord Cochrane (the founder of the Chilean navy), Admiral Manuel Blanco Encalada, Diego Portales, and of course Prat himself.

Located on a hilltop on Paseo 21 de Mayo, the museum is reached by the Ascensor Artillería from the Plaza Aduana (also known as Plaza Wheelwright). It is open daily from 10 am to 12.30 pm, and 3 to 6 pm. Admission costs about US$0.30.

La Sebastiana (Fundación Neruda)

Pablo Neruda's least known and least visited house (☎ 233759) is at Pasaje Collado 1, Cerro Florida. It has recently been restored and is open to the public daily except

Monday from 10.30 am to 2.30 pm and 3.30 to 6 pm. Admission is US$2. Take the Ascensor Bellavista near the Plaza Victoria and ask directions. The more famous Neruda house, with the extensive collection of maritime memorabilia, is at Isla Negra (see under that heading, later in this section).

Muelle Prat

This recently redeveloped pier, at the foot of Plaza Sotomayor, is a very lively place on weekends, with a good handicrafts market, the Feria de Artesanías. Several boats offer harbour tours for about US$1.50. (Do not photograph any of the numerous Chilean naval vessels at anchor.) For US$2 some take passengers all the way to Viña del Mar – a nice change of pace from the bus.

Congreso Nacional

Chile's imposing new Congress building, mandated by the 1980 constitution, geographically separates the legislature from the president and has proved to be a notable inconvenience since the return to democratic government – rapid physical communication between the two is only possible by helicopter. When Congress is in session, the building is open to the public Fridays from 3 to 5 pm. It's at the junction of Avenida Pedro Montt and Avenida Argentina, opposite the bus terminal.

El Mercurico Building

Festival

April 17 is the city's annual official day. It is the day the documents authorising the cabildo arrived in Valparaíso in 1791 – the glacial Spanish bureaucracy and slow communications across the Atlantic had delayed receipt of the authorisation for more than three years.

Places to Stay

There is relatively little accommodation near the bus terminal itself, but there is a very modest, unnamed hospedaje (☎ 235840) at Independencia 2312, corner of Francia. Also close to the bus terminal is a quiet, comfortable *casa familiar* belonging to Monica Villegas (☎ 215673), Avenida Argentina 322 near the corner of Chacabuco. Try also the appealing *Residencial Veracruz*, opposite the new Congreso Nacional at Pedro Montt 2881.

Most cheap hotels are near the Plaza Sotomayor. Try *Residencial Lily* (☎ 255995), Blanco 866 next to the Bar Inglés, or *Hotel Reina Victoria* (☎ 212203), Plaza Sotomayor 190. The latter has singles for around US$6 to US$8, with doubles at US$12 to US$15 including breakfast. It's an old building in a central location, with spacious rooms and hot water, but one disgruntled reader claimed that upper-storey rooms are cheaper only because the rats are more numerous.

Similarly priced, the *Garden Hotel* at Serrano 501 is just off Plaza Sotomayor, opposite the Ascensor Cordillera. It has large, clean rooms, with good showers and toilets, as well as a restaurant. On Cerro Concepción, reached by the Ascensor Turri, is *Residencial Latina* (☎ 252350), a family-oriented place at Pasaje Templeman 51, which comes highly recommended at US$7 per person.

For upscale accommodation you'll have to go to Viña del Mar, but you can try *Hotel Prat* (☎ 253081) at Condell 1443 or *Hotel Condell* (☎ 212788) at Pirámide 557, off Condell, both of which have singles/doubles for about US$23/31. *Hotel Lancaster* (☎ 217391), Chacabuco 2362, is slightly dearer.

Places to Eat

Traditionally, visitors dine in Viña del Mar, but a recent gastronomic revival has made Valparaíso an equally good place to eat. One of my best meals ever in Chile was at *Café Turri*, on Paseo Gervasoni at the upper exit of Ascensor Turri, with superb seafood in an agreeable setting, attentive but unobtrusive service, and panoramic views of Valparaíso and the harbour from the 3rd floor balcony – the waiters bring binoculars while you await your meal. Although not really cheap, it is exceptional value for money. For cheap eats, try the area around the bus station.

Getting There & Away

Air The nearest commercial airport is in Santiago. LAN-Chile (☎ 251441) has an office at Esmeralda 1048. Ladeco (☎ 216355) is at Esmeralda 973.

Bus – regional & long-distance Nearly all bus companies have offices at Valparaíso's Terminal Rodoviario, Avenida Pedro Montt 913 at the corner of Rawson, across from the new Congreso Nacional.

From Santiago, the most frequent and convenient bus company for Valparaíso (about 1¾ hours) and Viña del Mar (about two hours) is Tur Bus at the Terminal de Buses Sur, which leaves often between 6.30 am and 10 pm.

From Valparaíso (☎ 256425) and Viña del Mar (☎ 680424), buses leave between 6 am and 9 pm. Some Viña del Mar buses go direct to Santiago, while others go via Valparaíso, but the fare is identical at about US$2.50 one way and US$4 return. Cóndor Bus (☎ 214637 in Valparaíso, (☎ 685468 in Viña) offers similar services.

Buses La Porteña (☎ 210273), Molina 366, covers coastal and interior destinations in the northern sector of the Fifth Region, as far as Pichidangui and Los Vilos.

Sol del Pacífico (☎ 281029), Galvarino 110, Playa Ancha, serves destinations on the Ruta Panamericana from Santiago as far south as Los Angeles, plus the region's northern beaches as far as Zapallar and Papudo. Buses Zambrano (☎ 258986) follows the Panamericana north to Arica and intermediate stops, as do Pullman Bus (☎ 256898), Tramaca (☎ 250811) Flota Barrios (☎ 253-6764), and Chile Bus (☎ 881187 in Viña). Incabus Lasval (☎ 214915, 684121 in Viña) serves the cities of the Norte Chico as far as Chañaral and the mining town of El Salvador.

Fénix Pullman Norte (☎ 257993) serves all destinations on the Panamericana from Arica in the north to Temuco and Villarrica in the south. Other companies serving the south include Buses Lit (☎ 253948, 882348 in Viña), which also goes as far north as La Serena, and Buses Sol del Sur (☎ 252211), with service to Talca, Chillán and Concepción.

Bus – international Valparaíso and Viña both have direct services to Argentina, usually bypassing Santiago. Except when noted, all these buses leave between 8 am and 9 am. Buses which leave from Valparaíso also stop in Viña; see also Getting There & Away in the Viña del Mar section.

Fénix Pullman Norte leaves daily for Mendoza, Tuesday and Thursday for Buenos Aires. Buses El Rápido (☎ 252921) goes daily to Mendoza, where it makes connections for Córdoba and Buenos Aires. It also has Saturday and Sunday service to Mendoza at 10.30 am.

Buses CATA (☎ 258322) has daily departures for Mendoza at 8.30 am and 1.30 pm, with train connections to Buenos Aires. Buses TAC (☎ 257587) goes daily to Mendoza and Tuesday and Friday to Buenos

Aires (24 hours). Tas Choapa (☎ 252921) goes daily to Mendoza, with connections in Mendoza for Buenos Aires, and has a 12.45 pm bus to Córdoba Wednesday, Thursday, Saturday and Sunday.

Fares to Mendoza are about US$18, to Córdoba about US$50, and to Buenos Aires about US$60.

Train Valparaíso's Estación Puerto (☎ 217108) is at Plaza Sotomayor 711, corner of Errázuriz. At the end of 1991, Ferrocarriles del Estado renewed rail service between Valparaíso and Santiago's Estación Central for the summer months only, but it is uncertain whether this will continue. For details, see Getting There & Away in the Santiago chapter.

There are regular trains between the Valparaíso/Viña area and intermediate stations en route to the city of Los Andes, on the international highway to Portillo and Mendoza (Argentina).

Getting Around

Valparaíso and Viña del Mar are only a few km apart, connected by countless local buses for about US$0.25; it is also possible to take the local commuter train (see above). From Muelle Prat, tourist boats will take you to Viña for US$2.

Car Rental Try Asté Rent-a-Car (☎ 256597) at Avenida Francia 340 or Comveg (☎ 256583) at Avenida Argentina 850. Most agencies have their offices in Viña del Mar.

VIÑA DEL MAR

Viña del Mar (or Viña for short) is Chile's premier beach resort. Only a short bus ride north of Valparaíso, it is popularly known as the Ciudad Jardín (Garden City), for reasons obvious to any visitor – its manicured subtropical landscape of palms and bananas contrasts dramatically with the colourful disorder of its neighbour. Many wealthy Chileans and other wealthy Latin Americans own houses here – Viña is not cheap, but neither is it impossibly dear.

In the colonial era, much of Viña was the hacienda of the prominent Carrera family, but in the mid-19th century it was purchased by a Portuguese businessman named Alvarez, whose daughter and sole heir later married into the Vergara family, who have bestowed their name upon many of the city's landmarks. Soon thereafter, Viña's history as the country's Pacific playground began as the railroad linked Valparaíso with Santiago – the *porteños* of Valparaíso, many of them foreigners, now had easy access to the beaches and broad green spaces to the north and soon built grand houses and mansions away from the cramped harbour city. With construction of hotels and the subdivision of the sector north of the Estero Marga Marga, Viña became an increasingly attractive destination for the inhabitants of Santiago, though recently it has lost popularity to competing resorts like La Serena.

Orientation

Viña is about 10 km north of Valparaíso via the shoreline Avenida España. It consists of two distinct sectors, a long-established and prestigious area south of the Estero Marga Marga and a newer and more regular residential grid to its north. Several bridges, most notably the Puente Libertad, connect the two sectors. North of the Marga Marga, most streets are identified by number and direction, either Norte (north), Oriente (east), or Poniente (west). Avenida Libertad separates the ponientes from the orientes. These streets are usually written as a number, but are sometimes spelt out eg 1 Norte is also written as Uno Norte.

The commercial and activity centres of Viña are south of the Marga Marga, on the Plaza Vergara and the avenidas Arlegui and Valparaíso, which parallel the river. South of Alvarez is a zone of turn-of-the-century mansions which belonged to the Santiago/Viña elite, the centrepiece of which is the famous Quinta Vergara. Once the residence of the wealthy Alvarez-Vergara family, it is now a public park and one of the city's great attractions. Viña's main attraction, of course, is the white-sand beaches, which stretch northward from Caleta Abarca to the suburbs of Reñaca and Concón. The city's very limited industry is several km inland.

A pleasant way of getting to know Viña is an hour's ride around town in a horse-drawn carriage, leaving from the Plaza Vergara, about US$15 for two people.

Information

Tourist Office The municipal tourist office, the Central de Turismo e Informaciones (☎ 883154) is near the junction of Libertad and Arlegui, just off the Plaza Vergara. It's open weekdays from 9 am to 7 pm, Saturday from 9 am to 2 pm and 3 to 7 pm, and Sunday from 9 am to 2 pm. It distributes an adequate map, and a monthly flyer entitled *Todo Viña*, which includes useful information and a calendar of events.

The regional office of Sernatur, the national tourism organisation, (☎ 882285) is at Avenida Valparaíso 507, 3rd floor, but the entrance is a little difficult to find and the staff are more oriented toward businesses than individuals.

Money For US cash or travellers' cheques,

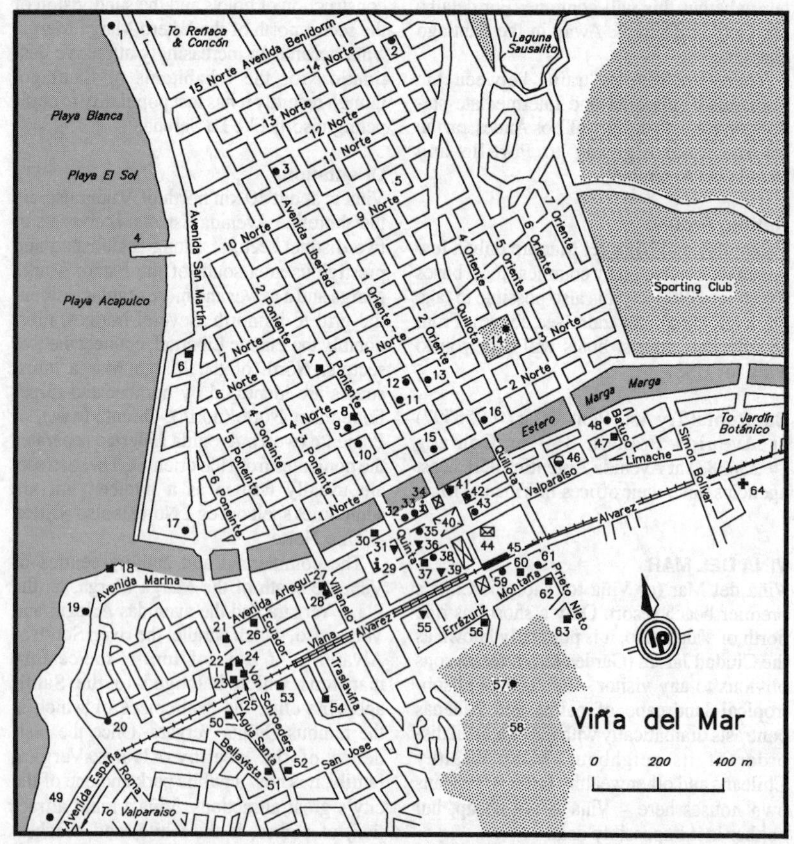

try Cambios Symatour at Arlegui 684/686, Cambios Afex at Arlegui 641, or Inter-Cambio at 1 Norte 655-B. Since many Argentines come to Viña, you should be able to exchange leftover Argentine currency as well.

Post & Telecommunications Correos de Chile is at Valparaíso 846. CTC has long-distance telephone offices at 14 Norte 1184, Avenida Valparaíso 628 near the plaza, and at the corner of Valparaíso and Villanelo.

Cultural Centres Viña has an active cultural life. There are frequent exhibitions of art and sculpture at the Centro Cultural Viña del Mar (☎ 689481), Avenida Libertad 250, which is open weekdays from 10 am to 1 pm and 2 to 5.30 pm, Saturday from 9 am to 1 pm and 4 to 8 pm, and Sunday from 10 am to 2 pm. The Sala Viña del Mar (☎ 680633), Arlegui 683, has similar programmes. It's open daily from 10 am to 7 pm except Sundays, when hours are 10.30 am to 1.30 pm.

Special exhibitions are shown at the Sala

■ PLACES TO STAY

6 Hotel San Martín
7 Residencial 555
8 Residencial Helen Misch
18 Hotel Cap Ducal
21 Residencial Verónica
22 Residencial Marbella
23 Residencial Victoria
24 Residencial Blanchait
25 Residencial Caribe
26 Residencial Villarrica
27 Residencial Oxarón
30 Residencial Magallanes
37 Residencial Ona Berri
41 Hotel O'Higgins
47 Hospedaje Calderón
50 Residencial Agua Santa & Residencial Patricia
51 Residencial La Montaña
52 Residencial Lausanne
53 Residencial Casino
54 Residencial Palace
56 Hotel Rondó
60 Residencial France
62 Residencial Edhison
63 Residencial La Gaviota

▼ PLACES TO EAT

31 Cafetería Anayak
36 Confitería Samoiedo
39 Restaurant Panzoni & El Naturista
55 Centro Español

OTHER

1 Reloj de Sol (Sun Dial)
2 CTC (Telephone)
3 Rent-a-Car Mach
4 Muelle Vergara
5 Instituto Chileno-Británico
9 CONAF
10 Instituto Chileno-Norteamericano
11 Centro Cultural/Viña del Mar
12 Museo Arqueológico Fonck
13 Instituto Chileno-Británico
14 Museo Palacio Rioja
15 Rentauto
16 Automóvil Club de Chile
17 Casino Municipal
19 Museo de la Cultura
20 Reloj de Flores del Mar (Clock of Flowers)
28 CTC (Telephone)
29 Sernatur
32 Cambios Afex (Money Exchange)
33 Sala Viña del Mar
34 Central de Turismo e Informaciones, Municipalidad
35 Cambios Symatour (Money Exchange)
38 CTC (Telephone)
40 Plaza Vergara
42 Sala Municipal de Exposiciones
43 Teatro Municipal
44 Post Office
45 Railway Station
46 Terminal Rodoviario
48 Mercado Municipal
49 Disco Scala
57 Palacio Vergara, Museo de Bellas Artes
58 Quinta Vergara
59 Bert Rent-a-Car
61 Disco Spa
64 Hospital Gustavo Fricke

Municipal de Exposiciones (☎ 680689), Arlegui 777, open weekdays from 9 am to 2 pm and 3 to 5.30 pm.

Viña has several international cultural centres, including the Instituto Chileno-Norteamericano (☎ 686191) at 3 Norte 532, the Instituto Chileno-Británico at 1 Oriente 252 (☎ 971440) and 3 Norte 824 (☎ 971061), and the Alianza Francesa (☎ 685968) at Alvarez 314.

Art Galleries Viña also has many private art galleries which are open to visitors, including the Galería de Arte Modigliani at Valparaíso 363, Local 105; Arte Gallery at Valparaíso 335; and Andrew Richard Gallery at 1 Poniente 724.

Travel Agencies The Automóvil Club de Chile (ACCHI, ☎ 689505) is just across the Marga Marga at 1 Norte 901.

Medical Services Hospital Gustavo Fricke (☎ 680041) is east of downtown at Viana Alvarez 1532, on the corner of Cancha.

National Parks CONAF (☎ 976589) is at 3 Norte 541.

Museums

Specialising in Mapuche silverwork and Rapa Nui (Easter Island) culture, the **Museo Arqueológico Fonck**, at 4 Norte 784, is open Tuesday to Friday from 10 am to 6 pm and weekends from 10 am to 2 pm, and charges US$0.65. If you lack the big bucks to fly to Easter Island, there's a *moai* (statue) on the museum grounds, accessible even when the museum itself is closed.

Two blocks east, at Quillota 214, is the **Museo Palacio Rioja**, another turn-of-the-century mansion which is now a municipal museum. It's open daily except Monday from 10 am to 2 pm and 3 to 6 pm; admission is US$0.30.

On Avenida Marina on the south bank of the Estero Marga Marga, the **Museo de la Cultura del Mar**, housed in the Castillo Wulff, is open Tuesday to Saturday from 10 am to 1 pm and 2.30 to 6 pm, Sundays and holidays from 10 am to 2 pm. Admission is US$0.40, except on Sundays and holidays when it's free.

Quinta Vergara

Now a public park, the magnificently landscaped Quinta Vergara contains the Venetian-style **Palacio Vergara**, former residence of the Alvarez-Vergara family, built in 1908. It houses the **Museo de Bellas Artes** (fine arts museum), which is open daily except Monday from 10 am to 6 pm, extended to 7 pm in summer. Admission is about US$0.30.

Frequent summer concerts complement the famous Festival de la Canción (see below). The grounds, whose only entrance is on Errázuriz at the south end of Calle Quinta, are open daily from 7.30 am to 6 pm, extended to 8 pm in summer.

Jardín Botánico Nacional

Chile's national botanical garden comprises 61 hectares of native and exotic plants which, since 1983, is slowly but systematically being developed as a research facility with an expanded nursery, library, educational programmes and plaques for identification of individual specimens. CONAF has restricted the entry of automobiles, and recreational activities such as football and picnicking, but it is still an interesting and relaxing place to spend an afternoon.

From Calle Viana in downtown Viña, take Bus No 20 east to the end of the line, then walk across the bridge about ten minutes; the Jardín is on your left. Admission is about US$1; the grounds are open daily except Monday from 8.30 am to 6.30 pm.

Festival Internacional de la Canción

Viña del Mar's most wildly popular attraction is the yearly Festival Internacional de la Canción (International Song Festival), held every February in the theatre of the Quinta Vergara. This ostentatious competition of the kitschiest artists from the Spanish-speaking world (for balance, there's usually at least one really insipid Anglo performer) resembles the Eurovision Song Contest; every evening for a week, everything stops as ticketless Chileans stare transfixed at TV sets in their homes, cafés, restaurants and bars. Patient and discriminating listeners may hear some worthwhile folk groups. The Latin American TV network Univisión broadcasts the better-known acts in the USA and elsewhere.

Beaches

Many of Viña's beaches are either crowded or contaminated, but those in the northern suburbs are far better – from Calle 2 Norte, take Bus No 9 north to Reñaca and Concón, for example. For more information, see the Around Viña del Mar section, below.

Organised Tours

Aguitur, Viña's Asociación de Guias de Turismo (☎ 681882), operates out of the same building as the municipal tourist office. It can arrange tours of Viña and Valparaíso (three hours, US$10 or four hours, US$16), Zapallar (eight hours, US$25), Isla Negra (eight hours, US$25), or Santiago (10 hours, US$30), as well as a three-hour night tour of Viña and Valparaíso for US$25. English, French, German and Italian-speaking guides are available.

Places to Stay

Accommodation is so plentiful in Viña that it would be impossible to list everything, but the entries below are a good sample. There are few bargains in summer, but outside the peak months of January and February supply exceeds demand and prices drop. March is an especially good month, when the weather is still ideal but most Chileans have finished their holidays.

Places to Stay – bottom end

In early 1992, hostel accommodation was available at *Residencial La Montaña* (☎ 622230), Agua Santa 153, for about US$5 per person.

For low-budget travellers, there are several alternatives on or near Agua Santa and Von Schroeders, and in the town centre near the bus terminal on Valparaíso. Off-season prices run to about US$5 per person, in season twice that or more. One Lonely Planet reader strongly endorsed *Residencial Verónica*, Von Schroeders 150, for about US$6. *Residencial Agua Santa* (☎ 901351), Agua Santa 36 in an attractive blue Victorian building, charges US$7 per person off-season and US$10 in peak season. Almost next door, at Agua Santa 48, is *Residencial Patricia* (☎ 663825), where singles cost US$8. Further south, *Residencial Lausanne*, at Agua Santa 181, is a pleasant family-run place but the front rooms can be very noisy, since buses from Viña to Santiago have to gear down to climb the steep hill.

One highly recommended place is *Hospedaje Calderón* (☎ 970456), a block from the bus terminal at Batuco 147, at US$7 per person. *Residencial France* (☎ 685976), on the 'wrong side of the tracks' (in Viña, at least) at shady Montaña 743, is a bit ragged, but very friendly for US$7 per person. Some rooms are small and boxy, but there are pleasant common areas. *Residencial Edhison* (☎ 680756), up the street at Montaña 890, is very slightly dearer. Near the grounds of the Quinta Vergara is *Residencial La Gaviota* (☎ 974439), Alcalde Prieto Nieto 0332, a bargain at US$8 with shared bath, US$10 with private bath.

Another recommendation is the very central *Residencial Oxarón* (☎ 882360) at Villanelo 136, a quiet location between Arlegui and Valparaíso, with very clean rooms, hot showers and breakfast for US$11 per person. *Residencial Blanchait* (☎ 974949), at Valparaíso 82-A, charges US$11/20 for a single/double with shared bath. *Residencial Ona Berri* (☎ 688187), upstairs at Valparaíso 618, has rooms for US$12 per person with shared bath, US$14 with private bath. *Residencial Victoria* (☎ 977370), Valparaíso 40, is comparable to both the Blanchait and the Ona Berri.

Places to Stay – middle

Generally more central, several fine places fall into the US$15-plus per person category, including: *Residencial Caribe* (☎ 976191), at Von Schroeders 46; *Residencial Villarrica*, at Arlegui 172; *Residencial Magallanes* (☎ 685101), at Arlegui 555 (slightly dearer with private bath); and *Residencial Casino* (☎ 662753) at Alvarez 110.

Residencial Palace (☎ 663134), Paseo Valle 387, charges US$20 per person, while rates at *Residencial Helen Misch* (☎ 971565), 1 Poniente 239, are US$20/37 for a single/double. *Residencial 555* (☎ 972240), 5 Norte 555 (apparently their lucky number), charges US$27/37. *Residencial Marbella* (☎ 978770) at Valparaíso 78 has doubles for US$41, while at the upper end of the range is the enthusiastically recommended *Hotel Rondó* (☎ 685073), Errázuriz 690, with an English-speaking owner whose rates are US$43/60 with breakfast.

Places to Stay – top end

One indignant reader called *Hotel San Martín* (☎ 689191), San Martín 667, a 'rip-off' at US$60 single, even with its view of Playa Acapulco. If you have the money, you could try *Hotel Cap Ducal* (☎ 626655), on an old ship set on a foundation in the surf at Avenida Marina 51, for US$87/100. But my choice would be the venerable and dignified *Hotel O'Higgins* (☎ 882016), on the Plaza Latorre (between the Plaza Vergara and Puente Libertad). Rates start at US$71/103, but you can pay up to US$100/131 and accumulate a huge room service bill without even working up a sweat.

Places to Eat

Like most upscale beach resorts, Viña is sinking under the weight of its hotels and restaurants, but there are good values for diners. Several correspondents have recommended *Restaurant Puerto Montt* on Valparaíso for large portions of well prepared and reasonably priced fish, although the wine is overpriced.

There is friendly service, excellent atmosphere and good, reasonably priced Italian and Middle Eastern food at *Panzoni*, which is small and very popular for lunch. It's at Pasaje Cousiño 12-B – Cousiño is easy to miss; it's a small passageway off Valparaíso, near the Plaza Vergara. On the same block is *El Naturista*, a vegetarian restaurant with a bargain fixed-price lunch for about US$2.

For coffee and desserts, try *Cafetería Anayak* at Quinta 134 or, especially, *Confitería Samoiedo* at Avenida Valparaíso 637.

Entertainment

Cinemas First-run movies often hit Viña even before Santiago. Try Cine Arte at Plaza Vergara 42, Cine Olímpo at Quinta 294, Cine Premier at Quillota 898, and Cine Rex at Avenida Valparaíso 758.

Discos There's a place in Antofagasta called 'Disco Hell', but Viña and its suburbs may take away the title with venues like Scala, at Caleta Abarca; Scratch, at Bohn 970; Spa, at Montaña 879; and Arenna at Bohn 770-A. In Reñaca, try Topsy Topsy, at Santa Luisa 501; and Yo Claudio, at Avenida Borgoño 15263. In Concón there's César, on Playa Amarilla.

It's not really a disco, but the Hotel Alcázar, Alvarez 646, holds a *noche de tango* every Saturday from 9 pm. There is also dancing on Friday and Saturday evenings at the Hotel O'Higgins, and at Restaurante Don Giacomo, Villanelo 135.

Casino The Casino Municipal de Viña del Mar, overlooking the beach on the north side of the Estero Marga Marga, offers the opportunity to squander your savings on slot machines, bingo and card games, in between dinner and cabaret entertainment. At San Martín 199, it's open daily from 6 pm.

Getting There & Away

Viña's Terminal Rodoviario (bus terminal) is at Valparaíso and Quilpué, two long blocks from the Plaza Vergara. Most long-distance buses from Valparaíso pick up passengers here as well (see Getting There & Away in the Valparaíso section).

Buses J M (☎ 883184), has frequent buses to Los Andes, plus daily service to Concepción (US$13, 10 hours) and Talcahuano. Buses Alfa 3 goes from Valparaíso and Viña to San Felipe and Los Andes via Concón, every 10 minutes in summer.

Bus – international Nuevo O'Higgins San Martín (☎ 681585) goes daily at 10 am to Mendoza, continuing to Buenos Aires on Thursday, Saturday and Sunday. Chile Bus (☎ 881187) departs daily at 11 am for Mendoza, with Monday and Friday service to Buenos Aires at 1 pm. See also Getting There & Away in the Valparaíso section.

Getting Around

Frequent local buses, marked 'Puerto' or 'Aduana', link Valparaíso with Viña, and can be caught anywhere along Arlegui; from the Muelle Vergara, you can also catch a launch to the Plaza Sotomayor in Valparaíso for US$2.

Taxis are twice as expensive in Viña as in Santiago.

Car Rental For cheapest rates, try Bert Rent-a-Car (☎ 685515) at Alvarez 750, across from the railway station. There are many others, including: Rent-a-Car Mach (☎ 972526), at Libertad 1098; Cars Rent-a-Car (☎ 684994), at Bohn 837; Rentauto (☎ 970888), at 1 Norte 741; Euro Rent-a-Car (☎ 882016) at the Hotel O'Higgins; and Kovacs Rent-a-Car (☎ 971580) at Jorge Montt 2300.

AROUND VIÑA DEL MAR

To the north of Viña are several less celebrated but more attractive beach towns. Many are merely suburbs, such as **Reñaca**, which has its own tourist office (☎ 900499) at Avenida Borgoño 14100, plus the most extensive beach in the area. Unfortunately, there is little or no budget accommodation.

Another popular balneario, **Concón**, is 15 km from Viña and equally exclusive in terms of accommodation.

Another 23 km beyond Concón is **Quintero**, a peninsular beach community which was once part of a hacienda belonging to Lord Cochrane. There is reasonable accommodation at *Residencial María Alejandra* (☎ 930266), Lord Cochrane 157, where singles with shared bath cost about US$6 and those with private bath are only slightly costlier.

Further north of Viña is the working port of **Horcón**, something of an artists' colony, where the beach is nothing to speak of but the seafood is among the best in the region. Take the Sol del Pacífico bus from Viña.

A more upscale resort is **Zapallar**, about 80 km north of Viña. The oceanside *Hotel Internacional Playa Amarilla* (☎ 811915), Subida Labarca 6, has been recommended at US$50. **Papudo**, 10 km further north, has a much wider range of accommodation.

ISLA NEGRA

Pablo Neruda's Pacific Ocean house, even more outlandish than La Chascona in Santiago, sits on a rocky headland between Valparaíso and Cartagena. Once vandalised and boarded up by the military government, it houses the Museo Neruda, with the poet's collections of bowsprits, ships-in-bottles, nautical instruments, wood carvings and other memorabilia. Isla Negra is *not*, by the way, an island.

In summer, Isla Negra (☎ (035) 212284) is open for visits weekdays from 10 am to 7.45 pm, but advance reservations are imperative, since there are up to 40 tours daily with guides whose interest and competence vary greatly. Admission and tour charges are US$2 per person. Although the tour lasts only half an hour, you can hang around and photograph the grounds as long as you like. From the Alameda terminal in Santiago, buses to the yachting centre of Algarrobo continue to Isla Negra via El Quisco, leaving pilgrims almost at the door.

The Southern Heartland

RANCAGUA

Founded in 1743 on lands 'ceded' by Picunche Indian cacique Tomás Guaglén, Rancagua played an important role in Chilean independence when, in 1814, it was the site of the Desastre de Rancagua (Disaster of Rancagua), in which Spanish Royalist troops vanquished Chilean patriots, many of whom were exiled to the Juan Fernández Islands. Chilean leader Bernardo O'Higgins went into exile in Mendoza, Argentina, but the battle was only a temporary setback for criollo self-determination.

1 Hotel Rancagua
2 Mercado Central
3 Bavaria Restaurant
4 Restaurant Casas Viejas
5 Hotel España
6 Hotel Camino del Rey
7 Iglesia de La Merced
8 CONAF
9 Post Office
10 CTC (Telephone)
11 Plaza Los Héroes
12 Sernatur (Tourist Office)
13 Railway Station
14 Bus Terminal
15 Hotel Turismo Santiago
16 CTC (Telephone)
17 Cobre Tour
18 Fincard (Exchange)
19 Museo Histórico Regional
20 Casa del Pilar de Esquina
21 Automóvil Club de Chile
22 Casa del la Cultura

Capital of the Sixth Region, Rancagua is mostly an agricultural service centre, but the regional economy also depends on the copper of the huge El Teniente mine, in the mountains to the east. One popular mountain attraction is the Reserva Nacional Río de los Cipreses, administered by CONAF.

Orientation

Rancagua (population about 160,000), on the north bank of the Río Cachapoal, is 86 km south of Santiago. Like most cities of colonial origin, it has a standard grid pattern centred on the Plaza Los Héroes, around which cluster most of the major public buildings. There is an equestrian statue of Bernardo

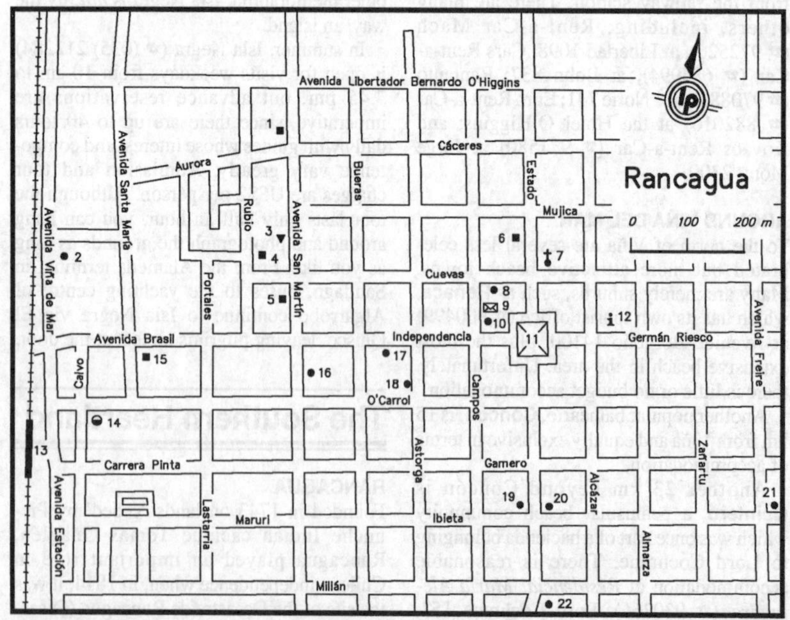

O'Higgins. The Carretera Pan-americana skirts the city centre to the east.

Information

Tourist Office Sernatur (☎ 230413) is at Germán Riesco 277, 1st floor. Try also the Automóvil Club de Chile (☎ 239930), Ibieta 09 at the corner of Freire.

Money Try Fincard, Astorga 485, for foreign exchange.

Post & Telecommunications Correos de Chile is on Campos between Cuevas and Independencia. CTC has long-distance offices at Campos 344 and San Martín 440.

Cultural Centres On Millán, about four blocks south of the plaza, the Casa del la Cultura was the headquarters of Royalist Colonel Mariano de Osorio during the battle for Rancagua. Administered by the municipality, it now holds regular exhibitions of paintings and photographs.

Travel Agencies Cobre Tour (☎ 224761) is at Independencia 634, Local 06.

National Parks CONAF (☎ 233769) is at Cuevas 480.

Iglesia de La Merced

At the intersection of Estado and Cuevas, this national monument dates from the mid-18th century, when it was the Convento y Templo de La Merced de Rancagua. During the battle of Rancagua, it served as headquarters for O'Higgins' patriots.

Casa del Pilar de Esquina

At Estado and Ibieta, this late-colonial house belonged to Fernando Errázuriz Aldunate, an important figure in the Chilean independence movement and one of the drafters of the constitution of 1833.

Museo Histórico Regional

In another colonial house, across Estado from the Casa del Pilar de Piedra, the regional museum focusses on O'Higgins' role in Chilean independence. It also contains a selection of colonial religious artwork. It's open weekdays except Monday from 9 am to 12.30 pm and from 2.30 to 6.30 pm, weekends and holidays from 9 am to 1 pm.

Festivals

In early autumn (March or April), the Campeonato Nacional de Rodeo (national rodeo championship) takes place at the Medialuna de Rancagua, on Avenida España, the northward extension of Avenida San Martín.

Places to Stay

Several travellers have recommended *Hotel España* (☎ 230141), San Martín 367, which has singles/doubles for US$11/18 but may have cheaper rooms with shared bath. *Hotel Rancagua* (☎ 232663), San Martín 85, is slightly dearer.

Hotel Turismo Santiago (☎ 230855), Avenida Brasil 1036 between Santa María and Lastarria, charges US$22/27, while *Hotel Camino del Rey* (☎ 239765), Estado 275, is the cream of the crop at US$25/43.

Places to Eat

Bavaria, a popular country-wide chain, is at San Martín 255. *Restaurant Casas Viejas*, Rubio 216, has been recommended.

Getting There & Away

Bus The Terminal de Buses a Santiago y Sur is on O'Carrol near Calvo. There is a very frequent service to the capital for about US$2, while many buses which cover the Panamericana between Santiago and the Lake District stop in Rancagua.

Train Rancagua's railway station is on Viña del Mar between O'Carrol and Carrera Pinto. The regular passenger services which connect Santiago with Temuco and other points south stop at Rancagua, but there are also frequent commuter trains to the capital.

AROUND RANCAGUA

El Teniente

At Sewell, 25 km east of Rancagua, El Teniente belonged to Kennecott Copper Corporation until its expropriation under the Unidad Popular, and is now part of the state-owned Codelco mining enterprise. It is the world's largest subsurface mine.

Theoretically, El Teniente is closed to the public, but if you want to visit, try to convince Codelco, on Calle Millán in Rancagua or at Huérfanos 1270 in Santiago, of your specialist's interest (it may be sufficient to be a schoolteacher).

Termas de Cauquenes

Only 28 km east of Rancagua, the thermal baths at Cauquenes have received such celebrated visitors as Bernardo O'Higgins and Charles Darwin, who wrote that the buildings consisted of 'a square of miserable little hovels, each with a single table and bench'. Since Darwin's day there have been sufficient improvements that *Hotel Termas de Cauquenes* (☎ 297226 in Rancagua, ☎ 483841 in Santiago) can now charge from US$63/109 for a single/double room in an area which, Darwin acknowledged, was 'a quiet, solitary spot with a good deal of wild beauty'.

If you can't afford to stay at Cauquenes, you can still spend the afternoon by taking a bus from the Mercado Central in Rancagua. Empresa Micro Termas de Cauquenes leaves Andén (Platform) No 8 on weekdays at noon and 5.30 pm, and on weekends and holidays at 11 am and 5 pm.

Reserva Nacional de los Cipreses

Ranging in elevation from 900 metres to the 4900-metre summit of Volcán Palomo in the upper drainage of the Río de los Cipreses, 37,000-hectare Los Cipreses contains a variety of volcanic landforms, hanging glacial valleys with waterfalls, and fluvial landscapes.

Los Cipreses has extensive forests of cypress, olivillo and other native tree species. Its wildlife includes guanaco, fox, vizcacha, condor and many other species of bird. There are petroglyphs at several sites, and camping is permitted at Los Maitenes, 12 km from the park entrance. Several hiking trails exist, and it is possible to rent horses from local people.

Los Cipreses, in the foothills and cordillera of the Andes, is 50 km south-east of Rancagua. No direct public transport exists, but visitors can take a bus as far as Termas de Cauquenes (see the previous section) and walk another 15 km to the park entrance. With luck and persuasion, it may be possible to arrange transport with CONAF in Rancagua.

Lago Rapel

In truth a reservoir rather than a lake, Lago Rapel was formed by the Central Hidroeléctrica Rapel, which inundated the basins of the Cachapoal and Tinguiririca rivers in 1968. It is, however, a popular site for water sports such as wind-surfing, water-

Zorro culpeo (fox)

skiing and fishing. There are many camping areas east of El Manzano, on the south shore of the northern arm of the reservoir, plus reasonable accommodation at *Hostería y Camping Playa de Llaullauquén*, on the eastern shore of its southern arm, for US$8 per person.

Lago Rapel is about 100 km west of Rancagua via Peluquén, on the Carretera Panamericana. It can also be reached from Santiago (147 km) with Buses Navidad from the Terminal Borja, Alameda 3250.

Pichilemu

Reached most easily by bus from the city of San Fernando (55 km south of Rancagua), Pichilemu has been the Sixth Region's most popular beach resort since the turn of the century. It's very crowded in season, but reasonable accommodation is available – try *Residencial Las Salinas* (☎ 681071), Aníbal Pinto 51, which has singles with shared bath for US$7, or *Residencial San Luis* (☎ 681040), Angel Gaete 27, for about US$10.

About 20 km south of Pichilemu is the smaller beach resort and fishing village of **Bucalemu**, where several residenciales on Avenida Celedonio Pastene have singles for about US$7.

Surfing In summer, the Campeonato Nacional de Surf (national surfing championship) takes place at Punta de Lobos, 6 km from town.

CURICÓ

Founded in 1743 by José Antonio Manso de Velasco, Curicó is a pleasant, attractive city of 65,000 which is a service centre for surrounding orchards and vineyards. While not a major attraction in its own right, it's a good base for excursions into the countryside, to coastal areas such as Vichuquén, and to parts of the Andes which few travellers see, such as Radal Siete Tazas.

Orientation

Beside the Río Guaiquillo, 195 km south of Santiago, Curicó lies just west of the Carretera Panamericana. Entering town from the Panamericana, the broad, tree-lined Avenida Manso de Velasco skirts the eastern edge of Curicó's central quadrangle. At the northern end of Manso de Velasco, Cerro Carlos Condell is a verdant, scenic overlook with a swimming pool to beat the summer heat.

Curicó's Plaza de Armas, surrounded by palms, is one of the prettiest in all of Chile, with a wonderful, turn-of-the-century wrought-iron bandstand and cool fountains with imperturbable black-necked swans. On its south side, a local artist has carved a tree trunk into a sculpture of a Mapuche warrior.

Information

Tourist Office Curicó has no formal tourist office, but the private Cámara de Turismo (☎ 310086) operates out of the government office on Carmen, on the east side of the Plaza. Open from 9 am to 6.30 pm, it's understaffed and lacks space, but does its best. Also try the especially helpful branch of the Automóvil Club de Chile (☎ 311156), at Chacabuco 759.

Money Curi Cambio at Merced 255, Oficina 106, is open weekdays from 9.30 am to 1.30 pm and 3.30 to 6 pm.

Post & Telecommunications Correos de Chile is at Carmen 556, opposite the Plaza de Armas. CTC has long-distance offices at Peña 650 and at Camilo Henríquez 414. ENTEL, at Prat 373 near Yungay, is open until midnight.

Cultural Centres The Centro Cultural Universidad Católica, Merced 437, offers films and concerts on a regular basis, and also has a small but good bookstore.

Travel Agencies Turismo Bucalemu (☎ 312089), Yungay 621, is helpful and a good source of information.

Vineyards

One of Chile's best-known vineyards,

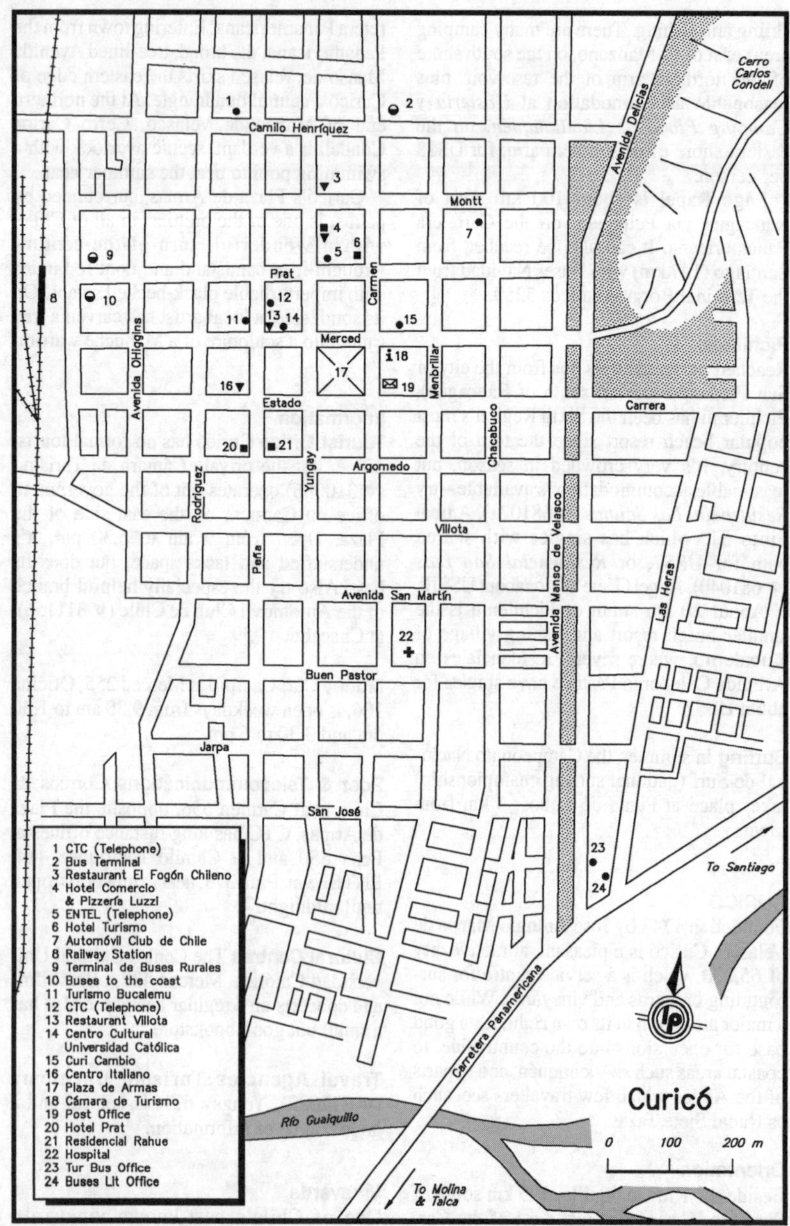
Cerro Carlos Condell
Avenida Delicias
Camilo Henríquez
Montt
Prat
Carmen
Merced
Menbrillar
Avenida OHiggins
Estado
Carrera
Argomedo
Yungay
Rodríguez
Chacabuco
Villota
Peña
Avenida Manso de Velasco
Avenida San Martín
Las Heras
Buen Pastor
Jarpa
San José
To Santiago
Carretera Panamericana
Río Gualquillo
To Molina & Talca
Curicó
0
100
200 m
1 CTC (Telephone)
2 Bus Terminal
3 Restaurant El Fogón Chileno
4 Hotel Comercio & Pizzería Luzzi
5 ENTEL (Telephone)
6 Hotel Turismo
7 Automóvil Club de Chile
8 Railway Station
9 Terminal de Buses Rurales
10 Buses to the coast
11 Turismo Bucalemu
12 CTC (Telephone)
13 Restaurant Villota
14 Centro Cultural Universidad Católica
15 Curi Cambio
16 Centro Italiano
17 Plaza de Armas
18 Cámara de Turismo
19 Post Office
20 Hotel Prat
21 Residencial Rahue
22 Hospital
23 Tur Bus Office
24 Buses Lit Office

Top : Church at Parinacota, Atacama Desert (AS)
Bottom : El Tatio geysers (WB)

Top Left : Fish market, Antofagasta (WB)
Top Right : Torre Reloj, Plaza Prat, Antofagasta (WB)
Bottom : Beach, Antofagasta (WB)

Bodega Miguel Torres (☎ 310455), is on the Carretera Panamericana, south of Curicó. Phone ahead, and take a taxi colectivo from Camilo Henríquez and Rodríguez toward the village of Molina. The winery is open daily from 8.30 am to 1 pm and 2.30 to 6.30 pm.

On the same route, near the village of Lontué, is **Viña San Pedro** (☎ 491517), a vineyard which dates from the early 18th century. Its hours are much more limited – in summer, Tuesday to Friday from 10.30 to 11.30 am and 3.30 to 4.30 pm; in winter, Tuesday to Thursday from 10 to 11.30 am and 3.30 to 4.30 pm.

Places to Stay

Friendly *Hotel Prat* (☎ 311069), only two blocks from the Plaza at Peña 427, is the the pick of budget accommodation at US$4 per person with shared bath, although the rooms vary – some are large, bright and comfortable, with high ceilings, while others are dark and a bit drab. The hot showers are fine, and there is a shady grape arbor over the patio. *Residencial Rahue*, across the street at Peña 410, is comparably priced and perfectly satisfactory.

At the tranquil *Hotel Comercio* (☎ 310014), Yungay 730, rates start at about US$14/18 for a single/double, but better rooms with private bath cost US$25 a single. *Hotel Turismo* (☎ 310823, formerly Hotel Luis Cruz Martínez), set on very attractive grounds at Carmen 727, has rooms from US$29/43.

Places to Eat

Restaurant Villota, Merced 487, has a fine fixed-price lunch in very pleasant surroundings for about US$4. For parrillada, try *El Fogón Chileno* at Yungay 802. Pizzas, sandwiches and a variety of snacks are available at *Pizzería Luzzi*, Yungay 720. Try also the *Centro Italiano*, Estado 531.

Getting There & Away

Bus The long-distance bus terminal is on Camilo Henríquez, three blocks north of the Plaza. Most north-south companies have their offices here. Two exceptions areBuses Lit (☎ 310554), at Las Heras 0195, and Tur Bus (☎ 312115) at Manso de Velasco 0106, which have buses leaving from those offices. Buses to Santiago leave about every half hour, and cost US$4. Buses Pullman del Sur (☎ 310387) has international services to Buenos Aires on Monday and Thursday at 1 pm (US$57).

For local and regional services, the Terminal de Buses Rurales is at the west end of Calle Prat, across from the railway station. Companies which operate bus services from there include Buses Bravo (☎ 312193), which goes to Lago Vichuquén and the coastal resort of Iloca; Buses Díaz (☎ 311905) and Ilomar (☎ 310358) also serve the coast. Buses Hernández goes to interior destinations such as Molina and Radal Siete Tazas.

Train Curicó's railway station is at the west end of Calle Prat, five blocks from the plaza. Trains between Santiago and Temuco stop here regularly.

AROUND CURICÓ

Radal Siete Tazas

In the cordillera south-east of Molina, 7600-hectare Radal Siete Tazas is an *área de protección* in the upper basin of the Río Claro. Ranging in elevation from 600 to 2150 metres, its major scenic attraction is a stunning series of falls (the highest of which is about 30 metres) and pools. Ecologically, it marks a transition between the drought-tolerant Mediterranean vegetation of the north, and the moist evergreen forests to the south. There are good, scenic hiking trails up Cerro El Fraile and at Valle del Indio, with camping at the Radal and Parque Inglés sectors.

CONAF maintains a visitor centre at Parque Inglés, 50 km from Molina by gravel and dirt road. This can be reached from Curicó and Molina by Buses Hernández. In summer, buses leave daily at 5 pm from the market in Molina; for the rest of the year they go only three times weekly. *Hostería Flor de la Canela* (☎ 491613), near the park headquarters, offers accommodation from December to March, for US$14 per person with shared bath, US$17 with private bath.

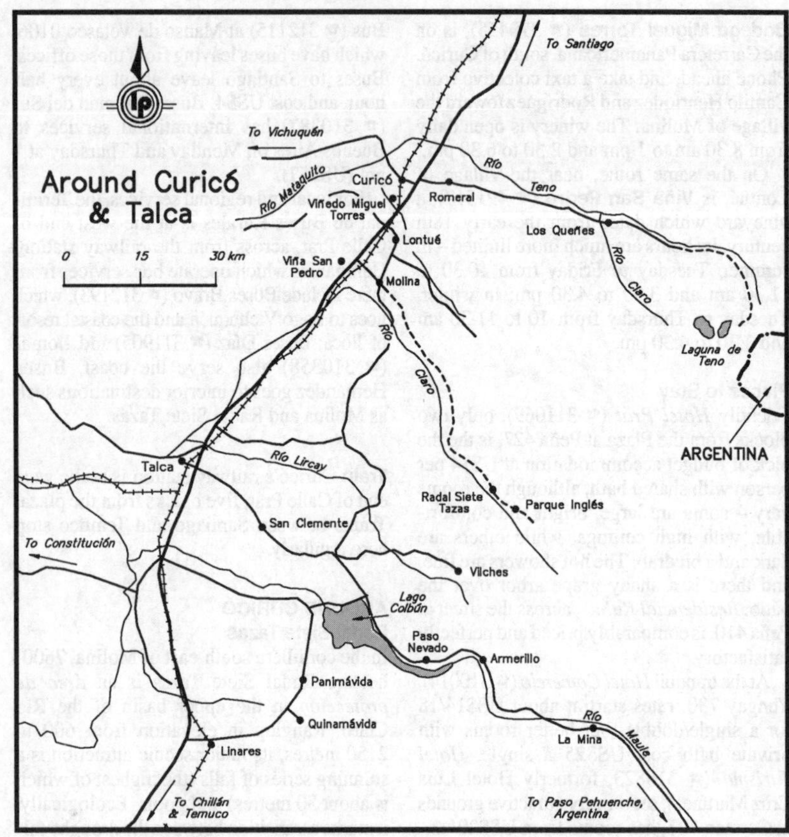

It has a restaurant, and there is also a kiosk where basic supplies are available.

Lago Vichuquén

In the coast range only a short distance from the Pacific, 110 km from Curicó, Lago Vichuquén is a natural lake which is a popular centre for water sports. Nearby is **Reserva Nacional Laguna de Torca**, a 600-hectare reserve which features breeding populations of black-necked swans and other birds. In especially wet years, the two lakes join to form a single extensive coastal wetland.

TALCA

Founded in 1690 but refounded in 1742 after a major earthquake, Talca witnessed the declaration of Chilean independence in 1818. Since its earliest days, it has been the residence of landowners and an important commercial centre in a prosperous agricultural region. It is capital of the Seventh Region of Maule.

Orientation

Talca (population about 140,000) is 257 km south of Santiago via the Carretera Panamericana, which skirts the city's eastern border, while the Río Claro limits its westward expansion. Talca's street plan is no less regular than most cities founded in the colonial era; streets north of the Plaza de Armas begin at 1 Norte, those to the south at 1 Sur, those to the east at 1 Oriente, and those to the west at 1 Poniente. Frequently '1' is spelled out as 'Uno', but nearly all other streets use the figure except for 4 Norte, a divided boulevard known as Avenida Bernardo O'Higgins. O'Higgins crosses the Río Claro to the Cerro de la Virgen, which offers fine views of the city.

Information

Tourist Office Sernatur (☎ 233669) is at 1 Poniente 1234. The Automóvil Club de Chile (☎ 232774) is virtually across the street at 1 Poniente 1267.

Post & Telecommunications Correos de Chile is opposite the Plaza, on 1 Oriente. CTC has long-distance offices at 1 Sur 1156 and 10 Oriente 1041, while ENTEL is at 4 Sur 1177.

Cultural Centres The Universidad de Talca's Salón Abate Juan Ignacio Molina (Salón Molina), at 1 Poniente 1351, offers various cultural events, including films, lectures and exhibitions of artwork.

Travel Agencies Bontour (☎ 234003) is at 5 Oriente 1080.

Medical Services The Hospital Regional (☎ 242406) is eleven blocks east of the plaza on 1 Norte, just across the railway tracks.

National Parks CONAF (☎ 234023) is at 2 Poniente 1180.

Museo O'Higginiano

In this late-colonial house, Bernardo O'Higgins officially signed Chile's declaration of independence in 1818. The house dates from 1762, and is handsomely furnished in period decor. It also contains archaeological and numismatic exhibits, as well as collections of Chilean and foreign painting and sculpture. It's open from Monday to Thursday from 9 am to 12.45 pm and 2.30 to 6.45 pm, on Friday from 9.30 am to 12.45 pm and 3 to 6.45 pm.

Galleries

Talca has a multitude of public and private art galleries which occasionally host films, concerts and other events as well. The **Sala de Arte** in the basement of the Hotel Plaza, 1 Poniente 1141, is open weekdays from 9.30 am to 1 pm and 3 to 7 pm. The **Sala Futrone**, in the post office on the plaza, is open weekdays from 9 am to 1 pm and 3 to 6.30 pm, while the **Pinacoteca Universidad de Talca**, 1 Oriente 1031, is open weekdays from 10 am to 1 pm and 3 to 7 pm. There are also the Municipalidad's **Casa del Arte**, 1 Norte 931, and the **Galería del Arte**, 1 Poniente 1261, whose opening hours are weekdays from 9.30 am to 1 pm and 3 to 7 pm, Saturdays from 9.30 am to 1 pm only.

Museo Bomberil

Travellers with more incendiary tendencies can visit the firemen's museum, in the main fire station at 2 Sur 1172. Its collections of antique fire-fighting equipment, photographs and miscellanea are open to the public so long as there's not a serious blaze raging across town.

Villa Cultural Huilquilemu

Once an important fundo but now property of the Universidad Católica, this complex of restored 19th-century buildings, 10 km east of Talca, houses a variety of galleries and museums (including a fine collection of farm machinery), chapels and regional crafts. It's open on Tuesday to Saturday from 3.30 to 6.30 pm, Sundays and holidays from 11 am to 2 pm.

Places to Stay

Near the railway station, *Hotel Alcázar*, 2 Sur 1359, is a clean and cheap alternative at about US$6 per person with shared bath. Across the street at 2 Sur 1360, *Residencial Cordillera* (☎ 221817) has singles with shared bath for US$8, while singles with

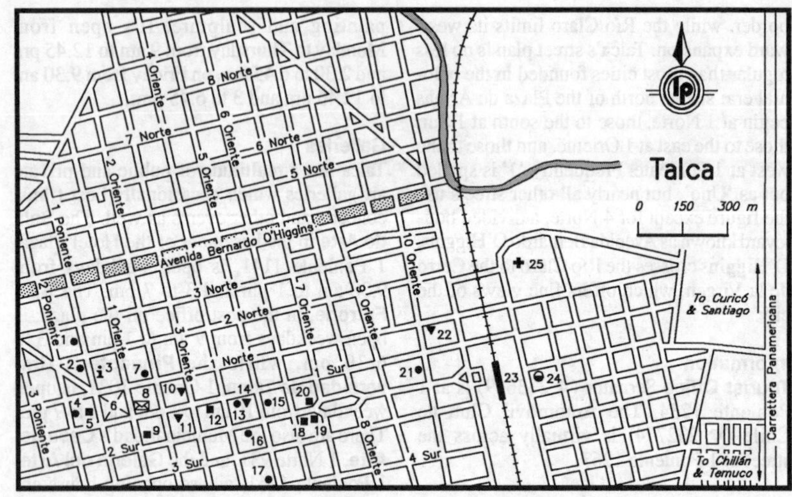

■ **PLACES TO STAY**	**OTHER**
5 Hotel Plaza	1 Salón Molina
9 Hotel Marcos Gamero	2 Automóvil Club de Chile
12 Hotel Claris	3 Sernatur
18 Hotel Napoli	4 CONAF
19 Hotel Cordillera	6 Plaza de Armas
20 Hotel Alcázar	7 Museo O'Higginiano
	8 Post Office
▼ **PLACES TO EAT**	13 CTC (Telephone)
	15 Bontour
10 Centro Español	16 Museo Bomberil
11 Restaurant Mykonos	17 ENTEL (Telephone)
14 Restaurant Ibiza	21 CTC (Telephone)
22 El Gallo Marino	23 Railway Station
	24 Bus Terminal
	25 Hospital

private bath go for US$14. *Hotel Claris* (☎ 226207), more central at 1 Sur 1026, is only slightly dearer with shared bath, but US$18/25 for a single/double with private bath.

Mid-range hotels start at about US$25/38, such as the *Hotel Napoli* (☎ 227373), 2 Sur 1314. For near-luxury, try *Hotel Plaza* (☎ 226150) at 1 Poniente 1141 or *Hotel Marcos Gamero* (☎ 223388) at 1 Oriente 1070. Both charge around US$35/45.

Places to Eat

Talca has several restaurants worth trying, including the *Centro Español* at 3 Oriente 1109, *Restaurante Ibiza* (which also has a take-away rotisserie) at 1 Sur 1168, *El Gallo*

Marino at 1 Norte 1718, and *Restaurante Mykonos* at 1 Sur 942.

Getting There & Away

Bus Talca's bus terminal (☎ 243270) is at 2 Sur 1920, directly behind the railway station. Many buses between Santiago and points south stop here, at least briefly. If the Paso Pehuenche has opened to Malargue and San Rafael in Argentina, this would be a very interesting and unusual way of crossing the Andes.

Train The railway station (☎ 226116) is at 11 Oriente 1000, at the eastern end of 2 Sur. All trains from Santiago's Estación Central to Temuco and points south stop here en route.

Getting Around

Car Rental American Rent-a-Car (☎ 233242) is at 1 Norte 1546.

AROUND TALCA

Vilches

In the Andean foothills between 600 and 2448 metres above sea level, Vilches is a 17,000-hectare 'área de protección' administered by CONAF. It's 65 km from Talca, and there is no formal camping site. It's possible to camp in the upper basin of the Río Lircay and make excursions on trails to Laguna El Alto, Laguna Tomate, and up the canyon of the Valle del Venado. Buses Vilches goes twice daily except Sunday from Talca, at 1 and 5 pm.

Six km from the park entrance in Vilches Alto, *Hostería Rancho los Canales* (☎ 223164 in Talca) has comfortable lodging for US$26 single and a restaurant as well.

CHILLÁN

Chillán is the birthplace of Chilean liberator Bernardo O'Higgins. It also marks the approximate northern border of La Frontera, that area over which Spain, and Chile, never really exercised effective control until the state finally subdued the Mapuche in the late 19th century. Founded in 1565 as a military outpost, destroyed and refounded several times more after earthquakes and Mapuche sieges, it moved to its present site in 1835, although the old city, nearby Chillán Viejo, has never really died. Of all the cities along the Carretera Panamericana between Santiago and Temuco, Chillán probably most deserves a stopover.

Orientation

Chillán (population 125,000), 400 km south of Santiago and 270 km north of Temuco, sits on an alluvial plain between the Río Ñuble and its smaller southern tributary, the Río Chillán. The city's focus is an area 12 blocks square, bounded by the divided, tree-lined avenidas Ecuador, Brasil, Collín and Argentina; the centre proper is the Plaza de Armas, bounded by Libertad, 18 de Septiembre, Constitución and Arauco.

Avenida O'Higgins connects the city with the Carretera Panamericana (which passes the city to the north-west) and the suburb of Chillán Viejo (the city centre until the earthquake of 1835). From Chillán Viejo there is alternative access to the Panamericana, southbound.

Information

Tourist Office Sernatur (☎ 223272), in the Edificios Públicos 422 off the plaza, is open on weekdays from 9 am to 1 pm and 3 to 7 pm, Saturdays from 9 am to 1 pm only. It is less than helpful, and reluctant to give out names and addresses for budget accommodation. Sernatur also maintains an office in Chillán Viejo, at the corner of O'Higgins and Serrano.

The Automóvil Club de Chile (☎ 216410) is at Libertad 455, Oficina 308.

Money Biotour, at Constitución 550, Local 9, should change US cash and travellers' cheques. At a pinch, try Banco del Estado, 18 de Septiembre 601, but its rates are lower than exchange houses.

Post & Telecommunications Correos de Chile is at Libertad 505. CTC long-distance offices are at Arauco 625, while ENTEL is at 18 de Septiembre 746.

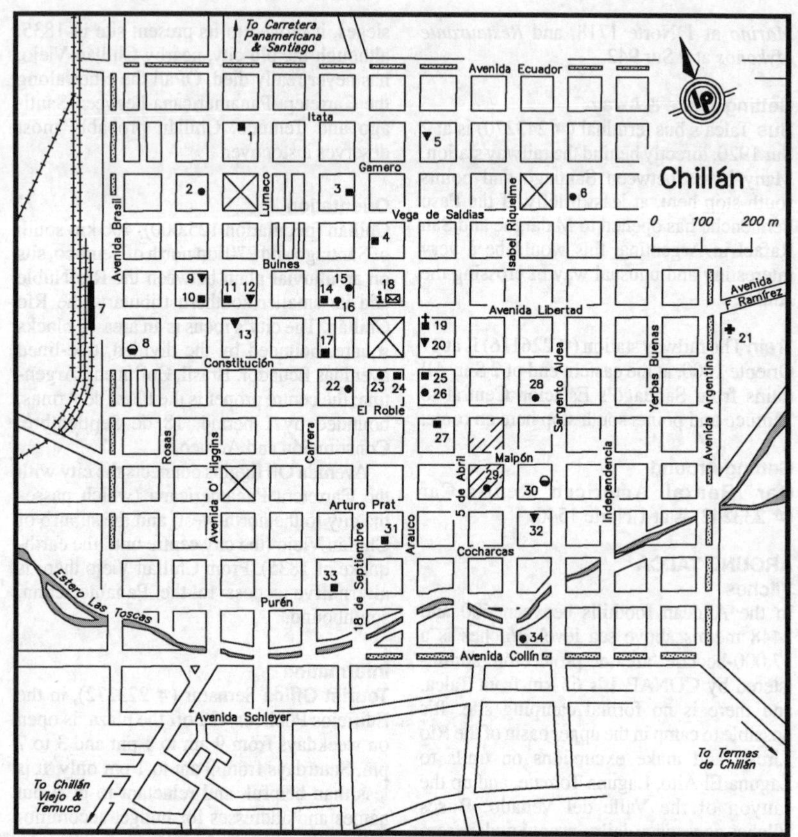

Cultural Centres The Pinacoteca Chillán Viejo, in the old town, holds art exhibitions and concerts. Normal opening hours are weekdays from 8.30 am to 1 pm and 2.30 to 7 pm.

Travel Agencies Chillán has several travel agencies, including Centrotur (☎ 221306) at 18 de Septiembre 656, Hispanotur (☎ 222399) at El Roble 845, and Alto Nivel (☎ 225267) at Arauco 683.

Medical Services Chillán's hospital (☎ 212345) is six blocks south-east of the Plaza, on the corner of Avenida Francisco Ramírez and Avenida Argentina.

Escuela México

After an earthquake in 1939 devastated Chillán, killing 15,000 people, the Mexican government of President Lázaro Cárdenas donated a new school to the city. Before its completion, at the urging of Pablo Neruda, the famous Mexican muralist David Alfaro Siqueiros decorated the library with spectacular murals honouring both indigenous and post-Columbian figures from the history of

■ PLACES TO STAY

1 Hospedaje Sonia Segui
3 Hotel Floresta
4 Claris Hotel
10 Hotel Martín Ruiz de Gamboa
11 Hotel Real
14 Hotel Americano
17 Hotel Rucamanqui
24 Gran Hotel Isabel Riquelme
25 Hotel Cordillera
27 Hotel Quinchamalí
31 Hospedaje Su Casa
33 Hospedaje Tino Rodríguez Sepúlveda

▼ PLACES TO EAT

5 Planka
9 Kuranepe
12 Taipe
13 Jai Yang
20 Centro Español
32 Cocinerías del Mercado

OTHER

2 Escuela México (Murals)
6 Museo Franciscano
7 Railway Station
8 Terminal de Buses Inter-regionales
15 ENTEL (Telephone)
16 Automóvil Club de Chile
18 Sernatur & Post Office
19 Catedral
21 Hospital
22 Centrotur
23 Biotour (Money Exchange)
26 CTC (Telephone)
28 Hispanotur
29 Feria
30 Terminal de Buses Rurales
34 Museo Naval Arturo Prat

the two countries. The northern wall is devoted to Mexico and the southern wall to Chile. Siqueiros' countryman Xavier Guerrero also participated in the project, his own simple but powerful murals 'Hermanos Mexicanos' (Mexican brothers) flanking the staircase to the library.

While this is still a functioning school, the staff welcome visitors who don't repeat my mistake of arriving during a major cleanup the day before the Mexican ambassador's ceremonial visit. It's at O'Higgins 250, between Gamero and Vega de Saldias.

Feria de Chillán

Chillán's open-air market, one of the most colourful in all of Chile, is a sprawling affair offering a great selection of local crafts and mountains of fresh produce. Chilean playwright Antonio Acevedo Hernández writes that the scene:

> ... at once produces the sensation of a broken rainbow fallen on the Feria, or of a fragment of the solar spectrum captured in a glorious instant, or perhaps the delirium of a mad painter projected on a massive pallet. The colour is something that shouts, whirls, absorbs the light, and overwhelms the vision.

Open daily, but especially lively on Saturday, the Feria occupies the entire Plaza de la Merced, bounded by Maipón, 5 de Abril, Arturo Prat and Isabel Riquelme, but spills over into adjacent streets as well. In the recently remodelled permanent market, across Maipón, there are many good and reasonable places to eat.

Museo Franciscano

Chillán's Franciscan museum displays historical materials of the order which, from 1585, proselytised among the Mapuche in 15 missions from Chillán to Río Bueno. It's on Sargento Aldea between Gamero and Vega de Saldias. Admission is free, and it's open daily except Sundays.

Museo Naval Arturo Prat

Arturo Prat, the naval officer who tried to sink a Peruvian ironclad with his sword in the harbour of Iquique, was born in the village of Ninhue, north-west of Chillán. This museum in his honour, at Isabel Riquelme 1173, is open Tuesday to Friday from 10 am to 12.30 pm and 3 to 7 pm. Admission is free.

Parque Monumental Bernardo O'Higgins

In Chillán Viejo, only a short bus or cab ride from the centre, a tiled mural 60 metres long marks the birthplace of O'Higgins and illustrates scenes from his life. Its grounds and the associated **Centro Histórico y Cultural** are open on weekdays from 9 am to 1 pm and 3 to 7 pm from April to November; during the rest of the year the schedule is 9 am to 1 pm and 2.30 to 7.30 pm on weekdays and 9 am to 1 pm Saturdays.

Places to Stay – bottom end

Chillán has a good selection of bottom-end accommodation from about US$4 per person, the cheapest of which is *Hospedaje Sonia Segui* (☎ 214879), Itata 288, where the rate includes breakfast. *Hospedaje Su Casa* (☎ 223931) at Cocharcas 555 is comparable. Try also *Hospedaje Tino Rodríguez Sepúlveda* (☎ 216181), Purén 443, which charges US$6.

Hotel Americano (☎ 221175), Carrera 481, has singles with shared bath for US$5, while the *Claris Hotel* (☎ 21980), 18 de Septiembre 357, costs about the same with shared bath, but is dearer with private bath at US$10/16 for a single/double. *Hotel Real* (☎ 221827), Libertad 219, has rooms with shared bath for US$7/12, and *Hotel Martín Ruiz de Gamboa* (☎ 221013), O'Higgins 497, charges US$10/13 with shared bath, US$11/16 with private bath.

Places to Stay – middle

Mid-range accommodation starts at about US$20/30 – try *Hotel Floresta* (☎ 222253) at 18 de Septiembre 278 or *Hotel Quinchamalí* (☎ 223381) at El Roble 634.

Places to Stay – top end

Hotel Cordillera (☎ 215211), Arauco 619, and *Hotel Rucamanqui* (☎ 222927), Herminda Martín 590, both charge around US$27/40. *Gran Hotel Isabel Riquelme* (☎ 213663), Arauco 600, is Chillán's most prestigious and dearest accommodation, starting at US$45/55.

Places to Eat

Several simple but excellent restaurants can be found in the *Cocinerías del Mercado* at Prat 826, 2nd floor; these may move as the central market is remodelled. The *Centro Español* is at Arauco 555; others worth a try are *Planka* at Arauco 103, and *Kuranepe* at O'Higgins 420. For Chinese food, there is *Taipe* at Libertad 299 or *Jai Yang* at Libertad 250.

Things to Buy

Chillán is one of the major artisans' zones of central Chile. Especially good are the ceramics from the nearby villages of Quinchamalí, Paine and Florida. Leatherwork, basketry, horsegear and weavings are available in the Feria.

Getting There & Away

Bus Chillán's Terminal de Buses Interregionales (☎ 221014) is at Constitución 01, on the corner of Avenida Brasil. Tur Bus (☎ 212502) has 17 northbound buses daily to Talca and Santiago (six hours, about US$9); southbound, it goes to Concepción (twice daily, US$2), Los Angeles (twice daily, US$2), Angol (daily, US$4), Temuco (daily, US$5), Valdivia (daily, US$7), and Puerto Montt (daily, US$11).

Tas Choapa has regular services north and south along the Panamericana, direct services to Valparaíso and Viña del Mar, and combinations to northern Chile and Argentina from Santiago. It also offers direct service to Bariloche, Argentina daily for US$32. Buses Lit runs similar routes, and also goes to destinations in the coastal range behind Viña del Mar, such as Quilpué and Villa Alemana. Igi Llaima has direct services to Neuquén, Argentina, via San Martín de Los Andes and Zapala.

Línea Azul has 20 buses daily to Concepción for US$2, plus two daily to Santiago for US$7. Chevalier has five daily to Santiago for the same price. Buses J B, Constitución 55, has seven daily to Salto del Laja and Los Angeles, while Biotal, Constitución 82, has three to Los Angeles, four to Concepción, and seven to Talca.

For local and regional services, the Terminal de Buses Rurales (☎ 223606) is on Sargento Aldea, south of Maipón.

Train Trains between Santiago and Temuco arrive and depart from the station (☎ 222424) on Avenida Brasil.

Getting Around

Car Rental First Rent-a-Car (☎ 211218) is at 18 de Septiembre 380.

AROUND CHILLÁN

Termas de Chillán

Long renowned for its thermal baths, and more recently for its skiing, Termas de Chillán is 80 km east of Chillán, at 1800 metres on the slopes of Volcán Chillán. Most of the road is paved. In 1991, the old hotel burned down, but the new *Hotel Pirigallo* appears ready to satisfy the demand, with singles/doubles with full pension for US$60/80. Reservations can be made at their office in Chillán (☎ 223887) at Libertad 1042, or in Santiago (☎ 251-2685) at Avenida Providencia 2237.

Parador Jamón, Pan y Vino (☎ 222682), 18 de Septiembre, Oficina 1 in Chillán, offers week-long fishing, hiking and camping excursions in the cordillera in and around the Termas. Doubles normally cost US$68.

CONCEPCIÓN

Concepción's industry, convenient energy resources, port facilities and universities make it the second most important city in Chile after Santiago. It is the capital of the Eighth Region of Biobío. Subject to earthquakes throughout its history, practically nothing remains of the city's colonial past. The modern centre has managed to integrate commerce, industry and education without sacrificing its human scale.

History

Founded in 1551 by Pedro de Valdivia but menaced constantly by Indians and devastated by earthquakes in 1730 and 1751, Concepción moved several times before reaching its present site in 1764. After a major Mapuche uprising in 1598, Spain did not seriously contest their control of the area south of the Biobío, and Concepción remained one of the Spanish Empire's southernmost fortified outposts. The fine harbours of Talcahuano and San Vicente were major reasons for the city's location, facilitating sea-borne communication with Santiago via Valparaíso.

From accounts of the late colonial period, Concepción much resembled other Chilean cities, where the dwellings reflected clear distinctions between social classes. A British visitor in 1804 wrote:

> The houses are commonly one storey high, but some are two, built of... *adoves*, large sun-dried bricks, and all of them are tiled. The largest have a courtyard in front, with an entrance through arched porches, and heavy folding doors... The windows have iron gratings, with many parts of them gilt, and inside shutters, but no glass. This article has been too dear, and it is consequently used only in the windows of the principal dwelling apartments of the richer classes. On each side of the court, or *patio*, there are rooms for domestics, the younger branches of the family, and other purposes...
>
> The dwellings of lower classes are on the same plan, except that they have no courts or patios, the fronts being open to the street, but they usually have a garden at the back, where the kitchen is built separately from the house, as a precaution against fire.

This type of construction made the city especially susceptible to earthquake damage, while its low-lying site exposed it to the power of seismic seawaves (or tsunami, often incorrectly called tidal waves). After experiencing a major quake near Valdivia in 1835, Darwin entered the Bahía de Concepción to find, as a result of the ensuing tsunami:

> ... the whole coast being strewed over with timber and furniture as if a thousand ships had been wrecked. Besides chairs, tables, book-shelves etc in great numbers, there were several roofs of cottages, which had been transported almost whole. The store-houses at Talcahuano had been burst open, and great bags of cotton, yerba, and other valuable merchandise were scattered on the shore.

After independence, Concepción's isolation from Santiago, coupled with the presence of lignite (brown coal) on the Lebú Peninsula near Lota, enabled it to develop an autonomous industrial tradition. The export of wheat for the California gold rush market further spurred the area's economic growth, and secondary industries emerged later in the form of glass-blowing, timber, and woollen and cotton textiles. The railway reached Concepción in 1872 and, after the Mapuche threat receded, the government bridged the Biobío to improve access to the mines and give the city a strategic role in the colonisation of La Frontera, the present-day Lake District.

Mining of coal, a scarce resource in South America, now takes place in westward-sloping seams as much as three km beneath the sea. Since WW II, the major industrial project to benefit Concepción has been the steel plant at Huachipato, built with US assistance. Inexpensive shipping and local energy make the industry competitive despite the fact that the iron ore comes from Coquimbo, 800 km north, and limestone comes from the Madre de Diós islands, 1500 km south.

Despite Concepción's industrial importance, wages and standards of living are relatively low. This, coupled with activism at the Universidad de Concepción, made the city and its industrial hinterland the focus of a highly politicised labour movement which was a bulwark of support for Salvador Allende and the Unidad Popular. As a centre of leftist opposition, the area suffered more than other regions under the military dictatorship of 1973-89.

Orientation

Concepción sits on the north bank of the Río Biobío, Chile's only important navigable waterway. Cerro Caracol, a scenic overlook, blocks any eastward expansion so that Concepción and its port of Talcahuano, 15 km north-west on the sheltered Bahía de Concepción, are rapidly growing together. Concepción proper has a population of about 270,000, but with Talcahuano the metropolitan area has nearly half a million.

Concepción's standard grid centres on the Plaza Independencia, a pleasantly landscaped space with an attractive fountain. Few older buildings have survived – the modern, utilitarian and rather plain buildings on the surrounding streets Aníbal Pinto, Barros Arana, Caupolicán and O'Higgins reflect the city's vulnerability to earthquakes. The Plaza is a bustling place, with frequent impromptu performances by actors and street musicians.

Only four blocks east of the plaza, Parque Ecuador is a pleasant refuge from the busy city centre. The park's border, Avenida Lamas, becomes Esmeralda south west of Prat and leads to the Puente Viejo (old bridge). This road continues south to the *Costa del Carbón* (Coast of Coal), where cities such as Coronel and Lota supply the energy for Concepción's industry. A newer and better bridge, the Puente Nuevo, is further west.

Information

Tourist Office Sernatur (☎ 227976) is at Aníbal Pinto 460. It is well stocked with maps and brochures and has a helpful and well informed staff. It's open daily in summer from 8.30 am to 8 pm; the rest of the year on weekdays only from 8.30 am to 1 pm and 3 to 6.30 pm.

ACCHI (☎ 226554), the Automóvil Club de Chile, at San Martín 519, is also a good source of information.

Money Try Inter-Santiago, Caupolicán 521, Local 58.

Post & Telecommunications Correos de Chile is at O'Higgins 799, on the corner of Colo Colo. CTC has long-distance offices at Colo Colo 487 and Barros Arana 673, Local 5. ENTEL is at Caupolicán 567, Local A.

Consulates Concepción has a surprisingly large number of foreign delegations, so it can be a good place to get a visa. Argentina has a consulate (☎ 222644) at San Martín 472, 5th floor. The Peruvian Consulate (☎ 224644) is at Barros Arana 348, Oficina 2. The UK Consulate (☎ 225655) is at Castellón 317. The German consulate (☎ 230973), at O'Higgins 445, is open weekdays from 9 am to 1 pm.

Cultural Centres Concepción has a glut of bi-national cultural centres: the Instituto Chileno-Norteamericano (☎ 225506) at Caupolicán 315, the Instituto Chileno-Británico (☎ 223778) at San Martín 531, the Instituto Chileno-Alemán (☎ 229287) at Chacabuco 840, the Instituto Chileno-Francés (☎ 222060) at Colo Colo 1, and the Instituto Chileno-Español at Trinitarias 165.

Travel Agencies Around the Plaza Independencia it's hard to walk any distance in any direction without passing a travel agency. One recommended choice is Pawulska Tour (☎ 238720), Aníbal Pinto 367, but there are countless others.

Bookshops As a university town, Concepción has a good selection of bookshops. Try Librería Manantial at Caupolicán 48 or Librería Paz on the south side of the Plaza Independencia.

Medical Services Concepción's Hospital Regional (☎ 237445) is at San Martín and Avenida Roosevelt, eight blocks north of the Plaza Independencia.

National Parks CONAF (☎ 233131) is at Serrano 529, 3rd floor.

Galería de Historia

This very fine museum, on the edge of Parque Ecuador on the corner of Victor Lamas and Lincoyán, features vivid, realistic dioramas depicting local and regional history, including: pre-Columbian Mapuche subsistence activities; the arrival of the Spaniards and battles between the two peoples (with fine representations of Mapuche tactics); construction of fortifications at Penco (the city's original site); signing of treaties; literary figure Alonso de Ercilla; Chile's declaration of independence; the 1851 battle of Loncomilla; the devastating 1939 earthquake (15,000 houses destroyed); and an especially finely detailed model of a local factory.

The museum is open daily except Monday from 10 am to 1 pm and 2 to 7 pm. There is no admission charge.

Casa del Arte

In the Barrio Universitario, at Chacabuco and Larenas, the art museum's highlight is the massive mural *La Presencia de América Latina* by Mexican artist Jorge González Camarena, a protegé of José Clemente Orozco. There are also two rooms of landscapes and portraits. Opening hours are Tuesday to Friday from 10 am to 7 pm, Saturday from 10 am to 7 pm, and Sunday from 10 am to 1 pm. Admission is free.

Museo de Concepción

Also known as the Museo de Historia y Artesanía Carlos Oliver Schneider, the city's museum has exhibits on the Mapuche and samples of local crafts. On the Plaza Acevedo at the north end of Maipú, it's open Tuesday to Saturday from 10 am to 5 pm and Sunday from 3 pm to 5.30 pm. Admission is normally US$0.40, but it's free on Sundays and holidays.

Museo Huascar

Built in Birkenhead in 1865 and captured from the Peruvian navy in 1879, the *Huascar* was one of the earliest ironclad battleships in the world. It is more an object than a proper museum, despite a series of naval portraits. It is in a remarkable state of preservation thanks to the labour of the navy's conscripts, whose spit-and-polish maintenance work never ends.

From Concepción, take any bus with 'Base Naval' on its placard to the Apostadero Naval, beyond the Club de Yates on Avenida Villaroel. You must leave your passport at the gate; photography is permitted, but only with the port of Talcahuano or the open sea as background – do *not* photograph other naval vessels or any part of the base itself. Opening hours are daily except Monday from 9.30 am to noon and 2 to 6 pm. Admission is US$0.30.

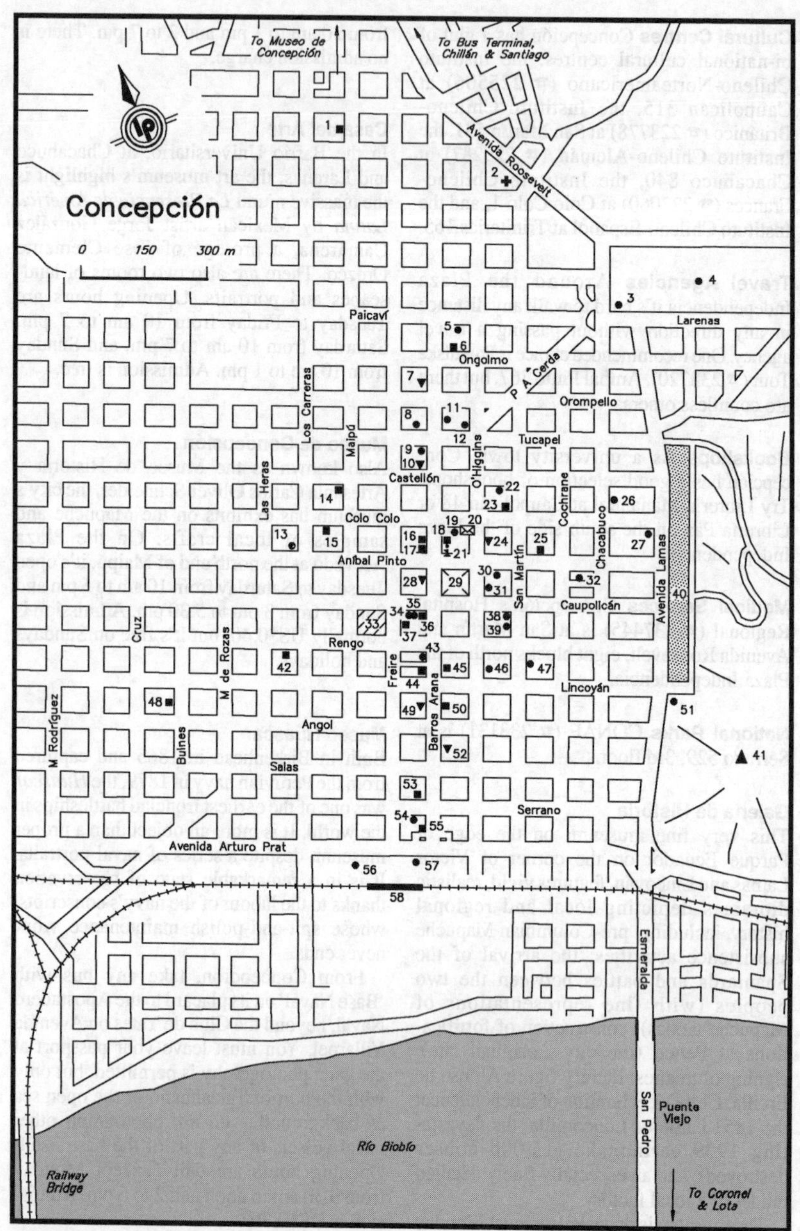
To Museo de Concepción
To Bus Terminal, Chillán & Santiago
Avenida Roosevelt
Concepción
0 150 300 m
Paicaví
Larenas
Ongolmo
P A Cerda
Orompello
Tucapel
Los Carreras
Maipú
Las Heras
O'Higgins
Castellón
Cochrane
Chacabuco
Avenida Lamas
Colo Colo
San Martín
Aníbal Pinto
Caupolicán
Rengo
Cruz
M de Rozas
Freire
Barros Arana
Lincoyán
M Rodríguez
Bulnes
Angol
Salas
Serrano
Avenida Arturo Prat
Esmeralda
San Pedro
Puente Viejo
Río Biobío
Railway Bridge
To Coronel & Lota

■ PLACES TO STAY

1 Hospedaje María Inés Jarpa
6 Residencial
14 Hotel Cruz del Sur
15 Residencial Colo Colo
16 Residencial Antuco & Residencial San Sebastián
17 Hotel Ritz
18 Hotel Tabancura
23 Hotel Alonso de Ercilla
25 Hotel de la Cruz
36 Hotel Araucano
37 Residencial Concepción
42 Casa de Huéspedes
44 Hotel Alborada
45 Residencial Metro
48 Casa Familiar González
50 Hotel El Dorado
53 Apart Hotel Concepción
55 Hotel Cecil

▼ PLACES TO EAT

7 China Town
24 Pastelería Suiza & Salón Inglés
28 Centro Español
49 El Naturista
52 Chungwa

OTHER

2 Hospital
3 Casa del Arte
4 Barrio Universitario
5 Buses Varmontt
8 Tur Bus & Bus Chevalier
9 Buses Cruz del Sur
10 Centro Italiano
11 Buses Tas Choapa
12 Buses Igi Llaima
13 Buses Biobío
19 CTC (Telephone)
20 Post Office
21 Sernatur
22 UK Consulate
26 Instituto Chileno-Alemán
27 Instituto Chileno-Francés
29 Plaza Independencia
30 Pawulska Tour
31 Teatro Concepción
32 Instituto Chileno-Español
33 Mercado Central
34 Inter-Santiago (Money Exchange)
35 ENTEL (Telephone)
38 Instituto Chileno-Norteamericano
39 Automóvil Club de Chile
40 Parque Ecuador
41 Cerro Caracol
43 Ladeco
44 LAN-Chile
46 German Consulate
47 Argentine Consulate
49 Peruvian Consulate
51 Galería de Historia
54 CONAF
56 Buses Los Alces
57 Buses J Ewert
58 Railway Station

Festivals

Organised by the universities, Concepción's Fiesta de la Primavera (Festival of Spring) lasts an entire week in early October, commemorating the founding of the city.

Coronel, an important mining town south of Concepción, has recently begun a Muestra Cultural de Folklore (folklore festival) in early February, during its traditional Semanas Culturales de Coronel.

Places to Stay – bottom end

Although a bit north of the centre, *Hospedaje María Inés Jarpa* (☎ 226238), Maipú 1757, is the best bargain in town at US$4 single, US$9 with three meals. Call ahead because of its limited space and its attractiveness to students from the nearby university. A standard, generic *Casa de Huéspedes* (☎ 244152), at Rengo 855, charges US$5 per person, with hot water and use of laundry and kitchen.

Residencial Concepción (☎ 223502), opposite the market at Freire 552, is technically no longer a residencial, but still offers accommodation for US$6 per person. *Residencial Metro* (☎ 225305), Barros Arana 464, has rooms for US$7 per person, while *Residencial O'Higgins*, O'Higgins 457, charges the same but includes breakfast. There is another central but nameless *residencial* (☎ 242340) at Ongolmo 486.

Residencial Colo Colo (☎ 234790), Colo Colo 743, is a very fine and friendly place at

US$11 per person. Similarly priced is *Casa Familiar González* (☎ 244939), at Bulnes 367, Casa 3.

Places to Stay – middle

If the train's late, try *Hotel Cecil* (☎ 230677), across from the station at Barros Arana 9, where single/doubles cost US$17/20. *Residencial Antuco* (☎ 235485) Barros Arana 741, Departamento 28, charges US$20/28 with breakfast. At the same street address, the *Residencial San Sebastián* (☎ 221366), Barros Arana 741, Departamento 55, has comparable service and prices. At *Hotel Ritz* (☎ 226696), Barros Arana 721, rates are US$27/37.

Toward the upper end of the range is *Hotel Alonso de Ercilla* (☎ 227984), Colo Colo 334, at US$30/45. *Hotel de la Cruz* (☎ 240016), Aníbal Pinto 240, is a fine place on a quiet street but still very central, at US$31/39.

At *Hotel Tabancura* (☎ 238348), Barros Arana 786, rates are US$34/46, while *Apart Hotel Concepción* (☎ 228851), Serrano 512, charges US$37/50. Try also *Hotel Cruz del Sur* (☎ 235655), which includes breakfast for US$48/70.

Places to Stay – top end

Hotel El Dorado (☎ 229400), Barros Arana 348, is the next step up at US$57/74. Concepción has two downtown luxury hotels, *Hotel Alborada* (☎ 242144) at Barros Arana 457 and *Hotel El Araucano* (☎ 230606) at Caupolicán 521. Both charge around US$80 single, but doubles cost only a few dollars more.

Places to Eat

Concepción's Mercado Central, occupying an entire block bounded by Caupolicán, Maipú, Rengo and Freire, has a multitude of cheap and excellent eating places, although the waitresses are more than just verbally aggressive – some literally try to drag customers into their venues. There's not much difference between these places in price, quality or decor, but *Don José* offers a superb pastel de choclo, a regional speciality which is a meal in itself.

Pastelería Suiza, O'Higgins 780, has a fine fixed-price lunch for about US$2. The *Salón Inglés*, next door, is similarly appealing. *El Naturista*, Barros Arana 342, serves vegetarian food, while *El Novillo Loco*, Pasaje Portales 539, is for carnivores. *Dino's*, Barros Arana 533, is a branch of the popular southern Chilean chain. For Chinese cuisine, visit *Chungwa* at Barros Arana 262 or *China Town* at Barros Arana 1115. The *Centro Español* at Barros Arana 675 and the *Centro Italiano* at Barros Arana 935 add a bit of European flavour.

For a cheap stand-up cappuccino or other coffee, try *Café Haití* at Caupolicán 511 or *Café Caribe* at Caupolicán 521.

Entertainment

Cinemas Unlike many Chilean towns where video has meant the demise of the cinema, Concepción still has four movie theatres: the Concepción at O'Higgins 650, the Regina at Barros Arana 340, and the Ducal and the Romano at Barros Arana 780. There are also frequent films at the university and at the various cultural institutes (see above).

Theatre & Music Concepción has several important venues for plays and concerts, so check the schedule for the Teatro Concepción (☎ 227193) at O'Higgins 650, the Aula Magna at Caupolicán 470, the Sala Andes (☎ 227264) at Tucapel 374, or the Casa del Arte (☎ 234985) in the Barrio Universitario.

Things to Buy

Local and regional crafts are on display in the Mercado Central, and also at La Gruta at Caupolicán 521, Local 64, Antumalal at Aníbal Pinto 450, Local 10, and Minga del Biobío at Barros Arana 1112. Look for woollens, basketry, ceramics, wood carvings and leather goods.

Getting There & Away

Air Aeropuerto Carriel Sur is five km northwest of downtown. Both LAN-Chile and

Ladeco operate vans to the airport, leaving from Hotel El Araucano and Hotel Alborada, costing US$2.50.

LAN-Chile (☎ 240025), Barros Arana 451, has two flights a day to Santiago (US$72) except on Friday (when there are four) and on weekends (when there is one per day). On Friday evenings it also has a flight to Punta Arenas for US$191. Ladeco (☎ 243261), Barros Arana 401, has two flights to Santiago every day except Sunday. Fares are virtually identical with LAN-Chile's.

Bus Concepción's bus terminal (☎ 310896) is on the outskirts of town at Tegualda 860, a side street off Avenida General Bonilla on the road to Chillán. All the buses leave from here, but because of its inconvenient location, many companies maintain a more central office as well as one at the terminal.

Tur Bus (☎ 222404), Tucapel 530, has 13 buses daily to Santiago, Buses Lit (☎ 230722) another 10, but many other companies cover the same route. Of these, Tas Choapa (☎ 230720), Barros Arana 1010, has excellent connections to northern Chile and to Argentina, along with Bus Chevalier (☎ 310896), Tucapel 516. Sol del Pacífico also has frequent services to Santiago and Valparaíso.

Buses Varmontt (☎ 230779) at Paicaví 427, Buses Igi Llaima (☎ 312498) at Tucapel 432, and Buses Cruz del Sur (☎ 314372) at Barros Arana 935, Local 9, as well as Tur Bus and Buses Lit, head south to Temuco and Puerto Montt. Buses Biobío (☎ 242751), Aníbal Pinto 822, has the most frequent service to Temuco; Igi Llaima is the most frequent to Los Angeles.

For services down the coast to Coronel, Lota, Arauco, Lebu, Cañete and Contulmo, try Buses Los Alces (☎ 221712) at Prat 699 or Buses J Ewert (☎ 222586) at Prat 535.

Charges vary considerably among companies, but typical fares from Concepción include Chillán or Los Angeles US$2, Angol US$3, Talca US$4, Temuco US$5, Santiago US$10, Valparaíso US$12, and Puerto Montt US$12.

Train Concepción's railway station (☎ 227777) is on Avenida Prat at the end of Barros Arana, but there is also a ticket office (☎ 225286) at Pinto 450, Local 16.

There are four trains daily to Santiago, at 8.30 and 9.15 am and 1 and 10 pm, taking about nine hours. The lowest fare is about US$11, while the salón service costs US$14. A sleeper on the night train costs from US$19 (cama baja) to US$26 (cama alta).

Getting Around

Car Rental Concepción has several rental agencies to choose among: the Automóvil Club de Chile (☎ 226554) at San Martín 519; Galerías (☎ 241790) at Colo Colo 379, Oficina 407; First Rent-a-Car (☎ 223121) at Cochrane 862; Budget (☎ 225377) at Barros Arana 541; and Avis (☎ 235837) at Aurelio Manzano 538.

AROUND CONCEPCIÓN

La Costa del Carbón

As an advertising slogan, the 'Coast of Coal' seems unappealing, but the area south of the Biobío draws substantial crowds to beaches in and around Coronel (which reeks of fishmeal), Lota, Arauco and the Lebú Peninsula. Probably the best day trip is to Lota, site of the 14-hectare **Parque Isidora Cousiño**, designed for the influential Cousiño family by an English landscape architect between 1862 and 1872. Now maintained by the state coal company ENACAR, it is open to the public in summer from 8 am to 8 pm Monday to Saturday, 10 am to 9 pm Sundays and holidays; in winter it closes at 6 pm. Admission is US$0.75.

One unusual excursion is a tour of ENACAR's undersea mine at Lota, in which you put on a hard hat, ride in a mine cart, and chip off a hunk of coal with a pneumatic drill. These tours, which cost US$17, take place daily at 10.50 and 3 pm every day, all year. For further information, contact the Parque Isidora Cousiño (☎ 249039), Carlos Cousiño 199 in Lota Alto, between 8 am and 6 pm weekdays.

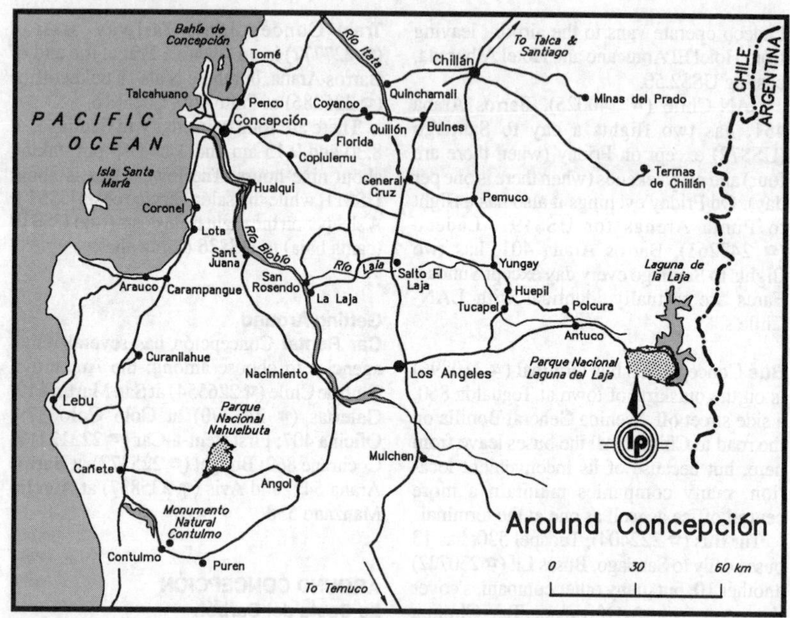

Ruta de la Araucana
Local and regional tourist authorities are establishing a series of historical markers showing famous sites from the epic poem *La Araucana*, by the soldier-poet Alonso de Ercilla y Zuñiga. The poem honours the bravery of the Mapuche in their resistance to the Spanish invasions of the 16th century. The first two markers have been placed near Punta Escuadrón, 22 km south of Concepción, and near Arauco, about two km west of the town of Carampangue.

Escuadrón is the site of the **Hito Histórico Galvarino**, which marks the battle of Lagunillas (1557), where the Mapuche *toqui* (chief) Galvarino had both hands severed by the swords of the Spaniards, after which he placed his own head on the block. The Spaniards refrained from executing him, but he swore revenge and continued to resist. On being recaptured years later, he may have been executed, though some historians believe he killed himself to avoid Spanish retribution.

The **Hito Histórico Prueba y Elección de Caupolicán** commemorates the site where Mapuche leader Colo Colo chose Caupolicán to lead the resistance battle which took place at Tucapel on the upper reaches of the Río Laja. They routed the Spaniards and executed Pedro de Valdivia in 1553.

At Cañete, 135 km south of Concepción, is the disappointing **Museo Araucano Juan Antonio Ríos**. It's named after a 20th-century Chilean president born nearby, rather than for any of the Mapuche people it presumably honours. Exhibits stress historical antecedents, economic activities, funerary customs and art, particularly silverwork. It also includes a small garden of native plants and a model replica of a Spanish fortification. It's open daily except Monday from 10 am to 12.30 pm and 2 to 6

Ercilla & the Araucanian Wars

In the early colonial era, armed conflict between the Spaniards and the Indian peoples of Chile was so bloody, protracted and pervasive that Chilean historian Alvaro Jara entitled his history of the period *Guerra y Sociedad en Chile* (War and Society in Chile). Yet, in spite of frequent brutality, the adversaries did not lack respect for each other and some even managed to see the broader picture and tragedy of the era even as they participated in it. The most prominent of these was Spanish soldier-poet Alonso de Ercilla, whose epic poem *La Araucana* is one of the classics of colonial Latin American literature.

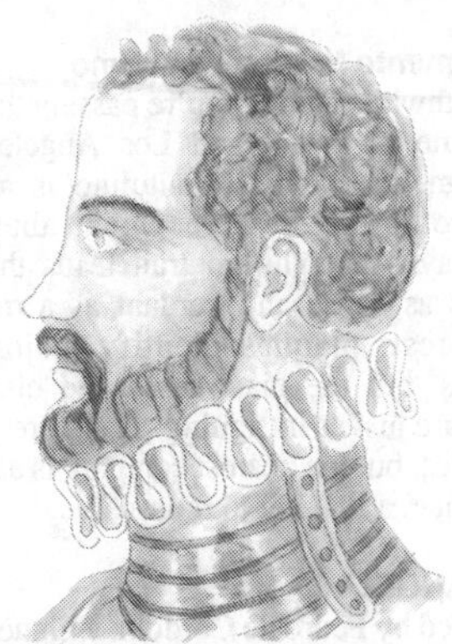
Alonso de Ercilla

Born into a noble Basque family in 1533 and educated in the classics, Ercilla entered the service of the Spanish royal family at the age of 15. At 21, on a visit to London, he heard of Pedro de Valdivia's death at the hands of the Araucanians and resolved to participate in the Spanish campaign against them. He spent seven years in the New World, including more than 1½ years exploring Chile and fighting the Indians. In 1563 he returned to Spain and his lengthy poem, based on personal experience, was published in three parts over two decades from 1569. While the epic form is itself romantic and Ercilla expresses the values of the Spanish elite, the poem is notable for its fidelity to historical events and its regard for, and analysis of, an opponent which most Spaniards both feared and denigrated. While the Araucanians bedevilled Ercilla and his countrymen, he could still admire their courage, tactics, and adaptability.

Araucanian tactics were unconventional and difficult to counter. To offset their opponents' mobility, they retreated into the forest, lured the Spaniards into swampy areas where horses were ineffective, and dismounted the riders with ropes and clubs. When possible they fought in the midday heat, quickly exhausting the heavily armoured Spaniards, and they set traps with sharpened stakes where (in Ercilla's words) surprised soldiers would die 'impaled...in agony'.

Like the Plains Indians of North America, the Araucanians became expert horsemen themselves, raiding the Argentine pampas for mounts, taming them and driving them back across the Andes to aid the resistance. One of the major factors in Araucanian success was their organisation, or rather their lack of it – the Spaniards had a hierarchical system of command which discouraged initiative and improvisation, but in the more egalitarian Indian society no single leader was indispensable. Also, Spain's commitment to dominating the region south of the Biobío was less than it might have been had the economic incentives been greater – there were no great bonanza mines to grab the Crown's attention.

Ercilla openly praised the intelligence and bravery of Indian leaders such as Lautaro, Caupolicán and Colo Colo, some of whom distinguished themselves at a very young age. Lautaro was captured by the Spanish at the age of 15. After three years' forced service as a scout, he escaped to play a leading role at the battle of Tucapel (where Colo Colo's forces killed Pedro de Valdivia), and became an important military leader until his death at the hands of the Spaniards in 1557, at the age of 22. Caupolicán, named *toqui* by the older Colo Colo, also helped defeat the Spaniards at Tucapel. He died a gruesome but stoic death when the Spaniards impaled him on a sharpened wooden pole – although legend says the disdainful cacique threw them off the platform and sat down of his own volition. The cacique Galvarino quietly suffered the amputation of both his hands but escaped to help lead his people against the Spanish invaders.

Ercilla's literary legacy still permeates all facets of Chilean society, from popular culture and tourism to revolutionary politics. The country's most popular soccer team is known simply as Colo Colo. A new series of historical markers on the coastal highway south of Concepción marks the Ruta de La Araucana, immortalising the bravery of the caciques. And one of Chile's most troublesome guerrilla movements, which has not ceased its resistance despite the return to democracy, has adopted the name of Lautaro.■

pm. Admission is US$0.70, but it's free on Sundays.

Monumento Natural Contulmo

A worthwhile stop if you're passing through en route to Angol and Los Angeles, the Monumento Natural Contulmo is an 84-hectare forest preserve which abuts the highway. An eight-km trail leads through woods as dense and verdant as a tropical rainforest; plaques identify major tree species, but the giant ferns and climbing vines are just as intriguing. There are picnic facilities, but the nearest camping is at Lago Lanalhue, a few km to the west.

LOS ANGELES

Founded by Pedro de Córdoba y Figueroa in 1739 as a bulwark against the Mapuche, Santa María de Los Angeles is not Hollywood, and the closest thing to a freeway is the two-lane Carretera Panamericana which skirts the town to the east. It does, however, have good access to the upper reaches of the Río Biobío and to Parque Nacional Laguna del Laja, which includes the 2985-metre Volcán Antuco.

Orientation

Los Angeles (population 115,000) is an agricultural and industrial service centre 110 km south of Chillán. The Estero Quilque, two blocks north of the Plaza de Armas, flows through the city into parklands on its western edge. East of the Plaza, the Avenida Alemania provides access to the Caraterra Panamericana.

Information

Tourist Office There's an information kiosk on the Plaza de Armas. Another dependable source of information is the Automóvil Club de Chile (☎ 314209), Caupolicán 201.

Money Change money elsewhere if possible, since Banco del Estado, Colón 160, pays very poor rates.

Post & Telecommunications Correos de Chile is on Caupolicán, on the south side of the Plaza de Armas. CTC's long-distance offices are at Paseo Quilpué, just west of Valdivia between Colo Colo and Rengo, and at the bus terminal.

Medical Services Los Angeles' Hospital Regional (☎ 321456) is on Avenida Ricardo Vicuña, just east of Los Carrera.

Places to Stay

Bottom-end accommodation is in short supply. At the very central *Hotel Mazzola* (☎ 321643), Lautaro 579, rates are US$19/25 for a single/double. *Gran Hotel Muso* (☎ 313183) at Valdivia 222, and *Hotel Mariscal Alcázar* (☎ 311725) at Lautaro 385, both charge around US$43/55.

Places to Eat

For parrilla, the best choice is *El Arriero*, Colo Colo 235, but for more varied fare try the *Centro Español* at Colón 482. One correspondent praised the Italian menu at *Di Leone*, Colón 285.

Things to Buy

For local and regional crafts, visit the Galería Centro Español, Colón 482, Local 7 & 8, or the Mercado Los Angeles at Villagrán and Tucapel.

Getting There & Away

Bus Los Angeles' bus terminal is on the corner of Caupolicán and Valdivia, on the south-west corner of the Plaza de Armas. Not all companies which connect Santiago with Puerto Montt enter Los Angeles, but you can catch these at the junction of Avenida Alemania and the Panamericana.

There are very frequent buses between Los Angeles and Concepción with Mini Pullman, Trancyl, Biobío, Igi Llaima and Los Alces. Buses J B has 14 buses a day to Angol, the gateway to Parque Nacional Nahuelbuta, via Renaico for US$1.50.

Train The railway station is on Caupolicán, three long blocks west of the Plaza. All trains between Santiago and Temuco stop at Los Angeles.

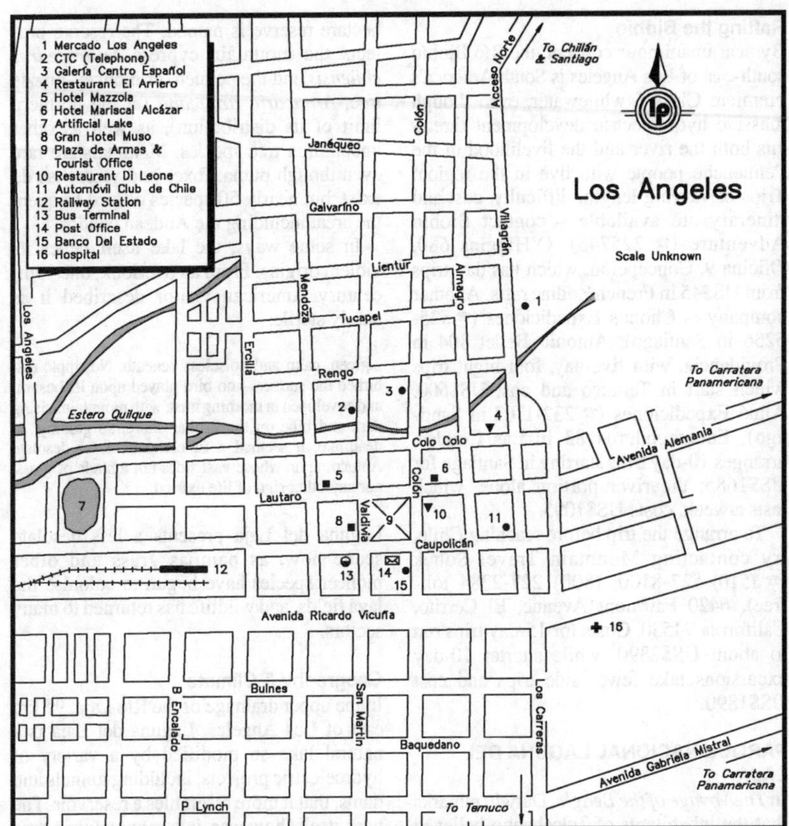

Getting Around

First Rent-a-Car (☎ 313812) is at Caupolicán 350. The Automóvil Club (☎ 314209) is at Caupolicán 201.

AROUND LOS ANGELES

Salto del Laja

Just east of the Carretera Panamericana, 25 km north of Los Angeles en route to Chillán, the Río Laja drops nearly 50 metres over a steep escarpment to form a miniature Iguazú before joining the Biobío at La Laja, 40 km to the west. Salto del Laja is a very popular recreation area, perhaps as much for its accessibility as its scenery.

Camping is possible at *Camping Río Huaqui* (open December to March) or at *Camping Curanadu* (open all year), both of which charge about US$6 per person. There is also conventional accommodation: *Motel Curanadu* (☎ 222372 in Los Angeles) for US$30 for four persons, *Hotel Los Manantiales* (☎ 323606 in Los Angeles) for US$27/33 a single/double, and *Hotel Salto del Laja* (☎ 321706 in Los Angeles) from US$36/43.

Rafting the Biobío

By near unanimous consent, the Río Biobío south-east of Los Angeles is South America's premiere Class 5 whitewater, even though massive hydroelectric development threatens both the river and the livelihood of the Pehuenche people who live in the region. Trips of varying length, difficulty, cost and itinerary are available – contact Biobío Adventure (☎ 225745), O'Higgins 680, Oficina 9, Concepción, which has day trips from US$45 in French Zodiac rafts. Another company is Chonos Expediciones (☎ 525-6256 in Santiago), Antonio Bellet 304 in Providencia, with five-day, four-night trips which start in Temuco and cost US$600. Altué Expediciones (☎ 232-1103 in Santiago), Encomenderos 83 in Las Condes, arranges 10-day trips starting in Santiago for US$1685; the river portion alone, which lasts a week, costs US$1095.

To arrange the trip before reaching Chile, try contacting Mountain Travel Sobek (☎ (510) 527-8100, (800) 227-2384 toll-free), 6420 Fairmont Avenue, El Cerrito, California 94530. Costs for 15-day trips run to about US$2390, while shorter 10-day excursions take fewer side trips and cost US$1890.

PARQUE NACIONAL LAGUNA DEL LAJA

In *The Voyage of the Beagle*, Darwin remarks that the inhabitants of Talcahuano believed that Concepción's great earthquake of 1835 'was caused by two Indian women, who being offended...stopped the volcano of Antuco'. Whether or not suppressed vulcanism triggered that quake, 2985-metre Antuco and its lava flows have dammed the Río Laja to form the Laguna, after which this 11,600-hectare reserve is named. The reserve protects the mountain cypress *Austrocedrus chilensis* and the pehuén, or monkey-puzzle tree, *Araucaria araucana* (at the northern limit of its distribution), as well as other uncommon tree species. Mammals are rare even though puma, foxes and vizcachas do exist, but nearly 50 species of bird frequent the area, including the Andean condor.

Condor

In some ways, the lake itself belies its violent origins. From an overlook, one 19th-century American visitor described it as nearly sterile:

> ...green, calm and noiseless beneath. No ripple disturbed the surface – no bird played upon its bosom; and enveloped in morning mist, with mountains rising dark and blue on the farther shore, so gloomy, so deathlike, it seemed a fit companion for desolate Antuco, upon whose vast sides not a blade of grass, nor any other sign of life existed.

Laguna del Laja presents a less desolate scene now, as pampas grass and other pioneer species have begun to colonise the lava fields, and wildlife has returned to many sectors.

Geography & Climate

In the upper drainage of the Río Laja, 95 km east of Los Angeles, Laguna del Laja is a natural lake so modified by a variety of hydroelectric projects, including tunnels and dams, that it more resembles a reservoir. The park itself, however, is a mountainous area ranging from 1000 to nearly 3000 metres above sea level. Its salient feature is the symmetrical cone of Antuco, but the higher Sierra Velluda to the south-west, beyond the park boundaries, offers a series of impressive glaciers.

Summer is fairly dry, but more than two metres of precipitation accumulate as rain and snow the rest of the year. The ski season lasts from June to October.

Trekking

Laguna del Laja has many trails which are suitable for either day hikes or longer excursions; the best is the circuit around Volcán Antuco, which provides views of both the

Sierra Velluda and the lake. For details, consult Lonely Planet's *Trekking in Patagonian Andes*.

If trekking or camping, buy all your supplies in Los Angeles, where selection is far better and prices are much lower.

Places to Stay & Eat

There are no formal campgrounds within the park itself, but near the entrance, at Km 90 on the road from Los Angeles is *Cabañas y Camping Lagunillas* (☎ 323606, Caupolicán 332 in Los Angeles). It offers 30 sites with electricity, hot showers, fire pits, and picnic tables for US$10 per site, plus US$1 per person. The cabañas charge US$50 per night for up to six persons. There is a restaurant as well.

In winter, for about US$9 per person, it is possible to stay at the ski lodge operated by the Dirección General de Deportes y Recreación, at the base of Volcán Antuco. It has beds for 50 skiers, a restaurant, and it rents ski equipment. It *may* open in summer. For reservations, contact DIGEDER (☎ 229054) at O'Higgins 740, Oficina 23, in Concepción.

Try also the *Refugio Municipal* of the Municipalidad of Los Angeles (☎ 322333, Avenida Colón in Los Angeles) or the *Departamentos Canchas de Esquí*, which belongs to the Club de Esquí de Los Angeles.

Getting There & Away

Between 8.30 am and 7.15 pm, Buses Antuco operates half a dozen buses per day from the terminal in Los Angeles to the village of Abanico. Return buses from Abanico leave between 6.45 am and 5.30 pm. The trip takes only about 1½ hours, but it takes another several hours to walk the 11 km to Chacay, where CONAF maintains administrative offices and a small visitor centre. Hitching is possible, but vehicles are few except on weekends.

ANGOL

Founded in 1553 by Pedro de Valdivia as a strategic frontier outpost – and destroyed half a dozen times over three centuries in the Mapuche wars – Angol de los Confines finally survived the Indian resistance after 1862. Easily reached by southbound travellers from Los Angeles but also from Temuco, it provides the best access into Parque Nacional Nahuelbuta, a mountainous forest reserve which features the largest remaining stands of Araucaria pines (monkey-puzzle trees) in the coastal range.

Orientation

Angol (population 43,000), 65 km south-west of Los Angeles and 127 km north of Temuco but off the Panamericana, straddles the Río Vergara, an upper tributary of the Biobío formed by the junction of the Ríos Picoiquén and Rehue. The older core of the city, centred on a particularly attractive Plaza de Armas, lies west of the river. Farther west, the nearby Cordillera Nahuelbuta rises to nearly 1600 metres.

Information

Tourist Office Angol's municipal tourist office (☎ 712046) is near the bridge across the Río Vergara, on the east side of the river. Open weekdays from 9 am to 1 pm and 3 to 6 pm, it has limited maps and brochures but a hard-working and well informed staff.

Money Angol has no formal cambios, but Boutique Boston, on Sepúlveda between Prat and Lautaro, will change US cash on weekdays from 9 am to 1 pm and 3 to 7 pm. You could also try Banco de Chile, Lautaro 2 at Ilabaca, or Banco del Estado at Chorrillos 398.

Post & Telecommunications Correos de Chile is on the corner of Lautaro and Chorrillos, at the north-east corner of the Plaza de Armas. CTC has offices offering long-distance telephone services at Lautaro 491, east of the river, and O'Higgins 297, west of the river.

National Parks CONAF has an office at Prat and Chorrillos which may be able to offer suggestions for transport to Parque Nacional Nahuelbuta.

Convento San Buenaventura

Built in 1863, this Franciscan convent is the oldest church in the region and well worth a visit. It's on Covadonga between Vergara and Dieciocho.

El Vergel & Museo Dillman S Bullock

The Escuela Agrícola El Vergel is an agricultural college which originated in the 19th century as a plant nursery and gardens. It was developed by Manuel Bunster, a Chilean of English descent. Acquired by Methodist missionaries in 1920, it has acquired a national reputation for training gardeners and farmers. Five km east of Angol but easily reached by taxi colectivo No 2 from the Plaza de Armas, the grounds are open to the public daily from 9 am to 8 pm.

The Museo Bullock has a very fine collection of natural history specimens and archaeological artefacts. It is the legacy of El Vergel's founder, North American Methodist missionary Dillman S Bullock. Bullock spent nearly 70 years in Chile, learning the Mapuche language and publishing a wide variety of articles on the region's biology, natural history and archaeology. It's open daily except Monday from 10 am to 1 pm and 3 to 6 pm. Admission is US$0.60.

Festivals

In the second week of January, the Municipalidad de Angol sponsors Brotes de Chile, a folk song festival with prizes ranging up to US$2500. It has become one of the most important festivals in Chile for nearly a decade and it features music, dance, food and crafts.

Places to Stay – bottom end

Angol has plenty of reasonable accommodation, starting with the *Casa del Huésped*, Dieciocho 465, for US$4 per person; *Pensión Chorrillos*, Chorrillos 724, is slightly more expensive but also serves good lunches for less than US$2. *Residencial Olímpia* (☎ 711162), Caupolicán 625, charges US$7/12 a single/double, while *Hostería Las Araucarias* (☎ 711096), Prat 499, has singles with breakfast for US$7.

Places to Stay – middle

Pensión Prat, Prat 364, has singles for US$10, as does *Pensión Vergara* (☎ 711964), Vergara 240. At both *Hotel Olímpia* (☎ 711517), Lautaro 194, and *Pensión Dieciocho*, Dieciocho 868, rates are about US$10/17. *Hotel Millaray* (☎ 711517), Prat 420, has rooms with shared bath for US$13/18, but with private bath rates nearly double.

Places to Stay – top end

Give it a French name and you can charge US$71 a single, like *Hotel Chez Mayatte* (☎ 711336), Vergara 569.

Places to Eat

Café Stop, Lautaro 176, offers sandwiches and parrillada, while *Pizzería Sparlatto* at Lautaro 418 has, obviously, pizza. For a wider selection, try *Las Totoras* at Ilabaca and Covandonga, or the *Club Social*, Caupolicán 498.

Things to Buy

Angol is renowned for its ceramics, produced at small factories which you can visit. Cerámica Serra is at Bunster 153, while Cerámica Lablé is at Purén 864.

Getting There & Away

For long-distance services, Angol's Terminal Rodoviario is at Caupolicán 200, a block north of the Plaza. Buses Biobío (☎ 711777) has more than a dozen buses daily to Temuco for about US$2.50, plus another five to Concepción for US$1.50. Tur Bus (☎ 711655) has morning and evening departures for Santiago (US$11), while Buses Lit (☎ 711549) has a nightly departure to the capital. Igi Llaima (☎ 711920) goes to Los Angeles and Concepción (twice daily) and Santiago (nightly). Trans Tur has morning and evening buses to the capital.

The Terminal Rural, for local and regional services, is at Ilabaca and Lautaro. Buses Thiele (☎ 711854) has extensive regional services, connecting Angol to the Costa del Carbón via Contulmo, Cañete, and Lebú (US$3), and to Concepción via Nacimiento and Santa Juana. Buses J B has 14 buses a day to Los Angeles (US$1.50) via Renaico.

Buses Angol goes from Angol to Vegas Blancas (US$1.75), seven km from the entrance to Parque Nacional Nahuelbuta, Monday, Wednesday and Friday at 7 am and 4 pm, returning at 9 am and 6 pm. For details of tours to the Parque Nacional Nahuelbuta, see the following section.

PARQUE NACIONAL NAHUELBUTA

Between Angol and the Pacific and covered with Araucaria pines, the coastal range rises to nearly 1600 metres. The Parque Nacional Nahuelbuta was created in 1939 to protect one of the last Araucaria forests outside the Andes. The Araucaria pine is also known as *puhuén*, or the monkey-puzzle tree, and the largest specimens can reach 50 metres in height and two metres in diameter. The 1600-hectare park also features notable stands of *Nothofagus* (southern beech). Rare animals such as puma, the Chiloé fox and the miniature Chilean deer known as the pudú can also be sighted.

At Pehuenco, on the road from Angol, CONAF maintains a Centro de Informaciones Ecológicas, with a small museum, where rangers offer audiovisual presentations on the local environment. Admission to the park is US$1.75.

Geography & Climate

In the province of Malleco in the Ninth Region, Nahuelbuta is about 35 km west of Angol. On a mostly flat or undulating plain, some 950 metres above sea level, permanent streams have cut deep canyons, while jagged peaks rise abruptly, up to 1565 metres on the summit of Alto Nahuelbuta. Unlike the Andes, the coastal range is granitic rather than volcanic in origin.

The park enjoys warm, dry summers, but snow falls at higher elevations in winter. May to September tends to be a very wet period. November to April is the best time for a visit.

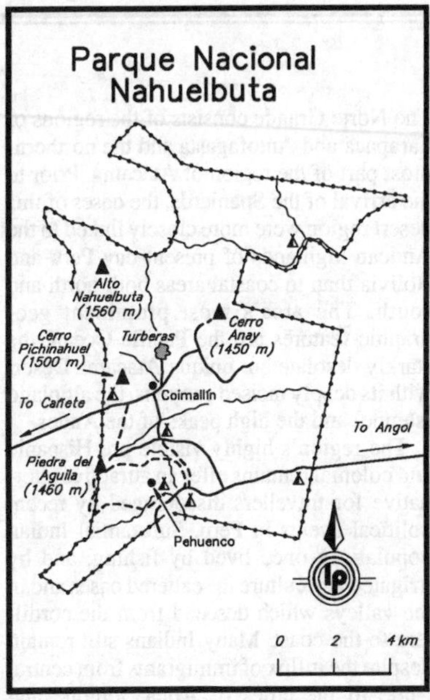

Things to See & Do

Nahuelbuta has 30 km of roads and 15 km of footpaths, so car-touring, camping and hiking are all possible. **Piedra del Aguila**, a four-km hike from Pehuenco, is a 1400-metre overlook with views to the Andes and the Pacific. **Cerro Anay**, 1450 metres, has similar views.

Places to Stay

CONAF charges US$5 per site at campgrounds at Pehuenco and at Coimallín.

Getting There & Away

For US$1.75, Buses Angol goes to Vegas Blancas which is seven km from the park entrance, Monday, Wednesday and Friday at 7 am and 4 pm. It also offers Sunday tours of the park for US$8 per person, leaving from Angol's Terminal Rural at 7 am.

Norte Grande & the Atacama Desert

The Norte Grande consists of the regions of Tarapacá and Antofagasta and the northernmost part of the region of Atacama. Prior to the arrival of the Spaniards, the oases of this desert region were more closely linked to the Andean highlands of present-day Peru and Bolivia than to coastal areas both north and south. The area's most prominent geographic features are the Pacific Ocean, the starkly desolate but unique Atacama Desert with its deeply incised canyons, the altiplano (steppe) and the high peaks of the Andes.

The region's highly visible pre-Hispanic and colonial remains offer an attractive alternative for travellers discouraged by recent political events in Peru. Substantial Indian populations once lived by fishing, and by irrigated agriculture in scattered oases and in the valleys which descend from the cordillera to the coast. Many Indians still remain despite the influx of immigrants from central Chile to the cities of Arica, Iquique and Antofagasta.

Indian peoples left impressive monuments, including huge stylised designs (geoglyphs) made by covering the light sands of the surrounding barren slopes with darker stones. Representations of llama trains illustrate the importance of the transverse canyons as transport routes in the pre-Columbian era. Coastal peoples exchanged products such as fish and guano for maize and charqui (sun-dried llama or alpaca meat) with the Andean Indians.

The Atacama is the most 'perfect' of deserts; some coastal stations have never recorded measurable rainfall, although infrequent 'El Niño' events can bring brief but phenomenal downpours. Otherwise, the only precipitation comes from the convective fogs known as *camanchaca* or *garúa*, which sometimes condense at higher elevations and support the scattered vegetation of the *lomas* (coastal hills).

Farther inland, rainfall and vegetation increase with elevation and distance from the sea. In the precordillera, or Andean foothills, Aymara farmers still cultivate the terraces which have covered the hillsides for millennia, although alfalfa fodder for livestock has largely replaced *quinoa* (a native Andean grain) and the myriad varieties of potato. Cultivation reaches as high as 4000 metres; above this level, the Aymara pasture llamas, alpacas and a handful of sheep, on the grasslands of the *puna* (highlands).

Until the late 19th century, the Norte Grande belonged to Peru and Bolivia. Treaty disputes, the presence of thousands of Chilean workers in the Bolivian mines, and Bolivian attempts to increase taxation on mineral exports led to the War of the Pacific (1879-1884) against Bolivia and Peru. Within those five years, Chile overpowered its rivals and annexed the copper-and nitrate-rich lands that are now the regions of Tarapacá and Antofagasta.

Most cities in the Atacama, such as Iquique and Antofagasta, owe their existence to minerals, especially nitrates and copper. Nitrate oficinas like Humberstone flourished during the boom of the early 20th century, withered when petroleum-based fertilisers superseded mineral nitrates, and are now ghost towns. Only a handful continue to operate, as newer methods make processing lower grade ores profitable.

One of the chief beneficiaries of the War of the Pacific was British speculator John Thomas North, the most important single figure in the history of the nitrate industry. In 1875, prior to the war, Peru expropriated nitrate holdings and issued bonds to their former owners. During the war, the value of these bonds plummeted and North, using capital from Chilean banks, bought as many as he could. When, after the war, Chile decided to restore ownership to bondholders, it was a windfall for North, who moved to gain control of all other industries on which the nitrate industry depended. Along with a handful of other entrepreneurs, he largely controlled the region's economy.

Chile's economic dependence on nitrates

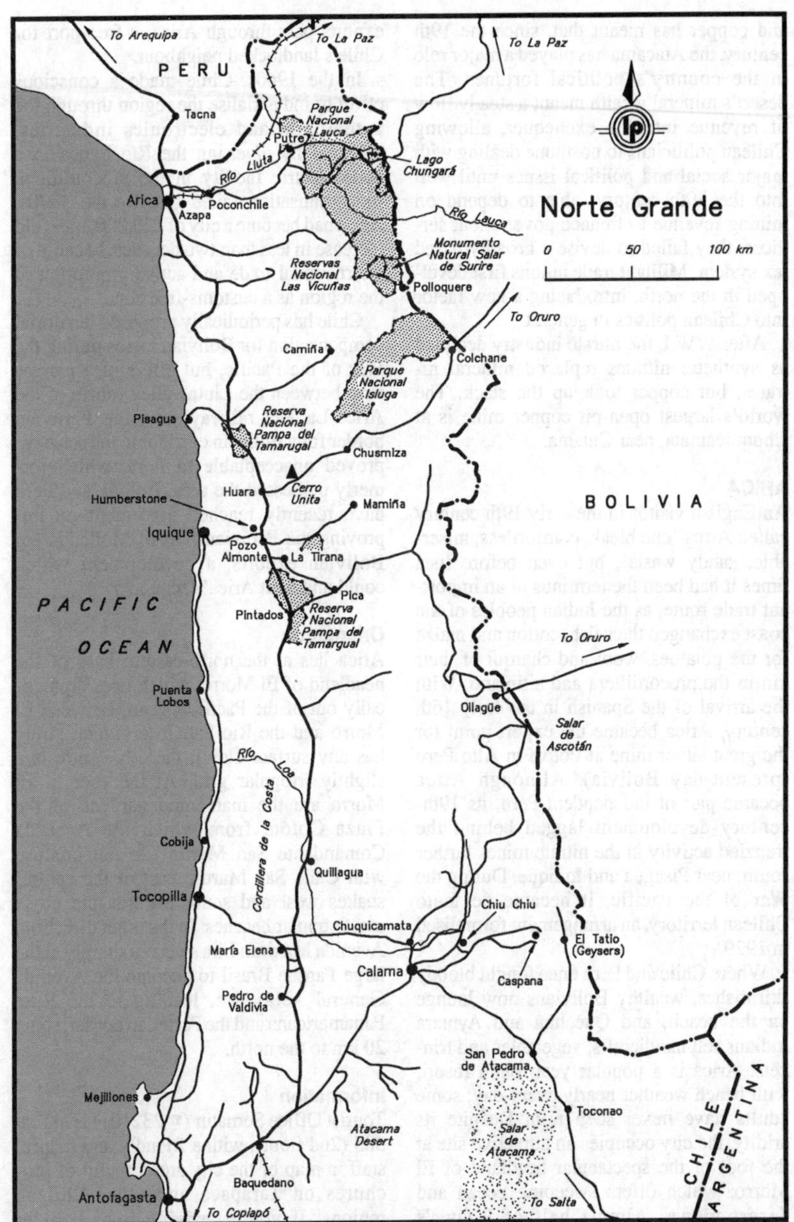
Norte Grande
0 50 100 km
To Arequipa
To La Paz
To La Paz
PERU
Tacna
Parque Nacional Lauca
Putre
Lago Chungará
Río Lluta
Arica
Azapa
Poconchile
Río Lauca
Monumento Natural Salar de Surire
Reservas Nacional Las Vicuñas
Polloquere
To Oruro
Colchane
Camiña
Parque Nacional Isluga
Pisagua
Reserva Nacional Pampa del Tamarugal
Chusmiza
Cerro Unita
Huara
Humberstone
Mamiña
BOLIVIA
Iquique
Pozo Almonte
La Tirana
Pica
PACIFIC OCEAN
Pintados
Reserva Nacional Pampa del Tamargual
To Oruro
Ollagüe
Salar de Ascotán
Puenta Lobos
Río Loa
Cobija
Cordillera de la Costa
Quillagua
Tocopilla
Chiu Chiu
Chuquicamata
El Tatio (Geysers)
María Elena
Calama
Caspana
Pedro de Valdivia
San Pedro de Atacama
Mejillones
Toconao
Atacama Desert
Salar de Atacama
CHILE
ARGENTINA
Baquedano
Antofagasta
To Copiapó
To Salta

and copper has meant that, since the 19th century, the Atacama has played a major role in the country's political fortunes. The desert's mineral wealth meant a steady flow of revenue into the exchequer, allowing Chilean politicians to postpone dealing with major social and political issues until well into the 20th century; able to depend on mining revenue to finance government services, they failed to devise a broadly based tax system. Militant trade unions first developed in the north, introducing a new factor into Chilean politics in general.

After WW I, the nitrate industry declined as synthetic nitrates replaced mineral nitrates, but copper took up the slack. The world's largest open-pit copper mine is at Chuquicamata, near Calama.

ARICA

An English visitor in the early 19th century called Arica 'one bleak, comfortless, miserable, sandy waste', but even before Inca times it had been the terminus of an important trade route, as the Indian peoples of the coast exchanged their fish, cotton and maize for the potatoes, wool and charqui of their kin in the precordillera and altiplano. With the arrival of the Spanish in the early 16th century, Arica became the export point for the great silver mine at Potosí in Alto Peru (present-day Bolivia). Although Arica became part of independent Peru, its 19th-century development lagged behind the frenzied activity in the nitrate mines farther south, near Pisagua and Iquique. During the War of the Pacific, it became de facto Chilean territory, an arrangement formalised in 1929.

Where Chile and Peru once fought bloody skirmishes, wealthy Bolivians now lounge on the beach, and Quechua and Aymara Indians sell handicrafts, vegetables and trinkets. Arica is a popular year-round resort, with beach weather nearly every day; some adults have never seen rain. Despite its aridity, the city occupies an attractive site at the foot of the spectacular headland of El Morro, which offers sweeping ocean and desert views. Almost half of Bolivia's exports pass through Arica, a free port for Chile's landlocked neighbour.

In the 1960s, Chile made a conscious effort to industrialise the region through the automobile and electronics industries, powered by diverting the Río Lauca to a hydroelectric facility in the precordillera. Industrialisation failed but, by the 1970s, Arica had become a city of 120,000, a sixfold increase in less than two decades, because of international trade and active promotion of the region as a customs-free zone.

Chile has periodically proposed territorial compensation for Bolivian losses during the War of the Pacific, but offers of a narrow strip between the Lluta valley (north of the Arica-La Paz railway) and the Peruvian border for a Bolivian corridor to the sea have proved unacceptable to Peru, which formerly possessed the area. Bolivia and Peru have recently reached agreement on improving the Peruvian port of Mollendo for Bolivian exports, a development which could undercut Arica's economy.

Orientation

Arica lies at the north-eastern base of the headland of El Morro, which rises dramatically out of the Pacific Ocean. Between El Morro and the Río San José (which rarely has any surface flow), the city centre is a slightly irregular grid. At the foot of El Morro are the manicured gardens of the Plaza Colón, from which the Avenida Comandante San Martín (do not confuse with Calle San Martín, east of the centre) snakes west and south towards the city's most popular beaches. In the other direction, Avenida Máximo Lira swerves sharply at the large Parque Brasil to become the Avenida General Velásquez, leading to the Ruta Panamericana and the Peruvian border, some 20 km to the north.

Information

Tourist Office Sernatur (☎ 232101) is at Prat 305 (2nd floor), with a friendly and helpful staff, a map of the city and a fistful of brochures on Tarapacá and other Chilean regions. If you're arriving from Peru or

Bolivia, this is a good place to orient yourself. The office is open weekdays from 8.30 am to 1 pm and 3 to 6.30 pm, Saturday from 8.30 am to 7 pm. There's also a municipal tourist kiosk on the Avenida 21 de Mayo near the intersection with Colón, open late into the evening.

The Automóvil Club de Chile (☎ 237780), at Chacabuco 460, offers free information and sells maps. It's open weekdays from 9 am to 1 pm and 4 to 8 pm, Saturdays from 9 am to 1 pm.

National Parks CONAF's regional office (☎ 231559) occupies the 3rd and 4th floors at Sotomayor 216, just off the Plaza Colón. For information on climbing, contact the Grupo Andino Cóndor de Arica, 18 de Septiembre 889, which meets on Mondays from 8.30 to 10.30 pm.

Money Arica has the best rates and least bureaucracy for changing money north of Santiago. If you're heading south, be sure to change money here, since it is very difficult or impossible to cash travellers' cheques in Calama and San Pedro de Atacama, and not easy to exchange cash dollars even at Calama's banks.

Reliable street moneychangers hang out at the corner of 21 de Mayo and Colón; there are several permanent exchange houses on 21 de Mayo, where you can change US cash and travellers' cheques, as well as Peruvian, Bolivian and Argentine currency. Try Yanulaque at 21 de Mayo 175, Marta Daguer at 18 de Septiembre 330, or Daniel Concha at Chacabuco 300. The latter is open late Saturday evening, but all are closed on Sundays – try the street moneychangers or the larger hotels (where rates will be less favourable).

Post & Telecommunications Correos de Chile and Telex-Chile are in the same building as the tourist office at Prat 305. For long-distance phone calls, go to ENTEL at Baquedano 388, near the corner with 21 de Mayo, or CTC at Colón 476 (which, however, does not permit international collect calls). In the alcove outside the tourist office, there is a fibre optic line with direct connection to overseas operators, including the USA, but it is accessible only during regular business hours.

Consulates Argentina no longer maintains a consulate here. The Peruvian Consulate (☎ 231020), at San Martín 220, is open from 9 am to 2 pm weekdays, while the Bolivian Consulate (☎ 231030), at 21 de Mayo 575 near the corner with General Lagos, is open from 9 am to 1 pm weekdays. The UK Consulate (☎ 231098) is at Baquedano 350.

Visas To replace a lost tourist card or extend a visa, go to the Departamento de Extranjería (☎ 231397) at 7 de Junio 188, 3rd floor.

Medical Services The Hospital Dr Juan Noé (☎ 231331) is at 18 de Septiembre 1000, a short distance from downtown.

Things to See

El Morro de Arica Overlooking the city, with outstanding views of the port and the Pacific, the Morro is an historical monument and open-air museum commemorating a crucial battle between Chilean and Peruvian forces in the War of the Pacific. It is accessible by car or by a footpath which leads from the southern end of Calle Colón.

Railway Memorabilia The 1924 German locomotive which once pulled trains on the Arica-La Paz line now stands in the Plazoleta Estación (also called the Parque General Baquedano), at the corner of 21 de Mayo and Pedro Montt. There is also a railway museum in the station.

Iglesia San Marcos de Arica Alejandro Gustavo Eiffel (yes, the same!) designed the newly repainted church of San Marcos de Arica, opposite the Plaza Colón, in 1875. Apart from his famous tower, Eiffel's achievements also include Arica's recently restored Aduana (customs building) on the Plaza Colón and Santiago's Estación Central.

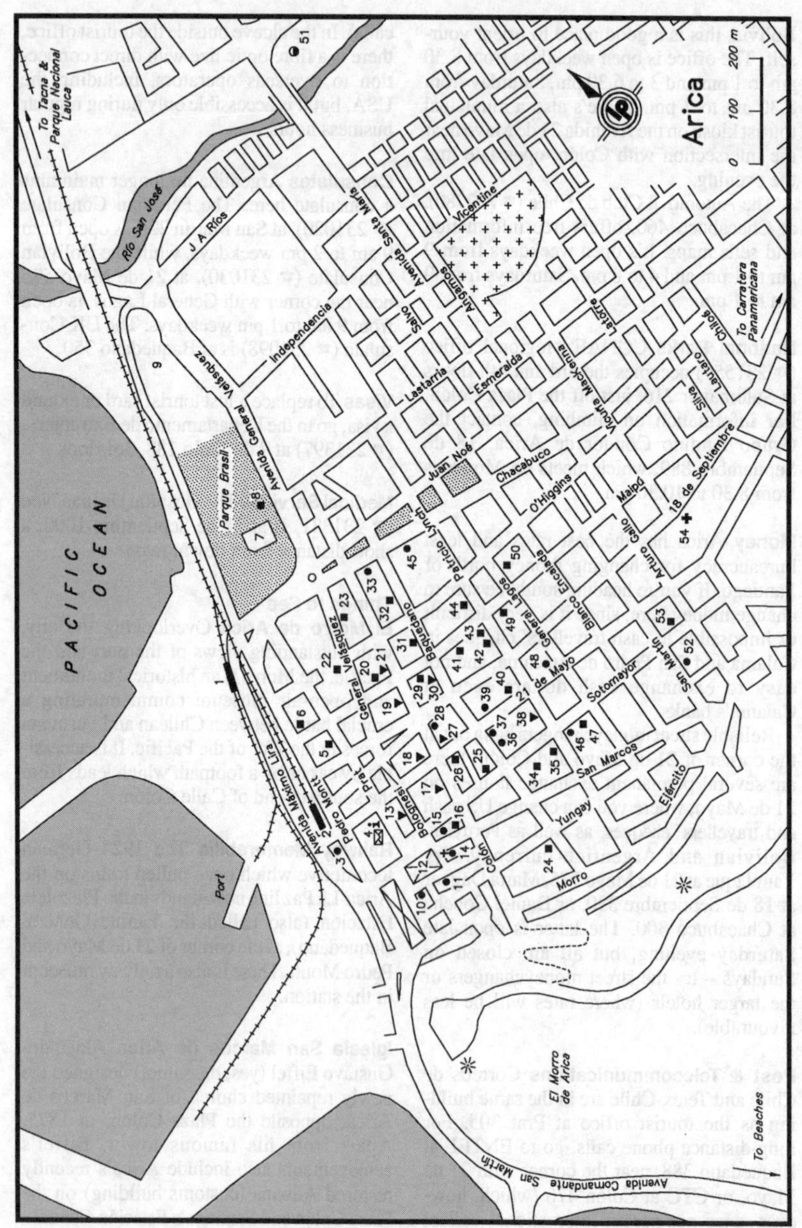
Arica
0 100 200 m
PACIFIC OCEAN
To Tacna & Parque Nacional Lauca
Río San José
J A Ríos
Avenida Santa María
Independencia
Salvo
Vicentine
Avenida General Velásquez
Parque Brasil
Lastarria
Esmeralda
Juan Noé
Chacabuco
O'Higgins
Maipú
18 de Septiembre
Vicuña Mackenna
Latorre
Silva
To Carretera Panamericana
Patricio Lynch
Baquedano
General Lagos
Blanco Encalada
Arturo Gallo
San Martín
21 de Mayo
Sotomayor
General Velásquez
Prat
Pedro Montt
Avenida Máximo Lira
Bolognesi
Colón
Yungay
San Marcos
Ejército
Morro
Port
El Morro de Arica
Avenida Comandante San Martín
To Beaches

■ PLACES TO STAY

5 Residencial Las Parinas
6 Residencial Durán
8 Hotel El Paso
16 Hotel Plaza Colón
20 Residencial Patricia
22 Residencial Velásquez
23 Residencial Chillán
24 Hotel Savona
25 Hotel San Marcos
26 King Hotel
29 Hotel Aragón
31 Residencial Madrid
32 Residencial Venecia
34 Residencial Sotomayor
35 Hotel Diego de Almagro
40 Residencial 21
41 Residencial La Blanquita
42 Residencial Muñoz
43 Hotel Lynch
44 Residencial Chungará
47 Hotel Tacora
49 Residencial Sur
50 Residencial El Cobre
53 Hostal Jardín del Sol

▼ PLACES TO EAT

13 Restaurant Natura
17 Restaurant Casino La Bomba
18 Restaurant El Arriero
19 El Rey del Marisco
21 Café Bavaria
27 Café 21
30 Buen Gusto No 2
38 Chifa Chin Huang Tao

OTHER

1 Railway Station (Arica-Tacna)
2 Railway Station (Arica-La Paz)
3 Plazoleta Estación
4 Sernatur (Tourist Office), Post Office & Telex-Chile
7 Casino
8 Hertz
9 University of Chile
10 LAN-Chile
11 Departamento de Extranjería (Visas)
12 Plaza Colón
14 Iglesia San Marco de Arica
15 CONAF
28 CTC (Telephone)
33 Colectivos to Tacna
36 UK Consulate
37 ENTEL (Telephone)
39 Ladeco
45 Automóvil Club
46 Lloyd Aéreo Boliviano
48 Bolivian Consulate
51 Bus Terminal
52 Peruvian Consulate
54 Hospital

Pasaje Bolognesi A narrow passageway off Plaza Colón between Sotomayor and 21 de Mayo, Pasaje Bolognesi has a lively artisan's market in the evenings.

Poblado Artesanal On the outskirts of Arica, at Hualles 2025 near the Ruta Panamericana to Iquique, the Poblado Artesanal (☎ 222683) is a replica of an altiplano village, including a church and bell tower. It is a good place to shop for artisanal goods, including ceramics, weavings, musical instruments, carvings and similar crafts, and has a good restaurant, *El Tambo*. Taxi colectivo No 3 will drop you near the entrance. It's open Tuesday to Sunday from 9.30 am to 1 pm and 3.30 to 7.30 pm, and there's a peña at 10 pm on Friday and Saturday.

Museo Arqueológico San Miguel de Azapa In the Azapa valley, 12 km from Arica, the Museo Arqueológico San Miguel de Azapa is an attractive building with a superb collection of exhibits of regional cultures from the 7th century BC to the Spanish invasion. There are numerous worthwhile archaeological sites in the Azapa valley which the staff can point out – ask about the geoglyphs at Alto Ramírez and Cerro Sagrado.

The museum is open Tuesday to Friday from 10 am to 6 pm, Saturday from 11 am to 6 pm. To get there, take a taxi colectivo from the corner of Maipú and Patricio Lynch; the cost is about US$1. Some local tour companies include the museum on their itineraries.

Beaches

Arica is one of Chile's best beach resorts,

since the water is warm enough for comfortable bathing. The finest beaches are along the Avenida Comandante San Martín, south of town, where there are a number of sheltered coves. There are others along the highway north to Tacna.

Organised Tours

Many companies offer trips around the city, the Azapa valley, and to Parque Nacional Lauca. Among them are Turismo Payachatas (☎ 251514) at Prat 484, Vicuña Tour (☎ 222971), in the Galería El Morro at 18 de Septiembre 399, Turismo Jurasi (☎ 251696) at Bolognesi 360, and Inti Tour (☎ 251354) at Prat 336. Tours to Lauca cost about US$20, leave around 7.30 am and return about 8.30 pm; there is presumably a legal requirement to carry oxygen for those who suffer from soroche at high altitudes, but there have been some complaints in this regard.

Festivals

Arica celebrates Carnival in February, the local Semana Ariqueña in June, and the Concurso Nacional de Cueca, a folkloric dance festival, the same month in the Azapa valley.

Places to Stay – bottom end

In 1992 there was an inexpensive *Albergue Juvenil* (☎ 222943) at Las Acacias 2124, but the address changes from year to year, so phone first.

Arica has lots of cheap accommodation, but many bottom-end places are cramped and smelly, and some lack hot water. Among the cheapest is *Residencial Sur* (☎ 252457, formerly *Residencial Nuñez)*, at Maipú 516 near the corner with Patricio Lynch, where rooms are US$4 per person. It's basic, with hot water and clean sheets, but very drab. *Residencial Muñoz*, at Patricio Lynch 565 near the intersection with 18 de Septiembre, is ultra-basic and rundown, but friendly and tolerable at US$4 per person. Others in this price range include *Residencial Chillán* (☎ 251677) at General Velásquez 719; *Residencial Sotomayor* (☎ 252336) at Sotomayor 442; *Residencial Venecia* (☎ 252877) at Baquedano 739; and *Residencial Patricia* at Maipú 269.

Recommended by many travellers, *Residencial Madrid* (☎ 231479) at Baquedano 685 has singles/doubles at US$5/9, but it is sometimes noisy and the manager can be brusque. *Residencial La Blanquita* (☎ 232064) at Maipú 472 is clean and has hot water; at US$7 per person, it's one of the better bottom-end choices.

Residencial Chungará (☎ 231677), Patricio Lynch 675, is probably the pick of this category – it's clean, bright, friendly and quiet (except for the front rooms nearest the TV), although some rooms are rather small. Rates are US$7 per person. *Residencial Velásquez*, at Velásquez 669 (☎ 231989), and *Residencial 21*, 21 de Mayo 487, charge about the same. Try also *Residencial Durán* (☎ 252975), Maipú 25 or *Residencial Las Parinas* (☎ 231971), Prat 541.

Camping There is free camping at Playa Corazones, at the end of Avenida Comandante San Martín eight km south of Arica. Basic supplies are available but no fresh water, which has to be brought from Arica. Beach camping is also possible north of town.

Places to Stay – middle

Hostal Jardín del Sol (☎ 232795), Sotomayor 841, is a step up at US$13/17 including breakfast. *Hotel Plaza Colón*, at San Marcos 261, costs US$18/24. *Hotel Tacora* (☎ 251240), Sotomayor 540, charges US$19/24.

One of Arica's best values is *Hotel Lynch* (☎ 231581), Patricio Lynch 589, where simple but clean rooms with shared bath start at US$11/17; with private bath, expect about US$22/27. It's a large place built around a central courtyard. *Hotel Diego de Almagro* (☎ 232927), at Sotomayor 490 near the corner with Patricio Lynch, has bright, clean rooms with private bath, TV, telephone and double beds for US$23/30.

Similar to the Diego de Almagro, the *King Hotel* (☎ 232094), at Colón 376 near the intersection with 21 de Mayo, has rooms for

US$23/32. Rates are about the same at *Hotel Savona* (☎ 232319), Yungay 380, which is popular with tour groups.

Hotel Aragón (☎ 252088), at Maipú 344 near the corner with Colón, offers bright motel-style rooms for US$22/29, all with private bath, but can be very noisy. Similar, but better situated, is *Hotel San Marcos* (☎ 232149) at Sotomayor 367 near the corner with Baquedano. Somewhat costlier but very convenient is *Hotel Central* (☎ 252575), 21 de Mayo 425.

Places to Stay – top end

On the beach at the south end of town, try the *Hostería Arica* (☎ 231201), Avenida Comandante San Martín 599, starting at US$43/51 and rising fast. Top of the list is *Hotel El Paso* (☎ 31965), set in pleasant gardens at General Velásquez 1109, with rooms at US$61/74.

Hotel Saint Gregory (☎ 221914), at Diego Portales 3221 on the road to the restful Azapa valley, has luxury accommodation starting at US$44/53 but beware – rates are higher if you pay in dollars. Farther out the valley, try the *Hotel Azapa Inn* (☎ 222512), Guillermo Sánchez 660, where rates start at US$54/65.

Places to Eat

There are numerous cafés and restaurants along 21 de Mayo, 18 de Septiembre, Maipú, Bolognesi and Colón. One popular meeting place is *Café 21*, at 21 de Mayo 201 near the corner with Colón, which serves hamburgers, sandwiches, snacks, coffee and excellent lager beer. Many foreign travellers congregate here. *Café Bavaria*, at Colón 611, is another decent snack bar. For breakfast, try the sandwiches and licuados at the very modest but excellent *Buen Gusto No 2*, Baquedano 559.

Restaurant Casino La Bomba, inside the fire station at Colón 357, is an Arica institution for its excellent, inexpensive midday meals and attentive service, plus the best and hottest fresh ají in Chile. If you can't find it, listen for its deafening siren at noon.

For seafood, there's *El Rey del Marisco* at Colón and Maipú, 2nd floor. *Restaurant Natura*, Bolognesi 367, is a vegetarian café. *El Arriero*, at 21 de Mayo 385 near the intersection with Colón, is an outstanding parrilla with pleasant atmosphere and friendly service, but it's closed Mondays. For typical Chilean food, try *El Tambo* at the Poblado Artesanal on the outskirts of town (see Poblado Artesanal under the Things to See section for details), or the *Club de Huasos*, open on Sundays only at Km 3.5 in the Azapa valley.

Like other coastal towns in northern Chile, Arica has several Chinese restaurants of decent quality. Try *Chifa Chin Huang Tao*, Patricio Lynch 317, or *Restaurant Shanghai*, at Maipú 534 near the corner with Patricio Lynch.

Getting There & Away

From Arica you can head north across the Peruvian border to Tacna and Lima, south toward Santiago, or east to Bolivia.

Air Chacalluta Airport (☎ 222831) is 18 km north of Arica, just south of the Peruvian border. Both Ladeco and LAN-Chile offer transportation to Chacalluta coordinated with their flight schedules.

Ladeco (☎ 252021) is at 21 de Mayo 443, while LAN-Chile (☎ 224738) is at 7 de Junio 148, opposite Plaza Colón. Ladeco flies daily from Arica to Iquique, Antofagasta and Santiago. LAN-Chile has a similar schedule, with fewer flights stopping in Antofagasta. The flight between Arica and Santiago is one of the most spectacular in South America, with awesome views of the northern coastal desert and the Andes, but be sure to sit on the left side southbound and the right side northbound. Fares to Santiago are about US$180, but if your schedule is flexible you may get a discount seat for about half that fare.

Lloyd Aéreo Boliviano (☎ 251919), at Patricio Lynch 298 near the intersection with Sotomayor, has three flights a week from Arica to La Paz. Aero Perú (☎ 232852) has an agent at 7 de Junio 148, downstairs from LAN-Chile.

Bus & Colectivo – domestic Arica's Terminal de Buses (☎ 241390), Diego Portales 948 at Santa María, is some distance from the centre but quickly reached by taxi colectivo from 18 de Septiembre. All major bus companies have their offices there. Except during holiday periods, advance booking should not be necessary.

To Iquique (four hours, US$5), try Buses Carmelita (☎ 241209) or Cuevas y González (☎ 241090). Taxi colectivos to Iquique, faster than buses, charge about US$8 per person. The major companies are Tamarugal (☎ 222609), Turis Auto (☎ 222673), Colectivos Taxi Norte (☎ 224806), and Turis Taxi (☎ 222671).

Fénix Pullman Norte (☎ 222457) goes to Antofagasta, La Serena and Santiago, with connections to the Lake District and other points in southern Chile. Chile Bus (☎ 222217) goes to the same destinations and also to Viña del Mar, as does Flecha Norte (☎ 241099), whose safety record has been questioned. Buses Zambrano (☎ 241587) serves Viña and Valparaíso.

Fichtur (☎ 222817) and Flota Barrios (☎ 223587) also go to Santiago. Tramaca (☎ 241198) goes to Calama (11 hours), Antofagasta and Santiago, while Geminis (☎ 241647) also has service to Calama and Antofagasta, with international connections to Salta, Argentina (see below).

Typical fares to Calama are about US$9, to Antofagasta US$13, to Viña del Mar and Valparaíso about US$30, and to Santiago US$32.

For the altiplano destinations of Parinacota (in Parque Nacional Lauca), Visviri and Charaña (on the Bolivian border), contact Buses Martínez (☎ 232265), Pedro Montt 620, or Transporte Humire (☎ 231891), Pedro Montt 662. Martínez leaves Tuesday and Friday at 10 am, while Humire departs half an hour later. Fares to Parinacota are about US$6, to Visviri US$7.50.

Buses La Paloma (☎ 222710), Germán Riesco 2071, accepts phone reservations to the precordillera villages of Socoroma (US$2), Putre (US$3) and Belén five times weekly, departing Arica at 6.45 am. To reach the terminal, take bus No 7 to German Riesco or arrange for their special taxibus to come to your hotel for US$0.40.

Bus Lluta serves Poconchile from the corner of Chacabuco and Vicuña Mackenna in Arica, four times daily starting at 6 am; if hitching to Parque Nacional Lauca, it is easiest to take this bus and proceed from the Carabineros checkpoint at Poconchile.

Bus & Colectivo – international Adsubliata (☎ 241972) offers frequent bus service (US$2) to Tacna (Peru). Several companies operate taxi colectivos to Tacna for about US$3.50 per person; these leave from Avenida Chacabuco, between Baquedano and Colón, whenever they are full, taking about an hour including a tedious Peruvian customs inspection.

TEPSA (☎ 222817) operates services to Lima (Peru) for US$30, Quito (Ecuador) for US$68, Bogotá (Colombia) for US$114, and Caracas (Venezuela) for US$158. It is generally cheaper to take a bus to Tacna and then buy a separate ticket to Lima or elsewhere in Peru.

Buses Litoral (☎ 251267), Chacabuco 454, run buses from Arica to La Paz (Bolivia) on Tuesday and Friday at 1 am, taking about 18 hours (longer or not at all in the rainy season) for US$20 one way. One LP reader reports that they are not keen about dropping passengers in Parque Nacional Lauca and will charge the full Arica-La Paz fare for this relatively short distance.

Tramaca makes connections in Calama with Atahualpa buses from Antofagasta to Salta (Argentina) on Friday at 9.30 pm. Ostensibly more comfortable than Litoral, Buses Géminis (☎ 241647) goes to La Paz on Wednesday (US$30) and to Salta weekly (28 hours, US$45) via Calama. These latter services are heavily booked and generally operate in summer only.

Train Arica has a regular train service to Tacna (Peru), but services to La Paz (Bolivia) have recently changed and there is no ordinary passenger train between the two cities.

The Ferrocarril Arica-Tacna (☎ 231115) is at Máximo Lira 889. Departures are usually around noon and 6 pm (turn up about half an hour earlier for exit formalities), and the journey takes about 1½ hours. The fare is about US$1.75, but taxi colectivos (see above) are faster and more convenient.

The Ferrocarril Arica-La Paz (☎ 231786) is opposite the Plazoleta Estación, at 21 de Mayo 51 near the corner with Pedro Montt. The new *El Dorado de los Andes* service leaves Monday and Thursday at 8 am, and costs US$50 for *coche salón* (with a reclining seat) and US$60 for *coche dormitorio* (a sleeper coach).

The Ferrobus-Arica La Paz (☎ 232844), which is a sort of bus on rails, operates weekly, taking about 11 hours and costing US$49, accepted only in US currency. Both services pass through very high and cold country, so dress warmly.

Car Rental Rental cars are available from Hertz (☎ 231487), on the grounds of Hotel El Paso at General Velásquez 1109, American (☎ 252234) at General Lagos 559, and Viva (☎ 251121) at 21 de Mayo 821.

Getting Around

Local buses and taxi colectivos connect the town centre and the main bus terminal. Taxi colectivos, only slightly more expensive than buses, are much faster and more frequent. Destinations are clearly marked on an illuminated sign on top of the cab.

Only taxi colectivos serve the Azapa valley. Between 7 am and 10 pm daily, they leave frequently from the corner of Maipú and Patricio Lynch, and cost about US$1.

AROUND ARICA

There are varied sights and recreational opportunities in and near Arica. Most are easy day trips, especially with a car, but some of the more distant ones would be more suitable as overnighters.

Lluta Geoglyphs

About 10 km north of Arica, the Ruta Panamericana intersects Ruta 11, which leads east up the valley of the Río Lluta to Poconchile. A short distance inland, a series of restored pre-Columbian geoglyphs cover an otherwise barren slope on the right. These figures, made by grouping dark stones over light-coloured sand, include representations of llamas, and recall the importance of pre-Columbian pack trains on the route to Tiahuanaco, a traffic which only recently disappeared with the construction of good motor roads.

Poconchile

Built in the 17th century, reconstructed in the 19th, and restored earlier this century, the **Iglesia de San Gerónimo** is one of the oldest churches in Chile. To get there, take the bus from Arica to the Carabineros checkpoint in Poconchile. It is possible to camp along the Río Lluta.

If you are driving beyond Poconchile, the Carabineros will record details of the vehicle and the driver, and give you a small ticket which you have to surrender on your return; this will expedite your passing through on the way back. If you are taking an alternative route back to Arica, let them know. There is some drug smuggling from Bolivia to Arica, so take care not to arouse suspicion.

Copaquilla

As the paved highway zigzags up the desolate mountainside, there are exceptional views of the upper Lluta valley. Along the route you'll see the appropriately named 'candle-holder' cactus *(cactus candelabros* or *Browningia candelaris)*, which grows just five to seven mm a year and flowers for 24 hours just once a year. These cacti and other plants absorb moisture from the camanchaca (fog) which penetrates inland.

At Copaquilla, overlooking a spectacular canyon, is the 12th-century **Pukará de Copaquilla**, a fortress built to protect Indian farmlands below – notice the abandoned terraces, evidence of a much larger pre-Columbian population. The fortress has been restored by the Universidad de Tarapacá. Tours to Parque Nacional Lauca normally make a brief stop here.

Socoroma

On the colonial pack route between Arica and Potosí, Socoroma is an Aymara farming village which features cobbled streets, the 17th-century **Iglesia de San Francisco**, and other colonial remains. Buses to Putre (see below) leave the highway and stop here briefly.

PUTRE

Putre, 150 km east of Arica by an excellent paved highway, sits 3500 metres above sea level in the precordillera; it's a charming Aymara village which, in the 16th century, was a *reducción* (a settlement established by the Spanish to facilitate control of the Indians). Many of its houses still contain elements from the colonial period.

Local farmers raise alfalfa for llamas, sheep and cattle on extensive stone-faced agricultural terraces, many of great antiquity. In 1994, in early November, Putre will be directly on the path of a total solar eclipse which will last more than six minutes; since the weather is almost always clear, it should be an outstanding place to view this event. It is also the gateway to Parque Nacional Lauca.

Iglesia de Putre

Dating from 1670, the adobe church of Putre was restored two centuries later. To visit its interior, which contains many valuable colonial artefacts, ask for the keys and leave a small donation.

Places to Stay & Eat

Restaurant Oasis, at Cochrane near the corner with O'Higgins, offers basic accommodation for US$3 per person and good plain meals. At the foot of O'Higgins, opposite the army camp, CONAF has a comfortable refugio which offers lodging when space permits for about US$8 (slightly cheaper for Chilean nationals).

Hostería Las Vicuñas (☎ 224997) caters to personnel from the nearby gold mine at Choquelimpie, but has a number of rooms available to the general public from US$47/63, breakfast included. Prices may drop when the mine closes. It also offers other meals.

Getting There & Away

Buses La Paloma (☎ 222710), Germán Riesco 2071 in Arica, serves Putre five times weekly. The bus departs Arica at 6.45 am, goes via Socoroma to Putre, then continues south to Belén, and returns the following day. Buses to Parinacota, in Parque Nacional Lauca (see below), pass by the turn-off to Putre, which is five km from the main highway. At 6 am, try hitching a lift with the mine trucks, which leave from the hostería and pass the Las Cuevas entrance to the park before turning off to Choquelimpie.

PARQUE NACIONAL LAUCA

One of Chile's most accessible parks, Parque Nacional Lauca is a world biosphere reserve which supports vicuña, condor, vizcacha and more than 150 species of bird, plus cultural and archaeological landmarks and Aymara herders of llamas and alpacas. Among its spectacular features is Lago Chungará, one of the highest lakes in the world, at the foot of the dormant twin Pallachata volcanos. Slightly to the south, Volcán Guallatire smokes ominously.

Lauca is 160 km north-east of Arica, near the Bolivian border. It comprises 138,000 hectares of altiplano, between 3000 and 6300 metres above sea level. Adjacent to the park, but more difficult of access, are the Reserva Nacional Las Vicuñas and the Monumento Natural Salar de Surire. Once part of the park, they now constitute technically separate units but are still managed by CONAF and are described below.

The park's altitude, well above 4000 metres in most parts, requires the visitor to adapt gradually. Do not exert yourself at first and eat and drink moderately; if you suffer anyway, try a cup of tea made from the common Aymara herbal remedy *chachacoma*, readily gathered around the settlements. Keep water at your bedside, as the throat is likely to desiccate in the arid climate, and wear sun protection in the daytime – the tropical sun can be truly brutal at this altitude.

Geography & Climate

Beyond Copaquilla, Ruta 11 climbs steadily but gradually through the precordillera to the park entrance at Las Cuevas, where the altiplano proper begins. Rainfall and vegetation increase with altitude and distance from the coast; it can snow during the summer rainy season, known as *invierno boliviano* (Bolivian winter).

Along the highway and at Las Cuevas, you will see remarkably tame specimens of the vicuña *(Vicugna vicugna)*, a wild relative of the llama and a major success story for Chilean wildlife conservation. Pay special attention to the ground-hugging, bright green *llareta (Laretia compacta)*, a densely growing shrub with a deceptive cushion-like appearance which belies the fact that it is nearly as hard as rock – the Aymara Indians need a pick or mattock to break open dead llareta, which they collect for fuel.

The local Aymara pasture their llamas and alpacas on verdant *bofedales* (swampy alluvial grasslands) and the lower slopes of the surrounding mountains, and sell handicrafts woven from their wool in the village of Parinacota.

Las Cuevas

At the western entrance to the park, Las Cuevas has a permanent ranger station which is a good source of information and an excellent place to view and photograph the vicuña, which have become exceptionally tame over the past decade of protection. Their numbers have increased from barely a thousand in the early 1970s to more than 27,000 today. Don't miss a soak in the rustic thermal baths nearby, where camping may be possible.

Ciénegas de Parinacota

On the north side of Ruta 11, the Ciénegas de Parinacota are the bofedales between the tiny settlements of Chucuyo and Parinacota, where most of the Aymaras' domestic livestock graze. They also harbour an exceptional amount of wildlife and some interesting cultural relics – there is a colonial chapel just below Restaurant Matilde. *Guallatas* (Andean geese) and ducks drift on the Río Lauca and nest on the shore, while the curious mountain vizcacha *(Lagidium viscacia)*, a relative of the domestic chinchilla, peeks out from numerous rockeries which rise above the swampy sediments. Look for the ruins of another centuries-old chapel about half an hour's walk from Parinacota.

Parinacota

Five km off the international highway, Parinacota is a very picturesque Aymara pastoral village with an fascinating 17th century colonial church, reconstructed in 1789. The surrealistic murals on its interior walls, the work of artists from the Cuzco school, recall Hieronymus Bosch's 'Sinners in the Hands of an Angry God', but note also the depiction of the soldiers bearing Christ to the cross as Spaniards. Ask caretaker Cipriano Morales for the key, and leave a small donation.

CONAF has a refugio, built originally for a high altitude genetic research project, at Parinacota (see below for information on accommodation). Ask the rangers for information on surrounding sights, such as Laguna Cotacotani and Cerro Guane Guane. Lorenza Calle, who lives in the first house on the right as you face the church from the plaza, offers excellent alpaca woollen goods, including caps, socks and pullovers.

Cerro Guane Guane

Immediately north of Parinacota, Cerro Guane Guane is a 5300-metre peak with extraordinary panoramic views of the park and beyond. It is climbable along its eastern shoulder, but the last 500 metres in particular are a difficult slog through porous volcanic sand – one step forward, two steps back. The climb takes about four hours from the village. Ask advice from CONAF's rangers, and do not attempt to climb Guane Guane in threatening weather, since there is no shelter from lightning.

Laguna Cotacotani

Laguna Cotacotani is the source of the Río

Guanacos & Vicuñas, Llamas & Alpacas

Unlike the Old World, the Western Hemisphere had few grazing mammals after the Pleistocene, when mammoths, horses and other large herbivores disappeared for reasons which are not entirely clear, but appear linked to hunting pressure by the earliest inhabitants of the plains and pampas of North and South America. For millennia, however, Andean peoples have relied on the New World camels – the wild guanaco and vicuña, the domesticated llama and alpaca – for food and fibre.

Vicuña

Guanaco and vicuña are few today, but are the likely ancestors of the domesticated llama and alpaca. In fact, they were among very few potential New World domesticates – contrast them with the Old World cattle, horses, sheep, goats, donkeys and pigs which have filled so many vacant niches in the Americas. Of the major domesticated animals from across the Atlantic, only the humped camels have failed to achieve an important role here. While the New World camels have lost ground to sheep and cattle in some areas, they are not likely to disappear.

The guanaco *(Lama guanicoe)* ranges from the central Andes to Tierra del Fuego, at elevations from sea level up to 4000 metres or more. In the central Andes, where the human population is small but widely dispersed and domestic livestock are numerous, guanaco numbers are small, but on the plains of Argentine Patagonia and in reserves like southern Chile's Parque Nacional Torres del Paine, herds of rust-coloured guanaco are still a common sight. Native hunters ate its meat and dressed in its skins.

By contrast the vicuña *(Vicugna vicugna)* occupies a much smaller geographical range, well above 4000 metres in the puna and altiplano from south-central Peru to north-western Argentina. While not as numerous as the guanaco, it played an critical role in the cultural life of pre-Columbian Peru which assured its survival – its very fine golden wool was the exclusive property of the Inca kings. Spanish chronicler Bernabé Cobo wrote that the ruler's clothing 'was made of the finest wool and the best cloth that was woven in his whole kingdom...most of it was made of vicuña wool, which is almost as fine as silk'.

Strict Inca authority protected the vicuña, but the Spanish invasion destroyed that authority and made the species vulnerable to hunting pressure over the past 500 years. By the middle of this century, poaching reduced its numbers from two million to perhaps 10,000 and caused its placement on Appendix I of the Endangered Species List. Conservation programmes such as that at Parque Nacional Lauca have achieved so impressive a recovery that economic exploitation of the species may soon benefit the communities of the puna. In Lauca and surrounding areas, vicuña numbers grew from barely a thousand in the early 1970s to more than 27,000 two decades later.

The communities of the puna and altiplano – in northern Chile, mostly Aymara Indians – still depend on llamas and alpacas for their livelihood. While the two species appear very similar, they differ in several important respects. The taller, rangier and hardier llama *(Lama glama)* has relatively coarse wool which serves for blankets, ropes and other household goods, and is also a pack animal, though llama trains are rare in Chile since the penetration of good roads into the altiplano. It can survive or even flourish on relatively poor, dry pastures, while the smaller, more delicate alpaca *(Lama pacos)* is not a pack animal and requires well-watered grasslands to produce a much finer wool with great commercial value. Both llama and alpaca meat are consumed by Andean households and even sold in urban markets – visit the Mercado Benedicto in Arica for 'churrasco de alpaca'.

Meagre earnings from wool and meat have not been sufficient to stem the flow of population from the countryside to cities like Arica and Iquique, but the commercialisation of vicuña wool might help do so, if international agreement permits it. According to a recent CONAF study, production and sale of vicuña cloth at a price of nearly US$290 per linear metre could earn more than than US$300,000 per annum for reinvestment in one of Chile's most remote and poorest regions. If, as intended, CONAF involves the area's inhabitants and respects their needs and wishes, it would set a precedent which many Latin American governments might emulate in tropical rainforests and other threatened environments. ■

Llama

Lauca, although unfortunate diversions by ENDESA, the national electric company, have caused fluctuations in lake levels and undermined its ecological integrity. Still, along its shores you will see extensive bird life and scattered forests of *queñoa (Polylepis tarapacana)*, one of the world's highest elevation trees, reaching about five metres in height. Though you are not likely to see puma, tracks are not unusual, and foxes are fairly common. You will also see extensive lava flows and cinder cones. Follow the road along the south bank of the Río Lauca from Parinacota.

Lago Chungará

More than 4500 metres above sea level, Lago Chungará is a shallow body of water formed when a lava flow dammed the snowmelt stream from 6350-metre Volcán Parinacota, which dominates the lake to the north. About 28 km from Las Cuevas, Chungará has abundant and unusual bird life, including the Chilean flamingo *(Phoenicopterus chilensis)*, the *tagua gigante* or giant coot *(Fulica gigantea)*, and the Andean gull *(Larus serranus)*. You can reach the west end of the lake from Parinacota on foot in about two hours, but most of its wildlife is more distant, near the Chilean customs station on the highway.

Because of Arica's insatiable appetite for hydroelectricity and the Azapa valley's thirst, ENDESA has built an intricate system of pumps and canals which may compromise the ecological integrity of Lago Chungará. Since Chungará is so shallow, any lowering of its level would dramatically reduce its surface area and impinge on those parts on which wading birds such as the flamingo and giant coot feed and nest.

Places to Stay & Eat

While there is no commercial accommodation in the park, there are several reasonable alternatives. In a pinch, the *CONAF refugio* at Las Cuevas may offer a bed.

In Chucuyo, directly on the highway to Bolivia near the junction to Parinacota, the *casa familiar* of Matilde and Máximo

Puma

Morales usually has an extra bed at a very reasonable price. Matilde will prepare alpaca steaks and other simple meals for about US$1, and there are two other inexpensive restaurants. You can also buy some supplies here, but it is cheaper and more convenient to bring whatever you need from Arica.

In Parinacota, CONAF has a very comfortable if sparsely furnished *refugio* which offers beds for US$8 per night, slightly cheaper for Chilean nationals, but you should bring your own sleeping bag. There are showers, but hot water depends on the sporadic arrival of gas canisters from Arica. Two small tent campsites are available nearby for US$4.

At Lago Chungará, CONAF charges US$4 per site for its lakeside *campground*, which has picnic tables and some shelter. At 4500 metres above sea level, it gets very cold at night.

Getting There & Away

The park straddles the Arica-La Paz highway, which is paved to the park entrance and will be paved all the way to the Bolivian border by 1995; the trip from Arica takes about four hours. From Arica, there is regular passenger service with Buses Martínez (☎ 232265), Pedro Montt 620, or Transporte Humire (☎ 231891), Pedro Montt 662. Martínez leaves Tuesday and Friday at 10 am, while Humire departs half an hour later. Fares to Parinacota are about US$6, to Visviri US$7.50.

Several travel agencies in Arica offer tours to the park – for details, see 'Organised Tours' in the Arica section, above. Although tours provide a good introduction, you spend most of the time in transit, so try to arrange a longer stay at Chucuyo, Parinacota, or Chungará – one alternative is to rent a car in Arica and drive to the park, which would also enable you to visit more remote sites like Guallatire, Caquena and the Salar de Surire (the latter only with a high-clearance vehicle since it involves fording the Río Lauca several times). Carry extra fuel in cans – most rental agencies will provide them – but fuel may be available from Matilde Morales in Chucuyo. Do not forget warm clothing and sleeping gear.

RESERVA NACIONAL LAS VICUÑAS

South of Lauca is the Reserva Nacional Las Vicuñas, consisting of 210,000 sparsely inhabited hectares. Once part of the park, it was reclassified in the mid-1980s to permit reopening of the gold mine at Choquelimpie, but this is scheduled to close again shortly as the historical tailings have been exhausted. Few Aymara shepherds inhabit this area, where the once endangered vicuña has proliferated. There is no public transport, but it may be possible to catch a lift with mining trucks.

Sixty km from Parinacota by road, at the base of smoking Volcán Guallatire, is the village of the same name, which features a 17th-century church. South of Guallatire, on the road to Surire, are the interesting ruins of a colonial silver mill.

Farther south, there are several fords of the Río Lauca which should not be attempted with a low-clearance vehicle – or by any vehicle if the river is high in the summer rainy season. If uncertain, scout your route by wading across (the water is surprisingly warm), taking special care to avoid sandbars; should you get stuck, there are Carabineros in Guallatire and Chilcaya (farther south) with 4WD vehicles who *may* be able to help.

MONUMENTO NATURAL SALAR DE SURIRE

En route to Surire, 126 km from Putre and 108 km from Parinacota, you are likely to see flocks of the sprinting *ñandú* (the ostrich-like rhea, *Pterocnemia pennata)*, as well as numerous vicuña. The monument itself comprises 12,000 hectares around a sprawling salt lake with breeding colonies of three species of flamingos, including the rare James flamingo *(parina chica* or *Phoenicoparrus jamesi)*. Again, there is no public transport, but it may be possible to hitch a lift

Nandú

with trucks from the nearby sulphur mine or with CONAF, which maintains a refugio here. Camping is possible at Polloquere, where there are rustic thermal baths.

Although most visitors return to Putre and Arica, it is possible to make a southerly circuit through Parque Nacional Isluga and back to Arica via Camiña or Huara. Do not attempt this without consulting with CONAF and/or the Carabineros.

IQUIQUE

Prior to the Spanish invasion, Iquique was a minor concentration of coastal Chango Indians who exchanged fish and guano from offshore islands for maize, potatoes and other products of the precordillera and the altiplano. During the colonial era, guano grew in importance, but the region's real wealth stemmed from the Huantajaya silver mine in the coast range, second only to the bonanza vein at Potosí.

During the 19th century, Tarapacá's minerals and nitrates were shipped by narrow-gauge railways through ports like Iquique, once little more than a collection of shanties at the base of the barren headlands. In 1835 Darwin wrote that Iquique:

> ...contains about a thousand inhabitants, and stands on a little plain of sand at the foot of a great wall of rock two thousand feet in height, here forming the coast. The whole is utterly desert. A light shower of rain falls only once in very many years; and the ravines consequently are filled with detritus, and the mountain-sides covered by piles of fine white sand, even to a height of a thousand feet...The aspect of the place was most gloomy; the little port, with its few vessels, and small group of wretched houses, seemed overwhelmed and out of all proportion with the rest of the scene.

In a few years, Darwin would barely have recognised Iquique. As the nitrate industry grew, its population exceeded 5000 in 20 years and 40,000 by the turn of the century. Not all the nitrate ports survived, but in those that did, like Iquique, nitrate barons built opulent mansions (many of them still standing), while authorities piped in water from the distant cordillera and imported topsoil for public plazas and private gardens. Iquique reflects this 19th-century boom, its Plaza de Armas complete with clock tower and theatre with corinthian columns, and many stately wooden Victorian mansions. Nearby ghost towns like Humberstone and Santa Laura, with their rusting machinery, recall the source of the wealth.

Now a city of more than 140,000, Iquique is still one of the Norte Grande's largest ports, but fishing has supplanted mining as its most important industry – Iquique ships more fishmeal than any other port in the world. Establishment of an ultra-modern zona franca (duty-free zone) in 1975 has made it one of the most prosperous cities in the country. The centre, though, retains the atmosphere of a 19th-century port, with its ramshackle wooden houses, sailors' bars, and street life.

Orientation

Iquique sits on a narrow terrace at the foot of the coastal range, which abruptly rises 600 metres above the city, 1853 km north of Santiago and 315 km from Arica by the roundabout Ruta Panamericana. Blocked by the mountains, Iquique has spread north and south along the coast.

The city's focus is the Plaza Prat, the renovation of which should be complete by the time this book appears. The Avenida Baquedano, which runs north-south along the east side of the Plaza, is the main thoroughfare, while the Calle Tarapacá runs east four blocks to the Plaza Condell, a secondary centre of downtown activity. Most points of interest are within a roughly rectangular area marked by Sotomayor to the north, the Avenida Costanera to the west, Amunátegui to the east, and Manuel Bulnes to the south. The main beaches are south of downtown, along Avenida Balmaceda and its extension Avenida 11 de Septiembre.

Information

Tourist Office Sernatur (☎ 411523, 427686) is at Aníbal Pinto 436, next to Ladeco and opposite the Hotel Phoenix. Open weekdays from 8 am to 1 pm and 2.30 to 6.15 pm, it

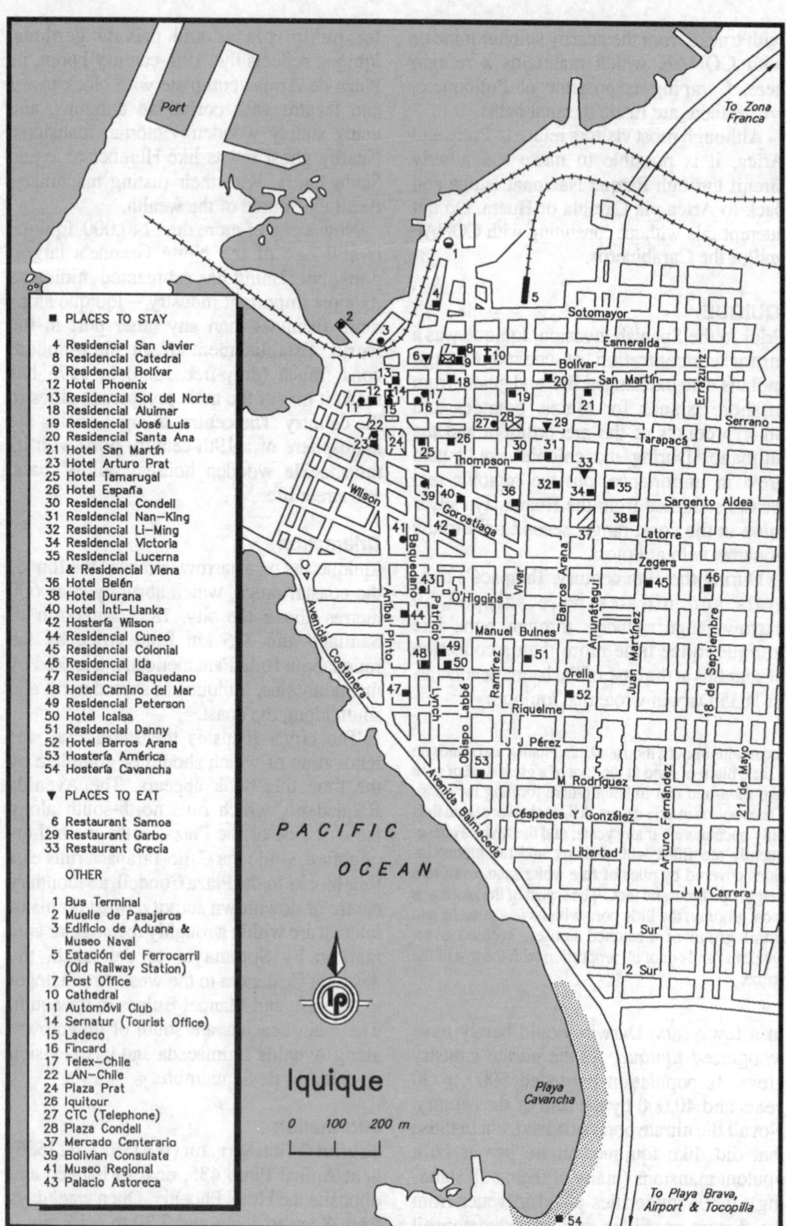
Iquique
■ PLACES TO STAY
4 Residencial San Javier
8 Residencial Catedral
9 Residencial Bolívar
12 Hotel Phoenix
13 Residencial Sol del Norte
18 Residencial Aluimar
19 Residencial José Luis
20 Residencial Santa Ana
21 Hotel San Martín
23 Hotel Arturo Prat
25 Hotel Tamarugal
26 Hotel España
30 Residencial Condell
31 Residencial Nan-King
32 Residencial Li-Ming
34 Residencial Victoria
35 Residencial Lucerna & Residencial Viena
36 Hotel Belén
38 Hotel Durana
40 Hotel Inti-Llanka
42 Hostería Wilson
44 Residencial Cuneo
45 Residencial Colonial
46 Residencial Ida
47 Residencial Baquedano
48 Hotel Camino del Mar
49 Residencial Peterson
50 Hotel Icalsa
51 Residencial Danny
52 Hotel Barros Arana
53 Hostería América
54 Hostería Cavancha
▼ PLACES TO EAT
6 Restaurant Samoa
29 Restaurant Garbo
33 Restaurant Grecia
OTHER
1 Bus Terminal
2 Muelle de Pasajeros
3 Edificio de Aduana & Museo Naval
5 Estación del Ferrocarril (Old Railway Station)
7 Post Office
10 Cathedral
11 Automóvil Club
14 Sernatur (Tourist Office)
15 Ladeco
16 Fincard
17 Telex-Chile
22 LAN-Chile
24 Plaza Prat
26 Iquitour
27 CTC (Telephone)
28 Plaza Condell
37 Mercado Centerario
39 Bolivian Consulate
41 Museo Regional
43 Palacio Astoreca
Port
To Zona Franca
Sotomayor
Esmeralda
Bolívar
San Martín
Errázuriz
Serrano
Tarapacá
Thompson
Wilson
Gorostiaga
Sargento Aldea
Latorre
Zegers
O'Higgins
Manuel Bulnes
Orella
Riquelme
J J Pérez
M Rodríguez
Céspedes Y González
Libertad
J M Carrera
1 Sur
2 Sur
Baquedano
Aníbal Pinto
Patricio Lynch
Obispo Labbé
Ramírez
Vivar
Barros Arana
Amunátegui
Juan Martínez
Arturo Fernández
18 de Septiembre
21 de Mayo
Avenida Costanera
Avenida Balmaceda
PACIFIC OCEAN
Playa Cavancha
To Playa Brava, Airport & Tocopilla
0 100 200 m

provides a free leaflet which tells what's on in Iquique, including concerts, films, sports and other events, but is less well stocked than its counterparts in other Chilean cities. It has a branch office at the Zona Franca (see below), north of the city centre.

Another dependable source of information is the Automóvil Club de Chile (☎ 422422) at Serrano 154.

Money Fincard, Serrano 372, is the only formal exchange house downtown, open weekdays from 9 am to 2 pm and 5 to 6.30 pm. There is also a cambio at the Zona Franca.

Banco de Chile, at Plaza Prat 660, will change foreign currency and travellers' cheques from 9 am to 2 pm weekdays.

Post & Telecommunications Correos de Chile, at Bolívar 458 between Obispo Labbé and Patricio Lynch, is open weekdays from 8.30 am to 12.30 pm and 3 to 7 pm, Saturday from 9 am to 1 pm.

Iquique has several telephone offices, including CTC at Ramírez 587 and at the Zona Franca, Módulo 212, 2nd level. ENTEL is at Gorostiaga 287, while Telex-Chile, San Martín 387, also offers international telephone services.

Consulates The Bolivian Consulate (☎ 421777) is at Latorre 399, Oficina 41-A. The Peruvian Consulate (☎ 431116) is at Los Rieles 131.

Medical Services The Hospital Regional Doctor Torres (☎ 422370) is at the corner of Serrano and Avenida Héroes de la Concepción.

Things to See

Because of its 19th-century heritage, derived from foreign exploitation of nitrates, Iquique's architecture resembles that of few other Latin American cities. There are many landmarks on or near the Plaza Prat, including the **Torre Reloj** (1877) clocktower; the **Teatro Municipal** (Municipal Theatre), a neo-classical structure which has hosted opera, theatre and other cultural activities since 1890; and the Moorish-style **Centro Español** (1904), now a club and restaurant whose interior features murals and oil paintings based on themes from *Don Quijote* and from Spanish history. South of the Plaza, Avenida Baquedano is a zone of preservation for Georgian-style buildings dating from 1880 to 1930.

The old **Estación del Ferrocarril**, the train station which linked Iquique with the nitrate oficinas of the interior is at the Sotomayor and Vivar intersection, four blocks north of the Plaza Condell.

Museo Regional The Regional Museum has moved to Baquedano 951, once the Iquique courthouse. It features a mock altiplano village with adobe houses and mannequins in traditional Aymara dress, plus a large collection of Neolithic artefacts, including raft and canoe paddles, fish hooks and sinkers, rope, harpoons, arrows, and quivers made of animal hide. There's also an exhibition of Indian ceramics and weaving, photos of the early days of Iquique, and a fascinating display on the nitrate industry, including a scale model of Oficina Peña Chica, east of Iquique, just north of Humberstone (see Around Iquique).

The museum is open weekdays from 9 am to 1 pm and 3 to 7 pm, and on Saturday from 10 am to 1 pm. Admission is a modest US$0.45.

Edificio de Aduana Built in 1871, the colonial-style Customs Building, on Esmeralda between Aníbal Pinto and Baquedano, is a two-storey structure with metre-thick walls, an octagonal tower and an attractive interior patio.

Museo Naval The Naval Museum, at Aníbal Pinto near the corner with Esmeralda, is a monument to the famous Battle of Iquique during the War of the Pacific. It's open Tuesday to Saturday from 9.30 am to 12.30 pm and 2.30 to 6 pm, Sundays and holidays from 10 am to 6 pm. Admission costs about US$0.30.

Muelle de Pasajeros Just west of the Edificio Aduana is the passenger pier which dates from 1901. Tours of the harbour leave from here; they pass the buoy which marks the site of Arturo Prat's sunken corvette *Esmeralda*, from the Battle of Iquique,.

Palacio Astoreca Now a museum and cultural centre which exhibits paintings by local artists, this 1904 nitrate tycoon's Georgian-style mansion, at the intersection of Patricio Lynch and O'Higgins, matches the opulence of the wool barons of Punta Arenas. It has a fantastic interior of enormous rooms with elaborate woodwork and high ceilings, massive chandeliers, stained glass windows, a gigantic billiard table and balconies. It's open daily from 10 am to 1 pm and weekdays only from 3 to 8 pm. Admission is about US$0.45.

Zona Franca Created in 1975, this monstrous monument to modern consumerism is the reason most Chileans visit Iquique and many have moved here. The entire First Region of Tarapacá is technically a customs-free zone, but its nucleus is this sprawling shopping centre for imported electronics, clothing, automobiles and almost anything else. The *zofri*, as it is commonly known, has made Iquique's unemployment rate the lowest in the country.

To see this feeding frenzy of voracious consumers, and maybe replace a lost or stolen camera, take any northbound taxi colectivo from the centre. It's open weekdays from 9.30 am to 1 pm and 4.30 to 9 pm, Saturdays from 9.30 am to 1 pm only.

Beaches

Playa Cavancha, beginning at the intersection of Balmaceda and Amunátegui, is Iquique's most popular beach, good for swimming but sometimes crowded. Farther south, along the Avenida 11 de Septiembre, the Playa Brava's crashing waves make it too rough for swimming, but it's fine for sunbathing. The easiest way to get there is by taxi colectivo from the centre of town – US$0.40 per person. Toward the hills, look for the massive dunes of Cerro Dragón, which looks like a set for a science fiction film.

Much farther south, toward and beyond the airport, the beaches are excellent and much less crowded, but public transport is very limited. Renting a car to explore this area, most of which is served by a superb paved highway, is an attractive option.

Organised Tours

Iquitour (☎ 422009), at Tarapacá 465-B next to the Hotel España, offers many tours of the city and its interior, but several readers have complained of poor service – one called their city tour 'horrible' – and failure to live up to contracts. Tours are conducted daily except Sunday, at about 9.30 am, they include visits to Pica, Humberstone, Santa Laura, Museo Pozo Almonte, La Tirana, La Huayca and Matilla for about US$25 including lunch. They also offer tours to Termas de Mamiña. Another possibility is Turismo Lirima (☎ 422049), Baquedano 823, which is more expensive but may be more dependable.

Instead of a formal tour, it may be equally reasonable and more convenient to hire a taxi with driver from the stand at the north-west corner of the Plaza Prat.

Places to Stay – bottom end

There's a cluster of seedy residenciales on Amunátegui between Sargento Aldea and Thompson, all charging about US$4 or less per person, including *Residencial Victoria* at 770, *Residencial Lucerna* at 723, and *Residencial Viena* at 729 (spartan and, according to one reader, 'absolutely filthy'). Another possibility is *Residencial Sol del Norte* (☎ 421546), Juan Martínez 852, for US$5 per person, but it lacks hot water. *Residencial Ida* (☎ 425833), 18 de Septiembre 1054, charges US$6 per person with shared bath; doubles with private bath cost US$18. *Residencial Baquedano*

(☎ 422990), Baquedano 1315, is slightly dearer. One reader enjoyed a nameless *hospedaje* at Gorostiaga 451 even though it lacked hot water.

Other bottom-enders include *Residencial Peterson*, Patricio Lynch 1257, where a double costs US$9 and *Hotel España* (☎ 411068), at Tarapacá 465 near Plaza Prat, which is not recommended although it may be tolerable for a night or two – consider a room with private bath, since the common baths are rather dirty. The rooms themselves are flimsy cubicles for US$5/10 single/double; those with private bath cost US$8/13.

Two budget lodgings near the bus station are *Residencial Esmeralda*, at Esmeralda and Patricio Lynch, and *Residencial Aluimar*, San Martín 486 between Patricio Lynch and Obispo Labbé. A step up is *Residencial José Luis*, San Martín 601 at Ramírez, which gets short-stay trade. Singles are US$7 and doubles US$10, with private bath; its cool, clean rooms all have large, comfortable double beds.

Probably the best bottom-end accommodation is tidy *Residencial Catedral* (☎ 423395), Obispo Labbé 233 opposite the cathedral, where singles/doubles with shared bath cost US$9/17 and doubles with private bath cost US$24. Very highly recommended, it has two levels of rooms around a pleasant courtyard and garden.

If it's full, the rambling *Residencial Bolívar*, around the corner at Bolívar 478, is a less obviously appealing but perhaps friendlier alternative at US$8 per person. One reader found *Residencial Condell*, Thompson 684, 'most hospitable', while *Residencial Santa Ana* (☎ 425375), Bolívar 741, is comparably priced.

Several other places charge around US$8 per person, including *Residencial Danny* (☎ 414161) at Vivar 1236; *Residencial Nan-King* (☎ 413311) at Thompson 752; *Residencial Li-Ming* at Barros Arana 705; *Hostería America* (☎ 427524) at Manuel Rodríguez 550; and *Residencial Cuneo* (☎ 428654) at Baquedano 1175. Most of these have doubles with private bath for about US$20-plus. Try also the *Residencial Colonial* (☎ 426097), Juan Martínez 1020, *Hotel Belén* (☎ 413644), Vivar 803, or *Hotel de La Plaza* (☎ 428394), Plaza Prat 302.

Places to Stay – middle

Iquique's best middle-range accommodation is the very central *Hotel Phoenix* (☎ 411349), Aníbal Pinto 451, with a friendly staff and simple but clean and bright rooms for US$20/30, including private bath and breakfast. Its ground floor offers a restaurant and billiard hall. Others in this category include *Hostería Wilson* (☎ 423789) at Wilson 422, the *Hostería Camino Real* (☎ 429521) at Zegers 1611, *Hotel Camino del Mar* (☎ 420465) at Orella 340, *Hotel Durana* (☎ 418085) at San Martín 294, and *Hotel San Diego* (☎ 413445) at Orella 1665.

Although less central, *Hotel Barros Arana* (☎ 412840) at Barros Arana 1330 near the corner with Orella, repays the effort of getting there. Rooms with private bath are US$27/34. Highly recommended, all its rooms are clean and fresh-looking, with TV and private bath. Comparably priced are *Hotel San Martín* (☎ 412260) at San Martín 823 and *Hotel Inti-Llanka* (☎ 413858) at Obispo Labbé 825.

Places to Stay – top end

Hotel Tamarugal (☎ 412833), at Tarapacá 369 near Plaza Prat, has rooms with private bath and TV for US$40/51, but one correspondent called it 'grubby and overpriced', though more central than the Barros Arana. *Hotel Icaisa* (☎ 412324) at Orella 434 charges US$57/60. One of Iquique's top hotels is the *Hotel Arturo Prat* (☎ 411067), on Aníbal Pinto 695 opposite the Plaza Prat, with rates of US$57/71. Because of its central location, it can be very noisy.

At Playa Cavancha is the *Hostería Cavancha* (☎ 431007), Los Rieles 250, which has rooms from US$60/70. Rooms facing the beach cost US$95/107, including breakfast.

Places to Eat

Despite its unprepossessing appearance, one of Iquique's best eating places is the

Mercado Centenario, the market on Barros Arana between Sargento Aldea and Latorre, where several upstairs restaurants offer a variety of excellent seafood at very reasonable prices. Another good, cheap choice is *Restaurant Grecia* at Thomson 865. A reader has recommended *Restaurant Samoa*, Bolívar 396, for a fine fixed-price lunch.

Unfortunately, the *Jugoslavenski Dom Club Social* (Yugoslav Club) on the Plaza Prat has recently closed, but check to see if it reopens. Not to be missed, but also not cheap, is the ornate *Club Español*, two doors away, with its Moorish interior and artwork. It's excellent value for money, but if you can't afford a meal, at least peek through the windows or have a drink inside.

The *Restaurant Circolo Italiano*, Tarapacá 477, specialises in pasta. Try the *Sociedad Protectora de Empleados de Tarapacá*, Thompson 207, for economical fixed-price meals. Iquique's trendiest snack bar is *Restaurant Garbo*, on Tarapacá between Barros Arana and Vivar.

Chinese restaurants are numerous – *Chifa Chai-Wha*, Thompson 917, is very cheap, with a simple Chinese meal for around US$3 per person. Others include *Chifa Tung Fong*, Tarapacá 835 between Barros Arana and Amunátegui, and the *Chifa Ming Wang*, at Barros Arana 668 near the intersection with Thompson.

Things to Buy

For arts and crafts from Iquique's altiplano, where some of Chile's most traditional Andean peoples live, check the Programa Artesanía Aymara in the Sala Lapeyrouse at the Museo Regional (see above), Baquedano 951. Savuña Aimara at Obispo Labbé 772 and CEMA-Chile at Plaza Prat 570 are also worth a visit.

Getting There & Away

Air Iquique's Diego Aracena Airport is 30 km south of town; Ladeco and LAN-Chile run taxi colectivos or minibuses coordinated with their flight schedules, for about US$4 per person.

Ladeco (☎ 412956), at Prat and Serrano half a block north of Plaza Prat, has two flights daily to Antofagasta and Santiago except on Thursday, when there is only one; its morning flight from Santiago continues to Arica. LAN-Chile (☎ 412540), at Pinto 444 facing Plaza Prat, has eight flights weekly to Santiago, four of which stop over in Antofagasta. Flights from Santiago continue to Arica.

Bus – domestic The bus terminal is at the north end of Patricio Lynch, but most companies have a more convenient office near the Mercado Centenario, so there's no need for a special trip to the bus station for tickets. Buses leave from the station, but passengers can board at the ticket offices. Services north and south are frequent.

To Arica (four hours, US$5), try Buses Carmelita (☎ 423156) at Barros Arana 841, Cuevas y González (☎ 422149) at Sargento Aldea 850, or Fénix Pullman Norte (☎ 422051) at Aníbal Pinto 531. Taxi colectivos, faster than buses, charge about US$8 per person. The major companies are Tamarugal (☎ 424856) at Sargento Aldea 783, Turis Auto (☎ 423137) at Serrano 724, and Turis Taxi (☎ 424428) at Barros Arana 897-A.

To Calama, Antofagasta and intermediate points, try Tramaca (☎ 420127) at Sargento Aldea 988, Kenny Bus (☎ 427807) at Latorre 944, Flota Barrios (☎ 426941) at Sargento Aldea 987, and Géminis (☎ 425931) at Obispo Labbé 187.

Numerous companies serve Santiago, including Carmelita, Flota Barrios, Fénix Pullman Norte, Buses Evans (☎ 424532) at Vivar 955, Chile Bus (☎ 428171) at Latorre 773, and Ramos Cholele (☎ 421648). Fichtur (☎ 425280), Aníbal Pinto 865, offers costlier but more comfortable bus cama service. Ramos Cholele, Chile Bus and Buses Zambrano (☎ 422428), Sargento Aldea 742, operate between Iquique and Viña del Mar/Valparaíso.

Buses San Andrés (☎ 413953), Sargento Aldea 798, goes daily to Pica, Arica, and Santiago. Buses Lirima (☎ 413094), Baquedano 823, goes to interior destinations like Pica, Mamiña and Matilla. Buses Julita

Santa Rosa (☎ 426368), Latorre 973, goes daily to Pica and, except on Sundays, to Mamiña. Other companies which serve Mamiña include Flonatur (which also serves Chusmiza) at Sargento Aldea 790, Transportes Rojas (☎ 424856) at Sargento Aldea 783, and Turismo Mamiña (☎ 420330) at Latorre 779. Taxitur (☎ 422044), at Sargento Aldea 791, has taxi colectivos to Mamiña and Pica.

Typical domestic fares from Iquique are: Arica, US$5; Calama, US$6; Antofagasta, US$11; La Serena, US$24; Valparaíso, Viña del Mar and Santiago, US$37.

Bus – international Besides its domestic services, Buses Géminis offers weekly direct service to Oruro and La Paz in Bolivia (US$26 and US$29), leaving at 1 am Saturday and taking 24 hours. On Tuesdays, in summer, Géminis also offers service via Calama to Salta, Argentina, for US$46.

Kenny Bus serves the border town of Colchane (US$6), in the altiplano of Iquique, Tuesday and Friday at 10 pm, arriving the following day at 6 am.

Car Rental For rental vehicles, try Hertz (☎ 426316) at Souper 650, Rent's Procar (☎ 424607) at Serrano 796, or Reátegui (☎ 429490) at General H Fuenzalida 1064.

Getting Around

As in Arica, taxi colectivos are the easiest way to get around town. Destinations are clearly marked on an illuminated sign on top of the cab.

AROUND IQUIQUE

Inland from Iquique are numerous geoglyphs, including the sprawling murals on the eastern slope of the coastal range at Pintados, and the enormous image of a man on Cerro Unita, a hillside in the Quebrada de Tarapacá, east of Huara. Also worth seeing are the nitrate ghost towns of Humberstone and Santa Laura, the important regional shrine of La Tirana, the Reserva Nacional Pampa del Tamarugal, precordillera villages like Chusmiza, Pica and Mamiña (all with hot springs), and altiplano villages like Colchane, in Parque Nacional Isluga.

Unfortunately, there is no regular public transportation along the coastal highway between Iquique and Tocopilla (in the Second Region, Antofagasta). The excellent paved surface of this road has reached Punta Lobos and should reach the mouth of the Río Loa, the southern limit of the Tarapacá Region, by the time this book appears. There is spectacular coastal desert scenery in one of the most tranquil parts of South America, although the steeper sections north of Tocopilla are vulnerable to slides – ask the Carabineros at the Río Loa checkpoint before committing yourself to going south. On the Antofagasta side of the Loa, the road is a washboard surface which is always passable but requires slow, careful driving.

Humberstone & Santa Laura

Once a huge nitrate oficina and now an eerie ghost town, Humberstone is on the Iquique-Arica highway about 45 km due east of Iquique. Nearly deserted but for scrap metal merchants and a handful of curious tourists, it is one of the best preserved and most accessible of the former mining settlements, with a main plaza flanked by a large theatre, church and market.

Almost all the original buildings are still standing; most are starting to crumble, but others such as the church are being restored. For recreational purposes, there were tennis and basketball courts. Don't miss the enormous swimming pool, built of cast iron from a shipwreck in Iquique harbour – but don't take the plunge off the diving board either. At the western end of town, the electrical generating plant still stands, along with the remains of the narrow gauge railway to the older Oficina Santa Laura, across the highway.

Nitrate oficinas could be hazardous places to work – one now-faded sign reminded miners that 'One accident could destroy all your hopes'. Another warned that workers' contracts prohibited sheltering anyone not associated with the company, which provided housing, health care, food and merchandise. Goods were normally purchased only with *fichas*, tokens which took the place of cash and were worthless elsewhere. Union organisers were not welcome.

Humberstone took its name from its British manager James Humberstone, who arrived in Pisagua in 1875 under contract to the San Antonio Nitrate & Iodine Company. Perfecting the 'Shanks system' for extracting a larger proportion of nitrates from the raw *caliche* (hardpan) of the pampas, he also became an important administrator and builder of the nitrate railways. Upon his retirement in 1925, Oficina La Palma was renamed in his honour; he died in Santiago in 1939.

Any bus from Iquique will drop you off at the ruins, at the junction of the Ruta Panamericana, and it is easy to hitch or catch a return bus. Take food, water and camera, since it is easy to spend many hours exploring the town. Early morning hours are the best time for wandering around, although afternoon breezes often moderate the midday heat.

El Gigante de Atacama

The Giant of the Atacama, 14 km east of Huara on the southern slope of Cerro Unita, is the largest prehistoric representation of a human figure in the world – a massive 86 metres long!

From the figure's head (which is square and supported by a thin neck) emanate a dozen rays – four from the top and four from each side. The eyes and mouth are square, the torso long and narrow, the arms bent (one hand appears to be an arrowhead). The size of the feet suggest the figure is wearing boots, and there are odd protrusions from the knees and thighs. Alongside the giant is another odd creature with what appears to be a tail – perhaps a monkey, although a reptile would seem more likely in the desert environment. The two figures are set amidst a complex of lines and circles, and on one side of the hill (facing the Huara-Chuzmisa road, visible as you approach the hill) there are a number of enormous clearings. The entire figure – including the head – is visible if you stand several hundred metres back from the base of the hill, which is isolated on the desert pampa. Avoid climbing the hill, which damages the pictures.

The Huara-Chuzmisa road is surfaced, as is the Arica-Iquique highway. Only the very short stretch (about one km) from the Huara-Chuzmisa road to the hill itself crosses the desert. Infrequent buses leave Iquique at inconvenient hours, so the best way to visit the site is to hire a car or taxi – hitching is impossible.

Chusmiza

At 3200 metres in the Quebrada de Tarapacá, 106 km from Iquique, Chusmiza is a thermal baths resort which also bottles one of Chile's most popular mineral waters. The only formal accommodation is the relatively pricey *Hostería Chusmiza* (☎ 422179 in Iquique for reservations). Flonatur, Sargento Aldea 790 in Iquique, has buses to Chusmiza. Kenny Bus serves the altiplano border town of Colchane (US$6 – see below), Tuesday and Friday at 10 pm, arriving the following day at 6 am.

Colchane & Parque Nacional Isluga

On the Bolivian border at 3750 metres, Colchane is the southern entrance to Parque Nacional Isluga. This is one of Chile's most isolated and traditional areas of indigenous people, though the village itself is a recent creation. It is possible to cross the border and catch a truck or bus to Oruro, Bolivia.

Parque Nacional Isluga, 175,000 hectares, is 19 km north of Colchane and 228 km from Iquique. It contains many natural and cultural features similar to those of Parque Nacional Lauca (see the Parque Nacional Lauca section), but is much less visited. CONAF maintains a refugio at the village of Enquelga and a campground at nearby Aguas Calientes, where there are thermal baths. From Isluga, it is possible to travel north to the Salar de Surire and Parque Nacional Lauca and west to Arica, but inquire about the state of roads, especially in the summer rainy season, and do not attempt it without a high-clearance vehicle.

Pintados

This is one of the most elaborate archaeological sites in the world – more than 400 individual geoglyphs blanket a large hillside in the coast range. From close up it is difficult to discern what most of them represent, but from a distance images of people, llamas, circles, squares, chequerboard patterns and even a gigantic arrow become apparent.

Pintados lies seven km west of the Pan American highway, between Iquique and Antofagasta, nearly opposite the eastward turn-off to Pica. It's actually a derelict nitrate railyard with a number of ruined buildings and rusting rolling stock. It is a long, dry and dusty but not impossible walk from the highway – figure about 1½ to two hours each way, with a possible detour to avoid the caretaker's junkyard dogs. Don't forget to bring food and water. The only other way to visit the site is by car, taxi or tour from Iquique.

La Tirana

La Tirana, 72 km from Iquique at the north end of the Salar de Pintados in one of the sections of the Reserva Nacional Pampa del Tamarugal, is one of northern Chile's most important religious shrines. Every year between 12 and 18 July more than 30,000 pilgrims overrun the tiny village (permanent population – 250) to pay homage to the Virgin of Carmen by dancing in the streets with spectacular masks and costumes in a Carnival-like atmosphere,

The **Santuario de La Tirana** consists of a broad ceremonial plaza on which sits one of Chile's most unusual, even eccentric, churches. Although there are several restaurants around the plaza, there are no hotels or residenciales – pilgrims camp in the open spaces east of town. Have a look at the **Museo del Salitre** on the north side of the plaza, which has a wild, haphazard assortment of artefacts from the nitrate oficinas. Enter through the Almacén El Progreso.

RESERVA NACIONAL PAMPA DEL TAMARUGAL

The desolate pampas of the Atacama would seem an unlikely place for an extensive forest, but the dense groves of trees on both sides of the Ruta Panamericana, south of Pozo Almonte, are not a mirage. Although not a natural forest, the trees are in fact a native species – the tamarugo *(Prosopis tamarugo)* – which covered thousands of square km of the Pampa del Tamarugal until the species nearly disappeared under the pressures of woodcutting for the nitrate mines of the Norte Grande.

CONAF manages the reserve, and has restored much of the forest, which survives despite very saline soils and provides fodder for livestock and fuelwood for local people. Although there is no surface water, seedlings are planted in holes dug through the salt hardpan; after a few months' irrigation, they are able to reach the groundwater which has seeped down from the Andean foothills.

The 108,000-hectare Reserva Nacional Pampa del Tamarugal actually comprises three separate sections; the southern one is the largest. CONAF's visitor centre is 24 km south of Pozo Almonte, on the east side of the Ruta Panamericana, with excellent exhibits on the biology and ecology of the tamarugo and the pampas. On the west side it maintains a campground (shaded sites with tables and benches cost US$4 per night), while it also offers a limited number of beds in its guest house for US$8 per person. Despite the highway which bisects the reserve, it's a very pleasant and restful stopover.

MAMIÑA

Mamiña, 73 km east of Pozo Almonte at 2700 metres in the precordillera, has been a popular hot springs resort for residents of the region since the days of the nitrate boom, although it is much older than that. The **Pukará del Cerro Inca** is a prehispanic fortress on Cerro Ipla, while the **Iglesia de Nuestra Señora del Rosario** is a national historical monument dating from 1632. Its twin belltower is unique in Andean Chile.

Places to Stay

As a resort, Mamiña has no shortage of

accommodation in a variety of price ranges. *Residencial Sol de Ipla*, Calle Ipla s/n, is the most economical, charging US$11 per person with shared bath. *Hotel Tamarugal* (☎ 424365 in Iquique), also on Ipla, costs about US$17, as does *Hostería El Tambo de Mamiña*, Calle El Tambo s/n. The town's best is the historic *Hotel Refugio del Salitre* (☎ 420330 in Iquique), built during the nitrate era, where rates are US$24 per person. There are at least half a dozen alternatives for bathing.

Getting There & Away

From Iquique, numerous companies operate bus service to Mamiña, including Buses Lirima (☎ 413094) at Baquedano 823, Julita Santa Rosa (☎ 426368) at Latorre 973, Flonatur (weekdays at 4 pm) at Sargento Aldea 790, Transportes Rojas (☎ 424856) at Sargento Aldea 783, Turismo Mamiña (☎ 420330) at Latorre 779. Taxitur (☎ 422044) at Sargento Aldea 791 has taxi colectivos weekdays at 4 pm.

PICA

Pica, 119 km south-east of Iquique on the road from La Tirana, is another popular hot springs resort. Spanish conquistador Diego de Almagro skirmished with local Indians on his expedition to Chile in 1535, but later in the colonial era the area became famous for its wines and fruits, which supplied the mines at Huantajaya and beyond. In the 19th century, it supplied wheat, wine, figs, raisins and alfalfa to the nitrate mines of the pampas.

Pica was so dependent on outside water for its livelihood that the Spaniards developed an elaborate system of more than 15 km of tunnels, like the ganats of the Middle East, to carry ground water to the village. In the 1920s, American geographer Isaiah Bowman observed that:

> Unlike most desert towns Pica stands in the midst of the desert without the green valley that elsewhere gives a natural basis for settlement. From its wells and springs and a reservoir in the course of a small stream descending from the piedmont the closely compacted gardens of the village are watered with scrupulous economy.

When Iquique boomed with nitrate exports, the Tarapacá Water Company piped water from Pica to the coast to accommodate the city's growth. At the same time, the town became a sort of 'hill station' for the nitrate barons. Now it is a more democratic destination, with several hotels and restaurants. Its **Iglesia de San Andrés**, barely a century old, is built on the ruins of two earlier churches, destroyed by earthquakes.

Places to Stay & Eat

Pica has cheap accommodation at the *Hostería O'Higgins* (☎ 741322), Balmaceda 6, and the *Hotel San Andrés* (☎ 741319), Balmaceda 197, both of which charge about US$6 per person. *Motel El Tambo* (☎ 741320), General Ibañez 68, and *Motel Turismo* (☎ 741316), General Ibañez 57, are costlier alternatives. There are several inexpensive restaurants.

Camping *Camping Miraflores* (☎ 741333), the municipal site at Miraflores 4, charges about US$3 per person, but has been reported to be in disrepair.

Getting There & Away

From Iquique, Flonatur at Sargento Aldea 790 offers bus services to Pica at 9.30 am. Santa Rosa (☎ 426368), at Latorre 973, leaves daily at 5.30 pm while Taxitur (☎ 422044), at Sargento Aldea 791, has taxi colectivos in the morning.

Antofagasta Region

In pre-Columbian times, the sea was the main source of subsistence for the Changos Indians who populated the coast of the present-day Antofagasta region. A Spanish visitor to Cobija in 1581 counted more than 400 Changos, who fished from sealskin canoes and hunted guanaco in those areas where condensation from the winter camanchaca renewed pastures in the coastal range. This small population, though, could not support encomiendas and colonial Spaniards largely ignored the area. Moreover, the population could be hostile, often attacking Spanish naval parties which came ashore in search of water at scattered coastal oases.

The interior of the region was different. Although the landscape was utterly barren for nearly 200 km to the east – in all the Norte Grande, the meandering Río Loa is the only river whose flow consistently reaches the Pacific Ocean – irrigated agriculture sustained relatively large sedentary populations in oases like Calama, on the Loa, and San Pedro de Atacama. At higher elevations shepherds grazed llamas, but the area was generally too dry for the more delicate alpaca. In the very high and arid Puna de Atacama, however, there was too little moisture to support any permanent human habitation – even the 5916-metre peak of Licancábur has no permanent snow cover.

In the early 18th century, the Spaniards started Cobija, 130 km north of modern Antofagasta, as a customs house; after the wars of independence, this remote outpost became Bolivia's outlet to the sea, despite its poor and scanty fresh water supply. Nearly destroyed by an earthquake and tsunami in 1877, followed by the development of mineral nitrates from the interior, it was superseded by Antofagasta.

Nitrates brought Antofagasta into the modern world. Nineteenth and 20th-century nitrate ghost towns line both sides of the Ruta Panamericana and the highway to Calama, and the oficinas of María Elena and Pedro de Valdivia still function, but copper has supplanted nitrates in the regional and national economy. Chuquicamata, the largest open-pit mine in the world, dominates the mining sector, but fishing and tourism are growing in importance.

Books About the Atacama

There is a wealth of outstanding travel literature on the Atacama. Although much of it is out of print and not widely known, it is worth checking university libraries for books like American geographer Isaiah Bowman's *Desert Trails of Atacama* (New York, American Geographical Society 1924). Bowman travelled by mule over the length of the Norte Grande and across the high Andean passes between Chile and Argentina and Bolivia, recording his impressions and speculations, and photographing towns and villages off the beaten track. Decades later William Rudolph, for many years the chief engineer at Chuquicamata, followed Bowman's footsteps in *Vanishing Trails of Atacama* (American Geographical Society, 1963), which chronicled the changing human landscape of the desert. John Aarons and Claudio Vita-Finzi published an entertaining account of a Cambridge expedition to the Atacama in *The Useless Land* (London, Robert Hale, 1960).

ANTOFAGASTA

With a population of 221,000, Antofagasta is the Norte Grande's largest city. Its port handles most of the minerals from the Atacama, especially the copper from Chuquicamata, and is still an important import-export centre for Bolivia, which lost the region to Chile during the War of the Pacific.

Founded in 1870, the port of La Chimba (later renamed Antofagasta) replaced Cobija as the region's most important settlement after nitrate exploitation began in the Salar del Carmen, a short distance inland, and it became apparent that it provided the easiest rail route to the east. By 1877, the railroad reached halfway to Calama, but it was not completed to Oruro until after the War of the Pacific, when Chile acquired the territory.

After the war, Antofagasta exported tin and silver from Bolivia, borax from the Salar de Ascotán, as well as nitrates from the pampas. The latter commodity underwent a major expansion after the turn of the century, when Antofagasta's port proved inadequate and the nearby harbour of Mejillones took up much of the slack. Later, however, infrastructural improvements restored Antofagasta's pre-eminence and it came to handle the highest tonnage of any Pacific port in South America.

Like the rest of the Norte Grande,

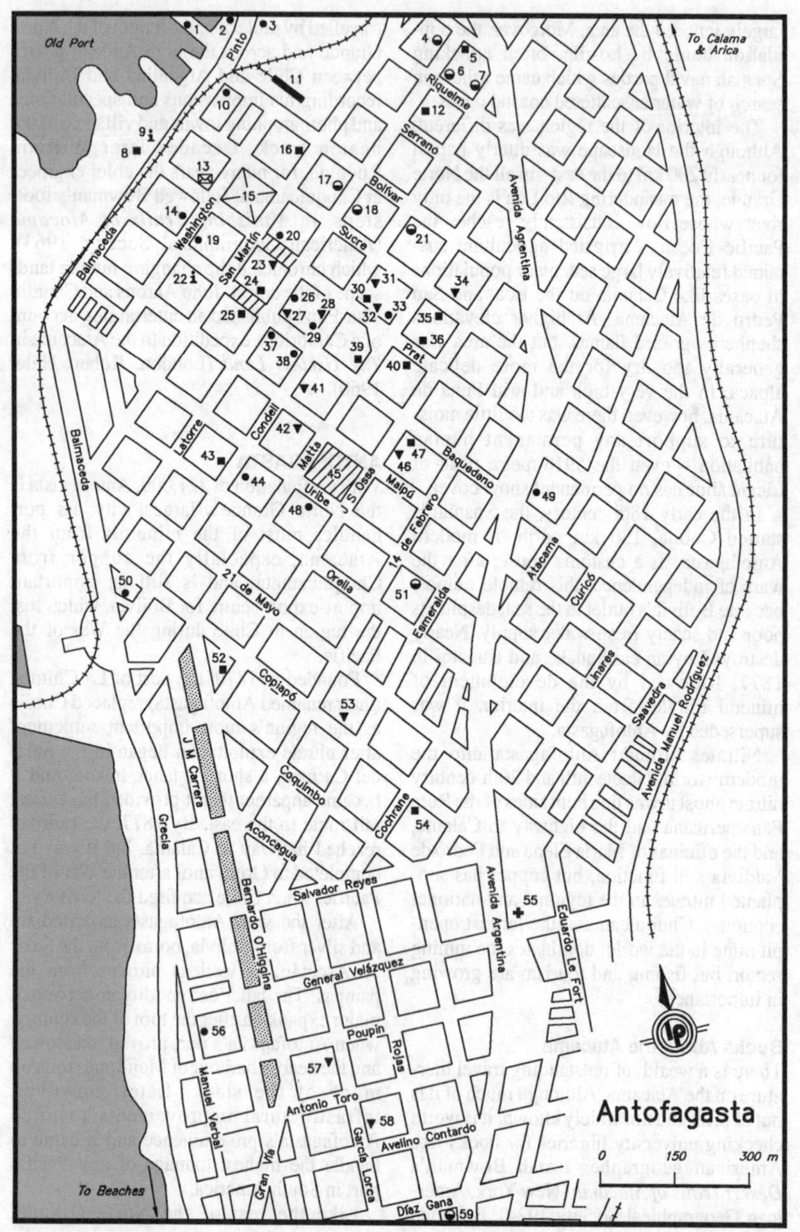
Old Port
To Calama & Arica
To Beaches
Antofagasta
0
150
300 m
Pinto
Balmaceda
Washington
San Martín
Latorre
Condell
Matta
Uribe
S Ossa
Maipú
Prat
Baquedano
Bolívar
Sucre
Serrano
Riquelme
Avenida Argentina
14 de Febrero
Esmeralda
Atacama
Curicó
Jinares
Saavedra
Avenida Manuel Rodríguez
21 de Mayo
Orella
Copiapó
Coquimbo
Aconcagua
J M Carrera
Grecia
Cochrane
Salvador Reyes
Bernardo O'Higgins
General Velázquez
Poupin
Rojas
Antonio Toro
Manuel Verbal
García Lorca
Gran Vía
Avelino Contardo
Díaz Gana
Eduardo Le Fort
Avenida Argentina
1
2
3
4
5
6
7
8
9
10
11
12
13
14
15
16
17
18
19
20
21
22
23
24
25
26
27
28
29
30
31
32
33
34
35
36
37
38
39
40
41
42
43
44
45
46
47
48
49
50
51
52
53
54
55
56
57
58
59

Antofagasta rarely receives any rainfall, but infrequent meteorological events can be catastrophic. In late 1991, a heavy storm caused a flash flood which obliterated the southern access road between the Ruta Panamericana and the city. In general, though, the city has an ideal climate, clear and dry, neither too hot nor too cold at any time of year. In the day, beach weather is the rule and at night, in the words of poet Neftalí Agrella, 'The moon hangs its lantern over Antofagasta'.

Orientation

Like Iquique, Antofagasta sits on a terrace at the foot of the coastal range, some 1350 km north of Santiago and 700 km south of Arica. The north-south Ruta Panamericana passes inland, east of the city, but there are paved northern and southern access roads (the latter a gravelled detour since the 1991 storms).

The western boundary of downtown Antofagasta' is the north-south Avenida Balmaceda, immediately east of the modern port, which veers north-east at Calle Uribe and eventually becomes Aníbal Pinto; to the south, it becomes Avenida Grecia. Within this central grid, bounded also by Bolívar and J S Ossa, streets trend from south-west to north-east; its focus is the Plaza Colón, the landmark clocktower of which is a replica of Big Ben (down to the sound of its bell), presented by the British community. In the area round the Plaza Colón there's a pleasant pedestrian mall.

■ PLACES TO STAY

5 Residencial Libertad
8 Hotel Antofagasta
12 Hotel San Marcos
16 Hotel San Martín
24 Hotel Plaza
25 Residencial Riojanita
30 Hotel Diego de Almagro
35 Hotel Rawaye
36 Residencial El Cobre
39 Hotel Astore
40 Residencial Paola
43 Hotel San Antonio
47 Hotel Rinconada
52 Hotel Brasil
54 Hotel América

▼ PLACES TO EAT

23 Café Caribe & Café Haití
27 Fiori di Gelatto
28 Pizzería D'Alfredo
31 Restaurant El Arriero
32 Restaurant Apoquindo
34 Casino de Bomberos
41 Restaurant Shanghai
42 Rincón Don Quijote
46 Restaurant Bavaria
53 Restaurant Un Dragón
57 Chifa Chong Hua (1)
58 Chifa Chong Hua (2)

OTHER

1 Muelle Salitrero
2 Terminal Pesquero (Fish Market)
3 SOQUIMICH
4 Buses Géminis
6 Buses Rurales
7 Buses Fichtur
9 Tourist Kiosk
10 Museo Regional
11 Railway Station
13 Post Office & Telex-Chile
14 Ladeco
15 Plaza Colón
17 Buses Flecha Dorada
18 Buses Fénix Pullman Norte
19 LAN-Chile
20 Fincard
21 Buses Flota Barrios
22 Sernatur (Tourist Office)
26 Cambio Inter-Santiago
29 CTC (Telephone)
33 ENTEL
37 Banco del Estado
38 Teatro Pedro de la Barra
44 Automóvil Club
45 Mercado Central
48 CTC (Telephone)
49 CONAF
50 Bolivian Consulate
51 Buses Tramaca
55 Hospital Regional
56 Argentine Consulate
59 Bus Terminal

Information

Tourist Office Sernatur has a very helpful office (☎ 264044) upstairs at Baquedano 360, open weekdays from 8.30 am to 1 pm and 3 to 7.30 pm. In addition, there is an information kiosk (☎ 224834) on Balmaceda at Prat, in front of the Hotel Antofagasta, open daily except Sunday from 9.30 am to 1.30 pm and 4.30 to 7.30 pm. On Sunday, it's open from 10.30 am to 2 pm.

Another good source of tourist information is the Automóvil Club de Chile (☎ 225332), Condell 2230.

Money It can be surprisingly difficult to change money in Antofagasta, but try Fincard, Prat 427 (open weekdays only) or Inter Santiago, Latorre 2528, No 12. Banco del Estado de Chile, at San Martín and Prat, seems to be the only bank which will change US dollar travellers' cheques and cash, but one reader was able to do both at Botillería Marcos, Latorre 2478.

Post & Telecommunications Correos de Chile is at Washington 2613, opposite the Plaza Colón, Telex-Chile next door at Washington 2601. CTC long-distance services are at Uribe 746 and at Condell 2527, while ENTEL is at Prat 649 close to the intersection with Matta.

Consulates The Argentine Consulate (☎ 222854), Manuel Verbal 1632, is open from 9 am to 2 pm, as is the Bolivian Consulate (☎ 221403), at Grecia 563, Oficina 23.

Cultural Centres For theatre and other performing arts, check the Teatro Pedro de la Barra, Condell 2495 at Baquedano.

National Parks For information on natural attractions of the region, contact CONAF (☎ 222250) at Avenida Argentina 2510.

Travel Agencies Antofagasta has a glut of travel agencies, including Turismo Cristóbal (☎ 224710) at Balmaceda 2575, Tatio Travel Service (☎ 263562) at Latorre 2579, No 20, and North Gate Tour (☎ 221565) at Baquedano 498, Nos 14 and 15. For less conventional destinations and tours, try Chile Turismo Aventura (☎ 221835) at Sucre 379, Dept 41-C, or Atacama Desert Expeditions (☎ 228141) at Esmeralda 2898.

Medical Services The Hospital Regional (☎ 269009) is at Avenida Argentina 1962.

Things to See

Like Iquique, Antofagasta is a 19th-century city whose architecture is not stereotypically Latin American – the British community has left a visible imprint not just through the **Torre Reloj** replica of Big Ben and the bandshell of the **Plaza Colón**, but also in the **Barrio Histórico** between the Plaza and the old port, which features many wooden Victorian and Georgian buildings. The **Muelle Salitrero** (Nitrate Pier) at the foot of Bolívar, for instance, was the work of Melbourne Clark, an early partner in the Tarapacá Nitrate Company. At the entrance to the pier is the former **Resguardo Marítimo** (Coast Guard), built in 1910.

A short distance to the south, at Balmaceda and Bolívar, is the former **Gobernación Marítima** (Port Authority), which houses the **Museo Regional** (Regional Museum), closed for remodelling in early 1992; it should reopen by the time this book appears. Across the street is the former **Aduana** (Customs House), originally erected in Mejillones in 1866 by a Chilean mining company and transported to its present site in 1888. Across Bolívar is the old **Estación Ferrocarril**, the terminus of the Antofagasta-La Paz railway, which is also being restored. It dates from 1887, though its 2nd storey was added in 1900.

To the north, across from the colourful **Terminal Pesquero** (Fish Market), is the **Casa de Adminstración** (Administrative Office) of the Sociedad Química de Chile (SOQUIMICH), once the Lautaro Nitrate Company and then the Anglo Lautaro Nitrate Company before its nationalisation in 1968.

Festivals

February 14, anniversary of the founding of

Antofagasta, is a major local holiday. There are fireworks at the Balneario Municipal, at the south end of Avenida Grecia.

Places to Stay – bottom end

Residencial Paola (☎ 222208), Prat 766, is a friendly, clean and quiet place, with rooms arranged around a central lounge for US$5 per person. Across the street, *Residencial El Cobre* (☎ 225162) at Prat 749 has clean but barren rooms for US$4 per person. It's funky but friendly, attracting many budget travellers. Others in this range include *Residencial Lautaro* (☎ 223727) at Latorre 3202, *Residencial Ríojanita* (☎ 268652) at Baquedano 464, and *Hotel Brasil* (☎ 228237) at J S Ossa 1973.

Hotel Rawaye (☎ 225399) at Sucre 762 is friendly, clean and excellent value at US$6/10 for a single/double with shared bath. *Residencial Libertad* (☎ 221509), Latorre 3064, is comparably priced.

Camping South of Antofagasta, there are campsites at Km 9 *(Camping Las Garumas,* (☎ 247758) and Km 11 *(Camping Rucamóvil,* (☎ 231913). Both charge around US$8 per site.

Places to Stay – middle

Hostal del Sol (☎ 228302), Latorre 3162, charges US$11/17, while *Hotel América* (☎ 263703), Copiapó 1208, is slightly dearer. About the same price is the unusual *Hotel Tatio* (☎ 244761), Avenida Grecia 1000, built of reconditioned tour buses with shared baths.

At *Hotel Rinconada* (☎ 261139), Baquedano 810, *Hotel San Antonio* (☎ 268857), Condell 2235, and *Hotel San Martín* (☎ 263503), San Martín 2781, rates are about US$17/24. *Hotel San Marcos* (☎ 251763), Latorre 2946, has rooms for US$20/30 with private bath. It's clean, with hot water and its own restaurant.

Places to Stay – top end

At *Hotel Diego de Almagro* (☎ 268331), at Condell 2624 near the corner with Prat, and *Hotel Astore* (☎ 267439), Matta 2537, rates are about US$26/34, while *Hotel Plaza* (☎ 269046), Baquedano 461, charges US$28/43 with private bath and TV. It also has its own restaurant and bar and is a fairly quiet place. *Hotel Antofagasta* (☎ 268259), on the beachfront at Balmaceda 2575, is the city's largest hotel, with rooms from about US$40/49.

Places to Eat

For my money, the best choice is the unpretentious *Terminal Pesquero* at the north end of the old port, where a collection of stands peddle tasty fresh shellfish. It is especially lively on Saturday mornings, but if you find sea urchins unappealing, the masses of pelicans which crowd the pier for scraps should at least prove amusing. Try also the *Mercado Central* on Ossa between Maipú and Uribe. Carnivores will find *El Arriero* at Condell 2644 a fine parrilla, with excellent service. The *Casino de Bomberos*, Sucre 763, has good set lunches for about US$2.

The popular *Apoquindo*, Prat 616, resembles the Dino's chain of southern Chile, serving a range of drinks, sweets and snacks. Another dependable but uninspired chain is *Bavaria*, J S Ossa 2428. For snacks, coffee, superb ice cream and other desserts, try *Fiori di Gelatto*, Latorre 2500. Another good choice for cakes and snacks is *Cari*, on Matta between Baquedano and Prat. For coffee better than soluble Nescafé, try *Café Caribe* at Prat 486 or *Café Haití* at Prat 482.

Like other northern Chilean cities, Antofagasta has an array of good and inexpensive Chinese restaurants, including *Chifa Wai Ming* at Las Cruces 784 and Avenida Ejército 086, *Un Dragón* at Copiapó 951, *Shanghai* at Latorre 2426, and *Chifa Chong Hua* at García Lorca 1468 and 1569.

Other recommended places include *Rincón Don Quijote* at Maipú 642, *Casa Vecchia* at O'Higgins 1456, and *La Papa Nostra* at Medina 052. *D'Alfredo*, at Condell 2539, has many varieties of pizza. About 15 minutes' walk from the centre is the good, inexpensive *Restaurant Los Andes*, 14 de Febrero 1945.

Getting There & Away

Air Antofagasta's Cerro Moreno Airport is 25 km north of the city, at the south end of the Mejillones Peninsula. Ladeco's airport bus (US$1) leaves one hour before flight time, or you can share a taxi to either LAN-Chile or Ladeco flights from the stand opposite LAN-Chile's downtown offices for US$2.

LAN-Chile (☎ 265151), at Washington 2552, has 10 flights a week from Santiago, four of them continuing to Iquique and Arica. There are 13 flights from Antofagasta to Santiago, four of them originating in Calama and four in Arica (with stopovers in Iquique). The remainder stop over in Copiapó.

Ladeco (☎ 269170), at Washington 2589 near the corner with Prat, has flights from Santiago every morning (continuing to Iquique and Arica) and every afternoon (except Thursday). On Tuesday, Friday and Saturday its afternoon flights continue to Calama, and some to Iquique. Return schedules are similar.

Bus The Terminal Rodoviario is at Avenida Argentina 1155, in the south end of town, but most companies operate out of their own terminals in the centre. Many have buses to Santiago, Arica and intermediate destinations.

Buses Tramaca (☎ 261770), at Uribe 936 near the intersection with 4 de Febrero, has frequent buses to Calama, plus daily service to Arica, Iquique, Santiago and intermediate points. Tramaca also handles tickets for the Calama-Oruro (Bolivia) railway.

Buses Atalhualpa, operating from the same office, crosses the Andes to Salta, Argentina, Saturday afternoons at 4 pm in summer. The fare is about US$33. Géminis (☎ 263968), Latorre 3055, also goes to Salta. Buses to Argentina fill rapidly, so buy your ticket as far in advance as possible.

Flota Barrios (☎ 261875), Condell 2764 between Bolívar and Sucre, has daily buses to most of the same destinations. Buses Flecha Dorada (☎ 264487, Latorre 2751, serves Calama, Santiago and Arica. Fénix Pullman Norte (☎ 225293), San Martín 2717, runs nearly identical routes. Fichtur (☎ 222431), Condell 3043, offers luxurious bus cama service to Copiapó, La Serena, and Santiago.

Several companies operate from the Buses Rurales terminal at Riquelme 513, including Fepstur (☎ 227345) and Chadday (☎ 266724), both of which go to Mejillones, and Chile Bus (☎ 251741), which covers most major stops on the Ruta Panamericana between Arica and Iquique. Buses Libac (☎ 247569), at the Terminal Rodoviario, connects Antofagasta with Calama and southerly destinations on the Ruta Panamericana, as far as Santiago.

Three lines go to Tocopilla, including Buses Camus (☎ 247536) and Turis Norte (☎ 247564) at the Terminal Rodoviario, and Incatur (☎ 247566) at Maipú 554. If Turis Norte is operating the coastal route from Tocopilla to Iquique, take advantage of this route just to see the coastline.

Typical fares from Antofagasta are: Calama US$4, Iquique US$10, Arica US$13, and Santiago US$24. Fichtur's bus cama to Santiago costs US$46.

Car Rental Rental cars are available from Hertz (☎ 269043), Balmaceda 2566; Budget (☎ 251745), Prat 206; Galerias (☎ 268311), Orella 964; S Izquierdo (☎ 263788), Prat 801; and American's (☎ 222803), Condell 2707.

AROUND ANTOFAGASTA

North of Antofagasta, a paved highway leads to Mejillones and Tocopilla, beyond which a spectacular but sometimes rugged highway goes to Iquique – if you have time and any possibility of taking this road, do not hesitate to do so. Between Mejillones and Tocopilla are the fascinating ghost towns of Cobija and Gatico.

La Portada

Probably the most photographed sight on the Antofagasta coast, La Portada is an offshore stack in which the stormy Pacific has eroded an impressive natural arch. It is about 16 km north of Antofagasta, on a lateral off the highway before Cerro Moreno airport. Take colectivo No 20 from Latorre and Prat, 20 minutes before every even-numbered hour.

Minas de Plata

Above the city are the remains of a 19th-century British-Bolivian silver refining plants; take colectivo No 3 and ask for Minas de Plata.

MEJILLONES

Once an important port in its own right, Mejillones is now a weekend bathing resort for residents of Antofagasta, 60 km to the south. Its permanent population is about 4000. At one time the residents mined fossil guano from the hills above the town and transported it to the port by an aerial tramway.

Mejillones has inexpensive accommodation at *Residencial Elizabeth* (☎ 621568), Almirante Latorre 440. For bus service from Antofagasta, try Fepstur (☎ 227345) and Chadday (☎ 266724), both of which are at the terminal at Riquelme 513.

Cobija & Gatico

Only a few km apart, 130 km north of Antofagasta and 60 km south of Tocopilla, Cobija and Gatico are desolate ghost towns whose few remaining families eke out a living from fishing and collecting seaweed. In the early 19th century, though, Cobija was a flourishing settlement which was Bolivia's outlet to the Pacific, serving the mines of the altiplano despite its precarious water supply, whose distribution reflected the early republican hierarchy. According to Isaiah Bowman:

> The best well close to the shore was reserved for the government officials and garrison. The rest of the populace was supplied with water from springs in the hills back of town, conducted in pipes and kept under lock and key, the daily quota being delivered to each family. More water might be purchased from a carrier who brought it from the interior. In those days the present of a barrel of sweet water from southern Chile or Peru was highly esteemed.

So was fresh produce. In 1851, when Cobija had a population of 1500, a North American seaman recorded the eagerness with which the settlement's residents greeted a shipment of supplies from the north:

> It was a matter of no little interest to witness the avidity of the population on landing the garden-stuff brought from Arica. Probably within ten minutes after the first boat-load of bags had been landed, all over town Indians, including soldiers, might have been seen stripping the rind from green sugar-cane...housekeepers bearing away piles of maize, sweet potatoes...an hour later the beach – which had served as the impromptu market-place – was again bare.

Today, if you visit Cobija, bring your own supplies. After an earthquake and tsunami nearly obliterated the town in 1877, its population declined rapidly; by 1907, it had only 35 inhabitants and now there are even fewer. You may be able to purchase fish, but everything else is at a premium except for camping among the atmospheric adobe walls overlooking the sea. In only a few places are the ruins obvious, such as the plaza, the church and the cemetery (with its wooden fences and crosses and a few crumbling adobe crypts), but for the most part the visitor has to guess the identity of any given building. Offshore stacks, stained white with guano, look like distant snow peaks across the ocean, especially at sunset.

TOCOPILLA

Tocopilla, with 22,000 inhabitants, is 190 km north of Antofagasta. Despite its isolation, it is an important nitrate port for the still operating oficinas of Pedro de Valdivia and María Elena. Since 1929, it has been the site of Codelco's thermoelectric plant, which serves the copper mining complex of Chuquicamata. Fishing is also an important industry. While Tocopilla has no major attractions in its own right, it is the last town on the spectacular coastal highway to Iquique, which is well worth the extra time and trouble it entails.

Tocopilla does have a **Museo Arqueológico** at Avenida Pinto and 21 de Mayo, 2nd floor. Cheap residenciales include *Residen-*

cial Royal (☎ 811488) at 21 de Mayo 1988 and *Residencial Sonia* (☎ 813086) at Washington 1329, both of which charge about US$4. Slightly upscale are *Hotel Chungará* (☎ 811036) at 21 de Mayo 1440, which charges US$13 per person, and *Hotel Vucina* (☎ 813088), at 21 de Mayo 2069, at US$17 per person. The best restaurant is the *Club de la Unión*.

Buses Turis Norte, 21 de Mayo 1348, operates between Tocopilla and Antofagasta, and sometimes on the coastal route to Iquique – inquire at their offices in Antofagasta. Hitching may not be totally impossible, but it certainly would be difficult.

María Elena, Pedro de Valdivia & the Nitrate Ghost Towns

Just 10 km east of the point where the Ruta Panamericana crosses the Tocopilla-Chuquicamata highway is María Elena (population 7700), founded in 1926 and now one of the last operating nitrate oficinas in the Atacama. Built on a orderly plan which looks better on paper than in practice, its streets form a pattern like the Union Jack.

Built as a company town (though it is now a municipality), María Elena offers such amenities as a theatre, supermarket, library, hospital, market and administrative offices. There is also a museum, open Monday to Saturday from 8 am to 1 pm and 2 to 8 pm Monday to Saturdays, Sunday from 10 am to 1 pm. Tours of the nitrate plant are possible with a week's advance notice to the SOQUIMICH public relations office (☎ 632731) in María Elena.

From Antofagasta, Buses Tramaca (☎ 261770), Uribe 936, has buses to María Elena which continue to Calama. Flota Barrios (☎ 261875), Condell 2764 in Antofagasta, also goes to María Elena. While there is no lodging in town, there is good camping on the Río Loa on the east side of the Ruta Panamericana. Decent food is available at the *Restaurante Yerco* and the *Restaurante Club Social*.

Pedro de Valdivia, slightly larger than María Elena, is 40 km to the south. Founded in 1930, it is open to visits by the public; inquire at the gate. Meals are available at the *Club Pedro de Valdivia*. Buses Tramaca and Flota Barrios connect the town with Antofagasta.

There are dozens of nitrate ghost towns in the Antofagasta region, lining both sides of the highway between Baquedano and Calama, and along the Ruta Panamericana north of the Tocopilla-Chuquicamata highway.

Baquedano

Halfway between Antofagasta and Calama, Baquedano was a major rail junction where the *Longino* (Longitudinal Railway) met the Antofagasta-La Paz line. The **Museo Ferroviario** is an open-air railroad museum, but a freight line still runs from here to the Argentine border at Socompa, where it is possible to make connections for Salta. This train is sporadic, agonisingly slow and truly filthy, but it will take really persistent passengers.

Quillagua

Quillagua is an oasis on the Río Loa, marking the border between the regions of Antofagasta and Tarapacá, 281 km northwest of the city of Antofagasta. For travellers, it is most noteworthy for thorough and tiresome customs checks southbound, since Tarapacá is a customs-free zone. Agricultural inspections are also time-consuming – do not carry any fresh fruit or meat.

CALAMA

Calama (population 120,000), 220 km from Antofagasta, claims to be the highest altitude city in Chile and the commercial centre for the world's largest open-pit copper mines at nearby Chuquicamata, whose perpetual plume of eastward-blowing dust and smoke gives its location away from a great distance in the cloudless desert. Calama is the starting point for visits to 'Chuqui' (a company town which is in fact higher than Calama), indigenous villages like Chiu Chiu, the oases of San Pedro de Atacama and Toconao, and the El Tatio Geysers. It's now the terminus of passenger service on the Calama-Oruro

(Bolivia) railway, which formerly ran all the way to Antofagasta.

Orientation

Calama sits 2700 metres above sea level, on the north bank of the Río Loa, the only Chilean river between the Peruvian border and Copiapó to reach the sea. Though it has sprawled with the influx of labourers who prefer its slightly milder climate to that of Chuquicamata, its central core is pedestrian-friendly. The modest Plaza 23 de Marzo, named for the date of its occupation by Chile in the War of the Pacific, is the focus of the centre, but most visitors will be interested in the sights of the Atacama outback.

Information

Tourist Office The municipal tourist office (☎ 212654, extension 60) is at Latorre 1689, near the corner with Vicuña Mackenna. It's open weekdays from 8.30 am to 1 pm and 3 to 6 pm (though it sometimes stays open later), and is very well informed on local matters.

Another good source of information is ACCHI, the Automóvil Club (☎ 212770), at Avenida Ecuador 1901.

Money Changing money has been difficult in Calama, but according to recent reports Raúl Villaroel González has opened a new cambio at Sotomayor 1818, with good rates and no commission for travellers' cheques.

One LP correspondent successfully cashed travellers' cheques at a clothing store called Valle de La Luna, on Ramírez, while another suggested the Casatel electronic shop at Ramírez 1183. Still, it is a good idea to arrive in Calama with some Chilean cash.

If desperate, try Banco de Chile, at Vivar 1995 near the corner with Vargas, the Banco de Crédito at Sotomayor 2002, or Banco O'Higgins at Sotomayor 2080.

Post & Telecommunications Correos de Chile is at Vicuña Mackenna 2167. CTC has long-distance telephone offices at Abaroa 1756, Abaroa 1987, and Vargas 1927. ENTEL is at Hurtado de Mendoza 2139.

Consulate The Bolivian Consulate (☎ 211976) is at Vicuña Mackenna 2020. It's open weekdays from 9.30 am to 12.30 pm, and from 4.30 to 6.30 pm.

Travel Agencies Calama has numerous travel agencies which arrange excursions to the more remote parts of the desert – though some of these trips can be arranged more cheaply from San Pedro de Atacama. Among them are Turismo El Sol (☎ 210152) at Abaroa 1781; Talikuna (☎ 212595) at General Velásquez 1948; Copper Tour (☎ 212414) at Sotomayor 2016; Tuyaj Tour (☎ 312864) at Latorre 1724; Loa Desert Adventure (☎ 212200) at Bañados Espinosa 2191; Tourism Adventure Desert (☎ 212242) at Latorre 1602; and Turismo Quitor (☎ 314159), Ramírez 2116, 2nd floor. For itineraries, see Organised Tours below.

Medical Services Calama's hospital (☎ 212347) is at Avenida Granaderos near the corner with Cisterna, a few blocks north of Plaza 23 de Marzo.

Things to See

Parque El Loa Newly built at the south end of town, Parque El Loa features a scale-model of the famous church at Chiu Chiu, with its twin belltowers, and a riverside swimming pool. It also includes the **Museo Arqueológico y Etnológico** (Museum of Archaeology & Ethnology), with exhibits on the peoples of the Atacama.

Organised Tours

Several popular circuits are available from or through the travel agencies listed above. Itineraries vary slightly, but the most complete goes from Calama to the El Tatio Geysers and back via traditional villages like Chiu Chiu, Caspana, Ayquina and Toconce, costing about US$25. It is possible to take a separate tour from Calama to these villages, all of which feature traditional Andean churches.

Other tours go to San Pedro de Atacama via the Valle de La Luna (Valley of the Moon), then spend the night in San Pedro

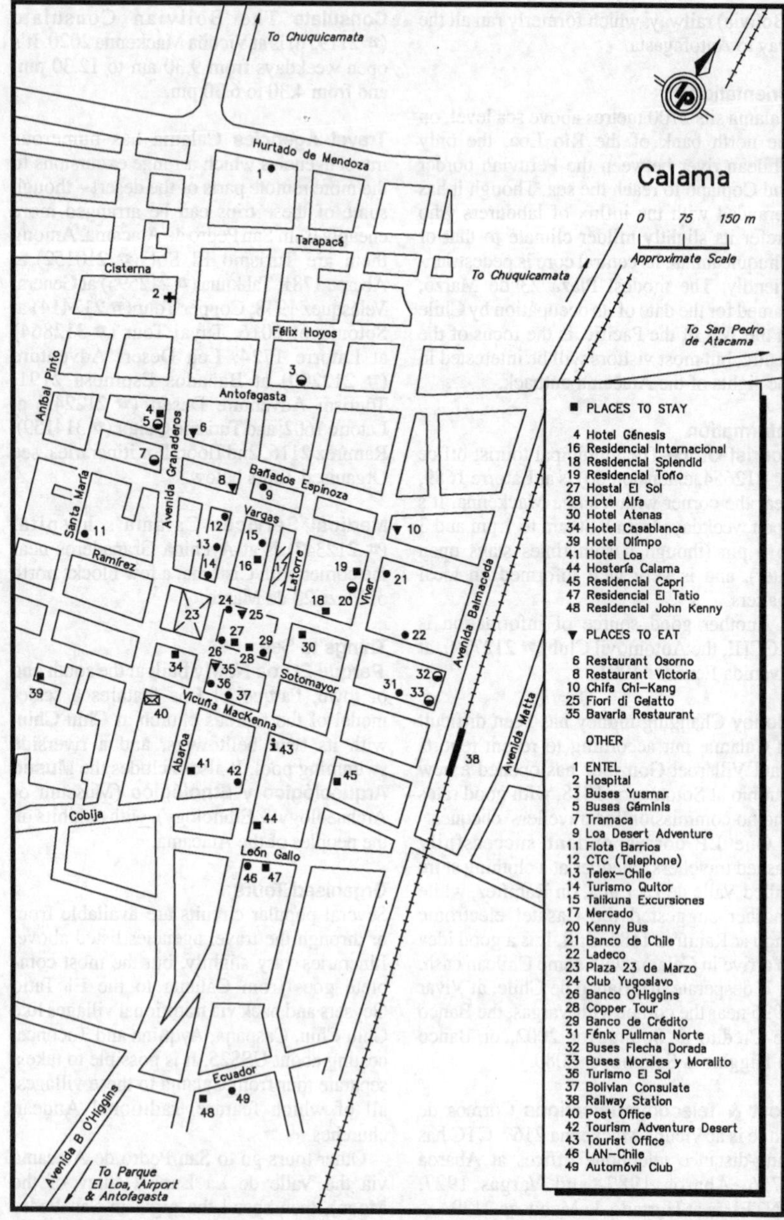

Calama
0 75 150 m
Approximate Scale
To Chuquicamata
To Chuquicamata
To San Pedro de Atacama
To Parque El Loa, Airport & Antofagasta
Hurtado de Mendoza
Tarapacá
Cisterna
Félix Hoyos
Antofagasta
Bañados Espinoza
Vargas
Ramírez
Latorre
Vivar
Sotomayor
Vicuña MacKenna
Abaroa
Cobija
León Gallo
Ecuador
Aníbal Pinto
Santa María
Avenida Granaderos
Avenida Balmaceda
Avenida Matta
Avenida B O'Higgins
PLACES TO STAY
4 Hotel Génesis
16 Residencial Internacional
18 Residencial Splendid
19 Residencial Toño
27 Hostal El Sol
28 Hotel Alfa
30 Hotel Atenas
34 Hotel Casablanca
39 Hotel Olímpo
41 Hotel Loa
44 Hostería Calama
45 Residencial Capri
47 Residencial El Tatio
48 Residencial John Kenny
PLACES TO EAT
6 Restaurant Osorno
8 Restaurant Victoria
10 Chifa Chi-Kang
25 Fiori di Gelatto
35 Bavaria Restaurant
OTHER
1 ENTEL
2 Hospital
3 Buses Yusmar
5 Buses Géminis
7 Tramaca
9 Loa Desert Adventure
11 Flota Barrios
12 CTC (Telephone)
13 Telex-Chile
14 Turismo Quitor
15 Talikuna Excursiones
17 Mercado
20 Kenny Bus
21 Banco de Chile
22 Ladeco
23 Plaza 23 de Marzo
24 Club Yugoslavo
26 Banco O'Higgins
28 Copper Tour
29 Banco de Crédito
31 Fénix Pullman Norte
32 Buses Flecha Dorada
33 Buses Morales y Moralito
36 Turismo El Sol
37 Bolivian Consulate
38 Railway Station
40 Post Office
42 Tourism Adventure Desert
43 Tourist Office
46 LAN-Chile
49 Automóvil Club

before visiting the El Tatio Geysers and returning via Caspana and Chiu Chiu for about US$35, including a box lunch but not accommodation in San Pedro. Another alternative visits the Salar de Atacama, including the picturesque village of Toconao, for US$20 from San Pedro de Atacama. In general, it seems cheaper and more convenient to make arrangements for El Tatio in San Pedro rather than in Calama, not only are they slightly cheaper from San Pedro, but are also shorter and a bit less tiring. Remember that tours to El Tatio leave as early as 4 am.

Festivals

Calama's major holiday is March 23, when the city celebrates the arrival of Chilean troops during the War of the Pacific with fireworks and other events.

Places to Stay – bottom end

Residencial Capri (☎ 212870), Vivar 1639, is tolerable by low-budget standards, with rooms at US$3 per person, but some travellers avoid it. *Residencial Toño* (☎ 211185), Vivar 1970, has been popular with foreign visitors for years. It has clean sheets and provides lots of blankets for US$4 per person, and is fairly quiet if nothing special. Also, try the nearby *Hotel Los Andes*. In the same range is *Hotel Génesis* (☎ 212841), at Avenida Granaderos 2148.

Residencial El Tatio, (☎ 212284), León Gallo 1987, has reasonably good rooms at US$7 per person, but has plumbing problems and sometimes lacks hot water. Clean, secure and recently renovated *Residencial Splendid* (☎ 212141), Ramírez 1960, is popular with travelling salespeople and the like. Singles/doubles with shared bath cost US$7/10, while more expensive rooms have private baths. Rates are similar at *Residencial Internacional*, at General Velásquez 1976 near the intersection with Vargas, which several travellers have recommended as good value. *Hotel Atenas* (☎ 212666), Ramírez 1961, has small, neat rooms for US$8/11 with shared bath. *Hotel Loa* (☎ 211693), Abaroa 1617, offers rooms with shared bath for US$8/12.

Places to Stay – middle

At *Residencial John Kenny* (☎ 211430), Ecuador 1991, rates start at US$9/17, while rooms with private bath cost US$12 per person. A step up is *Hostal El Sol* (☎ 211235), Sotomayor 2064, at US$22/27, while *Hotel Olímpo* (☎ 212389), Avenida Santa María 1673, charges US$24/30. Also worth trying is *Hotel Casablanca* (☎ 211722), opposite the Plaza 23 de Marzo at Sotomayor 2161, which has bright, neat rooms for US$26/32.

Places to Stay – top end

Hotel Alfa (☎ 211565), Sotomayor 2016, charges US$39/47. Near the top of the range is the very pleasant if now a bit rundown *Hostería Calama* (☎ 211115), Latorre 1521. At US$48/60, its rates include private bath and breakfast. On the southern outskirts of town, near the airport, is the new luxury *Hotel Topotel* (☎ 212208), Camino al Aeropuerto 1392, which is over the top at US$83/111.

Places to Eat

One of the more interesting places is the local market, on Latorre between Ramírez and Vargas – try the typical Chilean cheese known as 'quesillo'. *Restaurant Victoria*, at Vargas 2102 near the corner with Abaroa, is an ordinary budget restaurant, as is *Restaurant Osorno*, upstairs at Granaderos 2013B near the corner with Espinoza. For Chinese food, try *Chifa Tong Fong*, on Ramírez between Granaderos and Santa María, and *Chifa Chi-Kang* at Vivar 2037 near the corner with Espinoza.

Club Yugoslavo, Abaroa 1869 facing the Plaza 23 de Marzo, is a slightly more upmarket place. Around the corner is the *Bavaria Restaurant*, Sotomayor 2035, part of a dependable but uninspiring nation-wide chain. Near the market, *Restaurant Sándolo*, Vivar 1982, is a parrilla which also offers fish and other seafood.

For fine ice cream, other desserts, sandwiches and coffee, head to *Fiori di Gelatto* at Ramírez 2099, on the Plaza.

Getting There & Away

From Calama you can head north to Iquique and Arica, south-west to Antofagasta, east by train to Bolivia, or by bus to Salta, in Argentina.

Air Aeropuerto El Loa (☎ 212348) is a short cab ride south of Calama, but there are reports it is difficult to get a cab from the airport to town.

Ladeco (☎ 312626), Ramírez 1937, has Monday, Tuesday, Thursday and Saturday flights from Calama to Antofagasta and Santiago; from Santiago there are Tuesday, Friday and Saturday flights, which continue to Iquique, and a Thursday flight which does not. LAN-Chile (☎ 211394), at Latorre 1499 near the corner with León Gallo, has Monday, Wednesday, Friday and Sunday flights from Calama to Antofagasta and Santiago; from Santiago, on the same days, it stops over in Copiapó.

Bus – domestic Calama has no central bus terminal, but most bus companies are fairly central and within a few blocks of each other.

Tramaca (☎ 312587), Avenida Granaderos 3048, has frequent buses to Antofagasta, plus several daily to Santiago, Arica and Iquique. Flecha Dorada (☎ 212472), Ramírez 1802 at Balmaceda, has daily buses to Santiago via Antofagasta and Copiapó, and to Iquique and Arica. Flota Barrios (☎ 211497), Ramírez 2298, serves the same destinations along the Ruta Panamericana, as does Fénix Pullman Norte (☎ 211282), Sotomayor 1808. Kenny Bus (☎ 212514), Vivar 1954, serves Iquique via María Elena and Pozo Almonte.

Buses Géminis (☎ 211536), at Avenida Granaderos 2034 near the corner with Espinoza, has daily buses to Santiago, Antofagasta, Arica and Iquique. It also has buses to San Pedro de Atacama on Sundays only. Buses Morales y Moralito (☎ 212671), Sotomayor 1802 at Balmaceda, goes to San Pedro three times weekly. Buses Yusmar (☎ 212173), Antofagasta 2041, goes intermittently to Toconao for US$4.

Typical fares from Calama are: San Pedro de Atacama US$2.50, Toconao US$4, Antofagasta US$4, Iquique US$7, Arica US$9, and Santiago US$24.

Bus – international In summer, every Wednesday at 6.30 pm, Géminis crosses the Andes to Salta, Argentina, for US$40 single. Tramaca covers the same route, leaving Wednesdays at 4.30, for US$45. These buses are invariably full, so make reservations as far in advance as possible.

Train Every Friday at 11 pm there is an ordinary train service from Calama to Ollagüe, on the Bolivian border, with connections to Uyuni (US$11) and Oruro (US$18). Tickets are available either at Tramaca or at the Calama train station (☎ 212004), Balmaceda 1777 at Sotomayor; you may also be able to purchase tickets at the Tramaca office at the Terminal Norte in Santiago. Show your passport when buying tickets and be sure to obtain a Bolivian visa if you need one (see above for consulate information). Temperatures can drop well below freezing on this route, so bring warm clothing and sleeping gear.

Getting Around

There are a number of car rental agencies in Calama, including Hertz (☎ 211380) at Latorre 1510, Budget (☎ 211076) at Punta de Diamante s/n, Automotríz Miranda (☎ 211175) at Granaderos 2625, Maxo (212285) at Abaroa 2070, and Comercial Maipo (☎ 331592) at Balmaceda 3950. To visit the El Tatio Geysers, rent a Jeep or pickup truck – ordinary passenger cars lack sufficient clearance for the rugged roads in the area.

Taxi colectivos to Chuquicamata leave from Abaroa, between Vicuña Mackenna and Sotomayor. The fare is about US$0.75.

CHUQUICAMATA

Chuquicamata (or just Chuqui) is a company town, 16 km north of Calama, with enormous copper reserves which have made Chile the world's greatest producer of that commodity. Foreign capital originally financed the exploitation of its relatively low-grade ores, with open-pit techniques originally developed in the western USA. Today, it is the world's largest open-pit copper mine – nearly 400 metres deep – and its largest single supplier of copper. Despite Chile's attempts at economic diversification, Chuqui still provides half the country's total copper output and at least 25% of its annual export income. In total, copper accounts for 40% of Chilean exports.

Prospectors discovered the Chuquicamata deposits in 1911, but the original North American owner sold it to the Guggenheim brothers of New York City, who in turn sold it to the US Anaconda Copper Mining Company, which began excavations in 1915. Out of nothing, the company created a city (current population 30,000), with housing, schools, cinemas, shops, a hospital and clinics, and many other amenities, although many accused the company of taking out much more than it put back into the country. At the same time, labour unrest added to the resentment felt toward the huge, powerful corporation.

By the 1960s, Chile's three largest mines (the others were Anaconda's El Salvador, in the Atacama Region, and Kennecott's El Teniente, in Rancagua) accounted for more than 80% of copper production, 60% of total exports, and 80% of tax revenues. Anaconda, although it paid a greater percentage of its profits in taxes than other mining companies, became the target of those who advocated nationalisation of the industry.

Leftists in Congress – including Salvador Allende – had introduced nationalisation bills since the early 1950s, but support for nationalisation grew even amongst Christian Democrats and other non-leftists. During the Christian Democratic government of President Frei in the late 1960s, Chile gained a majority shareholding in the Chilean assets of Anaconda and Kennecott, partly because the companies feared expropriation under a future leftist regime.

In 1971 Congress approved nationalisation of the industry by a large majority, which even included rightist elements. After Allende's overthrow in 1973, the new military junta agreed to compensate companies for loss of assets, but retained ownership through the Corporación del Cobre de Chile (Codelco), although it has encouraged the return of foreign capital.

Chuquicamata is a clean, well ordered company town whose landscape is a constant reminder of its history. The modern football stadium is the **Estadio Anaconda**, while the **Auditorio Sindical** is a huge theatre, the interior mural of which commemorates a strike in the 1960s in which several workers died. A prominent statue near Relaciones Públicas honours the workers who operated equipment like the monstrous power shovel which towers nearby and created the huge excavations and the gigantic piles of tailings which surround the town.

Copper-Processing Given Chuqui's low-grade ore, only large quantities make production economical. The ore is quarried by blasting and power shovels; at the mining stage, material is classified as ore or waste depending on its copper content. Sufficiently rich material is dumped into a crusher, which reduces it to fine particles. The metal is then separated from the rock by a flotation process.

This flotation process separates and concentrates the copper through chemically induced differences in surface tension, carrying it to the surface of pools of water – the large pools of blue solution at the processing works are the concentrators where this process takes place. The copper concentrate becomes a thick slurry from which smelting extracts the final product.

Places to Eat

Good lunches are available at the *Club de Empleados* and the *Arco Iris Center*, both across from the plaza on Avenida J M Carrera, and the *Club de Obreros*, on Mariscal Alcázar two blocks south of the stadium. Try also *Restaurant Carloncho*, on the Avenida Comercial O'Higgins.

Organised Tours

Relaciones Públicas (The Public Relations Office) offers three-hour tours of the mine and smelter plant on weekdays. Report to the Oficina Ayuda a la Infancia, at the top of Avenida J M Carrera, by 9.45 am, bringing your passport for identification and making a modest donation of about US$0.50. If demand is sufficient there may be afternoon tours as well. Demand is very high in January and February, so get there early. Do not arrange the tour through travel agencies in Calama, which charge up to US$10 in lieu of Codelco's nominal fee.

Tours may not begin if the group does not meet a minimum size, perhaps as many as 35. Children under age 12 are not permitted. To enter the smelter building, you must wear sturdy footwear, long trousers and a long-sleeved jacket, but the mine will provide jackets, as well as helmets and protective eyewear. Allow at least three hours for the complete tour.

Getting There & Away

From Calama, take a taxi colectivo from Abaroa between Vicuña Mackenna and Sotomayor, just south of the Plaza 23 de Marzo, which leaves you at the taxi rank in Chuqui; it is a short walk uphill to the Oficina Ayuda a la Infancia. There are also public buses from Calama to Chuqui, leaving Calama from Granaderos and Ramírez, but they also go only to the Chuqui bus terminal.

All the long-distance bus companies have offices and terminals in Chuqui, so you could tour the mine and get a bus straight back to Antofagasta without hanging around Calama. Check departure times and expect the tour to run longer than anticipated.

SAN PEDRO DE ATACAMA

San Pedro de Atacama (San Pedro for short) is an oasis village at the northern end of the Salar de Atacama, a saline lake which has almost completely evaporated. To the east of the Salar rise immense volcanos, some active but most extinct. Symmetrical Licancábur, at 5916 metres, is one of the most visible – believe it or not, someone has dragged a mountain bike to the summit. Very near San Pedro is the colourful Valle de la Luna (Valley of the Moon), one of the Atacama's most scenic places.

San Pedro is just one of many oases in the area, but it is the most important. Some 120 km south-east of Calama, it sits 2440 metres above sea level and has a population of about 1000. Nearly all the houses are adobe, in separate compounds with adobe walls. First visited by Pedro de Valdivia in 1540, in the early 20th century it was a major stop on cattle drives from the Argentine province of Salta to the nitrate oficinas of the desert. Isaiah Bowman, in 1924, observed that:

> It takes thirteen to fourteen days for cattle to be driven from Salta to San Pedro de Atacama. They wait at San Pedro one or two days, according to the need for beef at the nitrate establishments, as well as their own condition, which depends largely upon the weather they have experienced in crossing the Puna. The days of waiting are called 'la tablada'. In this time the cattle are fed liberally, and if any of them are ailing or footsore they receive the attention of a veterinary. From San Pedro it takes three days to drive them to the nitrate establishments...

Bowman also chronicled the decline of San Pedro as the construction of the railroad across the Andes made stock drives obsolete:

> The fame that San Pedro has long enjoyed and the facilities it has for accommodating transient herds and droves attract the stockmen of Catamarca, La Rioja, San Luis, and Córdoba. For years they have sent droves of mules to be sold in the nitrate oficinas of the coastal desert farther north, but...completion of the Antofagasta railroad has greatly disturbed this traffic. In place of mule transport there is now railroad transport...

No longer on the cattle trail, in recent years San Pedro has become a popular destination on the 'gringo trail', but many young Chileans also spend their holidays in the picturesque colonial village. Still, despite increasing tourist trade, it remains an affordable and attractive place. Other sources of local employment are irrigated farming and the nearby sulphur mine.

Travellers to and from Argentina clear immigration with the Policía Internacional, as well as customs and agricultural inspections, on the road to Toconao.

Orientation

San Pedro is small and very compact, with almost everything of interest within easy walking distance of the plaza. While the streets do have names, few villagers use them; very few buildings have numbers. Finding your way by street names can be complicated, so you may have to ask.Calle O'Higgins is also known as Caracoles

Information

Tourist Office San Pedro's tourist office is in the Municipalidad, on the north side of the plaza. Open weekdays only, its hours are a bit irregular, but the staff are very knowledgeable and helpful.

Post & Telecommunications Correos de Chile is on Padre Le Paige, opposite the museum; San Pedro's eccentric postmaster is a landmark in his own right. CTC's long-distance telephone office, at O'Higgins (Caracoles) 43 half a block south of the plaza, is open from 8.30 am to 8 pm.

Things to See

Museo Gustavo Le Paige If ordinary deserts are paradise for archaeologists, the Atacama is total nirvana because of its nearly

1 Residencial y Restaurant Chiloé
2 Buses Morales y Moralito & Puna Expediciones
3 Residencial La Florida/Turismo Florida
4 Residencial El Pukará
5 Residencial Andacollo
6 Police Station
7 Church (Iglesia San Pedro)
8 Municipalidad
9 Museo Gustavo Le Paige
10 Plaza
11 Post Office
12 House of Pedro de Valdivia
13 Camping Turi
14 Buses Yusmar
15 CTC (Telephone)
16 Restaurant Juanita
17 Artesanía
18 Residencial Porvenir
19 Turismo Sánchez
20 Hostal Takha Takha
21 Tambo Cañaveral
22 Hostería San Pedro

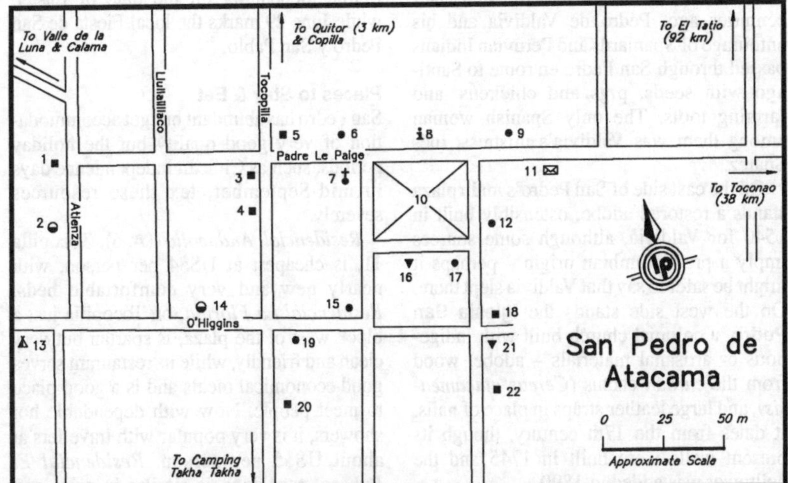

rainless environment, which preserves artefacts and other materials for millennia. In 1955, Belgian priest and archaeologist Gustavo Le Paige, assisted by the villagers of San Pedro and the Universidad del Norte (in Antofagasta), began to organise one of South America's finest museums, offering an overview of the area's cultural evolution through an extraordinary collection of pre-Columbian artefacts. Though primarily an archaeological museum, it also includes exhibits on the Inca conquest, the Spanish invasion and even the social anthropology of the area.

Some of the most interesting displays are the mummies of paleo-Indians, including a child buried in a pottery urn, and skulls which show deliberate malformation. There are also fragments of ancient weavings, pottery, tools, jewellery, and even paraphernalia for preparing, ingesting and smoking psychedelic plants and mushrooms.

Half a block from the plaza, the museum charges an admission fee of US$0.85. Student identification brings a substantial discount. Opening hours are weekdays from 8 am to noon and 2 to 6 pm, weekends from 10 am to noon and 2 to 6 pm.

Around the Plaza More than four and a half centuries ago, Pedro de Valdivia and his entourage of Spaniards and Peruvian Indians passed through San Pedro en route to Santiago with seeds, pigs and chickens, and farming tools. The only Spanish woman among them was Valdivia's mistress, Inés Suárez.

On the east side of San Pedro's main plaza stands a restored adobe, ostensibly built in 1540 for Valdivia, although some sources imply a pre-Columbian origin – perhaps it might be safer to say that Valdivia slept there. On the west side stands the **Iglesia San Pedro**, a colonial church built with indigenous or artisanal materials – adobe, wood from the *cardón* cactus *(Cereus atacamensis)*, and large leather straps in place of nails. It dates from the 17th century, though its present walls were built in 1745 and the belltower was added in 1890.

Iglesia San Pedro

Organised Tours

Since the tourist boom of the last decade, there are numerous operators who organise tours around San Pedro, the Valle de la Luna, the El Tatio Geysers, Toconao and the Salar de Atacama, and other sites. Normally, without a minimum of six persons, there are additional charges. For more detailed information, see the 'Around San Pedro de Atacama' section below.

Festivals

San Pedro celebrates Carnival in February or March, depending on the date of Easter, while June 29 marks the local Fiesta de San Pedro y San Pablo.

Places to Stay & Eat

San Pedro has abundant budget accommodation of very good quality but the holiday periods, such as Chilean independence days in mid-September, tax these resources severely.

Residencial Andacollo (☎ 6), Tocopilla 11, is cheapest at US$4 per person, with nearly new and very comfortable beds. *Residencial La Florida*, on Tocopilla just a block west of the plaza, is spartan but very clean and friendly, while its restaurant serves good economical meals and is a good place to meet people. Now with dependable hot showers, it is very popular with travellers at about US$5 per person. *Residencial El Pukará*, next door, is similar in price and quality. As you enter San Pedro from Calama, at Padre Le Paige and Atienza, you pass *Residencial Chiloé* (☎ 17), slightly more expensive but good value at about US$6 per person.

A block south of the plaza is *Residencial Porvenir* (☎ 8), which has doubles with private bath for US$7 per person. It's very basic, but clean and agreeable. The comparable *Hostal Takha Takha* (☎ 28) has moved to Calle Tocopilla, just south of O'Higgins. There are mixed reviews on the *Hostería San Pedro* (☎ 11), operated by an Australian woman and her Chilean husband – some love it and others think it mediocre. Rooms start at a relatively modest US$23/29 single/double, including private bath, plus swimming pool, restaurant and solar-heated showers. It's popular with many classes of visitors, though, from backpackers and tour groups to foreign film crews shooting at Valle de la Luna. Its restaurant has drawn praise for both quality and size of portions.

Besides the hotel restaurants, try *Restaurant Juanita* (which also has cheap accommodation) on the plaza and the excellent *Tambo Cañaveral*, which doubles as San Pedro's hottest night spot. For bread, cheese, fruit, vegetables, wine, beer and canned food there are numerous shops, including the Hostería's *Llamaroo*.

Camping *Camping Turi*, at the west end of O'Higgins, charges US$2 per person. *Camping Takha Takha*, on Tocopilla south of town, charges about US$3.

Things to Buy

There is a good craft shop on the plaza, with cardón carvings and ponchos of llama and alpaca wool. Crafts are also available at Hostería San Pedro and at the village of Toconao.

Getting There & Away

Buses Géminis has buses from Calama to San Pedro on Sundays only. Buses Morales Moralito has buses from Calama to San Pedro (US$3) daily and Toconao (US$4) three days a week. Return buses leave San Pedro at 8 am, 12.30 pm and 6 pm. Yusmar goes twice daily to Calama and four days a week to Toconao.

AROUND SAN PEDRO DE ATACAMA

Most of San Pedro's attractions are more than walking distance from the town, but several operators offer reasonably priced tours. Among the best-established are Turismo Ochoa (☎ 22) on Calle Toconao, south of the plaza, Turismo Roberto Sánchez (☎ 40) on O'Higgins, Turismo Florida (☎ 21) in the Residencial La Florida, and Atacama Desert Expeditions (☎ 35) on the plaza. The Hostería San Pedro also organises tours, and Turismo Nativa visits some out-of-the-way places such as the Salar de Uyuni in Bolivia and a weather station at 5750 metres on Cerro Sairecábur.

It is possible to reach the Bolivian border at Portezuelo del Cajón with sulphur trucks and continue by foot to Lago Verde, on the Bolivian side – about a two-hour walk. Get an exit stamp in San Pedro the day before, since these trucks leave about 5 am; they charge about US$5 to the border and, at the mining camp, there is a very basic 'guest room' with lodging for US$3.

Pukará de Quitor & Catarpe

Just three km north-west of San Pedro, on a promontory overlooking the Río San Pedro, are the ruins of a 12th-century Indian *pucará* (fortress). From the top of the fortifications, part of the last bastion against Pedro de Valdivia and the Spanish, you can see the entire oasis. Archaeologists have reconstructed parts of its ruined walls. Three km north, on the east side of the river, are the ruins of Catarpe, a former Inca administrative centre.

Valle de la Luna

About 15 km west of San Pedro, the Calama highway passes through an area of polychrome desert landforms left by flood and wind. Every place where the desert leaves a few odd formations, Latin Americans seem to call 'Valley of the Moon' – there are others in Bolivia and Argentina – but this area still

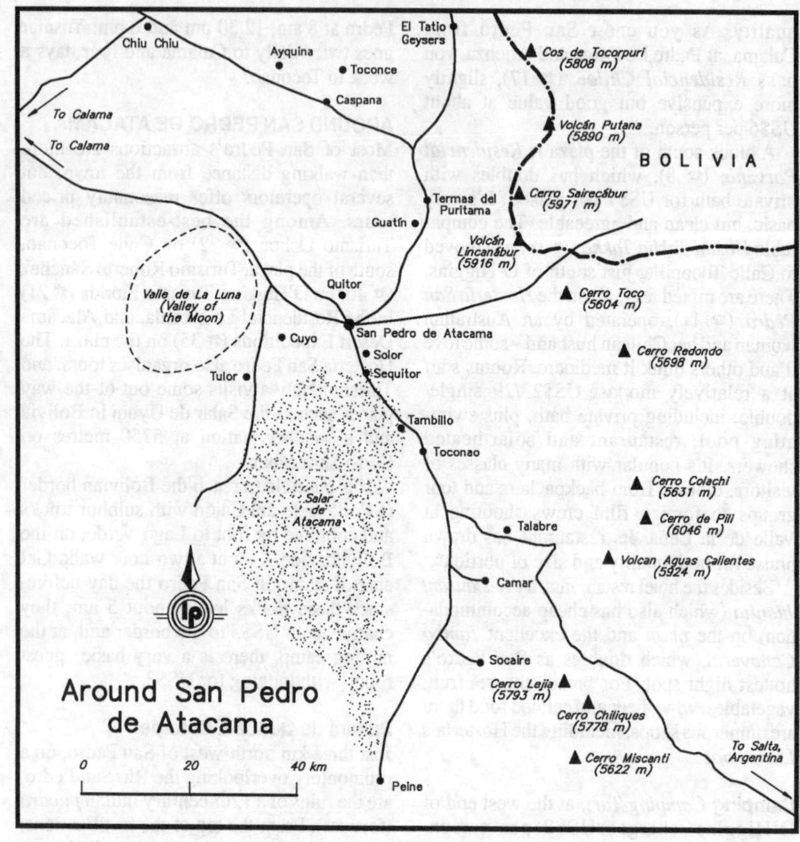

merits a visit. If driving, leave the highway to explore the dirt roads and box canyons to the north, but take care not to get stuck in the sand. You can hitch to the desert and hike around, but take plenty of water and food, and smear yourself with heavy sunblock. Some visitors enjoy the view and solitude at night under a full moon, in which case you should take warm clothing – at this altitude, nights are cool at any time of year, but especially in winter.

Termas de Puritama

About 30 km from San Pedro, en route to El Tatio, are the Termas de Puritama (or Baños de Puritama), a volcanic hot springs. There are no buses so, unless you have your own vehicle, arrange transport with the drivers of the sulphur mine trucks, which leave San Pedro early every morning. For a modest charge, you get a rough ride in the back of the truck for about an hour before the driver lets you off at the signed junction for the springs, on the west (left-hand) side of the road.

From the junction, it's a 20-minute walk along an obvious gravel track into a small canyon – if driving, leave your car at the junction. The temperature of the springs is about 33°C and there several falls and pools. Bring food and water. Camping is possible, but there's little fuel for a fire – and it gets very cold! There are a number of ruined buildings for shelter. Rain is unlikely.

Unless you intend to stay, return to the main road by 1 pm and flag down the first available truck. On the way back, the driver may drop you at the mine's Polán crushing plant, six km short of San Pedro, so you'll have to walk the rest of the way.

El Tatio Geysers

At 4300 metres, 95 km north of San Pedro, the El Tatio Geysers are the highest geyser field in the world and a probable future national park, although there is also pressure to develop them for geothermal energy. While the entire field is less spectacular than, say, the intermittent explosions of Yellowstone, the visual impact of the steaming fumaroles at sunrise in the azure clarity of the altiplano is unforgettable, and the individual structures formed when the boiling water evaporates and leaves behind dissolved minerals are strikingly beautiful.

Early morning, about 6 am, is the best time to see the geysers; after about 8.30 am, morning winds disperse the steam, although most tours leave by that hour and you can enjoy the large thermal pool in virtual privacy. There is no public transport, but several companies operate tours from Calama and San Pedro – San Pedro has better access and the tours tend to be a bit cheaper, at around US$20 including lunch and a stop at the Termas de Puritama.

If driving, leave San Pedro no later than 4 am to reach the geysers by sunrise. The route north from San Pedro is signed, but in the dark it may be easier to follow the tour agencies' jeeps and minibuses. Do not attempt the road, which is very rough, without a high clearance pickup or jeep. If you have rented a car in Calama, it is possible to return via the indigenous villages of Caspana, Toconce, Ayquina, and Chiu Chiu (see above, under Calama) rather than via San Pedro. Some tours from Calama take this route as well.

It is possible to camp at the geysers, but the nights are very cold at this elevation. Remember to watch your step – in some places, people have fallen through the thin crust into underlying pools of scalding water and suffered very serious burns.

TOCONAO

The village of Toconao, about 40 km south of San Pedro, is known for its finely hewn volcanic stone, the material for most of its houses. The **Iglesia de San Lucas**, with a separate belltower, dates from the mid-18th century.

Toconao, a locally important fruit-growing oasis with an intricate irrigation system, is noted for grapes, pomegranates, apples and herbs. Most of these orchards and fields are in the Quebrada de Jeria, a delightful place for a walk or even a swim – its water is of such high quality that, in Bowman's time, affluent families from San Pedro sent peons with mules to Toconao to fetch casks of drinking water. In the village proper, local women sell very fine products of llama wool, including ponchos, pullovers, gloves and socks, as well as souvenirs cut from local stone.

Toconao has several inexpensive residenciales and restaurants near the plaza. Buses from Calama to Toconao, via San Pedro, arrive in Toconao late at night. Hitching is possible from San Pedro (virtually every southbound truck goes to Toconao), but leave early in the day and be prepared to return early or stay the night, since return traffic is sparse.

Norte Chico

South of the Atacama proper is the Norte Chico (Little North), a semi-arid region of transition to the Mediterranean climate of the central valley. Once known as the 'region of 10,000 mines', it was a great silver mining zone and is still important for copper and iron. Several notable rivers make irrigated agriculture a productive industry, although the region contains only a small percentage of Chile's total arable land.

Politically, the Norte Chico consists of the Third Region of Atacama (capital Copiapó) and the Fourth Region of Coquimbo (capital La Serena), which is the area covered in this chapter.

For most travellers, the Norte Chico's major attraction will be its pleasant coastal climate, attractive beaches and colonial cities like La Serena. Off the beaten track of the Ruta Panamericana, there are intriguing villages and spectacular mountain scenery in areas where foreign travellers are still a novelty. Not far off the Panamericana are two interesting national parks, Pan de Azúcar and Fray Jorge, which only a handful of people ever visit.

HISTORY

In pre-Columbian times the coastal Norte Chico, like the Norte Grande, was home to Chango fisherfolk, while sedentary Diaguita farmers inhabited the fertile river valleys beyond the littoral and even parts of the less fertile uplands. The Diaguita, who crossed the Andes from present-day Argentina at an undetermined date, cultivated and irrigated maize. They also raised a variety of complementary crops, such as potatoes, beans, squash and quinoa at different altitudes, and they may have herded llamas. While their numbers were smaller and their political organisation less complex than the major civilisations of Peru and Bolivia, they could mobilise sufficient labour to build agricultural terraces and military fortifications. Some decades before the European invasion, the Inca Empire began to expand its influence among the Diaguita and other southern Andean peoples, but the area remained peripheral to the Central Andean civilisations.

Europeans first saw the region in 1535, when Diego de Almagro's expedition from Cuzco crossed the Paso San Francisco from Salta. Their first impressions were less than positive. Surviving phenomenal hardship, a member of Almagro's party left a graphic, gruesome account of the miserable 800-km march over the Puna de Atacama (which took 20 days in the best of times), reporting that both men and horses froze to death and that later expeditions, finding the undecomposed horses, 'were glad to eat them'.

In the lowlands, at least food and water were available, but Almagro and his men passed quickly through the Copiapó valley and turned south to the Río Aconcagua before returning to Cuzco through Copiapó and the oases of the Norte Grande. A few years later Pedro de Valdivia's party, following Almagro's return route to establish a permanent Spanish settlement at Santiago, met stiff resistance from Indian warriors at Copiapó; of one party of 30 which Valdivia had ordered back to Cuzco, only the two officers survived.

In the course of his travels, Valdivia founded the city of La Serena in 1541, but Copiapó lagged well behind until its 18th-century gold boom. When gold failed, silver took its place and Copiapó really boomed, tripling its population to 12,000 after a bonanza strike at Chañarcillo in 1832. But the Norte Chico was still very much a frontier zone. Darwin vividly described the behaviour of the region's miners:

> Living for weeks together in the most desolate spots, when they descend to the villages on feast-days, there is no excess or extravagance to which they do not run. They sometimes gain a considerable sum, and then, like sailors with prize-money, they try how soon they can contrive to squander it. They drink excessively, buy quantities of clothes, and in a few days return penniless to their miserable abodes, there to work harder than beasts of burden.

Silver declined by the late-19th century but copper soon took its place, with Anaconda's huge mine at Potrerillos later supplanted by El Salvador. Recently, the area around La Serena and the northern sector around Bahía Inglesa have undergone tourist booms (in some ways La Serena has overtaken traditional holiday destinations like Viña del Mar), but mining continues to be significant. The region is also important in Chilean cultural life – Nobel Prize poet Gabriela Mistral, for instance, was a native of the village of Vicuña in the Elqui valley, east of La Serena. Irrigated agriculture has always been important, but in recent years the Copiapó, Huasco and Elqui valleys have become notable contributors to Chile's booming fruit exports.

COPIAPÓ

Despite much earlier encomiendas and land grants and its founding in the mid-18th century, Copiapó is really a 19th-century city. Were it not for Juan Godoy's discovery of silver at Chañarcillo, it might have lagged even farther behind the rest of the country. Darwin, visiting Copiapó in 1835, noted the economic distortion which the mining boom had brought to an area whose agriculture sufficed to feed it for only three months a year:

> The town covers a considerable space of ground, each house possessing a garden; but it is an uncomfortable place and the dwellings are poorly furnished. Everyone seems bent on the one object of making money, and then migrating as quickly as possible. All the inhabitants are more or less directly concerned with the mines; and mines and ores are the sole subjects of conversation. Necessaries of all sorts are extremely dear; as the distance from the town to the port is eighteen leagues, and the land carriage very expensive. A fowl costs five or six shillings; meat is nearly as dear as in England; firewood, or rather sticks, are brought on donkeys from a distance of two and three days' journey within the cordillera; and pasturage for animals is a shilling a day: all this for South America is wonderfully exorbitant.

As it happened, the mining industry provided Copiapó with a number of firsts: the first railroad in South America (built between 1849 and 1852 from Copiapó to the port of Caldera), Chile's first telegraph and telephone lines and its first gas works. In the early decades of this century, Copiapó so impressed Isaiah Bowman that he described it as:

> ...beautifully kept, with clean streets, well repaired buildings, and a thoroughly businesslike air, whether

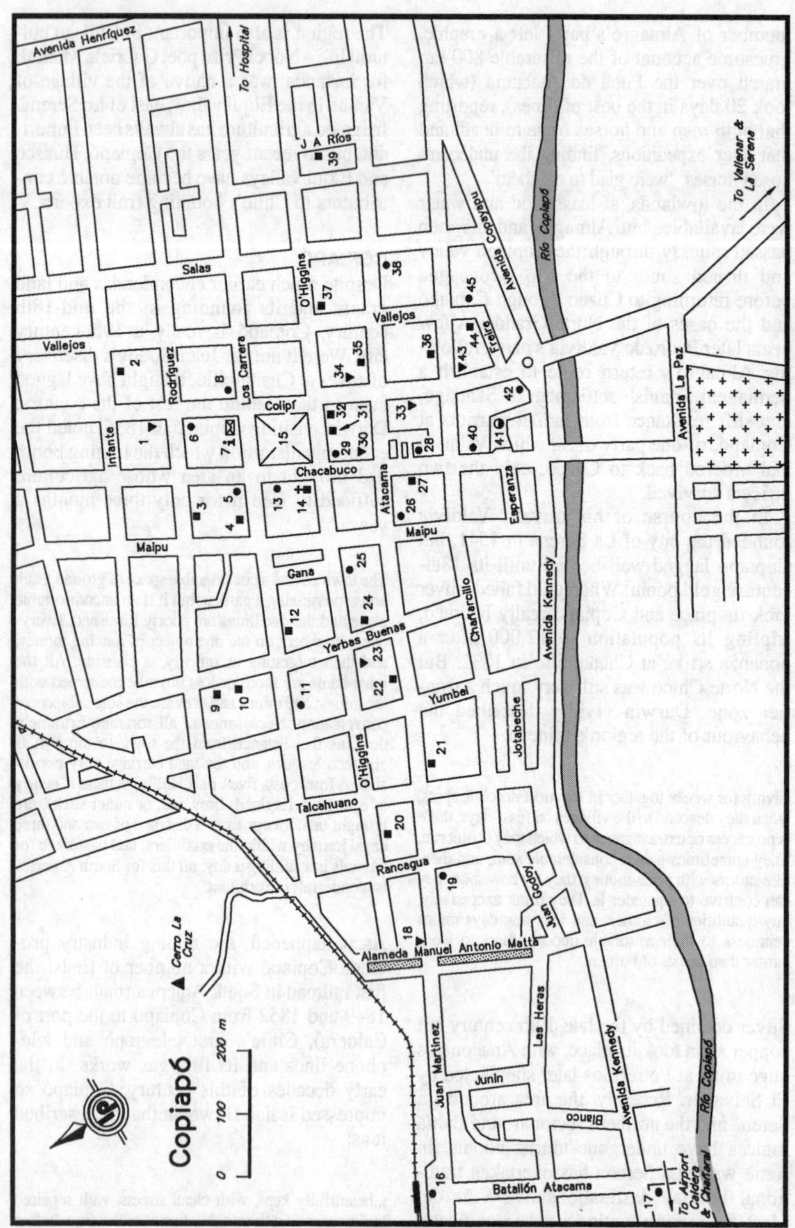
Avenida Henríquez
To Hospital
J A Ríos
Salas
O'Higgins
Vallejos
Vallejos
Rodríguez
Los Carrera
Colipí
Infante
Chacabuco
Atacama
Maipu
Maipu
Gana
Yerbas Buenas
O'Higgins
Talcahuano
Rancagua
Alameda Manuel Antonio Matta
Cerro La Cruz
Copiapó
0 100 200 m
Juan Martínez
Junín
Las Heras
Blanco
Batallón Atacama
Avenida Kennedy
Avenida Kennedy
Río Copiapó
Río Copiapó
To Airport Caldera & Chañaral
Juan Godoy
Jotabeche
Yumbel
Chañarcillo
Esperanza
Freire
Avenida Copayapu
Avenida La Paz
To Vallenar & La Serena

■ PLACES TO STAY

2 Hotel Montecatini
3 Residencial Rodríguez
4 Hotel San Francisco de la Selva
9 Hotel Edy Maryros
10 Hotel España
12 Residencial Cristi
20 Hotel La Casona
21 Residencial Torres
22 Hotel Inglés
24 Hotel Derby
27 Residencial Chacabuco
31 Hotel Diego de Almeida
32 Residencial Plaza
35 Hotel Palace
36 Residencial Chañarcillo
37 Anexo Residencial Chañarcillo
39 Youth Hostel
44 Hotel Archi

▼ PLACES TO EAT

1 Restaurant Galería
18 Il Pirón de Oro
23 Restaurant Tong Fan
30 Restaurant El Pollo
33 A Chau
34 Hao Hwa
43 Mei Lam

OTHER

5 CTC (Telephone)
6 Museo Mineralógico
7 Sernatur & Post Office
8 ENTEL (Telephone)
11 Club Social Libanés
13 Banco Concepción
14 Catedral
15 Plaza Prat
16 Museo de Ferrocarriles
17 Palacete Viña de Cristo
19 Museo Histórico Regional
25 Avis Rent-a-Car
26 CTC (Telephone)
28 Buses Flecha Dorada
29 Municipalidad
38 CONAF
40 Buses Tas Choapa
41 Bus Terminal
42 Pullman Bus
45 Rodaggio Rent-a-Car

we consider the management of its mines, the appearance and administration of its famous college and its still more famous school of mines, or the excellent administration of land and water rights.

Copiapó's population has fluctuated with the mining booms, but today it is a city of some 69,000 inhabitants which retains many of the attributes Bowman described. While not a major destination for international travellers, its pleasant climate and historical interest make it a worthwhile stopover on the Ruta Panamericana between La Serena and Antofagasta.

Orientation

Copiapó nestles in the narrow valley floor on the north bank of the Río Copiapó, 330 km north of La Serena, 800 km north of Santiago, and 565 km south of Antofagasta. Plaza Prat (also called Plaza de Armas), three blocks north of Avenida Kennedy (which is the Ruta Panamericana), marks the historical centre of the city. Overlooking the town from the north-west is the landmark Cerro La Cruz. Most areas of interest to the visitor are found in or near a roughly rectangular area delimited by the Calle Rodríguez on the north-east, the Alameda Manuel Antonio Matta on the north-west, the Avenida Henríquez on the south-east, and the Río Copiapó on the south-west.

Information

Tourist Office Sernatur (☎ 212838) occupies what appears to be a misplaced bomb shelter on the north side of Plaza Prat, directly in front of the Intendencia Regional at Los Carrera 691. Once you locate the entrance, the staff are exceptionally congenial and helpful. They are very well informed and can provide a list of accommodation in the city, an excellent free map and many brochures. It is open weekdays between 8.30 and 1 pm and 2.30 and 6.50 pm.

Money Banco Concepción at Chacabuco 485 will change cash dollars only.

Post & Telecommunications Correos de Chile is in the Intendencia Regional on the plaza. CTC has long-distance phone offices at Atacama 566 and on the northern corner of Los Carrera and Chacabuco, on Plaza Prat. ENTEL is at Colipí 500, on the eastern corner of the plaza.

Travel Agencies Copiapó's main travel agency is Turismo Atacama (☎ 214776) at Los Carrera 716.

National Parks For information on protected areas, including Parque Nacional Pan de Azúcar north of Chañaral, visit CONAF (☎ 213404) at Atacama 898.

Medical Services Copiapó's hospital (☎ 212023) is at the intersection of Los Carrera and Vicuña, about eight blocks east of Plaza Prat.

Museo Mineralógico

Founded in 1857 and supported by the Universidad de Atacama (successor to Copiapó's famous school of mines), the mineralogical museum is very literally dazzling, a tribute to the raw materials to which the city owes its very existence. Its exhibition hall displays more than 2000 samples organised according to chemical elements and structure, and a number of mineral curiosities. At the corner of Colipí and Rodríguez, a block from Plaza Prat, it's open Monday to Saturday from 10 am to 1 pm and weekdays only from 3.30 to 7 pm. Admission costs US$0.60.

Museo Histórico Regional

Closed for remodelling as of early 1992, the regional history museum, at Atacama 98 near Rancagua, should reopen by the time this book is published. Built in the 1840s, the building itself belonged to the influential Matta family. Hours are daily except Monday from 10 am to 1 pm, Tuesday to Friday from 3.30 to 7 pm, and Saturday from 3 pm to 6.15 pm. Admission is US$0.70.

Museo de Ferrocarriles

South America's oldest railroad, the Copiapó-Caldera line, opened on Christmas Day 1851 to carry the produce of the silver mine at Chañarcillo. North American shipping pioneer William Wheelwright attracted investors who formed a virtual who's who of the Chilean mining elite of the time, including Doña Candelaria Goyenechea, Agustín Edwards, Matías Cousiño, Vicente Subercaseaux and others. Though passenger trains no longer carry *copiapinos* (citizens of Copiapó) to the beach, Wheelwright's handiwork is on display at the railroad museum, in the old station on Juan Martínez, opposite Batallón Atacama. It is open weekends only from 11 am to 1 pm and 4 to 7 pm.

Things to See

Copiapó has a number of attractive buildings from its mining heyday, including the **cathedral** and the **municipalidad** (once a private house) on the Plaza de Armas. West of downtown, the **Alameda Matta** is an attractive, tree-lined street with a series of monuments dedicated to local figures (including Manuel Antonio Matta and prospector Juan Godoy, who discovered the Chañarcillo silver deposits) and pretty older buildings in unfortunate decline.

At the southern end of Batallón Atacama is Apolinario Soto's **Palacete Viña de Cristo**, built in 1860 of European materials and once the town's most elegant mansion. A few blocks west, on the grounds of the **Universidad de Atacama** (formerly the historic Escuela de Minas), is the Norris Brothers locomotive which was the first to operate on the Caldera-Copiapó line.

Festivals

Copiapó and the Atacama region celebrate numerous festivals. December 8 marks the founding of the city, while February 1 is the Festival de Candelaria. Throughout the region, August 10 is Día del Minero (Miner's Day).

Places to Stay – bottom end

During the summer, Copiapó has a *youth hostel* at Juan Antonio Ríos 371.

Otherwise, *Residencial Chacabuco* (☎ 213428), Chacabuco 271, is the cheapest in town at just under US$5 per person, but twice that for rooms with private bath. *Residencial Chañarcillo* (☎ 213281), Chañarcillo 741, has small but clean rooms for US$5/9 a single/double, but avoid being too close to the TV room. *Anexo Residencial Chañarcillo* (☎ 212284), run by the same management at O'Higgins 804, is funky but friendly at US$6/11; hot water is available from 7 to 11 am only.

Other budget alternatives include *Residencial Torres* (☎ 211385) at Atacama 230, *Residencial Cristi* (☎ 211700) at Los Carrera 440, *Residencial Rodríguez* (☎ 212861) at Rodríguez 528, and *Residencial Plaza* (☎ 212671) at O'Higgins 670.

Places to Stay – middle

Mid-range accommodation starts at about US$14/26 at places like *Hotel Derby* (☎ 212447), Yerbas Buenas 396, *Hotel Edy Maryros* (☎ 211408) at Yerbas Buenas 593 and *Hotel Inglés* (☎ 212797) at Atacama 337.

One of Copiapó's best values is *Hotel Palace* (☎ 212852), Atacama 741, with very attractive rooms around a delightful garden patio for US$20/29 with private bath. Other comparable places are *Hotel Montecatini* (☎ 211363; not to be confused with the much pricier Hotel Montecatini II) at Infante 766 and *Hotel España* (☎ 217197) at Yerbas Buenas 571.

Places to Stay – top end

Copiapó has a disproportionate amount of upscale accommodation, starting with the *Hotel Archi* (☎ 212983), Vallejos 111, at about US$27/34. Probably the best choice is the colonial-style *Hotel La Casona* (☎ 217278), O'Higgins 150, which offers accommodation in a beautiful garden setting for US$39/53, although the spiffy new *Hotel San Francisco de la Selva* (213255), Los Carrera 525, also deserves a look at US$46/56. Top of the line is the four-star *Hotel Diego de Almeida* (☎ 212075), O'Higgins 656, which charges US$61/69.

Places to Eat

Restaurant El Pollo, Chacabuco 340 between O'Higgins and Atacama, has a very good three-course lunch for about US$4. *Restaurant Bavaria*, Chacabuco 487, has decent but overpriced sandwiches. For seafood, try *Restaurant Galería* at Colipí 635 or *Il Pirón de Oro* at Atacama 1. Other interesting alternatives include Middle Eastern food at the *Club Social Libanés*, Los Carrera 350, and Italian food at *Villa Rapallo*, Chañarcillo 705.

Hao Hwa, Colipí 340, is one of the better Chinese restaurants in northern Chile, with good food, a very pleasant atmosphere and attentive service. Other Chinese restaurants include *A Chau* at Colipí 261, *Mei Lam* at Chañarcillo 700, and *Tong Fan* at O'Higgins 390.

For ice cream, try *Helados Diavoletto*, Henríquez 431A, whose standard and fruit flavours are both excellent.

Getting There & Away

Air Aeropuerto Chamonate (☎ 214360) is seven km west of Copiapó, just north of the Ruta Panamericana. LAN-Chile (☎ 213512), O'Higgins 640 near the Municipalidad, has flights to Calama and Antofagasta on Monday, Wednesday, Friday and Sunday, and to Santiago on Monday, Wednesday and Friday. LAN-Chile operates its own minibus from downtown to the airport.

Bus Conveniently close to the Ruta Panamericana, the Copiapó bus terminal (☎ 212577) is at the southern end of Chacabuco, three blocks south of Plaza Prat and just north of the river. Virtually all north-south buses stop here, as well as many to interior destinations. All the bus companies have offices here (some of them shared) but some have downtown offices as well.

Ramos Cholele (☎ 213113) connects Copiapó with the northern Atacama destinations of Antofagasta, Iquique and Arica, as do Zambrano, Evans and Carmelita. They all operate from the same office. Carmelita also goes south to La Serena, Coquimbo, Ovalle and Santiago (three times daily). Buses Tramaca (☎ 213979) covers the same Panamericana route, plus two buses daily to Calama and half a dozen to Taltal. Andes Mar Bus (☎ 213166) and Buses Libac (☎ 212237), O'Higgins 640, go to Santiago and intermediate points. Tas Choapa (☎ 213793), Chacabuco 180, works the same routes, with connections as far as Puerto Montt in southern Chile. They also go to Argentina, Uruguay and Paraguay.

Flecha Dorada (☎ 213050), Chacabuco 249, also operates on the Panamericana between Arica and Santiago. Flota Barrios (☎ 213645), Chacabuco 189, has similar itineraries, plus buses to Calama, Tocopilla and Viña del Mar. Pullman Bus (☎ 211039), Colipí 109, covers the Panamericana and serves Viña as well as southerly destinations off the Panamericana, including Illapel and Salamanca. They also go to northern mining towns such as Diego de Almagro, El Salvador, and Potrerillos. Inca Bus (☎ 213488) runs virtually the same routes.

Approximate fares from Copiapó include Arica US$24, Iquique US$22, Tocopilla or Calama US$16, Antofagasta US$12, Coquimbo or La Serena US$7, and Santiago or Viña del Mar US$14. Beyond Santiago, it costs about US$30 to Temuco, US$37 to Osorno and US$39 to Puerto Montt.

Pullman Bus, Libac, Flecha Dorada, Tramaca and Los Diamantes de Elqui run more expensive but more comfortable salón cama services to Santiago and Viña. Fares are about US$22.

Regional carriers include Recabarren (☎ 216991), Muñoz (☎ 213166) and Casther (☎ 218889), all of which run frequently to Caldera and Bahía Inglesa for a little more than US$1. Casther and Abarcia serve destinations in the upper Copiapó valley, such as Nantoco and Pabellón, Los Loros, Viña del Cerro and Tranque Lautaro. Fares are about US$2 at the maximum.

Car Rental There are several car rental agencies in Copiapó, including Hertz (☎ 213522) at Avenida Copayapu 173, Avis (☎ 212827) at O'Higgins 480, Galerías (☎ 212147) at Panamericana Sur 260, and Rodaggio (☎ 212153) at Vallejos 152.

AROUND COPIAPÓ

Up the valley of the Río Copiapó there are many worthwhile sights which are accessible by public transport from Copiapó. Farther inland, there are more challenging destinations, specifically the famous peak of Ojos del Salado on the Chilean-Argentine border.

Nantoco & Jotabeche

Nantoco is the former hacienda of Apolinario Soto. It is in the upper Copiapó valley, 23 km from the city, and is open to the public on request. A few km beyond Nantoco is the **Hacienda Jotabeche** which belonged to the notable Chilean essayist José Joaquín Vallejo. Better known by his pseudonym Jotabeche, Vallejo was a pioneer of Chilean literature and a keen observer of his country's customs.

Pabellón

Pabellón, 38 km from Copiapó, occupies a site in the midst of a vineyard zone which also offers basic camping.

Los Loros

Los Loros, 64 km from Copiapó, is a picturesque village in a rich agricultural zone which produces excellent grapes, watermelons, citrus and other fruits.

Viña del Cerro

This archaeological monument, on a spur off the main valley road, consists of the restored remains of a Diaguita-Inca copper foundry, with associated houses and other constructions, including more than 30 ovens.

Ojos del Salado

At 6893 metres above sea level, 222 km from Copiapó, Ojos del Salado is arguably the highest peak in South America (Argentines claim it is not as high as Aconcagua).

Because it is on the border, climbers must obtain authorisation from the Dirección de Fronteras y Límites (DIFROL; ☎ 671-4110, fax 698-3502), Bandera 52, 4th floor, in Santiago, which oversees activities in the border area. They must also report to the Carabineros in Copiapó before proceeding to the area. At the 5100-metre level, the Universidad de Atacama maintains a refugio which can shelter a dozen climbers; at 5750 metres, there is another with a capacity of 24.

Two guides in Copiapó may be able to help with arrangements: Giancarlo Fioco of Turismo Ojos del Salado at the Hotel La Casona and Marco Román at Hotel San Francisco de la Selva (see earlier for addresses). There is no public transport to the area.

CALDERA & BAHÍA INGLESA

A minor colonial port, Caldera grew dramatically after silver strikes east of Copiapó and the construction of the railroad in the mid-19th century. The railway also gave the residents of Copiapó easy access to the beach. Along with nearby Bahía Inglesa, it is

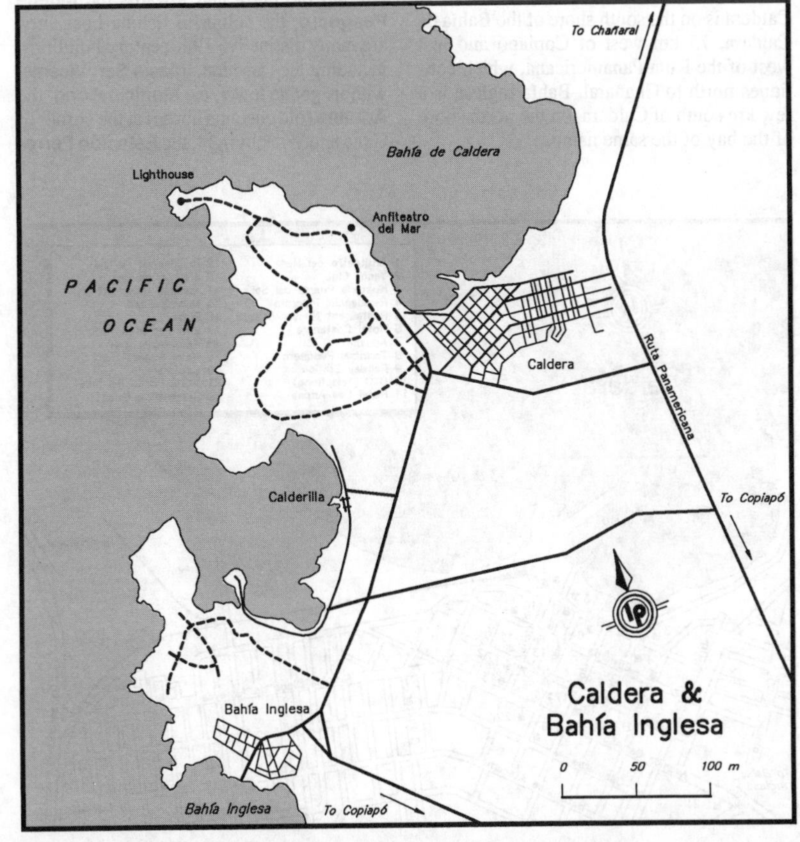

still the Third Region's most important beach resort. Although Bahía Inglesa's beaches are more sheltered and attractive, Caldera is livelier and much cheaper.

Bahía Inglesa was a refuge for British privateers during the colonial period. Now popular with visitors from central and northern Chile, it is very crowded during the January-February peak season, but during the off-season, when the weather is just as good, it is slightly cheaper.

Just north of Caldera there is a fruit inspection checkpoint; eat your produce before arrival or it will be confiscated.

Orientation

Caldera is on the south shore of the Bahía de Caldera, 75 km west of Copiapó and just west of the Ruta Panamericana, which continues north to Chañaral. Bahía Inglesa is a few km south of Caldera, on the north shore of the bay of the same name.

Information

Tourist Office Caldera ostensibly has a tourist office on the south-west side of the plaza, but there was no sign of it in early 1992.

Telecommunications CTC's long-distance telephone office is at Edwards 360, near the intersection with Cousiño.

Things to See

At the eastern entrance to town, along Avenida Diego de Almeyda, is the **Cementerio Laico**, the first non-Catholic cemetery in Chile, with interesting forged ironwork. Around the plaza and towards the **Muelle Pesquero**, the colourful fishing boat jetty, are many distinctive 19th-century buildings, including the cathedral, **Iglesia San Vicente**, with its gothic tower, the **Municipalidad**, the **Aduana** (old customs house) at the corner of Gana and Wheelwright, the **Estación Ferro-**

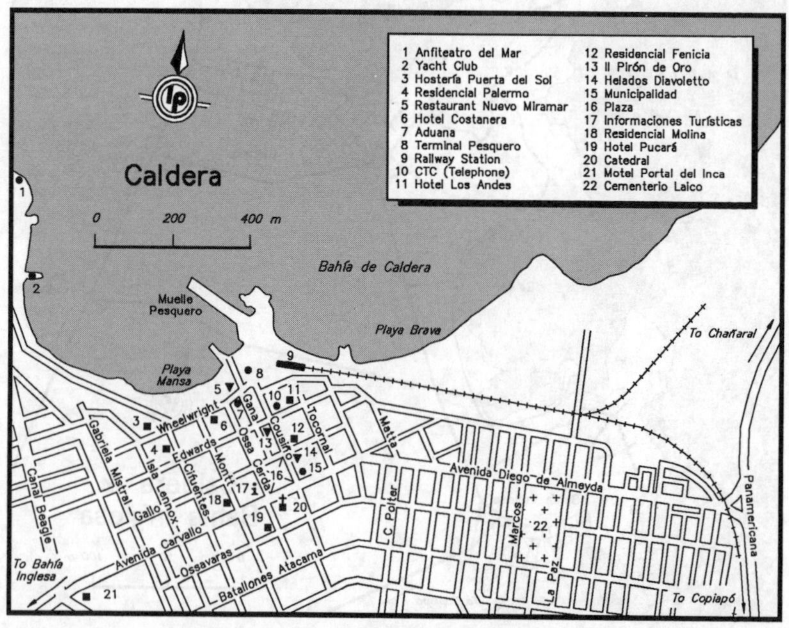

carriles (train station) for the line which linked Caldera with Copiapó, and several private houses.

Activities

Besides swimming and sunbathing, windsurfing is a popular pastime at Bahía Inglesa, with rental equipment available.

Festivals

In January the Festival del Cantar Juveníl de Caldera, a song festival, takes place in the open-air Anfiteatro del Mar, overlooking the sea west of the port.

Places to Stay

The cheapest options are *Residencial Molina* (☎ 315941) at Montt 346 and *Hotel Los Andes* (☎ 315220) at Edwards 360, both of which charge about US$6 per person. *Residencial Fenicia* (☎ 315594), Gallo 370, has singles/doubles with shared bath for US$10/18; with private bath, add about 50% more.

At *Residencial Palermo* (☎ 315171), Cifuentes 150, and *Hotel Costanera* (☎ 316007), Wheelwright 543, rates are about US$20/30 – the latter a bit dearer with private bath. *Hotel Pucará* (☎ 315258), Ossa Cerda 460, charges US$26/35 for rooms with private bath.

At the upper end of the scale is the *Hostería Puerta del Sol* (☎ 315205) at Wheelwright 750, where rates start at US$30/45. Even more upscale is the *Motel Portal del Inca* (☎ 315252) at Avenida Carvallo 945, on the road to Bahía Inglesa. Midway between Caldera and Bahía Inglesa is the *Motel Umbral de Bahía Inglesa* (☎ 315200), which charges US$100 per night for up to six persons.

Camping *Camping Bahía Inglesa*, on Playa Las Machas just south of Bahía Inglesa, has good facilities, but costs nearly US$20 per site in high season. It also has cabañas starting at US$28 for up to five persons with shared bath.

Places to Eat

Seafood is the only reasonable choice at Caldera. There is a branch of the Copiapó restaurant, *Il Pirón de Oro*, at Cousiño 218. Try also *Nuevo Miramar* at the northern end of Gana, overlooking the fishing pier. *Helados Diavoletto* has a branch at Cousiño 315, on the plaza, with excellent ice cream.

In Bahía Inglesa, the upscale *El Coral* at El Morro 564 offers superb seafood, including scallops which are now cultivated locally. It's expensive, but it you order carefully you may be able to eat here without shattering the budget.

Getting There & Away

There are frequent buses from Caldera to Copiapó, leaving from offices near the plaza. To catch a through bus north or south on the Panamericana, it may be easier to wait at the turnoff at the east end of Avenida Diego de Almeyda, as most do not enter Caldera.

Getting Around

Everything in Caldera is easily accessible on foot. Buses and taxi colectivos shuttle visitors between Caldera and Bahía Inglesa in about 10 minutes.

CHAÑARAL

Chañaral is a dilapidated but intriguing mining and fishing port set among the rugged headlands of the Sierra de las Animas, 165 km north-west of Copiapó and 400 km south of Antofagasta. It dates from 1833, almost a decade after Diego de Almeyda discovered the nearby Las Animas copper mine, but the area's economic powerhouse is the huge copper mine at El Salvador, in the mountains to the east.

For the people of Chañaral though, El Salvador, which provides their livelihood, has been a mixed blessing. In 1988 they had to go to court to force Codelco to construct a holding facility to prevent contamination by toxic runoff of the Río Salado and Chañaral's broad sandy beach. Chañaral's successful environmental action was the first of its kind in Chile.

Just north of Chañaral is the scenic coastal

Parque Nacional Pan de Azúcar (see separate entry later in this chapter), which straddles the border between the Second and Third Regions and is probably the best reason for a stopover in the area.

Orientation

Chañaral has two sections: the industrial port which sprawls along the shoreline and the residential area which scales the hills south of the Ruta Panamericana. The Panamericana turns sharply eastward at the southern entrance to town. Steep sidewalks link the streets of the highly irregular terrain, whose natural contours Chañaral has respected rather more than most other Chilean cities have.

Information

Tourist Office Chañaral's tourist office is on the Panamericana, at the southern entrance to town. It's open weekdays during the summer high season only.

Telecommunications CTC's long-distance offices are at Merino Jarpa 506.

Barquito

Barquito, two km south of Chañaral proper, contains the mechanised port facilities through which the copper of El Salvador passes. In a ramshackle way, it's an interesting landscape, with a large railway yard and many antique cars amongst the steep headlands.

Places to Stay

Hotel Jiménez, Merino Jarpa 551, is the cheapest accommodation at US$4 per person, while *Hotel Nuria*, Avenida Costanera 302, charges US$8 per person. At *Hotel Miní* (☎ 480079), San Martín 528, rates are US$20/22 a single/double. The best in town is the very appealing *Hostería Chañaral* (☎ 480055), Miller 268, where rooms start at US$22/24.

Places to Eat

For a town of its size, Chañaral has a number of surprisingly good, if modest, restaurants. *Restaurant Nuria*, on the plaza at Yungay 434, offers well prepared and reasonably priced seafood, salads and snacks, with friendly and attentive service. *Restaurant La Playa* at Merino Jarpa 546 and *El Rincón Porteño* at Merino Jarpa 567 are also worth a visit. There are also several places on the Panamericana if you're just passing through.

Getting There & Away

Chañaral's bus terminal is on Merino Jarpa between Conchuela and Los Baños, but many buses bypass town on the Panamericana, although most will stop to pick up passengers. Buses Pullman, which serves Diego de Almagro and El Salvador, and Flota Barrios have offices along Merino Jarpa.

Getting Around

For car rental, contact Rodrigo Zepeda (☎ 480015) at San Martín 407, who may also arrange excursions to Parque Nacional Pan de Azúcar.

PARQUE NACIONAL PAN DE AZÚCAR

Only 30 km north of Chañaral, Pan de Azúcar comprises 44,000 hectares of coastal desert and cordillera, with beautiful coves, white sandy beaches, stony headlands, abundant wildlife and a unique flora. There is excellent camping in some coastal areas.

Geography & Climate

Altitudes in the park range from sea level to 900 metres. In the coastal zone, the cold Humboldt Current supports a variety of marine life, such as otters and sea lions, and many birds, including pelicans, cormorants, and the Humboldt penguin.

At higher elevations, moisture from the camanchaca nurtures a unique vegetation of more than 20 species of cacti and succulents. Farther inland, guanacos and foxes are a common sight.

Isla Pan de Azúcar

In the twilight, as the camanchaca advances inland, the island of Pan de Azúcar seems to float on the ocean. Humboldt penguins and

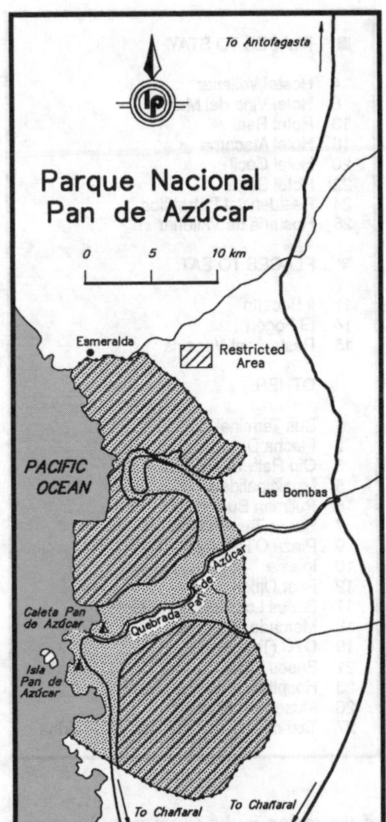

other seabirds nest in abundance; with a good pair of binoculars you can see them from the shore. Only 100 hectares in size, the island itself is a restricted area, but you can approach it by boat – ask the fishermen at Caleta Pan de Azúcar about a circumnavigation.

Places to Stay

CONAF operates camp sites with basic facilities, including picnic tables and welcome shade, at Cerro Soldado, Playa Piqueros and Caleta Pan de Azúcar. Charges are US$3 per site. Water is scarce, however, and it is best to bring your own. While the nearest supplies are at Chañaral, you may be able to purchase fish from the families at Caleta Pan de Azúcar.

Getting There & Away

While there is no regular public transportation to the park, a decent road leads north from the Panamericana near the cemetery at the east end of Chañaral. It should be possible to arrange a taxi from Chañaral for about US$20 if you want to camp, although you'll have to pay the driver both ways – double that amount if you make arrangements to be picked up. Although it may be possible to hitch from Chañaral, especially on a weekend, carrying the amount of provisions you'll need might be a problem, since water is so scarce.

CONAF collects an admission charge of about US$1 at the southern approach to the park. If you're driving and approaching from the direction of Antofagasta, there is also a park entrance at Las Bombas, 45 km north of Chañaral on the Panamericana, where a road follows the Quebrada Pan de Azúcar to the coast.

VALLENAR

Vallenar (population 38,000) lies in the valley of the Río Huasco, 145 km south of Copiapó and 190 km north of La Serena. It dates from the late 18th century, when colonial Governor Ambrosio O'Higgins applied the transliterated name of his native Ballenary, Ireland, to the area. Darwin later visited the area on horseback during his travels aboard the *Beagle*. After serious earthquake damage in 1922, Vallenar was rebuilt with wood instead of adobe, but the city's buildings still rest on unconsolidated sediments.

Like the rest of the Norte Chico, Vallenar developed on the basis of mining, but irrigated agriculture is also critically important. With the construction of new upstream reservoirs, assisted by Japanese capital, local farmers expect to be able to compete with their counterparts in the nearby Copiapó and Elqui valleys in the Chilean fruit export boom.

Orientation

Even motorists usually bypass Vallenar because the Puente Huasco (Huasco Bridge) which spans the valley does not drop down into the town, readily visible below. At the south end of the bridge, the Vallenar-Huasco highway leads east into town, crossing the river via the Puente Brasil.

The centre of town is the Plaza O'Higgins, also called Plaza de Armas, at the intersection of Prat and Vallejos. Everything in town is within easy walking distance of there.

Information

Tourist Office Vallenar's tourist office is a kiosk at the junction of the Panamericana and the Vallenar-Huasco highway, at the south end of the Puente Huasco. From December to March, it's open daily from 10 am to 1 pm and 4 to 8 pm.

Post & Telecommunications Correos de Chile is at the north-east corner of the Plaza de Armas. CTC's long-distance office is at Prat 1035.

Medical Services The Vallenar hospital (☎ 611202) is at the corner of Merced and Talca.

Museo del Huasco

Located at Sargento Aldea 742, Vallenar's history museum has a modest collection of local artefacts and materials, including an excellent photo collection. Admission is about US$0.35; opening hours are daily except Monday from 10 am to 1 pm, and Tuesday to Friday from 3.30 to 7.30 pm, although knowledgeable curator Jorge Zambra will often admit visitors even when the museum is closed.

Festivals

January 5 is a holiday celebrating the founding of the city, while later in the month the local song festival, Festival Vallenar Canta, takes place. In the village of San Félix, 58 km up the valley of the Río Huasco, the annual grape harvest in February is occasion for the Festival de la Vendimia. A speciality of the region is the sweet wine known as *parajete*, available in Vallenar wine shops.

■ PLACES TO STAY

4 Hostal Vallenar
8 Hotel Viña del Mar
13 Hotel Real
16 Hotel Atacama
20 Hotel Cecil
22 Hotel Segal
24 Residencial Potrerillos
25 Hostería de Vallenar

▼ PLACES TO EAT

11 Il Bocatto
14 El Fogón
15 Restaurant Venecia

OTHER

1 Bus Terminal
2 Flecha Dorada
3 Old Railway Station
5 Municipalidad
6 Pullman Bus
7 Buses Tas Choapa
9 Plaza O'Higgins
10 Iglesia
12 Post Office
17 Buses Los Conquistadores
18 Mercado Municipal
19 CTC (Telephone)
21 Buses Libac
23 Hospital
26 Museo del Huasco
27 Taxi colectivos to Huasco & Freirina

Places to Stay

Residencial Potrerillos, Sargento Aldea 940, is the cheapest in town at US$4, but the best value is *Hotel Viña del Mar* (☎ 611478), a cheerful family-run place at Serrano 611, which charges US$7 per person for rooms with shared bath. Slightly cheaper is *Hotel Atacama* (☎ 611426) at Serrano 873. *Hotel Segal* (☎ 614927), at Prat 1190-A, has singles/doubles with shared bath for US$13/16, while rooms with private bath cost US$17/24.

In the US$30/40 range, try *Hotel Cecil* (☎ 614071) at Prat 1059, *Hotel Real*

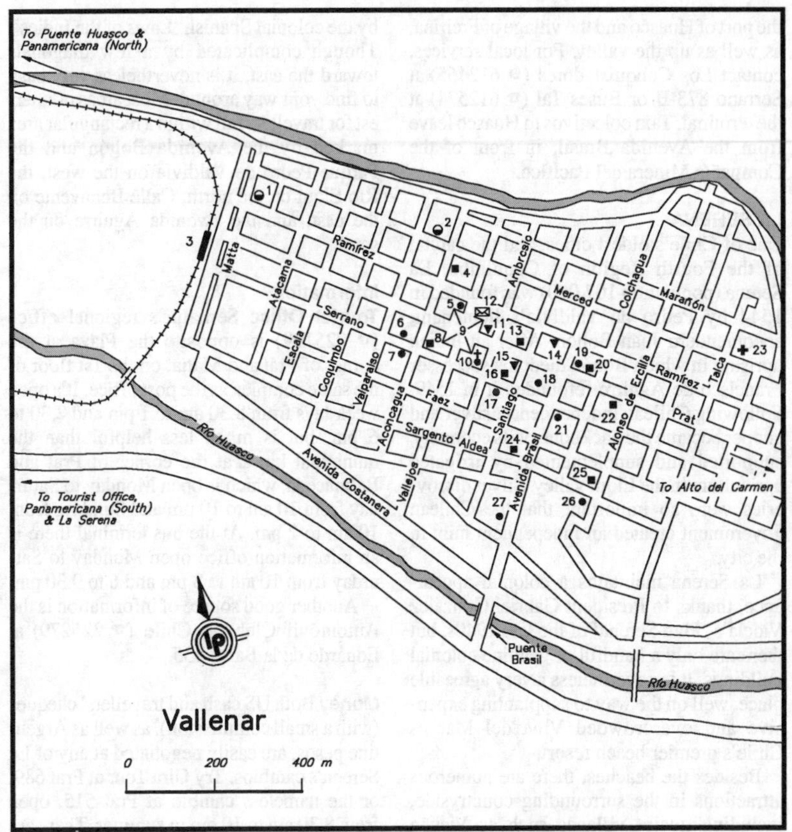

(☎ 613963) at Prat 881, or *Hostal Vallenar* (☎ 611266) at Aconcagua 455. The finest in town is the *Hostería de Vallenar* (☎ 614538) at Alonso de Ercilla 848, which also has a topnotch restaurant.

Places to Eat

One good, inexpensive place to eat is the *mercado municipal* (municipal market), at the corner of Serrano and Santiago. *Il Bocatto*, on Plaza de Armas, has small but good pizzas and snacks. For parrillada, try *El Fogón* at Ramírez 934. *Venecia*, at Santiago 654, serves Italian food.

Getting There & Away

Vallenar's bus terminal is on Matta, at the west end of Ramírez, but many companies have more convenient offices downtown. Flecha Dorada (☎ 611738) is at Merced 561, while Libac (☎ 611331) is at Brasil 715. Pullman (☎ 611612) is at Serrano 551 and Tas Choapa (☎ 611167) at Serrano 580. Flota Barrios (☎ 612483), Tramaca (☎ 612075), and Diamantes de Elqui (☎ 612574) are at the terminal.

North-south transport schedules closely resemble those of Copiapó, but buses and taxi colectivos also connect the town with the port of Huasco and the village of Freirina, as well as up the valley. For local services, contact Los Conquistadores (☎ 612465) at Serrano 873-B or Buses Tal (☎ 612574) at the terminal. Taxi colectivos to Huasco leave from the Avenida Brasil, in front of the Compañía Minera del Pacífico.

LA SERENA

One of Chile's oldest cities, and the capital of the Fourth Region of Coquimbo, La Serena (population 107,000) was founded in 1544 by Pedro de Valdivia's lieutenant, encomendero Juan Bohón. After an Indian uprising in which Bohón died, his successor Francisco de Aguirre refounded it in 1549. Following Chilean independence, silver and copper became the backbone of its economy, supported and supplemented by irrigated agriculture in the Elqui valley. Silver discoveries were so important that the Chilean government created an independent mint in the city.

La Serena maintains a colonial appearance, thanks to President Gabriel González Videla's 'Plan Serena' of the late 1940s, but there are only a handful of genuine colonial buildings. It is nevertheless a very agreeable place, well on the way to supplanting expensive and overcrowded Viña del Mar as Chile's premier beach resort.

Besides the beaches, there are numerous attractions in the surrounding countryside, including quaint villages such as Vicuña (birthplace of Nobel Prize poet Gabriela Mistral), with its nearby vineyards, and several important international astronomical observatories which take advantage of the region's exceptional atmospheric conditions.

Orientation

La Serena lies on the south bank of the Río Elqui, about two km above its outlet to the Pacific Ocean, 470 km from the capital of Santiago. The Carratera Panamericana, known as Avenida Juan Bohón, skirts the western edge of town.

The city plan, centred on the Plaza de Armas, is an extremely regular grid dictated by the colonial Spanish 'Laws of the Indies'. Though complicated by a few diagonals toward the east, it is nevertheless very easy to find your way around. Most areas of interest for travellers fall within a rectangular area marked by the Avenida Bohón and the Parque Pedro de Valdivia on the west, the Río Elqui on the north, Calle Benavente on the east, and the Avenida Aguirre on the south.

Information

Tourist Office Sernatur's regional office (☎ 225199) is opposite the Plaza at the corner of Prat and Matta, on the 1st floor of the same complex as the post office. It's open weekdays from 8.30 am to 1 pm and 2.30 to 6 pm, but is much less helpful than the municipal kiosk at the corner of Prat and Balmaceda, which is open Monday to Saturday from 10 am to 10 pm and Sundays from 10 am to 2 pm. At the bus terminal there is an information office open Monday to Saturday from 10 am to 3 pm and 6 to 9.30 pm.

Another good source of information is the Automóvil Club de Chile (☎ 225279) at Eduardo de la Barra 435.

Money Both US cash and travellers' cheques (with a small commission), as well as Argentine pesos, are easily negotiated at any of La Serena's cambios. Try Gira Tour at Prat 689, or the nameless cambio at Prat 515, open from 8.30 am to 10 pm in summer. There are several others in the same neighbourhood.

Symatour, in the Copec petrol station at the intersection of the Panamericana with Avenida Aguirre, also changes money at reasonable rates.

Post & Telecommunications Correos de Chile is at the corner of Matta and Prat, opposite Plaza de Armas. CTC has long-distance phone offices at Cordovéz 446 and in the Mercado La Recova building. ENTEL is at Prat 571.

Travel Agencies La Serena's numerous travel agencies include Viajes Valle La Serena (☎ 224927) at Prat 540, Viajes

Serena Oriente (☎ 212284) at Balmaceda 460 Local 6, Viajes Torremolinos (☎ 226 403) at Balmaceda 431, Turismo Aerocrom (☎ 224193) at Cienfuegos 420, and Gira Tour (☎ 223535) at Prat 689.

Bookshop La Serena's best bookstore is Librerías Universitarias, Cordovéz 470.

National Parks For information on national parks and other reserves in the Fourth Region, visit CONAF (☎ 215073) at Cordovéz 281.

Medical Services La Serena's hospital (☎ 225569) is at Balmaceda 916.

Churches

Many of La Serena's key features are on or near the beautifully landscaped Plaza de Armas. On the east side is the **Catedral** which dates from 1844. South-west of the plaza, facing onto another smaller but attractively landscaped plaza, is the colonial **Iglesia Santo Domingo**, a relic of the mid-18th century.

Museo Histórico Gabriel González Videla

González Videla, a native of La Serena, was president of the republic from 1946 to 1952. A controversial figure, he took power with the support of the Communist Party but soon outlawed it, driving poet Pablo Neruda out of the Senate and hounding him into exile. Exhibits on González Videla's life omit these episodes, but the museum includes other worthwhile materials on regional history and numerous paintings by Chilean artists.

The museum is at Matta 495 opposite the Plaza. Admission, which costs about US$0.70, is also valid for the city's archaeological museum (see below). Both are open Tuesday to Saturday from 9 am to 1 pm and 4 to 7 pm, Sunday from 10 am to 1 pm. The adjacent **Plaza González Videla**, between the museum and the post office, is the site of the annual book fair (see below).

Museo Arqueológico

La Serena's archaeological museum repeats many of the same themes of the González Videla museum. In addition, the archaeological museum has a valuable collection of Diaguita Indian artefacts from before the Inca conquest which limited the autonomous cultural development of the Chilean coast. There is a good map of distribution of Chile's aboriginal population.

At the intersection of Cordovéz and Cienfuegos, the museum's hours are identical to those of the González Videla museum. Save your ticket, since admission to one admits you to the other as well.

Museo Colonial de Arte Religioso

Occupying an annexe of the colonial **Iglesia San Francisco** at Balmaceda 640, this museum features polychrome sculptures from the Cuzco School and paintings from 17th-century Quito (Ecuador). The church itself, built in 1627 but reconstructed several times, contains 18th-century carvings on the beams of the sacristy.

Admission is US$0.60; opening hours are Tuesday to Saturday from 11 am to 1 pm and 4 to 7 pm, Sundays from 10 am to 1 pm only.

Museo Mineralógico

The Museo Mineralógico Ignacio Domeyko, La Serena's mineral museum, is one of the best in a country whose economy traditionally lives or dies by mining (the mineral museum in Copiapó is probably even better). Opening hours are weekdays from 9 am to noon. It's on Anfión Muñóz between Benavente and Infante.

Beaches

On a two-week vacation in La Serena, you can visit a different beach every day, but strong rip currents make some of them unsuitable for swimming. Safe beaches include Playa Canto del Agua, Playa Las Gaviotas, Playa El Pescador, Playa La Marina, Playa La Barca, Playa Mansa, Playa Los Fuertes, Playa Blanca, Playa El Faro (Sur) and Playa Peñuelas (Coquimbo). Suitable only for sunbathing and paddle-ball are

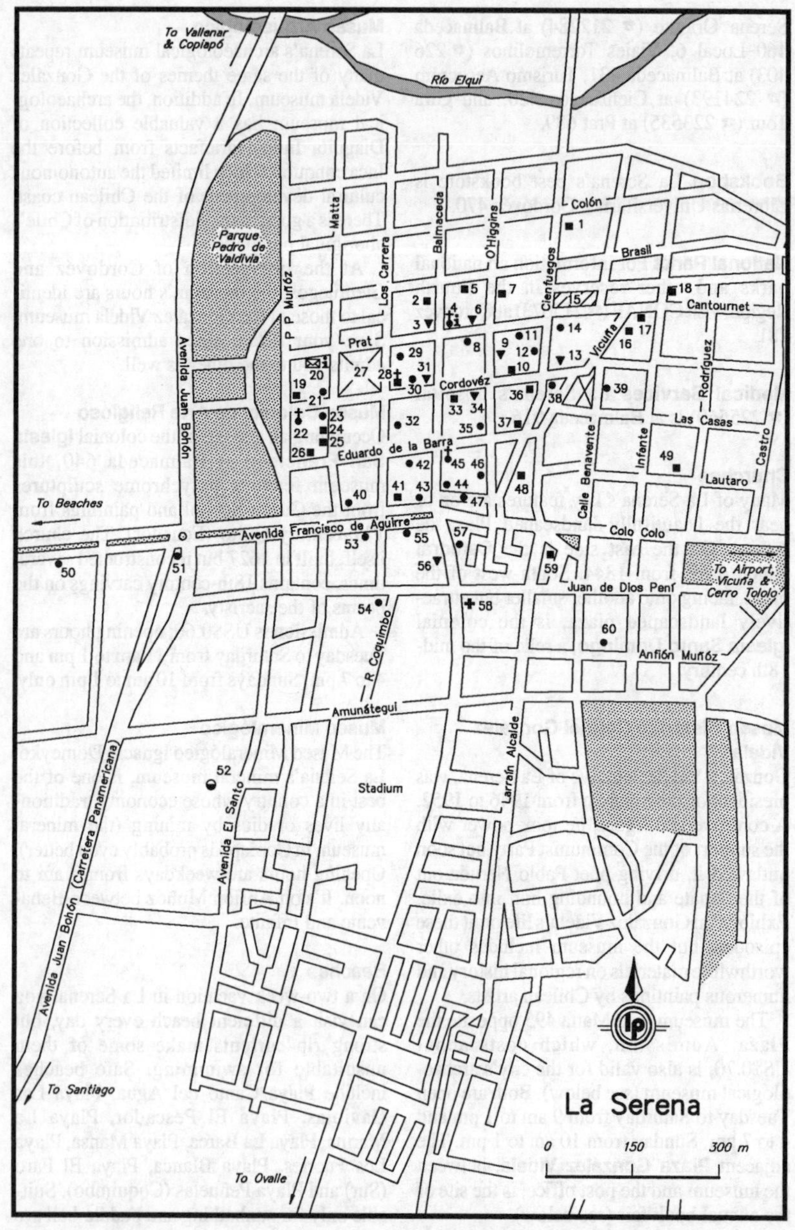
To Vallenar & Copiapó
Río Elqui
Parque Pedro de Valdivia
Matta
P P Muñoz
Los Carrera
Balmaceda
O'Higgins
Colón
Cienfuegos
Brasil
Cantournet
Vicuña
Rodriguez
Prat
Cordovéz
Las Casas
Infante
Castro
Eduardo de la Barra
Calle Benavente
Lautaro
Colo Colo
Juan de Dios Pení
Anfión Muñoz
To Beaches
Avenida Juan Bohón
Avenida Francisco de Aguirre
To Airport, Vicuña & Cerro Tololo
R Coquimbo
Amunátegui
Larraín Alcalde
Stadium
Avenida El Santo
Avenida Juan Bohón (Carretera Panamericana)
To Santiago
To Ovalle
La Serena
0 150 300 m

Playa Cuatro Esquinas, Playa El Faro (Norte), Playa Changa (Coquimbo), Playa Punta de Teatinos, Playa Los Choros, Playa Caleta Hornos, Playa San Pedro and Playa Chungungo. All of these have regular bus and taxi colectivo service from downtown La Serena.

To reach Tongoy, a popular resort south of La Serena, take a taxi colectivo from Calle Domeyko, a block-long street near the corner of Aguirre and Balmaceda.

Organised Tours

Diaguita Tour (☎ 212110), Balmaceda 836, runs a series of tours in the Limarí and Elqui valleys to sites like Valle del Encanto, Parque Nacional Fray Jorge, Termas de Socos, Vicuña, the Pichasca petrified forest, and the beaches of the Fourth Region. Prices for full-day tours run about US$30, except for the shorter La Serena city tour, which costs about half that. Try also Gira Tour (☎ 223535) at Prat 689.

Festivals

La Serena holds an annual book fair in February, displaying the latest work by national and foreign publishing houses. Many prominent Chilean authors visit the city and give public lectures during this time.

Activities

Besides swimming and sunbathing, other popular activities include sailing (if you

■ PLACES TO STAY

1 Pensión Matús
2 Hotel Pucará
5 Residencial Brasilia
7 Residencial El Loa
10 Gran Hotel La Serena
16 Hotel Casablanca
17 Pensión López
18 El Hostal del Turismo
19 Hotel Francisco de Aguirre
24 Residencial Lido
25 Residencial Chile
26 Hotel Pacífico
33 Hotel Berlín
36 Hotel Mediterráneo
37 Residencial Petit
41 Hotel Alameda
48 Residencial Norte Verde
49 Turismo 2000
59 Hotel Los Balcones de Alcalá

▼ PLACES TO EAT

3 Boccaccio
6 Restaurant Domingo Domingo
9 La Pizza Mía
13 Restaurant Mai Lan Fan
31 La Crísis
34 Restaurante Naturista Maracuyá
56 Yugoslav Club

OTHER

4 Iglesia La Merced & Tourist Kiosk
8 ENTEL (Telephone)
11 Gira Tour
12 LAN-Chile
14 Iglesia San Agustín
15 Mercado La Recova
20 Sernatur/Post Office
21 Museo Histórico González Videla
22 Iglesia Santo Domingo
23 CONAF
27 Plaza de Armas
28 Catedral
29 Municipalidad
30 CTC (Telephone)
32 CEMA-Chile Gallery
35 Buses Tas Choapa
38 Museo Arqueológico
39 Teatro Municipal
40 Buses Flecha Dorada
42 Automóvil Club de Chile
43 Línea Ruta 41
44 Buses Tal
45 Iglesia San Francisco & Museo Colonial de Arte Religioso
46 Buses Expreso Norte
47 Calle Domeyko, colectivos to Tongoy, Andacollo & Ovalle
50 Hertz Rent-a-Car
51 Symatour (Money Changing)
52 Bus Terminal
53 Buses Tramaca
54 Buses Frontera Elqui
55 Buses Libac
57 Diaguita Tour
58 Hospital
60 Museo Mineralógico

meet a member of the yacht club) and windsurfing. Wind-surfers who do not respect the rights of swimmers within 200 metres of the beach may run afoul of the Gobernación Marítima.

Places to Stay – bottom end

Many families who house students from the university rent to tourists only in summer, but may also have a spare bed at other times. One to recommend is that of *Pensión López* (☎ 226439), Cantournet 815, which has spacious singles with comfortable beds and excellent hot showers for about US$5. Other comparable places include *Pensión Matús* (☎ 214588) at Cienfuegos 230, *El Hostal del Turismo* at Infante 380, and *Turismo 2000* at Lautaro 960.

Residencial El Loa, O'Higgins 362, charges US$7 per person with shared bath, as does *Residencial Lido* (☎ 213073), Matta 547, which is very good value. *Residencial Norte Verde* (☎ 213646), Cienfuegos 672, is a friendly but unimpressive place for US$8 per person with shared bath, US$11 with private bath. At *Residencial Petit* (☎ 212536), Eduardo de la Barra 586, singles cost US$8 per person. *Residencial Chile* (☎ 211694), near the Plaza at Matta 561, is recommended at US$11/20 a single/ double.

Places to Stay – middle

Hotel Pacífico (☎ 225674), recommended as very comfortable and friendly at Eduardo de la Barra 252, has rooms for US$15/21 with breakfast. *Residencial El Silo* (☎ 213944), a long way out of the centre at Larraín Alcalde 1500, charges US$16/27 for rooms with private bath, while *Hotel Berlín* (☎ 222927) at Cordovéz 535 is slightly dearer. Rates at *Gran Hotel La Serena* (☎ 222975), Cordovéz 610, start at US$20/25 with private bath, as do those at *Hotel Alameda* (☎ 213052), Avenida Aguirre 452. *Residencial Brasilia* (☎ 211 883), Brasil 555, charges US$22/38.

Places to Stay – top end

One LP reader has endorsed *Hotel Los Balcones de Alcalá* (☎ 225999), Aguirre 781, where singles cost US$34. The very central *Hotel Mediterráneo* (☎ 225837), Cienfuegos 509, has rooms with private bath for US$37/54. At the very attractive *Hotel Casablanca* (☎ 212062), Vicuña 414, the same cost US$50/53, while *Hotel Pucará* (☎ 211966) at Balmaceda 319 charges US$48 for a single or double. Only slightly more expensive is the highly recommended, four-star *Hotel Francisco de Aguirre*, at Cordovéz 210 but fronting on the Parque Pedro de Valdivia.

Places to Eat

For superb seafood, any of the restaurants in the Mercado La Recova complex at the corner of Cienfuegos and Cantournet is a good choice, although I would especially recommend *Restaurant Caleta Hornos*, Local 220. The *Yugoslavenski Dom* (Yugoslav Club) at Balmaceda 871 has decent fixed price lunches for about US$3, although the food is really far from Yugoslavian. *Restaurante Naturista Maracuyá* is a vegetarian restaurant at Cordovéz 533, with very fresh ingredients. *Mai Lan Fan*, Cordovéz 740, has decent Chinese food. One reader strongly recommended *Domingo Domingo* at Prat 568.

Coffee, ice cream and desserts are outstanding at *Boccaccio*, at the corner of Prat and Balmaceda. *La Crisis*, Balmaceda 487, is another popular ice cream parlour and snack bar. For coffee, snacks and sandwiches, try *Café do Brasil* at Balmaceda 465. For pizza, try *La Pizza Mía* at O'Higgins 460.

Things to Buy

Check the La Recova market for musical instruments, woollens and dried fruits from the Elqui valley. Other crafts are available at the CEMA-Chile artisans' gallery, Los Carrera 562.

Getting There & Away

Air La Serena's Aeropuerto La Florida is a short distance east of downtown, on the highway to Vicuña and the Elqui valley.

Ladeco (☎ 225753), at Cordovéz 484,

flies to Santiago daily except Saturday. Schedules in the other direction are similar, except for a Saturday flight which continues to Calama and Iquique. LAN-Chile (☎ 225981) has offices at Cienfuegos 463, but no flights out of La Serena.

Bus La Serena's bus terminal (☎ 224573), which also serves nearby Coquimbo, is on the outskirts of town, at the intersection of Amunátegui and Avenida El Santo. They have frequent services to both regional and inter-regional destinations. Since the terminal is a distance from the centre, many companies have downtown offices as well.

Buses – regional Via Elqui (☎ 225240) has five buses daily to Vicuña. Frontera Elqui (☎ 221664), at Juan de Dios Pení and Coquimbo, serves the upper Elqui valley destinations of Vicuña, Rivadavia, Paihuano, Monte Grande, Pisco Elqui and Horcón daily, plus Chapilca and Huanta on Mondays and Fridays, and goes to Hurtado, south of Vicuña, on Saturdays. Los Diamantes de Elqui (☎ 225555) goes to Vicuña and Ovalle, as does Expreso Norte (☎ 224857, 225503), O'Higgins 675. Tas Choapa (☎ 224915, 225959), O'Higgins 599, Inca Bus (☎ 226088, 224795), Buses Tal (☎ 226148, 225555), Balmaceda 594, and Buses Palacios (☎ 224448), Amunátegui 251, also serve Ovalle. Postal Bus and Buses Carlos Araya, operating from the offices of Frontera Elqui, both have frequent service to Andacollo. Fares to regional destinations range from US$1 to US$3.

Buses – inter-regional Many companies ply the Panamericana routes, from Santiago to points north. Those which serve Santiago, taking about seven hours, include Inca Bus (☎ 226088), Tramaca (☎ 226071) at Avenida Aguirre 375, Buses Lit (☎ 224880) at Balmaceda 1302, Flota Barrios (☎ 225936) at Domeyko 550, Los Diamantes del Elqui (☎ 226148), Tas-Choapa (☎ 224915) at O'Higgins 599, Buses Palacios, Flecha Dorada (☎ 225880) at Avenida Aguirre 344, Expreso Norte, Buses Libac (☎ 226101) at Avenida Aguirre 452, and Pullman Bus (☎ 225284), O'Higgins 663. Los Corsarios (☎ 212942), Inca Bus (☎ 226088) and Pullman Bus all serve Valparaíso and Viña del Mar. Inca Bus and Pullman go daily to Illapel and Salamanca in the upper Choapa valley, north-east of Los Vilos.

For Copiapó and other northern destinations as far as Iquique and Arica, try Inca Bus, Flecha Dorada, Flota Barrios, Libac, Pullman, Tramaca, Chile Bus (☎ 225823), Carmelita (☎ 221664) or Fénix Pullman Norte (☎ 225555).

Typical fares from La Serena include: Santiago or Viña/Valparaíso US$9, Los Vilos US$6, Illapel/Salamanca US$7, Copiapó US$7, Chañaral US$10, Antofagasta US$15, Calama US$19, Iquique US$23, and Arica US$25.

Bus – international In the summer months, Wednesdays and Sundays at 12.30 am, Covalle Bus (☎ 213127) connects La Serena with Mendoza and San Juan in Argentina via the Libertadores pass. Fares are about US$30 for the 16-hour run to San Juan.

Taxi Colectivo Many regional destinations are more frequently and rapidly served by taxi colectivo. Anserco, which goes to Andacollo, and Nevada and Sol Elqui, both of which go to Vicuña, share an office (☎ 224428) at Domeyko 524, near Cienfuegos and Avenida Aguirre. Línea Ruta 41 (☎ 224517), Avenida Aguirre 460, goes to destinations in the upper Elqui valley such as Vicuña, El Molle, Paihuano, Rivadavia, Chapilca, and La Higuera. Secovalle, operating from the same offices, goes to Ovalle.

Car Rental For rental cars, try the Automóvil Club de Chile (☎ 225279) at Eduardo de la Barra 435, Hertz (☎ 225471) at Avenida Aguirre 0225 (west of the Panamericana), Budget (☎ 225312) at Matta 389, or Dollar (☎ 224726) at Avenida Aguirre 337. Lesser known local agencies include Rally (☎ 222323) at Matta 670, Daire (☎ 211568) at Prat 645 and El Faro (☎ 225745) at Avenida Aguirre 0660.

AROUND LA SERENA

Coquimbo

Coquimbo (population 106,000), the bustling port of La Serena, takes its name from a Diaguita word meaning 'place of calm waters'. Even Darwin remarked that it was 'remarkable for nothing but its extreme quietness'. Coquimbo no longer suffers the voracious fleas which plagued Darwin during his visit. It's in the hills of the rocky Península Coquimbo, between the Bahía de Coquimbo and the smaller Bahía Herradura de Guayacán. It is quaint and rather lively, especially on a Saturday night, but it's a less attractive place to stay than La Serena

Half-hour boat tours of the harbour depart from the Avenida Costanera daily between 10 am and 8 pm, charging US$1 for adults and US$0.50 for children. There are very popular beaches between Guayacán and La Herradura, easily reached from either Coquimbo or La Serena.

For a gastronomic change of pace, try the *Restaurant Arabe* at Alcalde 527, Chinese food at *Mai Lan Fan*, Avenida Ossandón 1, or Italian at *Tavola Calda*, Bilbao 451. For seafood visit *La Picada* on the Avenida Costanera or, for parrillada, *El Brasero* at Avenida Alessandri 113.

Observatorio Cerro Tololo

At 2200 metres above sea level, 88 km southeast of La Serena, Cerro Tololo is one of the most important observatories in the Southern Hemisphere. A joint project of the Universidad de Chile and several North American universities, it contains the second-largest telescope in the world.

To visit Cerro Tololo, make reservations by calling the office in La Serena (☎ 225415). There is no public transport; hitching is not impossible from the junction along the highway to Vicuña, but give yourself plenty of time.

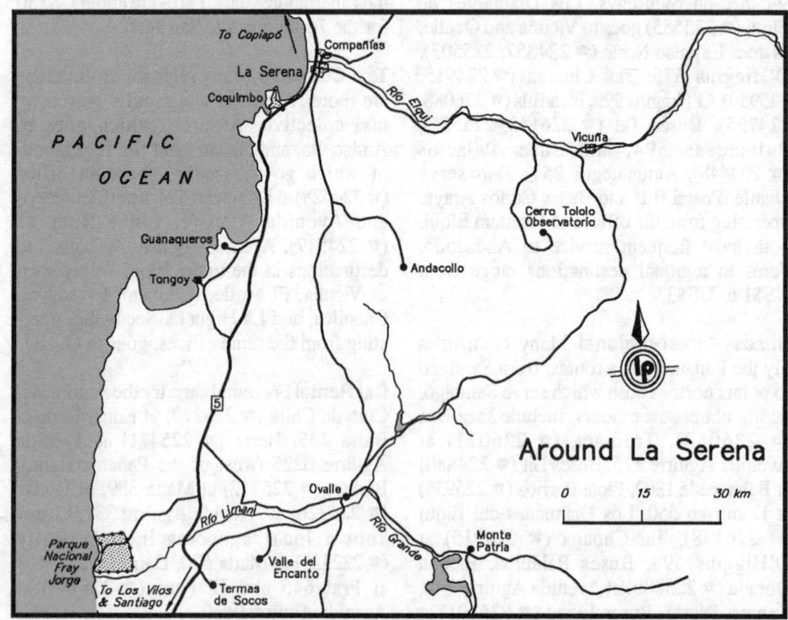

VICUÑA

Vicuña (population 7000) is a quiet village of adobe houses in the upper Elqui valley, 62 km from La Serena, in an area which produces grapes, avocados, papayas and other fruits. Suitable either for a day trip or a few days' stay, the village and its surrounding area have acquired something of an oddball reputation with the arrival of several groups convinced that UFOs frequent the area.

1 Hospital
2 Hostería Vicuña
3 Post Office
4 Torre Bauer (Informaciones Turísticas)
5 Iglesia de la Inmaculada Concepción
6 Plaza de Armas
7 Banco del Estado
8 Galería CEMA-Chile
9 Buses
10 CTC (Telephone)
11 Telex Chile
12 Restaurant Yo y Soledad
13 Gran Hotel Yasna
14 Residencial La Moderna
15 Hotel Sol del Valle
16 Museo Gabriela Mistral

Orientation

On the north bank of the Río Elqui, across a narrow bridge from the La Serena highway, Vicuña has a very regular town plan centred on the Plaza de Armas. Avenida Gabriela Mistral, running east-west off the plaza, is the main commercial street, but every important service or feature is within easy walking distance.

Information

Tourist Office The Municipalidad has an information office in the Torre Bauer (see below), opposite the plaza.

Money Vicuña's sole bank is the Banco del

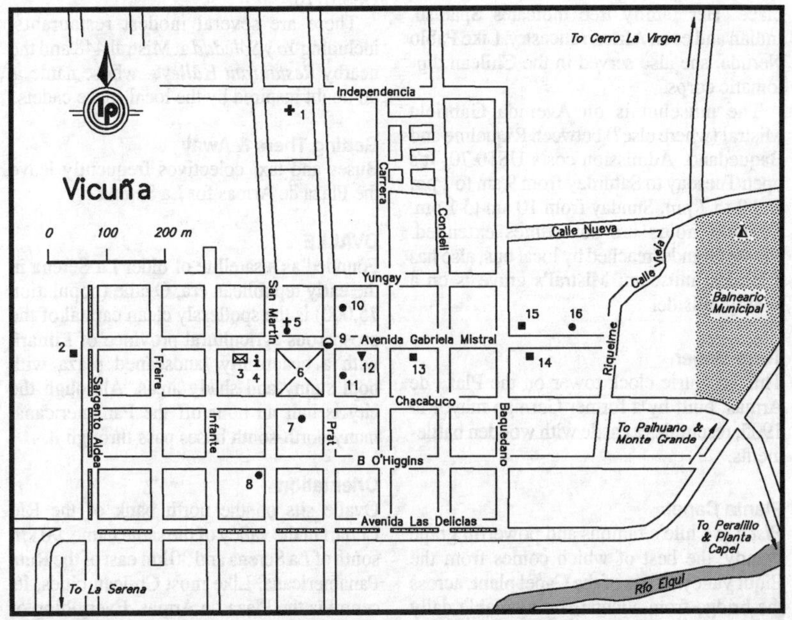

Estado, which offers notoriously poor rates; it is much better to change in La Serena.

Post & Telecommunications Correos de Chile is in the Municipalidad, at the corner of Mistral and San Martín. CTC's long distance office is at Prat 378, half a block off the plaza.

Medical Services Vicuña's hospital is at the corner of Independencia and Prat, a few blocks north of the plaza.

Museo Gabriela Mistral

Vicuña's museum is a tangible eulogy to one of Chile's most famous literary figures, born Lucila Godoy Alcayaga in 1889, in the nearby village of Monte Grande. In addition to a bust that makes her seem a particularly strict and severe schoolmarm, exhibits include a very handsomely presented photographic history of her life, plus modest personal artefacts such as her desk and a bookcase, and a replica of her adobe birthplace. Her family tree indicates Spanish, Indian and even African ancestry. Like Pablo Neruda, she also served in the Chilean diplomatic corps.

The museum is on Avenida Gabriela Mistral (where else?) between Riquelme and Baquedano. Admission costs US$0.70. It's open Tuesday to Saturday from 9 am to 1 pm and 3 to 7 pm, Sunday from 10 am to 1 pm. Summer hours are sometimes extended. Monte Grande, reached by local bus, also has a modest museum; Mistral's grave is on a nearby hillside.

Torre Bauer

This eccentric clock tower on the Plaza de Armas, built by a former German mayor in 1905, resembles a castle with wooden battlements.

Planta Capel

Pisco is Chile's famous and powerful grape brandy, the best of which comes from the Elqui valley. Tours of the Capel plant, across the bridge from Vicuña, are available daily except Sunday, every half-hour in summer and every hour the rest of the year.

Festival de la Vendimia

Vicuña holds its annual grape harvest festival in February.

Places to Stay & Eat

Vicuña has no shortage of reasonable lodging. *Residencial La Moderna*, on Mistral near Baquedano, is the cheapest at US$4 per person. *Gran Hotel Yasna* (☎ 411266), at Mistral 542, also charges US$4 per person for rooms with shared bath and US$7 with private bath (one reader reported plumbing problems). *Hotel Sol del Valle*, almost next door to the museum, charges US$6 a single, and also has a good restaurant. Camping is possible at the *Balneario Municipal*, which has a good restaurant and a swimming pool.

Vicuña's ritziest accommodation is the *Hostería Vicuña* (☎ 411144) at Sargento Aldea 101, where singles/doubles cost US$51/76.

There are several modest restaurants, including *Yo y Soledad* at Mistral 448 and the nearby *Restaurant Halley* – whose name is no doubt inspired by the local space cadets.

Getting There & Away

Buses and taxi colectivos frequently leave the Plaza de Armas for La Serena.

OVALLE

Founded as a satellite of older La Serena in the early republican era, Ovalle (population 75,000) is the spotlessly clean capital of the prosperous agricultural province of Limarí, with a beautifully landscaped plaza with both sunny and shady areas. Although the city is half an hour off the Panamericana, many north-south buses pass through it.

Orientation

Ovalle sits on the north bank of the Río Limarí in the valley of the same name, 90 km south of La Serena and 30 km east of the Ruta Panamericana. Like most Chilean cities, its centre is the Plaza de Armas. Everything of interest is within easy walking distance of the plaza.

1 CTC (Telephone)
2 Municipalidad
3 Hotel Turismo
4 Tourist Information
5 Plaza de Armas
6 Post Office
7 Club Comercial
8 Iglesia San Vicente Ferrer
9 Hotel Francia
10 Club Social Arabe
11 Automóvil Club
12 Hotel Roxy
13 Pullman Bus
14 Hospital
15 Hotel Quisco
16 Museo del Limarí
17 Mercado
18 Buses Carmelita
19 Inca Bus
20 Taxicolectivos Monterrey

Information

Tourist Office Ovalle's tourist office is a kiosk opposite the plaza on Victoria, between the Hotel Turismo and the Banco de Chile. In theory, its hours are Monday from 10 am to 2 pm, Tuesday to Friday from 10.30 am to 2.30 pm and from 4 to 8 pm, and Saturday from 10 am to 2 pm and 3.30 to 7.30 pm; in practice, things are not so precise.

Should the kiosk be abandoned, go to the Automóvil Club (☎ 620001) at Libertad 144, whose staff are friendly, helpful and competent.

Money It's better to change elsewhere, but try the Banco de Chile, on Victoria opposite the plaza, for US cash only.

Post & Telecommunications Correos de Chile is opposite the plaza, on Vicuña Mackenna between Victoria and Miguel Aguirre. CTC's long-distance phone office

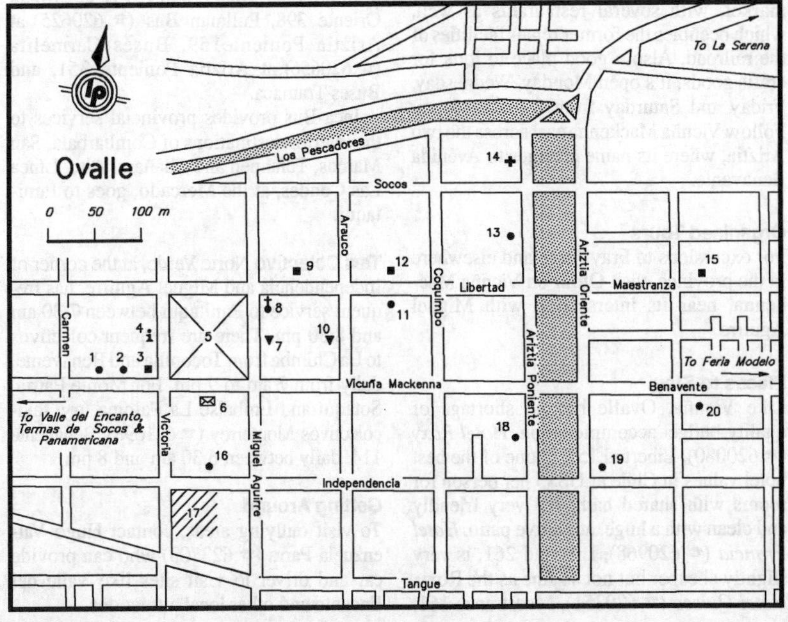

is at Vicuña Mackenna 499, a block west of the plaza.

Medical Services Ovalle's hospital is at the north end of Ariztia Poniente, between Socos and Los Pescadores.

Museo del Limarí

Ovalle's archaeological museum is a modest endeavour which stresses the trans-Andean links between the Diaguita peoples of coastal Chile and north-west Argentina, although there are also pieces from the earlier Huentelauquén and Molle cultures. Some of the larger ceramics are in exceptionally fine condition.

At Independencia 329, the museum is open Tuesday to Friday from 9 am to 1 pm and 3 to 7 pm, Saturday from 9 am to 6 pm, and Sunday from 10 am to 1 pm. Admission costs US$0.85.

Feria Modelo de Ovalle

This is Ovalle's lively fruit and vegetable market, with several restaurants as well, which occupies the former repair facilities of the railroad. Also a good place to look for crafts goods, it's open Monday, Wednesday, Friday and Saturday from 8 am to 4 pm. Follow Vicuña Mackenna east across the two Ariztia, where its name changes to Avenida Benavente.

Organised Tours

For excursions to Fray Jorge and elsewhere in the province, visit Olitur on Vicuña Mackenna, near its intersection with Miguel Aguirre.

Places to Stay

Like Vicuña, Ovalle has no shortage of quality budget accommodation. *Hotel Roxy* (☎ 620080), Libertad 155, is one of the best hotel values in Chile at US$5 per person for rooms with shared bath. It's very friendly and clean with a huge, attractive patio. *Hotel Francia* (☎ 620968), Libertad 261, is very slightly cheaper but not so fine as the Roxy. *Hotel Quisco* (☎ 620351), Maestranza 161, has singles for US$7 with shared bath, US$10 with private bath.

Ostensibly Ovalle's finest, *Hotel Turismo* (☎ 621025), at the corner of Victoria and Vicuña Mackenna, charges US$28/36 a single/double, but it's certainly not six times better than the Roxy.

Places to Eat

For a good fixed-price lunch, try the *Club Comercial* at Aguirre 244, opposite the plaza. Another interesting prospect is the *Club Social Arabe*, Arauco 255 between Libertad and Vicuña Mackenna, which offers Middle Eastern specialities like stuffed grape leaves. There are many reasonable places to eat along Calle Independencia, near the municipal market.

Getting There & Away

Bus North-south bus services closely resemble those from La Serena, though some companies which use the Panamericana bypass Ovalle. Those with offices in Ovalle include Inca Bus (☎ 621574) at Ariztia Oriente 398, Pullman Bus (☎ 620625) at Ariztia Poniente159, Buses Carmelita (☎ 620656) at Ariztia Poniente 351, and Buses Tramaca.

Inca Bus provides provincial services to the interior destinations of Combarbalá, San Marcos, Tulahuen and Chañaral Alto. Línea Las Condes, at the Mercado, goes to Punitaqui.

Taxi Colectivo Norte Verde, at the corner of Independencia and Miguel Aguirre, has frequent service to Punitaqui between 7.30 am and 8.30 pm. There are frequent colectivos to La Chimba from Tocopilla and Benavente, daily from 7 am to 9 pm. For Monte Patria, Sotaquí and Embalse La Paloma, try Taxicolectivos Monterrey (☎ 621698), Benavente 114, daily between 6.30 am and 8 pm.

Getting Around

To visit outlying areas, contact Hugo Valenzuela Parra (☎ 623703) who can provide car and driver to visit sites like Valle del Encanto and other local attractions.

AROUND OVALLE

Valle del Encanto

Just 19 km from Ovalle, Valle del Encanto is a rocky tributary canyon of the Río Limarí, with a remarkable density of Indian petroglyphs, pictographs and mortars from the El Molle culture, which inhabited the area from the 2nd to the 7th century AD. Views of the rock art are best in the early afternoon, when shadows are fewer, but it can be very hot.

Under the protection of the Municipalidad of Ovalle, the Monumento Arqueológico Valle del Encanto charges US$0.85 admission. Both picnicking and camping are possible. To get there, take any westbound bus out of Ovalle toward Termas de Socos and disembark at the highway marker, from which it is an easy five-km walk along a clearly marked road; with luck someone will offer a lift. Bring water for the hike, although there is potable water in the canyon itself. On weekends, a concessionaire sells sandwiches and snacks.

Termas de Socos

Termas de Socos, a short distance off the Panamericana at Km 370, 100 km south of La Serena and 33 km west of Ovalle, has great thermal baths and swimming pools. Private tubs cost US$4 per person for an hour's hot soak.

Camp sites, including pool access, cost US$20 for up to five persons; a rustic cabaña with two beds costs US$23. There is *very* upscale accommodation at the *Hotel Termas de Socos* (☎ 621373), with reservations available in Santiago (☎ 681-6692).

PARQUE NACIONAL FRAY JORGE

Moistened by the camanchaca of the Pacific Ocean, Parque Nacional Fray Jorge is an ecological island of Valdivian cloud forest in an otherwise semi-arid region, 110 km south of La Serena and 82 km west of Ovalle. Where Illapel, for instance, gets only about 150 mm rainfall per annum, Fray Jorge receives up to 10 times that to support a vegetation which more closely resembles the verdant forests of southern Chile than the Mediterranean scrub which covers most of the Norte Chico. Elevations range from sea level to 600 metres.

Of Fray Jorge's 10,000 hectares, there are only 400 hectares of this truly unique vegetation – enough to make it a UNESCO International Biosphere Reserve. Consequently, it is an area of great interest to scientists, and it is open to the public on a limited scale. Some believe that this relict vegetation is evidence of dramatic climate change, but others argue that these once-extensive forests were largely destroyed by humans for fuel, farming and timber.

The first recorded European visitor was a Franciscan priest named Fray Jorge in 1672. Darwin, surprisingly, overlooked the area when he turned inland from the coastal road and passed through Illapel instead. What he missed, at elevations above 450 metres where the effect of the ocean fog is most pronounced, were stands of *olivillo (Aetoxicon punctatum)*, *arrayán* (myrtle, *Myrceugenia correaeifolia)*, *canelo (Drimys winteri)*, plus countless species of shrub and epiphyte. Mammals are few and include two species of fox *(Dusicyon culpaeus* and *Dusicyon griseus)*, skunks and otters. There are some 80 species of bird, including the occasional Andean condor.

Fray Jorge is open to the general public in summer (January 1 to March 15) from Thursday to Sunday, plus holidays, from 8.30 am to 6 pm (though no one is admitted after 4 pm); the rest of the year, it is open on weekends only. Park admission is US$1.50 for Chilean citizens and US$3 for foreigners. There is a visitor centre in the process of development, with interesting photographic displays, a picnic area, and two interpretative nature trails.

Places to Stay

The only option in the park itself is to camp at El Arrayancito, where there are 13 sites with fireplaces (fuel wood is available), picnic tables, potable water and toilets, for US$4. Note that, because of staff limitations, the road opens at 8.30 am and closes at 6 pm, so it is impossible to leave outside these hours.

Getting There & Away

Fray Jorge is reached by a westward lateral off the Ruta Panamericana, about 15 km north of its junction with the paved road to Ovalle and about two km north of a Carabineros checkpoint. There is no regular public transport, but several agencies offer tours out of La Serena and Ovalle (see the respective city entries). North-south buses can drop you at the clearly marked junction, which is 22 km from the park itself – walking it is no picnic, but hitching may be feasible. Hitching out may be easier than hitching in, so ask tour companies if you can leave the tour and perhaps even return another day.

LOS VILOS

Los Vilos is a working-class beach resort of some 8000 permanent residents, a short distance off the Panamericana about midway between Santiago and La Serena. It has plenty of inexpensive accommodation and fine seafood, but tends to be very crowded in summer, when as many as 20,000 Chileans flock to the town. It is especially lively on Sunday mornings, when the fish market at Caleta San Pedro offers live fresh crab, dozens of kinds of fish, a roving hurdy-gurdy man and thousands of colourful balloons.

Orientation

Los Vilos consists of two distinct areas, an older part with a regular grid west of the railroad tracks, and a newer, less regular part between the tracks and the Panamericana. Although it has a central plaza, the Avenida Costanera, leading to the beach, is a much more important focus of activity, while most hotels and restaurants are along the Avenida Caupolicán, which links the town with the Panamericana.

Information

Tourist Office In summer, Los Vilos has a tourist information kiosk on Caupolicán between Talcahuano and Rengo, open from

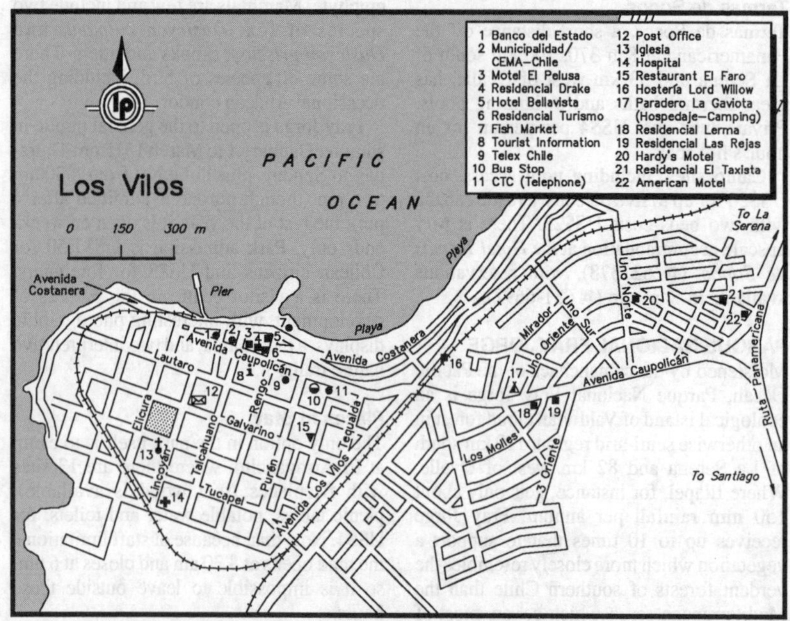

9 am to 2 pm and 4 to 9 pm. The staff are very competent and helpful.

Money Banco del Estado is on Caupolicán near the pier, but foreign visitors are few and rates are poor, so it's better to change in Santiago or La Serena.

Post & Telecommunications Correos de Chile is opposite the plaza, at the corner of Lincoyán and Galvarino. CTC's long-distance offices are on Caupolicán between Purén and Tequalda.

Medical Services Los Vilos' hospital is on Lincoyán, two blocks south of the plaza.

Places to Stay

Residencial Drake, on Caupolicán between Talcahuano and Rengo, is the cheapest of the central hotels at US$4 per person. *Residencial El Taxista*, near the highway at Tilama 247, is distant from the beach, but has comfortable singles with TV and shared bath for US$5. Although the entrance is through a bar, it is friendly and quiet, and not a bad place at all. The hospedaje *Paradero La Gaviota* (☎ 541236), at Caupolicán 1259, has singles/doubles for US$4/7, as well as campsites for US$1 per person (with a four-person minimum). Inspect your room first at *Residencial Lerma*, on Caupolicán near its intersection with Los Molles, where singles cost US$4, and watch for overcharging at nearby *Residencial Las Rejas*, which should cost about US$5.

Hotel Bellavista (☎ 541073), popular and central at Rengo 020, charges US$6 per person with breakfast and shared bath; it also has a very fine restaurant, with huge portions. There are good reports on *Residencial Turismo* (☎ 541176), Caupolicán 437, which charges US$7 per person.

Hostería Lord Willow (☎ 541037), Avenida Los Vilos 1444, has singles/doubles from US$20/29. The *American Motel*, in shady grounds at the junction of Caupolicán and the Panamericana, charges US$25/33, while *Hardy's Motel* (☎ 541098), Avenida Uno Norte 248, charges US$28/36. At *Motel El Pelusa* (☎ 541041), more central at Caupolicán 411, rates are US$28/48.

Places to Eat

Besides the restaurant at Hotel Bellavista (see above), *Restaurant El Faro* at Colipí 224 is also highly regarded. The beachfront cafés along the Avenida Costanera are cheap and good, especially *El Refugio del Pescador*.

Getting There & Away

Few buses enter Los Vilos proper, but it is easy to flag a bus either north or south from the junction of Avenida Caupolicán with the Panamericana – if you get hungry waiting, there's a good snack bar at the Copec petrol station. Companies which do stop in town include Pullman Bus (to Santiago), Inca Bus (to La Serena), and Tas Choapa (to Illapel and Salamanca). All of them have their offices along Avenida Caupolicán.

PICHIDANGUI

Thirty km south of Los Vilos, Pichidangui is a small, pleasant but more exclusive beach resort with many hotels and camping grounds. *Residencial Lucero*, besides accommodation for US$20 per person, has an excellent seafood restaurant with reasonable prices. Conspicuously tight security in the town probably means that General Pinochet is staying at his beachfront house.

La Araucanía & the Lake District

Few landscapes surpass or even equal the scenery beyond the Río Biobío. Perfect volcanic cones, blanketed by glaciers, tower above deep blue lakes, ancient forests, and verdant farmland. Outside the cities, the loudest sound is the roar of waterfalls spilling over cliffs into limpid pools, but it was not always so tranquil. In the early 17th century, Mapuche resistance reduced Spanish settlements south of the Biobío to ashes and ruin.

In this region, the most important cities are Temuco, Valdivia, Osorno and Puerto Montt, but about half the population still lives in the countryside. Tourism plays a major role in the economy, but forest products, cereals, dairy farming and livestock are also important. Local industries, such as sawmills and leather works, rely largely on these primary products.

Mapuche Indian

Temuco, in the Ninth Region of La Araucanía, is the starting point for exploring the area. From Temuco, you can visit Parque Nacional Conguillío and the upper reaches of the Biobío, head south to Lago Villarrica and Pucón, work your way to Licán Ray beside Lago Calafquén, on to Lago Panguipulli, and then to Futrono on Lago Ranco.

Farther south, east of Osorno, the Lago Puyehue route offers an easy land crossing to Argentina via Parque Nacional Puyehue, while Puerto Varas and Ensenada, on Lago Llanquihue, are stops on the route to Lago Todos Los Santos (most beautiful of all the lakes) in Parque Nacional Vicente Pérez Rosales, with a ferry from Petrohué to Peulla. From Peulla, it is possible to cross to Bariloche (Argentina) on a combination of boats and buses.

Puerto Montt, on the Golfo de Reloncaví, is the capital of the Tenth Region of Los Lagos and the gateway to Chiloé Island and Chile's remote and even more enthralling regions of Aisén and Magallanes. Despite construction of a new highway from Puerto Montt, the southern mainland of the Tenth Region, around Lago Yelcho, is more easily accessible from the city of Esquel, in the Argentine province of Chubut.

Travellers intending to visit the many national parks in the Araucanía and the Lake District should acquire Lonely Planet's *Trekking in the Patagonian Andes* (1992), which covers many extended walks in Conguillío, Huerquehue, Villarrica, Puyehue, Vicente Pérez Rosales and Alerce Andino. It also includes parts of the nearby Argentine Lake District.

HISTORY

South of Concepción, Spanish conquistadors found small gold mines, good farmland and

a large potential workforce of Indians; some lands were so tempting that conquistadors surrendered their encomiendas in the central valley for grants south of the Biobío. Despite their optimism, this area was a dangerous frontier and its settlements were constantly under the threat of Mapuche Indian attack or natural hazards. Spanish soldier-poet Alonso de Ercilla y Zuñiga immortalised the Mapuche resistance in his epic *La Araucana*, a classic of its genre and of Spanish literature.

The Mapuche constantly attacked settlements like Osorno and Valdivia, especially in the general rebellion of 1598. By the mid-17th century, the Spaniards abandoned most of the area except for a resettled and heavily fortified Valdivia in 1645-46; another century passed before the Spanish reclaimed settlements south of the Biobío. In the early 19th century, foreign travellers commonly referred to 'Arauco' as a separate country and it was not until the 1880s that treaties with the Mapuche made the area safe for European settlement. Eventually, the Mapuche lost much of their land to large estates and were restricted to small reserves.

Today, several hundred thousand Mapuche live in the provinces between the Biobío and the Río Toltén, still known as La Frontera. Deprived of land by colonial Spaniards and republican Chileans, they now earn a precarious livelihood from agriculture and crafts. From 1965 to 1973, land reform programmes improved their status, but the military coup of 1973 reversed many of these gains. Since the restoration of democracy in 1989, Mapuche peoples have been militant in seeking return of their lands and have, on several occasions, been successful.

German immigrants in the 19th century started many local industries, including breweries, tanneries, brick and furniture factories, bakeries, machine shops and mills. Their influence is still visible in cities like Valdivia and Osorno, which have many central-European style buildings, but visitors should not overestimate the German influence in the region. American geographer Mark Jefferson, writing in the 1920s, found the claims of German domination questionable:

> Puerto Montt was said to speak German and read German newspapers. I was even told I should find people there who were born in the country but could speak no Spanish. All this is exaggeration of the grossest sort...I found two persons who spoke no Spanish, but both were German-born. No street in the city has a German name, nor is German used on signs.

Chileans of German descent have perhaps left their greatest mark in architecture, food, and the agricultural landscape of dairy farms, but few have more than a romantic attachment to central Europe.

TEMUCO

Founded in 1881, after a famous treaty signed on Cerro Ñielol between the Chilean government and the Mapuche, Temuco (population 220,000) is now the fastest growing city in Chile. Supporting a range of industries, including steel, textiles, food processing and wood products, it is a service centre for a large hinterland.

With an increasing tourist industry, Temuco is the starting point for visits to the Lake District or to Mapuche villages in the surrounding countryside, as well as a market town for the Mapuche and their fine handmade woollens. Many Indians sell their produce and handicrafts in the city's markets.

Orientation

On the north bank of the Río Cautín, Temuco is 675 km south of Santiago via the Carretera Panamericana. Despite its late founding, it still conforms to the conventional grid of the Spanish colonial city, but the Panamericana (known as Avenida Caupolicán through town) slices diagonally through the centre from north-east to south-west. To the north, across the Avenida Balmaceda, historic Cerro Ñielol overlooks the city and the river. While the city is growing, travellers can still easily reach most sites of interest on foot.

Information

Tourist Office Sernatur's regional office (☎ 211969) is at Manuel Bulnes (or Bulnes) 586, corner of Claro Solar, opposite the Plaza de Armas Aníbal Pinto. It has city maps and many free leaflets, including a very useful *Datos Utiles Temuco*, but the staff can be remarkably indifferent or even hostile to any inquiry which goes beyond the most routine. In January and February, it is open on weekdays from 8.30 am to 8.30 pm, Saturdays from 9 am to 1 pm and 2 to 7 pm, and Sundays from 10 am to 1 pm; from March to December it is open on weekdays only from 9 am to 1 pm and 3 to 6 pm.

ACCHI (☎ 215132), the Automóvil Club, is also a good source of information at Bulnes 763.

Money Temuco has several exchange houses. Change US cash and travellers' cheques at Turismo Money Exchange at Bulnes 655, Local 1; Turcamb at Claro Solar 733; and Christopher Money Exchange, Arturo Prat 696, Oficina 419.

Post & Telecommunications Both Correos de Chile and TELEX-Chile are at the corner of Diego Portales and Prat. CTC long-distance offices are at Prat 565, Bulnes 368, and on Avenida Caupolicán at Manuel Montt.

Cultural Centres The Centro Cultural Municipal, at the junction of Avenida Balmaceda, Caupolicán and Prat, contains the Temuco library, two auditoriums for shows and concerts, and an exhibition hall. The Instituto Chileno-Norteamericano is on General Mackenna between Manuel Montt and Claro Solar.

Travel Agencies Larra-Tour (☎ 237913), Bulnes 307, Oficina 203, operates excursions ranging from city tours to visits to Mapuche villages and the national parks of the cordillera. Try also Anahi Turismo (☎ 211155) at Aldunate 235, International Tours (☎ 212745) at Prat 427, or many others in the central zone.

Bookshops For materials on the Mapuche and regional history, visit Librería Universitaria, Portales 861.

Medical Services Temuco's Hospital (☎ 212525) is at Manuel Montt 115, six blocks west and one block north of the Plaza de Armas.

National Parks CONAF (☎ 238900) is at Avenida Bilbao 931, 2nd floor.

Mercado Municipal

Three blocks north of the Plaza and bounded by Bulnes, Portales, Aldunate and Rodríguez, the municipal market building dates from 1929. One of the most popular attractions in central Temuco, it integrates service to the community (food and clothing) with tourist appeal (restaurants and crafts). It's open Monday to Saturday from 8 am to 7 pm, Sunday from 8.30 am to 2 pm.

Monumento Natural Cerro Ñielol

Because of the presence of natural concentrations of the copihue *(Lapageria rosea*, Chile's national flower), this 85-hectare urban park, administered by CONAF, merits the highest protection possible under Chilean forestry regulations. However, it is really a park of historical importance because it was at the tree-shaded site known as La Patagua that Mapuche leaders ceded land for the founding of Temuco in 1881.

Cerro Ñielol is a popular place for local outings, with its many picnic sites, a small lagoon, footpaths and an environmental information centre. There is an admission charge of US$0.35 per pedestrian and US$2 per car. The 800-seat *Restaurant La Cumbre* serves meals from noon to midnight.

Museo Regional de la Araucanía

Housed in an attractive colonial building at Alemania 084, this museum has permanent exhibits retelling the history of the Mapuche Indians before, during, and after the Spanish invasion. There is also material on European colonisation, maps of the city and the region,

Copihue

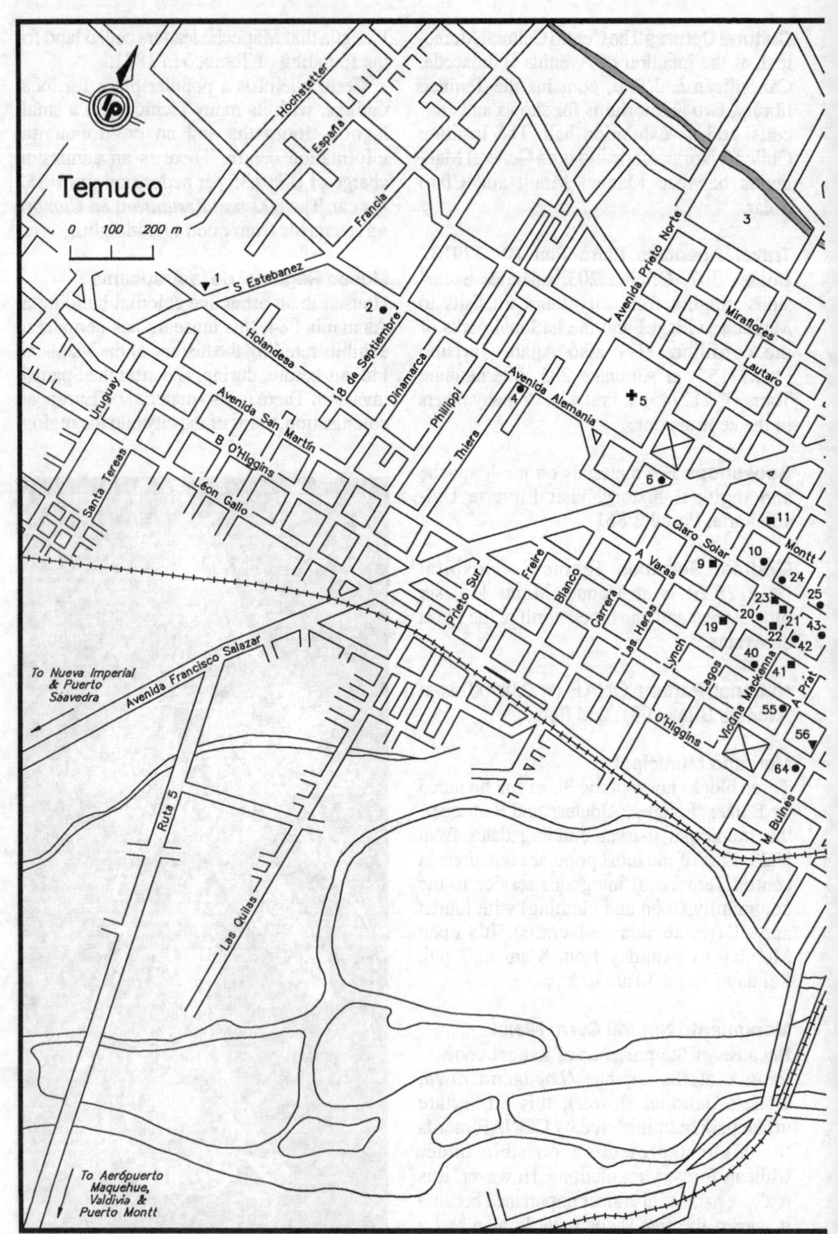
Temuco
0 100 200 m
Hochstetter
España
Francia
S Estebanez
Holandesa
18 de Septiembre
Dinamarca
Phillippi
Thiers
Avenida Prieto Norte
Miraflores
Lautaro
Avenida Alemania
Uruguay
Avenida San Martín
B O'Higgins
Santa Tereas
León Gallo
Claro Solar
Montt
A Varas
Freire
Blanco
Carrera
Prieto Sur
Las Heras
Lynch
Lagos
Vicuña Mackenna
A Prat
O'Higgins
M Bulnes
Avenida Francisco Salazar
Ruta 5
Las Quilas
To Nueva Imperial & Puerto Saavedra
To Aerópuerto Maquehue, Valdivia & Puerto Montt
1
2
3
4
5
6
9
10
11
19
20
21
22
23
24
25
40
41
42
43
55
56
64

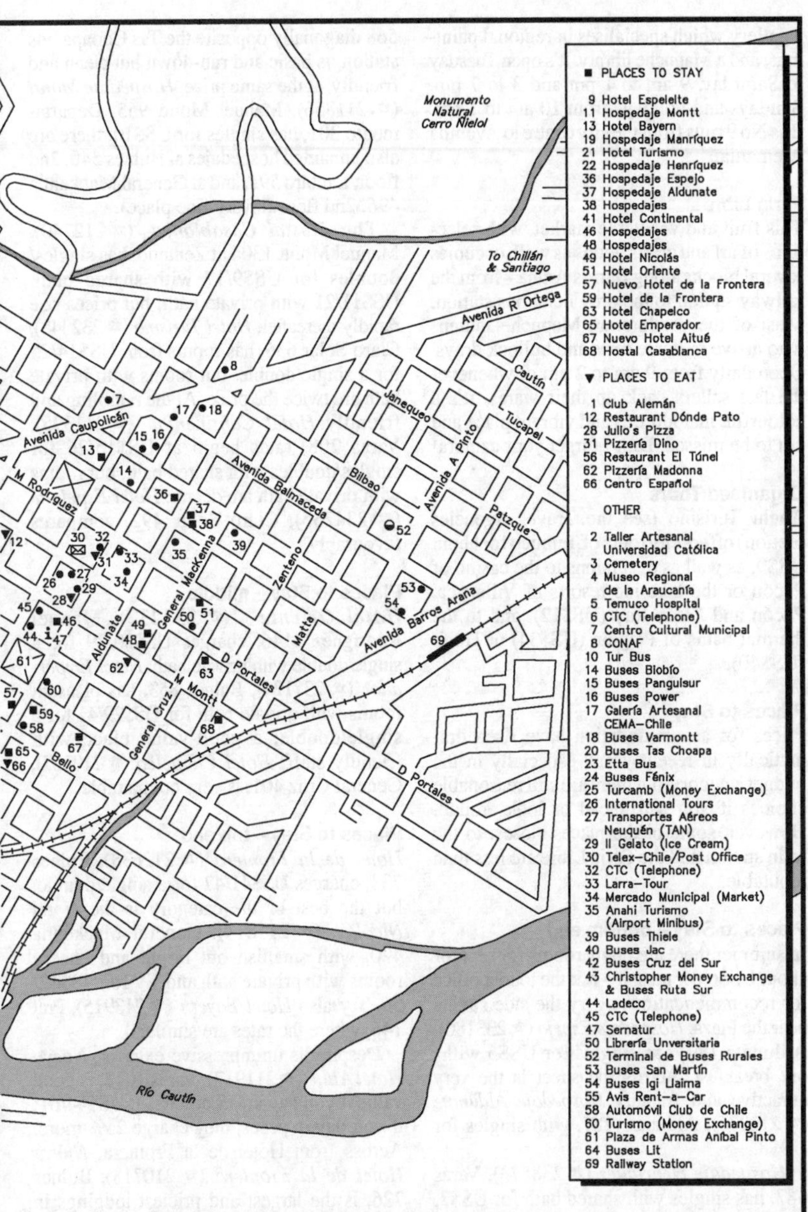

Monumento Natural Cerro Ñielol
To Chillán & Santiago
Avenida R Ortega
Cautín
Tucapel
Janequeo
Avenida A Pinto
Bilbao
Patzque
Avenida Caupolicán
M Rodríguez
Avenida Balmaceda
General MacKenna
Zenteno
Matta
Avenida Barros Arana
Aldunate
General Cruz
M Montt
D Portales
Bello
Río Cautín
■ PLACES TO STAY
9 Hotel Espelette
11 Hospedaje Montt
13 Hotel Bayern
19 Hospedaje Manríquez
21 Hotel Turismo
22 Hospedaje Henríquez
36 Hospedaje Espejo
37 Hospedaje Aldunate
38 Hospedajes
41 Hotel Continental
46 Hospedajes
48 Hospedajes
49 Hotel Nicolás
51 Hotel Oriente
57 Nuevo Hotel de la Frontera
59 Hotel de la Frontera
63 Hotel Chapelco
65 Hotel Emperador
67 Nuevo Hotel Aitué
68 Hostal Casablanca
▼ PLACES TO EAT
1 Club Alemán
12 Restaurant Dónde Pato
28 Julio's Pizza
31 Pizzería Dino
56 Restaurant El Túnel
62 Pizzería Madonna
66 Centro Español
OTHER
2 Taller Artesanal Universidad Católica
3 Cemetery
4 Museo Regional de la Araucanía
5 Temuco Hospital
6 CTC (Telephone)
7 Centro Cultural Municipal
8 CONAF
10 Tur Bus
14 Buses Biobío
15 Buses Pangulsur
16 Buses Power
17 Galería Artesanal CEMA-Chile
18 Buses Varmontt
20 Buses Tas Choapa
23 Etta Bus
24 Buses Fénix
25 Turcamb (Money Exchange)
26 International Tours
27 Transportes Aéreos Neuquén (TAN)
29 Il Gelato (Ice Cream)
30 Telex-Chile/Post Office
32 CTC (Telephone)
33 Larra-Tour
34 Mercado Municipal (Market)
35 Anahi Turismo (Airport Minibus)
39 Buses Thiele
40 Buses Jac
42 Buses Cruz del Sur
43 Christopher Money Exchange & Buses Ruta Sur
44 Ladeco
45 CTC (Telephone)
47 Sernatur
50 Librería Unversitaria
52 Terminal de Buses Rurales
53 Buses San Martín
54 Buses Igi Llaima
55 Avis Rent-a-Car
58 Automóvil Club de Chile
60 Turismo (Money Exchange)
61 Plaza de Armas Aníbal Pinto
64 Buses Lit
69 Railway Station

a gallery which specialises in regional paintings, and a Mapuche library. It's open Tuesday to Saturday, 9 am to 1 pm and 3 to 7 pm, Sundays and holidays from 10 am to 1 pm. Bus No 9 runs from the city centre to Avenida Alemania.

Feria Libre

This fruit and vegetable market, with selections of art and crafts goods as well, occupies several blocks along Barros Arana – from the railway station to the provincial bus station. Most of the vendors are Mapuche Indians who arrive in horse carts and bullock drays. Open daily from 9 am to 2 pm or whenever the last sellers pack up their wares, it's a colourful, malodorous and vibrant place and not to be missed. Don't forget your camera!

Organised Tours

Anahi Turismo (see the Travel Agencies section) offers city tours of Temuco for about US$9, as well as excursions to the casino of Pucón or the lakeside resorts of Villarrica, Pucón and Licán Ray (US$12), and to the thermal baths of Palguín (US$34) or Huife (US$40).

Places to Stay

Prices for accommodation have risen dramatically in recent years, especially in the budget category, but there are still reasonable choices if you call ahead or look around. However, some of the places closest to the train station and the Feria Libre are less than reputable.

Places to Stay – bottom end

In summer there are many rooms for rent for about US$6 per person – ask the tourist office for recommendations or try the side streets near the Plaza. *Hospedaje Espejo* (☎ 233186), Aldunate 124, has singles for US$5 without breakfast. Across the street is the very attractive and friendly *Hospedaje Aldunate* (☎ 212976), Aldunate 187, with singles for US$8.

Hospedaje Henríquez (☎ 238673), Varas 687, has singles with shared bath for US$7, while the *Hospedaje Manríquez*, at Varas 568 diagonally opposite the Tas Choapa bus station, is basic and run-down but clean and friendly, at the same price. *Hospedaje Montt* (☎ 211856), Manuel Montt 965, Departamento 301, has singles for US$10; there are also unnamed hospedajes at Bulnes 540, 2nd floor, Lautaro 591, and at General Mackenna 496, 2nd floor (a very fine place).

The *Hostal Casablanca* (☎ 212740), Manuel Montt 1306 at Zenteno, has singles/doubles for US$9/17 with shared bath, US$11/21 with private bath, but prices rise rapidly thereafter. *Hotel Turismo* (☎ 232348), Claro Solar 636, has rooms from US$14/25 for a single/double, but rooms with private bath are twice the price. At the rambling and friendly *Hotel Continental* (☎ 211395), Varas 708, rates begin at US$15/26 for singles/doubles with shared bath, but rooms with private bath are dearer. *Hotel Espelette* (☎ 234255), Claro Solar 492, compares favourably.

Places to Stay – middle

Hotel Oriente (☎ 233232), Manuel Rodríguez 1146, charges US$20/29 for a single/double with private bath. *Hotel Emperador* (☎ 237124), Bulnes 853, has pleasant rooms with private bath for US$29/41 for a single/double; a good-value place with friendly staff. *Hotel Chapelco* (☎ 210367), General Cruz 401, is very comparable.

Places to Stay – top end

Hotel de la Frontera (☎ 212638), Bulnes 733, charges US$41/47 for a single/double, but the best of the category is the *Hotel Nicolás* (☎ 211813), General Mackenna 420, with smallish but bright and cheery rooms with private bath and TV for US$42/56. Try also *Hotel Bayern* (☎ 213915), Prat 146, where the rates are similar.

Despite its unimpressive exterior, *Nuevo Hotel Aitué* (☎ 211917), Varas 1048, is good value if you pay in US dollars, at US$44/61; if you pay in pesos, they charge 25% more. Across from Hotel de la Frontera, *Nuevo Hotel de la Frontera* (☎ 210718), Bulnes 726, is the largest and priciest lodgings in town. Rates are US$65/80.

Places to Eat

Temuco's cheapest food is available at small restaurants and snack bars around the train station and the Terminal de Buses Rurales, but the best value is the seafood at various *puestos* (stands) in the Mercado Municipal market at Portales and Aldunate – don't leave Temuco without trying it. *Restaurant Caribe*, Puesto 45 in the market, is outstanding value for money, but a Chilean-American resident also highly recommends the slightly more formal and upscale *La Caleta* for a splurge. *Don Yeyo*, Puesto 55, and *El Turista*, Puesto 32, are other possible choices.

For good-quality fast food, try the spiffy *Pizzería Dino* at Bulnes 360, *Pizzería Madonna* at Manuel Montt 670, or the more up-market *Julio's Pizza* at Bulnes 478. *Restaurant El Túnel*, Bulnes 846-A, is a prime parrilla which stays open until 2 am. Another central parrilla is *Dónde Pato*, Portales 680.

For Mediterranean food, check out the *Centro Español* at Bulnes 883 but for more hearty middle-European fare the *Club Alemán*, the German club, is at Senador Estébanez 772. *Il Gelato*, Bulnes 420, has very fine ice cream.

Things to Buy

The Mercado Municipal has the city's best selection of handicrafts. Despite a lot of junk and kitsch products, it's a good place for Mapuche woollen ponchos, blankets and pullovers – many women also hawk these goods on the streets. Look for jewellery, pottery, polished stone mortars and musical instruments such as *zampoñas* (pan pipes) and drums.

Other good places to look for crafts are the Taller Artesanal Universidad Católica at Avenida Alemania 0422 and the Galería Artesanal CEMA- Chile, at Caupolicán and Balmaceda. Items here have price tags, so you can get some idea of the price range when bargaining in the market.

Getting There & Away

Air Temuco's Aeropuerto Maquehue is six km south of town, just off the Panamericana. Taxis from the front of Banco Osorno, on the

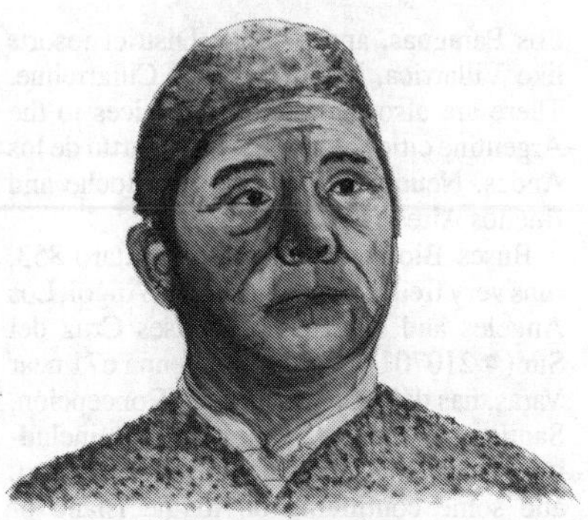

Mapuche holy man

Plaza de Armas, will take passengers for US$4. Anahi Turismo(☎ 211155), Aldunate 235, runs minibuses to the airport in coordination with flight schedules.

LAN-Chile (☎ 211339), Bulnes 657 near Antonio Varas, has one flight per day from Santiago; the Monday, Wednesday and Thursday flights continue to Osorno. Return schedules are very similar.

Ladeco (☎ 213180), near the Plaza at Prat 565, Local 2, has more flights and a wider range of destinations. Of its nine weekly flights, seven continue to Puerto Montt, four to Balmaceda/Coihaique, and the Wednesday flight, to Punta Arenas. Return schedules are also very similar.

Transportes Aéreos Neuquén (TAN, ☎ 210500), Portales 840, connects Temuco with Neuquén in Argentina on Tuesday and Thursday at 5 pm. The fare is US$91.

Bus – domestic Temuco is a major transport hub. The Terminal de Buses Rurales (☎ 210494) is at Avenida Balmaceda and Avenida Pinto; for local and regional destinations not mentioned in this section, check the schedules of the many companies at the terminal. Most long-distance companies have their offices in or near the centre.

Besides destinations on or near the Panamericana between Santiago and Puerto Montt, there are frequent connections to nearby national parks like Conguillío and

Los Paraguas, and to Lake District resorts like Villarrica, Licán Ray and Curarrehue. There are also international services to the Argentine cities of Zapala, San Martín de los Andes, Neuquén, Mendoza, Bariloche and Buenos Aires.

Buses Biobío (☎ 210599), Lautaro 853, runs very frequent bus services to Angol, Los Angeles and Concepción. Buses Cruz del Sur (☎ 210701), Vicuña Mackenna 671 near Varas, has daily bus services to Concepción, Santiago and many to Puerto Montt, including intermediate destinations like Osorno, and some continuing on to the island of Chiloé. It also offers more than a dozen daily trips to Valdivia.

Tas Choapa (☎ 212422), Varas 609, has a daily service to Valdivia and Puerto Montt and three buses to Santiago, all with intermediate stops, and also goes to La Serena. It also has a nightly direct service (at 11.15 pm) to Valparaíso and Viña del Mar without transfer in Santiago. Buses Fénix (☎ 212582), Claro Solar 609, has three night bus services to Santiago, with connections to northern Chilean destinations like Copiapó, Antofagasta, Iquique and Arica.

Tur Bus (☎ 234349), Lagos 538, has two buses daily to Concepción, three to Chillán, five to Osorno and to Valdivia, two to Puerto Montt, and nine to Santiago. Buses Lit (☎ 211483), San Martín 894, goes daily to Concepción, Valdivia, Osorno and Puerto Montt, and has four buses to Chillán and five to Santiago.

Buses Igi Llaima (☎ 210364), Miraflores 1551, goes daily to Chillán, twice daily to Santiago, and offers seven buses daily to Concepción, eight to Valdivia, and four to Osorno and Puerto Montt. Varmontt buses (☎ 211314), Bulnes 45, goes daily to Valdivia, Concepción, Osorno, Puerto Montt and Santiago.

Buses Power (☎ 236513), Bulnes 178, has three nightly buses to Santiago. Etta Bus (☎ 213451), Vicuña Mackenna 648, has two daily bus services to Concepción, two to Osorno and Puerto Montt, and three to Valdivia, plus a daily service to Santiago.

Buses Jac (☎ 210313), Vicuña MacKenna 798 near Varas, offers about 24 buses daily to Villarrica and Pucón, plus four daily buses to Santiago, three to Licán Ray and Coñaripe, and a daily service to Curarrehue. Buses Panguisur (☎ 211560), Miraflores 871, has seven buses daily to Panguipulli, plus three buses nightly to Santiago.

Buses Thiele (☎ 238632), Miraflores 1136, has three buses a day to Cañete, continuing on to Lebú, on the Costa del Carbón, and Concepción. Flota Erbuc (☎ 210219), at the Terminal de Buses Rurales, has three buses daily to Lonquimay, on the upper Biobío near the Argentine border.

Prices can vary considerably, so shop around, but typical fares from Temuco are: Coñaripe US$1.50; Villarrica US$2; Angol, Pucón or Licán Ray US$2.50; Valdivia, Los Angeles or Lonquimay US$3; Chillán or Currarehue US$4; Concepción or Osorno US$5; Puerto Montt US$7; and Santiago US$10. Times and frequencies of departures change throughout the year, with fewer buses in winter.

Bus – international Buses Fénix connects Temuco with Buenos Aires on Mondays and Wednesdays via the Paso Libertadores, north-east of Santiago, for US$70. Both Fénix and Tas Choapa buses have nightly services to Mendoza, with Santiago as a transfer point, for US$30.

Buses Jac, Igi Llaima and San Martín (☎ 234017), Balmaceda 1598, connect Temuco with Junín de los Andes, San Martín de Los Andes, and Neuquén, usually via the Paso Mamuil Malal east of Pucón but occasionally over the Paso Pino Hachado, directly east of Temuco via Curacautín and Lonquimay, along the upper Biobío. Buses Ruta Sur (☎ 210079), Claro Solar 692, and Igi Llaima both go to Neuquén via Zapala. Typical fares are Junín or San Martín US$15, Zapala US$23, and Neuquén US$29. Each of these services runs about three times a week in summer only.

Tas Choapa and Cruz del Sur have bus services to Bariloche, via Paso Puyehue east of Osorno, daily for US$27.

Train Daily trains from Temuco go north to Santiago (all year) and south to Puerto Montt (in summer only), stopping at various stations (see the Getting Around chapter). The quicker *La Frontera* train, leaving at 8.45 pm, takes about 10 hours to Santiago, while the slower *Puerto Montt* departs at 1.10 am, taking about 12 hours.

Buy train tickets either at the station (☎ 233416), eight blocks west of the Plaza on Avenida Barros Arana, or at the downtown office of Ferrocarriles del Estado (☎ 233522), Bulnes 582 near Claro Solar.

Getting Around

While Temuco has begun to sprawl, with the railway station and main bus terminal some distance from the centre, any taxi colectivo will quickly take you there. Bus No 1 runs from the city centre to the train station.

Car Rental Rental cars are available from the Automóvil Club (☎ 215132) at Bulnes 763, Hertz (☎ 235385) at Bulnes 750, Avis (☎ 211515) at Prat 800, First (☎ 233890) at Varas 1036, and Budget (☎ 214911) at General Mackenna and Varas. Car rental is worth considering for easy access to the surrounding national parks and Indian settlements.

AROUND TEMUCO

Chol Chol

Chol Chol is a dusty village of wooden, tin-roofed bungalows and dirt roads plied by Indian bullock carts. With traditional Mapuche *rucas* (houses) on its outskirts, it has the atmosphere of a frontier town where time has stood still, or at least run slowly.

From Temuco's Terminal de Buses Rurales, Buses Epaza and Huinca Bus (☎ 210494) take about 1½ hours to Chol Chol, the former via Nueva Imperial and the latter direct, for US$0.65. The bus is likely to be jammed with Indians returning from the market with fruits and vegetables.

PARQUE NACIONAL CONGUILLÍO

Created in 1950, Conguillío protects more than 60,000 hectares of alpine lakes, deep canyons, forests and the 3125-metre Volcán Llaima, which has experienced 28 violent eruptions since 1640, most recently in 1957. Some 12,000 years ago, a lava flow off Llaima's northern flank dammed the Río Truful Truful to form Lago Conguillío.

The Parque Nacional Conguillío now includes Sector Los Paraguas. It was created to protect the Araucaria pine, or monkey-puzzle tree, which is known to Spanish-speakers as 'the umbrella' (paragua) because of its unusual shape. The Mapuche, who named it the *pehuén*, have traditionally gathered nuts from its cones as food. At lower elevations are forests of southern beech (*Nothofagus* species). Conguillío's woodlands are more open than the denser Valdivian rainforest to the south.

Geography & Climate

In the province of Cautín in the Ninth Region, Conguillío is about 80 km east of Temuco. Its centrepiece is Volcán Llaima, but there are many other volcanic landforms and the glaciated peaks of the Sierra Nevada, north of Lago Conguillío, consistently exceed 2000 metres. In places, elevations drop to 900 metres.

The park experiences warm summers, but up to three metres of snow can accumulate in winter. Mean annual precipitation is about 2000 mm, falling almost entirely between May and September. December to April is the best time for a visit.

Things to See & Do

CONAF's visitor centre at Lago Conguillío offers a variety of programs from November to March, including slide shows and ecology talks, hikes to the Sierra Nevada and for children, boat excursions on the lake. Of course, independent travellers can undertake many of these same activities.

Experienced climbers can tackle Volcán Llaima from the west side, where there is a refugio on the road from Cherquenco. In the winter, when the road to Lago Conguillío is closed by snow, there is skiing in this sector. Contact the Escuela de Ski (☎ 235193) in Temuco, which offers classes and ski rental equipment.

Travellers with an interest in geology should visit the shores of the Río Truful-Truful where the canyon presents an insight into the park's evolution through the colourful strata which the rushing waters have exposed.

Places to Stay

Cabañas y Camping Conguillío (☎ 220254 in Temuco), a concessionaire authorised by CONAF, operates the accommodation at Lago Conguillío and is open from mid-December to early March. The cabañas, which sleep six, are built around the trunks of the pehuén trees and cost US$50 per night. Campsites are not cheap at US$17 for two tents with up to five persons, though some other campgrounds may be less expensive. The other alternative is to head into the back-country.

At the Los Paraguas sector, the *Refugio Escuela Ski* (☎ 235193 in Temuco) has 40 beds and a restaurant.

Getting There & Away

There are several ways to approach the park. To reach the Los Paraguas sector from Temuco's Terminal de Buses Rurales, take one of Flota Erbuc buses (☎ 210129). Four buses run daily to the village of Cherquenco (US$1), from where it is necessary to walk or hitch 17 km to the ski lodge. Nar Bus (☎ 211611) also runs eight buses daily to Cherquenco.

It is possible to approach the Conguillío sector from either the north or south. The northern route takes the Panamericana to Victoria, then the paved highway east to Curacautín, which is 42 km from the park headquarters (an alternative to Curacautín goes via a gravel road from Lautaro). Erbuc has six buses a day via Victoria (US$1.75) and four via Lautaro (US$2) but from Curacautín it is necessary to hitch.

The southern route to Conguillío sector passes through the villages of Cunco and Melipeuco. Nar Bus has half a dozen buses daily to Melipeuco (US$2), and from Hostería Hue-Telén in Melipeuco there are buses to the park headquarters. If you can afford to rent a car, it's easy to combine these two routes in a loop trip from Temuco.

VILLARRICA

One of La Araucanía's most popular resorts, Villarrica shares its name with the lake beside which it sits, and the smouldering, snow-capped volcano which dominates its skyline. Founded in 1552 by Gerónimo de Alderete as Santa María Magdalena de Villarrica, the settlement failed to survive repeated Mapuche attacks during the colonial period. According to one commentator in late colonial times, the Indians were well beyond Spanish authority:

> The ruins of this city are yet visible, particularly those of the walls of orchards and of a church. The town stood on the side of a lake...about 25 miles in circumference, and abounding with fish. The soil is very fertile, and the Indians raise maize, potatoes, quinoa, peas, beans, barley and wheat. Apple, pear, peach and cherry-trees are seen growing where they were planted by the Spaniards before the destruction of the city. The Indians neither admit missionaries nor comisario. They have all kinds of cattle and poultry, which they exchange with other tribes for ponchos, flannels, &c being very averse to trade with the Spaniards.

Not until 1883 did the Mapuche toqui Epuléf

allow the Chilean state, in the person of Colonel Gregorio Urrutia, to keep a permanent presence in the territory. German colonists have left a visible legacy, and the area has become one of the region's most popular holiday destinations.

Orientation

Villarrica sits on the south-west shore of Lago Villarrica, 86 km south-west of Temuco at the point where the Río Toltén drains the lake, starting its journey to the Pacific at Nueva Toltén. The city itself (permanent population 20,000) displays a fairly regular grid pattern, bounded by the irregular lakeshore on the north, Avenida J M Carrera to the west, the diagonal Presidente J A Ríos on the south, and Aviador Acevedo to the east. The important commercial streets are Avenida Pedro de Valdivia (the major thoroughfare) and Camilio Henríquez (which becomes Alderete south of Bilbao).

Information

Tourist Office The tourist office (☎ 411162) is at Pedro de Valdivia 1070 near Aviador Acevedo. Between January 1 and March 15, it is open from 8.30 am to 11 pm while during the rest of the year, hours are 8.30 am to 1 pm and 1.30 to 6.30 pm. The staff are exceptionally helpful and knowledgeable and there are many leaflets, including the very useful *Datos Utiles Villarrica* and an up-to-date list of accommodation and prices.

Money Turcamb, Valentín Letelier 704, will change US and Argentine cash, as well as US travellers' cheques. Try also Carlos Huerta, Anfión Muñoz 417.

Post & Telecommunications Correos de Chile is on General Urrutia, near Anfión Muñoz. CTC long-distance offices are at Henríquez 430, while ENTEL offers lower rates at a nearby facility which operates only in the high season.

Travel Agencies Peskytour (☎ 411385) is at Valentín Letelier 386, while Turismo Trigal (☎ 411078) is at Pedro Montt 365. Both organise climbing trips of Volcán Villarrica and other excursions to the national parks.

Medical Services Villarrica's hospital (☎ 411169) is at San Martín 460.

Museum

Next to the tourist office, there is a museum which exhibits Mapuche artefacts, including jewellery, musical instruments and several roughly hewn wooden masks – powerful carvings despite their simplicity. On the grounds in front of the museum is a Mapuche ruca, oblong with thatched walls and roof. Most of the time there is a staff member who explains the construction and function of the house, traditionally built by four men in four days under a reciprocal labour system known as *minga*. Reeds from the lake provide the thatch, so skilfully intertwined that water cannot penetrate even in this very rainy climate.

The museum is open daily from 9 am to 1 pm and 6 to 9 pm except Sunday, when it is open from 6 to 9 pm only. Admission is US$0.40.

Feria Artesanal

On Aviador Acevedo, behind the tourist office, is Villarrica's artisans' market which has a fine selection of local crafts and it is one of the few places to taste traditional Mapuche food.

Fishing

Fishing is good near Villarrica, especially on the Río Toltén, but first obtain a licence from Sernap, Pedro Montt 541. Travellers have also recommended Señor Gastón Balboa, San Martín 348, as a well equipped and knowledgeable fishing guide.

Festivals

At the annual *Muestra Cultural Mapuche*, in January and February, local Mapuche artisans display their wares to the public.

Places to Stay – bottom end

Villarrica has a fine selection of accommodation in all categories and is notably

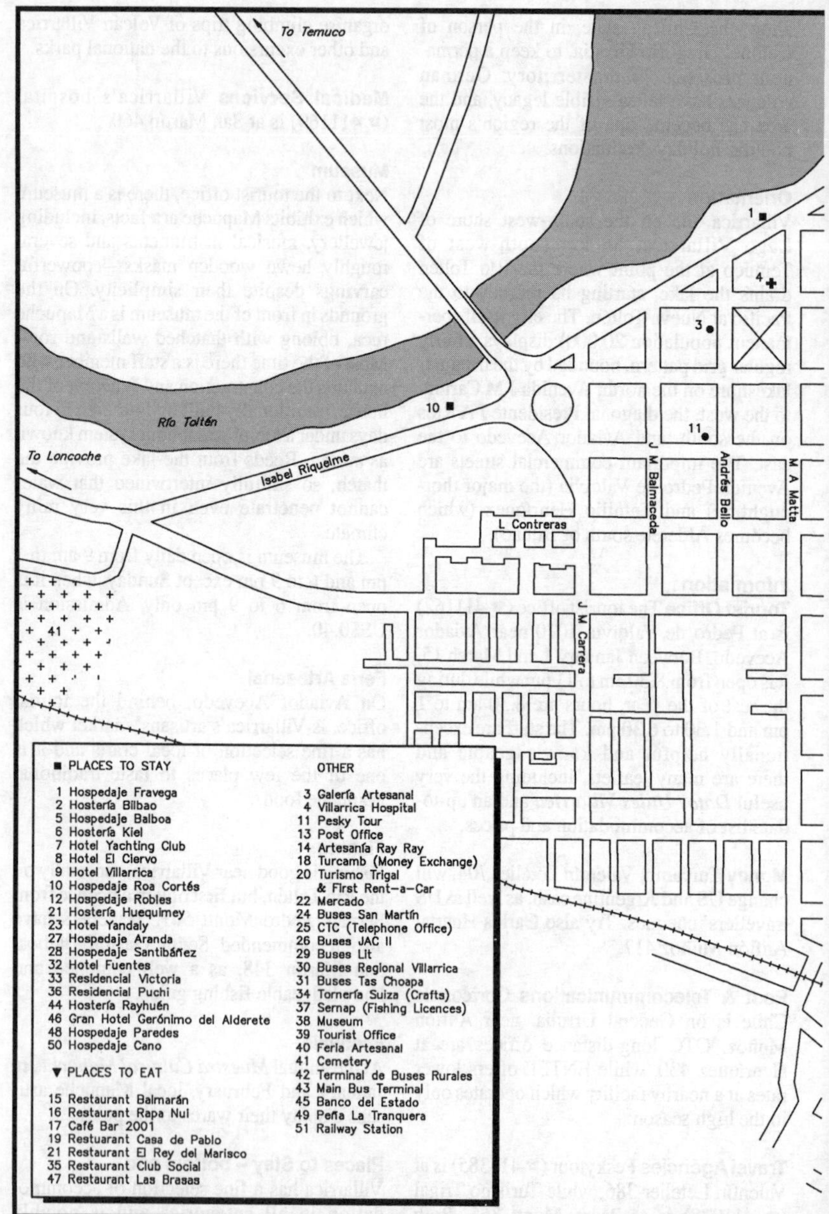
To Temuco
To Loncoche
Río Toltén
Isabel Riquelme
L Contreras
J M Balmaceda
Andrés Bello
M A Matta
J M Carrera
1
3
4
10
11
41
■ PLACES TO STAY
1 Hospedaje Fravega
2 Hostería Bilbao
5 Hospedaje Balboa
6 Hostería Kiel
7 Hotel Yachting Club
8 Hotel El Ciervo
9 Hotel Villarrica
10 Hospedaje Roa Cortés
12 Hospedaje Robles
21 Hostería Huequimey
23 Hotel Yandaly
27 Hospedaje Aranda
28 Hospedaje Santibáñez
32 Hotel Fuentes
33 Residencial Victoria
36 Residencial Puchi
44 Hostería Rayhuén
46 Gran Hotel Gerónimo del Alderete
48 Hospedaje Paredes
50 Hospedaje Cano
▼ PLACES TO EAT
15 Restaurant Balmarán
16 Restaurant Rapa Nui
17 Café Bar 2001
19 Restaurant Casa de Pablo
21 Restaurant El Rey del Marisco
35 Restaurant Club Social
47 Restaurant Las Brasas
OTHER
3 Galería Artesanal
4 Villarrica Hospital
11 Pesky Tour
13 Post Office
14 Artesanía Ray Ray
18 Turcamb (Money Exchange)
20 Turismo Trigal
& First Rent-a-Car
22 Mercado
24 Buses San Martín
25 CTC (Telephone Office)
26 Buses JAC II
29 Buses Lit
30 Buses Regional Villarrica
31 Buses Tas Choapa
34 Tornería Suiza (Crafts)
37 Sernap (Fishing Licences)
38 Museum
39 Tourist Office
40 Feria Artesanal
41 Cemetery
42 Terminal de Buses Rurales
43 Main Bus Terminal
45 Banco del Estado
49 Peña La Tranquera
51 Railway Station

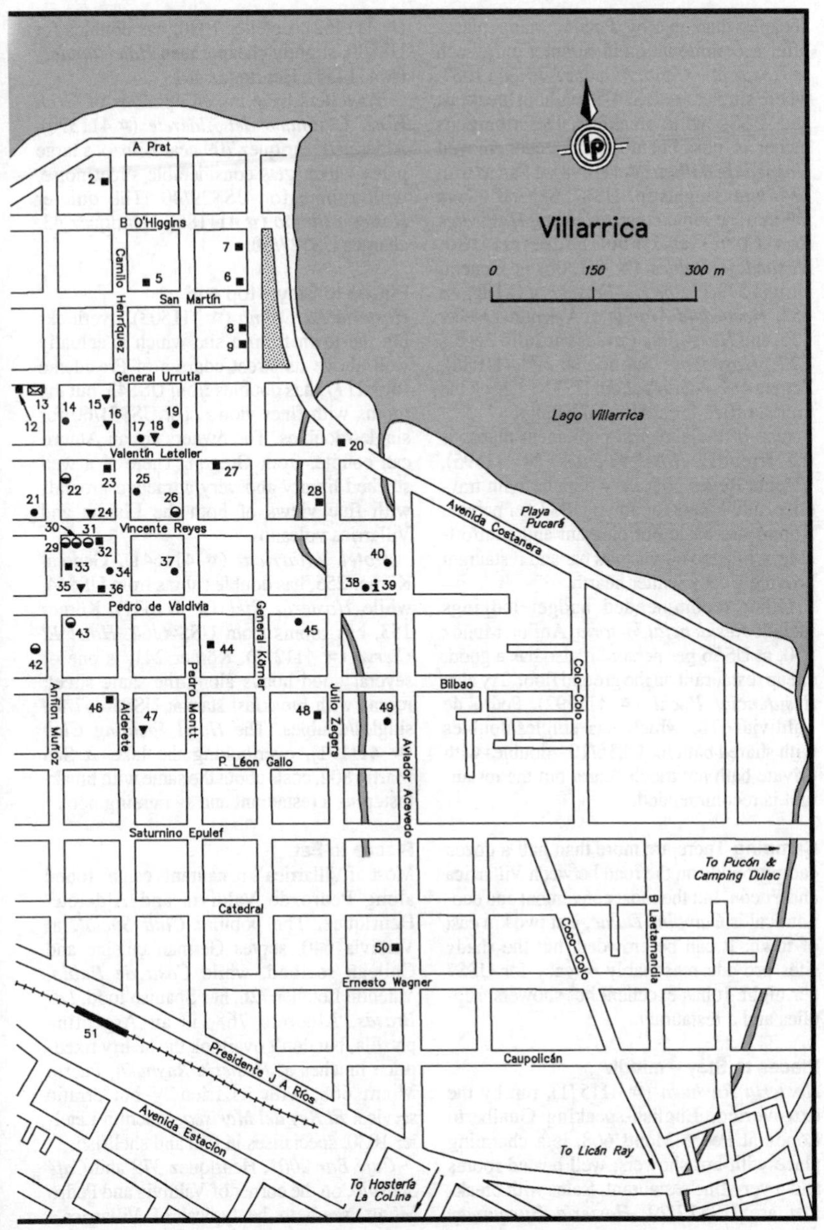
Villarrica
0
150
300 m
Lago Villarrica
A Prat
B O'Higgins
San Martín
General Urrutia
Valentín Letelier
Vincente Reyes
Pedro de Valdivia
Camilo Henríquez
General Körner
Pedro Montt
Julio Zegers
Anfion Muñoz
Alderete
Aviador Acevedo
P León Gallo
Saturnino Epulef
Catedral
Ernesto Wagner
Presidente J A Ríos
Avenida Estacion
Avenida Costanera
Playa Pucará
Colo-Colo
Bilbao
Coco-Colo
B Laetamandía
Caupolicán
To Pucón & Camping Dulac
To Licán Ray
To Hostería La CoLina
1
2
5
6
7
8
9
12
13
14
15
16
17
18
19
20
21
22
23
24
25
26
27
28
29
30
31
32
33
34
35
36
37
38
39
40
42
43
44
45
46
47
48
49
50
51

cheaper than nearby Pucón. Many places offer accommodation in summer only, such as *Hospedaje Cano*, Aviador Acevedo 1057, where singles are US$4.50 without breakfast and US$6 with breakfast. Describing its owner as 'nosy but nice', one reader enjoyed *Hospedaje Balboa* (☎ 411098) at San Martín 734, with singles for US$7. Several others fall into the same range, including *Hospedaje Roa Cortés* at Isabel Riquelme 130, *Hospedaje Robles* (☎ 411306) at General Urrutia 579, *Hospedaje Fravega* at O'Higgins 462, *Hospedaje Aranda* at Valentín Letelier 825, and *Hospedaje Paredes* at Julio Zegers 727. *Hospedaje Santibañez* (☎ 411086), Zegers 481, charges about US$10. Check the tourist office for additional listings.

One of the cheapest permanent places is the friendly *Hotel Fuentes* (☎ 411595), Vicente Reyes 665; very popular with travellers and hikers for about US$7 per person. Rooms are basic but pleasant and comfortable, while the downstairs bar and restaurant provide a cosy winter hearth.

Other recommended budget lodgings include *Residencial Victoria*, Anfión Muñoz 530, at US$6 per person; it also has a good, cheap restaurant on the ground floor. Try also *Residencial Puchi* (☎ 411392), Pedro de Valdivia 678, which has singles/doubles with shared bath for US$6/10 – doubles with private bath are much dearer but the restaurant is recommended.

Camping There are more than half a dozen campgrounds on the road between Villarrica and Pucón, but the most convenient and economical is *Camping Dulac*, just two km east of town. It can be crowded, but the shady sites provide reasonably privacy for US$7 per night. It has excellent hot showers, supplies and a restaurant.

Places to Stay – middle

Hostería Rayhuén (☎ 411571), run by the extroverted, English-speaking Gualberto López at Pedro Montt 668, is a charming place with hot showers, well heated rooms and a very fine restaurant. Rates with breakfast are US$17/29. *Hostería Huequimey* (☎ 411462), Letelier 1030, has doubles for US$30, slightly cheaper than *Hotel Yandaly* (☎ 411454), Henríquez 401.

Travellers have mixed opinions of *Gran Hotel Gerónimo del Alderete* (☎ 411370), Alderete/Henríquez 709 near Bilbao, a large place which gets considerable street noise, with rooms for US$29/40. The quieter *Hostería Bilbao* (☎ 411186), Henríquez 43, charges US$27/50.

Places to Stay – top end

Hostería La Colina (☎ 411503), overlooking the town from a site which is actually well above its street address of Presidente Ríos 1177, has doubles from US$43, but the rooms with finer views cost US$51/60 for singles/doubles. The owners are an American couple, from Oregon. There is a well stocked library and very attractive grounds with fine views of both the Llaima and Villarrica volcanos.

Hotel Villarrica (☎ 411641), General Körner 255, has double cabins from US$44, while *Hostería Kiel* (☎ 411631), Körner 153, has rooms from US$46/64. *Hotel El Ciervo* (☎ 411215), Körner 241, is one of several good hotels along the same street; rooms with breakfast start at US$56/67 for singles/doubles. The *Hotel Yachting Club* (☎ 411191), overlooking the lake at San Martín 802, costs about the same with breakfast, plus a restaurant and swimming pool.

Places to Eat

Most of Villarrica's restaurants can be found along Pedro de Valdivia and Alderete/Henríquez. The popular *Club Social*, at Valdivia 640, serves German cuisine and Chilean seafood, while *Casa de Pablo*, Valentín Letelier 726, has Spanish food. *Las Brasas*, Alderete 768, is an Argentine parrilla, but don't overlook the hearty fixed-price lunches at *Hostería Rayhuén*, Puerto Montt 668, with its friendly but erratic service. *El Rey del Marisco*, Valentín Letelier 1030, specialises in fish and shellfish.

Café Bar 2001, Henríquez 379 and *Café Scorpio*, on the corner of Valdivia and Pedro Montt, seem to be typical of Villarrica's tourist cafés, with their good selections of sandwiches and kuchen. *Baimarán*, Henríquez 331, serves fine Brazilian as well as Chilean food. *Rapa Nui*, Vicente Reyes 678, does not serve Polynesian food, but is good and cheap.

Entertainment

Peña La Tranquera, Acevedo 761 between Bilbao and Gallo, is a bar and folk club with live music as well as typical Chilean food.

Things to Buy

Besides the Feria Artesanal, there are several other places to look for Mapuche silverwork, baskets, woollens and carvings. Visit the Tornería Suiza at Henríquez 025, the Galería Artesanal at Andrés Bello 239, Artesaníu Ray-Ray at Muñoz 386, and Turismo Trigal at Pedro Montt 365.

Getting There & Away

Bus From Villarrica, there are frequent buses to Santiago, Puerto Montt and many Lake District destinations, plus regular international services to the Argentine towns of Zapala, Neuquén, San Martín de los Andes, Bariloche and Mendoza; fares are very similar to those from Temuco. The main bus terminal is on Pedro de Valdivia at Anfión Muñoz, but companies have offices scattered around the central area. For services to nearby destinations, the Terminal de Buses Rurales is at Anfión Muñoz 657.

Tur Bus (☎ 411534), Pedro de Valdivia 615, Buses Lit (☎ 411555), Vicente Reyes 623, and Buses Power (☎ 411121), Pedro de Valdivia 619 all offer daily services to Santiago. Igi Llaima (☎ 411516), Pedro de Valdivia 621, has buses Monday, Wednesday and Friday to San Martín de los Andes and Neuquén, Argentina. Tas Choapa (☎ 411595), Vicente Reyes 665, offers buses three days a week to Bariloche via Temuco and Osorno, as well as to Santiago and Puerto Montt.

Buses Jac (☎ 411447), at Vicente Reyes and Pedro Montt, has a frequent service to Santiago and Valdivia, plus buses on Monday, Wednesday and Friday to Neuquén (Argentina), via Junín de los Andes and San Martín de los Andes. Buses San Martín (☎ 411584), Anfión Muñoz 419, operates similar international services Tuesday, Thursday and Saturday. Buses Fénix (☎ 411313), Pedro de Valdivia 629, has buses to Santiago, with connections to Mendoza and Buenos Aires.

Buses Jac also goes to Temuco and Pucón every half hour, and offers ten departures daily to Licán Ray and six to Coñaripe. Buses Regional Villarrica, on Vicente Reyes next to Hotel Fuentes, has daily buses to Pucón and Curarrehue.

Getting Around

Car Rental First Rent-a-Car (☎ 411078) is at Pedro Montt 365.

PUCÓN

Unless the next major eruption of Volcán Villarrica obliterates it, Pucón will be a charming, upscale lakeside resort with fine accommodation and superb food, very much resembling Argentina's San Martín de los Andes. Villarrica may be cheaper (and safer – don't buy a condo in Pucón unless it's guaranteed lava-resistant), but a visit to Pucón is very worthwhile.

Orientation

Pucón (population 6000) is 25 km from Villarrica at the east end of the lake, between the estuary of the Río Pucón on the north and Volcán Villarrica on the south. It is a very compact town structured along a conventional grid system, bounded by the lake to the north, the Costanera Roberto Geis to the west, the flanks of the volcano on the south, and Avenida Colo Colo to the east. To the north-west, a wooded peninsula juts into the lake, forming the sheltered inlet La Poza at the west end of Avenida Libertador Bernardo O'Higgins, the main commercial street and thoroughfare.

Information

Tourist Office Pucón's municipal tourist office (☎ 441916), at Brasil 115 between Caupolicán and Lincoyán, is open in summer

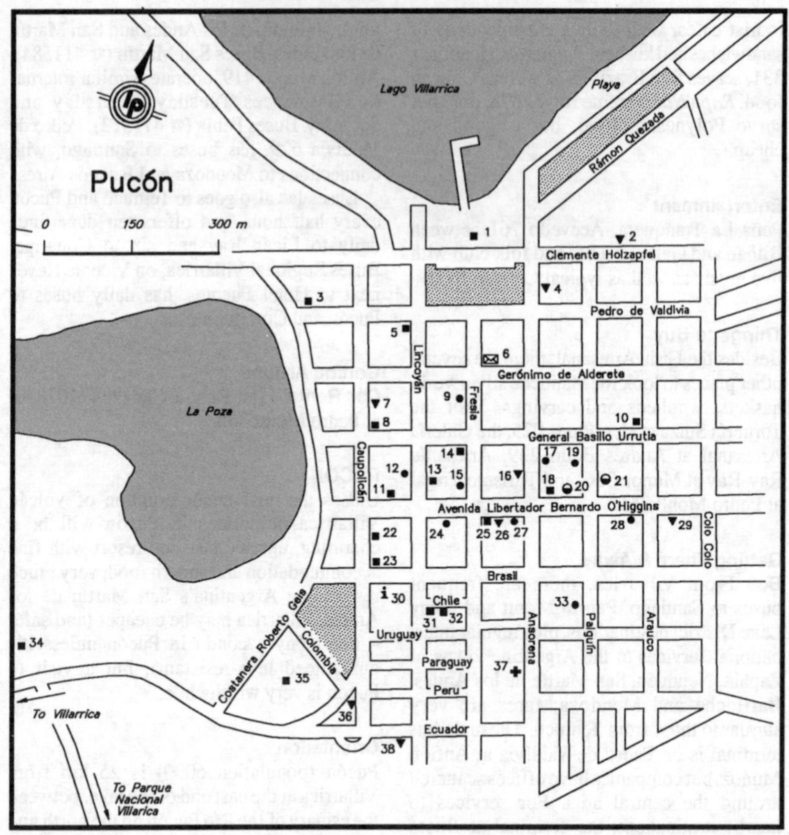

from 8 am to 10 pm Monday to Saturday, and from 10 am to 1 pm and 6 to 9 pm Sunday. In winter, it keeps weekday hours only from 8.30 am to noon and 2 to 6 pm. Fishing licences are available here for US$1 and are valid for a month.

Money Turcamb, O'Higgins 472, will exchange cash and travellers' cheques. Supermercado Eltit, O'Higgins 336, will also change cash.

Post & Telecommunications Correos de Chile is at the corner of Fresia and Gerónimo de Alderete. CTC long-distance offices are at Palguín 348.

Travel Agencies Pucón is the mecca for Chile's adventure travel industry, with several companies offering climbing, river rafting, mountain biking, horseback riding, fishing and similar activities. Among them are Sherpa's Expediciones, at Ansorena 335, Expediciones Trancura (☎ 441959) at O'Higgins 261, Altué Expediciones at O'Higgins 587 and Grado Diez (☎ 441113) at O'Higgins 371.

Prices do not vary greatly among these

■ PLACES TO STAY

1 Gran Hotel Pucón
3 Hotel Gudenschwager
5 Hotel La Posada
8 Hotel Araucarias
10 Hostería Don Pepe
11 Hostería Suiza
13 Residencial Lincoyán
14 Hostería El Principito
18 Hostería Millarahue
22 Hospedaje Joan Torres
23 Hospedaje Sonia
25 Hostería Salzburg
31 Hospedaje Lucía
32 Hospedaje Lucila
34 Hostería Antumalal
35 Hotel Interlaken

▼ PLACES TO EAT

2 Holzapfel Bäckerei
4 Restaurant Xing Hu
7 Trattoria Mangiare
16 Buffet Cordillera
26 Restaurant El Conquistador
29 Restaurant Club 77
36 Los Hornos de Pucón
38 Restaurant Marmonch

OTHER

6 Post & Telegraph Office
9 Autorentas del Pacífico (Car Rental)
12 CONAF
15 Banco del Estado
17 Sherpa's Expediciones
19 CTC (Telephone)
20 Buses Lit & Jac; Turcamb (Money)
21 Bus Terminal
24 Expediciones Trancura
27 Grado Diez (Travel Agency)
28 Altué Expediciones
30 Tourist Office
33 Bicycle Rental
37 Hospital

companies. To climb Volcán Osorno on a day trip if the weather holds, costs about US$35 per person while a three-hour rafting trip down the Río Trancura costs about US$10.

Medical Services The hospital (☎ 441177) is on Ansorena between Uruguay and Ecuador.

National Parks CONAF (☎ 441261) is at Lincoyán 372. Since there is no public transportation directly to Villarrica and Huerquehue national parks, CONAF personnel will sometimes carry passengers on their regular rounds if space is available.

Organised Tours

For a price (about US$270), Aerovía del Pacífico will take three passengers on a one-hour charter flight over the crater of Volcán Villarrica and other nearby sights. Contact Sol y Nieve Expediciones at O'Higgins and Lincoyán.

Places to Stay – bottom

Pucón has many hotels but not much budget accommodation, at least out of season. In summer, there are several inexpensive hospedajes, including *Hospedaje Sonia* (☎ 441269) at Lincoyán and Brasil, a good place to meet people, *Hospedaje Lucila* at Pasaje Chile 225, *Hospedaje Lucía* at Lincoyán 565, and *Hospedaje Juan Torres* (☎ 441248) at Lincoyán 443. All charge around US$6-7 single, some with breakfast or use of kitchen.

Perhaps the cheapest regular hotel is *Hostería Don Pepe*, at the corner of General Urrutia and Arauco; at US$11 per person, it's clean and quite pleasant. *Residencial Lincoyán* (☎ 441144), Lincoyán 323 between General Basilio Urrutia and O'Higgins, is similar in price and quality. In the same range is *Hostería Millarrahue* (☎ 441904), O'Higgins 460, whose restaurant has received a warm endorsement.

Places to Stay – middle

Mid-range accommodation starts at about US$17/32 for a single/double – try *Hostería Salzburg* (☎ 441907), on the corner of O'Higgins 311 and Fresia. Slightly more expensive are *Hostería El Principito* (☎ 441200) at Urrutia 291 and *Hostería Suiza* (☎ 441045) at O'Higgins 116. *Hotel La Posada* (☎ 441088), Pedro de Valdivia 191, has rooms with shared bath for US$28/42 for singles/doubles but those with private bath are notably dearer.

Near the top of the category is the very fine *Hotel Araucarias* (☎ 441286), Caupolicán 243, which charges US$31/55. The German influence is obvious in the Lake District's fine chalets, such as *Hotel Gudenschwager* (☎ 441156), at Pedro de Valdivia 12, which has double rooms with fine views across the lake for US$51.

Places to Stay – top end
Hotel Interlaken (☎ 441276), on Colombia near Costanera Geis, has doubles from US$75. For conspicuous luxury on the lakefront at Clemente Holzapfel 190, try the imposing *Gran Hotel Pucón* (☎ 441001), built by Ferrocarriles del Estado (the state railroad corporation) in the depths of the Great Depression in 1934. Rates start at US$80/120 for a single/double room but rise to US$126/171 if you want a lake view. For greater discretion, there's the expensive *Hotel Antumalal* (☎ 441011), camouflaged by lush, extensive gardens at Km 2 on the road to Villarrica. Singles/doubles are US$130/180 including breakfast.

Places to Eat
Most hotels have their own restaurants, but there are scores of other appealing places to eat although some of them are only open in summer. There are fine empanadas at *Los Hornos de Pucón*, Caupolicán 710 at the western approach to town. Nearby *Marmonch*, Ecuador 175 near Lincoyán, has a different, inexpensive fixed-price lunch daily. *El Fogón*, at O'Higgins 480 right by Buses Lit, is a parrilla. *El Conquistador*, O'Higgins 323, is highly regarded for its pizza, pancakes, meat and seafood.

For Italian food, try *Trattoria Mangiare*, Caupolicán 243. Chinese food is available at *Xing Hu*, Ansorena 83. *Club 77*, O'Higgins 635, offers traditional Chilean and regional specialities such as pastel de choclo, baked empanadas, and smoked trout. For really exquisite sweets, try the *Holzapfel Bäckerei*, Clemente Holzapfel 524, a restaurant which specialises in raspberry kuchen and other Germanic goodies. There is an all-you-can-eat smorgasbord at *Buffet Cordillera*, on Ansorena between Urrutia and O'Higgins.

Getting There & Away
Pucón's bus terminal is on Palguín between Urrutia and O'Higgins. Buses Jac has countless departures from Pucón to Villarrica, taking half an hour and costing about US$0.50. Long-distance connections to Santiago can be made from Pucón with Tur Bus, Fénix and Power.

Buses Cordillera services go to Paillaco on Lago Caburgua, near Parque Nacional Huerquehue, and to Termas de Huife, daily at 12.30 and 5 pm, for US$1. Also for US$1, Buses Regional Villarrica has five buses daily to Currarehue and Puesco, the last stop before the border crossing to Junín de los Andes in Argentina.

Getting Around
Car Rental Autorentas del Pacífico (☎ 441106), Fresia 224, is the local concessionaire for Hertz.

AROUND LAGO VILLARRICA

Casa Fuerte Santa Sylvia

In colonial times, the Villarrica region was one of the southernmost encomiendas in South America, but the area was abandoned and the forced labour system abolished after the general Mapuche uprising of 1599. Archaeological evidence from this site has revealed broken roof tiles apparently belonging to the encomendero's residence. A chapel, houses for the Mapuche servants, and several graves also exist. The Spaniards were lured here after the discovery of small gold deposits but they did not stay long in the face of determined Mapuche resistance.

Santa Sylvia is 18 km east of Pucón on the road to Termas de Huife; at the junction to Huerquehue, take the road to the right. It's open daily from 9 am to noon and 3 to 6 pm.

Termas de Huife

Hotel Termas de Huife (☎ 441222 in Pucón) is a hot springs chalet on the Río Liucura, 30 km north-east of Pucón, with singles/doubles for US$70/91, but day visitors can use the baths all day for US$7. Meals are available in the cafeteria.

From Pucón, Buses Cordillera (☎ 441903) goes every weekday to Huife at 12.30 and 5 pm; the latter bus returns the following day.

Termas de Palguín

Termas de Palguín, a mountain hot springs 30 km south-east of Pucón, features the attractive German-built chalet *Hotel Termas de Palguín* (☎ 441968 in Pucón), built in the mid-1940s on the Río Palguín. There are several pleasant walks and waterfalls in the area.

Accommodation starts at about US$33 per person with shared bath and all meals, while rooms with private bath cost around US$80/100 for a single/double with all meals, including access to two or four of the thermal baths. Day visitors can use the baths for US$6 and eat in the hotel's restaurant; camping is possible nearby. There is no regular public transport within 10 km of the baths but ask at travel agencies or the Pucón tourist office about day trips. A group should find it reasonable to hire a cab.

PARQUE NACIONAL HUERQUEHUE

Mountainous Huerquehue is a compact 12,500-hectare reserve of rivers and waterfalls, alpine lakes, and Araucaria and Nothofagus forests, with superb views across the the Río Pucón valley to Volcán Villarrica. There are occasional sightings of the Andean condor, but woodpeckers and thrushes are far more common.

Geography & Climate

On the western shore of Lago Caburgua, 35 km from Pucón, Huerquehue offers several pleasant hikes and good camping. Rushing snowmelt streams have cut deep canyons the flanks of which rise up to 2000 metres on Cerro Araucano.

The park enjoys warm summers, but snow accumulates at the higher elevations in winter. About 2000 mm of rain falls almost entirely between the months of May and September so November to April is the best time for a visit.

Carpinter Negro (woodpecker)

Lago Verde Trail

Leaving from the park headquarters at Lago Tinquilco, this is a very fine excursion for a day trip or overnight. The trail climbs from 700 to 1300 metres through dense forests of lenga (a deciduous southern beech) and past waterfalls. Frequent clearings in the forest reveal views of Volcán Villarrica in the distance. At upper elevations are solid stands of pehuén trees. The seven-km walk takes about two or three hours each way.

At the outlet of Lago Chico, the first of three clustered lakes, there are fine pools for swimming on warm days. Well marked trails head to Lago Toro and to Lago Verde, where CONAF maintains a refugio which may be available for overnight accommodation on request – ask at Lago Tinquilco.

Camping

At CONAF's 22-site campground on Lago Tinquilco, rates are about US$5 per site.

Getting There & Away

From Pucón, Buses Cordillera has two buses

daily to Paillaco, at the south end of Lago Caburgua, but it's another eight km on a dusty, winding road to the park entrance at Lago Tinquilco. Hitching may be feasible from Lago Caburgua, but it is probably wiser to start walking and hope for a lift.

One of CONAF's rangers delivers a long, tedious lecture on park etiquette (excluding ecology and environment) in a message-machine monotone before accepting your US$1.75 admission fee. Hopefully readers of this book will show a suitable respect for the environment and for other park users despite this uninspiring presentation.

PARQUE NACIONAL VILLARRICA

Spanish poet Alonso de Ercilla paid tribute to the awesome, smouldering cone of Volcán Villarrica,in his 16th-century epic *La Araucana*.

Great neighbour volcano,
The forge, they say, of Vulcan,
That belches continuous fire...

Created in 1940 to protect its extraordinary scenery, Parque Nacional Villarrica's centrepiece is still the smoking, 2850-metre Volcán Villarrica. One of Chile's most visible and accessible parks, its 60,000 hectares also contain other, inactive volcanoes such as 2360-metre Quetrupillán and, on the Argentine border, a section of the symmetrical cone of 3746-metre Lanín, which has given its name to an equally impressive park across the frontier.

Geography & Climate

Only 12 km from Pucón, Villarrica is an area of active vulcanism – a major eruption in 1971 opened a four-km fracture in Volcán Villarrica which emitted 30 million cubic metres of lava and displaced several rivers. One flow, down the Río Challupén, was 14 km long, 200 metres wide, and five metres in height.

At elevations of up to 1500 metres where lava flows have not penetrated, dense forests of southern beech and pehuén cover the mountain's flanks – Quetrupillán is the southern limit of the pehuén's natural range. The climate much resembles that of the nearby Parque Nacional Huerquehue, though it tends to rain more around Villarrica.

Trekking & Climbing Volcán Villarrica

Villarrica's accessibility makes it a mecca for hikers and climbers. The most popular trip is the climb to the summit of Villarrica, which is not technically demanding but requires equipment and either experience or someone who knows the route. Do not hesitate to turn back in bad weather.

Several adventure travel companies in Pucón rent equipment and lead guided excursions for about US$35 per person, requiring one full day – see Travel Agencies in the Pucón section. Several travellers have recommended an English-speaking guide named Aldo, who lives at Uruguay 650 in Pucón.

The most convenient of the treks is one that circles the southern flank of the volcano and finishes at the park at Termas de Palguín. From Termas de Palguín there is another route to Puesco, near the Argentine border, where there is public transport back to Pucón. Travellers Vivienne Mitchell and Paul Carter found CONAF rangers at the Puesco sector eager for company and very helpful and accommodating, leading them on some walks and pointing out others. For trekking details, see Lonely Planet's *Trekking in the Patagonian Andes*.

Skiing

The Refugio Villarrica accommodates skiers in the wintertime; for details, contact the Centro de Esqui in Pucón (☎ 441176).

Getting There & Away

Although Pargue Nacional Villarrica is very close to Pucón, there is no scheduled public transport to Sector Rucapillán, but a shared taxi should cost no more than a few dollars per head. To Sector Puesco, there is regular transport from Pucón with Buses Regional Villarrica.

LICÁN RAY

On the north shore of island-studded Lago Calafquén and surrounded by mountains, fashionable Licán Ray boasts one of the region's best beaches, the Playa Grande. It is a long strip of dark volcanic sand, jammed in the high season with refugees from Santiago. After the sun sets on summer nights, most visitors promenade on the main street, General Urrutia, filling the restaurants, hotels, cafés and billiard halls. Out of season, though, it is a restful sanctuary.

Orientation

Most of the main attractions in Licán Ray lie between the estuaries of the Río Muilpún and the Río Melilahuén. The town is 30 km south of Villarrica. General Urrutia, the main commercial street, is the southern extension of the Villarrica highway. Other roads go west to Panguipulli and east to Coñaripe. The Avenida Punuleff, which runs along the Playa Grande, is the western boundary while the Avenida Menquel, along the Playa Chica, is the southern limit.

Information

Tourist Office Licán Ray's municipal tourist office is on General Urrutia, between

1 Motel El Canelo
2 Camping Melilahuén
3 Telephone Office
4 Post Office
5 Posta Médica & Feria
6 Tourist Office
7 Motel El Canelo
8 Camping Licán Ray
9 Restaurant El Candil
10 Supermarket (Money Exchange)
11 Feria
12 Buses Jac
13 Chambres d'Hotel
14 Restaurant Ñaños
15 Hotel Refugio Inaltulafquén
16 Hostería Victor's Playa

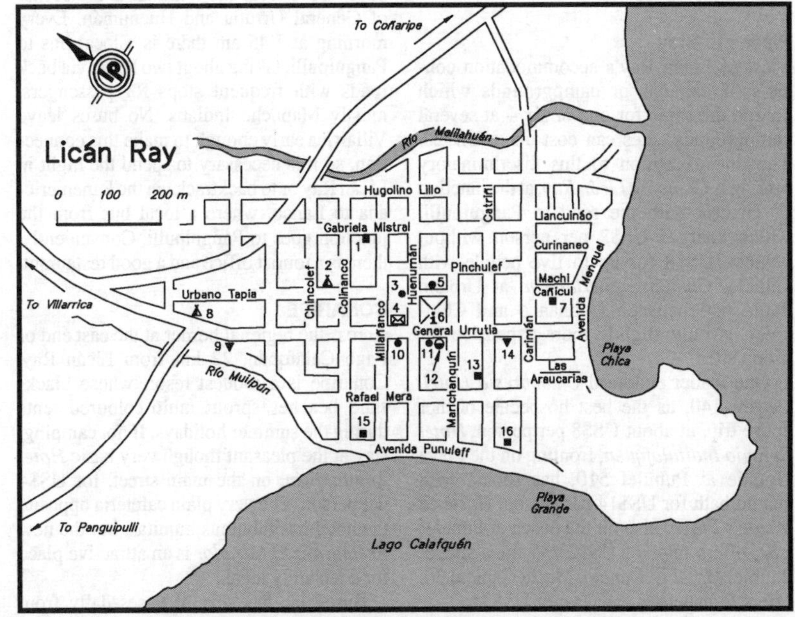

Huenumán and Marichanquín. It distributes maps, brochures and a list of hotels and during summer is open from 9 am to 9 pm weekdays, 9 am to 1 pm and 3 to 8 pm weekends.

Money Licán Ray has no exchange houses, but the supermarket on Urrutia, across from the post office, may change US cash.

Post & Telecommunications The Correos de Chile is on Urrutia between Millañanco and Huenumán. There is a telephone office around the corner on Huenumán, between Urrutia and Pinchulef.

Medical Services There is a *posta médica* (first-aid station) on Calle Esmeralda, behind the plaza.

Festivals

In the second week of February, the town celebrates the annual Semana de Licán Ray.

Places to Stay

Most of Licán Ray's accommodation consists of cabañas or campgrounds which charge the same for one or six – at several campgrounds, sites can cost up to US$20. The one exception to this discriminatory pricing is *Camping Licán Ray*, at the junction of Urrutia with the road to Panguipulli, which charges US$2 per person without vehicle, US$8 for up to five people with vehicle. *Camping Melilahuén*, at Urbano Tapia 640 between Colinanco and Chincolef, is only slightly more expensive for group sites.

One reader endorsed *Chambres d'Hotel*, Catriñi 140, as the best hospedaje on her entire trip, at about US$8 per person. *Hotel Refugio Inaltulafquén*, fronting on the Playa Grande at Punulef 510, has rooms with shared bath for US$14 per person. *Hostería Victor's Playa*, also on the beach at Punulef 120, offers rates of US$23/35 for a single/double. *Motel El Canelo*, Machi Cañicul 30, offers four-person cabañas for US$34.

Places to Eat

There are many cafés, restaurants and bars along General Urrutia and the Playa Grande. *El Candíl*, Urrutia 845, has good Spanish food and Chilean seafood specialities. *Ñaños*, on Urrutia between Catriñi and Carimán, is one of the town's most popular establishments.

Things to Buy

Licán Ray hosts two nightly crafts fairs. The first, on Calle Esmeralda behind the tourist office, consists of works by local artisans. The second, on Urrutia across from the tourist office, displays goods from other places in the region and around the country.

Getting There & Away

Bus From Villarrica, Buses Jac has frequent services to Licán Ray, taking about 45 minutes. There is also direct service to Santiago.

Although Buses Jac has its own terminal at General Urrutia and Marichanquín, most buses leave from the terminal at the corner of General Urrutia and Huenumán. Every morning at 7.45 am there is a local bus to Panguipulli, taking about two hours via back roads with frequent stops for passengers, mostly Mapuche Indians. No buses leave Villarrica early enough to make this connection, so it is necessary to spend the night in Licán Ray or to backtrack via the Panamericana to Lanco, where a local bus from the junction goes to Panguipulli. Conveniently, there is a tourist office and a good restaurant.

COÑARIPE

Across the regional border at the east end of Lago Calafquén, 22 km from Licán Ray, Coñaripe is a modest resort whose black-sand beaches sprout multi-coloured tents during the summer holidays. If not camping, stay at the pleasant though very basic *Hotel Antulafquén*, on the main street, for US$4 per person. The very plain cafeteria opposite the hotel has fabulous humitas, but the new *Restaurant El Mirador* is an attractive place for a leisurely meal.

Buses Jac has several buses daily from

Villarrica to Coñaripe via Licán Ray, costing about US$1.

VALDIVIA

On the orders of Pedro de Valdivia, Juan Pastene took formal possession of this area in 1544. Valdivia himself decreed the foundation of the city of Santa María La Blanca de Valdivia in early 1552, on the site of a Mapuche settlement known as Guadalauquén, but after Mapuche resistance obliterated it in 1599 and the Dutch even attempted to occupy the area, the city was eventually rebuilt as a military encampment. After languishing throughout the colonial era, it owes much of its present character to German immigration in the mid-19th century. Middle-European influence has since declined, but it can be detected in the city's architecture, the German surnames, and, in particular, the delicious regional cuisine.

Many older buildings, however, were destroyed in the earthquake of 1960 and replaced by modern concrete structures. However, there are still many European-style buildings and mansions along General Lagos, near the riverfront.

Orientation

Valdivia (population 110,000), 160 km south-west of Temuco and 45 km off the Panamericana, sits on the south bank of the Río Calle Calle (which becomes the Río Valdivia) near its confluence with the Río Cau Cau and the Río Cruces. Although Valdivia is shaped in part by the meandering river and is known as the City of the Rivers, it is, despite its colonial origins, far less regular than most other Chilean cities. Its central core is a very compact, triangular area between the Calle Arauco and the river.

Within this core, the riverfront Avenida Costanera Arturo Prat is a major focus of activity, but the most important public buildings are on the Plaza de La República. From the Panamericana, Avenida Ramón Picarte is the main eastern approach. To the west, the Puente Pedro de Valdivia crosses the river to Isla Teja, a leafy suburb which is the site of the Universidad Austral.

Information

Tourist Office Sernatur (☎ 213596) is on the riverfront at Avenida Costanera Arturo Prat 555 (commonly known as Avenida Prat), between Libertad and Maipú. Opening hours are weekdays from 9 am to 8.30 pm, Saturdays from 10 am to 4 pm, and Sundays from 10 am to 2 pm. There is also a branch at the bus terminal (☎ 212212), Anfión Muñoz 360, open daily from 8.30 am to 10 pm.

The Automóvil Club (☎ 212376), Caupolicán 475, is also a good source of information.

Money Valdivia has two exchange houses for both cash and travellers' cheques: Turismo is at Arauco 331, Local 23, while El Libertador is at Carampangue 325. Bank rates are less favourable for cash and involve a commission for travellers' cheques, but try Banco Concepción at Picarte 370, near the Plaza de la República.

Post & Telecommunications Correos de Chile is at O'Higgins 575, opposite the Plaza de la República. Telefónica del Sur has long-distance offices at San Carlos 107 near Yungay, but there are others at O'Higgins 386 and at Picarte 461, Local 2.

Cultural Centres The Centro Cultural El Austral (☎ 213658), Yungay 733, hosts public events in music and the arts. The Corporación Cultural de Valdivia, at Prat 549 just north of the tourist office, also promotes local cultural activities.

Travel Agencies Turismo Cochrane (☎ 212213), Caupolicán 544, arranges air and bus tickets, cashes travellers' cheques, and rents cars. Other similar agencies include Turismo Cono Sur (☎ 212757) at Maipú 129, Turismo Paraty (☎ 215585) at Independencia 640, and Turismo Valdivia (☎ 218524) at Caupolicán 588 just north of the restaurant La Bomba.

Bookshops Libros Chiloé, Caupolicán 410, has a good selection of books by Chilean and foreign authors.

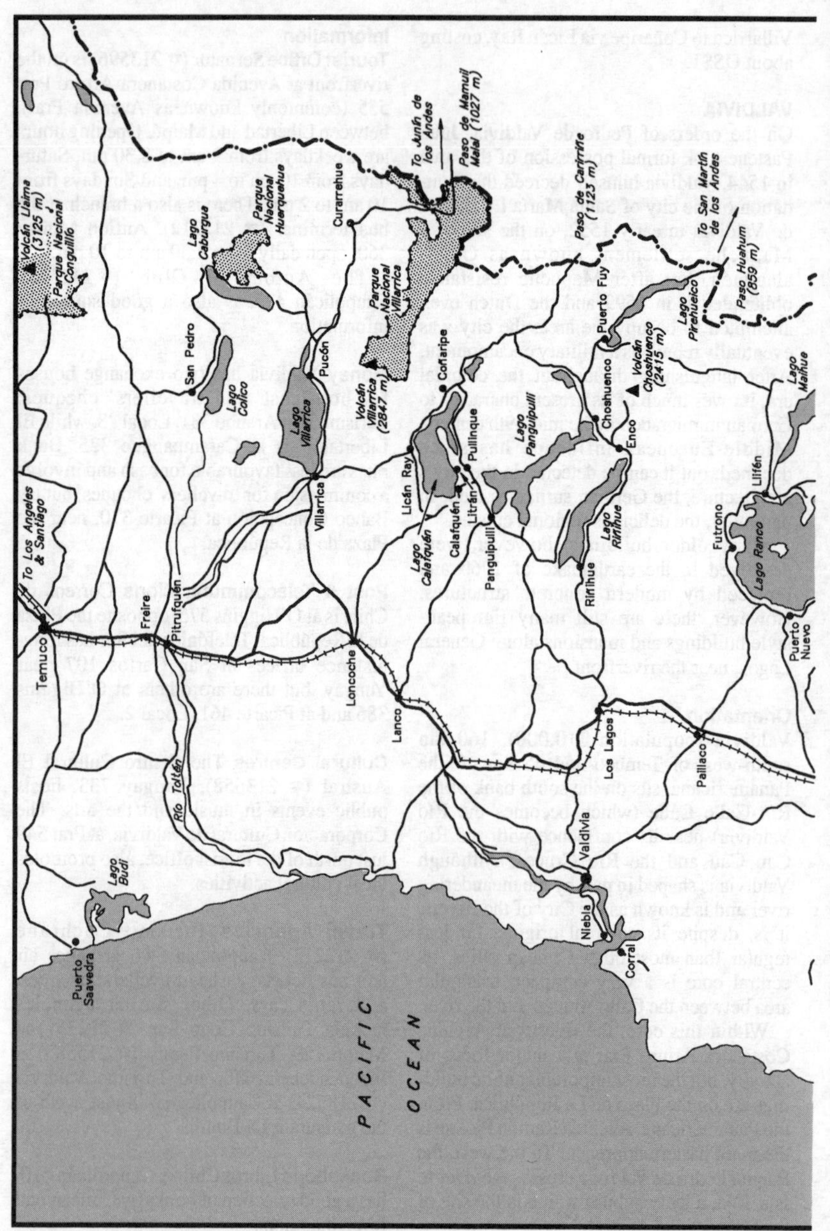
Volcán Llaima (3125 m)
Parque Nacional Conguillío
Lago Caburgua
Parque Nacional Huerquehue
Curarrehue
To Junín de los Andes
Paso de Mamuil Malal (1027 m)
Paso de Carirriñe (1123 m)
To San Martín de los Andes
Paso Huahum (859 m)
Lago Pirehueico
Puerto Fuy
Volcán Choshuenco (2415 m)
Choshuenco
Enco
Lago Maihue
Lago Panguipulli
Coñaripe
Pullinque
Parque Nacional Villarrica
Volcán Villarrica (2847 m)
Pucón
Lago Villarrica
Villarrica
San Pedro
Lago Colico
To Los Angeles & Santiago
Temuco
Freire
Pitrufquén
Loncoche
Lanco
Licán Ray
Lago Calafquén
Calafquén
Litrán
Panguipulli
Lago Riñihue
Riñihue
Llifén
Futrono
Lago Ranco
Puerto Nuevo
Paillaco
Los Lagos
Valdivia
Niebla
Corral
Río Toltén
Lago Budi
Puerto Saavedra
PACIFIC OCEAN

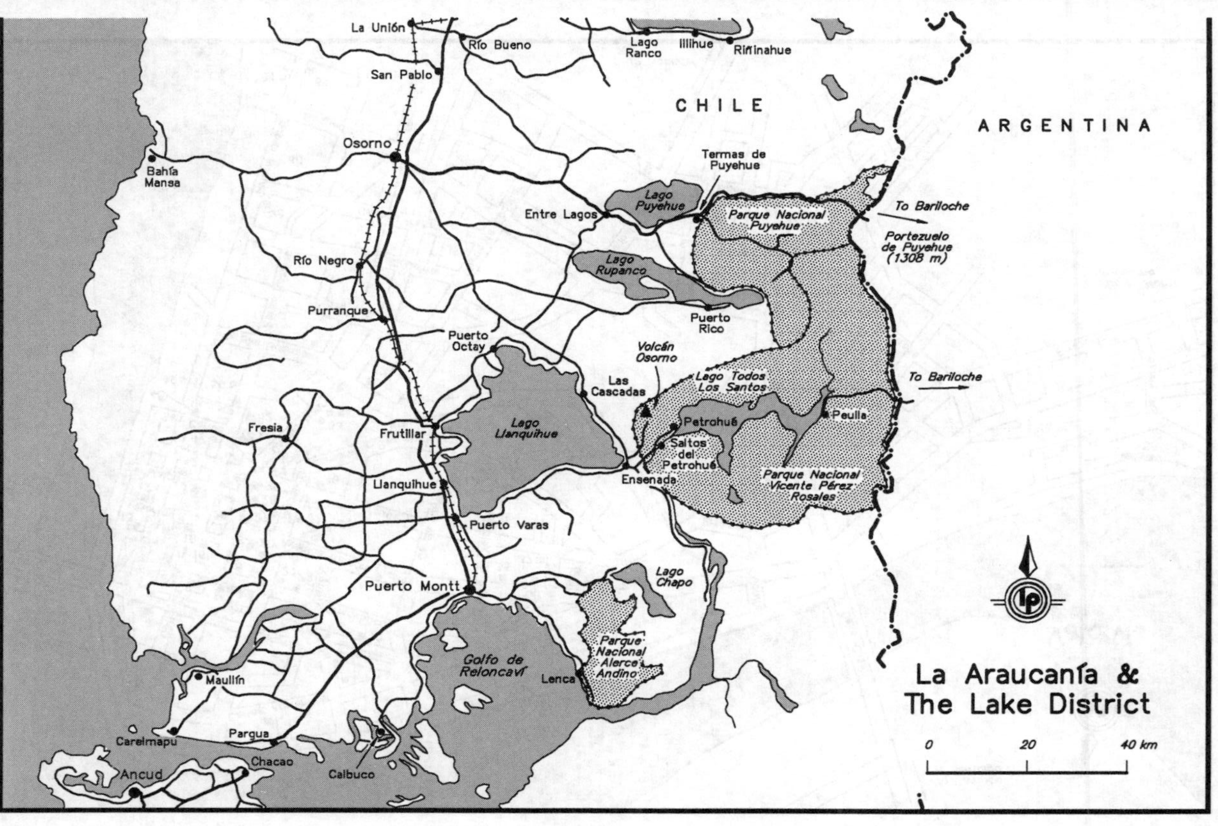
La Unión
Río Bueno
Lago Ranco
Illihue
Riñinahue
San Pablo
CHILE
ARGENTINA
Osorno
Bahía Mansa
Termas de Puyehue
Lago Puyehue
Entre Lagos
Parque Nacional Puyehue
To Bariloche
Portezuelo de Puyehue (1308 m)
Río Negro
Lago Rupanco
Purranque
Puerto Rico
Puerto Octay
Volcán Osorno
Lago Todos Los Santos
To Bariloche
Las Cascadas
Lago Llanquihue
Petrohué
Peulla
Fresia
Frutillar
Saltos del Petrohué
Ensenada
Parque Nacional Vicente Pérez Rosales
Llanquihue
Puerto Varas
Lago Chapo
Puerto Montt
Parque Nacional Alerce Andino
Golfo de Reloncaví
Lenca
Maullín
La Araucanía &
The Lake District
0
20
40 km
Carelmapu
Pargua
Chacao
Calbuco
Ancud

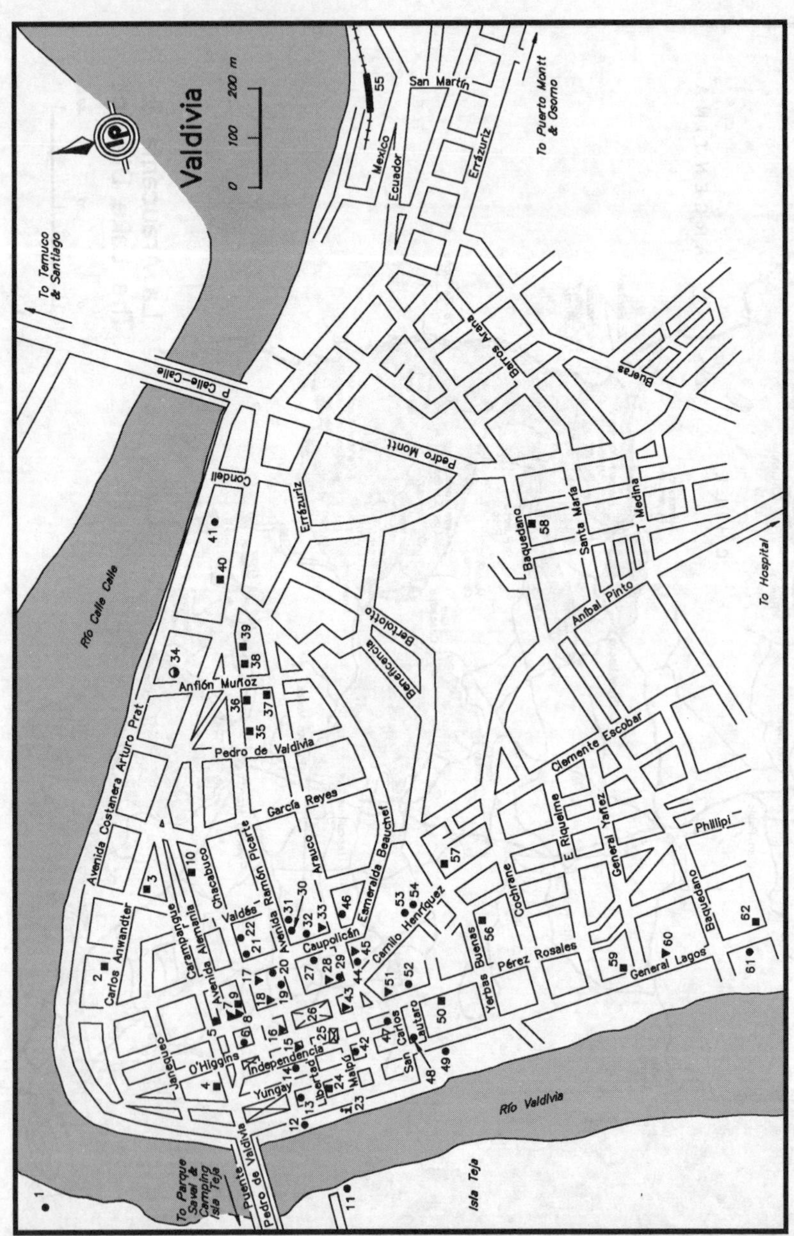
Valdivia
0
100
200 m
To Temuco & Santiago
To Puerto Montt & Osorno
To Hospital
To Parque Saval & Camping Isla Teja
Río Calle Calle
Río Valdivia
Isla Teja
P Calle-Calle
San Martín
Mexico
Ecuador
Errázuriz
Barros Arana
Bueras
Pedro Montt
Condell
Baquedano
Santa María
T Medina
Aníbal Pinto
Bertolotto
Beneficencia
Anfión Muñoz
Avenida Costanera Arturo Prat
Pedro de Valdivia
García Reyes
Ramón Picarte
Arauco
Esmeralda
Beauchef
Clemente Escobar
E Riquelme
General Yañez
Phillipi
Cochrane
Camilo Henríquez
Chacabuco
Avenida Alemania
Valdés
Caupolicán
Carampangue
Carlos Anwandter
Janequeo
O'Higgins
Independencia
Yungay
Libertad
Maipú
San Carlos
Lautaro
Yerbas Buenas
Pérez Rosales
General Lagos
Puente Valdivia
Pedro de Valdivia

Medical Services Valdivia's Hospital Regional (☎ 214066) is south of the centre at Bueras 1003, near Aníbal Pinto.

Torreón del Barro
East of Valdivia's bus terminal, the Torreón del Barro is the turret of a Spanish fort built in 1774. A second turret, built in the 17th century, stands at the corner of Yerbas Buenas and Yungay, facing the Río Valdivia.

Feria Fluvial
Valdivia's riverside market, north of the tourist office, is a great place to buy a bag of cherries and just watch the river flow. On Sundays, Valdivianos flock to the area to buy fish and fruit for the week, float downstream to Niebla and Corral, or just plain relax in the sun.

Museo Histórico y Arqueológico
Housed in a fine riverfront mansion on Isla Teja, at Los Laureles 47, this is one of Chile's most beautiful museums. Uniformly well labelled, its large collection covers the era from pre-Colombian times to the present, with particularly fine displays of Mapuche Indian artefacts and household items from the early days of German settlement. Well organised tours, in Spanish only, are a bit

■ PLACES TO STAY

2 Hospedaje Anwandter 482
3 Hospedaje Anwandter 601
4 Hotel Pedro de Valdivia
9 Hotel Palace
10 Hotel Melillanca
24 Hotel Unión
35 Hotel Montserrat
36 Residencial Aínlebu & Residencial Germania
37 Residencial Calle Calle
38 Hospedaje Picarte 953
39 Hotel Regional
40 Hostal Chalet Alemán
50 Hostal Centro Torreón
56 Hostal Villa Paulina
57 Hostal 403
58 Hospedaje Olivera
59 Hospedaje Turiños
62 Hotel Raitué

▼ PLACES TO EAT

7 Restaurant Shanghai
8 Establecimientos Delicias (Café)
15 Restaurant El Conquistador
16 Café Hausmann
17 Restaurant La Vie Claire & Pastelería La Baguette
18 Centro Español
28 Club de la Unión
33 Restaurant La Bomba
43 Café Palace
45 Restaurant El Patio
51 Gelatería Entrelagos (Ice Cream)
60 Restaurant Yang Cheng

OTHER

1 Universidad Austral
5 El Libertador (Money Exchange)
6 Telefónica del Sur
11 Museo Histórico y Arqueológico
12 Feria Fluvial
13 Mercado
14 London Pub Discotheque
19 Bánco Concepción
20 Automóvil Club de Chile
21 Libros Chiloé
22 Music Pub Gay-Lussac
23 Sernatur & Corporación Cultural de Valdivia
25 Post Office
26 Plaza de la República
27 Ladeco
29 Crafts Market
30 Chocolatería Camino de Luna
31 Telephone Office
32 Turismo Cochrane
34 Bus Terminal
41 Torreón del Barro
42 Turismo Cono Sur
44 Turismo (Money Exchange)
46 Discotheque Izma
47 Turismo Paraty
48 Telephone Office
49 Centro Cultural El Austral
52 First Rent-a-Car
53 Artesanía CEMA-Chile
54 Ruca Indiana
55 Railway Station
61 Asset y Méndez Rent-a-Car

rushed but the guides are happy to answer questions at the end.

To get to the museum, which sits across the Río Valdivia from the Puerto Fluvial, take the bridge over the Río Valdivia, turn left at the first intersection and walk about 200 metres; the entrance is on the left (east) side. Admission is about US$1.

Parque Saval

On Isla Teja, at the north end of Los Laureles, Parque Saval is a virtual botanical garden, pleasant and shady with a riverside beach. There is a pleasant trail along the Laguna de los Lotos (the Lotus Lake), which is covered with lily pads and a good place to see birds. Admission is US$0.30, but it is also possible to camp for US$4 per night in limited facilities.

Opposite the park entrance, the Universidad Austral operates a first-class dairy outlet which sells very fine ice cream, yoghurt, and cheese at bargain prices.

Places to Stay

Valdivia's accommodation scene is a bit unusual, with plenty of bottom-end places, at least in summer, relatively few in the mid-range, and some good value for money in the top-end category. For most of the year, students from the Universidad Austral monopolise the cheapest lodging, but many of these same places vigorously court tourists in summer. Most hospedajes take their name from the street on which they're located, so don't be surprised to find three or more with identical names – if someone recommends a place, be sure to get the exact street number.

Hospedajes are heavily concentrated on Avenida Ramón Picarte and Carlos Anwandter. Sernatur provides a very thorough list of seasonal accommodation, which does change from year to year.

Places to Stay – bottom end

Valdivia's cheapest accommodation is *Residencial Calle Calle*, south of the bus station at Anfión Muñoz 597, which costs about US$4 per person and is very good. *Hotel Regional*, Picarte 1005, is plain but clean, with hot water, a friendly staff, and a small restaurant for US$6 per person. The equally basic *Residencial Ainlebu*, Picarte 865, is not especially friendly, has sagging mattresses, and some rooms can be noisy. It's cold in winter, but it does have hot showers and decent meals; rates are US$9 with breakfast. Other places for around US$6 include *Hospedaje Anwandter 482* (☎ 215619) at Anwandter 482 and *Hospedaje Olivera* (☎ 214362) at Baquedano 1145. Very friendly, but not central, is the *Hospedaje Turiños* (☎ 215607) at General Lagos 1080.

Highly regarded *Hostal 403* (☎ 219389), at Yerbas Buenas 403, charges US$8 with breakfast. *Hotel Unión* (☎ 213819), convenient to the riverfront at Prat 514, is overpriced but clean at US$9 per head, with a downstairs bar and a rather brusque owner. *Hospedaje Picarte 953* (☎ 213055), Picarte 953 near the bus terminal, is very clean and attractive, for US$11/20 for a single/double including breakfast.

Residencial Germania, (☎ 212405), at Picarte 873 adjacent to Residencial Ainlebu, is a very decent place for US$11 per person with breakfast, hot showers, heated rooms and a restaurant. The owners are friendly and speak German. *Hospedaje Anwandter 601* (☎ 218587), also highly recommended at Anwandter 601, is comparably priced.

Another popular place is *Hotel Montserrat* (☎ 212032), a few doors down from the Germania at Picarte 849, with small but clean and bright rooms for US$9/16 for a single/double, including breakfast. Try also *Hostal Centro Torreón* (☎ 2312622), Pérez Rosales 783, for US$13 per person.

Camping *Camping Isla Teja* (☎ 213584) is about half an hour's walk across the Puente Pedro de Valdivia, at the end of Calle Los Robles and Los Cipreses. It's in a pleasant orchard setting – free apples in late summer – with good sanitary facilities and a riverside beach, for US$8 per site.

Cheaper but less comfortable camping is possible at Parque Saval.

Places to Stay – middle

Hotel Raitué (☎ 212503), south of the centre at General Lagos 1382, has singles/doubles with private bath for US$20/23. *Hostal Villa Paulina* (☎ 212445), Yerbas Buenas 389, charges US$30/38 for single/double rooms with private bath. *Hostal Chalet Alemán* (☎ 218810), Picarte 1134, and *Hotel Palace* (☎ 213319), Chacabuco 308, are slightly dearer for similar accommodation. Rooms at the Palace are small but pleasant, and it's very central.

One of the best value hotels in Valdivia, in a much more tranquil setting but still very convenient, is the appealing *Hotel Isla Teja* (☎ 215014), across the Puente Pedro de Valdivia at Las Encinas 220, for US$38/45.

Places to Stay – top end

At *Hotel Melillanca* (☎ 212509), Avenida Alemania 675, rates start at US$42/57 for a single/double, but one traveller thought it poor value for money. *Hotel Pedro de Valdivia* (☎ 212931), a pink palace with elaborate gardens at Carampangue 190, sits alone at the top of the category at US$67/80 for a single/double with breakfast.

Places to Eat

Valdivia has a wide variety of fine restaurants in all price categories. For inexpensive meals, try those on Arauco between Caupolicán and García Reyes, which are popular with locals. *El Patio* at Arauco 347 reportedly has good, cheap food. *Hostal 403*, Yerbas Buenas 403, has a different dinner special every night.

Restaurant El Conquistador, O'Higgins 477 facing the Plaza de la República, has a simple downstairs café and a fancier upstairs restaurant, with a balcony overlooking the Plaza. *Club de La Unión* (once the German Club), at Camilo Henríquez 540 on the Plaza, offers filling, well prepared three-course meals, with tea or coffee, for about US$4. Try also the *Centro Español* at Henríquez 436, and the *Restaurant La Bomba*, Caupolicán 594 at Arauco, which has good meals, reasonable prices and occasional live music. Valdivia has two Chinese restaurants, *Yang Cheng* at General Lagos 1118 and *Shanghai* at Henríquez 326. Vegetarians can visit *La Vie Claire* at Caupolicán 435-A, popular for both its food and atmosphere.

For coffee and snacks, check out *Café Palace*, Pérez Rosales 580 at Arauco, extremely popular with young people – on Saturday mornings in particular. For Valdivia's finest pastries and desserts, try *Establecimientos Delicias* at Henríquez 372 or *Café Hausmann* at O'Higgins 394. There are very fine kuchen at *Pasteleria La Baguette*, Caupolicán, and good ice cream at *Entrelagos*, Pérez Rosales 630.

Entertainment

Cinemas The Cine Cervantes, Chacabuco 210, is the only place to see first-run movies.

Discos Valdivia's several pubs and discos are within a few blocks of each other in the centre: Discotheque Izma at Arauco 425, Music Pub Gay-Lussac at Chacabuco 455, and London Pub Discotheque at Independencia 471.

Things to Buy

Chocolates are a regional speciality, with several different outlets including Chocolatería Entrelagos at Pérez Rosales 622, Confitería Sur at Henríquez 374, and Chocolatería Camino de Luna at Picarte 417.

There is a very interesting, informal crafts market in the evening at the north-east corner of Arauco and Henríquez. More conventional outlets for arts and crafts goods include Artesanía CEMA-Chile at Hen-ríquez 726, Ruca Indiana at Henríquez 758, Cerámica Terra at Caupolicán 544, and Cerámica y Porcelanas Lilián at Prat 507, Departamento 4.

Getting There & Away

Air Valdivia's Aeródromo Las Marías is north of the city via the Puente Calle Calle. LAN-Chile (☎ 213042) has offices at Henríquez 379, Local 9, but no flights. Ladeco (☎ 213392), Caupolicán 579, flies to Santiago on Monday and Tuesday mornings, Wednesday evening and Friday afternoon.

Bus From Valdivia's Terminal de Buses (☎ 212212), at Anfión Muñoz 360 on the corner of Anwandter, Tas Choapa, Buses Norte, Fénix and Cruz del Sur have frequent buses to destinations on or near the Panamericana between Puerto Montt and Santiago. Typical fares from Valdivia are: Temuco US$3.50; Puerto Montt US$5; Concepción US$8; and Santiago US$13.

Turibus and Buses Norte serve Bariloche in Argentina, for US$22. There are three buses weekly to Punta Arenas via Osorno and Argentine Patagonia for US$57 single.

Several companies serve Lake District destinations. Buses Línea Verde, Pirehueico, Valdivia and Chile Nuevo go to Panguipulli, while Línea Verde has daily buses to Futrono. Buses Jac has regular service to Villarrica and Temuco. Fares to Panguipulli and Villarrica are around US$2.50.

Train Valdivia no longer enjoys direct rail service, but rather a bus-train combination via Temuco. For tickets and information, go to Ferrocarriles del Estado (☎ 214978), Ecuador 2000, with any east-bound bus or taxi colectivo on Arauco or Picarte.

Getting Around

From the bus terminal or the train station, any bus marked 'Plaza' will take you to the Plaza de la República. Buses from the Plaza to the terminal go down Arauco before turning onto Picarte. There are also taxi colectivos.

Car Rental Rental cars are available from Hertz (☎ 218316) at Pedro Aguirre Cerda 1154, , the Automóvil Club (☎ 212376) at Caupolicán 475, Autowald (☎ 212786) at Camilo Henríquez 610, Assef y Méndez Rent-a-car at General Lagos 1335, and First Rent-a-Car (☎ 215973) at Pérez Rosales 674.

AROUND VALDIVIA

Corral, Niebla & Isla Mancera

Outside Valdivia, where the Río Valdivia and the Río Tornagaleones join the Pacific Ocean, there are 17th-century Spanish forts at Corral, Niebla and the island of Mancera. Largest and most intact is the **Fuerte de Corral**, built in 1645 and restored and expanded in the 18th century. The **Fuerte Castillo de Armagos**, a half-hour's walk north of Corral, sits on a crag above a small fishing village. Corral and Armagos are most easily reached by boat from Valdivia.

Sernatur's English-language description of the fortifications at the mouth of the river is perhaps more amusing than instructive:

> The disposition of the fortresses was with out any doubt, a unique completely different to it's similars in America. Due to the field of configuration it was necessary to recur to the expedient of many separated forts in order to defent navigation channel between Valdivia and the bay.

In 1820, a single Chilean warship under the direction of the Scotsman Lord Thomas Cochrane launched an audacious and successful assault on Spanish forces at what one of his subordinates later called the 'Gibraltar of South America'. Boldly seizing a Spanish vessel in the harbour, 300 musketeers were able to land and they took Corral by surprise – no mean feat since it was defended by more than 700 soldiers and 100 cannons.

Lord Cochrane himself had a colourful career. Convicted of fraud and jailed in Britain, he became one of the world's highest-ranking mercenaries, serving countries such as Chile, Brazil and Greece. Britain restored his rank in 1842 and even promoted him to Admiral in 1854.

A third fort, **Fuerte Niebla**, is on the north side of the river mouth and is accessible by bus or boat from Valdivia. Niebla is also a popular bathing resort for Valdivianos. It has a tourist office, open daily from 9 am to 1 pm and from 2.30 to 7 pm. One traveller has praised *Restaurant Canto del Agua*, which serves fish fresh off the boat. In Corral, which is a more tranquil place to stay, there

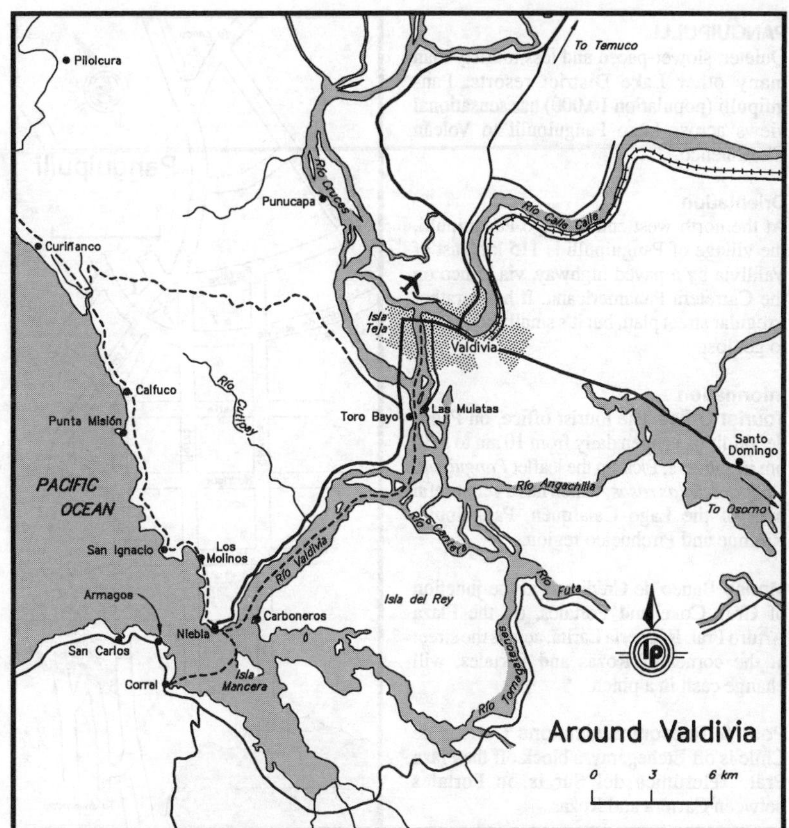

are several waterfront restaurants, some of which serve huge plates of curanto.

The fortifications on **Isla Mancera** can only be visited by boat.

Getting There & Away The best alternative is a leisurely cruise on the regular launches from the Puerto Fluvial, near the Valdivia tourist office, returning by bus in the afternoon. Departures vary according to the day and season; the trip takes about 2½ hours from Valdivia to Corral via Isla Mancera, Armagos and Niebla. Prices vary considerably, depending on the level of service. The *María Angélica* leaves daily for Corral at 10.15 am, returning at 6.30 pm, while the *Duby* leaves at 11.30 am and returns at 7 pm. Both cost about US$1.75 single. The *Pillanco*, which leaves at 12.30, charges US$7.

Leaving daily at noon, Tour Puerta al Pacífico includes lunch and visits to Corral, Niebla and Isla Mancera for US$13. All services are less frequent outside the summer high season.

Buses to Niebla leave from the corner of Yungay and Chacabuco in Valdivia. There are 21 launches daily across the river between Niebla and Corral for US$0.75.

PANGUIPULLI

Quieter, slower-paced and less touristy than many other Lake District resorts, Panguipulli (population 10,000) has sensational views across Lago Panguipulli to Volcán Choshuenco.

Orientation

At the north-west end of Lago Panguipulli, the village of Panguipulli is 115 km east of Valdivia by a paved highway, via Lanco on the Carretera Panamericana. It has a rather irregular street plan, but it's small enough not to get lost.

Information

Tourist Office The tourist office, on Pedro de Valdivia, is open daily from 10 am to 8.30 pm in summer. Pick up the leaflet *Panguipulli – capital de las rosas*, which has a very useful map of the Lago Calafquén, Panguipulli, Riñihue and Pirehueico region.

Money Banco de Crédito is at the junction of Cruz Coke and Portales, on the Plaza Arturo Prat. Rotisería Larita, across the street at the corner of Rozas and Portales, will change cash in a pinch.

Post & Telecommunications Correos de Chile is off Etchegaray, a block off the Plaza Prat. Telefónica del Sur is on Portales between Carrera and Rozas.

Festivals

In late January and early February, Panguipulli celebrates the founding of the town during the Semana de la Rosa.

Places to Stay

There are several hotels and residenciales in Panguipulli. One reader has endorsed *Hospedaje Berrocal* at J M Carrera 834. A nameless hospedaje on Pedro de Valdivia, directly opposite the bus terminal, charges only US$4 per person. At *Hostal España*, at the corner of O'Higgins and Rodríguez, rooms are US$11 per person with breakfast. *Cabañas Tío Carlos*, on Etchegaray below Freire, offers accommodation for US$13 per

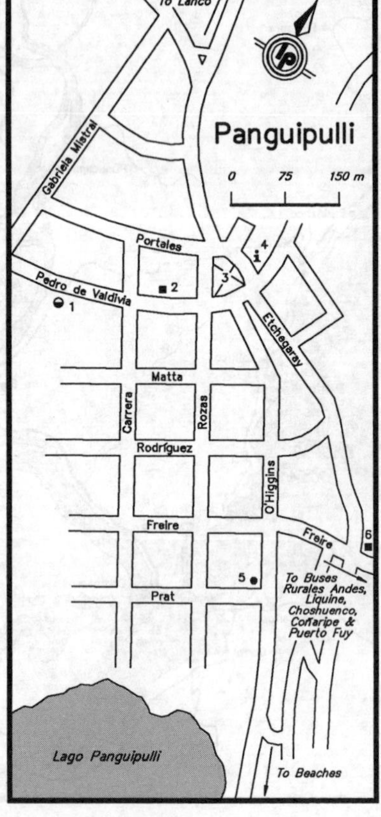

1	Bus Station
2	Hotel Central
3	Plaza Arturo Prat
4	Tourist Office
5	Banco Estado de Chile
6	Hostería Quetropillan

person but also rents cabins for US$57 for up to six persons.

Hotel Central, on Pedro de Valdivia between Carrera and Rozas, has airy rooms and clean bathrooms with hot water (even

Top Left : Port of Antofagasta (WB)
Top Right : Fishmonger, Los Vilos (WB)
Bottom : Political mural, Los Vilos (WB)

Top : Fishing boats, Río Bueno (WB)
Bottom : Volcán Osorno, Parque Nacional Vicente Pérez Rosales (GL)

bathtubs) for US$20/30, with a very friendly and helpful manager. Upstairs rooms are quieter and larger.

Prices are about the same at *Hostería Quetropillán* (☎ 348), Etchegaray 381, a quiet location on the corner with Freire. On the road to Lanco, 500 metres outside town, *Hotel Rayen Trai* (☎ 292) charges US$34/48.

Places to Eat

Try *Restaurant Chapulín* at Rozas 639, which has meat and seafood dishes, or *Girasol* on Rozas near Matta, recommended by a reader. Perhaps the most interesting choice is the *Restaurant Didáctico El Gourmet*, Ramón Freire 0394, a cooking school whose the graduate chefs seek jobs throughout the Lake District and Chile.

Getting There & Away

Bus Panguipulli has two main bus terminals. The larger one, on Pedro de Valdivia between Gabriela Mistral and Carrera, has regional and long-distance buses to Temuco, Valdivia and Santiago, plus local services to Choshuenco, Neltume and to Puerto Fuy on Lago Pirehueico.

Buses Pirehueico, Valdivia and Chile Nuevo each have daily buses to Valdivia, taking about 2½ hours; Tur Bus has its own terminal at Valdivia and Rozas. Buses Transpacar has several buses daily to Choshuenco, Neltume and Puerto Fuy; according to one account, the crowded bus to Choshuenco is like a 'mobile oven'. For up-to-date information on the ferry from Puerto Fuy to Puerto Pirehueico and the Argentine border at Paso Hua Hum, ask at the Hostería Quetropillán.

Ruta Andes uses the smaller terminal, on Freire near Etchegaray, for daily service to Coñaripe (US$1.75), with connections to Licán Ray and Villarrica.

CHOSHUENCO

Choshuenco, little more than two streets at the east end of Lago Panguipulli, survives on farming, a local sawmill and visitors who enjoy its attractive black-sand beach. There are many fine walks in the nearby countryside, at the foot of 2415-metre Volcán Choshuenco.

Farmer

Places to Stay & Eat

Hotel Rucapillán, next to the beach, is very clean, with heating, a good restaurant, hot showers and friendly staff. Rooms are about US$10 per person, with boats for hire as well. Another decent place is the basic but agreeable *Claris Hotel*, with rooms for US$6 per person. Slightly dearer is *Hotel Choshuenco*, which also has a restaurant.

Hostería Pulmahue, just out of town on the road to Enco, sits among gardens above the lake. Pleasant rooms with private bath cost US$50 per person, including all meals.

Getting There & Away

Buses from Panguipulli to Puerto Fuy pass through Choshuenco, taking about two hours and returning to Panguipulli early the next morning. From Puerto Fuy, Transportes Mariela takes passengers and vehicles to Puerto Pirehueico on Tuesday, Thursday, Saturday and Sunday at 9 am, and there are other services on Monday, Wednesday and Friday.

FUTRONO

Futrono is a small, quiet and dusty town overlooking Lago Ranco, 102 km from Valdivia via Paillaco, on the Panamericana. While the lake is attractive, public access is limited and difficult. The offshore islands are Mapuche reserves, sometimes accessible from the town of Lago Ranco, on the south side of the lake. The main street, Avenida Balmaceda, continues east to Llifén and Lago Maihue; although the road around the east side of Lago Ranco is very poor beyond Llifén, travellers to the town of Lago Ranco can make connections there.

Places to Stay & Eat

Hospedaje Futronhue, on Balmaceda near Manuel Rodríguez, is simple but clean, tidy and very friendly, with accommodation for US$4 per person. There are hot showers.

Hostería El Rincón Arabe (☎ 262), on a diagonal road off Balmaceda as you enter from Valdivia, overlooks the lake, with a swimming pool and a very fine restaurant. It has recently changed ownership, but there are still excellent Middle Eastern and Chilean meals, accompanied by wine and Middle Eastern music. Rooms are about US$9/16 for a single/double with breakfast.

Getting There & Away

Futrono's four bus companies have offices on Avenida Balmaceda. Buses Futrono, Buses en Directo, Buses Pirehueico and Buses Cordisur each operate several buses daily to Valdivia (US$2) via Paillaco. Cordisur continues to Llifén and Riñinahue, where there are connections for the town of Lago Ranco.

LLIFÉN

Llifén, at the east end of Lago Ranco via a rather poor road, is a more attractive but significantly more expensive resort than Futrono. The *Hostería Chollinco* (☎ 283), a short distance up the road to Lago Maihue, charges nearly US$20 for a campsite, not to mention US$40 per person for accommodation. Lodging is available at *Hostería Huequecura* or *Hostería Licán*, for half that price.

RÍO BUENO

On the Carratera Panamericana, 40 km north of Osorno, Río Bueno (population 12,000) is a crossroads for Lago Ranco. Its colonial **Fuerte San José de Alcudia**, dating from 1778, commands a bluff overlooking the river, while the **Museo Arturo Moller Sandrock**, Pedro Lago 640, contains Mapuche artefacts and documentation on German colonisation in the region. Both are worth a visit if you have time to kill.

Reasonable accommodation is available at *Hotel Richmond* (☎ 363), Comercio 755, for about US$5 a single. There are several buses a day to Lago Ranco with Obando, Buses del Sur, San Martín and Buses Ruta 5.

LAGO RANCO

The town of Lago Ranco (population 2000), 124 km from Valdivia via Río Bueno, on the south shore of its namesake lake, is a plain, inexpensive working-class resort in pleasant but unspectacular country. There is a strong indigenous presence as Isla Huapi, in the centre of the lake, is a Mapuche reserve.

Information

Tourist Office Staffed by young, friendly, enthusiastic and well informed locals, Lago Ranco's municipal tourist office has free maps and leaflets on the Lake District. It's on Avenida Concepción, the main road from Río Bueno, and is open daily from 8.30 am to 12.30 pm and 2.30 to 6.30 pm from January to March.

Post & Telephone Correos de Chile is at Curicó 105. There's a public phone on La Serena, half a block from Concepción.

Travel Agencies Turihott (☎ 201), Valparaíso 111, runs auto trips around Lago Ranco and has a launch for excursions to Isla Huapi.

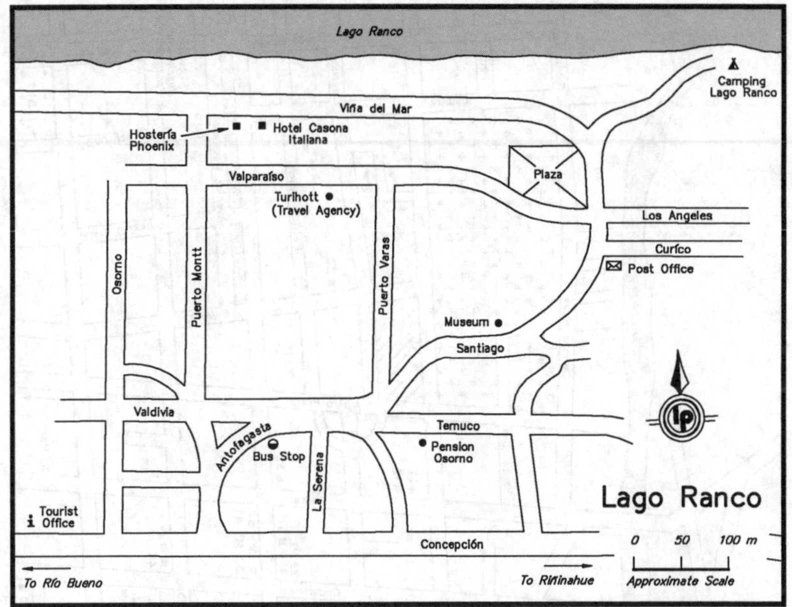

Festivals

Visitors are welcome to the Mapuche festival *Lepun*, which takes place on Isla Huapi in late January, but photography is strictly forbidden.

Places to Stay & Eat

Pensión Osorno, Temuco 103, is a spartan but tidy little hotel which costs about US$5 per person. *Hotel Casona Italiana* (☎ 225), on the lakefront at Viña del Mar 145, is a clean, bright place with moderate prices, about US$10 per person. Almost next door at Viña del Mar 141, *Hostería Phoenix* (☎ 226) charges US$20/28 for a single/double. At the other end of the spectrum, three km west of town, the *Lago Ranco Yacht Hotel* charges US$48 per person with full pension.

Camping Lago Ranco, on a crowded lakefront site with limited shade, charges US$4 per site with cold showers only.

Getting There & Away

On weekdays at 9 am, Buses Obando goes to Río Bueno, with connections both north and south on the Panamericana. Buses San Martín also goes to Río Bueno, while Buses Ruta 5 goes to Osorno via Río Bueno.

Buses Lagos del Sur also goes to Osorno and to Riñinahue, at the east end of Lago Ranco. Like Lagos del Sur, Obando also has buses to Riñinahue, with connections to Futrono which include crossing the Río Calcurrupe on a barge driven by the current.

OSORNO

Founded in 1558 by García Hurtado de Mendoza, San Mateo de Osorno had, by the end of the 16th century, a population of more than 1000 Spaniards and mestizos who were supported directly or indirectly by encomiendas of 80,000 Indians. The great Mapuche rebellion of 1599 forced the city's inhabitants to flee to Chiloé and it was not until 1796 that the Spaniards re-established the

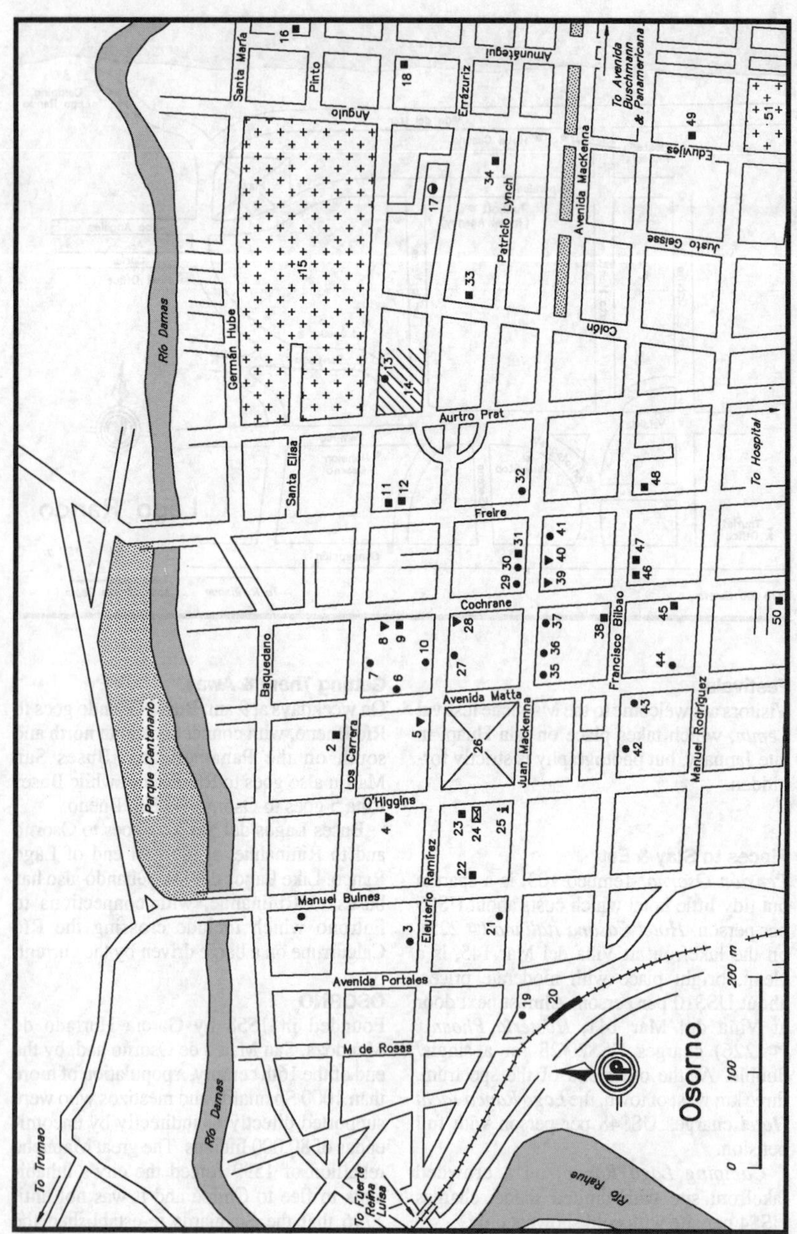
Santa María
Pinto
Angulo
Arrunátegui
Errázuriz
To Avenida Buschmann & Panamericana
Eduvijes
Patricio Lynch
Avenida MacKenna
Justo Geisse
Colón
Río Damas
Germán Hube
Aurtro Prat
Santa Elisa
To Hospital
Freire
Cochrane
Francisco Bilbao
Baquedano
Los Carrera
Avenida Matta
Juan Mackenna
Manuel Rodríguez
Parque Centenario
O'Higgins
Eleuterio Ramírez
Manuel Bulnes
Avenida Portales
M de Rosas
Río Damas
To Trumao
To Fuerte Reina Luisa
Río Rahue
Osorno
0
100
200 m

settlement. Even after Chilean independence from Spain, growth was slow, and overland communications were difficult and dangerous because of Mapuche control over the countryside.

Since the mid-19th century, German immigrants have left their mark on the city and the region, particularly in manufacturing and in dairy farming. By the turn of the century, the population reached 5000, the city had its first newspapers, and the railroad had arrived from Santiago. The city's economy still depends on agriculture and its subsidiary industries, but tourism is increasing significantly, thanks to the excellent communications to the north and south, and across the Andes to Argentina.

Orientation

Osorno (population 110,000), situated at the confluence of the Río Rahue and the Río Damas is 910 km south of Santiago and 110 km north of Puerto Montt. The city is a key road and rail transport hub, to Lago Puyehue, Lago Rupanco, Parque Nacional Puyehue, and Pajaritos (the major border crossing to Argentina).

Most places of interest to the traveller are within a few blocks of the Plaza de Armas, in an area bounded by the Río Rahue to the west, the Río Damas to the north, Avenida Francisco Bilbao to the south, and Calle Angulo to the east.

Information

Tourist Office Sernatur (☎ 234104) has moved to the 1st floor of the Edificio Gobernación Provincial, on the Plaza de Armas. It's well stocked with maps, pamphlets and information on Osorno and the

■ PLACES TO STAY

2 Hospedaje
9 Hotel Interlagos
11 Residencial Schulz
12 Residencial Aitué
16 Hospedaje Amunátegui
18 Hospedaje de la Fuente
22 Hotel Tirol
23 Gran Hotel Osorno
31 Hotel García Hurtado de Mendoza
33 Residencial Ortega
34 Hotel Rayantú
38 Residencial La Posada
45 Residencial Hein
46 Hotel Waeger
47 Residencial Bilbao
48 Residencial Stop
49 Hotel Villa Eduvijes
50 Residencial Riga

▼ PLACES TO EAT

4 Deutscher Verein
5 Dino's Restaurant
8 Pizzería Lucas
28 Pasterlería Rhenania
39 Restaurant Casa del Altillo
40 Pizzería Los Platos

OTHER

1 Automóvil Club de Chile
3 Cine Lido
6 Centro Cultural
7 Ñiltur Rent-a-Car
10 Galería Rombocól/Osorno Tour
13 Orlandina Regalos
14 Mercado Municipal/Terminal de Buses Rurales
15 German Cemetery
17 Main Bus Terminal
19 Disco Mario's
20 Railway Station
21 CONAF
24 Post Office
25 Sernatur
26 Plaza de Armas
27 Galería Catedral/Turismo Frontera
29 Telephone Office
30 Cambiotur (Money Exchange)
32 Los Detalles (Crafts)
35 Banco de Chile
36 First Rent-a-Car
37 German Consulate
41 Alta Artesanía
42 Hertz
43 Museo Histórico Municipal
44 LAN-Chile & Budget Rent-a-Car

entire region. *El Diario Austral*, Osorno's daily newspaper, publishes a monthly *Guía de Servicios*.

There is a private tourist information office (☎ 234149), coordinated with Sernatur, at the Terminal de Buses, Errázuriz 1400. Another good source of information is the Automóvil Club (☎ 232269), Manuel Bulnes 463.

Money Osorno has several convenient cambios, including: Turismo Frontera in the Galería Catedral, Ramírez 949, Local 5; Agencia de Viajes Mundial, in the same building just across the hall; and Cambiotur, Juan Mackenna 1010, which is open weekdays from 9.30 am to noon and 3.30 to 7 pm, Saturdays from 10 am to noon only. All three will change US and Argentine cash and US$ travellers' cheques.

Post & Telecommunications Correos de Chile is at O'Higgins 645, opposite the Plaza de Armas. Telefónica del Sur, Mackenna 1004 at Cochrane, is very efficient for overseas calls.

Consulates The German Consulate (☎ 232151) is in the Edificio Paillahue at Mackenna 987, Oficina 4.

Cultural Centres Osorno's Centro Cultural, Avenida Matta 550, offers regular exhibitions of painting, photography and other events. It's open daily from 9 am to 1 pm and 3 to 7.30 pm.

Travel Agencies Like other cities in the Lake District, Osorno has numerous travel agencies, including Turismo Frontera (☎ 236394), and Osorno Tour (☎ 238034), in the Galería Rombocol at Ramírez 952, Local 12.

Medical Services Osorno's Hospital Base (☎ 235572) is on Avenida Bühler, the southward extension of Arturo Prat.

National Parks CONAF (☎ 234393) is at Mackenna 674, 3rd floor.

Museo Histórico Municipal

Osorno's well arranged historical museum includes exhibits on Mapuche culture, the city's shaky colonial origins, German colonisation, the city's development in the 19th century, information about the local naval hero Eleuterio Ramírez. It also has natural history displays.

The museum holds several uncommon and noteworthy objects. A very unusual collection of antique firearms includes a pistol which seems to be attached to an early Swiss army knife. A historical photograph of the Termas de Puyehue depicts the modest origins of what is now a very elegant and expensive resort, east of Osorno. A display of Chilean banknotes contains Unidad Popular's 500 escudo note of 1971, which poignantly represents a rugged copper miner instead of the 'great men' who grace every other note.

The museum, at Matta 809, is open weekdays from 10 am to 12.30 pm and 3 to 6.30 pm, Saturdays from 11 am to 1 pm and 2 to 6 pm. There is no charge for admission.

Cementerio Católico

The Catholic cemetery, on Rodríguez, has some immense, ornate family crypts with numerous German surnames, reflecting the town's history from the 19th century to the present. There is also a Cementerio Alemán on Los Carrera.

Historical District

Between the Plaza de Armas and the railway station, Osorno has many buildings of historical interest, including a lot of obsolete factories and weathered Victorian houses. Many are deteriorating but others have been well restored.

Fuerte Reina Luisa

To the west of the railway station, the bulwarks of Osorno's Fuerte Reina Luisa, built in 1793 on the orders of the Governor of Chile, Don Ambrosio O'Higgins (father of Bernardo O'Higgins) once guarded the riverine access to Osorno. While the ruins are not spectacular, they are well restored and a pleasant site for a lunchtime breather.

Festivals

Osorno's Festival Regional del Folklore Campesino, for two days in mid-January, presents and promotes typical music, dance, crafts and food. Later, at the end of March, it hosts the Semana Osornina, a celebration of the city's colonial origins and Germanic heritage.

Places to Stay – bottom end

Hostel accommodation is available at *Residencial Stop* (☎ 232001), Freire 810, for US$4 including kitchen privileges. It's clean but ramshackle; some rooms are very small but the staff are friendly.

Hospedaje Amunátegui, three blocks from the bus terminal at Amunátegui 372 near Presidente Pinto, has very clean singles for US$4. After very amicable haggling, *Hospedaje de la Fuente* (☎ 239516), Los Carrera 1587, charges about US$4 per person. It's spotlessly clean but has sagging beds.

Residencial Ortega, at Colón 602, between Errázuriz and Patricio Lynch, is adequate at US$5 per person, including breakfast and hot showers, but it does need renovations. *Residencial Hein* (☎ 234116), Cochrane 843 between Francisco Bilbao and Manuel Rodríguez, has smaller but much better-maintained rooms. Its congenial German-Mapuche owner charges US$10/17 for a single/double with shared bath. A nameless *hospedaje* at Los Carrera 872, next to the Esso station, is very clean and comfortable at US$8 per person, including breakfast.

Camping *Camping Olegario Mohr*, on the south bank of the Río Damas just off the Panamericana, is a shady municipal site, with picnic tables and firepits, but it lacks hot water and has only two toilets each for men and women. However, it's free, and the attendants take orders for hot fresh bread – make your request in the evening for the next day's breakfast. Any taxi colectivo out to Avenida Buschmann will drop you at the Panamericana, within a few minutes' walk of the site.

Places to Stay – middle

Highly recommended, the clean and friendly *Hotel Villa Eduvijes* (☎ 235023), a few blocks south of the bus terminal at Eduvijes 856, is good value at US$13/23 for a single/double. *Residencial Aitué* (☎ 239922), Freire 546, is a very fine choice for US$14/26, with breakfast, TV and shared bath – slightly dearer with private bath. *Residencial Schulz* (☎ 237211), nearby at Freire 530, is a bit cheaper and well recommended. *Hotel Tirol* (☎ 233593), Bulnes 630, charges US$17/26 for a single/double.

Double/single room rates at *Residencial La Posada*, Bilbao 992, are about US$17/29, while nearby *Residencial Bilbao* (☎ 236755), Francisco Bilbao 1019, charges about US$23/34 for single/doubles, as does *Residencial Riga* (☎ 232945), Amthauer 1058 near Cochrane.

Places to Stay – top end

Top-end accommodation at the art-deco *Gran Hotel Osorno* (☎ 232171), facing the Plaza de Armas at O'Higgins 615, starts at about US$30/48 for singles/doubles. The rooms are simple, clean and neat with phones and private baths. The rooms are reasonable but not really grand. Try also *Hotel Interlagos* (☎ 234695) at Cochrane 551, with rates of US$34/51 for singles/doubles.

Hotel Waeger (☎ 233721), Cochrane 816 at Bilbao, is German-run and treated me well because I could speak passable German. Perhaps Osorno's most dignified hotel, it has rooms with private bath and breakfast for US$52/71 for singles/doubles, and a very good restaurant.

It's not the most expensive, though – several others charge in the range of US$60/80 for singles/doubles, including *Hotel Rayantú* (☎ 238114) at Patricio Lynch 1462, *Hotel García Hurtado de Mendoza* (☎ 237111) at Mackenna 1040, and *Hotel del Prado* (☎ 235020) at Cochrane 1162.

Places to Eat

The *Club Social Ramírez*, on Eduvijes almost next door to the Hotel Villa Eduvijes, offers generous portions of good cheap food.

Dino's, facing the Plaza at Ramírez 898, is good for drinks, snacks, grills and ice cream. *Pizzería Los Platos*, Mackenna 1027, has cheap lunchtime dishes for about US$2, but is perhaps most notable for not serving pizza! *Pizzería Lucas*, Cochrane 559, is bright, small, and so popular it may well move to larger quarters – go early to get a seat at lunch.

La Naranja, Local 13 in the Mercado Municipal at Prat and Errázuriz, has very good and inexpensive food, while there are fine pastries and light meals at *Pastelería Rhenania*, Eleuterio Ramírez 977. The *Deutscher Verein* (German Club), O'Higgins 563, is more typically Chilean than German, but offers very good food with fine service at reasonable prices. For a splurge, try *Casa del Altillo*, Mackenna 1011.

Entertainment

Cinema Osorno's only movie theatre is the Cine Lido, Ramírez 650.

Discos There are a number of central discos, including Mario's at Mackenna 555, Power 2000 in the Gran Hotel Osorno at O'Higgins 615, and Juan Salvador Gaviota, at the corner of Colón and Errázuriz.

Things to Buy

Local and regional crafts, including wood carvings, ceramics and basketry, are available at the Mercado Municipal, Errázuriz 1200, Locales 2 & 3; Alta Artesanía, Mackenna 1069; Los Detalles, Mackenna 1100; and Orlandina Regalos, Los Carrera 1233.

Getting There & Away

Air Osorno's Aeropuerto Carlos Hott Siebert (sometimes known as Cañal Bajo) is seven km east of downtown, across the Panamericana via Avenida Buschmann. LAN-Chile (☎ 236688), Matta 862, Block C, has recently begun flights to and from Santiago via Temuco. These leave Santiago on Monday morning, returning from Osorno at 6.45 pm, and on Wednesday and Thursday afternoons, returning at 7.50 pm.

Ladeco (☎ 234355) has offices at Cochrane 816, but its flights leave from Puerto Montt.

Bus Osorno has two bus terminals. For long-distance services, the Terminal de Buses (☎ 234149) is at Avenida Errázuriz 1400, near Angulo. Some buses to local and regional destinations leave from the Terminal de Buses Rurales in the Mercado Municipal, on the corner of Errázuriz and Prat. Several smaller destinations in the Lake District are most conveniently reached from Osorno.

Bus – rural Buses Puyehue (☎ 236541), at the Mercado Municipal, has several buses daily to Termas de Puyehue en route to Aguas Calientes (US$2), and to Chilean customs and immigration at Pajaritos (US$3), within Parque Nacional Puyehue. Across the Río Rahue, Bus Mar (☎ 236166), Tarapacá 799, and Buses Maicolpue (☎ 234003), Valdivia 501, connect Osorno with Bahía Mansa (two hours, US$2), the only easily accessible ocean bathing resort between Valdivia and the island of Chiloé. Buses Ruta 5 (☎ 237020), at the main bus terminal, serves Río Bueno with connections to Lago Ranco.

Buses Piedras Negras (☎ 234371), located in the offices of Igi Llaima at the main bus terminal, goes as far as Puerto Rico, on the south shore of Lago Rupanco. Transur, in the same offices, goes to Las Cascadas, on the eastern shore of Lago Llanquihue at the foot of Volcán Osorno. Buses Via Octay (☎ 230118), also in the main terminal, serves Puerto Octay and Frutillar on Lago Llanquihue.

Bus – regional & inter-regional Many companies offer services to Puerto Montt and other regional destinations, including Tas Choapa (☎ 233933), Varmontt (☎ 232732), Tur Bus (☎ 234170), ETC and Victoria Sur (☎ 233050), Intersur, Pullman Sur (☎ 232777), Etta Bus (☎ 236370), Igi Llaima (☎ 234371), Bus Norte (☎ 233319), and Cruz del Sur (☎ 232777). The fare is about US$2.

Most of the same companies cover destinations on the Panamericana between Osorno and Santiago – typical fares include Temuco US$4, Los Angeles or Concepción US$8, Santiago US$12, Viña del Mar or Valparaíso US$14. Many but not all of these services originate in Puerto Montt; for more details, see Getting There & Away in the Puerto Montt section.

Bus – international Osorno has convenient international services to Bariloche and other Argentine destinations via the Puyehue pass over the Andes. Tas Choapa has connections for Mendoza and Buenos Aires via the Libertadores pass. Buses to destinations in Chilean Patagonia, such as Coihaique, Punta Arenas and Puerto Natales also go via the Puyehue pass. Other principal companies are Bus Norte, Igi Llaima, Cruz del Sur, Río de La Plata and Turismo Lanín (☎ 233633). Most of these services originate in Puerto Montt; see Getting There & Away in the Puerto Montt section for more details.

Fares to Bariloche are about US$20, to Mendoza US$40, and to Buenos Aires, US$100.

Train Osorno's railway station (☎ 232991) is at the west end of Juan Mackenna, corner of Portales. The Santiago-Puerto Montt line has a summer service only but it's really pointless to take the train south since buses to Puerto Montt are so frequent and convenient. Northbound trains depart for Santiago at 11.20 am, taking 20 hours, and 7.12 pm, taking 17 hours.

Getting Around

Car Rental For rental cars, try First Rent-a-Car (☎ 233861) at Mackenna 959, Hertz (☎ 236000) at Bilbao 857, the Automóvil Club (☎ 232269) at Bulnes 463, Ñiltur (☎ 232356) at Los Carrera 951 or Budget (☎ 236128) at Matta 862, Block C.

AROUND OSORNO

Along with Puerto Montt, Osorno is one of the best centres for exploring the Chilean lakes. From Osorno, you can go east to Lago Puyehue with its thermal baths, and continue to Parque Nacional Puyehue. Going south takes you to Lago Llanquihue and the resorts of Puerto Octay and Frutillar.

Entre Lagos

Entre Lagos is a modest, pleasant resort, 50 km east of Osorno on the south-west shore of Lago Puyehue. For US$10, the very quiet and sheltered *Camping No Me Olvides* is one of the best facilities in the country with private sites large enough for two tents, abundant firewood, and excellent showers and toilets. For hotel accommodation, try *Hostería Entre Lagos* (☎ 647-225), Ramírez 65, which has singles/doubles for US$23/29.

Termas de Puyehue

One of Chile's most famous hot springs resorts, Termas de Puyehue is 76 km east of Osorno where the paved Ruta 215 forks; the north fork goes to Anticura and the Argentine border while the southern lateral leads to Aguas Calientes and ends in Antillanca, in Parque Nacional Puyehue.

Set in elegant grounds at the junction of the two roads, the baronial *Hotel Termas de Puyehue* (☎ 232157 in Osorno, ☎ 231-3417 in Santiago) truly resembles an old world alpine resort. It has singles/doubles for

…ith breakfast; half-pension and … are also available.

PARQUE NACIONAL PUYEHUE

Puyehue is Chile's most popular national park and receives the most visitors. Created in 1941 to protect 65,000 hectares of verdant montane forest and starkly awesome volcanic scenery, it has since expanded to 107,000 hectares and recently celebrated its 50th anniversary.

In Puyehue's lower Valdivian forest, the dominant tree species is the multi-trunked ulmo *(Eucryphia cordifolia)*, accompanied by olivillo *(Aextoxicon punctatum)*, tineo *(Weinmannia trichosperma)* and southern beech *(Nothofagus* species). The dense undergrowth includes the delicate, rust-barked arrayán *(Myrceugenella apiculata*, a member of the myrtle family), quila *(Chusquea* species; a genus of solid rather than hollow bamboos which make some areas utterly impenetrable), and wild fuchsia. At higher elevations, the southern beeches lenga and coihue dominate.

Pudú

In such dense forest, wildlife is hard to see but in more open areas there are occasional sightings of puma or pudú, but birds are the most common type of wildlife. On the peaks, you may glimpse the Andean condor; along the rivers, look for the Chilean torrent duck *(Merganetta armata, pato corta-corriente* in Spanish), which flourishes in the very rough whitewater of Class 5 rapids.

Geography & Climate

Mountainous Puyehue is about 75 km east of Osorno via Ruta 215, the international highway to Argentina, which is paved through the park as far as the Chilean border crossing at Pajaritos. Altitudes range from 250 metres on the delta of the Río Golgol where it enters Lago Puyehue, to 2236 metres on the summit of Volcán Puyehue.

The park has a humid temperate climate, with an annual rainfall of about 4200 mm at Aguas Calientes. The annual mean temperature is about 9°C, with a summer average of about 14°C, which falls to 5°C in winter. January and February, the driest months, are best for visiting the high country, but the park is open all year and skiing is fine in winter.

Despite Puyehue's moist climate, many areas north of Ruta 215 are relatively barren as plants have been slow to recolonise after a major eruption of Volcán Puyehue in 1960. On the western slopes of the volcano are many extinct fumaroles (vents which emit steam and gases) and very lively hot springs.

Aguas Calientes

One of the highlights at Aguas Calientes is the **Sendero El Pionero**, a steep 1800-metre nature trail which offers, at the end of the trail, splendid views of Lago Puyehue, the valley of the Río Golgol, and Volcán Puyehue. En route you will see the nalca *(Gunnera chilensis)*, resembling an enormous rhubarb, with edible stalks and with leaves almost large enough for umbrellas. There are exceptionally fine specimens of the multi-trunked ulmo, which grows to 45 metres and is covered with white flowers in summer. Chileans greatly prize *miel de ulmo*, the honey from the pollen which bees extract from these flowers.

Another easier nature trail is the **Sendero Rápidos del Chanleufú**, which follows the river for 1200 metres. For a longer excursion, take the 11-km trail to **Lago Bertín**, where there is a basic refugio. After hiking

along the nature trails, or returning from a longer trek, you can soak or swim in a heated pool filled with the therapeutic mineral waters. Aguas Calientes was named after these waters. This place is a more economical alternative than Termas de Puyehue.

CONAF's **Centro de Visitantes**, open daily from 9 am to 1 pm and 2.30 to 8.30 pm, has a simple but informative display on Puyehue's natural history and geomorphology, with slide presentations daily at 5 pm. It generally has basic maps and brochures, despite occasional shortages.

CONAF rangers also lead overnight backpack trips to Lago Paraíso, Volcán Puyehue, Lago Constancia and Pampa Frutilla. For schedules and reservations on these trips, which are free of charge, make arrangements with CONAF at the park or in Osorno. Bring your own tent, food, and raingear.

Antillanca

For some of the finest views of Puyehue and the surrounding area, visit Antillanca, a popular winter resort with a ski lodge, at the foot of Volcán Casablanca. This ski area has only three surface lifts, 460 metres of vertical drop, and a friendly, club-like atmosphere.

The ski season runs from early June to the end of October.

At the end of the 18-km road beyond Aguas Calientes, the lodge is also open in summer when there is good hiking and camping in the backcountry but the nearest formal campground is at Aguas Calientes.

Anticura

Anticura is the best base for exploring the wilder sectors of the park. The international highway follows the course of the Río Golgol but the finest scenery is the magnificently desolate plateau at the base of Volcán Puyehue, reached only by an overnight backpack from El Caulle, two km west of Anticura.

On the western slope of Puyehue, a steep morning-plus walk from El Caulle, CONAF has a well maintained refugio which is a good place to lodge or camp (ask CONAF at Anticura for the key). From the refugio it is another four hours or so through a moonscape of massive lava flows and extinct fumaroles to a spring with rustic thermal baths which is a fine and private place to camp. Trekkers can continue north to Riñinahue, at the south of Lago Ranco, or return to Anticura.

Some of Puyehue's most interesting backcountry lies in the remote area between Chilean customs and immigration at Pajaritos and the border, which was once heavily fortified when Argentina threatened war over the Beagle Channel in 1979. Signs of these preparations have disappeared, but to visit Pampa Frutilla, the upper reaches of the Río Golgol, and Lago Constancia, you need permission from the Carabineros as well as from CONAF (whose guided overnight trips into these areas simplify the process).

Another worthwhile sight, more easily reached from the highway, is the **Salto del Indio**, an attractive waterfall on the Golgol where, according to legend, a lone Mapuche hid to escape encomienda service in a nearby Spanish gold mine.

CONAF has a visitor centre at Anticura, although it's less well organised than the one at Aguas Calientes.

Places to Stay & Eat

CONAF charges US$4 per site for its rustic but very attractive campground at Catrue, near Anticura, which has fresh water, picnic tables, firepits and basic toilets. At Aguas Calientes, private concessionaires operate *Camping Chanleufú* (☎ 236988 in Osorno), which costs US$14 per site, and *Camping Los Derrumbes*, which costs US$11 for up to eight persons. Neither has hot showers, but fees entitle you to use the nearby thermal baths. In January and February, these latter sites are very crowded and noisy, making Catrue a much better alternative.

Hostería y Cabañas Aguas Calientes (☎ 236988 in Osorno) rents four-bed cabins for US$64 to US$76. It has a restaurant that offers breakfast for US$3.50 and lunch or dinner for US$7, and also has groceries and supplies (although supplies are much cheaper and more varied in Osorno).

Hotel Antillanca (☎ 235114 in Osorno, ☎ 233-3454 in Santiago), has single/double accommodation for US$36/52, breakfast included. Lunch or dinner costs an extra US$9. Its gymnasium, sauna, disco, boutique and shops seem badly out of place in a national park.

Getting There & Away

From Osorno's Mercado Municipal, at Errázuriz and Colón, Buses Puyehue (☎ 236541), has several buses daily to Termas de Puyehue en route to Aguas Calientes (US$2), and to Chilean customs and immigration at Pajaritos (US$3). In winter, the Club Andino de Osorno (☎ 232297) offers direct services to the ski lodge at Antillanca.

Traffic is heavy enough, so hitching from the eastern outskirts of Osorno should not be too difficult if the bus schedule proves inconvenient.

PUERTO OCTAY

Peaceful, attractive Puerto Octay, 50 km from Osorno at the north end of Lago

Llanquihue, resembles a middle-European village. It has about 2500 permanent residents, many of German descent. In the early days of German settlement, when roads were very poor and water transport was critical, it was a very important port on the route between Puerto Montt and Osorno.

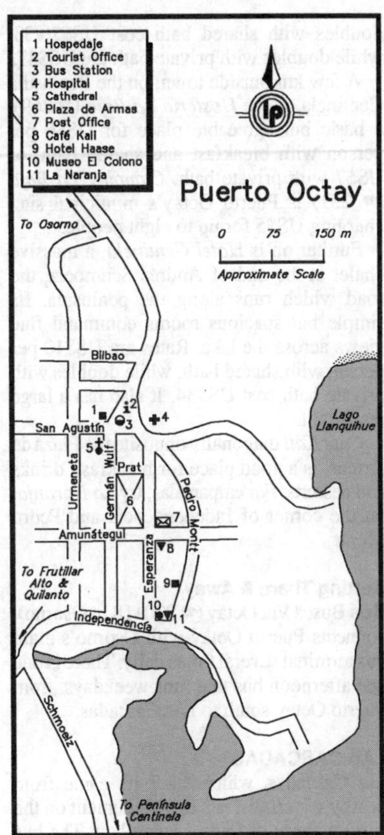

Information

Puerto Octay has a municipal tourist office (☎ 276) on Pedro Montt near San Agustín.

Museo El Colono

Puerto Octay's museum, on the corner of Independencia and Esperanza, displays antique farm machinery and other turn-of-the-century artefacts like old porcelain, rusting irons, ancient gramophone records and steam-driven telephones.

Festivals

Over the course of the summer, Puerto Octay sponsors several festivals which vary from year to year. In 1992, for instance, it hosted the Rodeo Libre, a celebration of southern Chile's huaso (cowboy) traditions, and the Degustación de Platos Típicos, a national culinary competition. Check the tourist office in Osorno for an updated list.

Places to Stay & Eat

Several travellers have complimented the clean, comfortable and friendly *hospedaje* upstairs at German Wulf 712, near the lakeshore and adjacent to the church, at US$8 per person with breakfast. The same folks run the *Restaurant Cabaña* across the road.

German-run *Hotel Haase* (☎ 213), Pedro Montt 344, is a rambling building with spacious interiors, high ceilings and three dining rooms. Soaring prices have carried it well above its former budget category– singles/

doubles with shared bath cost US$20/33, while doubles with private bath are US$47.

A few km outside town, on the Península Centinela, is the *Hostería La Baja* (☎ 269), a basic but agreeable place for US$6 per person with breakfast and shared bath, or US$7 with private bath. *Camping La Baja* (☎ 251) is Puerto Octay's municipal site, charging US$5 for up to eight people.

Further on is *Hotel Centinela*, a massive chalet at the end of Andrés Schmoelz, the road which runs along the peninsula. Its simple but spacious rooms command fine views across the lake. Rates are US$10 per person with shared bath, while doubles with private bath cost US$34. It also has a large restaurant.

Café Kali diagonally opposite the Plaza de Armas, is a good place for breakfast, drinks and desserts. For empanadas, try *La Naranja*, on the corner of Independencía and Pedro Montt.

Getting There & Away

Bus Buses Via Octay (☎ 230118 in Osorno), connects Puerto Octay with Osorno's main bus terminal several times daily. There is one late afternoon bus that runs weekdays, from Puerto Octay south to Las Cascadas.

LAS CASCADAS

Las Cascadas, which takes its name from nearby waterfalls, is a tiny settlement on the eastern shore of Lago Llanquihue. The bus ride from Puerto Octay offers grand views of Volcán Osorno as it passes through dairy country with many small farms and tiny, shingled churches – all painted yellow with red corrugated iron roofs. Las Cascadas fronts onto a black-sand beach on the lakeshore.

Places to Stay & Eat

Hostería Irma, one km south of town on the road to Ensenada, charges about US$12 per person. It has a bar, serves meals and is very pleasant and highly recommended. Diagonally opposite the hostería, alongside the lake, is a peaceful, quiet and free campsite with almost no facilities.

Camping Las Cañitas (☎ 235377 in Osorno), three km down the road towards Ensenada, charges US$5 per site for basic services, including cold showers. It also rents four-bed cabañas for US$25.

Getting There & Away

Bus There is one bus each weekday from Puerto Octay to Las Cascadas. Because of the poor road, there is no bus service beyond Las Cascadas, so you'll have to walk or hitch to Ensenada, the entry point to Parque Nacional Vicente Pérez Rosales – or return to the Panamericana and take the bus from Puerto Varas.

The bus from Puerto Octay arrives at Las Cascadas early in the evening, so unless you can hitch the 20 km to Ensenada (a four-hour walk) you'll have to spend the night in Las Cascadas.

FRUTILLAR

Frutillar, one the Lake District's most pleasant and popular resorts, has superb views of the snow-capped Volcán Osorno, seemingly floating on the horizon across Lago Llanquihue to the east. Noted for its meticulously preserved Germanic architecture, it consists of two distinct parts: the resort area by the lake is Frutillar Bajo (Lower Frutillar), while the part near the Carratera Panamericana is Frutillar Alto (Upper Frutillar), about two km west. Between them, the two have a permanent population of about 5000.

Orientation

Frutillar Bajo is about 70 km south of Osorno and 40 km north of Puerto Montt. The main street, Avenida Philippi, runs north-south along the lakeshore with most of the hotels and other points of interest along its west side, and fine sandy beaches on the east side. Avenida Carlos Richter connects Frutillar Bajo with Frutillar Alto.

Information

Tourist Office There is a helpful tourist kiosk (☎ 316) on the jetty, across Avenida Philippi from San Martín. Summer hours (January & February) are 9 am to 9 pm, while

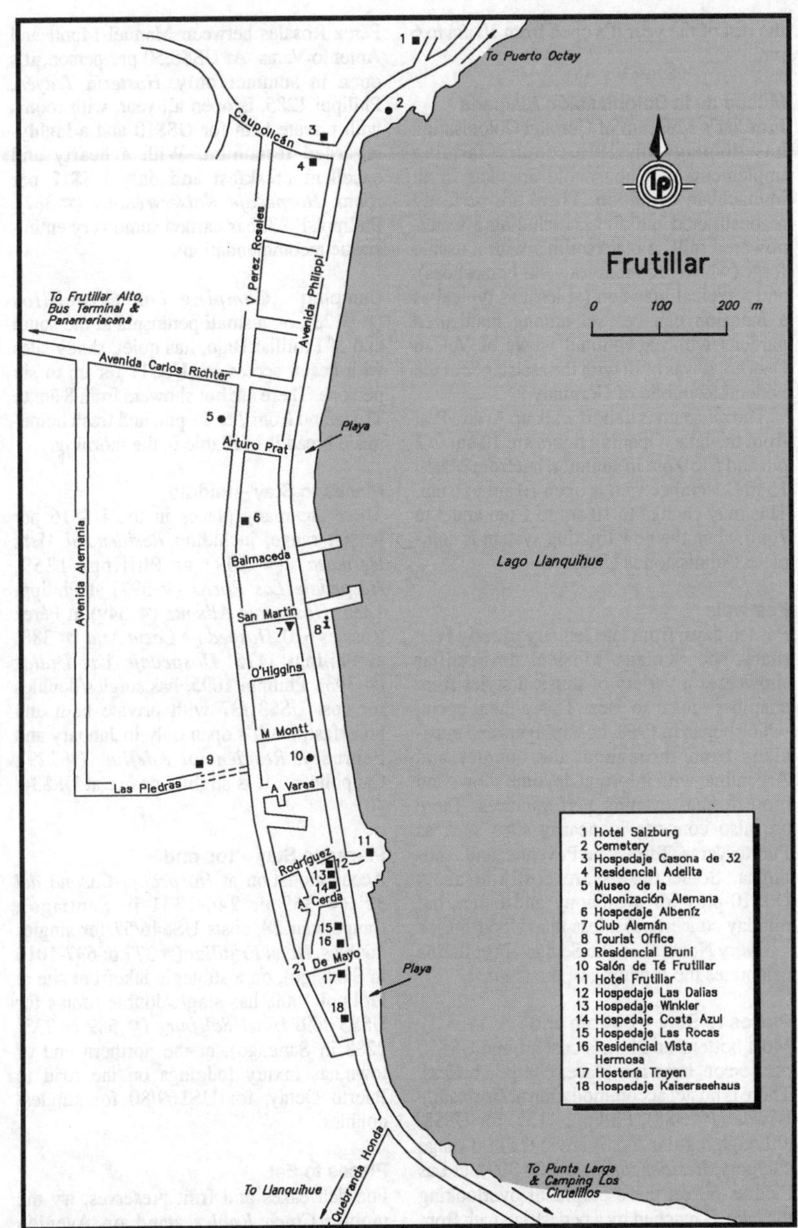

Frutillar
0
100
200 m
To Puerto Octay
Caupolicán
V Perez Rosales
Avenida Philippi
To Frutillar Alto, Bus Terminal & Panameriacana
Avenida Carlos Richter
Arturo Prat
Playa
Avenida Alemania
Balmaceda
San Martín
O'Higgins
M Montt
Las Piedras
A Varas
Rodríguez
A Cerda
21 De Mayo
Playa
Lago Llanquihue
To Llanquihue
Quebranda Honda
To Punta Larga & Camping Los Ciruelillos
1 Hotel Salzburg
2 Cemetery
3 Hospedaje Casona de 32
4 Residencial Adelita
5 Museo de la Colonización Alemana
6 Hospedaje Albeníz
7 Club Alemán
8 Tourist Office
9 Residencial Bruni
10 Salón de Té Frutillar
11 Hotel Frutillar
12 Hospedaje Las Dalias
13 Hospedaje Winkler
14 Hospedaje Costa Azul
15 Hospedaje Las Rocas
16 Residencial Vista Hermosa
17 Hostería Trayen
18 Hospedaje Kaiserseehaus

the rest of the year it's open from 10 am to 6 pm.

Museo de la Colonización Alemana

Frutillar's Museum of German Colonisation has displays on 19th-century farming implements and household artefacts in an immaculate condition. There are perfectly reconstructed buildings, including a water-powered mill, a blacksmith's with a usable forge (which produces souvenir horseshoes), and a typical mansion (at least as typical as a mansion can be) set among manicured gardens with exceptional views of Volcán Osorno. It was built with the assistance of the Federal Republic of Germany.

The museum is a short walk up Arturo Prat from the lake. Opening hours are 10 am to 2 pm and 5 to 9 pm in summer, but from March 15 to December 15 it is open 10 am to 6 pm. This may change to 10 am to 1 pm and 3 to 7 pm when the new lighting system is complete. Admission is US$1.

Festivals

For ten days, from late January to early February, the Semana Musical de Frutillar showcases a variety of musical styles from chamber music to jazz. This annual event, which began in 1968, hosts singers and musicians from throughout the country and Argentina, with informal daytime shows and more formal evening performances. There are also concerts in nearby sites such as Puerto Varas, Termas de Puyehue, and Antillanca. Some tickets are costly at about US$10-plus for symphony and ballet, but midday concerts cost less than US$1.50.

Every November, the Semana Frutillarina celebrates the founding of the town.

Places to Stay – bottom end

Most bottom-end hotels cost around US$10 per person, but a few places charge a bit less. There is hostel accommodation at *Hospedaje Winkler* (☎ 388), Philippi 1155, for US$8, although regular rooms are in the mid-range category. *Residencial Bruni* (☎ 309), at Las Piedras 60 on the escarpment overlooking the lake, is reached by a pedestrian path from Pérez Rosales between Manuel Montt and Antonio Varas. At US$8.50 per person, it's open in summer only. *Hostería Trayén*, Philippi 1285, is open all year, with rooms with private bath for US$10 and a highly-regarded restaurant. With a hearty and excellent breakfast and only US$12 per room, *Hospedaje Kaiserseehaus* (☎ 387), Philippi 1333, has earned some very enthusiastic recommendations.

Camping *Camping Los Ciruelillos* (☎ 9123), on a small peninsula at the south end of Frutillar Bajo, has quiet, shady sites with beach access for US$11 for up to six persons. There are hot showers from 8 am to 11 am and from 7 to 11 pm, and fresh home-made bread is available in the morning.

Places to Stay – middle

There are many places in the US$16 per person range, including *Residencial Vista Hermosa* (☎ 209) at Philippi 1259, *Hospedaje Las Rocas* (☎ 397) at Philippi 1235, *Hospedaje Albeníz* (☎ 349) at Pérez Rosales 610, *Hospedaje Costa Azul* (☎ 388) at Philippi 1175. *Hospedaje Las Dalias* (☎ 393), Philippi 1095, has singles/doubles for cost US$31/37 with private bath and breakfast, but it's open only in January and February. *Residencial Adelita* (☎ 229), Caupolicán 31, is slightly dearer at US$34/40.

Places to Stay – top end

Accommodation at *Hospedaje Casona del 32* (☎ 369 or 246-1331 in Santiago), Caupolicán 28, costs US$46/57 for singles doubles. *Hotel Frutillar* (☎ 377 or 697-1010 in Santiago), on a strategic lakefront site at Philippi 1000, has single/double rooms for US$57/69. *Hotel Salzburg* (☎ 589 or 233-2288 in Santiago), at the northern end of town,has luxury lodgings on the road to Puerto Octay, for US$69/80 for singles/doubles.

Places to Eat

For rich cakes and fruit preserves, try the mobile *Cinco Robles* stand on Avenida

Philippi. The *Club Alemán*, on San Martín off Philippi, has fixed price lunches for US$7. *Café del Sur*, Pérez Rosales 580, serves reasonable home-cooked lunches, while the restaurant at the *Hotel Frutillar* is the best choice for a splurge.

Things to Buy

Local specialities include fresh raspberries – delicious and cheap at about US$1.40 per kg in season – plus raspberry jam and kuchen. You can also get miniature wood carvings of the buildings at the museum.

Getting There & Away

Trains from Santiago to Puerto Montt stop at Frutillar Alto but you can also reach Frutillar by bus from Osorno or Puerto Montt. Buses Varmontt, on the corner of Alessandri and Carlos Richter in Frutillar Alto, has buses to Puerto Montt and Osorno every half hour between 7.10 am and 9.40 pm. Buses Cruz del Sur, also on Alessandri, has similar services.

Getting Around

Taxi colectivos cover the short distance between Frutillar Alto and Frutillar Bajo.

PUERTO VARAS

Puerto Varas is the gateway to Lago Todos Los Santos in Parque Nacional Vicente Pérez Rosales and the popular boat-bus crossing to Bariloche in Argentina. This town was an important lakeport during the 19th-century German colonisation, and is now a popular tourist destination.

Orientation

Puerto Varas lies on the south-east shore of Lago Llanquihue, only 20 km north of Puerto Montt. Unlike most Chilean cities, it has a very irregular street composition mainly because of its hilly topography and the curving shoreline of the lake. Most tourist services, however, are within a small grid bounded by Portales, San Bernardo, Del Salvador and the lakeshore. Outside this area, street numbers are disorderly to the point of chaos; on one street, three consecutive houses were numbered 62, 140, and 48.

The escarpment of Cerro Calvario, a steep hill south of downtown, has diverted Puerto Varas's growth to the east and west along the lakeshore. The Avenida Costanera, becomes paved Ruta 225 to Ensenada, Petrohué, and Lago Todos Los Santos.

Information

Tourist Office Puerto Varas's municipal tourist office (☎ 232437), at Del Salvador 328 near San Francisco, has free maps and brochures about the entire area, with a friendly and well informed staff. It's open daily from 9 am to 9 pm.

Money Banco de Chile and the Banco del Estado are both on Santa Rosa, opposite the Plaza de Armas. For better rates and longer opening hours, change cash and travellers' cheques at Turismo Los Lagos, Del Salvador 257, Local 11, which is open Monday to Saturday from 9 am to 1.30 pm and 3 to 8.30 pm, Sundays and holidays from 10.30 am to 1.30 pm.

Post & Telecommunications Correos de Chile is at San José 324. Telefónica del Sur's long-distance office, at Santa Rosa and Del Salvador, is open daily from 8 am to 11 pm.

Travel Agencies Puerto Varas is one of the major Lake District centres for *turismo aventura*, with numerous agencies offering trekking in Parque Nacional Vicente Pérez Rosales, climbing Volcán Osorno, birdwatching on the Río Maullín, and rafting on the Río Petrohué. Among them are Tranco Expediciones (☎ 233297) at Del Salvador 529, Ecotravel (☎ 233222) on the Avenida Costanera, and Pillán (☎ 232334) at Del Salvador 100.

For more conventional travel services, like the bus-boat excursion across the Andes to Argentina, try Andina del Sud (☎ 232511), Del Salvador 243.

Medical Services Puerto Varas's Hospital San José (☎ 232336) is at Dr Bader 810, on

Cerro Calvario near Del Salvador's westward exit from town.

Feria Artesanal

The local artisans fair, on Del Salvador near the lakefront, has a fine selection of local handicrafts.

Things to See & Do

The actual city of Puerto Varas doesn't have any really prominent attractions, but Lago Llanquihue and the surrounding area provide opportunities for recreational activities such as swimming, wind-surfing, and cycling. There are mountain bikes for rent at the Feria Artesanal for about US$14 per day. Check the adventure travel companies for rental equipment for other sports.

Turismo Nieve (☎ 233000), San Bernardo 406, runs daily excursions to various destinations around Lago Llanquihue, to Petrohué and Peulla in Parque Nacional Vicente Pérez Rosales, and as far afield as Chiloé Island.

Places to Stay – bottom end

A popular tourist destination, Puerto Varas has a wealth of accommodation in all categories, although one reader detected a prejudice against backpackers. The most reasonable are the many hospedajes, some of which are seasonal. *Hospedaje Novoa* (☎ 232906), San José 544, is a bit ramshackle and run-down, but has singles for US$5.50 without breakfast. *Hospedaje Hernández* (☎ 232353), Del Salvador 1025, is comparably priced.

Most of the other hospedajes are in the US$10-plus range, such as *Hospedaje Opitz* (☎ 232909) at Del Salvador 741, *Hospedaje Schwabe* (☎ 233165) at Ramón Ricardo Rosas 361, *Hospedaje Klein* (☎ 233109) at Eleuterio Ramírez 1255, *Hospedaje Vargas* (☎ 232364) at Del Salvador 329 opposite the tourist office, *Hospedaje Elsa* (☎ 232803) at Verbo Divino 427, *Hospedaje Sureño* (☎ 232648) at Colón 179, and *Hospedaje Bittner* (☎ 232201) at Walker Martínez 564. *Hospedaje Ceronni* (☎ 232016), at Estación 262, has been recommended.

Clean with hot showers and a decent restaurant, the very basic *Residencial Unión*, San Francisco 669 opposite the Varmontt bus terminal, has poor beds and is cold in winter. Rooms are US$8 per person with breakfast. *Residencial Hellwig* (☎ 232472), San Pedro 210 at Portales, is cheap with reasonably spacious rooms at US$10 per person despite an apparent motto of 'one room, one towel'.

Places to Stay – middle

Hostería La Sirena (☎ 232897), Santa Rosa 710, is a fine place with sweeping views of Puerto Varas and the lake. Doubles cost US$30 with private bath. *Hotel Loreley* (☎ 232226), Maipú 911, has doubles for US$34. *Country House Restaurant Hotel* (☎ 233105) at Walker Martínez 584, an attractive place with a very fine restaurant, charges US$34/46 for a single/double.

Places to Stay – top end

With all the style of a bomb shelter, *Gran Hotel Puerto Varas* (☎ 232524), Klenner 351, charges US$44/59 for singles/doubles. Alternatives include *Hotel Asturias* (☎ 232754, ☎ 335440 in Santiago) at Del Salvador 322 near the tourist office, where rates are US$48/59 for a single/double, or *Hotel Licarayén* (☎ 232305) at San José 114, which overlooks the waterfront and has doubles for US$62 – one reader called it the best in Chile. The dearest place in town is *Hotel del Lago* (☎ 232291), Klenner 195, at US$75/85 for singles/doubles.

Places to Eat

Café Real, upstairs from Turismo Los Lagos at Del Salvador 257, has cheap fixed price lunches, while the *Café Central* at San José 319 is the best place for coffee and desserts – *Café Asturias* at San Francisco 302 looks a bit rundown. *El Gordito* and *El Mercado*, both in the Mercado Municipal at Del Salvador 582, are very fine, if rather upscale, seafood restaurants. The *Club Alemán*, San José 415, is another good choice, as is *Il Gato Renzo*, Del Salvador 314 next to the tourist office. *Country House Restaurant Hotel*, Walker Martínez 584, has very appealing but rather expensive meals.

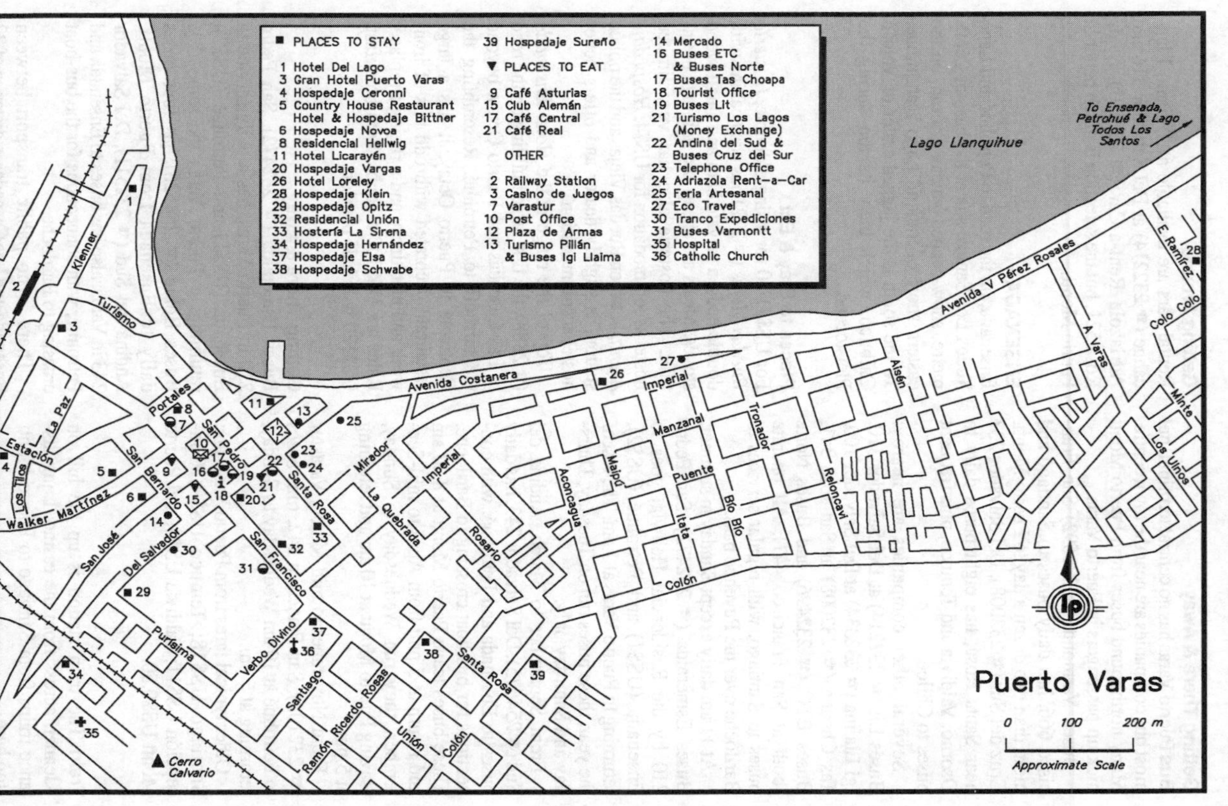
■ PLACES TO STAY
1 Hotel Del Lago
3 Gran Hotel Puerto Varas
4 Hospedaje Ceronni
5 Country House Restaurant
Hotel & Hospedaje Bittner
6 Hospedaje Novoa
8 Residencial Hellwig
11 Hotel Licarayén
20 Hospedaje Vargas
26 Hotel Loreley
28 Hospedaje Klein
29 Hospedaje Opitz
32 Residencial Unión
33 Hostería La Sirena
34 Hospedaje Hernández
37 Hospedaje Elsa
38 Hospedaje Schwabe
39 Hospedaje Sureño
▼ PLACES TO EAT
9 Café Asturias
15 Club Alemán
17 Café Central
21 Café Real
OTHER
2 Railway Station
3 Casino de Juegos
7 Varastur
10 Post Office
12 Plaza de Armas
13 Turismo Pillán
& Buses Igi Llaima
14 Mercado
16 Buses ETC
& Buses Norte
17 Buses Tas Choapa
18 Tourist Office
19 Buses Lit
21 Turismo Los Lagos
(Money Exchange)
22 Andina del Sud &
Buses Cruz del Sur
23 Telephone Office
24 Adriazola Rent-a-Car
25 Feria Artesanal
27 Eco Travel
30 Tranco Expediciones
31 Buses Varmontt
35 Hospital
36 Catholic Church
Lago Llanquihue
To Ensenada, Petrohué & Lago Todos Los Santos
Puerto Varas
0 100 200 m
Approximate Scale
Cerro Calvario
Avenida V Pérez Rosales
Avenida Costanera
E Ramírez
Colo Colo
A Varas
Minte
Los Ulmos
Aisén
Imperial
Manzanal
Tronador
Reloncaví
Puente
Bío Bío
Itata
Maipú
Aconcagua
Colón
Mirador
La Quebrada
Rosario
Santa Rosa
San Francisco
San Pedro
Portales
Turismo
Klenner
La Paz
Estación
Los Tilos
Walker Martínez
San Bernardo
San José
Del Salvador
Purísima
Verbo Divino
Santiago
Ramón Ricardo Rosas
Unión

Getting There & Away

Bus Puerto Varas has no central terminal, but most bus companies are near the town centre. Many northbound buses from Puerto Montt pick up passengers in Puerto Varas.

Buses Varmontt (☎ 232592) San Francisco 666, has daily buses to Santiago and more than two dozen a day to Puerto Montt. Cruz del Sur (☎ 233008), Del Salvador 237 near Santa Rosa, has eight buses daily to Osorno, Valdivia and Temuco, plus frequent buses to Chiloé.

Several other companies are nearby: Buses Lit (☎ 232214) at Del Salvador 310, Igi Llaima (☎ 232334) at Del Salvador 100, Tas Choapa (☎ 232008) at San José 341, Buses ETC (☎ 232496) and Buses Norte (both at San Francisco 447). All operate buses to Santiago, with regular services to Bariloche over the Puyehue pass.

At 11 am daily except Sunday in summer, Buses Esmeralda (☎ 232472), San Pedro 210 by the Residencial Hellwig, goes to Ensenada (US$1) and Petrohué (US$2), returning to Puerto Varas at 1 pm. The rest of the year, these buses run on Tuesday, Thursday and Saturday only.

From September to March, Andina del Sud (☎ 254675), Del Salvador 243, has daily buses to Ensenada and Petrohué, with connections for bus-boat crossing to Bariloche. These buses leave Puerto Montt at 8.30 am and return at 5 pm; from April to mid-September, they run Wednesday to Sunday, leaving Puerto Montt at 10 am and returning at 5 pm.

From November to mid-March, Varastur (☎ 232103), San Francisco 242, runs buses to Petrohué at 10 am Wednesday to Sunday, returning at 5 pm.

Other typical fares from Puerto Varas are: Santiago US$18; Temuco US$9; Concepción US$11; Valdivia US$4; and Puerto Montt US$0.50.

Train The train station is up the hill on Klenner, across from the casino. Long-distance trains from Santiago to Puerto Montt stop here.

Getting Around

Rental cars are available at Turismo Llancahue (☎ 232214) at Del Salvador 316 and Adriazola Rent-a-Car (☎ 233101), Santa Rosa 521, but the selection is much better in Puerto Montt.

ENSENADA

Ensenada, on the road to Petrohué and Lago Todos Los Santos, sits at the base of 2660-metre, snow-capped Volcán Osorno, on the eastern shore of tranquil Lago Llanquihue. To the south is the jagged crater of Volcán Calbuco, which blew its top during the Pleistocene.

Places to Stay & Eat

For US$11/20 for a single/double, *Hostería Ruedas Viejas* (☎ 312) has cosy cabins with double beds, a private bath and small wood stoves. Meals are cheap and helpings bountiful. The hostería also has very limited hostel accommodation for US$4. *Hospedaje Arena*, between Ruedas Viejas and the police station, is slightly dearer and offers better hostel accommodation.

Top of the range is the *Hotel Ensenada* (☎ 2888), the first large building on the road to Las Cascadas and Puerto Octay, beyond the turn-off to Petrohué. Resembling the Centinela in Puerto Octay, it has a large restaurant decorated with odd bits of ironwork and machinery and a raging fireplace. Rates are US$100 a double with breakfast, US$120 with half-pension.

Getting There & Away

Buses Esmeralda (☎ 232472), San Pedro 210 in Puerto Varas, has a daily service to Ensenada (US$1) and Petrohué (US$2), returning to Puerto Varas the same day. Buses Bohle (☎ 254526) has four buses daily to Ensenada from Puerto Montt. Andina del Sud (☎ 232511), Del Salvador 243 in Varas, also has buses to Ensenada and Petrohué, with connections for the bus-boat crossing to Bariloche.

There is no public transport between Ensenada and Las Cascadas, a distance of 22 km on the road to Puerto Octay, but hitching may be feasible.

PARQUE NACIONAL VICENTE PÉREZ ROSALES

Beneath the flawless cone of Volcán Osorno, Lago Todos Los Santos is the centrepiece of Parque Nacional Vicente Pérez Rosales and the jewel of the Lake District. A scoured glacial basin between thickly forested moraines (ridges of glacial debris), the lake offers dramatic views of the volcano. From here you can take the popular boat-bus route across the Andes to Argentina. The needle point of Volcán Puntiagudo lurks to the north while, to the east, prominent Volcán Tronador marks the Argentine border.

Established in 1926 to protect this extraordinary scenery, 251,000-hectare Pérez Rosales was Chile's first national park, ironically honouring a man who, according to Mark Jefferson, 'arranging the first important settlement of Germans near Lake Llanquihue...hired the Indians to clear away the woods by fire'. Ecologically, the park's Valdivian rainforest and other plant communities closely resemble those of Parque Nacional Puyehue, east of Osorno.

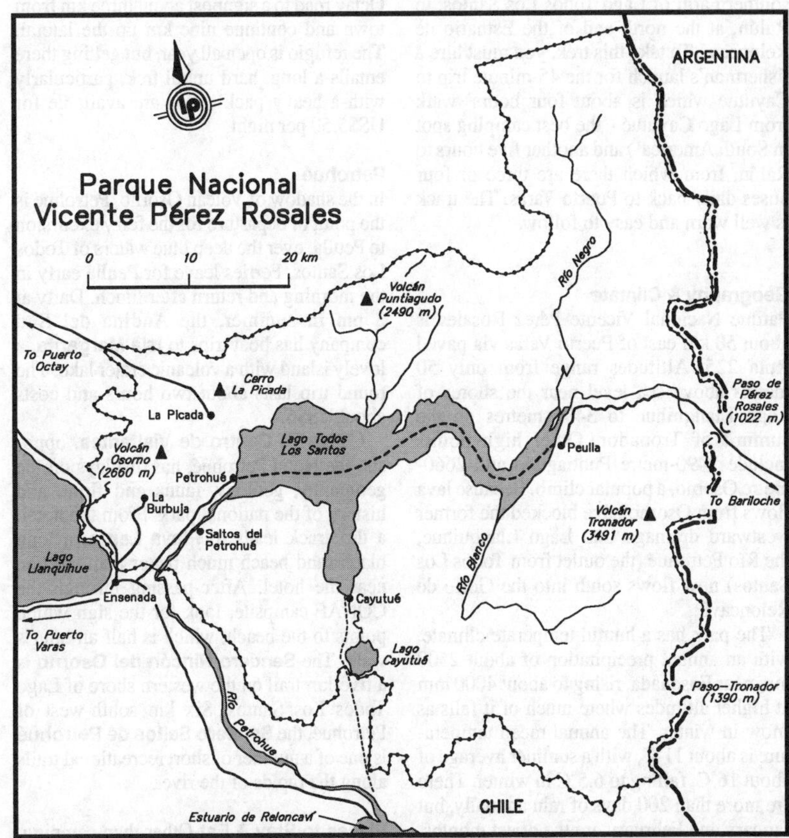

Pérez Rosales has a much longer history, however. In pre-Columbian times, the Camino de Vuriloche was a major trans-Andean crossing for the Mapuche. Later, the Jesuit missionaries used this route, starting at the island of Chiloé, continuing up the Estuario de Reloncaví and crossing the pass south of Tronador to Lago Nahuel Huapi, thus avoiding the riskiest crossings of the region's lakes and rivers. For more than a century after the Mapuche uprising of 1599, the Indians successfully concealed this route from the Spaniards.

One reader, Kevin Bell of Epping, Australia, suggests a trek from Cayutué, on the southern arm of Lago Todos Los Santos, to Ralún, at the north end of the Estuario de Reloncaví. To take this trek, you must hire a fisherman's launch for the 45-minute trip to Cayutué which is about four hours' walk from Lago Cayutué ('the best camping spot in South America') and another five hours to Ralún, from which there are three or four buses daily back to Puerto Varas. The track is well worn and easy to follow.

Geography & Climate

Parque Nacional Vicente Pérez Rosales is about 50 km east of Puerto Varas via paved Ruta 225. Altitudes range from only 50 metres above sea level near the shores of Lago Llanquihue to 3491 metres on the summit of Tronador. Other high points include 2490-metre Puntiagudo and 2660-metre Osorno, a popular climb. Because lava flows from Osorno have blocked the former westward drainage into Lago Llanquihue, the Río Petrohué (the outlet from Todos Los Santos) now flows south into the Golfo de Reloncaví.

The park has a humid temperate climate, with an annual precipitation of about 2500 mm near Ensenada, rising to about 4000 mm at higher altitudes where much of it falls as snow in winter. The annual mean temperature is about 11°C, with a summer average of about 16°C, falling to 6.5°C in winter. There are more than 200 days of rain annually, but January and February are the driest months.

Volcán Osorno

Many adventure travel companies in Puerto Varas and Puerto Montt offer guided climbs of Volcán Osorno, which requires snow and ice-climbing gear. Experienced, well equipped climbers should be able to handle it alone. In winter, skiing is very popular at the **Centro de Esqui La Burbuja** (☎ 2891), 1250 metres above sea level. For reservations in Puerto Montt, contact the Hotel Vicente Pérez Rosales (☎ 252571), Antonio Varas 447.

The *Teski Ski Club Refugio* (☎ 6490) is just below snow line, with excellent views of Lago Llanquihue. Take the Ensenada-Puerto Octay road to a signpost about three km from town and continue nine km up the lateral. The refugio is open all year, but getting there entails a long, hard uphill trek, particularly with a heavy pack! Beds are available for US$5.50 per night.

Petrohué

In the shadow of Volcán Osorno, Petrohué is the point of departure for the ferry excursion to Peulla, over the deep blue waters of Todos Los Santos. Ferries leave for Peulla early in the morning and return after lunch. Daily at 3 pm in summer, the Andina del Sud company has boat trips to **Isla Margarita**, a lovely island with a volcanic crater lake. The round trip lasts about two hours and costs about US$6.

CONAF's **Centro de Visitantes**, opposite the Hotel Petrohué, has displays on the geography, geology, fauna and flora, and history of the national park. From the hotel, a dirt track leads to **Playa Larga**, a long black-sand beach much better than the one near the hotel. After passing through the CONAF campsite, look for the sign which points to the beach, which is half an hour's walk. The **Sendero Rincón del Osorno** is a five-km trail on the western shore of Lago Todos Los Santos. Six km south-west of Petrohué, the **Sendero Saltos de Petrohué** is one of a number of short recreational trails along the rapids of the river.

Places to Stay & Eat Other than camping,

there are only two alternatives for lodging at Petrohué. Cheaper of the two is the *Casa Familiar Küscher*, across the river, for which you'll have to hire a rowboat. They rent rooms for about US$7.50 per person. *Hos-tería Petrohué* (% 258042), the other option, is very comfortable and has a restaurant. Rooms with private bath start at US$28/ 48 for a single/ double with breakfast only, US$35/64 with half-pension. Things are quieter after March 1, but facilities are open all year.

Camping is possible in the grounds of the Casa Familiar Küscher. The other campground, currently occupied by the army but perhaps available in a pinch, is on the lakefront, a few minutes' walk from the Hostería Petrohué. Buy food in Puerto Varas rather than in Petrohué, where the only shop charges premium prices.

Getting There & Away – bus In summer, Buses Esmeralda (☎ 232472), San Pedro 210 in Puerto Varas, has service daily except Sunday at 11 am to Ensenada (US$1) and Petrohué (US$2), returning to Puerto Varas at 1 pm. This bus arrives at Petrohué after the ferries to Peulla have left, so plan on a night at Petrohué. The rest of the year, buses run on Tuesday, Thursday and Saturday only.

From September to March, Andina del Sud (☎ 254675), Varas 947 in Puerto Montt, has daily buses to Ensenada and Petrohué via Puerto Varas, with connections for its own bus-boat crossing to Bariloche. They leave Puerto Montt at 8.30 am and return at 5 pm; from April to mid-September, they run Wednesday to Sunday, leaving Puerto Montt at 10 am and returning at 5 pm.

From November to mid-March, Varastur (☎ 232103), San Francisco 242 in Puerto Varas, has buses to Petrohué from Wednesday to Sunday at 10 am, returning at 5 pm.

Getting There & Away – boat Andina del Sud's ferry departs Petrohué early in the morning for Peulla, a three-hour trip which is the first leg of the journey to Bariloche. Purchase tickets at the kiosk near the jetty for US$7 single; the trip takes about three hours. Tickets are also available at Andina del Sud offices in Puerto Varas and Puerto Montt.

Peulla

Approaching Peulla, the deep blue of Lago Todos Los Santos becomes an emerald green. The tiny village, which has a hotel, a school and a post office, bustles in summer as tourists pass through customs and immigration en route to Bariloche.

There is an easy walk to **Cascada de Los Novios**, a waterfall just a few minutes from the Hotel Peulla. For a longer excursion, take the eight-km **Sendero Laguna Margarita**, a rugged but rewarding climb from Peulla.

Places to Stay & Eat One km from the dock is the *Hotel Peulla* (☎ 258041), which charges US$60/85 for singles/doubles with half-pension and, according to satisfied correspondents, is worth the splurge. There's a bar and restaurant, with a buffet (about US$10) during tourist season. Nearby is the more modest *Residencial Palomita*, which has rooms for US$12 per person with half-pension. Both places are open all year.

There's a campsite opposite CONAF, and it may also be possible to get a room with a local family – several readers have recommended the home of Elmo and Ana Hernández, on the right side as you leave the jetty, where your US$6 can include a good chess game!

PUERTO MONTT

Settled by German colonists in the mid-19th century, Puerto Montt is one of southern Chile's most important cities. Its older architecture is middle European, the houses faced with unpainted shingles, high-pitched roofs and quaint, ornate balconies. The city has a modern centre, but the cathedral on the Plaza de Armas, built entirely of redwood in 1856, is the oldest building.

As a major gateway to the southern Lake District, Chiloé and Chilean Patagonia, Puerto Montt has air, bus and train links in virtually all directions.

Orientation

Capital of the Tenth Region of Los Lagos,

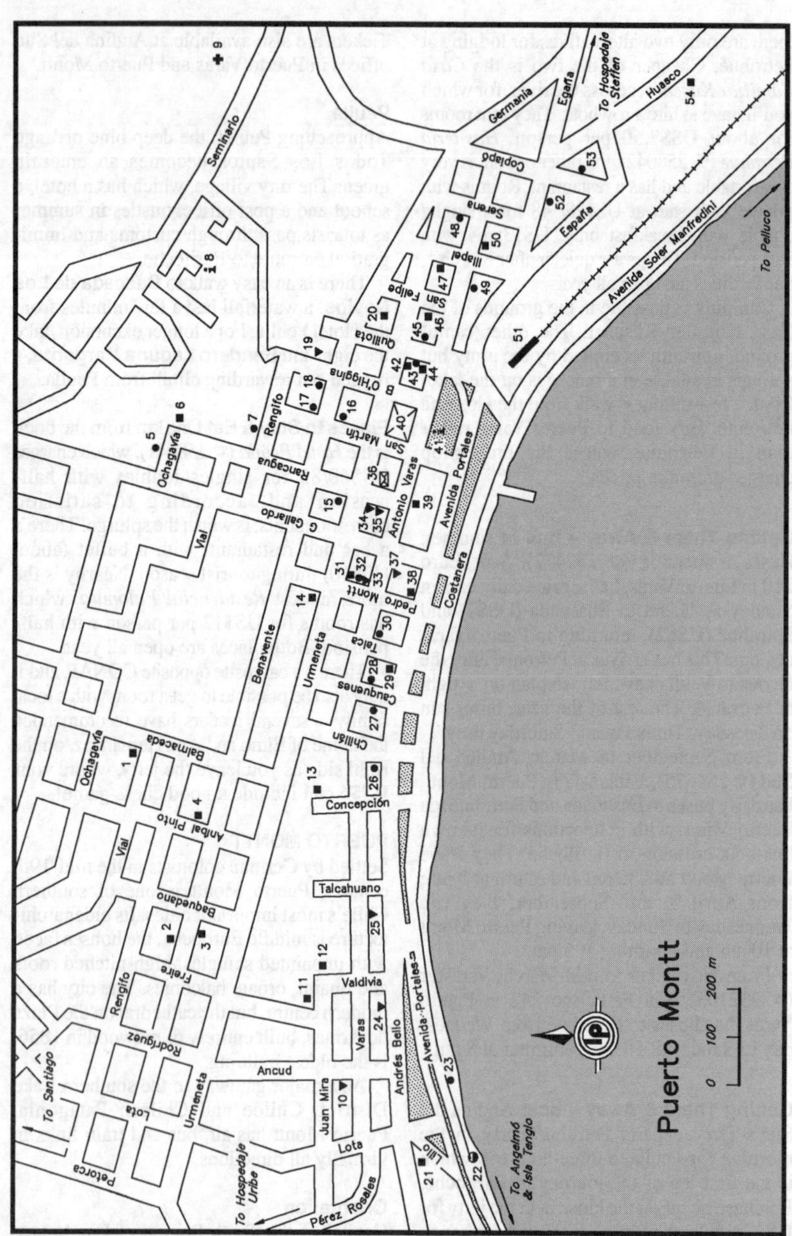
Puerto Montt
0 100 200 m
To Santiago
To Hospedaje Uribe
To Angelmó & Isla Tenglo
To Pelluco
To Hospedaje Steffen
Avenida Soler Manfredini
Avenida Portales
Avenida-Portales
Costanera
Seminario
Germania
Egaña
Huasco
Copiapó
Serena
España
Illapel
San Felipe
Quillota
O'Higgins
Rengifo
San Martín
Rancagua
Antonio Varas
Ochagavía
Vial
G. Gallardo
Benavente
Urmeneta
Pedro Montt
Talca
Cauquenes
Chillán
Balmaceda
Concepción
Aníbal Pinto
Talcahuano
Baquedano
Freire
Valdivia
Varas
Rodríguez
Ancud
Andrés Bello
Juan Mira
Lota
Lillo
Petorca
Pérez Rosales

Puerto Montt (population 90,000) is 1020 km south of Santiago via the Carratera Panamericana, which skirts the northern edge of the city as it continues to Chiloé. The city's spectacular setting at the north end of the Golfo de Reloncaví may remind visitors from Seattle or Vancouver of Puget Sound or the Strait of Georgia.

The city centre occupies a narrow coastal plain, behind which the hills rise very steeply. Along the waterfront, Avenida Portales heads west to the small fishing port of Angelmó, while to the east, Avenida Soler Manfredini continues to the bathing resort of Pelluco and connects with the rugged Camino Austral, a combination of ferries and gravel roads which ends far south, at Villa O'Higgins in the Eleventh Region of Aisén.

Information

Tourist Office Puerto Montt's municipal tourist office is a kiosk at Varas and O'Higgins, in front of the Plaza de Armas. It's open daily from 9 am to 2 pm and 3 to 9 pm.

Sernatur (☎ 252720) inconveniently overlooks the city from the 2nd floor of the annex of the Edificio Intendencia Regional, O'Higgins 480, a stiff climb from the waterfront but the staff are very helpful and have much more material than the municipal office. It's open weekdays from 8.30 am to 1 pm and 1.30 to 5.48 pm.

Money There are several cambios, including Turismo Los Lagos at Varas 595, Local 3; Cambio El Libertador at Urmeneta 529; Turismo Money Exchange at Urmeneta 300,

■ PLACES TO STAY

1 Hospedaje
2 Hospedaje Benavente
3 Hospedaje
4 Hospedaje
6 Hotel Le Mirage
11 Hospedaje Polz
12 Residencial Embassy
13 Raúl Arroyo's House (Hospedaje)
14 Hotel Gamboa
20 Residencial Urmeneta
21 Escuela No 1 (Youth Hostel)
29 Hotel Colina
31 Hospedaje Pedro Montt
38 Hotel Burg & Restaurant Amsel
39 Hotel Vincente Pérez Rosales
42 Gran Hotel Don Luis
44 Hotel Montt
46 Residencial Sur
47 Residencial Millantú
50 Hotel El Candil
54 Hospedaje El Toqui

▼ PLACES TO EAT

10 Restaurant Embassy
19 Centro Español
24 El Jabalí
25 Restaurant El Bodegón
33 Dino's Restaurant
35 Café Real
36 Café Central
37 Café Vicorella

OTHER

5 CONAF
7 Turismo Odisea
8 Edificio Intendencia Regional (Sernatur)
9 Hospital
15 Banco de Chile
16 Budget Rent-a-Car
17 LAN-Chile
18 Ladeco
22 Bus Terminal
23 Museo Juan Pablo II
26 Telefónica del Sur (Telephones)
27 Automóvil Club
28 Argentine Consulate & Pastelería Lisel
29 Colina Rent-a-Car
30 Turismo Los Lagos (Money Exchange)
32 Telefónica del Sur (Telephones)
34 Post Office
40 Plaza de Armas
41 Tourist Office
43 Transportes Aéreos Don Carlos
45 Casa del Arte Diego Rivera
48 Aerosur
49 Transmarchilay
51 Railway Station
52 Traucomontt Tours
53 Avis Rent-a-Car

Local 23; and La Moneda de Oro at the bus terminal.

Post & Telecommunications Correos de Chile is at Rancagua 126. Telefónica del Sur has long-distance offices at Pedro Montt 114, Chillán 98, and at the bus terminal on Portales.

Consulates The Argentine Consulate (☎ 253996) is at Cauquenes 94, 2nd floor, near Varas. Open weekdays from 8 am to 1 pm, it will issue visas for Argentina.

Travel Agencies Traucomontt Tours (☎ & fax 258555), at Egaña 82 around the corner from the train station, makes special efforts to cater to overseas travellers. Besides arranging guides and equipment for Volcán Osorno and other adventure trips, directors Caroline Caulfield-Giles and Adrian Turner sell IGM topographic maps and travel books (including *Lonely Planet* guides) and will reserve flights, rental cars, and ferry trips – ask for their advice in getting a Navimag cruise to Puerto Natales. They also operate a used paperback book exchange, and rent mountain bikes (US$13 per day) and even sea kayaks. Traucomontt Tours is open daily from 9 am to 8 pm, including Sundays and holidays.

Turismo Odisea (☎ 259725), Rengifo 430-A, offers a variety of similar excursions, including a five-day sea kayak voyage around Chiloé for about US$400, plus yacht cruises around Chiloé and the Gulf of Ancud, and to Hornopirén, for about US$360. Other agencies offering similar services include Altué Expediciones (☎ 254593) at Pedro Montt 162, Local 18, and Dufour (☎ 258277) at Benavente 305. Climbing Osorno costs about US$60 to $120, depending whether it's a one-day or overnight, while rafting on the Río Petrohué ranges from US$35 to US$55.

Medical Services Puerto Montt's hospital (☎ 253991) is on Seminario, which runs behind the Intendencia Regional, the building which houses Sernatur.

National Parks CONAF (☎ 254882) is at Ochagavía 464.

Cultural Centres

The upstairs gallery at the Casa del Arte Diego Rivera, a joint Mexican-Chilean project finished in 1964, displays work by local artists such as Jose Hugo Cárcamo, who paints oils and watercolour landscapes of the region. The gallery is at Quillota 116 near Antonio Varas. Admission to exhibitions is free.

The Casa del Arte also has a Sala de Espectáculos which offers a selection of quality films which change frequently.

Museo Juan Pablo II

Occupying a new waterfront building on Portales, the former Museo Vicente Pérez Rosales is a major disappointment which emphasises one transitory event, the Pope's 1984 visit, at the expense of the region's long and rich history. Some other exhibits are inappropriate for this museum, such as displays on Easter Island, and many of the poorly labelled and ill-displayed objects are replicas rather than originals. There are some good photographs of the 1960 earthquake and its aftermath.

Admission is US$1. The museum is open weekdays from 10 am to 1 pm and 3 to 7 pm, weekends and holidays from 11 am to 7 pm.

Angelmó

About three km west of the town centre by frequent local buses, the picturesque fishing port of Angelmó has an outstanding crafts market, with a range of goods including handmade boots, curios, copperwork, ponchos, woollen sweaters, hats and gloves. The waterfront cafés of Angelmó serve outstanding seafood specialities, especially curanto.

Isla Tenglo

Reached by launch from the docks at Angelmó, the island of Tenglo on the Gulf of Reloncaví is much quieter than the bustling Puerto Montt. For a meal, try *Restaurant Hoffman*.

Organised Tours

Different sorts of organised tours are available, from sedentary city tours to white-water rafting and climbing. Excursiones Turimontt (☎ 254402), Oficina 20 in the bus terminal, has bargain tours to Puerto Varas, Ensenada, Saltos del Petrohué and Lago Todos Los Santos, for US$9 including lunch. Departure time is 10 am.

Andina del Sud (☎ 257797), Varas 437 near the Hotel Vicente Pérez Rosales, offers regular city tours of Puerto Montt (US$7), Puerto Varas (US$11), Frutillar (US$13), Ancud (US$30), Puyehue (US$35) Petrohué (US$17) and Peulla. The Peulla tour includes an overnight stay at Hotel Peulla, with breakfast, for US$35 single. Varastur (☎ 252203), also at Varas 437, has a recommended day tour to Frutillar for US$20 which includes an English-speaking guide and a sumptuous lunch.

Places to Stay – bottom end

In summer, hostel accommodation is available for US$1.40 at *Escuela No 1*, at the corner of Lillo and Lota, opposite the bus terminal. Cold showers, an 11.30 pm curfew, and the requirement that you provide your own sleeping bag may deter some travellers.

Many visitors prefer hospedajes to hotels. One of the cheapest is an unnamed *hospedaje* at Gallardo 552, for just over US$4 with hot water and kitchen privileges. Another popular place is *Raúl Arroyo's Hospedaje*, Concepción 136, but recent visitors report that his resources are overtaxed and his standards have fallen. Singles are about US$6 per person.

Another *hospedaje*, at Aníbal Pinto 328, has been recommended as warm, clean, friendly and good value. *Hospedaje Polz* (☎ 252851), Juan Mira 1002, is slightly dearer. One popular choice is *Hospedaje Uribe*, at Trigal 312 (up Pérez Rosales from the bus terminal), whose amusing owner speaks both English and French.

Several readers have recommended *Hospedaje Steffen* (☎ 253823) at Serrano 286, reached by colectivo No 3 from Egaña, and an unnamed *hospedaje* at Vial 754, near Balmaceda. Another unnamed *hospedaje*, at Benavente 943, has singles for US$8.50 with breakfast. *Hospedaje Puerto Montt*, Pedro Montt 180, has similar facilities and prices, as does *Hospedaje El Toqui* (☎ 255824), Huasco 213.

Residencial Embassy (☎ 253533), Valdivia 130 near Varas, is a decent little place at US$9 per person. At the friendly but slightly gloomy *Residencial Urmeneta* (☎ 253262), Urmeneta 290 between Quillota and San Felipe, rates are US$8.50/12.50 for single/double rooms with shared bath. *Residencial Benavente* (☎ 253084), Benavente 948, is comparably priced. One reader has recommended *Residencial Sur* (☎ 252832), at San Felipe 183.

East of downtown, overlooking the Gulf of Reloncaví, *Hospedaje Balneario Pelluco* (☎ 259690), Juan Soler 96, is a very friendly and comfortable house with beach views and breakfast for US$9 single with shared bath, US$12 per person with private bath. Taxi colectivos from Puerto Montt's train station go almost to the front door.

Camping *Camping Los Paredes*, six km west of town on the road to Chinquehue, charges US$10 for pleasant sites with hot showers, but amiable haggling may reduce that to US$6. The proprietors are eager to please, providing extension cords and light bulbs, as well as barbecues. There is plenty of hot water in the showers which, however, are a little hard to regulate. Local buses from the bus terminal will drop you at the entrance.

Places to Stay – middle

Mid-range accommodation, starting around US$14 per person and ranging up to about US$19/29 for a single/double, is relatively scarce. Try places like *Hotel Gamboa* (☎ 252741) at Pedro Montt 157, *Residencial Millantú* (☎ 252758) at Illapel 146, or *Hotel El Candíl* (☎ 254886) at Varas 177.

Places to Stay – top end

At the *Hotel Le Mirage* (☎ 255125), Rancagua 350, single/double rooms cost US$44/

53 including breakfast and TV, and the hotel has a friendly staff. *Hotel Colina* (☎ 253502), Talca 81 at Portales, has good accommodation with a view and private bath for US$45/57. Some travellers like *Hotel Montt* (☎ 253651), Varas 301 at Quillota, which has small but cosy rooms for US$51/57, but others think it is poor value.

One reader complained that *Hotel Burg* (☎ 253813), Pedro Montt 56 at Portales, lacked running water despite charging US$70 for a double room. *Hotel Vicente Pérez Rosales* (☎ 252571), Varas 447, has long been the city's top hotel, charging US$77/89 for singles/doubles, but it has seen better days. The new *Gran Hotel Don Luis* (☎ 259001), at Urmeneta and Quillota, has made good first impressions for US$88/98.

Places to Eat

The *Restaurant El Bodegón*, Varas 931, is popular with locals and sometimes has live music at night, but some travellers have criticised its hygiene. For drinks, snacks and Streuselkuchen (highly recommended by a German correspondent), try *Café Central* at Rancagua 117, opposite the post office.

Another possibility is *Café Real* at Rancagua 137, while *Café Vicorella*, Varas 515, is a mecca for caffeine addicts, with capuccino, cortado and espresso. *Dino's* at Varas 550 has also been recommended. *Restaurant Amsel*, on the waterfront at Pedro Montt 56, is only so-so for both food and service. There is a fine bakery, *Pastelería Lisel*, at Cauquenes 82. *El Jabalí*, Andrés Bello 976, has been recommended as good and cheap – try the paila marina.

One LP reader hailed the paella at the *Centro Español*, O'Higgins 233, as the best he had ever eaten. The bathing resort of Pelluco, east of downtown via Avenida Juan Soler, is a good hunting ground for restaurants – try the parrillada at *El Fogón Criollo* or any of the other restaurants along the beach. Don't leave Puerto Montt without tasting curanto or other regional seafood specialities at the waterfront cafés of Angelmó – among the recommended choices are *Marfino*, Angelmó 1856, and especially, *Asturias*. Another fine seafood place is the *Restaurant Embassy*, Ancud 104 in Puerto Montt.

Getting There & Away

Air Local buses connect downtown Puerto Montt with Aeropuerto El Tepual, 16 km west of town, for all incoming and outgoing flights.

Ladeco (☎ 253002), at Benavente 350 near O'Higgins, has two flights a day to Santiago except Saturdays, when there is only one. Some of these proceed from Punta Arenas or Balmaceda (Coihaique) and stop in Temuco. It has flights to Punta Arenas daily except Saturday, when there is none, and Wednesday, when there are two. Ladeco also flies to Balmaceda on Monday, Thursday, Friday and Saturday.

LAN-Chile (☎ 253141), San Martín 200, has 15 flights weekly to Santiago; the Friday flight stops in Concepción. It also has eight flights weekly to Punta Arenas and nine to Coihaique.

Several smaller airlines operate out of Puerto Montt, some with discount fares. Inquire about Pacific Air, which offers three flights weekly between Santiago and Punta Arenas via Puerto Montt; these flights are often booked ahead for two to three weeks.

Transportes Aéreos Neuquén (☎ 255146), an Argentine provincial airline at Varas 445, flies to Bariloche, with connections to San Martín de los Andes and Neuquén. Another new Argentine carrier, Spasa, also flies to Bariloche for US$45. Air taxi services such as Transportes Aéreos Don Carlos (☎ 253219), Quillota 139, and Aerosur (☎ 252523), Serena 149, fly to Chaitén, Futaleufú and Palena.

Bus Puerto Montt's Terminal de Buses (☎ 253143) is on the waterfront, at Avenida Portales and Lota. There are services to all Lake District destinations, Chiloé, Santiago, Coihaique, Punta Arenas and Argentina. Services to the Camino Austral are limited.

Bus – rural At the time of writing, Buses Fierro (☎ 253022) has daily buses as far as

Hornopirén on the Camino Austral, but for the moment communications with the mainland port of Chaitén take place by ferry both from Puerto Montt and from the port of Quellón, on Chiloé. Since conditions and traffic on the Camino Austral are erratic, transport information changes rapidly. Check details on arrival in Puerto Montt.

Other important rural destinations include the coastal towns of Maullín and Carelmapu, served by Transporte Calbuco (☎ 253468) and Transporte Maullín (☎ 256253); and the towns of Ralún and Río Puelo (popular fishing areas on the Río Petrohué and the Estuario de Reloncaví), served by Buses Bohle (☎ 254526) and Buses Río Frio.

Bus – regional & inter-regional Cruz del Sur (☎ 254731) and Trans Chiloé (☎ 254934) have frequent services to Ancud, Castro and other destinations on Chiloé. Varmontt (☎ 254410), Igi Llaima (☎ 254519), Buses Lit (☎ 254011) and Etta Bus (☎ 257324) all go to Concepción and to various stops along the Panamericana as far as Santiago. Other companies which serve Santiago include Turibus (☎ 253245), Bus Norte (☎ 252783), Tas Choapa (☎ 254828), Tur Bus (☎ 253329), Via Tur (☎ 253133), and Inter Sur. Buses Lit and Tur Bus have daily service to Valparaíso and Viña del Mar.

For the long bus trip to Punta Arenas, which goes via the Atlantic coast of Argentina, contact Turibus, Bus Norte or Bus Sur (☎ 252926). Turibus also goes to Coihaique on Thursday and Saturday via Argentina, while Bus Sur's Saturday service goes to Puerto Natales as well as Punta Arenas.

Bus – international Bus Norte and Buses Río de La Plata (☎ 253841) have daily buses to Bariloche, Argentina, via the Puyehue pass. Igi Llaima goes four times a week to San Martín de Los Andes, continuing to Neuquén. Tas Choapa, Turismo Lanín (☎ 252203), and Cruz del Sur go to Argentina less frequently.

Buses Andina del Sud and Varastur (☎ 252203), both at Varas 437, offer daily bus-boat combinations to Bariloche, Argentina, via Ensenada, Petrohué and Peulla. These depart Puerto Montt in the morning, arriving in Bariloche early in the evening. With an overnight stay at Peulla, this costs about US$80.

Typical fares from Puerto Montt are: Puerto Varas US$0.50; Osorno US$3; Ancud US$4; Castro US$6; Quellón US$10; Concepción US$12; Chillán US$14; Santiago US$17; Bariloche US$20 via Osorno or US$33 via Lago Todos los Santos; San Martín de los Andes US$23; Coihaique US$40; and Punta Arenas US$57.

Train Puerto Montt's railway station (☎ 252922) is at the east end of Avenida Portales, when it becomes Soler Mefredini. In summer months only, daily trains to Santiago depart at 8.15 am and 4.30 pm, taking about 20 and 22 hours, respectively. Fares range from US$19 in clase económico and US$24 in salón, to US$30 in an upper berth, and US$40 in a lower berth. There is a 10% discount for return fares.

Boat The most appealing route to Chile's far south is by sea from Puerto Montt but, as one local resident puts it, 'The picture changes with each tide'. Information on maritime services should only be considered a general guide. Ferry or bus-ferry combinations connect Puerto Montt with Chiloé Island and Chaitén in the Tenth Region; ferries to Chiloé leave from the port of Pargua, on the Canal de Chacao, where other southbound ferries occasionally sail as well. Some continue to Puerto Chacabuco (the port of Coihaique) in the Eleventh (Aisén) region or go to Puerto Natales in the Twelfth (Magallanes) region.

Ferries also visit truly remote spots such as Puerto Edén and Laguna San Rafael. Information about these ferry trips is included in the Aisén chapter. Travellers prone to motion sickness may consider medication prior to crossing the Golfo de Penas, which is exposed to gut-wrenching Pacific swells.

Navimag (☎ 253754), at the Terminal de

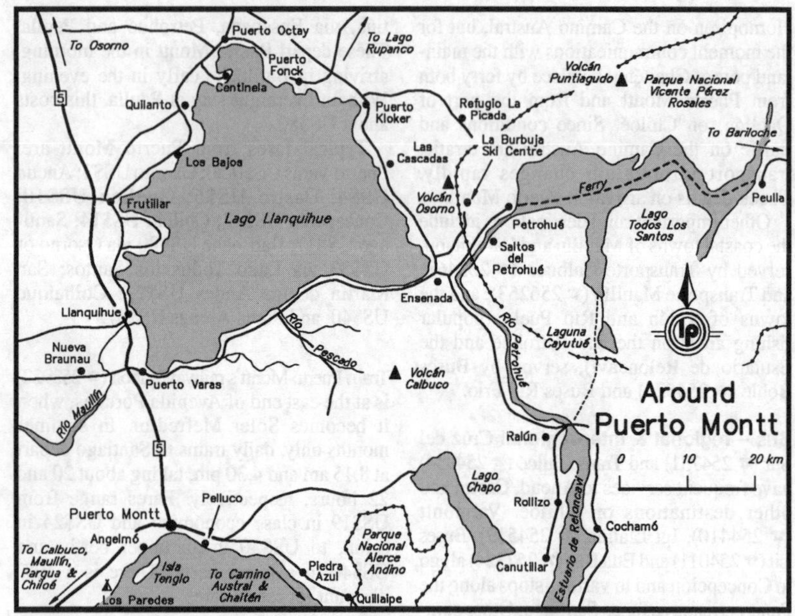

Transbordadores in Angelmó, sails to Puerto Chacabuco twice weekly on the ferry *Evangelistas*, and three times monthly to Puerto Natales, a spectacular three-day cruise through the Chilean fjords. Space is not always available – Navimag seems actively to discourage passengers on this route and allots only 16 places to them.

Fares from Puerto Montt to Puerto Chacabuco range from US$43 for a seat with no meals, to US$235/290 per single/double for a cabin with all meals included. Triple (US$110 per person) and quadruple (US$88 per person) cabins are also available. These sailings continue to Laguna San Rafael; see the Aisén chapter for more details.

Fares from Puerto Montt to Puerto Natales range from US$100 to US$150, or even more for cabins. If possible, try to book passages between Puerto Montt and Puerto Natales at Navimag's Santiago offices (☎ 696-3211, Miraflores 178, 12th floor. In Puerto Montt, Traucomontt Tours (see the Travel Agencies section above) has a good record for getting its clients a berth.

Transmarchilay (☎ 254654), Antonio Varas 215, sails from Puerto Montt to Chaitén (Tuesday, Friday and Sunday, 10 hours) and to Puerto Chacabuco (Tuesdays and Fridays, 26 hours). To Chaitén, fares range from US$10 for deck space to US$20 for a reclining seat and US$40 and up per person for a double cabin. Comparable accommodations to Chacabuco cost slightly less than double the fares to Chaitén.

Transmarchilay also operates auto-passenger ferries from Pargua, 60 km south-west of Puerto Montt, to Chacao, on northern tip of Chiloé Island (see the Chiloé chapter). Fares are about US$2 for passengers or US$10 per car, no matter how many passengers. There is no extra ferry charge for passengers on buses to Chiloé.

Getting Around

Many Lake District attractions, such as Lago

Llanquihue, Petrohué and Lago Todos Los Santos are most conveniently explored by car. Rental cars are available from the Automóvil Club (☎ 252968) at Cauquenes 75; Autowald (☎ 256355) at Portales 1330; Budget (☎ 254888) at San Martín 200; First Rent-a-Car (☎ 252036) at Urmeneta 883; Galerías (☎ 256434) at Benavente 575, Oficina 203; Hertz (☎ 252122) at Urmeneta 1036; Avis (☎ 256575) at Copiapó 43; Fama's (☎ 258060) at Rancagua 125, 2nd floor; and Colina (☎ 258328) at Talca 79.

AROUND PUERTO MONTT

Calbuco

In 1604, the Spanish settlers fleeing from Osorno founded Calbuco, 51 km south of Puerto Montt on a spur off the Panamericana. The island fishing village, connected to the mainland by a causeway, has a wealth of seafood restaurants and reasonable accommodation US$8 per person) at *Residencial Aguas Azules* (☎ 427), Avenida Oelckers 159. Buses Bohle, ETC and Aguas Azules provide transport from Puerto Montt.

Maullín

South-west of Puerto Montt, Maullín is a small, quiet port on the estuary of the Río Maullín, which in many ways is as much a highway as the paved route to Puerto Montt – people are constantly crossing from shore to shore, and up and down the river. *Residencial Toledo*, opposite the Copec petrol station at 21 de Mayo 147, has accommodation for US$4 per person, but *Paula Vargas*, Gaspar del Río 468, also provides lodging.

There is a very good restaurant in the bus terminal on the Costanera. Between them, ETM and ETC have buses to Puerto Montt about every half hour for US$2.

Only five km west of Maullín is the seaside resort of **Pangal**, where the *Complejo Turístico Pangal* (☎ 244) has singles/doubles for US$20/30 and a highly regarded restaurant. At the end of a gravel road, 17 km south of Maullín, is **Carelmapu**, a very picturesque fishing village with a couple of good restaurants, *Mi Rincón* and *La Ruca*, and modest lodging at a nameless *residencial* on O'Higgins. Camping is possible at *Mar Brava*, on a cliff overlooking the Pacific. On February 2, the village celebrates the fiesta of the Virgin of Candelaria. There are frequent buses from Maullín to Carelmapu for about US$0.80.

PARQUE NACIONAL ALERCE ANDINO

One of Chile's newest parks, 40,000-hectare Alerce Andino protects some of the last remaining forests of *Fitzroya cupressoides*, a conifer which resembles the giant sequoia of California in appearance and longevity. Though not as tall as the sequoia, reaching only 40 metres, a 3000-year-old specimen can reach four metres in diameter. Unfortunately, its attractive lumber has made the species vulnerable to commercial exploitation.

Geography & Climate

This mountainous park, rising from sea level to 1558 metres on the summit of Cerro Cuadrado, is only 40 km from Puerto Montt via the Camino Austral. Exposed to the Pacific frontal systems, it receives annual precipitation of 3300 to 4500 mm, often in the form of snow above 800 metres. The average temperature is 15°C in January and 7°C in July. There are several glacial lakes, the largest of which is Lago Chapo on the park's border, which is now unfortunately exploited for hydroelectricity and fish farming.

Trekking

The best reason for visiting Alerce Andino is to hike in the backcountry. Between the Río Chamiza and Río Chaica sectors of the park, there is a good trail, with several refugios along the route (see LP's *Trekking in the Patagonian Andes*). Several Puerto Montt travel agencies, including Traucomontt Tours and Turismo Odisea, will organise trips to the park.

Places to Stay

Camping is the only alternative. CONAF has a 10-site campground at the Río Chamiza, at the northern end of the park, and a three-site

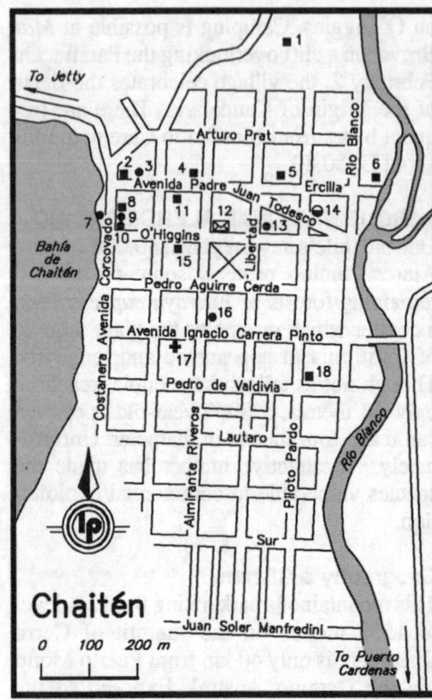

1 Hostería Mi Casa
2 Hotel El Triángulo
3 Aerotransportes Don Carlos
4 Hospedaje Sebastián
5 Hostal Puyuhuapi
6 Hospedaje Lo Watson
7 Transmarchilay
8 Hostería Schillng
9 Mercado Municipal
10 CNT (Telephone)
11 Hospedaje Gabriel
12 Post Office
13 Banco Del Estado
14 Bus Terminal
15 Hospedaje Mahurori
16 ENTEL (Telephone)
17 Hospital
18 Hospedaje Mary

campground at Lago Chaiquenes, at the head of the Río Chaica valley. For trekkers, back-country camping is another possibility.

Getting There & Away

There are two ways of getting to the park. From Puerto Montt, Buses Fierro has daily buses to the village of Correntoso, only three km from the Río Chamiza entrance on the northern boundary of the park, where there is hiking access into the backcountry. Fierro also has buses to the crossroads at Lenca, on the Camino Austral, where a lateral road climbs up the valley of the Río Chaica. This offers slightly better access to a number of lakes and peaks, and is probably a better choice for the non-trekker.

CHAITÉN

Fewer than 3000 people live in the pioneer settlement of Chaitén, a quiet port and military outpost towards the northern end of the Camino Austral. From Chaitén there are Transmarchilay ferries to Quellón, on the island of Chiloé, and to Puerto Montt.

Orientation

Chaitén consists of a few wide streets in a regular grid pattern between the Bahía de Chaitén and the Río Blanco. The Plaza de Armas, bounded by O'Higgins (formerly Independencia), Almirante Riveros, Pedro Aguirre Cerda and Libertad, is two blocks east of the bay, where the Costanera Avenida Corcovado (formerly O'Higgins) connects the town with the ferry port, about a ten-minute walk. Most other services – hotels, restaurants and shops – are between the Costanera and the Plaza.

Information

Tourist Office There is a tourist office in the Mercado Municipal, on the Costanera, which has a handful of leaflets and a list of hospedajes.

Money Change money before coming to Chaitén. Banco del Estado, on the corner of Libertad and O'Higgins, may change US cash but gives very poor rates.

Post & Telecommunications Correos de Chile is near the Plaza at Riveros and

Top : Fishing boats, Isla Chiloé (WB)
Bottom Left : Iglesia de San Francisco, Castro, Isla Chiloé (AS)
Bottom Right : Palafitos (houses on stilts), Castro, Isla Chiloé (WB)

Top Left : Waterfall & glacier, Parque Nacional Bernardo O'Higgins (GL)
Top Right : Cueva del Milodon, north of Puerto Natales (GL)
Bottom : Balmaceda glacier near Puerto Natales, Parque Nacional Bernardo O'Higgins (AS)

O'Higgins. CNT is on the Costanera at O'Higgins, while ENTEL is at Riveros 475.

Medical Services Chaitén's hospital (☎ 244) is on Avenida Iganacio Carrera Pinto between Riveros and Portales.

Places to Stay & Eat

For bottom-end accommodation, look for handwritten signs in the windows of private houses, some of which are open only in summer high season, from mid-December to the end of March. One of these is *Hospedaje Mahurori* (☎ 273), O'Higgins 141, which has doubles for US$9. Several places offer beds for US$4-6, including *Hospedaje Lo Watson* at Ercilla 580, *Hospedaje Mary* at Piloto Pardo 593, *Hospedaje Sebastián* (☎ 225) at Avenida Padre Juan Todesco 188, and *Hospedaje Gabriel* at Todesco 141. *Residencial Astoria* (☎ 263), Corcovado 442, has rooms for US$7 per person.

Hotel El Triángulo (☎ 312), Todesco 12 at Corcovado, has singles for US$10 with breakfast and common bath, as does *Hostal Puyuhuapi* (☎ 237) at Ercilla 354. *Hostería Schilling* (☎ 295), a few doors up from El Triángulo at Corcovado 243, has singles/doubles for US$20/34.

Chaitén's finest is the highly recommended *Hostería Mi Casa* (☎ 285), Avenida Norte 206, on a hill just north of town. It's a large place with its own restaurant and simple, but clean and spacious rooms costing US$29/46 for singles/doubles with breakfast.

For seafood and other local specialities, try the simple but appealing restaurants at the Mercado Municipal, on the Costanera Corcovado. Hotel El Triángulo's restaurant has also drawn praise.

Getting There & Away

Air Aerosur (☎ 228), on Corcovado, and Aerotransportes Don Carlos (☎ 275), Todesco 42, offer regional air services.

Bus Transport details for the Camino Austral change rapidly as the road undergoes improvements. Overland connections are best to the south: Buses Transaustral (once weekly) and Artetur (twice weekly) take the Camino Austral south to Coihaique (US$26, 12 hours), while Chaitur and Bus Yelcho go to Palena and Futaleufú (US$10), on the Argentine border.

Boat Transmarchilay (☎ 272) at Corcovado 266 near the Hostería Schilling, has eight ferries monthly to Quellón or Chonchi, on the island of Chiloé, and another eight to Puerto Montt or Pargua. At present, ferries to Chiloé leave Wednesday at noon and Saturday at 10 pm; those coming to Puerto Montt sail Monday at 10 pm and Thursday at 8 pm. Schedules change, so confirm them at any Transmarchilay office; for fares, see the section for Quellón, Chonchi and Puerto Montt.

FUTALEUFÚ

Futaleufú, 155 km from Chaitén via a necessarily indirect route around Lago Yelcho, is only a few km from the Argentine border, the towns of Trevelin and Esquel, and Parque Nacional Los Alerces. The town is at the confluence of the Río Espolón and the Río Futaleufú, renowned for fishing and for white-water rafting.

Reasonable accommodation is available from about US$4 to US$7 at *Residencial Carahue* (☎ 221), O'Higgins 332; *Hospedaje El Campesino* at Prat 107; *Hospedaje Cañete* (☎ 214) at Gabriela Mistral 374; and *Hotel Continental* (☎ 222) at Balmaceda 595. *Posada Campesina La Gringa* (☎ 260, (☎ 274-7964 in Santiago) is more upscale and much dearer at US$40 per person with breakfast. Chaitur, on Manuel Rodríguez, has buses to Chaitén on the Camino Austral for US$10.

Transporte Samuel Flores (☎ 213), Balmaceda 434, connects Futaleufú with Argentina in a Volkswagen Kombi.

PALENA

Palena, 150 km south-west of Chaitén on a lateral off the Camino Austral, is another alternative for crossing the border into Argentina, although there is no public transport. The route goes across the Paso Palena Carrenleufú to the Argentine town of Corcovado, south of Trevelin. For inexpensive accommodation, about US$4, try *Pensión Bellavista* at General Urrutia 785, *Hotel La Frontera* (☎ 240) at Pedro Montt 977, or *Residencial El Paso* (☎ 226) at Pudeto 661. Rather dearer, about US$10, is *Residencial La Chilenita* (☎ 212), Pudeto 681.

Bus Yelcho, on the Plaza de Armas, connects Palena with Chaitén.

PARQUE NACIONAL QUEULAT

Straddling the Camino Austral midway between Chaitén and Coihaique, 154,000-hectare Parque Nacional Queulat is an area of steep-sided fjords, rushing rivers, evergreen forests, creeping glaciers and high volcanic peaks. Created in 1983, it has rapidly gained popularity since completion of the highway, but still qualifies as an off-the-beaten-track destination.

Geography & Climate

This national park, 200 km south of Chaitén and 220 km north of Coihaique, rises from sea level on the Canal Puyuhuapi to 2225 metres. Moisture-laden Pacific frontal systems drop up to 4000 mm of rain per year on the park, nurturing southern beech forests at lower altitudes, and adding snow to sizeable glaciers at the highest elevations. Temperatures range from 4°C to 7°C, depending on elevation. Large streams, such as the Río Cisnes, and the glacial fingers of Lago Rosselot, Lago Verde and Lago Risopatrón offer excellent fishing.

Things to See & Do

Queulat has become a popular destination for adventure travel companies. It also presents superb hiking, camping and fishing opportunities for independent visitors, although heavy brush inhibits off-trail exploration. There is a good two-km trail to the **Ventisquero Colgante** (Hanging Glacier), 36 km south of Puyuhuapi, and another up the **Río Guillermo**. For ideas on other excursions, consult rangers at the guard stations at Pudú, Ventisquero, Puyuhuapi, El Pangue or La Junta.

Places to Stay

Queulat offers a multitude of camping alternatives in and around Puyuhuapi, some of which are operated by CONAF and others by private parties. *Camping El Pangue*, five km north of Puyuhuapi on Lago Risopatrón, charges US$5 per site, while *Camping Puyuhuapi* is within the town itself. *Camping Río Queulat*, 34 km south of Puyuhuapi, is a free site.

In Puyuhuapi itself there is reasonable accommodation at *Hostería Ludwig*, at the south end of town, for US$11/14 for a single/double, and mid-range lodging at the *Hostería Alemana*, Ubel 450, for US$23 per person. More economical accommodation is available at the village of La Junta, at the northern end of the park near the turnoff to Lago Rosselot and Lago Verde: *Hostería Copihue* at Lynch and Varas, and *Hostería Valdera*, on Varas, both charge about US$7-8 per person.

Back at Puyuhuapi, more upscale accommodation is offered at the *Hostería Puyuhuapi* at US$50/56, while the very luxurious *Hotel Termas de Puyuhuapi* (☎ 223-5567 in Santiago), a hot springs resort 11 km south of Puyuhuapi at Bahía Dorita, charges US$90/110 for singles/doubles in high season, but only US$68/83 the rest of the year. Full pension costs an extra US$35 per day.

Getting There & Away

Buses Artetur and Buses Transaustral connect Chaitén and Coihaique via the Camino Austral, and will drop passengers at La Junta, Puyuhuapi, or other points along the western boundary of the park. Renting a car in Coihaique gives much more flexibility, but this can be expensive without several people to share the costs.

Chiloé

About 180 km long but only 50 km wide, the Isla Grande de Chiloé is a well watered, densely forested island of undulating hills, with a temperate maritime climate. Its northern tip is linked to the Chilean mainland by frequent ferries across the Canal de Chacao. To the east of Chiloé island, the Golfo de Ancud and the Golfo de Corcovado are dotted with many smaller islands, known as archipelagic Chiloé. Politically, the province of Chiloé belongs to the Tenth Region of Los Lagos.

Prior to the arrival of the Spaniards in the 16th century, Huilliche Indians cultivated potatoes and other crops in its fertile volcanic soil. Spain took possession of Chiloé in 1567 and founded the city of Castro the following year. Jesuit missionaries were among the first settlers, but early 17th-century refugees from the Mapuche uprising on the mainland also established settlements. During the Wars of Independence, Chiloé was a Spanish stronghold, resisting criollo attacks in 1820 and 1824 from heavily fortified Ancud, until final defeat in 1826.

Distinctive shingled houses with corrugated metal roofs line the streets of Chiloé's towns and punctuate the verdant countryside. For much of the year, rain and mist obscure the sun which, when it finally breaks through the clouds, reveals majestic panoramas across the Golfo de Ancud to the snow-capped volcanos of the mainland.

Ancud and Castro are the only two sizeable towns. Some towns, most notably Castro, have picturesque neighbourhoods of *palafitos*, rows of houses built on stilts over the water, where boats can anchor at the back door on a rising tide. Other palafitos can be found at Ancud, Quemchi, Chonchi and smaller ports.

Do not miss the smaller villages, with more than 150 distinctive wooden churches up to two centuries old – nine of them national monuments. There are 18th-century churches at Achao, Chonchi, Quilquico, Quinchao and Villupulli, while those at Dalcahue, Nercón and Rilán date from the 19th century. Castro's gaudy Iglesia San Francisco was built this century.

Nearly all of Chiloé's 115,000 inhabitants (Chilotes) live within sight of the sea. More than half make their living from peasant agriculture, but many others depend on fishing for food and money. The nearly roadless western shores and interior still preserve extensive forests, while the densely settled eastern littoral contributes wheat, oats, vegetables and livestock to a precarious economy. Despite great natural beauty, there are still many contemporary parallels with the 19th century, when Chiloé was one of Chile's poorest areas and Darwin commented that:

> ...the climate is not favourable to any production which requires much sunshine to ripen it. There is very little pasture...and in consequence, the staple articles of food are pigs, potatoes and fish...The arts, however, are in the rudest state; – as may be seen in their strange fashion of ploughing, their method of spinning, grinding corn, and in the construction of their boats...Although with plenty to eat, the people are very poor: there is no demand for labour, and consequently the lower orders cannot scrape together money sufficient to purchase even the smallest luxuries. There is also a great deficiency of circulating medium. I have seen a man bringing on his back a bag of charcoal, with which to buy some trifle, and another carrying a plank to exchange for a bottle of wine.

Because of perpetual economic hardship, many Chilotes have reluctantly left the island for employment elsewhere, from the copper mines of the Norte Grande to the sheep estancias of Argentine and Chilean Patagonia. Although to metropolitan sophisticates, 'Chilote' is synonymous with 'bumpkin', the island has a rich tradition of folklore and legend which has made great contributions to Chilean literature.

In part, at least, Chiloé's reputation derives from its insularity – the waters of the Canal de Chacao were so rough that, in days of sail,

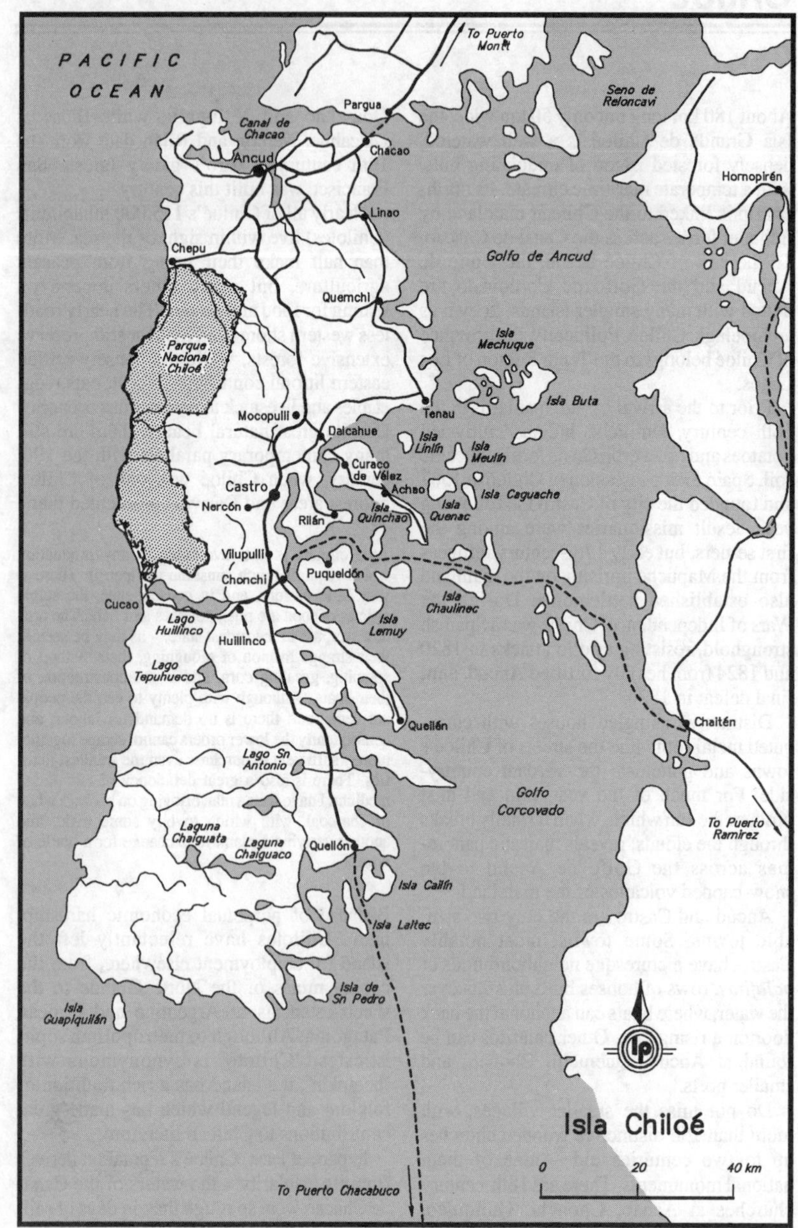
PACIFIC OCEAN
To Puerto Montt
Seno de Reloncaví
Pargua
Canal de Chacao
Chacao
Ancud
Hornopirén
Linao
Chepu
Golfo de Ancud
Quemchi
Parque Nacional Chiloé
Isla Mechuque
Tenau
Isla Buta
Mocopulli
Dalcahue
Isla Linlín
Isla Meulín
Curaco de Vélez
Castro
Achao
Isla Quinchao
Isla Caguache
Nercón
Isla Quenac
Rilán
Vilupulli
Puqueldón
Chonchi
Isla Chaulinec
Cucao
Lago Huillinco
Huillinco
Isla Lemuy
Lago Tepuhueco
Queilén
Chaitén
Lago Sn Antonio
Golfo Corcovado
Laguna Chaiguata
Laguna Chaiguaco
Quellón
To Puerto Ramírez
Isla Cailín
Isla Laitec
Isla de Sn Pedro
Isla Guapiquilán
Isla Chiloé
0
20
40 km
To Puerto Chacabuco

settlers crossed only reluctantly to and from the mainland. Nowadays, of course, ferries sail regularly from Pargua to Chacao, but there is no prospect of a bridge that would span the channel. This isolation has encouraged self-reliance but also an unexpected courtesy and hospitality towards visitors which has changed little since Darwin remarked, more than a century and a half ago, that 'I never saw anything more obliging and humble than the manners of these people'.

ANCUD

Founded in 1767 as a fortress to defend the Chilean coastline from foreign intrusion, Ancud (population 17,000) is now Chiloé's largest town, an attractive fishing port on a promontory overlooking the Bahía de Ancud.

Orientation

At the north end of the Isla Grande, Ancud sits on a small peninsula with the Golfo de Quetalmahue to the west. The Península de Lacuy, farther to the west, shelters the harbour from the swells and storms of the open Pacific.

Because of its irregular topography, Ancud has a very atypical street plan, but it's small and compact enough for directions to be easy to follow. Most points of interest are within a few blocks of the north-south Avenida Costanera and the Plaza de Armas, on the hill above it. Calle Aníbal Pinto provides access to the Carretera Panamericana, a branch of which runs onto Chiloé, ending at Quellón on the island 's southern tip.

Information

Tourist Office The tourist office (☎ 2665), at Libertad 665 opposite the Plaza de Armas, is open weekdays from 8.30 am to 12.30 pm and 2.30 to 8 pm, weekends from 10 am to 2 pm. It has plenty of brochures, maps of the town, and lists of hotels and residenciales.

Money It's better to change in Puerto Montt, but Banco de Crédito at Ramírez 257 and Banco del Estado at Ramírez 299 should help out.

Post & Telecommunications Correos de Chile is at the corner of Pudeto and Blanco Encalada. The Compañía Nacional de Teléfonos (CNT) is at Chacabuco 745.

Travel Agencies Turismo Ancud (☎ 3019) is at Pudeto 219.

Medical Services Ancud's hospital (☎ 2355) is at Almirante Latorre 405, on the corner of Pedro Montt.

Museo Regional Aurelio Bórquez Canobra

Colloquially known as the Museo Chilote, this building has towers and battlements like a small fortress. It houses ethnographic and historical materials (including an outstanding selection of photographs) and a fine natural history display. Its sunny patio displays representations of figures from Chilote folklore, such as the mermaid La Pincoya (symbol of the ocean's fertility) and the troll-like Trauco.

Among the fine exhibits are watercolours by local artist Francisco Vera Cárcamo, depictions of Chilote landscapes and architecture, as well as scale models of several of the island's shingled wooden churches. Note the variety of designs among the shingles. A very fine three-dimensional relief map of Chiloé indicates the major settlements.

There's also a replica of the schooner *Ancud*, which sailed the treacherous fjords and Straits of Magellan to claim Chile's southernmost territories in the mid-19th century. Chile's first fire engine, sent from Europe to Valparaíso in 1852, is also displayed. One of Ancud's most intriguing restaurants is the thatched-roof Chilote house on the museum's patio, whose traditional kitchen, dug into the earth through an opening in the floor, serves a fine curanto on weekends for about US$4. In addition, the museum is probably your best bet for seeing the *pudú*, the elusive miniature deer of the southern Chilean forests.

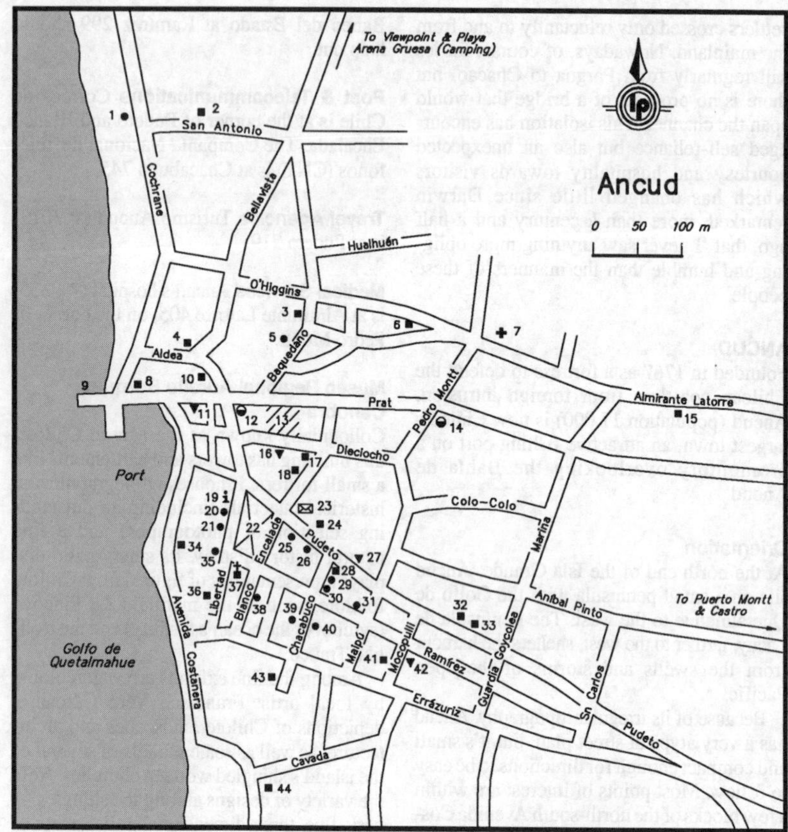

Admission is US$1. On Libertad just south of the Plaza de Armas, the museum is open weekdays from 9 am to 12.30 pm and 2.30 to 6.30 pm, Saturday from 10 am to 12.30 pm and 2.30 to 6 pm, and Sunday from 11 am to 12.30 pm and 2.30 to 5 pm.

Fuerte San Antonio
At the north-western corner of town, a short walk up Cochrane, are the early 19th-century remains of the Fuerte San Antonio, whose cannon still look down on the harbour. During the wars of independence, this was Spain's last outpost in Chile.

Festivals
For a week in January, Ancud observes the Semana Ancuditana. It includes the annual Encuentro de Folklore de Chiloé, which promotes the island's music, dance and cuisine.

Places to Stay – bottom end
Ancud has two hostels which offer very cheap accommodation in January and February. The *Albergue Juvenil* (☎ 2065) at Almirante Latorre 478 offers floor space for sleeping bags for US$1.50 per night, but also lets travellers pitch their tents in the patio for less than US$1. The *Casa del Apostulado*

■ PLACES TO STAY

2 Hostería Ancud
3 Hostal Montserrat
4 Hospedaje Bellavista
6 Hostal Marjessori
8 Residencial Wechsler
10 Residencial Madryn
15 Albergue Juvenil
17 Hospedaje Montenegro
18 Hospedaje
24 Hotel Lacuy
28 Hotel Lydia
32 Hospedaje Germania
33 Hospedaje Navarro
34 Hotel Polo Sur
36 Hotel Galeón Azul
41 Hospedaje Miranda
43 Casa del Apostulado
44 Hostería Ahuí

▼ PLACES TO EAT

11 Restaurant La Pincoya
13 Restaurant El Sacho
16 Restaurant El Cangrejo
27 Restaurant El Jardín
28 Café Lydia
34 Polo Sur Restaurant
42 Restaurant Capri

OTHER

1 Fuerte San Antonio
5 Artesanía Moai
7 Hospital
9 Pier
12 Bus Terminal
13 Mercado Municipal
14 Bus Terminal
19 Tourist Office
20 Transmarchilay
21 LAN-Chile
22 Plaza de Armas
23 Post Office
25 Turismo Ancud
26 Bus Norte
29 Buses Cruz del Sur
30 Banco de Crédito
31 Banco del Estado
35 Museo Regional Aurelio Bórquez Canobra
37 Catedral
38 Taller de Artesanía
39 CNT (Telephone)
40 Buses Trans Chiloé

(☎ 3256), on Chacabuco near Errázuriz, offers floor space for US$1.50, mattresses for US$2.50, and proper beds for US$3.50 per night. Visitors can use the kitchen from 6 to 10 pm.

Other than hostels, hospedajes provide the cheapest accommodation at about US$4 to US$5 per person – look for signs in the windows of private houses. Many are seasonal, but some which are open all year include *Hospedaje Navarro* at Pudeto 361, *Hospedaje Miranda* at Mocopulli 753, and an unnamed *hospedaje* at Blanco Encalada 541. For clean rooms and baths, hot showers and amiable hosts, the Miranda is an especially good choice.

Hospedaje Montenegro (☎ 2239), at Dieciocho 191, has singles with shared bath for around US$5. *Hospedaje Bellavista* (☎ 2384) at Bellavista 449 and the nearby *Residencial Madryn* (☎ 2128) at Bellavista 491 both charge around US$7 a single, but doubles are cheaper at the Madryn, which also includes breakfast

Recently renovated *Residencial Wechsler* (☎ 2318), Cochrane 480, has a reputation for Germanic austerity but is very well kept. Singles with shared bath cost US$8.50, while comfortable rooms with private bath cost US$14 per person, although the breakfast is nothing to write home about. At *Hospedaje Germania* (☎ 2214), Pudeto 357, singles/doubles are US$10/16 with shared bath, nearly double that with private bath. *Hostal Marjessori*, O'Higgins 274, charges US$13 per person with private bath.

Camping *Camping Arena Gruesa* (☎ 2975), six blocks from the Plaza de Armas at the north end of Bellavista, rents sites for US$10, including hot showers, picnic tables and barbecues and firewood. *Camping Playa Gaviotas*, north-east of Ancud, has similar facilities and good beach access, but little shade or shelter, for US$8 per site.

Places to Stay – middle

Despite its unimpressive exterior, *Hotel Lydia* (☎ 2990), at Pudeto 256, has a highly regarded restaurant and clean, agreeable rooms from US$13/20 a single/double; rooms with private bath cost nearly double that.

Hotel Lacuy (☎ 3019), Pudeto 219, comes recommended at US$23/30 for rooms with breakfast and private bath, but has thin walls and can be noisy. Rates for comparable accommodation at *Hotel Polo Sur* (☎ 2200), Costanera 630, are US$29/40, while the home-like *Hostal Montserrat* (☎ 2957), Baquedano 417, has slightly cheaper singles and slightly dearer doubles. At *Hostería Ahuí* (☎ 2415) on the southern outskirts of town, rates are US$36/41.

Places to Stay – top end

Hotel Galeón Azul, (☎ 2567, formerly the Hotel Quintanilla) at Libertad 751, charges US$53/59. Ancud's top hotel is *Hostería Ancud* (☎ 2340 or 713165 in Santiago), overlooking the sea and Fuerte San Antonio at San Antonio 30, with excellent views from the bar. Rooms cost US$54/69, including breakfast and private bath.

Typical Chiloén church

Places to Eat

Going to Chiloé without eating seafood is like going to Argentina without tasting beef. Good, reasonably priced local specialities are available at *El Sacho*, in the Mercado Municipal, on Dieciocho between Libertad and Blanco Encalada.

Other good seafood restaurants include *Polo Sur* at Avenida Costanera 630, *La Pincoya* at Prat 61 on the waterfront, and *Restaurant Capri* at Mocopulli 710. *El Cangrejo*, Dieciocho 155, gets more notice for its decor – business cards and other scrawls on the walls make it seem that just about every visitor to Ancud has eaten here.

Despite its appearance, *El Jardín*, Pudeto 263, has relatively modest prices for enormous slabs of meat. For good dinners, desserts and coffee, try *Café Lydia*, in the Hotel Lydia at Pudeto 256. One reader insists that the *Hamburgería*, Prat 94, is much better than its name would suggest, with fine seafood and good service.

Things to Buy

Ancud has a plethora of outlets for artisanal goods like woollens, carvings and pottery. Besides the museum, try Artesanía Moai at Baquedano 429, Francisquita at Libertad 530, and the Taller de Artesanía at Blanco Encalada 730.

Getting There & Away

Chiloé has no regular air services. All traffic to and from the island is by ferry between Pargua, on the mainland 56 km south-west of Puerto Montt, and Chacao, at the north-eastern corner of the island. Bus fares to and from the mainland include the half-hour ferry crossing; if you're hitching and walk on board you will have to pay US$2 for the privilege. The pier at Pargua is a good place to ask for a lift.

Bus Cruz del Sur (☎ 2265), at Chacabuco 672, has a dozen buses a day to Puerto Montt; some of these continue to Osorno, Valdivia, Concepción, Temuco and Santiago. It has a dozen buses a day to Castro and several more to Chonchi and Quellón. Varmontt (☎ 3049), on the Costanera, has buses to Puerto Montt and destinations on Chiloé as far as Quellón.

Buses Trans Chiloé (☎ 2876) at Chacabuco 750 has several buses daily to Castro, Chonchi, Quellón and Puerto Montt. Turibus (☎ 2289), at the corner of Dieciocho and Libertad, goes to Concepción and Santiago, Punta Arenas and Puerto Natales. Bus Norte, Pudeto 250, also has connections to Punta Arenas and Puerto Natales.

For buses to other destinations on Chiloé, go to one of the bus terminals; on Pedro Montt opposite Prat, and on the corner of Prat and Libertad. Buses Mar Brava has three buses weekly to Chepu, at the northern end of Parque Nacional Chiloé, for US$1.25.

Fares to Castro are US$2, to Chonchi US$3, and to Puerto Montt US$4.

Boat Transmarchilay (☎ 2317), at Libertad 669 alongside Sernatur, sails from Chonchi or Quellón to Chaitén, and to Puerto Chacabuco in the Aisén Region (see the entry for Quellón later in this chapter). It also runs ferries between Pargua and Chacao, as does Naviera Cruz del Sur (☎ 2506), at Chacabuco 672. For automobiles, the fare between Pargua and Chacao is about US$10, including as many passengers as you can fit in the car.

CASTRO

Founded in 1567 by Martín Ruiz de Gamboa, Castro is the capital of Chiloé province. When Darwin visited the city in 1834, he found it 'a most forlorn and deserted place' in which:

> The usual quadrangular arrangement of Spanish towns could be traced, but the streets and plaza were coated with fine green turf, on which sheep were browsing...The poverty of the place may be conceived from the fact, that although containing some hundred of inhabitants, one of our party was unable anywhere to purchase either a pound of sugar or an ordinary knife. No individual possessed either a watch or a clock; and an old man, who was supposed to have a good idea of time, was employed to strike the church bell by guess.

Castro has largely overcome the economic depression of the 19th century. Its most conspicuous attraction – the bright and incongruously painted wooden church opposite the Plaza de Armas – dates from 1906. The waterfront palafitos with their crafted *tejuelas* (shingles) add more than a touch of vernacular architectural distinction. Like Ancud, Castro is popular during the summer holidays, attracting many Chilean and Argentine tourists.

Orientation

On a sheltered estuary on the Isla Grande's eastern shore, 90 km south of Ancud, most of Castro (population 17,000) sits on a bluff above the water; only the Costanera Avenida Pedro Montt has direct access to the shore. Almost everything of interest to the traveller is within a few blocks of the Plaza de Armas, bounded by Gamboa, O'Higgins, Blanco Encalada and San Martín. Ruta 5, the Panamericana, enters town from the direction of Ancud and exits south toward Quellón, the end of the line for this branch of the international highway.

Information

Tourist Office Sernatur (☎ 5699) has recently opened an office at O'Higgins 549, 1½ blocks north of the Plaza. It's open weekdays from 8.30 am to 1.30 pm and 2.30 to 6.30 pm, and keeps a very complete list of accommodation, including inexpensive hospedajes.

Local businesses fund the private tourist office, underneath the stage of a small bandstand on the Plaza de Armas, which has town maps and some information on the surrounding countryside. It's open weekdays from 9 am to 1 pm and 3 to 7 pm, Saturdays from 9 am to 1 pm only.

Money Banco del Estado, at the corner of San Martín and Latorre, changes cash and

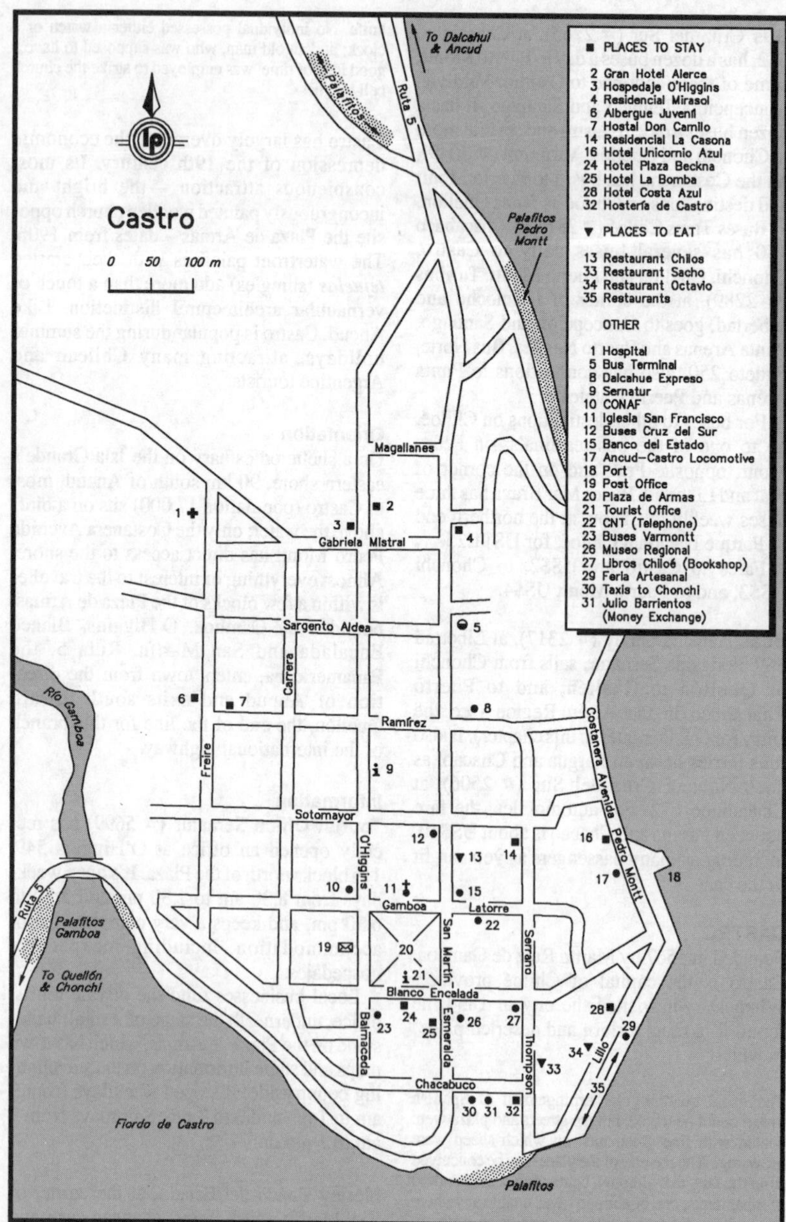

Castro
0 50 100 m
To Dalcahui & Ancud
Palafitos
Ruta 5
Palafitos Pedro Montt
Magallanes
Gabriela Mistral
Sargento Aldea
Carrera
Freire
Ramírez
Sotomayor
O'Higgins
Gamboa
Latorre
San Martín
Serrano
Blanco Encalada
Esmeralda
Balmaceda
Thompson
Chacabuco
Costanera Avenida Pedro Montt
Lillo
Río Gamboa
Palafitos Gamboa
To Quellón & Chonchi
Fiordo de Castro
Palafitos
PLACES TO STAY
2 Gran Hotel Alerce
3 Hospedaje O'Higgins
4 Residencial Mirasol
6 Albergue Juvenil
7 Hostal Don Camilo
14 Residencial La Casona
16 Hotel Unicornio Azul
24 Hotel Plaza Beckna
25 Hotel La Bomba
28 Hotel Costa Azul
32 Hostería de Castro
PLACES TO EAT
13 Restaurant Chilos
33 Restaurant Sacho
34 Restaurant Octavio
35 Restaurants
OTHER
1 Hospital
5 Bus Terminal
8 Dalcahue Expreso
9 Sernatur
10 CONAF
11 Iglesia San Francisco
12 Buses Cruz del Sur
15 Banco del Estado
17 Ancud-Castro Locomotive
18 Port
19 Post Office
20 Plaza de Armas
21 Tourist Office
22 CNT (Telephone)
23 Buses Varmontt
26 Museo Regional
27 Libros Chiloé (Bookshop)
29 Feria Artesanal
30 Taxis to Chonchi
31 Julio Barrientos (Money Exchange)

travellers' cheques (with a 10% commission), weekdays from 9 am to 2 pm. At other hours, or for better rates, try Julio Barrientos (☎ 5079) at Chacabuco 286.

Post & Telecommunications Correos de Chile is at O'Higgins 388, on the west side of the Plaza de Armas. For long-distance telephone services, go to CNT at Latorre 289.

Travel Agencies Castro has a more vigorous tourist industry and better infrastructure than Ancud. Several travel agencies offer tours to sights such as Parque Nacional Chiloé, the islands of Quinchao, Lemuy and Mechuque, and the market at Dalcahue. Contact Pehuén Expediciones (☎ 5254) at Lillo 119, or Chiloé Tours (☎ 2155) or Queilén Bus (☎ 2173), both at the bus terminal at San Martín 689.

Bookshops Libros Chiloé, Blanco Encalada 202, has a good selection of books on both regional and general Chilean subjects.

Medical Services Castro's hospital (☎ 2445) is at Freire 852, at the foot of Cerro Millantuy.

National Parks CONAF (☎ 2289) is on the 3rd floor of the Gobernación Provincial, at the corner of O'Higgins and Gamboa.

Iglesia San Francisco de Castro

Built in 1906 at the north end of the Plaza de Armas, Castro's San Francisco church assaults the vision with its dazzling exterior paint job – salmon with violet trim. The attractive varnished-wood interior is more soothing, despite some morbidly gruesome portrayals of the crucifixion and other religious statuary.

Ancud-Castro Locomotive

On the Avenida Pedro Montt, near the Hotel Unicornio Azul, stands the original, German-made locomotive from the narrow-gauge railway which connected Castro with Ancud via Pupelde, Coquiao, Puntra, Butalcura, Mocopulli and Pid Pid. According to local legend, the only difference between 1st and 3rd-class tickets was that the conductor would order 3rd-class passengers off the train to help push the locomotive over the crest of even gentle slopes. Service on this line ended with the earthquake and tsunami of 1960.

Palafitos

All around Castro, shingled houses on stilts stretch out into estuaries and lagoons; at high tide, resident fishermen tie their boats to the stilts, but from the street these houses resemble any other in town. This truly singular architecture, now the subject of determined preservation efforts, can be seen along the Costanera Pedro Montt at the north end of town, at the market on the south end (where some are restaurants), and at both ends of the bridge across the Río Gamboa, where Ruta 5 heads south to Quellón.

Museo Regional

Housed in new quarters on Esmeralda, half a block south of the Plaza, this museum houses an idiosyncratic but well organised collection of Huilliche relics, traditional farm implements, and exhibits on the evolution of Chilote urbanism. In summer (January to March), opening hours are weekdays from 9 am to 8 pm and Saturday from 9 am to 2 pm. The rest of the year, it's open weekdays from 8.30 am to 1 pm and 3 to 6 pm, Saturdays from 10 am to 1 pm. There is no charge for admission.

Feria Artesanal Mercado

This waterfront market has a fine selection of woollen ponchos and sweaters, caps, gloves and basketry. Note the bundles of dried seaweed and the rhubarb-like nalca plant, both eaten by the Chilotes, and the chunks of peat they use as fuel. The market has several excellent, inexpensive restaurants.

Festivals

In mid-February, Castro celebrates the Festival Costumbrista, a week-long party with folkloric music and dance and traditional foods.

Places to Stay – bottom end

For summer hostel accommodation, go to the *Albergue Juveníl* (☎ 2766), in the Gimnasia Fiscal at Freire 610, which charges about US$2 per person.

Castro has an abundance of hospedajes charging about US$5 a single, some of which are only seasonal – ask at Sernatur for a complete list or look for handwritten signs in windows along San Martín and O'Higgins, near Aldea.

Residencial Mirasol, San Martín 851, has singles for US$5, as does *Residencial La Casona* (☎ 2246), Serrano 496. Despite an unprepossessing appearance, *Hotel La Bomba* (☎ 2300), half a block from the Plaza at Esmeralda 270, has simple but bright and airy rooms for US$6 per person with private bath. Despite its attractive setting, *Hotel Costa Azul* (☎ 2440), above the Restaurant Octavio at Lillo 67, is 'damp and cold and a little bleak' for US$8.50 per person with shared bath, but don't hesitate to haggle a bit. *Hospedaje O'Higgins* (☎ 2016), O'Higgins 831, charges US$8.50 with shared bath, US$12 with private bath.

Camping *Camping Pudú*, north of Castro on the road to Dalcahue, charges US$8 per site for reasonable facilities, but is a bit far out of town.

Places to Stay – middle

Reports on the *Hotel Plaza Beckna* (☎ 5109), at Blanco Encalada 383 opposite the tourist kiosk on the Plaza, are indifferent at best. Singles/doubles with shared bath cost US$17/30, while others with private bath are much dearer; there is great variability, so ask to see the room first. *Gran Hotel Alerce* (☎ 2267), O'Higgins 808, is good value for US$35/44 for rooms with private bath, telephone and TV.

Places to Stay – top end

Hostal Don Camilo (☎ 2180), Ramírez 566, charges US$51 for a double. On the waterfront at Pedro Montt 228, *Hotel Unicornio Azul* (☎ 2359) is perhaps Castro's most appealing accommodation, named after a popular song by Cuban singer Silvio Rodríguez. Simple but attractive rooms cost US$53/59 with breakfast.

The *Hostería de Castro* (☎ 2301) at Chacabuco 202, conspicuous by its exaggerated chalet design, has good views of the harbour. Rooms are US$50/60 with private bath but without breakfast.

Places to Eat

The palafito restaurants at the waterfront market have the best food for the fewest pesos. *Brisas del Mar* and *Mariela* both have fixed-price lunches for less than US$2, as well as more expensive specialities. *Restaurant Octavio*, Lillo 67 across from the market, has three-course dinners for about US$3. *Restaurant Maucari*, Lillo 93, has curanto for US$4 per person.

Try *Chilos*, at San Martín 449, for meat and seafood, and *Sacho*, at Thompson 213, for curanto.

Getting There & Away

Bus From its central location, Castro is the major hub for bus traffic on Chiloé. The Terminal de Buses Rurales (bus terminal) is on San Martín near Sargento Aldea; most but not all long-distance companies have their offices nearby. Buses Arroyo (☎ 5604) has two to three buses a day to Huillinco and Cucao, the entrance to Parque Nacional Chiloé on the west coast, while Ocean Bus (☎ 5492) has two daily services on the same route. Since most of these buses leave early in the morning and return in the early evening, it is possible to visit the park on a day trip. The fare is about US$2 one-way.

Dalcahue Expreso (☎ 5164), Ramírez 233, has buses every half hour to Dalcahue on weekdays but fewer on weekends. Buses Cárdenas covers the same route less frequently, but also goes to smaller towns like Quetalco, San Juan and Calén. Buses Lemuy serves Chonchi and destinations on Isla Lemuy, including Puqueldón, while Buses Queilén, which also operates tours around

Chiloé, has regular service to Queilén and intermediate points. Cruz del Sur (☎ 2389), on the corner of San Martín and Sotomayor, has a dozen buses daily to Ancud and Puerto Montt, several of which continue to Osorno, Valdivia, Temuco, Concepción and Santiago. It also has several buses daily to Chonchi and Quellón, as does Regional Sur (☎ 2071), at the bus terminal. Buses Trans Chiloé (☎ (☎ 5152), also at the terminal, has several buses daily north to Ancud and Puerto Montt, and south to Chonchi and Quellón. Varmontt (☎ 2776), Balmaceda 289, connects Castro with Ancud, Puerto Montt and Santiago.

Castro enjoys direct bus service, via Argentina, to Punta Arenas and Puerto Natales, twice weekly with Buses Ghisoni (☎ 2358) and two to four times weekly with Bus Sur at the terminal. Turibus (☎ 5088), at Esmeralda 252, goes to Puerto Montt, Concepción and Punta Arenas. The run to Punta Arenas takes 36 hours and costs about US$51 in winter, US$63 in summer.

The fare from Castro to Quellón is about US$3, to Puerto Montt about US$6.

DALCAHUE

Dalcahue is a modest fishing port which takes its name from the *dalca*, the type of open canoe in which indigenous Chilotes went to sea. The tsunami of 1960 washed away Dalcahue's palafitos, but it still features a 19th-century church and the most important crafts market on Chiloé. The shipwrights at work in the harbour are worth a visit.

Orientation & Information

On the east coast of Chiloé, Dalcahue (population 1000) is 20 km north-east of Castro and opposite the island of Quinchao, to which there are ferry-bus connections.

Dalcahue's tourist office, in the Muni-

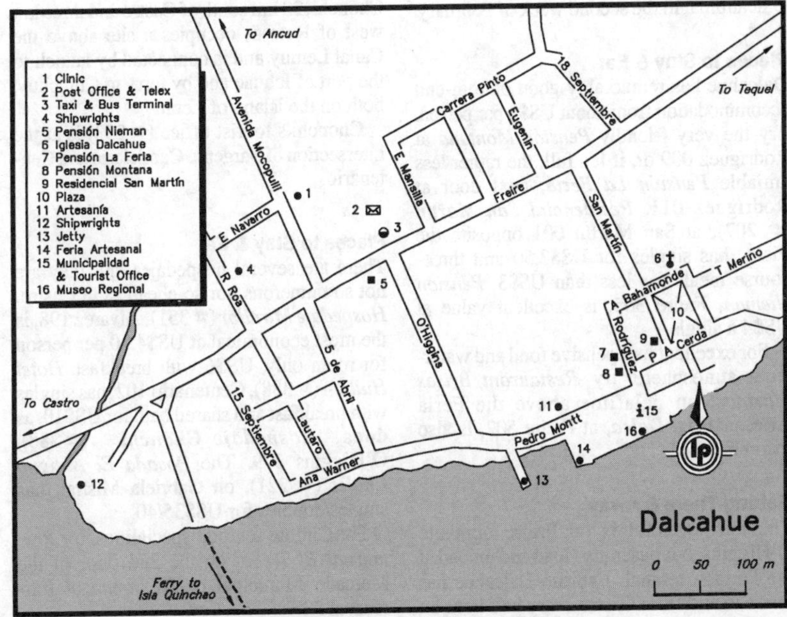

cipalidad near the Feria Artesanal, is open daily except Monday from 9.30 am to 1.30 pm and 3 to 7 pm.

Things to See & Do

Artisans from offshore islands travel great distances to Dalcahue's **Feria Artesanal**, which is casual and nonchalant, with a fine selection of woollens, wooden crafts, basketry and good cheap places to eat. Sellers will often drop their prices without even hearing a counter-offer. The nearby **Museo Regional** crams fossils, stuffed birds, a few good household implements and a rotting dalca into a single inadequate room.

On the plaza, two blocks east, the neoclassical **Iglesia Dalcahue**, with Doric columns, dates from 1854. It is not in especially good repair, but has a truly grisly statue of Christ, with movable arms attached with leather straps.

Festivals

Dalcahue's annual fiesta is the Semana Dalcahuina, in the second week of February.

Places to Stay & Eat

Dalcahue has remarkably good bottom-end accommodation from about US$3 per person. Try the very friendly *Pensión Montana* at Rodríguez 009 or, if it's full, the rather less amiable *Pensión La Feria*, next door at Rodríguez 011. *Residencial San Martín* (☎ 207), at San Martín 001 opposite the Plaza, has singles for US$3.50 and three-course meals for less than US$3. *Pensión Nieman*, Freire 305, is excellent value at US$4 a single.

For excellent inexpensive food and waterfront atmosphere, try *Restaurant Brisas Marinas*, on palafitos above the Feria Artesanal. *La Dalca*, at Freire 502, is also recommended.

Getting There & Away

The bus terminal is on Freire opposite O'Higgins, but buses also load and unload at the Feria Artesanal. Expreso Dalcahue has buses to and from Castro every half hour on weekdays, but there are only seven on Saturdays and four on Sunday market day, at 8 and 9.30 am and 2 and 5.30 pm. However, frequent taxi colectivos from Castro charge just over US$1 for the half-hour trip.

The motor launch *Ultima Esperanza* connects Dalcahue with the outlying Islas Chauques, Tuesday and Friday at 2 pm. There are also launches across the estuary to Isla Quinchao, with bus connections to the village of Achao and its landmark 18th-century church.

CHONCHI

Jesuits founded the town of Chonchi in 1767 and built the original church shortly thereafter, but the notable **Iglesia San Carlos de Chonchi**, with its three-storey tower and multiple arches, dates from the mid-19th century. There is other interesting vernacular architecture along Calle Centenario.

Orientation & Information

Chonchi, 23 km south of Castro and three km west of Ruta 5, occupies a site above the Canal Lemuy and is connected by launch to the port of Ichuac and by ferry to Chulchuy, both on the island of Lemuy.

Chonchi's tourist office (☎ 233) is at the intersection of Sargento Candelaria and Centenario.

Places to Stay & Eat

There are several hospedajes, but they are not so numerous nor so cheap as in Castro. *Hospedaje Mirador* (☎ 351), Alvarez 198, is the most economical at US$4.50 per person for room only, US$6 with breakfast. *Hotel Huildín* (☎ 388), Centenario 102, has singles with breakfast and shared bath for US$10, as does *Hospedaje Chonchi* (☎ 288), O'Higgins 379. The *Posada El Antíguo Chalet* (☎ 221), on Gabriela Mistral, has singles/doubles for US$35/40.

For Chilote seafood specialities, try *Restaurant El Trébol* on the 2nd floor of the Mercado Municipal or *La Sirena* at Irarrázaval 52.

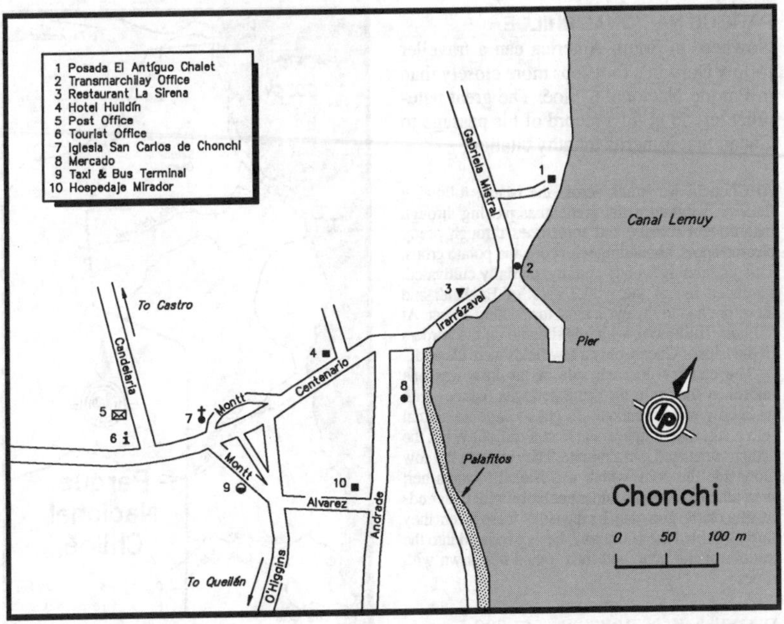

1 Posada El Antíguo Chalet
2 Transmarchilay Office
3 Restaurant La Sirena
4 Hotel Huildín
5 Post Office
6 Tourist Office
7 Iglesia San Carlos de Chonchi
8 Mercado
9 Taxi & Bus Terminal
10 Hospedaje Mirador

Gabriela Mistral
Canal Lemuy
Irarrázaval
To Castro
Candelaria
Centenario
Pier
Montt
Montt
Palafitos
Alvarez
Andrade
O'Higgins
To Quellén
Chonchi
0 50 100 m

Getting There & Away

Bus Cruz del Sur (☎ 218) and Trans Chiloé have several buses daily from Castro to Chonchi.

Boat The Transmarchilay office (☎ 319) is at the foot of the pier; at times ferries to Chaitén and Puerto Chacabuco leave from here, but see the Quellón entry, later in this chapter, for details.

There are launches to the port of Ichuac on the island of Lemuy. The ferry *El Caleuche* leaves every two hours between 8 am and 8 pm from Puerto Huichas, five km to the south, and lands at Chulchuy, with connections to Puqueldón.

Taxi The easiest way from Castro to Chonchi is by taxi colectivo. In Castro these leave from Chacabuco near Esmeralda, while in Chonchi they leave from Pedro Montt, opposite the Iglesia San Carlos. The fare is about US$1 one-way.

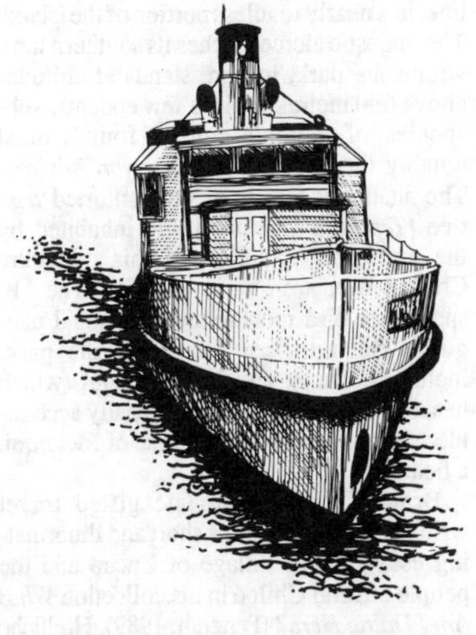

PARQUE NACIONAL CHILOÉ

Nowhere in South America can a traveller follow Darwin's footsteps more closely than in Parque Nacional Chiloé. The great naturalist left so vivid a record of his passage to Cucao that it merits lengthy citation:

> At Chonchi we struck across the island, following intricate winding paths, sometimes passing through magnificent forests, and sometimes through pretty cleared spots, abounding with corn and potato crops. This undulating woody country, partially cultivated, reminded me of the wilder parts of England, and therefore had to my eye a most fascinating aspect. At Vilinco (Huillinco), which is situated on the borders of the lake of Cucao, only a few fields were cleared...
>
> The country on each side of the lake was one unbroken forest. In the same periagua (canoe) with us, a cow was embarked. To get so large an animal into a small boat appears at first a difficulty, but the Indians managed it in a minute. They brought the cow alongside the boat, which was heeled towards her; then placing two oars under her belly, with their ends resting on the gunwale, by the aid of these levers they fairly tumbled the poor beast, heels overhead into the bottom of the boat, and then lashed her down with ropes.

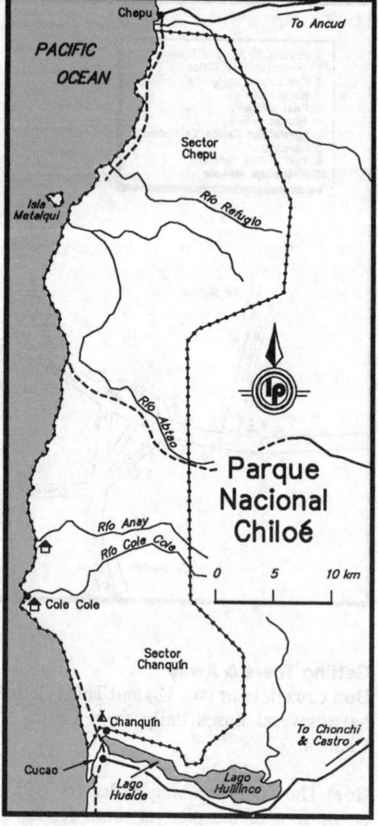

Established in 1982, the 43,000-hectare Parque Nacional Chiloé protects extensive stands of native coniferous and evergreen forest, plus a long and almost pristine coastline, in a nearly roadless portion of the island. The majestic alerce reaches its southern limit within the park, in pure stands at altitudes above 600 metres, while a few endemic subspecies of animals can be found, most notably the Chilote fox *Dusicyon fulvipes.* The shadowy forests of the contorted *tepú* tree *(Tepualia stimulais)*, are inhabited by the pudú, but sightings of this miniature Chilean deer are rare in the wild. The 110 species of bird include the occasional penguin. The northern sectors of the park, including Chepu and Isla Metalqui (which has a sea lion colony) are less easily accessible without a car or, in the case of Metalqui, a boat.

Bruce Chatwin, the late gifted travel writer and novelist, left a short and illuminating essay on the village of Cucao and the people of rural Chiloé in his collection *What Am I Doing Here?* (Penguin, 1989). Huilliche communities in and around the park resent CONAF's management plan which has restricted their access to traditional subsistence resources while permitting some commercial activities. Again, there are conspicuous parallels with Darwin's time, when the great scientist wrote that:

> The district of Cucao is the only inhabited part on the whole west coast of Chiloé. It contains about 30 or 40 Indian families, who are scattered along four or five miles of the shore. They are very much secluded from the rest of Chiloé, and have scarcely any sort of commerce, except sometimes in a little oil, which they get from seal-blubber. They are tolerably dressed in

clothes of their own manufacture, and they have plenty to eat. They seemed, however, discontented, yet humble to a degree which it was quite painful to witness. These feelings are, I think, chiefly to be attributed to the harsh and authoritative manner in which they are treated by their rulers.

Geography & Climate

On the island's Pacific coast, Parque Nacional Chiloé is about 30 km west of Chonchi and 54 km south-west of Castro, via the paved Ruta Panamericana and a decent gravelled lateral to Huillinco and Cucao. Altitudes range from sea level to 850 metres on the heights of the Cordillera de Piuchén. The annual average temperature in the temperate maritime climate is about 10°C, with a mean annual rainfall at Cucao of 2200 mm, evenly distributed throughout the year. The park is open all year, but fair weather is more likely in summer, which is the best time for a visit.

Sector Chanquín

Chanquín, across the suspension bridge from Cucao, is the starting point for almost all excursions into the park. CONAF's **Centro de Visitantes**, open daily from 9 am to 7.30 pm, has good displays on local flora and fauna, the indigenous Huilliche peoples, the early mining industry and island folklore. A short distance away is the **Museo Artesanal**, a typical Chilote-style house with a fine collection of farm and household implements, walls insulated by reeds, and a recessed fireplace in the floor – a building technique which has caused many such houses to burn to the ground. Outside are wooden carts and sleighs, used to haul heavy loads over wet ground in damp weather.

Near the Chanquín camping ground is the **Sendero Interpretivo El Tepual**, a short nature trail built on tree trunks, which loops through dense, gloomy forest where you might expect to meet the Trauco, a troll-like creature from Chilote folklore. There are several other trails, including the **Sendero Dunas de Cucao**, which goes from the visitor centre through a remnant of coastal forest to a series of dunes behind a long, white sandy beach. After the earthquake of 1960, a tsunami obliterated much of the coastal plant cover and the dunes have been advancing despite efforts to restore native vegetation. Except on very warm days, the water is too cold for swimming.

Day hikers or trekkers can follow the coast north on a three-km trail to **Lago Huelde**, where there is a Huilliche community. At Río Cole Cole, about 12 km north of Chanquín, and at Río Anay, another eight km north, there are rustic refugios in reasonably good condition, but a tent is not a bad idea in this changeable climate. Trekkers should acquire CONAF's 1:125,000 topographic map in Puerto Montt, or photocopy it at Sernatur's Ancud office. Wear water-resistant footwear and woollen socks since, in Darwin's words, 'everywhere in the shade the ground soon becomes a perfect quagmire'.

Places to Stay & Eat

Camping is possible on the green near the suspension bridge across the outlet from Lago Cucao, but there are no sanitary facilities. *Camping Chanquín*, across the bridge and 200 metres beyond CONAF's visitor centre, has very secluded sites with running water, firewood, cold showers and latrines for US$1.40 per person. At the refugios or along the trails, there is no charge for camping.

For those not wishing to camp, several hospedajes in Cucao are within easy walking distance of the park entrance. *Hospedaje El Paraíso* and *Hospedaje Pacífico* have B&B for US$4 per person, while *Posada Cucao* is slightly dearer at US$7. All offer reasonably priced meals. Limited supplies are available in Cucao, but everything except fresh fish and a few vegetables is cheaper in Castro.

Getting There & Away

Cucao is 54 km from Castro and 34 km west of Chonchi via a decent gravelled road. There is regular bus transport between Castro and Cucao with Ocean Bus (☎ 5492 in Castro), which leaves Castro weekdays at 8.30 am and 4 pm, returning from Cucao at 7.30 am (the following morning) and 6 pm.

On weekends, it leaves at 7.45 am, returning from Cucao at 7 pm.

Buses Arroyo (☎ 5604 in Castro) has early buses (5.45 am) to Cucao on Monday, Wednesday and Friday, plus weekday services at 11.30 am and 4 pm. Return services from Cucao are on Monday, Wednesday and Friday at 7.15 am, plus weekdays at 1.30 and 5.45 pm. On weekends, Arroyo leaves Castro at 8 am and returns at 5 pm, with an additional Sunday bus from Castro at 9 am and from Cucao at 3 pm.

Buses Mar Brava has three buses weekly from Ancud to Chepu, at the northern end of the park, for US$1.25.

QUELLÓN

Not to be confused with nearby Queilén, Quellón is 92 km south of Castro and the terminus of Ruta 5. It is also Isla Grande's southernmost port, from which Transmarchilay ferries sail to Chaitén and Puerto Chacabuco. There are fine views of the surrounding islands including Cailín, a former Jesuit estancia which, in Darwin's day, was the 'last outpost of Christianity'. At Rayen Anti, 22 km north of Quellón, the Huilliche Indian community of Huequetrumao sells woollens, wood carvings and basketry.

Places to Stay & Eat

On the waterfront at Pedro Montt 245, a few doors from the Transmarchilay office, is the *Anexo Hotel Playa* (☎ 278), a decent little place with rooms for US$5 per person. There's hot water and a good cheap restaurant.

Pensión Vera, Gómez García 18, is comparably priced. Despite its shabby exterior, it's OK inside – very spartan, but with hot water. *Hotel La Pincoya* (☎ 285), La Paz 64, is a comfortable place with friendly staff and hot water, charging US$26/31 a single/double with breakfast.

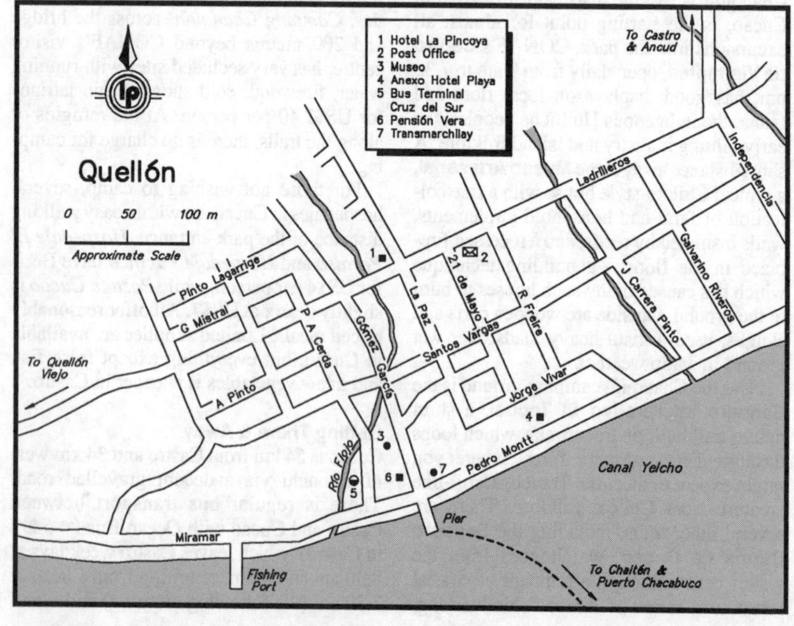

For a small town, Quellón has fine seafood in the waterfront restaurants near the jetty and at *Las Quilas* at La Paz 053, *Quilineja* at Pedro Montt 201, and *Estrella del Mar* at Gómez García 18.

Getting There & Away

Bus Buses Cruz del Sur is at Cerda 52, around the corner from the pier. The bus from Castro to Quellón takes about 1½ hours and costs about US$2.

Boat Transmarchilay (☎ 272) is at Pedro Montt 261, at the foot of the pier. You can reach the Aisén region by ferry from Quellón, either via Chaitén, or directly to Puerto Chacabuco (the port for Coihaique). Ferries run to a timetable but sometimes leave late, depending on how long it takes to load all the cars and trucks. Schedules also change seasonally, so verify the information given below at Transmarchilay offices.

The car ferry *La Pincoya* sails from Quellón to Puerto Chacabuco on Saturdays and alternate Mondays at 6 pm, taking 18 hours for the journey. Vehicle size determines the cost of transporting a car, which ranges from US$97 (shorter than four metres) to US$110 (longer than four metres).

There are several classes of ferry travel. To Puerto Chacabuco, a *camarote* (sleeper) costs US$63 per person, double occupancy, while a *butaca proa* (reclining aircraft seat) costs US$34 and a *butaca popa* (reclining bus seat) US$30. *Clase económica* costs US$20 and gives you a place indoors in a large room with tables and upright bench seats, while *pasaje general* costs US$14 and entitles you to deck or corridor space. Because of changeable weather, the latter is not recommended.

La Pincoya and *El Colono* alternate sailings on the six-hour crossing between Quellón and Chaitén, on Monday and Thursday afternoons. Sleepers are available for US$28 per person, although it seems pointless on this relatively short trip, while the cheapest pasaje general is about US$9. It costs from US$54 to US$64 to transport a car. From Chaitén you can bus south to Coihaique.

Aisén

Beyond Chiloé and Puerto Montt, the islands, fjords and glaciers of the Eleventh Region of Aisén (sometimes spelt Aysén; known also as the Región del General Carlos Ibáñez del Campo) mirror the landscapes of Alaska's Inside Passage, New Zealand's South Island, and Norway's subarctic coast. The recently opened Camino Austral Longitudinal (Southern Longitudinal Highway) awkwardly links Puerto Montt with widely separated towns and hamlets from Chaitén to Cochrane, and may extend as far south as Villa O'Higgins, but the most convenient connections are by air or ferry from Puerto Montt, ferry from Chiloé, or overland through the Argentine province of Chubut.

For thousands of years, the Chonos and Alacaluf Indians fished and hunted the intricate canals and islands of western Aisén, while their Tehuelche counterparts hunted guanaco and other game on the steppes of the mainland. Aisén's wild and rugged geography deterred European settlement for centuries even after Francisco de Ulloa first set foot up the Península de Taitao in 1553. Fortune seekers believed the legendary 'City of the Caesars' to be in Trapananda, as Aisén was first known, but Jesuit missionaries from Chiloé were the first Europeans to explore the region in detail. In the late 17th century, Bartolomé Díaz Gallardo and Antonio de Vea came upon Laguna San Rafael and the Campo de Hielo Norte, the northern continental ice sheet.

Recounting his experiences in the Guayanecos islands, shipwrecked British seafarer John Byron, grandfather of the famous poet Lord Byron, made it apparent why Europeans did not flock to the inclement region. From the shore, he wrote:

> ...a scene of horror presented itself: on one side the wreck...together with a boisterous sea, presented us with the most dreary prospect; on the other, the land did not wear a much more favourable appearance: desolate and barren, without sign of culture, we could hope to receive little other benefit from it than the preservation it afforded from the sea...Exerting ourselves, however, though faint, benumbed and almost helpless, to find some wretched cover against the extreme inclemency of the weather, we discovered an Indian hut...within a wood, in which as many as possible, without distinction, crowded themselves, the night coming on exceedingly tempestuous and rainy.

Several expeditions (including Fitzroy's British expedition on which Darwin served

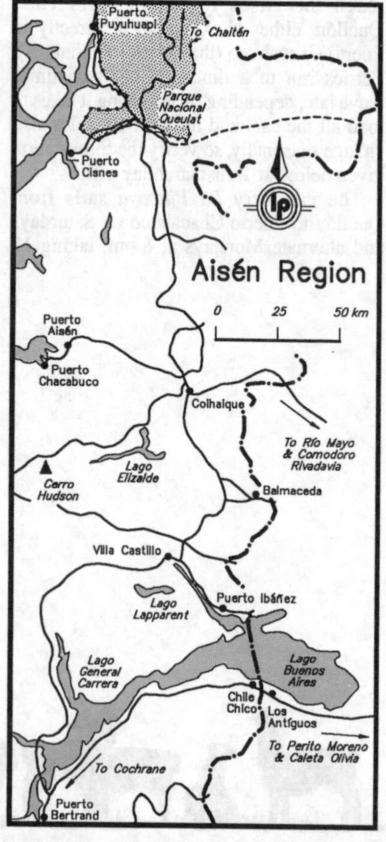

as a naturalist) visited the area in the late 18th and early 19th centuries, some in search of a protected passage to the Atlantic. Argentine expeditions investigated the area from the east, becoming the first non-native people to see Lago General Carrera (LagoBuenos Aires to Argentines). In the early 1870s, Chilean naval officer Enrique Simpson made the most thorough survey of the area to that time, mapping areas as far south as the Península de Taitao.

Not until the early-20th century did Chile

Carretera Longitudinal Austral Presidente Pinochet

On Puerto Montt's waterfront, where Avenida Diego Portales becomes Avenida Juan Soler Mefredini, in front of the railroad station, there is a fading, vandalised sign announcing the beginning of Ruta 7, the Carretera Longitudinal Austral Presidente Pinochet, more popularly referred to as the Camino Austral. Only a few km east, beyond the beach suburb of Pelluco, a smooth concrete roadway becomes the spine-rattling washboard surface of one of the most ambitious and, to this point, least productive, public works projects ever undertaken in Chile.

From Puerto Montt, the Instituto Geográfico Militar's stunningly beautiful map traces a solid yellow line of Ruta 7 for more than a thousand km to the pioneer settlement of Cochrane, between the Campo de Hielo Norte (the northern Patagonian icefield) and the Argentine border. The road is discontinuous, requiring several ferry crossings unlikely ever to be bridged or circumvented because of the phenomenal expense this would entail. Eventually, though, it will reach Villa O'Higgins, 220 km south of Cochrane at the foot of the Campo de Hielo Sur, and some have fantasised extending it through the fjords and islands of extreme southern Chile all the way to Punta Arenas.

The population of this entire region, from Puerto Montt to Villa O'Higgins, does not exceed 80,000 and nearly half of those people live in the city of Coihaique, the only sizeable population centre between Puerto Montt and Punta Arenas. Why then, would Chile invest US$102 million to serve so few people? While the public rationale is development, the real answer lies in geopolitics.

Like many other Southern Cone military men, General Augusto Pinochet Ugarte believes the state is an organic entity which must grow or die – that is, it must effectively occupy and develop all the territory within its formal boundaries or risk losing that territory to other states. In his textbook *Geopolítica* (Santiago, Editorial Andrés Bello, 1977), Pinochet explicitly asserts that the state is 'a superperson, the highest form of social evolution'. As an organic entity, it must maintain an integrated system of communications, which are 'the nerves which unite the different zones within and among themselves'. By Pinochet's logic, the longitudinal highway is the spinal cord of Chile, connecting the country's extremities to the brain in Santiago, the capital.

Chilean geopoliticians, Pinochet being the most significant, perceive Argentina as an expansionist threat in the thinly populated lands of the far south, and Argentine geopoliticans hold a similar view towards Chile. For Chileans, this interpretation is not unreasonable, since the two countries barely avoided armed conflict over the Beagle Channel in 1979 and Argentina, acting on its own geopolitical principles, invaded and occupied the British-held Falkland Islands for 2½ months in 1982. Since the restoration of civilian rule, relations between the two countries have been more cordial, but the military obsession with territorial security lurks in the background.

In the meantime, the near completion of the Camino Austral has had ironic consequences. To some degree it has encouraged economic development in forestry, fisheries and mining, but these are largely extractive industries which take out more than they leave. The several ferry links on the highway between Puerto Montt and Chaitén have proved inadequate for most commercial traffic, which still use the ferries between Chiloé and Puerto Chacabuco – as do most tourists. Meanwhile, the laterals off the Camino Austral have made communication with Argentina better than ever – in fact so much better that buses between Coihaique and Puerto Montt pass through the Argentine provinces of Chubut and Río Negro rather than use the much slower Chilean route. Argentine tourists flock across the border to Aisén and, should they ever need to, so could the Argentine military. This is probably not what Pinochet had in mind.

For adventurous travellers, though, the opening of the Camino Austral has paid dividends. Remote destinations like Chaitén and Coihaique, and national parks like Queulat are now readily accessible by road, even though public transport still tends to be minimal and sporadic. Though it is hard to see the benefits to the country as a whole, visitors who want to see a rugged, remote territory can now do so in relative comfort. ■

actively promote colonisation, granting the Valparaíso-based Sociedad Industrial Aisén a long-term lease for the exploitation of livestock and lumber. This measure fomented a wave of spontaneous immigration from mainland Chile and the Argentine province of Chubut which threatened the Sociedad's monopoly, but small-scale colonists successfully resisted ejection from the valley of the Río Simpson.

Still, the company controlled much of the land – nearly a million hectares in and around Coihaique – and dominated the regional economy. Part of its legacy is the destruction of much of Aisen's native southern beech forest in a series of fires which raged for nearly a decade in the 1940s. Encouraged by a Chilean law which rewarded clearance with land titles, the company and colonists burned nearly three million hectares of lenga forest which once covered Aisén. While this burning was intentional, some fires escaped control and the bleached trunks of downed trees now litter hillsides from Mañihuales to Puerto Ibáñez.

Since the agrarian reform of the 1960s, the influence of the Sociedad and other large landowners has declined. Improved maritime communications and the improved highway system have encouraged immigration into the area, which is still only sparsely populated.

COIHAIQUE

Founded in 1929, Coihaique (often spelt Coyhaique) was the first major town in the region. At first a service centre for the properties of the Sociedad Industrial, the city has outgrown its pioneer origins to become a modest but tidy city with a population of about 40,000.

Orientation

Situated at the foot of the basalt massif of Cerro Macay and at the confluence of the Río Simpson and the Río Coihaique, Coihaique is the capital of the Eleventh Region. Although linked by road to Puerto Chacabuco to the west, Puerto Ibáñez in the south and Chaitén in the north, it's also readily accessible from Argentine Patagonia. Most visitors, however, arrive at Puerto Chacabuco, either by ferry or by air from Puerto Montt, and continue overland to Coihaique.

For travellers who have become accustomed to the standard Latin American grid, Coihaique's unusual street plan can be disorienting. Its focus is the pentagonal Plaza de Armas, from which ten streets radiate like spokes from a wheel, but within a block or two in every direction this irregularity gives way to a more conventional pattern. Avenida Baquedano, which skirts the north-east side of the town, eventually connects with the paved road west to Puerto Chacabuco and a gravelled road east to the Argentine border at Coihaique Alto. Avenida Ogana heads south to Balmaceda, Puerto Ibáñez, and other southerly points on the Camino Austral.

Information

Tourist Office Sernatur (☎ 231752) is at Lord Cochrane 320, between Francisco Bilbao and Ramón Freire. Like everything else in Coihaique, its opening hours are 9 am to 1 pm and 3 to 7 pm. Another good source of information is the Automóvil Club (☎ 231649) at Bilbao 583.

Money Change cash and travellers' cheques at Cambio El Libertador at Arturo Prat 340, Oficina 207, or at Turismo Prado, 21 de Mayo 417.

Post & Telecommunications Correos de Chile is at Cochrane 202, near the pentagonal Plaza de Armas. CTC, at Moraleda 495, is open until 10 pm.

Travel Agencies Coihaique has several travel agencies, some of which will arrange fishing holidays or visits to Laguna San Rafael, but they can be surprisingly indifferent to anything unconventional. Among them are Turismo Prado (☎ 231271) at 21 de Mayo 417, Turismo Queulat (☎ 231441) at Dussen 340, Oficina 3, and Turismo Ñandú (☎ 233161) at Horn 40, Local 17. Expediciones Coihaique (☎ 232300), Bolívar 94,

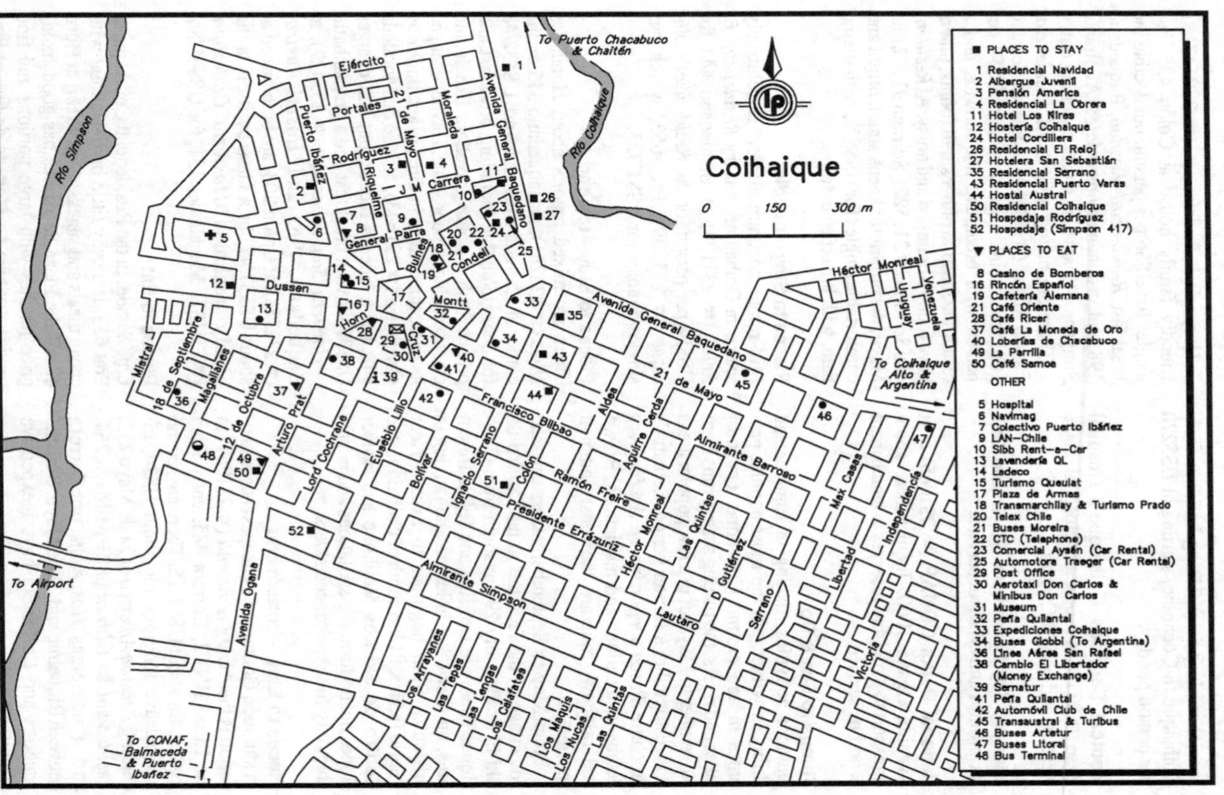
Coihaique
0 150 300 m
■ PLACES TO STAY
1 Residencial Navidad
2 Albergue Juvenil
3 Pensión America
4 Residencial La Obrera
11 Hotel Los Nires
12 Hostería Coihaique
24 Hotel Cordillera
26 Residencial El Reloj
27 Hotelera San Sebastián
35 Residencial Serrano
43 Residencial Puerto Varas
44 Hostal Austral
50 Residencial Coihaique
51 Hospedaje Rodríguez
52 Hospedaje (Simpson 417)
▼ PLACES TO EAT
8 Casino de Bomberos
16 Rincón Español
19 Cafetería Alemana
21 Café Oriente
28 Café Ricer
37 Café La Moneda de Oro
40 Loberías de Chacabuco
49 La Parrilla
50 Café Samoa
OTHER
5 Hospital
6 Navimag
7 Colectivo Puerto Ibáñez
9 LAN–Chile
10 Sibb Rent-a-Car
13 Lavandería QL
14 Ladeco
15 Turismo Queulat
17 Plaza de Armas
18 Transmarchilay & Turismo Prado
20 Telex Chile
21 Buses Moreira
22 CTC (Telephone)
23 Comercial Aysén (Car Rental)
25 Automotora Traeger (Car Rental)
29 Post Office
30 Aerotaxi Don Carlos & Minibus Don Carlos
31 Museum
32 Peña Quilantal
33 Expediciones Coihaique
34 Buses Giobbi (To Argentina)
36 Línea Aérea San Rafael
38 Cambio El Libertador (Money Exchange)
39 Sernatur
41 Peña Quilantal
42 Automóvil Club de Chile
45 Transaustral & Turibus
46 Buses Artetur
47 Buses Litoral
48 Bus Terminal
To Puerto Chacabuco & Chaitén
To Coihaique Alto & Argentina
To Airport
To CONAF, Balmaceda & Puerto Ibáñez
Río Simpson
Río Coihaique
Ejército
Portales
Puerto Ibáñez
Rodríguez
Riquelme
21 de Mayo
Moraleda
J M Carrera
Avenida General Baquedano
General Parra
Bulnes
Condell
Dussen
Horn
Montt
Cruz
Mistral
18 de Septiembre
Magallanes
12 de Octubre
Arturo Prat
Lord Cochrane
Eusebio Lillo
Bolívar
Ignacio Serrano
Francisco Bilbao
Colón
Ramón Freire
Presidente Errázuriz
Aldea
Aguirre Cerda
Almirante Barroso
Héctor Monreal
Las Quintas
D Gutiérrez
Serrano
Lautaro
Almirante Simpson
Avenida Ogana
Max Casas
Libertad
Independencia
Victoria
Uruguay
Venezuela
Los Arrayanes
Las Tepas
Las Lengas
Los Calafates
Los Maquis
Los Nucas

specialises in pricey fishing holidays from Coihaique to Cochrane, starting at US$270 per person per day.

Medical Services Coihaique's Hospital Base (☎ 231286) is on Calle Hospital, at the western end of J M Carrera.

Laundry Try Lavandería QL, Bilbao 160, for prompt and efficient service.

National Parks CONAF (☎ 231065) is at Avenida Ogana 1060. Inquire here about transport to parks and reserves to which there is no bus service.

Things to See & Do

Outdoor activities, fishing in summer and skiing in winter, are the most popular pastimes in and around Coihaique. On most lakes and rivers, the fishing season runs from November to May, but in a few popular areas it is restricted to a shorter period. Sernatur's brochure *Pesca Deportiva en Aysén* gives details of locations and restrictions. Brown and rainbow trout are the most common species.

From May to September, skiers can take advantage of the facilities at the **Centro de Ski El Fraile**, only 29 km south from Coihaique. There are two lifts and five different runs, up to two km in length and ranging in difficulty from beginner to expert. Near Puerto Ibáñez, 81 km south of Coihaique, the **Centro de Ski Los Maillines** has steeper slopes but no formal installations and is suitable only for experienced skiers.

Places to Stay – bottom end

In summer, Coihaique's cheapest accommodation is the *Albergue Juvenîl* (☎ 231961) in the Liceo BN- 2, Carrera 485, entry from Ibañez, for about US$1.75. There are several inexpensive lodgings for about US$4, including *Pensión America* at 21 de Mayo 233, *Residencial La Obrera* at 21 de Mayo 264, and a nameless *Hospedaje* on Carrera between Riquelme and 21 de Mayo. Both the América and La Obrera have inexpensive restaurants.

Hospedaje Rodríguez (☎ 232647), a friendly family house at Colón 495, has singles for US$6 per person, but decline the breakfast. *Residencial Navidad*, Baquedano 198, and an unnamed *hospedaje* at Almirante Simpson 417 are also worth checking out.

There are mixed reviews of *Residencial Puerto Varas* (☎ 231544), Ignacio Serrano 168. Some think it good value at US$7 per person with breakfast, hot showers and a restaurant, despite rather small rooms; others have found it cramped and noisy. At *Residencial Serrano* (☎ 211522), Serrano 91 at 21 de Mayo, the proprietor keeps small, bright and comfortable singles for US$8.50 with shared bath, with breakfast extra.

Places to Stay – middle

Mid-range accommodation is relatively scarce in Coihaique, but try *Residencial El Reloj* (☎ 231108) at Baquedano 444 for US$14 per person, or the *Residencial Coihaique* (☎ 231239), Prat 653, which has singles/doubles for US$17/23.

Places to Stay – top end

There are mixed reports about *Hotel Los Ñires* (☎ 222261), at Baquedano 315 on the corner of Carrera, where rates are US$32/48 for a single/double including breakfast and private bath – some travellers like it and others consider it poor value. Having changed its name three times in three years, the *Hotel Cordillera* (☎ 231643), at José de Moraleda 448, has a hideous facade, but still charges US$37/47 with breakfast and a private bath.

Hotelera San Sebastián (☎ 233427), at Baquedano 496, and *Hostal Austral* (☎ 232522), at Colón 203, are both priced at about US$37/47. In a class by itself is the highly regarded *Hostería Coihaique* (☎ 231137), Magallanes 131, for US$65/86.

Places to Eat

Café Samoa, in the Residencial Coihaique at Prat 653, is a cosy little bar/restaurant with cheap meals and snacks. *Café Ricer*, at Horn 48 off the Plaza de Armas has good fixed-price lunches with large portions and fine service; try also *La Moneda de Oro* at Prat

431. There are good desserts and light meals at *Café Oriente*, Condell 201. The more sedate *Cafetería Alemana*, at Condell 119, is a popular local hangout with similar fare.

Another good choice for fixed-price lunches is the *Rincón Español*, Prat 230, and the *Casino de Bomberos*, General Parra 365, also has very fine meals at reasonable prices. For seafood, go to *Loberías de Chacabuco*, Almirante Barroso 553. For meat, the obvious choice is *La Parrilla*, Prat 601.

Entertainment

To locate Peña Quilantál, which offers live folk music some nights, look for the bleached bovine skull above the entrance at Eusebio Lillo 145. La Parrilla, at Prat 601, also has live peña entertainment.

Things to Buy

Several crafts outlets sell woollens, leather goods, wood carvings and seashells. The Feria Artesanal de Coihaique and the Galería Artesanal de CEMA-Chile are both on the Plaza de Armas, while Agrotec Limitada is nearby at Dussen 360.

Getting There & Away

Air Coihaique is served by two airports. The Aeropuerto Teniente Vidal, about five km south of town, has a short runway and a steep approach. Luggage retrieval is awkward and inefficient. Shared cabs to downtown cost only about US$3; shared cabs to the airport leave from outside the LAN-Chile office or you can arrange to be picked up at an address of your choice. LAN-Chile (☎ 231188), General Parra 215, operates eight flights a week between Santiago, Puerto Montt and Teniente Vidal; three of these stop in Temuco as well.

There is also the military airfield at Balmaceda, 30 km south of Coihaique. It handles the larger aircraft flown by Ladeco (☎ 231300, on the corner of Prat and Dussen). It has three flights weekly to Puerto Montt and Santiago; one weekly flight from Puerto Montt continues to Punta Arenas. Until the road to Balmaceda is completely paved, Ladeco flights mean an extra hour on a rough bus ride with Buses Libertad (☎ 232244; at Coihaique's bus terminal).

Aerotaxi Don Carlos (☎ 232981), Cruz 63, flies small aircraft to Cochrane on Wednesdays and Fridays, to Villa O'Higgins on Wednesdays only, to Lago Verde on Tuesdays and Fridays, and to Chile Chico on Tuesdays and Saturdays. The fare to Chile Chico is US$27, to Cochrane US$43, and to Villa O'Higgins US$76. Línea Aérea San

Mapuche medicine woman

Rafael (☎ 233408), another air taxi service at 18 de Septiembre 469, flies daily to Chaitén for US$28.

Bus & Colectivo Coihaique's Terminal de Buses is at the corner of Lautaro and Magallanes, but only a handful of companies have their offices there. For frequent buses to Puerto Aisén, go to La Cascada (☎ 231413) at the terminal, Transaustral (☎ 231333) at Baquedano 1171, or Minibuses Don Carlos (☎ 232981) at Cruz 63. Transaustral has Thursday and Sunday buses to Puerto Chacabuco, while La Cascada bus services connect with arriving and departing ferries. Fares to Aisén and Chacabuco are about US$2. Rural buses are few, but Buses del Norte, at the terminal, runs eight buses weekly to Valle Simpson, Seis Lagunas, Lago Atravesado, Villa Frei and El Salto.

Northbound on the Camino Austral, Transportes Mañihuales, also at the terminal, has buses daily to Villa Ortega and Mañihuales (US$3) at 5 pm. Buses Litoral (☎ 232903), at Baquedano and Independencia, has buses on Tuesday and Saturday to Puerto Cisnes, on a lateral off the Camino Austral, for US$13. Colectivos Basoli (☎ 232596), at Pasaje Puyuhuapi 47, is slightly cheaper, departing on Wednesdays and Sundays. Buses Artetur (☎ 233368), Baquedano 1347, goes to Puyuhuapi (US$13) and Las Juntas (US$15) on Tuesdays and Saturdays; Transaustral, which serves the same destinations on Wednesdays and Saturdays, is slightly dearer. To Chaitén (12 hours, US$28), Transaustral and Artetur both have Saturday buses, while Artetur has an additional Tuesday service.

Southbound on the Camino Austral, Colectivo Puerto Ibáñez (☎ 233064), Presidente Ibáñez 30, sells a combination ticket with the ferry from Puerto Ibáñez to Chile Chico for US$8.50; Aerobus (☎ 231172) has Monday, Wednesday and Friday buses to Puerto Ibáñez for US$6. Buses Pudú (☎ 231008) goes twice weekly on Tuesdays and Saturdays, to Villa Cerro Castillo (US$7), Bahía Murta (US$14), Puerto Tranquilo (US$15), Puerto Guadal (US$17) and Cochrane (US$22). Aerobus covers most of these destinations on Mondays, Wednesdays and Fridays.

Long-distance bus services to Osorno and Puerto Montt, with connections to northern Chile, go via Argentina. Buses Moreira (☎ 231759), Local 5 in the Galería Barrientos on Condell, departs on Tuesdays and Fridays at 3 pm, while Turibus (☎ 231333) at Baquedano 1171 leaves Tuesdays and Fridays at 4 pm. Fares to Osorno are about US$36; to Puerto Montt US$38.

Buses Giobbi (☎ 232067), Bolívar 194, has buses three days a week to Comodoro Rivadavia, Argentina, via Río Mayo and Sarmiento. The fare is US$29 for the all-day trip, leaving Coihaique in the morning and arriving in Comodoro early in the evening.

Boat Ferries to Chiloé, Chaitén and Puerto Montt leave from Puerto Chacabuco, two hours west of Coihaique by bus.

Transmarchilay (☎ 221971), upstairs at 21 de Mayo 417, has ferries from Chacabuco to Chaitén and Puerto Montt on Monday at noon, Wednesday at 8 pm, and Saturday at 4 pm; fares range from US$17 to US$43, depending on the type of seat. To Quellón on the Isla Grande de Chiloé, there are sailings on Tuesday at 4 pm and Sunday at 6 pm. Fares range from US$13 to US$35, depending on the type of seat. Passengers should confirm these schedules which are subject to change.

Navimag (☎ 223306) with two offices; one at Presidente Ibáñez 347 and the other at Oficina 1, also sails from Puerto Chacabuco to Puerto Montt, on Tuesdays, Thursdays and Sundays at 4 pm. There is a single fare of US$43.

Getting Around

Car Because public transport in the Eleventh Region is infrequent, sometimes inconvenient and serves mostly major destinations along the Camino Austral, travellers should consider renting a car to see the countryside. Shop around because prices vary considerably, but try Comercial Aisén (☎ 233456) at Moraleda 420, Sibb Rent-a-Car (☎ 211044) at General Parra 95, Automotora Traeger (☎ 231648) at Baquedano 457, Automundo (☎ 211621) at Bilbao 510, or Turismo Prado (☎ 231271) at 21 de Mayo 417.

The Automóvil Club (☎ 221847) at Bilbao 583, is exceptionally friendly and helpful, meeting clients at the airport and picking up the car from there as well.

RESERVA NACIONAL COIHAIQUE

Despite its proximity to the city, barely an hour's walk away, this 2150-hectare reserve is very wild country, with exhilarating panoramas of the town and the enormous basalt columns of Cerro Macay behind it, and other nearby and distant peaks. Native southern beech forests of coihue and lenga, along with introduced species such as pine and larch, cover the hillsides of the reserve.

There are short nature trails at Laguna Verde and Laguna Venus but the reserve's real attractions are the extraordinary views. It is a convenient, popular retreat for the residents of Coihaique but is large enough so that it never feels oppressively crowded.

Geography & Climate

On the southern slopes of Cerro Cinchao, Reserve Nacional Coihaique is only five km from town, via the paved road toward Puerto Chacabuco and a steep dirt road to the entrance. Altitudes range from 400 to 1000 metres above sea level. Summers are warm and relatively dry, with a mean temperature of about 12°C. Most of the 1100 mm of annual precipitation, in the form of both rain and snow, falls in winter.

Places to Stay

It's easy enough to make this a day trip from Coihaique but with a tent you can stay at rustic CONAF campgrounds at Laguna Verde and El Brujo for US$3 per night. Facilities are very basic, but there are picnic tables, fresh water and firepits. Bring as much food as you need for the duration.

Getting There & Away

Local drivers can and do take ordinary vehicles up the very steep dirt road but it's not really a good idea without a jeep or other 4WD vehicle. It's a snail's-pace hike of about 1½ hours to the park entrance, where CONAF collects an admission fee of US$1, plus another hour to Laguna Verde.

MONUMENTO NATURAL DOS LAGUNAS

On the road to Coihaique Alto and the Argentine border, this 181-hectare wetland reserve has abundant bird life in an area which is ecologically transitional from southern beech forest to semi-arid plains. There are nature trails, a picnic area, and a CONAF visitor centre which is open daily from 9 am to 6 pm. While it lacks regular public transport, ask CONAF about transport.

RESERVA NACIONAL RÍO SIMPSON

Despite being downgraded from national park status, 41,000-hectare Río Simpson is an accessible, scenic combination of river, canyon and valley between Coihaique and its port city of Puerto Chacabuco. Along the paved road, streams from tributary canyons cascade over nearly vertical cliffs to join the broad valley of the Río Simpson. The native flora consist of evergreen forest, mostly southern beech species.

Geography & Climate

Reserva Nacional Río Simpson is only 37 km west of Coihaique, via the paved highway to Puerto Chacabuco. Altitudes range from 100 to 1900 metres above sea level. The climate is damp, with up to 2500 mm rainfall in some sectors, but summers are warm, with mean maximum temperatures of 15°C to 17°C.

Things to See & Do

CONAF's **Centro de Visitantes**, at Km 37 on the Chacabuco-Coihaique road, consists of a small natural history museum and botanic garden. It is a good introduction to region's ecology and wildlife, with well prepared specimens of taxidermy, including an Andean condor. There is a beach for swimming and many people take advantage of the river's proximity for fishing. A short distance from the visitors' centre is the **Cascada La Virgen**, a shimmering waterfall on the north side of the highway.

Near the confluence of the Río Simpson and the Río Correntoso, 22 km from Coihaique, there is a good hike up the canyon to Laguna Catedral which requires an overnight stay.

Places to Stay

Camping Río Correntoso (☎ 232005), 24 km west of Coihaique, has 50 spacious riverside sites for US$10.

Getting There & Away

There are frequent buses between Coihaique and Puerto Aisén with La Cascada, Transaustral and Minibuses Don Carlos; see the Coihaique entry for details. Since you can get on or off anywhere on the route, transport is really very easy.

PUERTO CHACABUCO

One of the most common ports of entry to the region is Puerto Chacabuco, connected to the regional capital of Coihaique by an excellent paved road. At the east end of a narrow fjord, Puerto Chacabuco can be reached by ferry from Chaitén or from the port of Quellón on Chiloé. Chacabuco displaced Puerto Aisén as the port of Coihaique when the harbour at Puerto Aisén silted up.

Places to Stay

Hotel Moraleda (☎ 351155), on O'Higgins just outside the harbour compound, has singles/doubles for US$8/11 and is convenient for late arrivals on the ferries. *Hotel Loberías de Aisén* (☎ 351115), J M Carrera 50, has upscale accommodation for US$39/42.

Getting There & Away

Bus Buses from Coihaique, 82 km from Puerto Chacabuco by paved highway, meet arriving and departing ferries (see the Coihaique entry). After the road passes through a narrow tunnel above the valley of the Río Simpson, Coihaique becomes visible in the distance, against a setting of impressive volcanic peaks.

Boat Navimag and Transmarchilay connect Puerto Chacabuco to Quellón or Chonchi on the island of Chiloé, and to Chaitén and Puerto Montt; for details, see the previous Coihaique section.

PARQUE NACIONAL LAGUNA SAN RAFAEL

Glaciers brush the sea in this 1.7 million hectare park at the edge of the Campo de Hielo Norte, the massive northern Patagonian ice sheet, which encompasses some of the most spectacular fjord and mountain scenery in the world. Established in 1959, the park is the most popular single attraction in the entire Eleventh Region, despite the difficulty and expense of getting there.

Dense with floating icebergs calved from the San Rafael glacier, this park is a memorable sight even beneath the sombre clouds which so often hang, like gloomy curtains, over the surrounding peaks.

Geography & Climate

Laguna San Rafael is a nearly-enclosed inlet of the sea and is 225 km south-west of Puerto Chacabuco via a series of longitudinal channels between the Chonos archipelago and the Península de Taitao on the west, and the Patagonian mainland on the east. Only the low-lying Istmo de Ofqui, linking Taitao with the mainland, impedes access to the Golfo de Penas. In the 1930s, the Chilean government began a canal to connect the two, but abandoned the project after proceeding only 300 metres.

Altitudes range from sea level to 4058 metres on the summit of Monte San Valentín, the highest peak in the southern Andes. The climate is damp and humid, with 3500 mm of precipitation in coastal areas. At higher elevations, more than 5000 mm of rain and snow nourishes the 19 major glaciers which coalesce to form the Campo de Hielo Norte which covers about 300,000 hectares. Because of the Pacific, the mean annual temperature is a relatively mild 8°C and the San

Rafael glacier (or Ventisquero San Rafael in Spanish) appears to be receding.

Things to See & Do

Sightseeing around the San Rafael glacier is clearly the major attraction, but fishing, climbing and hiking are also possible for well equipped travellers in top physical condition. Those travellers intending to hike should heed Darwin's caution that:

> The coast is so very rugged that to attempt to walk in that direction requires continued scrambling up and down over the sharp rocks of mica-slate; and as for the woods, our faces, hands and shin-bones all bore witness to the maltreatment we received, in attempting to penetrate their forbidding recesses.

Those who overcome these obstacles will see considerable wildlife, mostly birds, including flightless steamer ducks, black-browed and sooty albatross, and Magellanic penguins. Otters, sea lions and elephant seals also frequent the icy waters, while pudú, pumas and foxes inhabit the surrounding forests and uplands.

Places to Stay

No permanent accommodation exists at Laguna San Rafael. Most visitors stay on board the ships, but in cases of emergency, CONAF will permit people to stay in the unheated basement of an abandoned hotel which serves as the park's headquarters.

CONAF has recently instituted a entrance fee of about US$10 per visitor to the park. While this may seem steep, especially in comparison with similar fees for other parks, it is only a very small percentage of the cost of the entire trip and is well justified, given the cost of maintaining a permanent CONAF presence.

Getting There & Away

The only way to gain access to and from Laguna San Rafael is by air and sea so travel tends to be expensive and/or time-consuming.

Air Charter flights from Coihaique land at Laguna San Rafael's 775-metre gravel airstrip. Contact Línea Aérea Hein (☎ 232772) at Bilbao 968 or Línea Aérea San Rafael (☎ 233408) at 18 de Septiembre 469. These take five passengers for about US$370 return for the 1½ hour flight.

Boat There are several alternatives for sea access to Laguna San Rafael, roughly (in more than one sense!) a 16-hour trip from Puerto Chacabuco. The cheapest is Broom Austral's (☎ 351134 in Chacabuco) *Calbuco*, which sails on Fridays at 6 pm and returns Sundays at 7 am, and has reclining Pullman seats for US$86 and berths for US$114.

Broom also operates the *Patagonia Express*, a luxury catamaran with on-board accommodation which includes all meals, for US$300 in peak season (January to March) or US$240 (March to mid-April). It is possible to take this all the way from Puerto Montt for US$690 per person in peak season or US$552 in low season, but these fares do not include accommodation at Puyuhuapi, Chacabuco or Coihaique. For reservations in Santiago, contact Patagonia Travelling Service (☎ 223-5567) at Fidel Oteíza 1956, 10th floor, in Providencia, or in Puerto Montt (☎ 258460) at Portales 870.

Another relatively inexpensive alternative is the ferry *Evangelistas*, operated by Navimag (☎ 233306), Presidente Ibáñez 347 in Coihaique, which charges US$137 return and sails three times a month. From Puerto Montt, the cruise takes five days and four nights.

Transmarchilay (☎ 231971), 21 de Mayo 417 in Coihaique, runs the ferry *El Colono*, with fares from US$114 in clase económica, to US$143 butaca popa (bus-type seat), US$171 butaca proa (aircraft-type seat), and US$290 per person for a camarote (sleeper). In Santiago, the Transmarchilay office (☎ 335959) is at Agustinas 715, Oficina 514.

Sice Travel (☎ 233466), 21 de Mayo 461 in Coihaique, charters the motor launch *Patagonia* for US$4400, which works out to about US$366 per person for the 12-passenger maximum. Nueva Hammerfest (☎ 333156 in Puerto Aisén), operates the luxury yacht

Visund on four sailings a month for US$760 per person. Tourism Skorpios (☎ 338715), MacIver 484, 2nd floor in Santiago, sails between Puerto Montt and Laguna San Rafael on the 160-passenger *Skorpios* from September to April from US$1096 per double in low season to US$1560 in high season, but is considerably more expensive for better cabins. One correspondent who took the *Skorpios* found it good but not great, and was disappointed with the guides, whose background and interest in natural history was weak.

PUERTO INGENIERO IBÁÑEZ

Buried in volcanic ash by the 1991 eruption of Volcán Hudson, Puerto Ingeniero Ibáñez (or just Puerto Ibáñez), on the shores of the emerald-green Lago General Carrera, has recovered more quickly than other towns in the area affected by the volcano's eruption. Surrounded by steep mountains and barren hills, the town has regular ferries to Chile Chico and the Argentine border at Los Antíguos. Across the border, Lago General Carrera is known as Lago Buenos Aires.

Things to See

The town of Puerto Ingeniero Ibáñez is of little interest but the surrounding countryside is very worthwhile if you can afford to rent a car. From Puerto Levican, on the lake, there are panoramic views of the whole Río Ibáñez valley when dust from Volcán Hudson does not obscure the horizon.

Livestock – cattle and sheep – are the backbone of the local economy. You may see the local *huasos* driving their herds along the roads. Orchard crops do well in the low-altitude micro-climate along the lake. Long lines of poplars, planted as wind breaks, separate the fields, while black-necked swans and pink flamingos crowd the river and its shores.

Places to Stay & Eat

The two places to stay are both opposite the ferry dock. The *Residencial Ibáñez* (☎ 227), at Dickson 31, has unheated singles with plenty of extra blankets for about US$5 with breakfast; other meals are available. Next door at Dickson 29 is *Hotel Monica* (☎ 226), only slightly more expensive.

Getting There & Away

For transport from Coihaique to Puerto Ibáñez, see the earlier Coihaique section. Transmarchilay's car and passenger ferry sails on Tuesday, Wednesday and Saturday mornings to Chile Chico, on the southern shore of the Lago General Carrera – check exact departure times at Transmarchilay in Coihaique. The fare from Puerto Ibáñez to Chile Chico is US$3 per person. On alternate Tuesdays the ferry visits all the small ports along Lago General Carrera.

Cisne de cuello negro (black-necked swan)

RESERVA NACIONAL CERRO CASTILLO

Reserva Nacional Cerro Castillo, 75 km south of Coihaique, is a sprawling 180,000-hectare reserve of southern beech forests, overshadowed by the basaltic spires of Cerro Castillo, reaching nearly 2700 metres and flanked by three major glaciers on its southern slopes. This is very fine and rarely visited trekking country (not to be confused with the settlement of Cerro Castillo near Parque Nacional Torres del Paine, in the Twelfth Region of Magallanes).

Things to See & Do

Sightseeing, fishing and trekking are popular recreational alternatives. There is an excellent four-day trek from Km 75, at the northern end of the reserve, to Villa Cerro Castillo at the southern end, which is described in LP's *Trekking in the Patagonian Andes*.

Places to Stay

On the Camino Austral, 67 km south of Coihaique, CONAF operates the modest campgrounds *Laguna Chaguay* and *El Silencio* for US$3 per site, but camping with tents is free and spectacular in the backcountry, despite CONAF's US$1 admission charge. Be sure to check in with the ranger, since trekking is potentially hazardous on trails which can require fording rushing streams of glacial meltwater.

At Villa Cerro Castillo, at the south end of the reserve, on a short gravelled lateral from the Camino Austral about 10 km west of the Puerto Ibáñez junction, *Pension El Viajero* has a few rooms for US$3 per person, a bar and a cheap restaurant. Otherwise, the village itself is a typical pioneer settlement of cement block houses with corrugated metal roofs.

CHILE CHICO

Founded in 1928 by immigrant fortune-seekers of several nationalities – Argentine, Brazilian, Chilean, French, German and Italian – Chile Chico derived its early prosperity from copper, where blue-tinged ore is still visible in the rocky hills. One can imagine the optimism of the first settlers, but the only tangible reminder of their great expectations is the wide, dusty main street, built to accommodate streams of traffic that

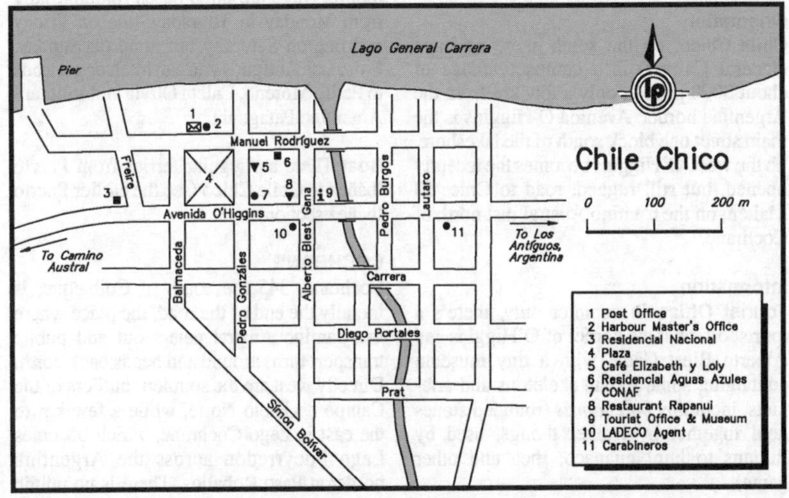

never arrived. When miners exhausted the copper, the economy declined but the cultivation of high-quality fruit in this unique climate has kept the town alive if not truly prosperous.

The warm and sunny weather has encouraged production of apples, pears, plums and cherries equal to those from the Chilean heartland. The primary market is Coihaique but the 1991 eruption of Volcán Hudson smothered the orchards of Chile Chico in ash, seriously jeopardising the town's future.

Even under ideal growing conditions fruit is not lucrative because markets other than Coihaique are distant and transport is difficult and expensive. Farmers cannot sell to Argentina, since growers across the Argentine border in Los Antíguos grow the same fruit. Much of the harvest falls and rots on the ground or is fed to pigs.

Because the town has no other industry, many people have left Chile Chico to work in Argentina. In the 1960s the population was 6000 but now is only about half of that. Remittances from expatriate workers, or those in other parts of Chile, are a main source of income, while some make a living catering to the minor tourist trade from Argentina.

Orientation

Chile Chico, on the south shore of Lago General Carrera, is a compact village of about 3000 people, only a few km from the Argentine border. Avenida O'Higgins is the main street one block south of the lakeshore. To the west, O'Higgins becomes the recently opened, but still rugged, road to Cruce El Maitén, on the Camino Austral just north of Cochrane.

Information

Tourist Office In summer only, there's a tourist office at the corner of O'Higgins and Alberto Blest Gana, with a tiny museum containing some Indian skeletons and artefacts, including *boleadoras* (rounded stones held together by leather thongs, used by Indians to hunt guanaco, rhea and other game).

Post & Telecommunications Correos de Chile is on the corner of Manuel Rodríguez and Balmaceda.

Police The Carabineros, O'Higgins 506 at Lautaro, keep a record of who's going to Argentina and may help arrange transport when buses are not available.

Places to Stay

Chile Chico has two small residenciales, both of which charge about US$7 per person with breakfast: *Residencial Nacional* (☎ 265) is at Freire 24, while *Residencial Aguas Azules* (☎ 320) is at Manuel Rodríguez 252.

Places to Eat

For snacks and drinks, try *Café Elizabeth y Loly* on Pedro Gonzáles, opposite the plaza. Also try the *Restaurant Rapanui* at the corner of O'Higgins and Blest Gana.

Getting There & Away

Air Aerotaxi Don Carlos has three flights weekly from Coihaique to Chile Chico. There is a Ladeco agent on O'Higgins.

Bus Transportes VH crosses the border to Los Antíguos, just nine km east, for US$3 return. There are three buses running daily from Monday to Thursday, one on Friday and one on Saturday but none on Sunday. From Los Antíguos you can hitch or get a bus to Perito Moreno, Caleta Olivia and southern Argentine Patagonia.

Boat There are regular ferries from Puerto Ibáñez to Chile Chico (see the earlier Puerto Ibáñez section).

COCHRANE

Cochrane, 345 km south of Coihaique, is literally the end of the road, the place where the Camino Austral peters out and public transport turns around and heads back north. Directly west are the southern outliers of the Campo de Hielo Norte, while a few km to the east is Lago Cochrane, which becomes Lago Pueyrredón across the Argentine border at Paso Roballos. There is no public

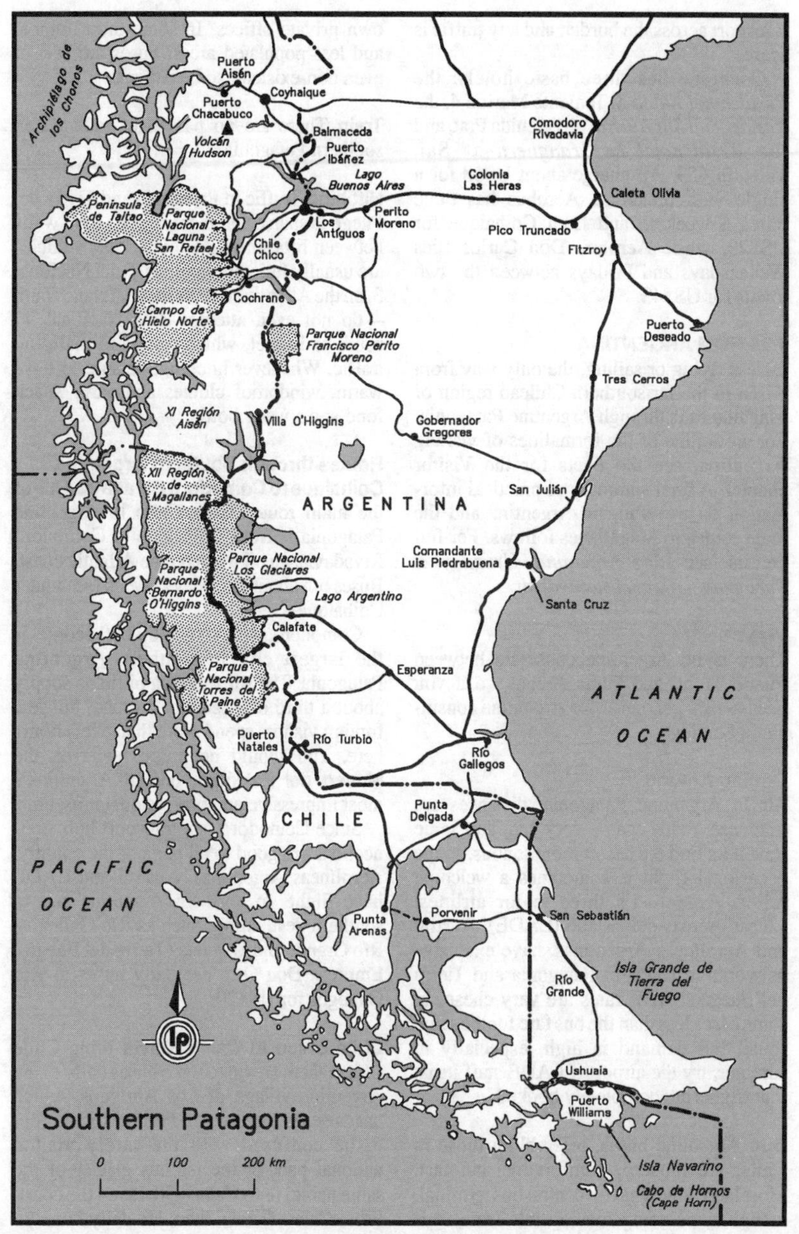

Archipiélago de los Chonos
Puerto Aisén
Coyhaique
Puerto Chacabuco
Volcán Hudson
Balmaceda
Puerto Ibáñez
Lago Buenos Aires
Península de Taitao
Parque Nacional Laguna San Rafael
Los Antiguos
Perito Moreno
Chile Chico
Cochrane
Campo de Hielo Norte
Parque Nacional Francisco Perito Moreno
XI Región Aisén
Villa O'Higgins
XII Región de Magallanes
Comodoro Rivadavia
Colonia Las Heras
Caleta Olivia
Pico Truncado
Fitzroy
Puerto Deseado
Tres Cerros
Gobernador Gregores
San Julián
ARGENTINA
Comandante Luis Piedrabuena
Santa Cruz
Parque Nacional Los Glaciares
Lago Argentino
Parque Nacional Bernardo O'Higgins
Calafate
Esperanza
Parque Nacional Torres del Paine
ATLANTIC OCEAN
Puerto Natales
Río Turbio
Río Gallegos
Punta Delgada
CHILE
PACIFIC OCEAN
Punta Arenas
Porvenir
San Sebastián
Isla Grande de Tierra del Fuego
Río Grande
Ushuaia
Puerto Williams
Isla Navarino
Cabo de Hornos (Cape Horn)
Southern Patagonia
0
100
200 km

transport across the border, and any traffic is scarce.

Cochrane has three basic hotels: the *Residencial Rubio* at Teniente Merino 4, the *Residencial Sur Austral* on Avenida Prat, and the *Residencial La Tranquera* at San Valentín 653. All charge about US$8 for a single with breakfast. Aerobus has three buses a week to and from Coihaique for US$23, while Aerotaxi Don Carlos flies Wednesdays and Fridays between the two towns for US$43.

TO/FROM ARGENTINA

Unless flying or sailing, the only way from Aisén to the far southern Chilean region of Magallanes is through Argentine Patagonia. For an outline of the formalities of visiting Argentina, see the Facts for the Visitor chapter. A brief summary of practical information on travelling in Argentina and the main routes to Magallanes follows. For full details, see LP's *Argentina, Uruguay & Paraguay – a travel survival kit.*

Visas

There is no Argentine consulate between Puerto Montt and Punta Arenas, so if you need a visa, get one at the Argentine consulate in Santiago.

Getting Around

Air In Argentine Patagonia, distances are immense, roads can be very bad, and some travellers find the desert monotonous, so the occasional flight is sometimes a welcome relief. Argentina's three major airlines, Líneas Aéreas del Estado (LADE), Austral and Aerolíneas Argentinas, have extensive networks in southern Patagonia and Tierra del Fuego. LADE fares are very cheap, in some cases less than the bus fare for the same route, but demand is high, especially in summer; try the airport if LADE staff insist that flights are completely booked.

Bus Argentine buses, resembling those in Chile, are modern, comfortable and fast. Most large towns have a central bus terminal, though some companies operate from their own private offices. In some more remote and less populated areas, buses are few or even non-existent, so be patient.

Train There are no passenger railways in southern Patagonia.

Hitching Traffic in Patagonia and Tierra del Fuego is sparse and there may be long waits between lifts, since the few private vehicles are usually full with families. Ruta Nacional 3, on the Atlantic coast, is the best route south – do not even attempt Ruta Nacional 40 south of Esquel, which carries virtually no traffic. Whenever hitching, be sure to have warm, windproof clothes and carry snack food and a water bottle.

Routes through Southern Argentina

Coihaique to Comodoro Rivadavia One of the main routes from Chile to Argentine Patagonia is from Coihaique to Comodoro Rivadavia, an oil town on the Atlantic coast. Buses run about three days a week (see under Coihaique).

Comodoro, with about 100,000 people, is the largest city in southern Argentine Patagonia. The surrounding oilfields supply about a third of Argentina's crude, but few foreign visitors spend more than a few hours here. You should not miss, however, the **Museo del Petróleo**, one of Argentina's most impressive and professional museums.

Since Comodoro is a transport hub, connections are good to all parts of the country. Aerolíneas Argentinas, Austral and LADE have flights to northern Argentina and to southern destinations such as Río Gallegos, Río Grande and Ushuaia (Tierra del Fuego). Empresa Don Otto has daily buses to Río Gallegos for US$20.

Chile Chico to Caleta Olivia From Chile Chico, there are up to three buses daily to the Argentine village of Los Antíguos, which has buses to the town of Perito Moreno (not to be confused with the rarely visited national park or the famous glacier of the same name) or to Caleta Olivia, on the coast. From Caleta Olivia, there are daily buses to

Río Gallegos and frequent buses on the short hop to Comodoro Rivadavia.

Like Chile Chico, Los Antíguos has suffered from the deposition of ash from the eruption of Volcán Hudson, but its site on Lago Buenos Aires is incomparably beautiful and its mild climate a pleasure. Perito Moreno is a frontier town where you still see elderly gauchos in riding gear. On Thursdays, LADE flights from Comodoro Rivadavia (US$23) stop here en route to Gobernador Gregores and Río Gallegos (US$38) in the morning and return by the same route in the afternoon.

Caleta Olivia is a miniature version of Comodoro Rivadavia, a plain but friendly oil town with frequent bus connections.

To/From Río Gallegos Río Gallegos, 800 km south of Comodoro Rivadavia, is a sizeable sheep-farming town which is the starting point for trips to Calafate, near Argentina's Parque Nacional Los Glaciares, and Ushuaia, on the island of Tierra del Fuego. From Río Gallegos there are daily buses to Puerto Natales and Punta Arenas in Chile. Aerolíneas Argentinas, Austral and LADE have daily flights to Comodoro Rivadavia, Río Grande and Ushuaia, while LADE has daily flights to Calafate.

Every four years or so in the Parque Nacional Los Glaciares, the advance of the 60-metre high Moreno glacier, more than a km wide at its base, blocks the Brazo Rico (Rico Arm) of Lago Argentino until the weight of the water behind it bursts the dam in a spectacular natural cataclysm. In addition to the glaciers, the nearby Fitzroy range is some of South America's finest trekking country.

There are daily buses to Calafate from Río Gallegos. During summer, there are buses about three days a week from Calafate to Puerto Natales, Chile, but this trip is difficult in winter, when snow sometimes cuts the road from Calafate to Chile. The road from Calafate to Puerto Natales passes through the spectacular Parque Nacional Torres del Paine.

Another crossing from Argentina to Chile is by bus from Río Gallegos to Puerto Natales, via the coal town of Río Turbio. Take one of the daily buses from Río Gallegos to Río Turbio, then catch one of the frequent worker's buses from Río Turbio to Puerto Natales. LADE has three flights a week between Río Turbio and Río Gallegos.

Magallanes & Tierra del Fuego

The Twelfth Region, Región de Magallanes y de La Antártica Chilena, takes in all Chilean territory south of about the level of Cerro Fitzroy. It includes the western half of the Isla Grande de Tierra del Fuego (the eastern half is Argentine), the largely uninhabited islands of the Tierra del Fuego archipelago, and the slice of Antarctica claimed by Chile.

Magallanes

Battered by westerly winds and storms which drop huge amounts of rain and snow on the seaward slopes of the Andes, Magallanes is a rugged, mountainous area, geographically remote from the rest of the country. It forms the southern part of Chilean Patagonia. Coming from Aisén or the Chilean mainland, Magallanes and its capital Punta Arenas are only accessible by road through Argentine Patagonia, or by air or sea.

Ona, Yahgan, Haush, Alacaluf and Tehuelche Indians, subsisting through fishing, hunting and gathering, were the region's original inhabitants. There remain very few individuals of identifiable Ona, Haush or Yahgan descent, while the Alacalufes and Tehuelches survive in much reduced numbers. Magellan, in 1520 the first European to visit the region, left it his name, but early Spanish attempts at colonisation failed. Tiny Puerto Hambre (Port Famine) at the southern end of the Strait of Magellan (Estrecho de Magallanes) is a reminder of these efforts. Nearby, the restored wooden bulwarks of Fuerte Bulnes recall Chile's first colonisation of 1843, when President Manuel Bulnes ordered the army south to the area, then only sparsely populated by indigenous peoples.

The California gold rush gave birth to Punta Arenas, and its initial prosperity depended on the maritime traffic which passed through the straits between Europe, on the one hand, and California and Australia on the other. With the opening of the Panama Canal and the reduction of traffic around Cape Horn (Cabo de Hornos), the port's international importance diminished. Later wealth derived from the wool and mutton industry which transformed both Argentine and Chilean Patagonia in the late-19th century. Besides wool, Magallanes' modern economy depends on commerce, petroleum development and fisheries, which have made it Chile's most prosperous region, with the country's highest levels of employment, housing quality, school attendance and public services. Its impressive natural assets, particularly Parque Nacional Torres del Paine, have made it an increasingly popular tourist destination.

PUNTA ARENAS

At the foot of the Andes on the western side of the Strait of Magellan, Punta Arenas has nearly 100,000 inhabitants. Its free port facilities have promoted local commerce and encouraged immigration from central Chile. Although the basic cost of living is high, luxuries such as automobiles and electronics are much less expensive here. As the best and largest port for thousands of km, it attracts ships from the burgeoning South Atlantic fishery as well as Antarctic research and tourist vessels. Elaborate mansions and other impressive buildings from the wool boom lend a turn-of-the-century atmosphere to the city centre.

History

Founded in 1848, Punta Arenas was originally a military garrison and penal settlement which proved to be conveniently situated for shipping en route to California during the gold rush. Compared to the initial Chilean settlement at Fuerte Bulnes, 60 km south, it had superior supplies of wood and water, and

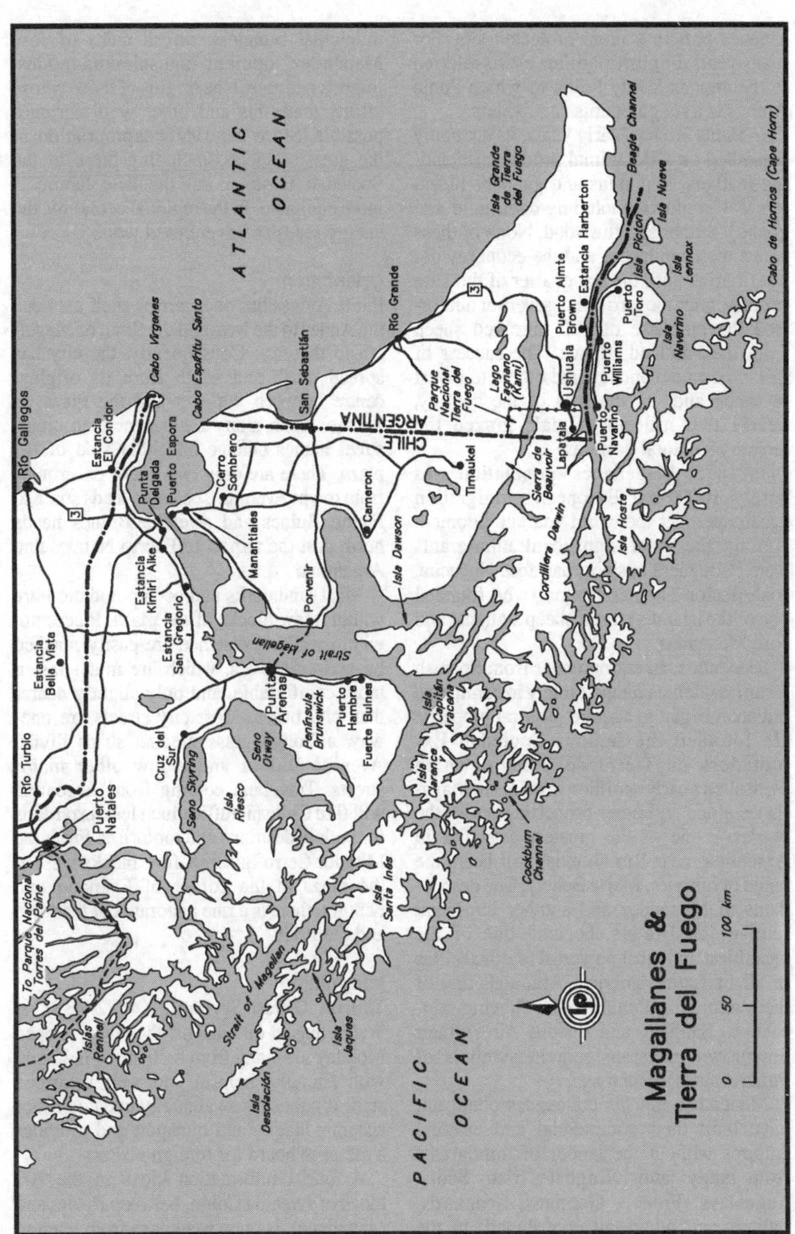
Magallanes &
Tierra del Fuego
0
50
100 km
PACIFIC
OCEAN
ATLANTIC
OCEAN
Río Gallegos
Estancia El Condor
Cabo Vírgenes
Punta Delgada
Puerto Espora
Cabo Espíritu Santo
Cerro Sombrero
San Sebastián
Río Grande
Isla Grande de Tierra del Fuego
ARGENTINA
CHILE
Estancia Kimiri Aike
Manantiales
Cameron
Timaukel
Estancia San Gregorio
Porvenir
Isla Dawson
Estancia Bella Vista
Río Turbio
Puerto Natales
To Parque Nacional Torres del Paine
Cruz del Sur
Punta Arenas
Strait of Magellan
Península Brunswick
Puerto Hambre
Fuerte Bulnes
Seno Otway
Seno Skyring
Isla Riesco
Isla Capitán Aracena
Isla Clarence
Cockburn Channel
Isla Santa Inés
Isla Jaques
Isla Desolación
Islas Rennell
Parque Nacional Tierra del Fuego
Lago Fagnano (Kami)
Sierra de Beauvoir
Cordillera Darwin
Lapataia
Ushuaia
Puerto Almte Brown
Estancia Harberton
Beagle Channel
Puerto Navarino
Puerto Williams
Puerto Toro
Isla Navarino
Isla Hoste
Isla Picton
Isla Nueva
Isla Lennox
Cabo de Hornos (Cape Horn)
3

a better port in a more protected site. For many years, English maritime charts referred to the area as Sandy Point, of which Punta Arenas is a rough Spanish equivalent.

In Punta Arenas' early years, its economy depended on wild animal products (including feathers, seal skins and guanaco hides) mineral products (including coal, gold and guano), timber and firewood. None of these was a major industry, and the economy did not flourish until the last quarter of the 19th century, after the territorial governor authorised the purchase of 300 purebred sheep from the Falkland Islands. The success of this experiment encouraged others to invest in sheep and, by the turn of the century, nearly two million animals grazed the territory's natural pastures.

In 1875, Magallanes' population was barely 1000, but European immigration accelerated as the wool market boomed. Among the most significant immigrants were Portuguese businessman José Nogueira, Irish doctor Thomas Fenton (who founded one of the island's largest sheep stations) and José Menéndez.

Menéndez, an entrepreneur from Spanish Asturias, at first engaged solely in commerce but soon began to acquire pastoral property. He founded the famous Sociedad Explotadora de Tierra del Fuego, which controlled nearly a million hectares in Magallanes alone and other properties across the border – one of the greatest estancias in Argentina, near Río Grande, still bears the name of his wife, María Behety. The descendants of Menéndez and another important family, the Brauns, became one of the wealthiest and most powerful regional elites in all of Latin America. Although few of them remain in Punta Arenas (having relocated to Santiago and Buenos Aires), their downtown mansions remain symbols of Punta Arenas' golden age.

Menéndez and his colleagues could not have built their commercial and pastoral empires without the labour of immigrants from many lands; English, Irish, Scots, Yugoslavs, French, Germans, Spaniards, Italians and others all contributed. In the municipal cemetery, on all sides of José Menéndez' opulent mausoleum, modest tombstones reveal the origins of those whose efforts made his and other wool fortunes possible. Since the 1960s expropriation of the great estancias (including those of the Sociedad Explotadora) the land tenure is more equitable. In the regional economy, the energy industry has eclipsed wool.

Orientation

Punta Arenas lies on a narrow shelf between the Andes to the west and the Strait of Magellan to the east. Consequently, the city has spread north and south from its original centre between the port and the Plaza de Armas. As in many Latin American cities, street names change on either side of the plaza. There are only two major exit routes from town: Avenida Costanera leads south to Fuerte Bulnes and Avenida Bulnes heads north past the airport to Puerto Natales and Argentina.

Most landmarks and accommodation are within a few blocks of the plaza. Places not within walking distance are easily reached by taxi colectivos, which are much faster, more comfortable, and only slightly dearer than city buses. Most city streets are one-way, although grass median strips divide Avenida Bulnes and a few other major streets. Travellers coming from Argentina will find Chilean traffic much less hazardous for both pedestrians and motorists. From the Mirador Cerro La Cruz, four blocks west of the plaza at the corner of Fagnano and Señoret, there is a fine panorama of the town and the strait.

Information

Tourist Office Sernatur (☎ 224435), at Waldo Seguel 689 just off the plaza, is open Monday to Friday from 8.30 am to 6.45 pm, with friendly, helpful and well informed staff. It publishes an annually updated list of accommodation and transport and provides a message board for foreign visitors.

A tourist information kiosk in the 700 block of Avenida Colón, between Bories and Magallanes, is open weekdays from 9 am to

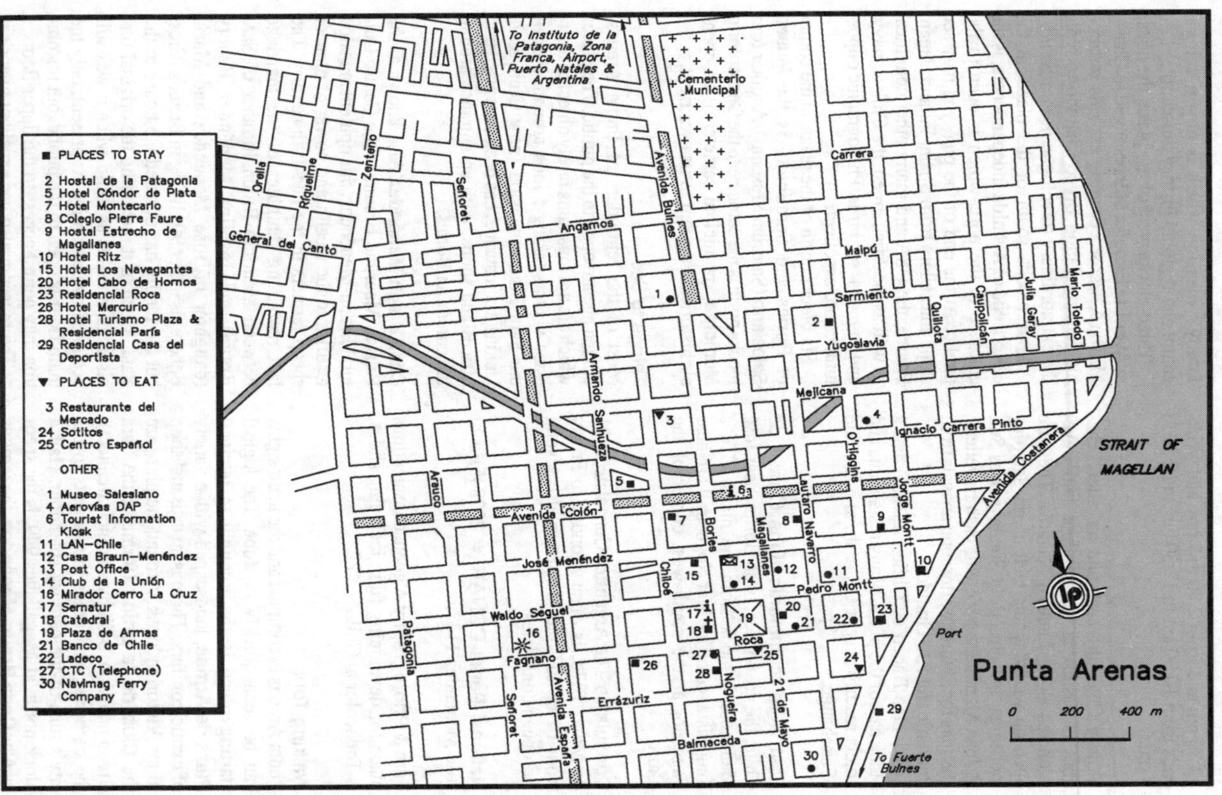
■ PLACES TO STAY
2 Hostal de la Patagonia
5 Hotel Cóndor de Plata
7 Hotel Montecarlo
8 Colegio Pierre Faure
9 Hostal Estrecho de Magallanes
10 Hotel Ritz
15 Hotel Los Navegantes
20 Hotel Cabo de Hornos
23 Residencial Roca
26 Hotel Mercurio
28 Hotel Turismo Plaza & Residencial París
29 Residencial Casa del Deportista
▼ PLACES TO EAT
3 Restaurante del Mercado
24 Sotitos
25 Centro Español
OTHER
1 Museo Salesiano
4 Aerovías DAP
6 Tourist Information Kiosk
11 LAN-Chile
12 Casa Braun-Menéndez
13 Post Office
14 Club de la Unión
16 Mirador Cerro La Cruz
17 Sernatur
18 Catedral
19 Plaza de Armas
21 Banco de Chile
22 Ladeco
27 CTC (Telephone)
30 Navimag Ferry Company
To Instituto de la Patagonia, Zona Franca, Airport, Puerto Natales & Argentina
Cementerio Municipal
Carrera
Orella
Riquelme
Zenteno
Señoret
Avenida Bulnes
Angamos
General del Canto
Maipú
Sarmiento
Yugoslavia
Quillota
Caupolicán
Julia Garay
Mario Toledo
Mejicana
Armando Sanhueza
O'Higgins
Ignacio Carrera Pinto
Avenida Costanera
STRAIT OF MAGELLAN
Arauco
Avenida Colón
Bories
Magallanes
Lautaro Navarro
Jorge Montt
José Menéndez
Chiloé
Pedro Montt
Waldo Seguel
Patagonia
Fagnano
Roca
Port
Punta Arenas
Nogueira
21 de Mayo
Errázuriz
Señoret
Avenida España
Balmaceda
0 200 400 m
To Fuerte Bulnes

12.30 pm and from 2.30 to 7 pm, and weekends from 10.30 am to 12.30 pm and 2.30 to 7 pm.

Money Changing cash and travellers' cheques is easiest at the cambios and travel agencies along Lautaro Navarro. They are open on weekdays as well as on Saturday mornings, but closed on Sundays. Bus Sur, at José Menéndez 556, will cash travellers' cheques for Saturday afternoon arrivals from Porvenir and Río Grande.

Try also Banco de Chile on Roca, half a block east of the plaza. Many restaurants and hotels readily accept US cash, at a fair rate of exchange.

Post & Telecommunications Correos de Chile, the post office, is on Bories, near José Menéndez a block from the plaza. CTC's long-distance office is at Nogueira 1116 near Fagnano, at the south-west corner of the plaza.

Consulates The Argentine Consulate, at 21 de Mayo 1878, is open Monday to Friday from 10 am to 2 pm. There are also several European consulates.

National Parks CONAF (☎ 227845) is at José Menéndez 1147.

Film & Photography A good, conscientious place for developing film, including slides, is Todocolor at Chiloé 1422.

Walking Tour

Punta Arenas is compact and the main sights can be seen quickly on foot. The logical starting place is the lovingly maintained **Plaza de Armas**, landscaped with a variety of exotic conifers. There is an artisans' shop in the Victorian kiosk. Around the plaza are the **Club de la Unión** (formerly the Sara Braun mansion, built by a French architect), the **catedral**, and other monuments to the city's turn-of-the-century splendour. Half a block north, at Magallanes 949, is the spectacular **Casa Braun-Menéndez**, the famous family's mansion which is now a cultural centre and regional history museum.

Three blocks west of the plaza, the house at **Avenida España 959** belonged to Charly Milward, whose eccentric exploits inspired his distant relation Bruce Chatwin to write the extraordinary travelogue *In Patagonia.*

Four blocks south of the plaza, at the eastern end of Avenida Independencia, is the entrance to the port, which is open to the public. At the end of the pier, you may see ships and sailors from Spain, Poland, Japan, France, the USA and many other countries, as well as local fishermen, the Chilean navy, and countless sea birds. Photographic opportunities are excellent.

Six blocks north of the plaza, at the corner of Bories and Sarmiento, is the **Museo Salesiano** (Salesian Museum). Another four blocks north is the entrance to the **Cementerio Municipal** (municipal cemetery), an open-air historical museum in its own right.

Things to See

Most of the reminders of Punta Arenas' golden age are open to the public. The places which are not museums rarely object to interested visitors taking a look around. Part of the Sara Braun mansion (now Club de la Unión), for instance, has been converted into offices and shops, with an entrance around the corner on Bories.

Casa Braun-Menéndez Also known as the Palacio Mauricio Braun, or the Centro Cultural Braun-Menéndez, this opulent mansion testifies to the wealth and power of pioneer sheep farmers in the late-19th century. The last remaining daughter of the marriage between Mauricio Braun (brother of Sara Braun) and Josefina Menéndez Behety (daughter of José Menéndez and María Behety) is in her 90s living in Buenos Aires, but the family has donated the house to the state. Much of it, including the original furnishings, remains as it did when it was still occupied by the family. At present, only the main floor is open to the public, but restoration may permit access to the upper floors.

The museum also has excellent historical

photographs and artefacts of early European settlement. Admission charges are modest, but there is an extra charge for photographing the interior. Hours are Tuesday to Saturday from 11 am to 4 pm and Sunday from 11 am to 1 pm. Access to the grounds is easiest from Magallanes, but the entrance is at the back of the house.

Museo Salesiano The Salesian museum (its full name is Museo Regional Salesiano Mayorino Borgatello), at Bulnes 374 near Sarmiento, features anthropological, historical and natural history exhibits of materials collected by a missionary order which greatly assisted European settlement of the region. In summer, the museum is open Tuesday to Sunday from 10 am to 1 pm and from 3 to 6 pm; in winter, weekday hours are from 3 to 6 pm only, while weekend hours are identical to summer ones.

Cementerio Municipal The walled municipal cemetery, at Avenida Bulnes 949, tells a great deal about Magallanes' history and social structure. The first families of Punta Arenas flaunted their wealth in death as in life – wool baron José Menéndez has one of the most extravagant tombs – but the headstones among the topiary cypresses also tell of English, German, Scandinavian and Yugoslav immigrants who supported these families with their labour. One monument pays tribute to the nearly extinct Onas. Open daily, the cemetery is about a 15-minute walk from the plaza, or you can take any taxi colectivo from the front gate of the Casa Braun-Menéndez on Magallanes.

Instituto de la Patagonia Part of the Universidad de Magallanes, the Patagonian institute features an interesting collection of early farm and industrial machinery imported from Europe, a typical pioneer house and shearing shed (both reconstructed), and a wooden-wheeled trailer which served as shelter for outside shepherds. Visitors can wander among the outdoor exhibits at will, but ask the caretaker at the library for admission to the buildings.

The library also has a fine display of historical maps, and a series of historical and scientific publications for sale to the public. A rather overgrown botanic garden, a small zoo, and experimental garden plots and greenhouses are also open to the public.

Opening hours are Monday to Friday from 8.30 am to 12.30 pm and 2.30 to 6.30 pm. Weekend visits may be possible by prior arrangement. Any taxi colectivo to the Zona Franca (duty-free zone, see below) will drop you across the street.

Organised Tours

Several agencies run trips to the important tourist sites near Punta Arenas, as well as to more distant destinations like Torres del Paine. Karú-Kinká (☎ 227868), Arauco 1792, offers guided excursions to the Club Andino (Andean Club, which offers winter skiing) for US$9, a city tour for US$15, and trips to the Otway penguin colony and Fuerte Bulnes for US$45 each. Guides speak German, French and Dutch. Torres del Paine excursions start at US$270, and include overnight camping or hotels. Up to four people per vehicle may split the cost.

Turismo Pali Aike (☎ 223301), José Menéndez 556, has slightly cheaper trips (including sandwiches and soft drinks) to the Otway penguin colony and Fuerte Bulnes. There is an additional itinerary to Río Verde, on Seno Skyring (Skyring Sound), for US$12. Arka Patagonia (☎ 226370), Roca 886, Local 7, also runs trips for similar prices. Buses Fernández (☎ 222313), Chiloé 930, is the only company with which it is possible to make trips to Seno Otway (Otway Sound) and Fuerte Bulnes in the same day, for about US$30 per person – one correspondent especially recommended Antonio Busolich as a guide.

Traveltur (☎ 228159), Roca 886, Local 25, arranges sailings to Parque Nacional Los Pingüinos between November and March (on request and weather permitting) and also visits Seno Otway, Fuerte Bulnes, and Torres del Paine. Enquire about prices.

For week-long luxury cruises of the Beagle Channel and the remote fjords of the

Cordillera Darwin on the *MV Terra Australis*, contact Cruceros Australis (☎ 696-3211), Miraflores 178, 12th floor, in Santiago.

Places to Stay – bottom end

Prices for accommodation have risen recently, but there is still good value around. One of the best places is the *Colegio Pierre Faure*, Lautaro Navarro 842, a private school which serves as a hostel during the summer months of January and February, although the staff may be able to accommodate visitors at other times of the year. Singles are US$5 with breakfast, but you can also pitch a tent in the rear garden for US$3 per person. All bathrooms are shared, but there is plenty of hot water. It is a good place to meet other travellers.

There are inexpensive hospedajes in the port area south of the downtown area, at Boliviana 238 (reported friendly but a bit dirty), and Paraguaya 150. One reader very much liked *Hospedaje Rivero*, Boliviana 366 (four blocks south of the plaza), at US$4 per person. Another reader has exuberantly recommended *Hospedaje Guisande*, a family house at J M Carrera 1270 near the cemetery, for US$6 per person.

Residencial Roca (☎ 223803), at Roca 1058 near O'Higgins, welcomes backpackers but is often full. In a well heated but leaky building, a single bed in a six-bed room costs US$5 without breakfast, while a private single costs US$9 when available. *Residencial Casa del Deportista* (☎ 222587), near the port at O'Higgins 1205, also charges US$5 per person for a shared room, but may have private rooms for couples. For the same price *Residencial Internacional*, Arauco 154, is popular but not especially clean, while *Residencial Rubio*, España 640, is good value at US$6.50 a single with breakfast. Another recommended *private house* is at Arauco 1514, with room and breakfast for US$5.

Residencial París (☎ 223112), at Nogueira 1116, 3rd floor, half a block off the Plaza de Armas, costs US$11 per person. *Hotel Montecarlo* (☎ 223448), a dilapidated but clean and spacious building at Colón 605 near Chiloé, has singles/doubles with shared bath at US$9/16, but rooms with private bath are more expensive.

Places to Stay – middle

Hostal Estrecho de Magallanes (☎ 226011), José Menéndez 1048, and the highly recommended *Hotel Ritz* (☎ 224422), Pedro Montt 1102, both have rooms for about US$20/28. Lonely Planet reader Pete Larrett describes the Ritz as:

> a labyrinth of entrance halls and corridors, décor from an Edwardian seaside boarding house, the mystique of an abandoned casino...[while the shared baths are] large enough for minor social functions.

At *Hostal de la Patagonia* (☎ 223521), O'Higgins 472, rates are US$27/35. *Hotel Turismo Plaza* (☎ 221300), one floor below Residencial Paris, charges US$37/46, while *Hotel Cóndor de Plata* (☎ 227987), Colón 556, is a comfortable modern place, at US$36/40 – better value than others charging twice the price. *Hotel Mercurio* (☎ 223430), at Fagnano 595, is also modern, clean and comfortable at US$35/41.

Places to Stay – top end

Perhaps the best place in town, *Hotel Los Navegantes* (☎ 224677), José Menéndez 647, has rooms for US$71/82, while the slightly more central *Hotel Cabo de Hornos* (☎ 222134), on the Plaza de Armas, charges US$94/110. The latter has a good but costly bar, and its solarium features a number of stuffed birds, including rockhopper and macaroni penguins, which visitors to local penguin colonies are unlikely to see.

Places to Eat

Punta Arenas offers the best of Chilean seafood – both finfish and shellfish are superb. *Sotitos*, at O'Higgins 1138, has an outstanding reputation for local specialities such as centolla (king crab), but is not cheap. The same holds for the nearby *Bar Grill Beagle*. Prices are moderate at *Restaurant Taberna de Silver*, O'Higgins 1037, which often has deep-fried fish. There are some very negative reports about *El Fogón*, next door.

The *Centro Español*, above the Teatro Cervantes on the Plaza de Armas, serves delicious conger eel and scallops, among other specialities. An extravagant meal, with wine, will cost about US$10, but midday specials should only cost half that.

The *Restaurante del Mercado*, upstairs on the corner of Mejicana and Chiloé, prepares a spicy ostiones al pil pil (scallops) and a delicate but filling chupe de locos (an abalone dish). Because of overexploitation and consequent harvest restrictions, locos may not be available. Other popular regional dishes include mussels and sea urchins but, if you are with a group, you may wish to order curanto.

Many restaurants, including all the above, serve more conventional parrilla dishes. *La Carioca*, on the corner of Chiloé and Menéndez, has good sandwiches and lager beer, although its pizzas are small and expensive. A good place for breakfast and onces (elevenses) is *Café Garogha*, Bories 817, where news junkies can watch CNN.

Recent readers' recommendations include *Venus*, on Pedro Montt half a block from Hotel Ritz, *Quijote* on the corner of Navarro and Pedro Montt, and *Monaco*, on Nogueira near the post office. One reader praised the *Golden Dragon*, a Chinese restaurant at Colón 529, as offering the best Chinese food they had eaten outside Asia.

Entertainment

Since the end of the military dictatorship, which regularly enforced a curfew, Chilean nightlife is more exuberant. Café Garogha, Bories 817, has a lively crowd late into the evening, and sometimes live entertainment. As in any port, there are numerous bars; try the Ñandú Café Grill, at Waldo Seguel 670, which also serves meals.

There are two cinemas, including the Teatro Cervantes on the plaza de Armas, which often show Chilean, North American and European films.

On the outskirts of the centre is the municipal racetrack. There is also a stadium where the local representative in the Chilean soccer league plays.

Things to Buy

The Zona Franca (duty-free zone) in Punta Arenas is a good place to replace a lost or stolen camera, and to buy film and other luxury items. Fujichrome slide film (36 exposures) costs about US$5 per roll without developing; print film is also cheap. Taxi colectivos are frequent from the centre to the Zona Franca, which is open daily except Sunday.

Chile Típico, Carrera Pinto 1015, offers items made by artisans in copper, bronze, and other materials.

Getting There & Away

The tourist office distributes a useful brochure with complete information on all forms of transportation and their schedules to and from Punta Arenas, Puerto Natales, and Tierra del Fuego, including those which go to or through Argentina.

Air Aeropuerto Presidente Carlos Ibáñez del Campo is 20 km north of town. Aerovías DAP runs its own bus service to the airport, while LAN-Chile and Ladeco use local bus companies.

LAN-Chile (☎ 223338), Lautaro Navarro 999 near Pedro Montt, flies to Puerto Montt (US$144) and Santiago (US$223) daily except Thursday. Children aged between two and 12 years travel for slightly more than half-fare. Ladeco (☎ 226100), at Roca 924 near O'Higgins, flies the same routes daily except Wednesday. Fares differ slightly from LAN's. The cut-rate carrier SABA has gone out of business, but its successor Pacific Air is attempting to fill the vacuum of bottom-end air services between Punta Arenas and Santiago.

Aerovías DAP (☎ 223958), O'Higgins 891, flies to Porvenir and back twice daily from Monday to Saturday for US$13.50 a single. On Tuesday, it goes to and from Puerto Williams, on Isla Navarino, for US$62 one way, slightly cheaper return. Children under six years old travel for half-price. In summer,

Aerovías DAP has weekly flights to the Falkland Islands (Islas Malvinas) for US$365 a single. During winter, these flights depart on alternative weeks. It also has monthly flights to Teniente Marsh air base in Antarctica for US$1000 a single, permitting one or two nights in Antarctica before returning to Punta Arenas.

The Chilean Air Force (FACh) has irregular flights to Puerto Montt which are cheaper than commercial flights. Enquire at the tourist office or airport.

Bus Punta Arenas has no central bus terminal; each company has its own office from which its buses depart, although most of these are fairly close together, on or near Lautaro Navarro. There are direct buses to Puerto Natales, Río Grande and Río Gallegos (Argentina) and mainland Chilean destinations via Argentina.

Buses Fernández (☎ 222313), Armando Sanhueza 745, has buses to Puerto Natales at 7 am and at 2.30 and 6.30 pm – and is very responsible. According to one reader, when two of Fernández' passengers lost tent poles on the trip to Puerto Natales, the company paid their passage back to Punta Arenas, put them in a hotel and paid their meals, and bought them a new tent.

Bus Sur (☎ 224864), José Menéndez 556, has buses to Puerto Natales daily, at 3 and 7 pm, for US$6. Buses Victoria Sur (☎ 226213), Colón 793, is slightly more expensive but offers excellent service. Buses depart daily at 8 am and 7.30 pm, except on Sunday when the only service is at 10 am. Buses Pacheco (☎ 225641) at Lautaro Navarro 601, has services on Monday and Thursday to Río Grande, in Argentine Tierra del Fuego, returning the following day. The fare, including the ferry crossing from Punta Arenas to Porvenir, is US$25. By walking fast in Río Grande, it is possible to make an immediate connection to Ushuaia.

There are numerous services to Río Gallegos in Argentina all for about US$15. The most frequent service is offered by Buses Pingüino (☎ 222396), Roca 915. Buses Ghisoni (☎ 222078), Navarro 975, and Agencia Taurus (☎ 222223), 21 de Mayo 1502, also have several departures. Buses Mansilla (☎ 221516), José Menéndez 556, offers services less frequently.

Fares to central Chile, via Argentina, are more variable. Ghisoni, Bus Sur, Buses Fernández, Bus Norte (☎ 222599) on the Plaza de Armas, Turibus (☎ 223795) at José Menéndez 647, and Ettabus (☎ 226370) at Roca 886, Local 7, all go to Osorno and Puerto Montt in the Chilean lake district. Fares to Santiago range from US$66 (Bus Norte) to US$100 (Bus Sur). These trips take as long as two days, but the buses are very comfortable and there are frequent meal and rest stops.

Boat Navimag (☎ 222593), which offers passage from Puerto Natales to Puerto Montt via the spectacular Chilean fjords, has an office at Avenida Independencia 830. For further information, see the Puerto Natales section.

Transbordador Austral Broom (☎ 228204) charges US$6 a single between Punta Arenas and Porvenir (US$35 per automobile). Their ferry departs from Tres Puentes, easily reached by taxi colectivo from the Casa Braun-Menéndez. On Sundays and holidays, when the ferry returns at 5 pm, it is possible to do this as a day trip without rushing.

There are reports of thefts from the cardeck, which is inaccessible to passengers during the crossing, so avoid leaving personal belongings such as bicycles or backpacks in the open.

The *Beaulieu*, a small cargo vessel, can take two or three passengers on its monthly trip to Puerto Williams, for US$300 per person return. Those with patience can sometimes obtain passage to Puerto Williams on board Chilean naval vessels. Enquire at Tercera Zona Naval, a beautiful Victorian building at Lautaro Navarro 1150.

Getting Around

Bus & Colectivo Although most places of interest are within easy walking distance of the centre, public transport is excellent to outlying sights like the Instituto de la

Patagonia and the Zona Franca. Taxi colectivos, which are much more comfortable and much quicker than buses, operate on numbered routes and are only slightly more expensive than buses (about US$0.30, a bit more late at night and on Sundays).

Car Rental In high season, book a car in advance if at all possible. Avis (☎ 227050) is at the airport as well as downtown at Navarro 1065, while Hertz (☎ 222013) is across the street at Navarro 1064. Budget (☎ 225696) and the Automóvil Club de Chile (☎ 221888) are at O'Higgins 964 and O'Higgins 931, respectively. First Rent-a-car (☎ 225729) is at Avenida Colón 798.

AROUND PUNTA ARENAS

Penguin Colonies

There are two substantial Magellanic penguin colonies near Punta Arenas. The one on Seno Otway north-west of the city, is easier to reach, while the larger and more interesting one is Parque Nacional Los Pingüinos, accessible only by boat. Several species of gulls and cormorants are also common, along with southern sea lions. Since there is no scheduled public transport to either penguin colony, it is necessary to rent a car or take a tour to visit them. For details, see the previous Organised Tours and Getting Around sections.

Also known as the Jackass penguin for its characteristic braying sound, *Spheniscus magellanicus* comes ashore in the southern spring to breed and lay its eggs in sandy burrows or under shrubs a short distance inland. Magellanic penguins are naturally curious and tame, although if approached too quickly they will retreat into their burrows or toboggan awkwardly across the sand back into the water. If approached too closely, they will bite and can inflict serious cuts, large enough to require stitches – *never* stick your hand or face into a burrow. The least disruptive way to observe the penguins is to seat yourself near a burrow and wait for their curiosity to get the better of them. With reasonable patience, good photographs are easy to take.

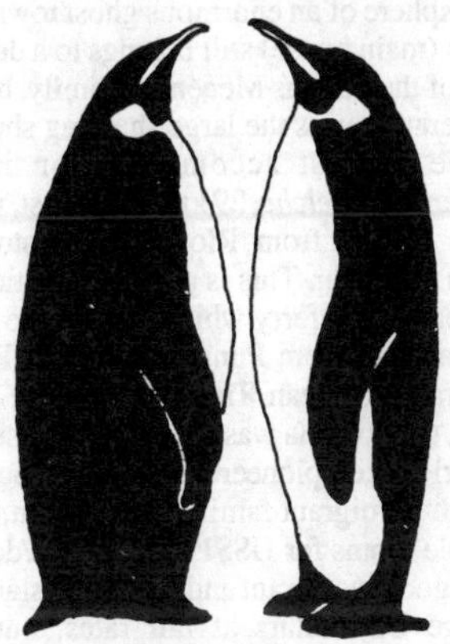

Penguins

Fuerte Bulnes

Named for Manuel Bulnes, the Chilean president who ordered the occupation of the territory in 1843, Fuerte Bulnes (Fort Bulnes) is a restored wooden fort, surrounded by a fence of sharp stakes, 55 km south of Punta Arenas. Only a few years after its founding it was abandoned because of its poor, rocky soil, inferior pasture, lack of potable water, and exposed site. To the east, across the Strait of Magellan, are Isla Dawson (Dawson Island, a 19th-century Salesian mission to the Yahgans and a notorious prison camp after the 1973 coup), and the spectacular Cordillera Darwin.

A gravel road runs from Punta Arenas to Fuerte Bulnes but there is no public transport. Several travel agencies offer half-day excursions to Fuerte Bulnes and the nearby fishing village of Puerto Hambre; for details, see the Organised Tours and Getting Around sections above.

Estancia San Gregorio

Some 125 km north-east of Punta Arenas, on the highway to Río Gallegos (Argentina) this 90,000-hectare estancia is now a cooperative. Since most buildings – employee housing, warehouses, chapel, and *pulpería* (company store) – have been abandoned, it presents the atmosphere of an enormous ghost town. The casco (main house) still belongs to a descendent of the famous Menéndez family, but the cooperative uses the large shearing shed.

The nearest accommodation is the *Hostería Tehuelche*, 29 km north-east, where buses to and from Río Gallegos stop for lunch or dinner. This is also the junction for the road to the ferry which crosses the Strait of Magellan from Punta Delgada to Puerto Espora in Chilean Tierra del Fuego. Until 1968, the hostería was the casco for Estancia Kimiri Aike, pioneered by the Woods, a British immigrant family. It has clean, comfortable rooms for US$13/22 a single/double, and a good restaurant and bar. Hotel staff will change US dollars at fair rates, but you should change your Argentine currency before leaving Río Gallegos.

PUERTO NATALES

Puerto Natales, a port town with 18,000 residents about 250 km north-west of Punta Arenas via a good paved road, lies on the eastern shore of Seno Ultima Esperanza (Last Hope Sound). Traditionally dependent on wool, mutton and fishing, it has become an essential stopover for hikers and other visitors en route to Parque Nacional Torres del Paine. It also offers the best access to Parque Nacional Bernardo O'Higgins and the famous Cueva del Milodón (Milodon Cave), and is the terminus for the Navimag ferry from Puerto Montt via the Chilean fjords. From here, you can also cross the Argentine border to the coal-mining town of Río Turbio, where many Chileans work, and to Parque Nacional Los Glaciares.

History

In search of a route to the Pacific, the first Europeans to visit Seno Ultima Esperanza were the 16th-century Spaniards Juan Ladrillero and Pedro Sarmiento de Gamboa, but their expeditions left no permanent legacy. In part because of Indian resistance, European settlers did not arrive until the late-19th century, when German explorer Hermann Eberhard established a sheep estancia near Puerto Prat, which was superseded by Puerto Natales. The dominant economic enterprise was the slaughterhouse and meat packing plant at Bories, operated by the Sociedad Explotadora, which drew livestock from south-western Argentina as well. This factory still functions, although its importance has declined.

Orientation

Puerto Natales itself is compact enough so that walking suffices for most purposes. Although its grid is more irregular than in many Chilean cities, most destinations are easily visible from the waterfront, where the Costanera Pedro Montt runs roughly north-south. Near the shore, notice the graceful black-necked swans, which are easily photographed with a medium telephoto lens. Gulls and cormorants blanket the old jetty pilings near the tourist office. The Cueva del Milodón and Bories are on the Torres del Paine highway north of town.

Information

Tourist Office The tourist office, which has maps and information about hotels, restaurants and transportation, is a chalet on the Costanera Pedro Montt at the intersection with the Phillipi diagonal. Its hours are Monday to Saturday from 9.30 am to 1 pm and 3 to 7 pm.

Money There are several cambios on Blanco Encalada near Eberhard, one block east of the plaza. Relojería Omega, the jewellery repair shop, will change travellers' cheques. All these places will exchange Argentine currency, unless the rates are too volatile.

Post & Telecommunications The post office is directly on the Plaza de Armas, at Eberhard 423 near Tomás Rogers. It also contains the offices of Telex Chile. CTC, on the corner of Blanco Encalada 23 and Phillipi, operates long-distance services from 8 am to 10 pm.

Organised Tours

Several travel agencies in Puerto Natales offer visits to the main local attractions.

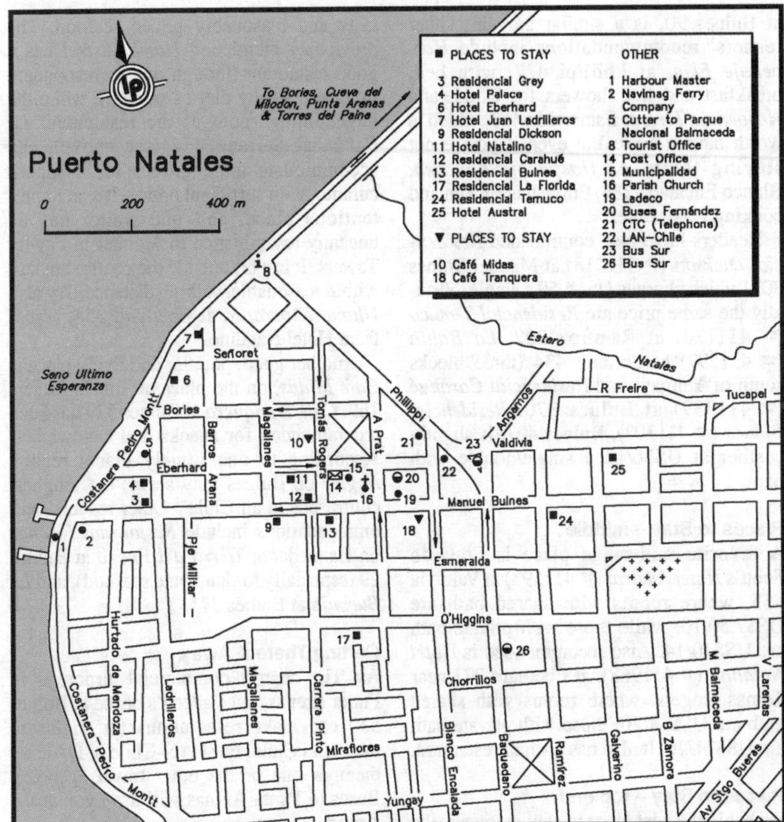

Eduardo Scott at the Hotel Austral speaks English and can take eight to 10 passengers to Torres del Paine and other destinations in his minibus. Andes Patagónicos (☎ 411594), Blanco Encalada 226, and Stop Cambios (☎ 411393), Baquedano 380, have similar services for about US$35 per person per day. Three-day excursions to Torres del Paine cost about US$120 per person with Buses Fernández.

Luis Díaz (☎ 411050), at Patricio Lynch 170, and Andes Patagónicos rent camping equipment, but check to be sure if tents are water-repellent.

Places to Stay – bottom end

Puerto Natales is popular with budget travellers and budget travellers are popular in Puerto Natales. When your bus arrives, you may be buried in business cards or slips of paper offering bottom-end accommodation. There is a highly recommended hostel at Bories 206 for US$3 with kitchen privileges. The owner, Sergio Nitrigual, goes out of his way to help travellers with bus and tour tickets.

Residencial La Florida (☎ 411361), O'Higgins 431, costs US$3 a single, while *Residencial Grey*, in a typical regional house at Bulnes 90, is a similar bargain. Other readers' recommendations include *Hospedaje Elsa*, at Phillipi 427, with bed, breakfast and hot showers for US$5, and *Hospedaje Teresa*, Esmeralda 463, which is worth having a meal at even if you're not staying there. At *Hospedaje Knudsen*, Blanco Encalada 284, English is spoken and cooking is possible.

Readers have also commended *Residencial Dickson* (☎ 411218) at Manuel Bulnes 307, which charges US$4.50 a single. Virtually the same price are *Residencial Temuco* (☎ 411120) at Ramírez 202, *La Bahía* (☎ 411297) at Serrano 434 (three blocks south of Yungay) and *Residencial Carahué* (☎ 411339) at Bulnes 370. *Residencial Bulnes* (☎ 411307), Bulnes 407, is slightly costlier at US$6/12 a single/double with bath.

Places to Stay – middle

A favorite mid-range place is Eduardo Scott's *Hotel Austral* (☎ 411593) at Valdivia 955, where rooms with shared bath are US$7.50/10, while those with private bath are US$10/14. Also recommended is *Hotel Natalino* (☎ 411968), at Eberhard 371 near Tomás Rogers, where rooms with shared bath are US$14/20; those with private bath are US$21/26. It also has a small restaurant.

Places to Stay – top end

Probably the best place to stay in town is the waterfront *Hotel Eberhard* (☎ 411208), at Pedro Montt 25 near Señoret, where rooms with private bath and breakfast start at US$52/56, although the bathrooms and showers are tiny. There is an excellent dining room with a panoramic view of Seno Ultima Esperanza, and an attractive 2nd-floor lounge with cable TV.

Slightly cheaper, but comparable, are the *Hotel Palace* (☎ 411134) at Ladrilleros 209 and *Hotel Juan Ladrilleros* (☎ 411652) at Pedro Montt 161.

Places to Eat

For a small provincial town, Puerto Natales has excellent restaurants, specialising in tasty and reasonably priced seafood. The previously mentioned *Hotel Austral* has a good restaurant (though one correspondent tired of a steady diet of salmon), while the huge dining room at the residencial *La Bahía*, at Serrano 434 (see above), can accommodate large groups for a superb curanto, with sufficient notice. It's an unpretentious place, and one waiter has an uncanny resemblance to Manuel in Fawlty Towers. It is a bit outside the centre, but still within reasonable walking distance. Try also *Ultima Esperanza* at Eberhard 354, across from Hotel Natalino.

Another good, popular and lively place is *Café Midas*, on the plaza at Tomás Rogers 169. *Café Tranquera* at Bulnes 579 has been recommended for snacks and sandwiches. According to one Lonely Planet reader, *Angies* on Bulnes may serve 'the toughest churrascos in all Chile'. Other readers' recommendations include *Restaurant Reymar* on Baquedano, *Tierra del Fuego* at Bulnes 29 (especially for lamb and seafood), and *La Burbuja* at Bulnes 371.

Getting There & Away

Air The nearest commercial airport is in Punta Arenas, but Ladeco's office at Bulnes 530 can make reservations for flights to mainland Chile. For LAN-Chile or DAP, try them or one of the other travel agencies. Buses to Punta Arenas will drop you at the airport.

Bus Puerto Natales has no central bus terminal. Buses Fernández (☎ 411111) is at Eberhard 555, while Bus Sur (☎ 411325) is at Baquedano 534. For details of services between Punta Arenas and Puerto Natales, see the Punta Arenas section.

In summer, Bus Sur also goes daily to Torres del Paine for US$7 a single, slightly cheaper return. It goes twice weekly to Río Gallegos in Argentina for US$15. Some of its buses continue from Torres del Paine to Calafate in Argentina, for US$45 a single. A two-day tour to Calafate and Parque Nacional Los Glaciares is available for US$70. Servitur, on Prat between Bulnes and

Esmeralda, offers daily minibus service to Paine at 7 am, returning from the administración (park headquarters) at 2 pm, and will collect passengers at their hotels. Buses JB, Bulnes 370, leaves for Paine at 6.30 am, returning from the administración at noon.

Turisur and Cotra have many buses daily from the corner of Phillipi and Baquedano to the Argentine coal mining town of Río Turbio for US$1. From there it is possible to make overland or air connections to Río Gallegos and to Calafate. Since flights with LADE, the Argentine air force's passenger service, are very inexpensive, this can be the cheapest way to Calafate, but there is only one flight a week, on Thursday at noon. There is, however, a daily bus from Turbio to Calafate for US$25.

Boat Services to Puerto Montt via the awesome Chilean fjords are very changeable. Navimag (☎ 411287), on the Costanera Pedro Montt, sails to Puerto Montt three times a month in summer, but appears to actively discourage passengers, for whom there are only 16 berths on the ferry *Evangelistas*. If you manage to secure a spot, the entire trip takes three days and four nights.

Including meals, passages range from US$100 with a reclining (Pullman) seat to US$150 with bunk and US$300 in a 1st-class cabin. It can be a rough trip not just because of rugged weather and the turbulent Golfo de Penas, but also because of hurried meals, insufficient sleeping space, inadequate sanitary facilities, and the powerful odour of the cattle and sheep on board. The crew, however, make a serious effort to keep everyone happy.

Car Rental Rental cars can be a reasonable alternative to buses if the expenses are shared. Andes Patagónicos offers mid-size cars for US$20 per day, plus US$8 insurance and US$0.20 per km. For US$60 plus insurance you are allowed 350 km per day, while larger cars cost about 15% more.

AROUND PUERTO NATALES

Bories

The **frigorífico** (meat-freezing factory), built in 1913 with British capital, is four km north of town. At one time, this factory processed huge amounts of meat, tallow, hides and wool from estancias in both Chile and Argentina for export to Europe, but its operations are now much reduced. There remain several interesting metal-clad buildings and houses, classic examples of hybrid Victorian/Magellanic architecture.

Parque Nacional Bernado O'Higgins

The southern end of Parque Nacional Bernado O'Higgins was formerly the Parque Nacional Balmaceda, but Balmaceda has now been incorporated into the much larger Parque Nacional O'Higgins. The area is largely inaccessible, but the southern tip can be reached on one of the spectacular cruises from Puerto Natales up Seno Ultima Esperanza. En route, there are glimpses of the frigorífico at Bories, several small estancias whose only access to Puerto Natales is across the sound, numerous glaciers and waterfalls, a large cormorant rookery, a smaller sea lion rookery, and sometimes you'll see Andean condors. It is four hours' sail to Puerto Toro, where a footpath leads from the jetty to the base of the Serrano glacier. On a clear day, the Torres del Paine are visible in the distance. The return trip follows the same route.

Weather permitting, the cutter *21 de Mayo* or the smaller and somewhat less comfortable *Trinidad* make the trip daily during summer and will go at other times if demand is sufficient. The cost is US$28 per person. Decent meals are available on board for about US$6, as are hot and cold drinks. For reservations, contact the owners (☎ 411176) at Ladrilleros 171. They can also arrange hiking and rafting excursions to Torres del Paine via Paso de los Toros and Río Serrano.

Cueva del Milodón

Cueva del Milodón (the Milodon Cave) is a national monument, administered by CONAF. It is 24 km north-west of Puerto Natales. The cave itself is the site where, in the 1890s, Captain Eberhard discovered the well preserved remains of the enormous ground sloth called the milodon.

The milodon was an herbivorous mammal which, like the mammoth and many other American megafauna, became extinct near the end of the Pleistocene. More than twice the height of a human, it pulled down small trees and branches for their succulent leaves. Within the cave, which is 30 metres high, 80 metres wide, and 200 metres deep, stands a full-size replica of the animal; well after its extinction, Indians took shelter here. Smaller caves nearby can be explored with a torch.

The milodon has generated many fanciful stories, including legends that Indians kept it penned as a domestic animal, and that some specimens remained alive into the last century. Bruce Chatwin's literary travelogue *In Patagonia* amusingly recounts these tales.

Although the closest hotel accommodation is at Puerto Natales, camping and picnicking are possible near the site. CONAF charges US$1.50 for admission, less for Chilean nationals and children. Buses to Torres del Paine will drop you at the entrance, which is several km walk from the cave proper. Alternatively, you can take a taxi or hitch from Puerto Natales.

PARQUE NACIONAL TORRES DEL PAINE

The Torres del Paine (Towers of Paine) are spectacular granite pillars which soar almost vertically for more than 2000 metres above the Patagonian steppe. The Torres and other high peaks, though, are only one feature of what may be South America's finest national park, a miniature Alaska of shimmering turquoise lakes, roaring creeks and rivers, cascading waterfalls, sprawling glaciers, dense forests and abundant wildlife. The issue is not whether to come here, but how much time to spend.

For hikers and backpackers, the 180,000-hectare park is an unequalled destination, with a well developed trail network as well as opportunities for cross-country travel. Strong westerlies make the weather changeable, but very long summer days make outdoor activities possible late into the evening. Good foul-weather gear is essential, and a warm sleeping bag and good tent are imperative for those undertaking the popular Paine circuit.

The area is now recovering from the over-exploitation of its pastures, forests and wildlife, which occurred for nearly a century before the creation of the park in 1959. The park now shelters large and growing herds of guanaco, flocks of the flightless rhea or ñandú, Andean condors, flamingos and many other species. Since 1978, it has been part of the United Nations' Biosphere Reserve system. For visitors from the northern hemisphere, almost everything will be new.

The park's outstanding wildlife conservation success has undoubtedly been the guanaco *(Lama guanicoe)*, which grazes the open steppes where its main natural enemy, the puma, cannot approach undetected. After more than a decade of effective protection from hunters and poachers, the guanaco barely flinches when humans or vehicles approach. The elusive huemul, or Chilean deer, is much more difficult to spot.

Guided day trips from Puerto Natales are possible, but permit only a superficial reconnaissance. It is better to explore the several options for staying at the park, including camping at both backcountry and improved sites, and staying at the guesthouses near the park headquarters and at Lago Pehoé.

Entry

At the park entrance on the north side of Lago Sarmiento, on the road from Puerto Natales, CONAF now charges an entry fee of US$8 per person (less for Chilean nationals). If you intend to hike the Paine circuit (see following), it is necessary to register with the ranger here or at park headquarters at Río Serrano. In fact, because of mishaps on the trail, rangers now collect passports and only return them when you finish the trek. Do not leave your passport in Puerto Natales or you will be sent to park headquar-

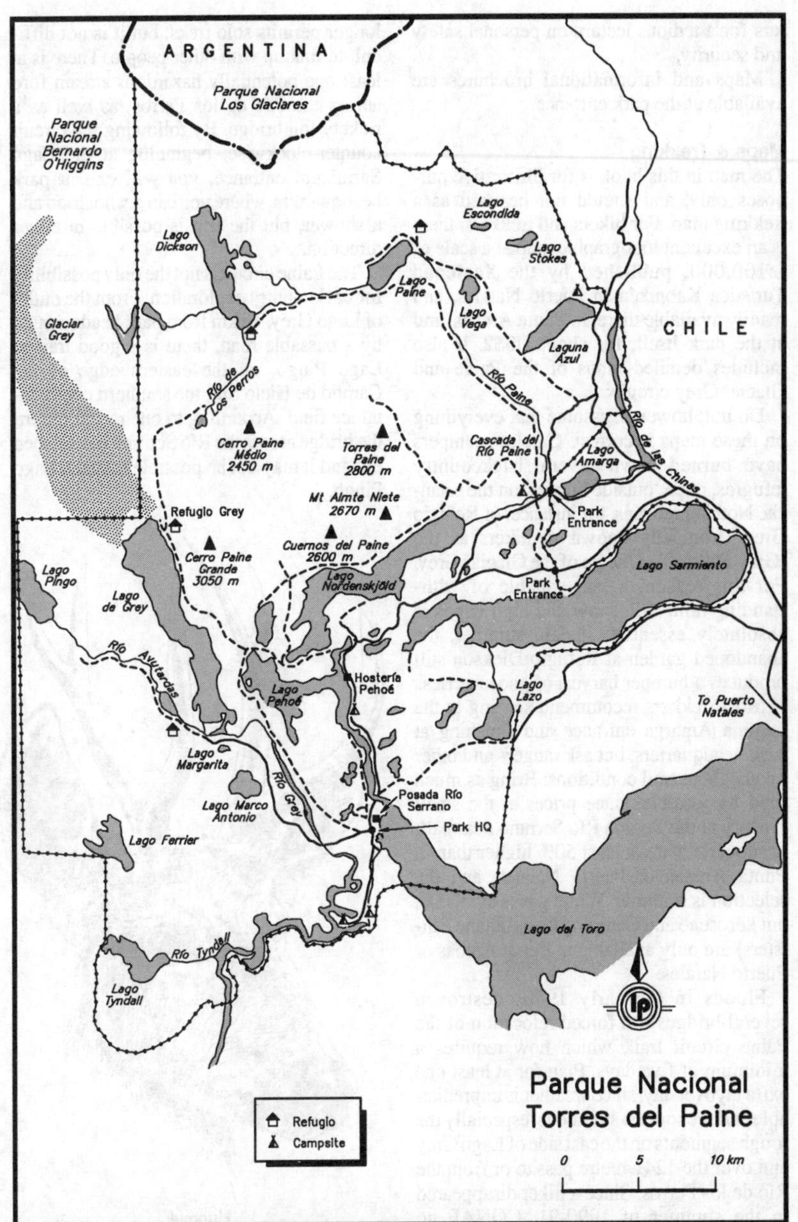
ARGENTINA
Parque Nacional Los Glaciares
Parque Nacional Bernardo O'Higgins
Lago Dickson
Lago Escondida
Lago Stokes
Lago Paine
Lago Vega
Laguna Azul
CHILE
Glaciar Grey
Río de Los Perros
Río Paine
Río de las Chinas
Cascada del Río Paine
Lago Amarga
Cerro Paine Médio 2450 m
Torres del Paine 2800 m
Mt Almte Nieto 2670 m
Park Entrance
Refugio Grey
Cerro Paine Grande 3050 m
Cuernos del Paine 2600 m
Lago Sarmiento
Lago Pingo
Lago de Grey
Lago Nordenskjöld
Park Entrance
Río Avutardas
Lago Pehoé
Hostería Pehoé
Lago Lazo
To Puerto Natales
Lago Margarita
Río Grey
Lago Marco Antonio
Posada Río Serrano
Park HQ
Lago Ferrier
Lago del Toro
Río Tyndall
Lago Tyndall
Parque Nacional Torres del Paine
Refugio
Campsite
0 5 10 km

ters for a tedious lecture on personal safety and security.

Maps and informational brochures are available at the park entrance.

Maps & Trekking

The map in this book is for illustrative purposes only, and should not be used as a trekking map. For hikers and trekkers, there is an excellent topographic map at a scale of 1:100,000, published by the Sociedad Turística Kaonikén in Puerto Natales, and readily available there, in Punta Arenas, and at the park itself, for about US$2. It also includes detailed maps of the Paine and Glaciar Grey circuits.

Do not, however, assume that everything on these maps is correct. Careless campers have burned down several backcountry refugios, once 'outside houses' on the estancia. Nothing remains, for instance, of Refugio Grey (ironically known to hikers as the 'Grey Hilton'), at the lip of the Glaciar Grey. For this reason, a tent capable of withstanding rain, hail, snow and high winds is absolutely essential. In late summer, the abandoned garden at Refugio Dickson still produces a bumper harvest of gooseberries.

Most trekkers recommend starting at the Laguna Amarga entrance and finishing at park headquarters, but ask rangers and other hikers about trail conditions. Bring as much food as possible, since prices at the small grocery at the Posada Río Serrano near park headquarters are at least 50% higher than in Punta Arenas or Puerto Natales, and the selection is minimal. White gas is available, but kerosene and Camping Gaz (butane canisters) are only available in Punta Arenas or Puerto Natales.

Floods in the early 1980s destroyed several bridges and forced relocation of the Paine circuit trail, which now requires a minimum of five days. Plan for at least one extra layover day, since weather is unpredictable and the route is strenuous, especially the rough segments on the east side of Lago Grey and over the 1241-metre pass to or from the Río de los Perros. Since a hiker disappeared in the summer of 1990-91, CONAF no longer permits solo treks, but it is not difficult to link up with other people. There is at least one potentially hazardous stream ford across the Río de los Perros, as well as a rickety log bridge. By following the circuit counter-clockwise, beginning at the Lago Sarmiento entrance, you will exit at park headquarters, where you can get hot food and a shower, but the trip is possible in either direction.

The Paine circuit is not the only possibility for backcountry exploration. From the outlet of Lago Grey, 18 km from park headquarters by a passable road, there is a good trail to Lago Pingo, on the eastern edge of the Campo de Hielo Sur, the southern continental ice field. According to one recent report, the bridge across the Río Serrano has washed out and it may not be possible to reach Lago Pingo.

Huemul

For more detailed information and maps, consult Clem Lindenmayer's *Trekking in the Patagonian Andes* (Lonely Planet Publications) and/or William Leitch's *South America's National Parks*, both of which feature extensive coverage of the park.

Places to Stay & Eat

There are two hotels, both often crowded in summer. At the *Hostería Pehoé*, on a small island in the lake of the same name and linked to the mainland by a footbridge, single/double rooms start at US$70/90 for views of the peaks called Cuernos del Paine (Horns of Paine) and Paine Grande, the highest point in the park. The hotel's restaurant and bar are open to the public. Bookings can be arranged in Punta Arenas (☎ 224223) or Puerto Natales (☎ 411442). Boat trips to the Glaciar Grey cost US$25 per person, weather permitting.

More economical is the *Posada Río Serrano*, a remodelled estancia building near park headquarters, where rooms start at US$24/31 with shared bath, but cost nearly double that with private bath. It has a reasonably priced restaurant and bar, with occasional, informal live entertainment. Arrange bookings in advance in Puerto Natales (☎ 411355).

Lower cost and even free accommodation exists. A short distance from Posada Río Serrano is a CONAF refugio for US$4 (including one hot shower), with floor space for your own sleeping bag. Other refugios, such as that at Pudeto on Lago Pehoé are free but *very* rustic. Organised camp sites, including those on Lago Pehoé and at Río Serrano, charge US$8 for up to six people, with firewood and hot showers (always available in the morning but in the evening by request only). At the more remote and rustic Laguna Azul site, which lacks showers, site charges are US$5 per night.

At Río Serrano, see Brigitte Buhoffer for horse riding for US$18 per day. Pack horses cost US$32 per day.

Getting There & Away

For details of public transportation to the park, see the Puerto Natales section above. Bus services leave passengers at the administración at Río Serrano, although you can disembark at Lago Sarmiento to begin the Paine circuit, or elsewhere upon request. Hitching from Puerto Natales is possible, but competition is considerable. A new and totally superfluous road is defacing the landscape between the Cueva del Milodón and the park entrance.

Summer bus services connect Torres del Paine and Calafate (Argentina) via the Río Don Guillermo border crossing and La Esperanza – enquire at the administración. If Calafate merchants drop their opposition, the much more convenient route via the Sierra Baguales, north of Laguna Azul, will permit direct travel to Parque Nacional Los Glaciares and its famous Moreno Glacier in only a few hours. At present, the trip requires a full day to Calafate alone.

PUERTO WILLIAMS

On Isla Navarino on the south side of the Beagle Channel, directly opposite Argentine Tierra del Fuego, Puerto Williams is a Chilean naval base and settlement with a population of about 1000. It was nearby that Fitzroy encountered the Yahgan Indians who accompanied the *Beagle* back to England for several years. Missionaries in the mid-19th century and fortune-seekers during the local gold rush of the 1890s established a permanent European presence.

A few people of Yahgan descent still reside near Puerto Williams. A territorial dispute over the three small islands of Lennox, Nueva and Picton, east of Navarino, nearly brought Argentina and Chile to war in 1978, but papal intervention defused the situation and the islands remain in Chilean possession.

Information

There is a cluster of public services, including telephone, post office, supermarket and tourist office, on President Ibáñez. Money exchange is possible at the only travel agency.

Things to See

The **Museo Martín Gusinde**, with exhibits on local natural history and anthropology, honours the German priest and ethnographer who worked among the Yahgans. It's open Monday to Friday from 9 am to 1 pm, and daily from 3 to 6 pm. East of town, at **Ukika**, live the few remaining Yahgans. There is good hiking in the surrounding countryside, but the changeable weather demands warm, water-resistant clothing.

Places to Stay & Eat

Residencial Onashaga, in the centre, is basic but clean and comfortable for US$9 a single. Near the up-market, highly recommended *Pensión Temuco*, it is possible to camp for US$9, or US$18 with meals. Winter prices may be negotiable at *Hostería Patagonia* (☎ 226100 in Punta Arenas), which has singles/doubles for US$75/90. Both hotels serve meals.

Getting There & Away

Air DAP flies to and from Punta Arenas on Tuesdays for US$62 a single, slightly cheaper return. Seats are limited and advance reservations essential. DAP flights to Antarctica make a brief stopover here.

Boat Chilean naval supply vessels, which sail irregularly between Punta Arenas and Puerto Williams, sometimes take passengers. On Saturdays, at least during summer, it is possible to cross from Ushuaia to Puerto Williams, or vice versa, for US$50. Enquire at the tourist office in either place.

Tierra del Fuego

From the 16th-century voyages of Magellan to the 19th-century explorations of Captain Robert Fitzroy and Charles Darwin on the *Beagle* and even to the present, Tierra del Fuego, this 'uttermost part of the earth', has held an ambivalent fascination for travellers from around the world. For more than three centuries, its climate and terrain discouraged

Ferdinand Magellan

European settlement, yet native people considered it a 'land of plenty'. Its scenery, with glaciers descending nearly to the ocean in many places, is truly enthralling.

Yahgan Indians, now nearly extinct, built the fires which prompted Europeans to give this region its name, now famous throughout the world.

Tierra del Fuego consists of one large island, Isla Grande de Tierra del Fuego, which is shared between Chile and Argentina, and many smaller islands which belong to Chile, only a few of which are inhabited. The Strait of Magellan separates the archipelago from the South American mainland.

History

While Magellan passed through the straits which bear his name in 1520, neither he nor anyone else had any immediate interest in the surrounding land and its people. Seeking a passage to the spice islands of Asia, early navigators feared and detested the stiff westerlies, hazardous currents, and violent seas which impeded their progress. Consequently the Ona, Haush, Yahgan and Alacaluf Indians who peopled the area faced no immediate competition for their lands.

All these groups were mobile hunters and gatherers. The Ona, also known as Selknam, and Haush subsisted primarily on land-based resources, hunting the guanaco and dressing in its skins, while the Yahgans and Alacalufes, known collectively as Canoe Indians, lived primarily on fish, shellfish, and marine mammals. The Yahgans, also known as the Yamana, consumed the fungus known as Indian bread *(Cytarria* species), which is a parasite on the ñire, a species of southern beech. Despite the usually inclement weather, the Yahgans used little or no clothing, but had constant fires, even in their bark canoes, to keep them warm.

The collapse of Spain's American empire opened the area to European settlement and brought about the rapid demise of the indigenous Fuegians, whom Europeans struggled to understand. Darwin, visiting the area in 1834, wrote that the difference between the Fuegians, 'among the most abject and miserable creatures I ever saw', and Europeans was greater than that between wild and domestic animals. On a previous voyage, Captain Fitzroy had abducted several Yahgans who, after several years of missionary education in England, he returned to their distant home.

From the 1850s, missionaries attempted to catechise the Fuegians. The earliest attempt ended in failure with the death by starvation of British evangelist Allen Gardiner. Gardiner's successors, working from a base at Keppel Island in the Falklands, were more successful, despite the massacre of one party by Fuegians at Isla Navarino. Thomas Bridges, a young man on Keppel Island, learned to speak the Yahgan language and became one of the first settlers at Ushuaia, in what is now Argentine Tierra del Fuego. His son Lucas Bridges, born at Ushuaia in 1874, left a fascinating memoir of his experiences among the Yahgans and Onas entitled *The Uttermost Part of the Earth*.

Although the Bridges family and others who followed them had the best motives, the increasing European presence exposed the Fuegians to diseases, such as typhoid and measles, to which they had little resistance. One measles epidemic wiped out half the native population in the district, and recurrent contagion nearly extinguished them over the next half century. Some early sheep ranchers made things worse with their violent persecution of the Indians, who had resorted to preying on domestic flocks as guanaco populations declined.

Since no European power had any interest in settling the region until Britain occupied the Falklands in the 1770s, Spain too paid little attention. The successor governments of Argentina and Chile felt differently. Chile's presence on the Strait of Magellan and increasing British missionary activity spurred Argentina to formalise its authority at Ushuaia in 1884, with the installation of a territorial governor the following year. International border issues in the area were only finally resolved in 1984, when an Argentine plebiscite ratified diplomatic settlement of a dispute over three small islands in the Beagle Channel, which had lingered on for decades and nearly brought the two countries to open warfare in 1979.

Despite minor gold and lumber booms, Ushuaia was for many years primarily a penal settlement for both political prisoners and common criminals. For a few people, sheep farming brought great wealth and it still provides the island's economic backbone, although the north-eastern sector near San Sebastián has substantial petroleum and natural gas reserves. Since the 1960s, the tourist industry has become so important that flights and hotels are often heavily booked during the summer. The spectacular mountain and coastal scenery in the immediate countryside of Ushuaia, including Parque Nacional Tierra del Fuego, attracts both Argentines and foreigners.

Geography & Climate

Surrounded by the South Atlantic Ocean, the Strait of Magellan and the south-easternmost part of the Pacific Ocean, the archipelago of Tierra del Fuego has a land area of roughly 76,000 sq km, about the size of Ireland or South Carolina. The Chilean-Argentine border runs directly south from Cabo Espíritu Santo, at the eastern entrance of the strait, to the Beagle Channel, where it trends eastward to the Channel's mouth at Isla Nueva. Most of Isla Grande del Tierra del Fuego belongs to Chile, but the Argentine side is more densely populated, with the substantial towns of Ushuaia and Río Grande. Porvenir is the only significant town on the Chilean side.

The plains of northern Isla Grande are a landscape of almost unrelenting wind, enormous flocks of Corriedale sheep, and oil derricks. The mountainous southern part of the island offers scenic glaciers, lakes, rivers and sea coasts. The maritime climate is surprisingly mild, even in winter, but its changeability makes warm, dry clothing important, especially when you're hiking or at higher elevations. The Cordillera Darwin and the Sierra de Beauvoir, reaching up to 2500 metres in the west, intercept Antarctic storms, leaving the plains around Río Grande much drier than areas nearer the Beagle Channel.

The higher southern rainfall supports dense forests of both deciduous and evergreen southern beech, while the drier north consists of extensive native pasture grasses and low-growing shrubs. Storms batter the bogs and truncated beeches of the remote southern and western parts of the archipelago. Guanaco, rhea and condor can still be seen in the north, but marine mammals and shore birds are the most common wildlife in the tourist destinations along the Beagle Channel.

Getting There & Around

Travelling overland, the simplest route to Argentine Tierra del Fuego is via Porvenir, across the Strait of Magellan from Punta Arenas. There is also a ferry across the narrows at Punta Delgada, but no public transportation to it. The principal border crossing is at San Sebastián, a truly desolate place about midway between Porvenir and Río Grande. Except in the towns themselves, all roads are gravelled, and some are in very bad condition.

For more information about the formalities required for a visit to Argentina, see the Facts for the Visitor chapter, early in this book. The nearest Argentine consulate is in Punta Arenas.

PORVENIR

Porvenir, founded less than a century ago to service the new sheep estancias across the Strait of Magellan from Punta Arenas, is the largest settlement on Chilean Tierra del Fuego. Its 6400 inhabitants include many of Yugoslav descent, to whom there are monuments commemorating the brief gold rush of the 1880s and their continuing presence in the area.

Porvenir only becomes visible as the ferry approaches its sheltered, nearly hidden harbour. The waterfront road, or costanera, leads from the ferry terminal to a cluster of corroding, metal-clad Victorians which belie the town's optimistic name ('the future'). The beautifully manicured plaza has a worthwhile museum, but for most travellers Porvenir is only a stopover en route to or from Ushuaia, on the Argentine side of Tierra del Fuego.

Tourist Office

For tourist information, visit the kiosk on the costanera between Mardones and Muñoz Gamero. Ferry tickets to Punta Arenas are also available, and the bus to the ferry terminal arrives and departs from here. There's also the Oficina de Informaciones, at Valdivieso 402, on the plaza

Museo Provincial

The museum, on the main plaza, has natural history, archaeological and historical exhibits, including one on early Chilean cinematography. Its hours are weekdays from 8.30 am to 12.30 pm and 2.30 to 6 pm.

Places to Stay & Eat

For its size, Porvenir has good accommodation and food. The cheapest rooms are at the *Residencial Colón* (☎ 580108), Damián Riobó 108, where rooms with shared bath cost around US$5 per person. Other reasonable choices are the *Hotel Rosas* (☎ 580088), Phillipi 296, at US$10.50/16.50 for a single/double, and the slightly dearer *Hotel Central* (☎ 580077), at Phillipi 298. For up-market comfort, try *Hostería Los Flamencos*

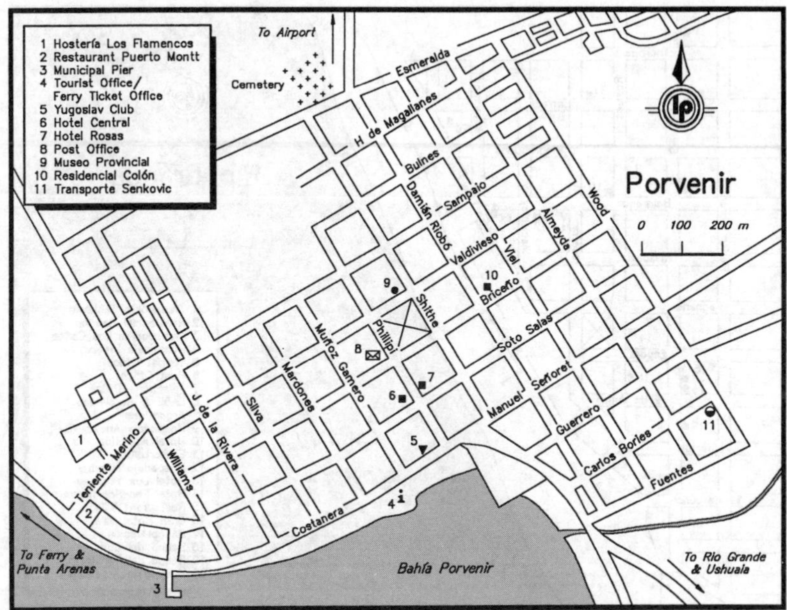

(☎ 580049), on Teniente Merino, where prices are US$53/62.

Hotel Rosas has a good, inexpensive restaurant specialising in seafood. The Yugoslav Club, on the costanera, has also been recommended, along with *Restaurant Puerto Montt*, on the costanera at Teniente Merino.

Getting There & Away

Air Aerovías DAP (☎ 580089), on Manuel Señoret, flies across the strait to Punta Arenas in 10 minutes for US$13.50, twice daily, from Monday to Saturday.

Bus Transporte Senkovic, Carlos Bories 295, departs on Tuesday and Saturday for Río Grande, in Argentine Tierra del Fuego, for US$11. From there it is possible to make connections to Ushuaia.

Boat Transbordadora Broom operates a car/passenger ferry to Punta Arenas; for details see the Punta Arenas section. The crossing takes about 2½ hours. The bus to the ferry terminal, leaving from the tourist kiosk about an hour before the ferry's departure, provides a farewell tour of Porvenir for US$0.75. Taxis cost at least four times as much.

RÍO GRANDE (Argentina)

Founded in 1894, Río Grande is a bleak, windswept petroleum and agricultural service centre on the estuary of its namesake river. Most visitors will pass through quickly en route to Ushuaia, but Río Grande is not completely without interest.

Orientation & Information

Most important services are close to the main plaza. For tourist information, visit the tourist office (☎ 21701) on the corner of Estrada and Lasserie. For money exchange, try Banco de la Nación Argentina (Banco Nación), on San Martín near 9 de Julio (do not confuse the similarly named streets 9 de

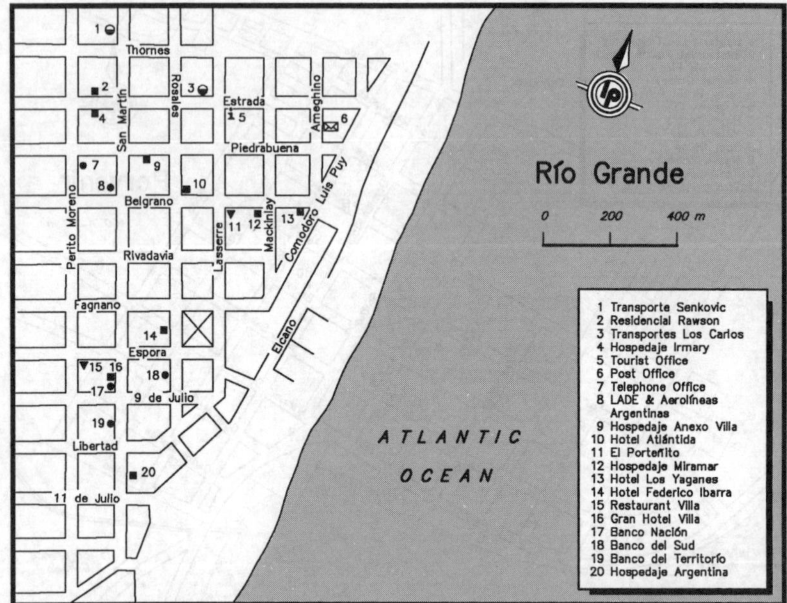

Julio and 11 de Julio, which are parallel but two blocks apart). The post office is at Ameghino 712, between Piedrabuena and Estrada, while telephone services are at Piedrabuena 787, on the corner of Perito Moreno.

Places to Stay

Because of its large number of single labourers, Río Grande is notorious for lack of hotel space, especially at the bottom end of the scale. Patience and perseverance are necessary to find acceptable accommodation, which may be a dormitory bed. Single women will probably prefer mid-range hotels.

Places to Stay – bottom end

Hospedaje Argentina (☎ 22365), at San Martín 64 between 11 de Julio and Libertad, is probably the best bargain in town, but its dormitory-style accommodation is often full. *Hospedaje Irmary*, at Estrada 743 between San Martín and Moreno, has singles at US$8, as does *Hotel Anexo Villa*, at Piedrabuena 641 between San Martín and Rosales.

Places to Stay – middle

Hospedaje Miramar (☎ 22462), Mackinlay 595 near Belgrano, one of the best hotels in town, has clean, well heated singles/doubles at US$8/11 with shared bath and US$11/15 with private bath. *Gran Hotel Villa* (☎ 22312), San Martín 277 between 9 de Julio and Espora, is comparable. It has a restaurant/confitería downstairs. *Residencial Rawson*, Estrada 750 across from Hospedaje Irmary, is slightly dearer.

Places to Stay – top end

All top-end hotels charge about the same, US$44/58. *Posada de los Sauces* (☎ 22895), Elcano 839, has been recommended enthusiastically. *Hotel Isla del Mar* (☎ 21518), Güemes 963, also has a good reputation. *Los*

Yaganes, Belgrano 319 (☎ 22372), belongs to the Automóvil Club Argentino (ACA) and offers a 30% discount to club members. Also in this category are *Hotel Federico Ibarra* (☎ 21071), on Rosales near Fagnano, and *Hotel Atlántida* (☎ 22592) at Belgrano 582.

Places to Eat

The previously mentioned hotels Gran Hotel Villa, Hotel Ibarra and Hotel Los Yaganes all have restaurants. You can also try *El Porteñito*, at Lasserre 566 near Belgrano. For short orders and sandwiches, there are many confiterías in and around the centre, including the one at Residencial Rawson. *Pizzería Colombia*, on Rosales across from the Hotel Atlántida, has good food and is open all night.

Getting There & Away

Air Aerolíneas Argentinas (☎ 22748, 22749) and LADE (☎ 21151) are both at San Martín 607, on the corner of Belgrano. Aerolíneas has daily flights to Buenos Aires. LADE flies daily to Calafate, Ushuaia (US$39), and Río Gallegos, with connections to Buenos Aires and northern Patagonian destinations such as Comodoro Rivadavia and Trelew. Líneas Aéreas Kaikén, a private airline, serves the same destinations as LADE.

Austral (☎ 21388) is at Perito Moreno 352. Its daily flights from Ushuaia continue to Río Gallegos, Comodoro Rivadavia, Bahía Blanca and Buenos Aires. Connections from the north are similar.

Bus Transportes Los Carlos (☎ 21188), Estrada 568, has two daily buses to Ushuaia during summer, at 12.30 and 7.30 pm, perhaps less frequently during winter when snow can close the Paso Garibaldi. The four-hour trip costs about US$20.

Transporte Senkovic (☎ 22345), San Martín 959, departs on Wednesday and Saturday at 6 am to Porvenir, in Chilean Tierra del Fuego, with ferry connections to Punta Arenas. The seven-hour trip costs about US$20, and tickets may not be available on the day of the trip. Buses Pacheco, Bilbao 813, is more expensive at US$34 a single to Punta Arenas (including the ferry across the Strait of Magellan). Reservations are essential.

Car Rental Given limited public transportation, fishing trips and other excursions outside town are much simpler with a rental car, available from A-1 (☎ 22657), on the corner of Belgrano and Ameghino.

AROUND RÍO GRANDE

Things to See

The historic **Museo Salesiano**, 11 km north of town on Ruta 3, was established by the missionary order which converted the Indians in this part of the island. The museum has exhibits on geology, natural history and ethnography. **Estancia María Behety**, 20 km west, features the world's largest shearing shed. The Río Grande meat-freezing plant or **frigorífico**, can process up to 2400 sheep per day. **Lago Kami** (Kami is the Indian name; it's also also known as Lago Fagnanoi), the huge glacial trough on Ruta 3 between Río Grande and Ushuaia, merits a visit. *Hostería Kaikén* offers lodging for US$14 per person.

Fishing

Fishing is a popular recreational activity in many nearby rivers. For information on guided trips on the Fuego, Menéndez, Candelaria, Ewan and MacLennan rivers, contact the Club de Pesca John Goodall. One highly recommended place is the *Hostería San Pablo*, 120 km south-east of Río Grande, where there is good fly fishing for trout and salmon on the Río Irigoyen.

USHUAIA (Argentina)

Argentines and Chileans dispute which is the world's southernmost city, but fast-growing Ushuaia clearly surpasses modest Puerto Williams. In 1870, the British-based South American Missionary Society made Ushuaia its first permanent outpost in the Fuegian region, but only artefacts, memories and Thomas Bridges' famous dictionary remain to tell of the Yahgan Indians who once flourished in the area. The nearby Estancia

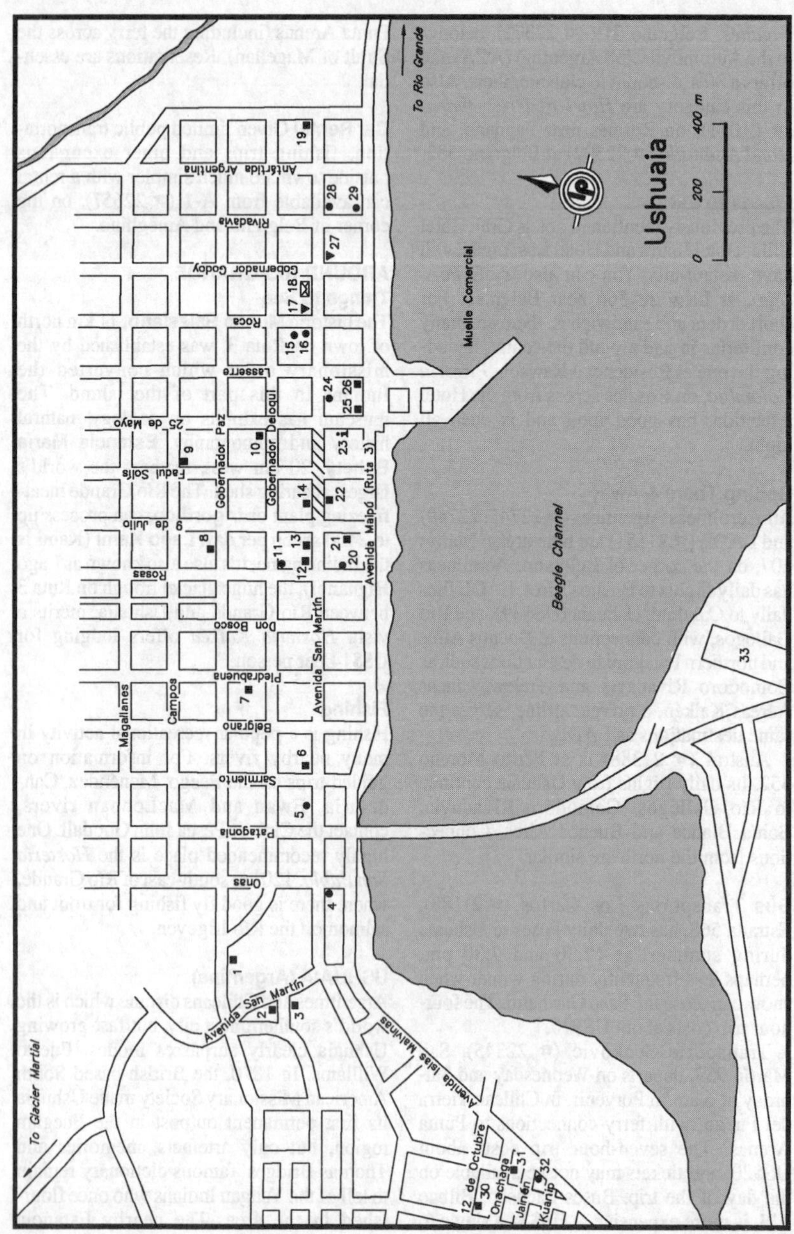
Ushuaia
0 200 400 m
To Rio Grande
To Glacier Martial
Muelle Comercial
Beagle Channel
Avenida Maipú (Ruta 3)
Avenida San Martín
Avenida Islas Malvinas
Gobernador Deloqui
Gobernador Paz
25 de Mayo
Fadul Solís
9 de Julio
Rosas
Don Bosco
Piedrabuena
Campos
Magallanes
Belgrano
Sarmiento
Patagonia
Onas
Antártida Argentina
Rivadavia
Gobernador Godoy
Roca
Lasserre
12 de Octubre
Onachaga
Jainén
Kuanip
1
2
3
4
5
6
7
8
9
10
11
12
13
14
15
16
17
18
19
20
21
22
23
24
25
26
27
28
29
30
31
32
33

■ PLACES TO STAY

1 Hospedaje América
2 Hotel Antártida
3 Hotel Las Lengas
6 Hostería Monte Cervantes
7 Hostería Mustapic
8 Pensión Rosita
9 Hospedaje Velásquez
10 Hospedaje Malvinas
12 Hotel Cabo de Hornos
13 Hospedaje No 845
14 Hospedaje César
19 Hotel Mafalda
21 Hospedaje Ona
22 Residencial Capri
25 Hotel Canal Beagle
26 Hotel Albatros
30 Hotel Maitén
31 Hospedaje Fernández

▼ PLACES TO EAT

17 Pizzería Ideal
27 Moustacchio

OTHER

4 Supermarket
5 Administración del Parque Nacional Tierra del Fuego
11 Laundrette
15 Telefónica Argentina
16 Aerolíneas Argentinas
18 Post Office
20 Transporte Los Carlos
23 Tourist Office
24 LADE & Austral
28 Banco de la Nación
29 Museo Territorial Fin del Mundo
32 Chilean Consulate
33 Airport

Harberton still belongs to descendents of the Bridges family.

Between 1884 and 1947, Argentina incarcerated many of its most notorious criminals and political prisoners here and on remote Isla de Los Estados (Staten Island). Since 1950, Ushuaia has been an important naval base, supporting Argentine claims to Antarctica, and in recent years it has become an important tourist destination. Wages are higher here than in central Argentina, but so are living expenses. Forestry, fishing, and tourism are the most important industries, although efforts to attract electronics assembly have had some success. Ushuaia is ostensibly a free port, but foreign visitors will find few real bargains compared with those in Punta Arenas.

Over the past two decades, the town itself has sprawled and spread from its original site on the Beagle Channel, but the setting is still one of the most dramatic in the world, with jagged glacial horns rising nearly 1500 metres above the sea. This surrounding landscape offers trekking, fishing and skiing, as well as the opportunity to go as far south as roads go. Ruta 3, Argentina's Atlantic coast highway, ends at Bahía Lapataia in Parque Nacional Tierra del Fuego, 3242 km from Buenos Aires.

Orientation

Ushuaia is on the north shore of the Beagle Channel, its harbor protected by the nearby peninsula on which the airport has been constructed. The shoreline Avenida Maipú, which becomes Avenida Islas Malvinas west of the cemetery, is also Ruta 3 and leads west to Parque Nacional Tierra del Fuego. The waterfront is a good place to watch shorebirds.

The principal commercial street is Avenida San Martín, one block north of Maipú. Most hotels and tourist services are within a few blocks of here. Unlike most Argentine cities, Ushuaia has no central plaza, but San Martín is a pedestrian mall between 9 de Julio and 25 de Mayo, with benches and a children's playground. North of San Martín, streets rise very steeply, providing good views of the Beagle Channel.

Several streets in central Ushuaia have been renamed in recent years, so ask for clarification if necessary.

Information

Tourist Office The tourist office (☎ 21423) has moved to new offices at 25 de Mayo 50, between Maipú and San Martín; there is also an entrance at San Martín 638. The friendly, patient and helpful staff speak some English, have a complete list of hotel accommodation and current prices, and will assist in finding a room with private families – although one correspondent reports they will only do so in high season, from mid-November to Easter, when all the hotels are full. There is a small airport branch, open for arriving flights.

Money Banco Nación is on San Martín near Rivadavia, but collects horrendous commissions on travellers' cheques – as much as 25% on a US$50 cheque. Other banks charge lower commissions, but even the most reasonable, Banco del Sud at Maipú 761, collects 8%. Try to change cash in the morning when banks are open, rather than in the afternoon when they are closed and informal rates are extortionate. The cambio at the tourist office, open from 4 to 7.30 pm daily, collects 10% on travellers' cheques.

Post & Telecommunications ENCOTEL, the Post office, is on Avenida San Martín on the corner of Gobernador Godoy. Telefónica Argentina is at Roca 154, just north of San Martín.

Consulates Chile has a consulate at Avenida Islas Malvinas 236, on the corner of Jainén. If you're crossing into Chile via Parque Nacional Tierra del Fuego, obtain authorisation here first.

Books & Bookshops Rae Natalie Prosser de Goodall's detailed bilingual guidebook *Tierra del Fuego* is essential for anyone spending more than a few days on the island. A new edition was due out in late 1991, and should be available both in Buenos Aires and local bookshops – try the museum or Librería del Sol, on 9 de Julio between San Martín and Maipú, which carries books in Spanish and English.

Museo Territorial Fin del Mundo

On the waterfront on the corner of Maipú and Rivadavia, this museum has an informed, enthusiastic staff which oversees exhibits on natural history, Indian life, the early penal colonies (complete with photographic rogues' gallery), and replicas of an early general store and bank. The museum also has a bookshop and a good specialised library. By request, the museum or the post office will put a special 'Ushuaia – Fin del Mundo' stamp in your passport.

Well worth the admission charge of US$1.50, the museum is open weekdays from 3 to 6 pm, and weekends from 4 to 8 pm. Hours may vary in winter. At 5 pm daily, museum personnel lead tours of the former prison, now part of the naval base at the east end of San Martín.

Glaciar Martial

Just within the borders of Parque Nacional Tierra del Fuego, Glaciar Martial is reached by a magnificent walk which begins from the west end of Avenida San Martín, passes the national parks office, and climbs the zigzag road (with many short cuts for hikers) to the ski run seven km north-west of town. It is possible to hitch or take a taxi to the chairlift which sometimes operates in summer (when it is functioning, the lift fare is about US$5 and saves an hour's walk). From the base of the lift, the glacier is about a two-hour walk, with awesome panoramas of Ushuaia and the Beagle Channel. Weather is very changeable, so take warm, dry clothing and sturdy footwear. Other options in the Parque Nacional Tierra del Fuego are described in the next section.

Organised Tours

Local operators offer tours to the principal tourist attractions in and around Ushuaia, including Parque Nacional Tierra del Fuego (see following). Among them are Rumbo Sur (☎ 21139) at San Martín 342, and Turismo Alternativo Caminante (☎ 22723), Deloquí 368, which specialises in trekking to destinations like Lago Fagnano. One reader has praised Aptatur on San Martín for close attention to travellers' wishes for the most inclusive itinerary at the most reasonable price.

Boat trips, with destinations including Isla de Pájaros, Isla Bridges, and the sea lion colony at Isla de los Lobos, are popular during summer and throughout the year. The catamaran *Ana B* leaves from the Muelle Comercial (commercial jetty) opposite Hotel Albatros, and costs about US$26 for a three-hour excursion. The most common species you'll see is the southern sea lion *Otaria flavescens*, whose thick mane will make you wonder why Spanish speakers call it *lobo marino* (sea wolf). Fur seals, nearly extinct because of over-exploitation during the past century, may be seen in small numbers. Isla de Pájaros has many species of birds, including extensive cormorant colonies. In summer, excursions may be extended to Lapataia, Estancia Harberton and Puerto Williams, across the channel in Chile.

One correspondent recommended the full-day boat trip on the *Tres Marías*, which includes a superb seafood dinner. Skipper Hector Monsalve (☎ 21897), Avenida Romero 514, speaks a bit of English and will take a minimum of four passengers and maximum of eight for US$60 per person.

Trips to historic Estancia Harberton, east of Ushuaia, can be arranged with sufficient notice, but no one should arrive unannounced. There are also city tours, excursions over Paso Garibaldi to Lago Fagnano and Río Grande, and various other cruises. The tourist office provides a useful descriptive brochure.

Fishing

Fishing is a popular pastime for both Argentines and foreigners. Get the required licence from the Gobernación in Ushuaia and enquire there for other regulations. Spinning and fly casting are the most common means of hooking brown trout, rainbow trout, Atlantic salmon, and others. The nearest site is Río Pipo, five km west of town. It is possible to visit the fish hatchery at Río Olivia, two km beyond. The tourist office has a good informational brochure with other recommendations.

Places to Stay – bottom end

Since the apparent closure of the truly squalid but very cheap *Hotel Las Goletas*, Maipú 857, there is little real budget accommodation in Ushuaia. If you're really desperate, check to see if it has reopened.

The next cheapest choice is *Hospedaje Ona*, 9 de Julio 27 near Maipú, where dormitory-style beds cost US$5. Weekly rates are slightly lower.

For a more family-oriented environment, try friendly *Hospedaje Velásquez* (beware the homemade jam), Fadul Solís 361 at Campos (ex-Colón), or *Pensión Rosita*, on Gobernador Paz between Rosas (ex-Triunvirato) and 9 de Julio, for about US$10 to US$12 per person. *Hospedaje América* (☎ 23858), Gobernador Paz 1600, has singles/doubles at US$12/16. Opinions of *Residencial Capri* (☎ 21833), San Martín 720, which charges US$15, per person, are tepid, as are the showers.

Proprietors of many *casas de familia* meet incoming flights, but the tourist office may also arrange such accommodation which is much cheaper than hotels. One place which has been highly recommended is that at Primer Argentino 176, outside the centre. Near the airport and the trail to Glaciar Martial, *Elvira's house* (☎ 23123) at Fuegia Basket 419 is slightly cheaper but also warmly recommended.

Camping There is a free municipal camp site at Río Pipo, five km west of town, but facilities are minimal. Other camp sites, including some free ones, are found at Parque Nacional Tierra del Fuego.

Places to Stay – middle

Mid-range hotels are easier to find, but still may be very crowded in summer. The enthusiastically recommended *Hospedaje Fernández* (☎ 21453), Onachaga 68, has doubles at US$19. Other possibilities in this range are *Hospedaje César* (☎ 21460) at San Martín 753 for US$17/27, *Hospedaje Malvinas* (☎ 22626) at Deloquí 609 for US$25/35, and *Hotel Maitén* (☎ 22745) at 12 de Octubre 140 for US$18/22.

Places to Stay – top end

Waterfront hotels have the finest views and

highest prices. Among them are *Hotel Albatros* (☎ 22504), Maipú 505 near Lasserre, at US$31/60 with breakfast, and ACA's *Hotel Canal Beagle* (☎ 21117), Maipú 599 near 25 de Mayo, at US$44/58. Also central are *Hotel Cabo de Hornos* (☎ 22187), San Martín near Rosas, for US$38/45 with breakfast, and the new and pleasant *Hotel Mafalda* (☎ 22373) at San Martín 15 for US$38/50, breakfast not included.

Outside the centre, but still within reasonable walking distance, are the Tudor-style *Hostería Monte Cervantes* (☎ 22153), San Martín near Sarmiento, and the highly recommended *Hotel Antártida* (☎ 21807) at San Martín 1600 for US$38/47.

At *Estancia Río Pipo* (☎ 23411), five km west of town, cabañas rent for US$78/88.

Places to Eat

Food which is both cheap and good is not easily available in Ushuaia and, at the more expensive restaurants, reservations are essential for groups of any size. The lively *Pizzería Ideal*, at San Martín 393 near Roca, is good, reasonable and open when many other places are closed. The previously mentioned *Hotel Mustapic* has fairly reasonable three-course meals.

Costlier, but good value with excellent food and service, is *Moustacchio* (☎ 23308), at San Martín 298. *Tante Elvira* (☎ 21982, 21249), San Martín 234, also has a good reputation. One reader praised *Parrilla Tío Carlos*, Campos 758, for high quality food and large portions. Beware the expensive but erratic *Casita Azul*, at San Martín near 9 de Julio.

Getting There & Away

Air Ushuaia has frequent air connections with Buenos Aires and with other parts of Patagonia. Aerolíneas Argentinas (☎ 21910) recently moved to Roca 116 between San Martín and Deloquí, flies to Buenos Aires with stopovers at various intermediate points, such as Río Gallegos, Trelew, and Bahía Blanca. On Monday, Wednesday, Friday and Saturday, departure time is 12.50 pm, while on Tuesday, Thursday and Sunday there are flights at 2.20 and 5.45 pm. Austral (☎ 23235), at San Martín 638, has daily flights to Río Gallegos and Buenos Aires at 10 am. One-way fares to Buenos Aires cost around US$250.

LADE (☎ 21123), San Martín 564, flies to Calafate via Río Grande (US$35) and Río Gallegos (US$60) on Tuesday and Thursdays. Líneas Aéreas Kaikén (☎ 23049), Antártida Argentina 75 near San Martín, serves the same destinations, plus Punta Arenas (US$105). It also operates charter overflights of Cape Horn. Flights to Punta Arenas leave on Tuesday, Thursday and Saturday at 8 am.

Ushuaia's airport is on the peninsula across from the waterfront, linked to town by a causeway. Cabs are reasonable, but there are also buses along Maipú and it's not even that far to walk unless you have very heavy or awkward baggage. The short runway, steep approach and frequent high, shifting winds make landing at Ushuaia an adventure which timid fliers may wish to avoid.

Bus Transporte Los Carlos (☎ 22337), Rosas 85, crosses the Paso Pass via Lago Kami to Río Grande, where connections can be made to Porvenir (Chile) and Punta Arenas. Buses leave daily at noon and at 7 pm. The four-hour trip costs about US$20. It is possible to get off the bus en route, for example at Paso Garibaldi or Lago Kami, and continue by a later bus, paying the driver for the second segment.

Buses Tolkeyén (☎ 21117), in the Hotel Canal Beagle at 25 de Mayo 45, goes directly to Punta Arenas on Thursday at 9.30 am, for US$45 a single, taking about 14 hours.

For transportation to Parque Nacional Tierra del Fuego, see the previous Organised Tours section.

Boat On Mondays and Saturdays, if demand is sufficient, a ferry takes passengers from Ushuaia across the Beagle Channel to Puerto Williams, on Navarino Island in Chile, for US$50. The crossing takes 1½ hours, but service is erratic, so confirm the details.

Top : Río Paine, Parque Nacional Torres del Paine (GL)
Bottom : Guanacos, Parque Nacional Torres del Paine (AS)

Top : Island children, Isla Robinson Crusoe (WB)
Bottom : Ruins at Puerto Inglés, Isla Robinson Crusoe (WB)

From Puerto Williams, there are weekly air and sea connections with Punta Arenas.

Car Rental Although rural public transport is better in Ushuaia than in Río Grande, it is still limited. There are, however, several rental car agencies. U-Rent-a-Car operates from the same offices as the previously mentioned Líneas Aéreas Kaikén. Other agencies include Rent Austral (☎ 22422) at Gobernador Paz 1022, and Autograd (☎ 22723) at Deloquí 368. Rental charges are very high, and can exceed US$100 per day.

PARQUE NACIONAL TIERRA DEL FUEGO (Argentina)

The 63,000-hectare Parque Nacional Tierra del Fuego, extending from the Beagle Channel in the south along the Chilean border to beyond Lago Kami (or Lago Fagnano) in the north, is the only coastal national park in Argentina. Just 18 km west of Ushuaia, its forests, bays, lakes, rivers, peaks and glaciers attract many visitors and hikers, both Argentine and foreign, although the park lacks the integrated network of hiking trails of Chile's Torres del Paine. There are, however, many shorter hiking trails and one major trek which deserve mention. The seven-km walk to Glaciar Martial is described in the Ushuaia section.

Three species of southern beech *(Nothofagus)* dominate the dense native forests. These trees are known by their common names coihue, lenga, and ñire. The evergreen coihue and the deciduous lenga thrive on the heavy coastal rainfall at lower elevations. The deciduous ñire tints the Fuegian hillsides during autumn. Other tree species are much less significant and conspicuous.

The *Sphagnum* peat bogs in some parts of the park support ferns, colourful wildflowers, and some insectivorous plants; these may be seen on the self-guided Laguna Negra nature trail. To avoid damage to the bog and danger to yourself, stay on the trail, part of which consists of a catwalk for easier passage across the swampy terrain.

Park mammals are few, although guanaco and foxes exist. Visitors are most likely to see two unfortunate introductions, the European rabbit and the North American beaver, both of which have caused ecological havoc and proved impossible to eradicate. The rabbits number up to 70 per hectare in some areas, while the beaver's handiwork is visible in the ponds and dead beeches along the Sendero de los Castores (Trail of the Beavers) to Bahía Lapataia. Originally introduced at Lago Kami in the 1940s, beavers quickly spread throughout the island.

Bird life is much more abundant, especially along the coastal section, including Lapataia and Ensenada bays. The Andean condor and the maritime black-browed albatross overlap ranges here, although neither is common. Numerous species of shore-birds such as cormorants, gulls, terns, oystercatchers, grebes, steamer ducks and kelp geese are common. The large, striking upland goose *(cauquén)* is widely distributed farther inland. Space prohibits a detailed description here, but an outstanding guide is Claudio Venegas Canelo's *Aves de Patagonia y Tierra del Fuego Chileno-Argentina* (Punta Arenas, 1986).

Marine mammals are most commonly seen on offshore islands.

Canquén

Trekking
Most park trails are relatively short, but at least two merit longer trips. With permission from the Chilean consulate and Argentine authorities in Ushuaia, it is possible to hike from Lapataia into Chile, along the north shore of Lago Roca.

There is also an extended trek up the Río Pipo, across the Montes Martial (Martial Mountains) to Lago Kami. This rugged trip, 30 km each way, begins at the Río Pipo camp site, and can also be done as a loop, returning to Ushuaia via the Río Carbajal and the Río Olivia. Experienced, independent hikers can undertake this trek on their own, but travel agencies in Ushuaia can also assist (see Organised Tours). Take warm, dry clothing, good footwear and a sleeping bag, a tent, and plenty of food.

Camping
Since the *Hostería Alakush* at Lago Roca burned down, camping is the only alternative for those wishing to stay here.

The only organised camp site within the park, also at Lago Roca, has hot showers, a confitería and groceries. At US$6 per person, it is not really cheap, but there are free camp sites without facilities at Lapataia, Ensenada and Río Pipo.

Getting There & Away
In summer, Línea Parque Nacional leaves daily in summer from Maipú 329 in Ushuaia, at 10 am, 3.30 and 7.30 pm, returning from the Lago Roca camping ground at 11 am, 4.30 and 8.30 pm. The round-trip fare is US$10, and you need not return the same day.

Hitching to the park is possible, although most Argentine families will have little room in their vehicles. The park admission fee, payable at the ranger station on Ruta 3, costs US$3 per person. There are also ranger stations at Lago Roca and Lapataia.

Juan Fernández Islands

Scottish maroon Alexander Selkirk left an odd legacy to the Juan Fernández Islands. Selkirk, who spent more than four years in utter isolation on Masatierra, was the real-life model for Daniel Defoe's fictional character Robinson Crusoe. In 1966 Isla Masatierra, the only inhabited island of the group, was renamed 'Isla Robinson Crusoe' in honour of literature's most renowned castaway. This name change was motivated explicitly by the tourist concerns of the Chilean government.

The history of the Juan Fernández Islands, though, is much more than just Selkirk, and Isla Robinson Crusoe is much more than a hermit's hideaway. Singularly tranquil, it is also a matchless national park, managed by CONAF, and a UNESCO 'World Biosphere Reserve', with much to offer the motivated traveller. Despite the Chilean government's motives, it is not a major holiday destination and is not likely to become one because of the near impossibility, and clear undesirability, of significantly expanding its tourist infrastructure.

HISTORY

Uninhabited when Spanish mariner Juan Fernández discovered them in November 1574, the islands as a group still bear his name, though the modest Fernández had named them the Islas Santa Cecilia. Two decades passed before Spain even attempted even a temporary occupation. For more than two centuries, the islands were largely a refuge for pirates and sealers who sought pelts of the endemic Juan Fernández fur seal *(Arctocephalus phillippi)*.

According to one account, North American sealers took nearly three million sealskins off one of the islands between 1788 and 1809. Single cargoes of 100,000 pelts were not unusual, bringing the species to the point of extinction by the early-19th century. When North American sealer Benjamin Morrell visited in 1824, he speculated curiously that the absence of these seals had to do with the establishment of a Chilean penal colony:

> Fur and hair-seals formerly frequented this island; but of late they have found some other place of resort, though no cause for the change has been assigned. Perhaps the moral atmosphere may have been so much affected by the introduction of three hundred felons as to become unpleasant to these sagacious animals.

Whether or not Morrell gave the fur seal too much credit for its virtue and wisdom, the Juan Fernández Islands were most renowned for the adventures of Scotsman Alexander Selkirk, who spent more than four years marooned on Masatierra after being put ashore, at his own request, from the privateer *Cinque Ports* in 1704. This was tantamount to a death sentence for most castaways who soon starved or shot themselves, but Selkirk survived by adapting to his new home and enduring his desperate isolation.

Ironically the Spaniards, who vigorously opposed the presence of privateers in the New World, had made his survival possible. Unlike many small islands, Masatierra had abundant water, but food could have been a problem if the Spanish had not introduced goats. Disdaining fish, Selkirk tracked the feral goats and attacked them with his knife, devoured their meat and dressed himself in their skins. Sea lions, feral cats and rats – the latter two, European introductions – were among his other companions.

Daily, Selkirk climbed to a lookout above Cumberland Bay (Bahía Cumberland) in hope of spotting a vessel on the horizon, but not until 1708 did his saviour, Commander Woodes Rogers of the privateers *Duke* and *Duchess*, arrive, with the famed privateer William Dampier as his pilot. Rogers recalled first meeting with Selkirk when the ship's men returned from shore:

> Immediately our Pinnace return'd from the shore, and brought abundance of Craw-fish, with a man Cloth'd in Goat-Skins, who look'd wilder than the first Owners of them.

After signing on with Rogers and returning to Scotland, Selkirk became a celebrity. Defoe's fictionalised account of his experiences, though set in the Caribbean, became the enduring classic novel for which Isla Robinson Crusoe is now named.

After Selkirk's departure, privateers *(persona non grata* on the South American mainland) frequented the islands even more for rest and relaxation, of a sort, and to hunt

---

Who Was Friday?

Europeans receive credit for many achievements which other peoples accomplished first. A Miskito Indian from Nicaragua spent several years' solitary exile on the Juan Fernández Islands decades before Alexander Selkirk was put ashore there, and well before Daniel Defoe made Robinson Crusoe an enduring figure in world literature.

Admittedly the young Miskito, Will, would never have seen the Juan Fernández islands without the 'help' of Europeans. He had met the famous English privateer William Dampier in the Caribbean, and accompanied him to the Pacific. Will was inadvertently left ashore when Spanish forces surprised Dampier's expedition at Cumberland Bay (Bahía Cumberland) in 1681, and for the next three years he successfully evaded Spanish detection because, as Dampier wrote:

> The Moskitos are in general very civil and kind to the English...but they do not love the French, and the Spaniards they hate mortally.

Even today, the Miskito of Nicaragua and Honduras prefer English to Spanish as a second language. Will's life in the Caribbean prepared him well for his isolation in the Juan Fernández islands. Knowing the ingenuity and adaptability of the Miskito, Dampier was unsurprised to find that Will had made the most of limited resources:

> He had with him his Gun and a Knife, with a small Horn of Powder and a few Shot; which being spent, he contrived a way by notching his Knife, to saw the Barrel of his Gun into small Pieces, wherewith he made Harpoons, Lances, Hooks and a long Knife, heating the pieces first in the Fire, which he struck with his Gunflint, and a piece of the Barrel of his Gun, which he hardened...The hot pieces of Iron he would hammer out and bend as he pleased with Stones, and saw them with his jagged Knife; or grind them to an edge by long labour, and harden them to a good Temper as there was occasion. All this may seem strange to those that are not acquainted with the Sagacity of the Indians; but it is no more than these Moskito Men are accustomed to in their own Country, where they make their own Fishing and Striking Instruments, without either Forge or Anvil...

In Central America, the Miskito lived by hunting, fishing, and gardening, and by gathering in the forests and on the shores of the western Caribbean. On Isla Masatierra, without a canoe or dory (a word adapted from Miskito into English), Will could not hunt the green turtle which formed the core of Miskito subsistence, but he could fish the inshore waters of the island. There were no wild deer in Masatierra's

seals. In response, Spain re-established itself at Bahía Cumberland in 1750, founding the village of San Juan Bautista. Occupation was discontinuous, though, until Chile established a permanent presence in 1877.

After the turn of the 19th century, Masatierra played a notorious role in the struggle for Chilean independence, as Spanish authorities exiled 42 Chilean patriots there after the disastrous Battle of Rancagua in 1814. The exiles, including prominent people like Juan Egaña and Manuel de Salas, neither accepted nor forgot their relegation to damp caves behind San Juan. For many years, the island remained a nearly inescapable political prison for the newly independent country. During WW I, it once again played a memorable historical role, as the British naval vessels *Glasgow* and *Orama* confronted and sank the German cruiser *Dresden* at Bahía Cumberland.

Since then, the Juan Fernández Islands have played a less conspicuous but perhaps more significant role in global history. In 1935 the Chilean government declared the islands a national park for preservation of their unique flora and fauna, later undertaking a programme to remove the feral goats (on whose predecessors Selkirk depended so much for his subsistence) in order to preserve a priceless part of the world's natural heritage.

GEOGRAPHY

Separated from Valparaíso by 670 km of the open Pacific, the Juan Fernández archipelago consists of Isla Robinson Crusoe (formerly Isla Masatierra), Isla Alejandro

---

dense forests, but he could track and kill the feral goats on which Selkirk later lived. In fact, wrote Dampier, Will was so comfortable that he could afford to be selective in his diet:

> He told us that at first he was forced to eat Seal, which is very ordinary Meat, before he had made Hooks: but afterwards he never killed any Seals but to make Lines, cutting their Skins into Thongs. He had a little House or Hut half a Mile from the Sea, which was lin'd with Goats Skins; his Couch or Barbecu of Sticks lying along about two foot distant from the Ground, was spread the same, and was all his Bedding...He saw our Ship the Day before we came to an Anchor, and did believe we were English, and therefore kill'd three Goats in the Morning...and drest them with Cabbage, to treat us when we came ashore.

Dampier's return also reunited Will with a countryman named Robin.

> These were names given them by the English, for they had no Names among themselves... [Robin] first leap'd ashore, and running to his Brother Moskito Man, threw himself flat on his face at his feet, who helping him up, and embracing him, fell flat with his face on the Ground at Robin's feet...

This was extraordinary, but the Miskito were no strangers to remote places.

It was no coincidence that Defoe placed Robinson Crusoe's fictional island in the Caribbean, where European interlopers had long depended on the Miskito for fishing, hunting and sailing skills by which 'one or two of them in a Ship, will maintain 100 Men...'

In reality, not just one but hundreds of Fridays helped thousands of Crusoes survive in unfamiliar surroundings in the New World. If the fictional Crusoe overshadowed the genuine Selkirk, Friday's real-life predecessor was more than just a product of Defoe's imagination. Few knew the names of Will and his countrymen except the English privateers and others 'of whom they receive a great deal of Respect'. ■

Daniel Defoe

Selkirk (formerly Isla Masafuera), and Isla Santa Clara. The original Spanish names are prosaic: Masatierra simply means 'closer to land', ie to the South American continent, while Masafuera means 'farther out' – it is another 170 km closer to Sydney. Tiny Isla Santa Clara, known to early privateers as Goat Island, is only three km off the southern tip of Isla Robinson Crusoe.

Land areas are small, very small, but the islands' topography is extraordinarily rugged as, geologically, the entire archipelago is a group of emergent peaks from a submarine mountain range known as the Juan Fernández Ridge, which trends east-west for more than 400 km at the southern end of the Chile Basin. Isla Robinson Crusoe comprises only an area of 93 sq km, with a maximum length of 22 km and a maximum width of 7.3 km, but reaches a maximum altitude of 915 metres on the peak of Cerro El Yunque (The Anvil), which hovers above the island's only settlement, the village of San Juan Bautista. Isla Alejandro Selkirk is even more mountainous, rising to 1650 metres on Cerro Los Inocentes, where snow has fallen.

The Pacific Ocean surrounds the islands, and the adjacent sea floor drops precipitously to more than 4000 metres below sea level on all sides. This leaves relatively little continental shelf to support marine fauna and flora – according to one estimate, the total area exploited for fishing is only about 325 sq km. Those maritime resources which are present, particularly the Juan Fernández lobster *(Jasus frontalis*, really a crayfish), are in great demand on the mainland and provide a substantial income for some of Isla Robinson Crusoe's residents.

CLIMATE

The archipelago is far enough from the continent for the subtropical water masses to moderate the chilly sub-Antarctic waters of the Peru (or Humboldt) Current, which flows northward along the coast of Chile. Nevertheless, the climate is distinctly Mediterranean, with clearly defined warm, dry summers and cooler, wet winters. At San Juan Bautista, February is the warmest month, with a mean daily maximum temperature of 21.8°C, while August is the coolest month, with a daily temperature averaging 10.1°C. Mean annual precipitation is 1000 mm, of which 70% falls between April and October; less than 10% falls in summer (December to February). Winds often exceed 25 knots.

Because of the islands' irregular topography, rainfall varies greatly over very short distances. In particular, the Cordón Chifladores (of which Cerro El Yunque is the highest point) intercepts most of the rainfall, and creates a pronounced rain shadow on the south-eastern portion of Isla Robinson Crusoe, which is no less barren than parts of the Atacama. By contrast, the area north of the cordón is dense rainforest, with a high concentration of the endemic species for which the islands became a national park and a biosphere reserve.

FLORA

As on many oceanic islands, the indigenous biota has suffered from the introduction of ecologically exotic species, particularly goats, which sustained Selkirk but devoured much of the original vegetation. More opportunistic plant species, resistant to grazing and to fires set by humans, colonised areas which the goats had degraded.

Still, a great deal remains in sectors of the island where even an invader as agile as the goat could neither penetrate nor completely dominate the native flora. In places, the terrain is so steep that one can only proceed by grasping branches of the nearly impenetrable foliage. Once, pursuing a feral goat, Selkirk plunged over a sheer cliff and survived only because the animal's body cushioned his fall.

The vegetation of the Juan Fernández Islands presents an extraordinary mixture of geographic affinities, from the Andes and sub-Antarctic Magallanes to Hawaii and New Zealand. In their oceanic isolation, though, the flora have evolved into something very distinct from their continental and insular origins. Of the 87 genera of plants on the islands, 16 are endemic, found nowhere else on earth; of 140 native plant species, 101 are endemic. These plants survive in three major communities: the evergreen rainforest, an evergreen heath, and an herbaceous steppe.

The evergreen rainforest is the richest of these environments, with a wide variety of tree species such as the endemic *luma (Nothomyrcia fernandeziana)* and the *chonta (Juania australis)*, one of only two palm species native to Chile. Perhaps the most striking vegetation, though, is the dense understorey of climbing vines and the towering endemic tree ferns *Dicksonia berteroana* and *Thyrsopteris elegans*. The forest was also a source of edible wild plants collected by the crews of visiting ships, as Rogers indicated by noting:

> The Cabbage Trees abound about three miles in the Woods, and the Cabbage very good; most of 'em are on the tops of the nearest and lowest mountains.

The evergreen heath replaces the rainforest on the thinner soils of the highest peaks and exceptionally steep slopes. Characteristic species are the tree fern *Blechnum cyadifolium* and various tree species of the endemic genus *Robinsonia*. The steppe, largely confined to the arid eastern sector of Isla Robinson Crusoe and to Isla Santa Clara, consists of perennial bunch grasses such as *Stipa fernandeziana*.

Visiting ships, seeking fresh provisions, collected edible wild species such as the cabbage and even planted gardens which they, and others, later harvested. Exotic plant species from the mainland have provided unfortunate competition for native flora. At lower elevations, the wild blackberry *(Rubus ulmifolius)* and the shrub *maqui (Aristotelia chilensis)* have proven to be aggressive colonisers despite concerted efforts to control them. Branches from the maqui are used to make lobster traps.

FAUNA

The most notable animal species is the only native mammal, the Juan Fernández fur seal. The seals were nearly extinct a century ago, but now about 2500 individuals breed on the islands. The southern elephant seal *Mirounga leonina*, hunted for its blubber, no longer survives here. There are 11 endemic bird species, of which the most eye-catching is the Juan Fernández hummingbird *(Sephanoides fernandensis)*. The male is conspicuous because of its bright red colour; the female is a more subdued green, with a white tail. Only about 250 hummingbirds survive, feeding off the striking Juan Fernández cabbage which grows in many parts of San Juan Bautista. However, the species does best in native forest.

Introduced rodents and feral cats have endangered nesting marine birds, such as Cook's petrel *(Pterodroma cookii defilippiana)*, by preying on their eggs or young. Another mammal which has proliferated since its introduction in the 1930s is the South American coatimundi (*coatí* in Spanish).

BOOKS

Available in many editions, Defoe's classic *Robinson Crusoe* is an obvious choice, but there are many accounts of voyages which stopped at least briefly in the islands. One of the most accessible is Captain Rogers' *A Cruising Voyage Round the World*, available in a Dover Publications facsimile edition (New York, 1970). Certainly the most thorough history in English is Ralph Lee Woodward's *Robinson Crusoe's Island* (Chapel Hill, University of North Carolina Press, 1969).

If you read Spanish and have a general interest in remote oceanic islands you may wish to obtain Juan Carlos Castilla's edited collection *Islas Oceánicas Chilenas* (Santiago, Ediciones Universidad Católica, 1988), which includes articles on various aspects of the natural history of the Juan Fernández Islands, Easter Island (Rapa Nui), San Félix and San Ambrosio (1000 km west of Chañaral, and inhabited only by the Chilean navy), and the uninhabited Sala y Gómez, 400 km west of Rapa Nui. There are summaries of all the articles in English.

GETTING THERE & AWAY

Air

From Santiago, two companies operate air taxi services to Juan Fernández, almost daily in summer but less frequently during the rest of the year. Flights normally depart from Santiago's Los Cerrillos airport, but are sometimes postponed when bad weather makes landing impossible on Isla Robinson Crusoe's dirt airstrip. Travel arrangements should be flexible enough to allow for an extra two or three days' stay on the island if necessary.

LASSA (☎ 273-4309), Avenida Larraín 7941 in the eastern Santiago suburb of La Reina, flies six-passenger air taxis from Los Cerrillos airport in Santiago. Their offices are actually in the Aeródromo Tobalaba, a small airfield at which some flights land. The other company is Transportes Aéreos Isla Robinson Crusoe (☎ 531-3772), whose offices are at Monumento 2570 in the southwestern Santiago suburb of Maipú. Both companies offer charter flights for up to five passengers, but on a per person basis these are no cheaper than regularly scheduled flights

One-way fares are around US$175, but do check with LASSA for discount packages which include accommodation and all meals from about US$570. Another company which arranges packages is DMC Tours (☎ 242-9042) in Santiago.

San Juan Bautista is about 1½ hours from the airstrip by a combination of 4WD (down a frighteningly precipitous dirt road) to the jetty at Bahía del Padre, and motor launch (the best part of the trip, sailing more than half way around the island's awesome volcanic coastal escarpments). Both the flight and the rest of the voyage, however, can be rough, so some travellers may want to consider preventative medication. Cost of the launch should be included in your air ticket, but check to be certain.

Boat

Without your own boat, it's not easy to sail to Juan Fernández, but quarterly naval supply ships will carry passengers for next to nothing, barely the cost of food. Unfortunately, it's hard to learn departure dates without hiring the CIA, since even the most innocuous Chilean naval movements are top secret – but try calling the Comando de Transporte (☎ 258457) at the Primera Zona Naval, opposite the Plaza Sotomayor in Valparaíso.

Another alternative is by the fishing boats which visit the islands on an irregular schedule. Contact Empresa Pesquera Chris in Santiago (☎ 681-1543) at Cueto 622, or in Valparaíso (☎ 216800) at Cochrane 445. These charge around US$85 for a one-way passage from Valparaíso to San Juan Bautista.

GETTING AROUND

Getting around Isla Robinson Crusoe presents no major problems but is not necessarily cheap, since it requires hiring a fishing boat or, perhaps more economically, accompanying the lobster catchers to their grounds. To arrange a launch, contact Polo González, at LASSA's office on the plaza, or at his cabañas; rates are fixed by the Municipalidad. A launch to Puerto Inglés, for example, costs US$14 for up to eight passengers. CONAF rangers visiting outlying sites in their launch may be willing to take along passengers.

Getting to and from Isla Alejandro Selkirk, rarely visited by any foreigner, presents serious problems, but fishing boats from the mainland will sometimes carry passengers. During the lobster season, a CONAF ranger stays on the island. If you should manage to get there, you may have to stay for months.

SAN JUAN BAUTISTA

San Juan Bautista, the only settlement on Isla Robinson Crusoe, has a permanent population of about 600, of whom perhaps 100 are transplanted mainlanders. With only two motor vehicles (not counting launches), neither of which is ordinarily in service, San Juan Bautista is one of the most tranquil places in all of Chile. Immigrants from the mainland soon adjust to the relaxed pace of island life. Most visitors to Juan Fernández

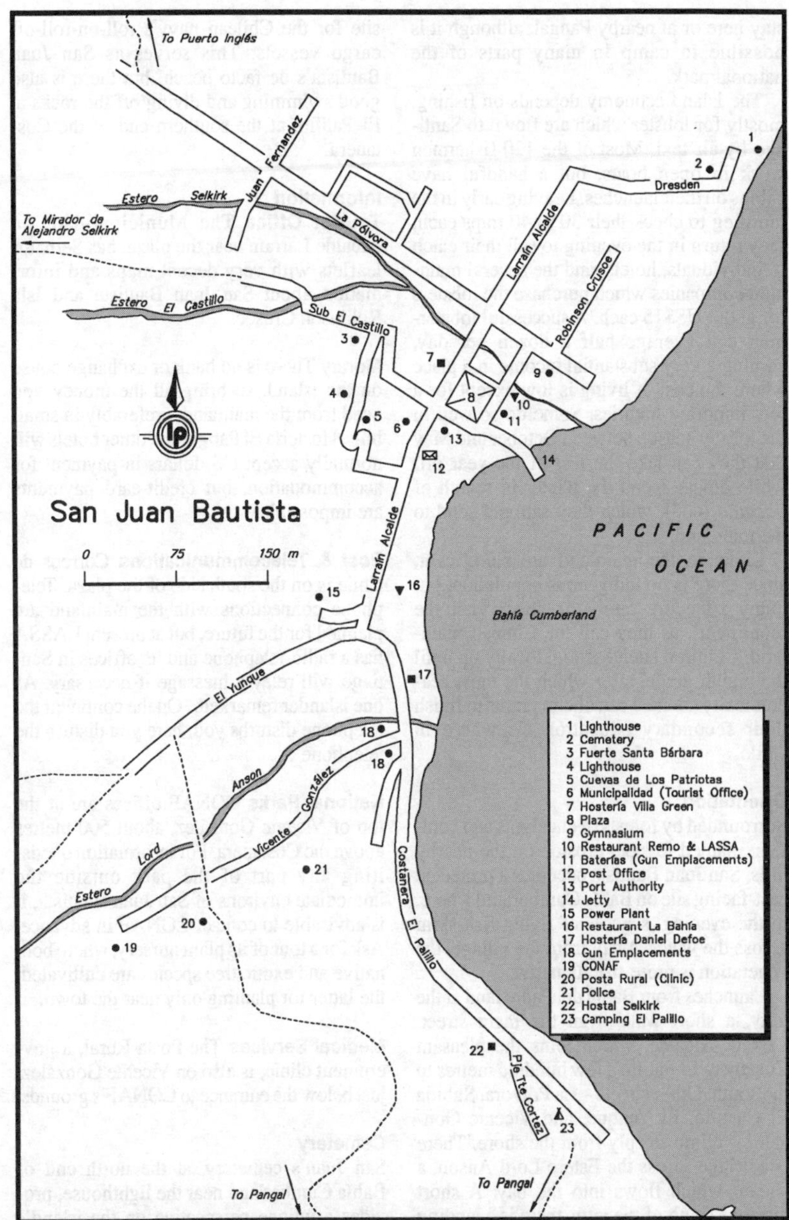
San Juan Bautista
To Puerto Inglés
To Mirador de
Alejandro Selkirk
Juan Fernández
Estero Selkirk
La Pólvora
Estero El Castillo
Sub El Castillo
Dresden
Larraín Alcalde
Robinson Crusoe
PACIFIC OCEAN
Bahía Cumberland
0 75 150 m
El Yunque
Anson
Vicente González
Lord
Estero
Costanera El Palillo
Pje Tte Cortez
To Pangal
To Pangal
1 Lighthouse
2 Cemetery
3 Fuerte Santa Bárbara
4 Lighthouse
5 Cuevas de Los Patriotas
6 Municipalidad (Tourist Office)
7 Hostería Villa Green
8 Plaza
9 Gymnasium
10 Restaurant Remo & LASSA
11 Baterías (Gun Emplacements)
12 Post Office
13 Port Authority
14 Jetty
15 Power Plant
16 Restaurant La Bahía
17 Hostería Daniel Defoe
18 Gun Emplacements
19 CONAF
20 Posta Rural (Clinic)
21 Police
22 Hostal Selkirk
23 Camping El Palillo

stay here or at nearby Pangal, although it is possible to camp in many parts of the national park.

The island economy depends on fishing, mostly for lobster which are flown to Santiago by air taxi. Most of the 120 fishermen work in open boats, but a handful have cabins on their launches. Leaving early in the morning to check their 30 to 40 traps each, they return in the evening to sell their catch to individuals, hotels, and the several mainland companies which purchase the lobsters for about US$15 each. A successful lobsterman can average half a dozen per day, earning a very substantial income in a place where the cost of living is low except for a few imported luxuries. Some do so well in the lobster season between October and May that they can take the rest of the year off, while others spend the winter in search of *bacalao* (cod), which they salt and send to the mainland.

Links to the mainland are significant, since there is no indigenous population, but many islanders rarely or never visit the 'continent', as they call the Chilean mainland. Children attend school locally up until the eighth grade, after which the most academically talented can obtain grants to finish their secondary education elsewhere in Chile.

Orientation

Surrounded by forests of eucalypts and conifers, planted to stem erosion on the nearby hills, San Juan Bautista occupies a protected east-facing site on Bahía Cumberland where, in the evening, schools of flying fish skim across the water. Away from the village, the vegetation is more strictly native.

Launches from Bahía del Padre land at the jetty, a short walk from the main street, Larraín Alcalde, which joins the pleasant Costanera El Palillo a few hundred metres to the south. Other streets – La Pólvora, Subida El Castillo, El Yunque, and Vicente González – climb steeply from the shore. There is a bridge across the Estero Lord Anson, a stream which flows into the bay. A short distance south of the jetty, there is a landing site for the Chilean navy's roll-on-roll-off cargo vessels. This serves as San Juan Bautista's de facto beach, but there is also good swimming and diving off the rocks at El Palillo, at the southern end of the Costanera.

Information

Tourist Office The Municipalidad, on Alcalde Larraín near the plaza, has Sernatur leaflets with very decent maps and information about San Juan Bautista and Isla Robinson Crusoe.

Money There is no bank or exchange house on the island, so bring all the money you need from the mainland, preferably in small bills. Hostería El Pangal and other hotels will normally accept US dollars in payment for accommodation, but credit-card payments are impossible.

Post & Telecommunications Correos de Chile is on the south side of the plaza. Telephone connections with the mainland are planned for the future, but at present LASSA has a radio-telephone and its offices in Santiago will relay a message if necessary. As one islander remarked, 'On the continent the telephone disturbs you; here you disturb the telephone'.

National Parks CONAF offices are at the top of Vicente González, about 500 metres above the Costanera. For information on visiting any part of the park outside the immediate environs of San Juan Bautista, it is advisable to contact CONAF in advance. Ask for a tour of its plant nursery, where both native and exotic tree species are cultivated, the latter for planting only near the town.

Medical Services The Posta Rural, a government clinic, is also on Vicente González, just below the entrance to CONAF's grounds.

Cemetery

San Juan's cemetery, at the north end of Bahía Cumberland near the lighthouse, provides a unique perspective on the island's history, with its polyglot assortment of Spanish, French and German surnames – the latter survivors of the sinking of the *Dresden*.

Cuevas de Los Patriotas

In these caverns behind San Juan Bautista, reached by a short footpath from Larraín Alcalde, Juan Egaña, Manuel de Salas and 40 other participants in the Chilean independence movement spent several years after their defeat in the Battle of Rancagua in 1814.

Fuerte Santa Bárbara

In 1767 a British visitor, surprised to learn that Spain had established a permanent presence at Bahía Cumberland, reported that:

> This fort, which is faced with stone, has eighteen or twenty embrasures, and within it a long house, which I supposed to be barracks for the garrison: five and twenty or thirty houses of different kinds are scattered round it...

Built in 1749 by Spain to discourage incursions by pirates, these fortifications were reconstructed in 1974. To get there, follow the path north along the Cuevas de los Patriotas, or else climb directly from the plaza via the Subida El Castillo.

Places to Stay & Eat

CONAF has a very quiet and pleasant camping ground, *Camping El Palillo*, which is free of charge with running water and a pit latrine. It's at El Palillo, at the south end of the Costanera. There is plenty of firewood, but the nearest shower, with cold water only, is a 15-minute walk away at the jetty. There is another convenient site at the previously mentioned *Plazoleta El Yunque*. Elsewhere in Parque Nacional Juan Fernández, camping is permitted just about anywhere except in the zona intangible, but in some areas you'll need to carry your own water.

Otherwise, accommodation in San Juan Bautista tends towards the costly, but usually includes all meals (remember that this includes lobster every day). *Hostería Daniel Defoe*, open all year on the Costanera near Vicente González, has shoreline cabins which appear a bit ramshackle but are really very comfortable, for US$50 to US$65 per person with all meals. Half-pension is possible, and the hotel also serves meals to non-guests, although the food is dearer and no better than that at Restaurant La Bahía (see following). The staff will, however, prepare lobster for one person.

Hostería Villa Green, on Larraín Alcalde opposite the plaza, charges US$65 a single, US$55 per person for a double, and US$45 per person for a triple. Polo González, LASSA's agent in San Juan Bautista, has excellent accommodation in beautiful grounds in his *Hostal Selkirk*, on the Costanera. Singles with full pension cost US$87 per day, doubles US$69 per person; suites cost about a third more.

LASSA runs *Hostería El Pangal*, an hour's walk south of San Juan Bautista with excellent views of the village and Cerro El Yunque en route, which can also be reached by launch from the jetty at San Juan Bautista. Unfortunately, the area around Pangal is less interesting, badly eroded, and has poorer access to the countryside. It can also be much more expensive at US$142 a single with all meals or US$118 per person for a double, but does have more economical bunks from US$40 a single without meals. However, they sometimes offer discount tours, including lodging and all meals for four days and three nights, for US$570 per person for a double.

If you're not staying at one of the few hotels, give restaurants several hours' notice if you wish to have lunch or dinner. *Restaurant La Bahía*, despite its modest appearance, is one of the best-value places in all of Chile. Owner Jorge Angulo has lived half his 60 years on the island, and prepares an extraordinary ceviche (cholera warnings in Chile do not extend to Juan Fernández so eating raw seafood should be safe). He also has succulent lobster for about US$11 per person, but he requires a two-person minimum so the other half of the lobster doesn't go to waste. Try also *vidriola*, an especially tasty fish which is much cheaper. Regular meals cost about US$5.

Restaurant Remo, on the north-east side of the plaza, serves only sandwiches and drinks, but has longer opening hours than other places.

PARQUE NACIONAL JUAN FERNÁNDEZ

Parque Nacional Juan Fernández includes every sq cm of the archipelago, a total of 9300 hectares, though the township of San Juan Bautista is a de facto exclusion. Like many oceanic islands, the national park is a storehouse of rare plants and (to a lesser degree) animals, evolved in isolation and adapted to very specific environmental niches.

Mirador de Selkirk

To see what Selkirk saw, hike to his lookout *(mirador)* above San Juan Bautista. The three-km walk, gaining 565 metres in elevation, takes about 1½ hours of steady walking but rewards the climber with views of both sides of the island, although sometimes obscured by clouds. Start as early in the morning as possible and take at least a light cotton shirt since it can be much cooler at the lookout (which is exposed to wind and weather) than it is at sea level.

On the saddle, there are two metal plaques commemorating Selkirk's exile on the island. The first, minted by John Child & Son of Valparaíso and placed there by officials of the Royal Navy, reads:

> In memory of Alexander Selkirk, Mariner, a native of Largo, in the county of Fife, Scotland, who lived on this island in complete solitude for four years and four months.
>
> He was landed from the *Cinque Ports* galley, 96 tons, 16 guns, AD 1704 and was taken off in the *Duke*, privateer, 12th Feb, 1709.
>
> He died lieutenant of *HMS Weymouth*, AD 1723, aged 47 years.
>
> This tablet is erected near Selkirk's lookout, by

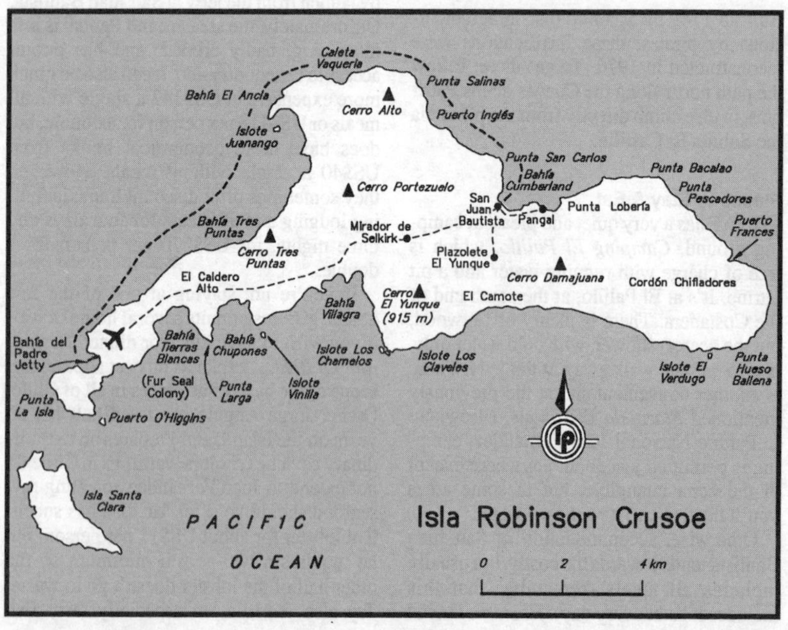

Commodore Powell and the officers of *HMS Topaze*, AD 1868.

More than a century later, a Scottish relative added his own tribute:

Tablet placed here by Allan Jardine of Largo, Fife, Scotland, direct descendant of Alexander Selkirk's brother David. Remembrance 'Till a' the seas gang dry and the rocks melt in the sun'. January 1983.

The trail to the lookout begins at the south end of the Plaza of San Juan Bautista, climbs the Subida El Castillo, and follows the north side of the Estero El Castillo before zigzagging up the Cerro Portezuelo to Selkirk's lookout – fill your canteen before continuing up the hillside through dense thickets of maqui and blackberry, which gradually give way to native ferns and trees. Beyond Selkirk's lookout, the trail continues to the airstrip. If you're camping west of the pass, it is possible to walk there to catch your flight back to the mainland, but make arrangements before leaving San Juan Bautista or you could lose your reservation.

Plazoleta El Yunque & El Camote

Plazoleta El Yunque, half an hour's walk from San Juan Bautista via a road-trail just beyond the power station at the south end of Larraín Alcalde, is a tranquil forest clearing, with picnic and camping areas. A German survivor of the *Dresden* once had a homestead here – the foundations of his house are still visible.

Beyond the plazoleta is a very difficult and poorly marked trail to a saddle at El Camote, which has a splendid view of the south coast of Isla Robinson Crusoe and the offshore Islote (islet) El Verdugo. This short but exhausting hike is very rewarding but, as part of the *zona intangible*, entry is restricted unless you have special permission. CONAF ranger Miguel García may accompany motivated hikers who, in any event, will not be able to locate the trail without him. Some of the park's best-preserved flora can be found in this area.

Puerto Inglés

Only a 15-minute boat ride from San Juan Bautista, Puerto Inglés offers a reconstruction of the shelter in which Selkirk passed his years on Masatierra. There are also ruins of a cowherd's shelter and adequate water for camping, but no firewood. If you don't care to pay up to US$14 for a very short boat ride, there is a steep, tiring trail from the top of Calle La Pólvora which will take you over the ridge in about two hours.

Bahía Tierras Blancas

Isla Robinson Crusoe's only breeding colony of Juan Fernández fur seals is at Bahía Tierras Blancas, a short distance east of the landing strip above Bahía del Padre. The trail which connects the airstrip with San Juan Bautista via the previously mentioned Mirador de Selkirk passes close to the colony, but there is no drinking water, so you must bring your own if you plan to camp. Fishermen will also take passengers to Tierras Blancas.

If you can't visit Tierras Blancas, you can still see pods of fur seals at Bahía del Padre on your arrival, or at the north end of Bahía Cumberland, just beyond the cemetery in San Juan Bautista. Although the seals will not come up on the rocks, you can get within about 10 metres of them.

Easter Island (Rapa Nui)

How Pacific Islanders arrived at Easter Island (Rapa Nui), the world's most remote inhabited island, is as much a mystery as how their descendants could design and sculpt hundreds of colossal *moai* from hard volcanic basalt, transport these tall and heavy statues great distances from quarry to coast, and erect them on great stone *ahu* (platforms).

Residents and visitors have applied various names to this small, isolated volcanic land mass. Polynesian settlers named it Rapa Nui, but the view of the seemingly infinite sea from the summit of Terevaka, the island's highest point, reveals why they also called it Te Pito o Te Henua – the Navel (Centre) of the World. From here, a vessel can sail more than 1900 km in any direction without sighting inhabited land.

Dutch mariner Jacob Roggeveen, the first European to sight the island, named it Easter Island after the date of his discovery; the Spaniards first called it San Carlos (after King Carlos III). Other mariners dubbed it Davis's Land after confusing it with territory identified by the 17th-century English pirate Edward Davis. Roggeveen's legacy survived among Europeans, however: English speakers call it Easter Island; Spanish speakers refer to Isla de Pascua, Germans to Osterinsel.

HISTORY

Prehistory

In archaeology and antiquity, Rapa Nui raises issues totally disproportionate to its size (only 117 square km) and population (about 2000). The nearest populated land mass, 1900 km west, is even tinier Pitcairn Island of *Bounty* fame, and the next nearest inhabited 'neighbours' are the Mangarévas (Gambier) islands, 2500 km west, and the Marquesas, 3200 km north-west. The South American coast is 3700 km to the east. Yet Rapa Nui is central to some very big questions.

The most obvious ones are where the original islanders came from, how they arrived at such an unlikely destination, what inspired them to build the imposing monuments for which Rapa Nui is so famous, and how they transported these from quarry to site. Even larger questions deal with the existence and frequency of trans-Pacific contacts, and cultural exchanges between peoples for whom the world's greatest ocean would presumably have been a massive barrier.

There is broad consensus that the first Americans were Asiatic peoples who crossed the Bering Strait into Alaska via a land bridge, which disappeared as sea level rose with the melting of the continental ice sheets at the end of the Pleistocene, about 12,000 years ago. Exact dates are in dispute (some people argue that crossings took place during even earlier glacial epochs), although no one doubts that such migrations ceased with the rising oceans. These immigrants reached the southernmost extremes of South America and created the great civilisations of Mexico and Peru. For millennia they were isolated from Asia.

But how isolated, and for how long? Among scholars of prehistory, there is a long-running debate between two major schools of thought: partisans of 'independent invention' assert that New World civilisations evolved in geographical isolation until the voyages of Columbus, while 'diffusionists' argue in favour of substantial evidence of contacts and cultural exchange across the Pacific long before 1492 . Important economic plants, such as the coconut for example, appear to have been present in both the eastern and western hemispheres when Europeans first saw the New World, while the sweet potato, a New World domesticate, was also a widely diffused Polynesian staple. Patterns of navigation and settlement in the Pacific are central to diffusionist arguments, and Rapa Nui is a key piece in a complex puzzle, the last possible stopover on eastbound

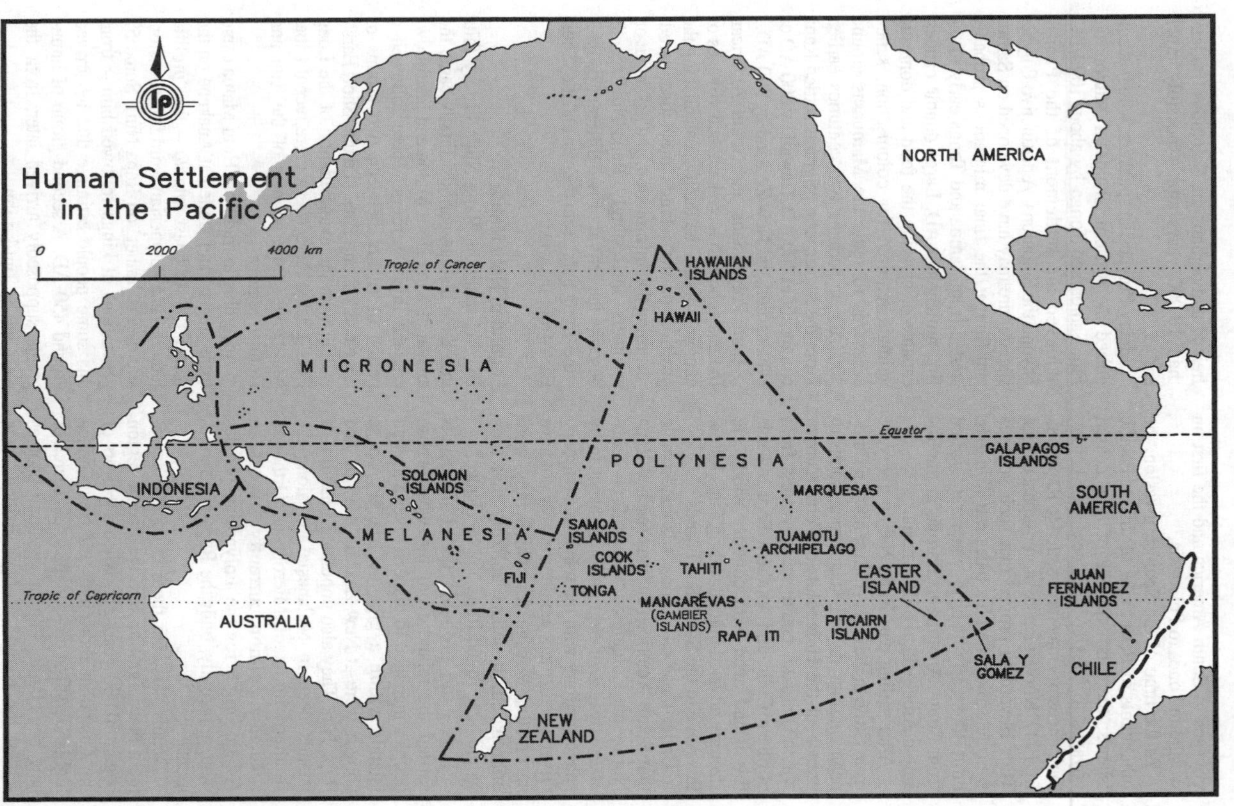
Human Settlement in the Pacific
0
2000
4000 km
NORTH AMERICA
Tropic of Cancer
HAWAIIAN ISLANDS
HAWAII
MICRONESIA
Equator
GALAPAGOS ISLANDS
POLYNESIA
SOLOMON ISLANDS
INDONESIA
MARQUESAS
SOUTH AMERICA
MELANESIA
SAMOA ISLANDS
TUAMOTU ARCHIPELAGO
COOK ISLANDS
TAHITI
EASTER ISLAND
JUAN FERNANDEZ ISLANDS
FIJI
TONGA
Tropic of Capricorn
MANGARÉVAS
(GAMBIER ISLANDS)
RAPA ITI
PITCAIRN ISLAND
AUSTRALIA
SALA Y GOMEZ
CHILE
NEW ZEALAND

voyages to South America and the first on westbound ones to Polynesia.

At the time of the Spanish invasion, the inhabitants of Peru knew of distant Pacific islands; there is evidence of long coastal voyages to Mexico and, centuries before, their ancestors may have sailed to Rapa Nui. In 1947 Norwegian explorer-archaeologist Thor Heyerdahl proved that such voyages were feasible when his balsa raft *Kon-Tiki*, built like early Pacific watercraft, sailed from South America to Raroia, in the Tuamotu Archipelago of Polynesia.

After sailing past Rapa Nui on a voyage from Chile in the early-19th century, a European mariner described a strong southern branch of the Humboldt (or Peru) Current which, he said, could speed vessels from northern Chile and southern Peru towards this island even with contrary winds. He strongly advised that all sailing ships follow this route to the South Sea Islands.

Under these conditions it is conceivable that South American Indians reached Rapa Nui by pre-Columbian watercraft on deliberate voyages of exploration rather than by chance drifting with the winds and currents. Given that drifters would probably not have survived a voyage for which they were unprepared, it seems unlikely that they would have found Rapa Nui by chance.

It is more probable that Polynesians settled the island from the west. These peoples managed to disperse over a myriad islands within a gigantic triangle whose corners were at New Zealand, Hawaii, and Rapa Nui. They also populated a handful of islands deep in Melanesia and along the southern limits of Micronesia. Orthodox academic opinion currently favours an Asiatic origin for the Polynesian peoples who, apparently, built the Rapa Nui monuments.

Details vary, but there is general agreement that migration into the Pacific region began 50,000 years ago when ancestors of the Australian aboriginals and New Guinea highlanders first crossed the sea in search of new homelands. Papuan-speaking peoples settled the islands of New Britain, New Ireland and perhaps the Solomons, no later than 10,000 years ago – possibly much earlier.

Malay-Polynesian speakers, who had colonised the western islands of Micronesia, Fiji, Samoa and Tonga by about 1000 BC, achieved the settlement of the Pacific beyond the Solomons. A distinctive Polynesian culture may have developed on Samoa and Tonga; the final migrations probably started from Samoa and Tonga early in the first millennium AD. Large double canoes, capable of carrying the food and domestic animals required for colonisation, sailed eastwards to settle the Marquesas around 300 AD or perhaps two centuries earlier. From the Marquesas, migrants settled Rapa Nui by about 400 AD, Hawaii by 800 AD or even earlier, and New Zealand by 900 AD.

Both Polynesians and South American Indians appear to have launched voyages of exploration into the Pacific, establishing the position of the islands they discovered, recording that information, and passing it on to others. Interestingly, Rapa Nui legends describe the arrival of two different peoples – the 'Long Ears' from the east and the 'Short Ears' from the west.

Legend of Hotu Matua

By oral tradition, Rapa Nui's history falls into three distinct periods. Firstly came the arrival of King Hotu Matua and his followers, the initial settlers. There followed a period of rivalry between two groups of people, the 'Long Ears' and the 'Short Ears', ending with the extermination of the Long Ears. Lastly, there was a more recent tribal war between the peoples of the Tuu and Hotu-iti regions.

According to tradition, Hotu Matua came from the east and landed at Anakena on the island's north coast (*matua* – the 'prolific father' – is a Polynesian word for 'ancestor' and means 'father' on Rapa Nui). Some 57 generations of kings followed him – from this some people estimate that he arrived around 450 AD. A second group of immigrants supposedly arrived later, from the west, led by Tuu-ko-ihu.

By the early 20th century, however, European visitors had recorded confused and contradictory versions of this legend. Hotu Matua's voyage had a number of starting points: the Galápagos Islands to the north-east, the Tuamotu Archipelago to the north-west, Rapa Iti to the west, and the Marquesas to the north-west. Some versions even have Tuu-ko-ihu arriving on Hotu Matua's boats.

Trying to date events using genealogies is difficult and uncertain; researchers have collected a number of different lists of kings descended from Hotu Matua. One, estimating 20 to 30 generations descended from Hotu Matua until the last native king died after a slave raid in 1862, concluded that Hotu Motua arrived at Rapa Nui as late as the 16th century.

Long Ears & Short Ears

In Rapa Nui oral tradition, a gap exists between the arrival of Hotu Matua and the division of islanders into Long Ear and Short Ear groups. One explanation is that Long Ear immigrants may have come from Polynesia, where some groups practised the custom of ear lobe elongation, but it's not impossible that arrivals from pre-Columbian Peru brought the custom.

In attempting to reconcile oral tradition with theories of migration, some have speculated that the Long Ears arrived with Hotu Matua from Polynesia, followed by the Short Ears under Tuu-ko-ihu from the west. Some suggest that the Long Ears built the great ahu (platforms for statues) and that the Short Ears carved the moai (the human-like stone statues of Easter Island) and placed them on the ahu, while others hold that the Long Ears carved the moai assisted by Short Ears.

At some time, though, conflict between the two groups resulted in the near extermination of the Long Ears – perhaps a single survivor remained. Calculating from genealogies of islanders claiming descent from the last Long Ear (who had married a Short Ear woman after the end of the war), one estimate placed that survivor in the second half of the 17th century. The reasons for this

Easter Islander – from Cook's 1774 visit

warfare appear to have been demographic and ecological, resulting in damage or destruction of many of Rapa Nui's stone monuments.

Toppling of the Moai

A long peace ensued after the Short Ears' victory over the Long Ears, but eventual dissension between different families or clans led to bloody wars in which cannibalism was practised, and many moai were toppled from their ahu. According to one account, tribes or clans were highly territorial and proud of their moai, while enemy groups would topple the moai to insult and anger their owners. The only moai standing today have been restored this century.

Arrival of the Dutch – 1722

Spanish vessels entered the Pacific from South America in the early 16th century, but in April 1772 a Dutch expedition under Admiral Jacob Roggeveen became the first Europeans to set foot on Rapa Nui.

Roggeveen recorded his observations in the ship's log, whilst another crew member, Carl Behrens, published an account of the voyage. Since they landed on Easter Day, according to common European custom, Rapa Nui acquired the name Easter Island.

The Dutch found the islanders, who subsisted primarily on produce from intensively cultivated gardens and secondarily on the limited wealth of the sea, very friendly. The great moai, though, baffled them despite their obvious religious significance. According to Roggeveen:

> What the form of worship of these people comprises we were not able to gather any full knowledge of, owing to the shortness of our stay among them; we noticed only that they kindle fire in front of certain remarkably tall stone figures they set up; and, thereafter squatting on their heels with heads bowed down, they bring the palms of their hands together and alternately raise and lower them.

Behrens recorded that the islanders:

> ...relied in case of need on their gods or idols which stand erected all along the sea shore in great numbers, before which they fall down and invoke them. These idols were all hewn out of stone, and in the form of a man, with long ears, adorned on the head with a crown...

Behrens mentioned that some islanders wore wooden blocks or discs in their elongated ear lobes – some of which were so long that, after removing the plugs, islanders hitched the lobe over the top of the ear to keep it from flapping. He concluded that those with blocks or discs who also shaved their heads, were probably priests. Those who did not cut their hair wore it long, either hanging down the back or else plaited and coiled on the top of the head.

Spanish Expedition – 1770

Not until 1770 did Europeans again visit Rapa Nui, when a Spanish party from Peru under Don Felipe González de Haedo claimed the island for Spain and renamed it San Carlos. The Spaniards noted that male islanders generally went unclothed, wearing only plumes on their heads, whilst a few wore a sort of coloured poncho or cloak. Women wore hats made of rushes, a short cloak around the breasts and another wrap from the waist downwards.

Most of the islanders dwelt in caves, but others lived in elliptical boat-shaped houses, probably the type seen by the Dutch. Their only weapons were sharp obsidian knives. The absence of goods and metal implements suggested no commerce with the outside world, but gardens with sugar cane, sweet potatoes, taro and yams provided a healthy subsistence. An officer of the expedition recorded that the islanders' appearance:

> ...[did] not resemble that of the Indians of the Continent of Chile, Peru or New Spain in anything, these islanders being in colour between white, swarthy and reddish, not thick-lipped nor flat nosed, the hair chestnut coloured and limp, some have it black, and others tending to red or a cinnamon tint. They are tall, well built and proportioned in all their limbs; and there are no halt, maimed, bent, crooked, luxated, deformed or bow legged among them, their appearance being thoroughly pleasing, and tallying with Europeans more than with Indians.

Captain Cook & Other Europeans

In 1774, the famous Englishman Captain James Cook led the next European expedition to land on Rapa Nui. Cook, familiar with the Society Islands, Tonga, and New Zealand, concluded that the inhabitants of Rapa Nui belonged to the same general lineage.

Cook believed that islanders no longer regarded the moai as idols, and he thought them to be monuments to former kings; the ahu appeared to be burial sites. His account is the first to mention that, though some moai still stood and carried their topknots, others had fallen and their ahu were damaged. Cook found the islanders poor and distressed, describing them as small, lean, timid, and miserable.

It seems probable then, that war had raged since the Spanish visit in 1770, reducing the population to misery and destroying some of the moai. Another theory is that the islanders, wary of foreigners, hid in caves from Cook's crew, but this contradicts Roggeveen's account of friendly islanders. It's possible that a number of moai had been toppled even before the Spanish and Dutch visits, but that those sailors did not visit the same sites as Cook.

Another 18th-century European, the Frenchman La Perouse, visited Rapa Nui. After his two ships crossed from Chile in 1786, he found the population of the island calm and prosperous, suggesting a quick recovery from any catastrophe. In 1804, a Russian visitor reported more than 20 moai still standing, including some at the southern coastal site of Vinapu. Accounts from ensuing years suggest another period of destruction, so that perhaps only a handful of moai stood a decade later.

In 1864 Eugene Eyraud, the first European missionary on the island, commented that:

> These savages are tall, strong, and well built. Their features resemble far more the European type than those of the other islanders of Oceania. Among all the Polynesians the Marquesans are those to which they display the greatest resemblance. Their complexion, although a little copper-coloured, does neither differ much from the hue of the European, and a great number are even completely white.

Population, Environment & Warfare

What was the reason for the warfare on Rapa Nui and the destruction of the moai? Recent research suggests a demographic explanation: islanders were few when Hotu Matua first landed at Anakena, but over the centuries the population grew, first slowly and then rapidly, so that sheer numbers threatened the natural resource base. Once intensively cultivated gardens yielded an agricultural surplus sufficient to support a priestly class, the artisans and labourers who produced the moai and their ahu, and even a warrior class.

There were limits to how intensively crops could be grown. Irrigation, for instance, was difficult or impossible in an environment which lacked surface streams. Forest resources, probably used for timber to move the moai to their ahu, were greatly depleted. This situation worsened when warriors used fire for military purposes. Food sources from the sea was too poor and too dispersed to provide more than a supplement to agriculture.

Conflict over land and resources erupted in warfare by the late-17th century, only shortly before Roggeveen's arrival. Alfred Metraux estimated a population of up to 4000 in the early 19th century, while Katherine Routledge speculated on a maximum population of about 7000, but other informed guesses range up to 20,000. Accounts by later European visitors, such as Cook, provide graphic images of the results of what must have been a protracted struggle in which the population had declined even before slave raids in the mid-19th century. Colonialism, a late arrival, delivered the final blow to an already struggling population.

Colonialism in the Pacific

Whether or not the people of Rapa Nui experienced a period of self-inflicted havoc, their discovery by the outside world almost resulted in their annihilation. The first catastrophe was the Peruvian slave raid of 1862, leading directly or indirectly to many deaths. Then followed a brief but violent period involving the transportation of many more islanders to foreign mines and plantations, the introduction of previously unknown diseases, emigration compelled by mission-aries, and the near-disintegration of local culture.

The Peruvian raid happened when, after the European voyages of the late 18th century, European and North American entrepreneurs saw the Pacific as an unexploited 'resource frontier'. First came the whalers – many of them North American – who ranged the Pacific from Chile to Australia. Then came planters who set out to satisfy increasing European demand for tropical agricultural products like rubber, sugar, copra and coffee. This often resulted in indigenous people becoming slaves or wage labourers on their own lands, or in the importation of foreign labour where local labour proved insufficient, inefficient or difficult to control.

Then came slavers who either kidnapped

Polynesians or, to give the trade a veneer of legitimacy, compelled or induced them to sign contracts to work in lands as remote as Australia and Peru. Many of the slavers' victims died from the rigours of hard labour, poor diet, disease, and maltreatment. Christian missionaries also entered the region bringing their imported culture which undermined and degraded the local customs.

Since the 1860s, local history on Rapa Nui consists of three periods: one in which a French sea captain ruled the island; a second, from 1888 to 1952, when a Chilean-Scottish sheep-grazing concern leased nearly the entire island; and the third with the active intervention of the Chilean state.

Peruvian Slave Raid – 1862

Violent encounters had occurred between Europeans and islanders ever since Roggeveen's landing, but the Peruvian raid was vicious and ruthless. Slavers kidnapped about 1000 islanders (including the king and nearly all the *maori* or 'learned men') and took them to work the guano deposits on Peru's Chincha Islands. After Bishop Jaussen of Tahiti protested to the French representative at Lima, Peruvian authorities ordered the return of the islanders to their homeland, but disease and hard labour had already killed about 900 of them. On the return voyage, smallpox killed most of the rest. The handful who survived brought an epidemic to the island which killed many of its remaining inhabitants, leaving perhaps only a few hundred people.

The first attempts at Christianising the island occurred after this disaster. Eugene Eyraud, of the Chilean branch of the French Catholic *Société de Picpus*, initially met resistance and left in 1864, but returned in 1866. With the assistance of other missionaries, he converted the islanders within a few years.

Dutroux-Bornier Period – 1870-1877

The first attempt at commercial exploitation of the island began in 1870, when Frenchman Jean-Baptiste Dutroux-Bornier settled at Mataveri, at the foot of Rano Kau. Importing sheep, he intended to convert the entire island into a ranch and expel the islanders to the plantations of Tahiti. The missionaries, who planned to ship the islanders to mission lands in southern Chile or the Mangarévas, opposed his claims to ultimate sovereignty over the island and its people.

Dutroux-Bornier armed local followers and raided the missionary settlements, burning houses and destroying crops, leaving many people dead or injured, and forcing the missionaries to evacuate in 1870 and 1871. Most islanders reluctantly accepted transportation to Tahiti and the Mangarévas, leaving only about a hundred people on the island. Dutroux-Bornier ruled until the remaining islanders killed him in 1877.

Annexation by Chile – 1888

Spain never pursued its interest in Rapa Nui and, in any event, lost all its South American territories early in the 19th century. On the advice of naval officer Policarpo Toro, who had visited the island as early as 1870, Chile officially annexed the island in 1888 during a period of expansion which included the acquisition of territory from Peru and Bolivia after the War of the Pacific (1879-84).

With its vigorous navy, Chile was capable of expanding into the Pacific. It valued the island partly for its agricultural potential, real or imagined, but mostly for geopolitical purposes; as a naval station, to prevent its use by a hostile power, for its location on a potentially important trading route between South America and East Asia, and for the prestige of having overseas possessions, any possessions, in an era of imperialism.

Williamson, Balfour & Company

Attempts at colonisation came to nothing and, with no clear government policy, by 1897 Rapa Nui fell under control of a single wool-growing company run by Enrique Merlet, a Valparaíso businessman who had bought or leased nearly all the land. Control soon passed into other hands, however.

In 1851 in Liverpool, three Scottish businessmen founded S Williamson & Company to ship British goods to the west coast of South America. Its Chilean branch, Williamson, Balfour & Company, officially came into being in 1863, by which time the company controlled a substantial fleet and had expanded its interests to include a wide range of products and countries. In the early 20th century, it acquired Merlet's Rapa Nui holdings, managing the island through its Compañía Explotadora de la Isla de Pascua (CEDIP), under lease from the Chilean government. The company became the island's de facto government, continuing its profitable wool trade until mid-century.

How islanders fared under this system is the subject of differing accounts, but there were several uprisings against the company. One result of foreign control was the genetic transformation of the islanders, as they intermarried with immigrants of many countries and, by the 1930s, perhaps three-quarters of the population were of mixed descent, including North American, British, Chilean, Chinese, French, German, Italian, Tahitian, or Tuamotuan stock.

In 1953, when Chile was seeking to consolidate its control over its far-flung and rather unwieldy territories, the government revoked CEDIP's lease. The navy took charge of the island, continuing the imperial rule to which islanders had been subject for nearly a century.

Chilean Colonialism

Rapa Nui continued under military rule until the mid-1960s, followed by a brief period of civilian government, until the military coup of 1973 once again brought direct control by the military. There is now, however, local self-government.

By the 1960s, the island was a colony pure and simple. Islanders' grievances included unpaid labour, travel restrictions, confinement to the Hanga Roa area, suppression of the Rapa Nui language, ineligibility to vote (Chilean universal suffrage did not extend to Rapa Nui) and arbitrary naval administration against which there was no appeal. However, increased contact with the outside world soon developed after the establishment of a regular commercial air link between Santiago and Tahiti in 1967, with Rapa Nui as a refuelling stop.

For a variety of reasons – including islanders' dissatisfaction, increased immigration from the continent, international attention and tourist potential, and the assumption of power by President Frei – the Chilean presence became more benevolent in the 1960s. There were advances in providing medical care, education, potable water and electricity.

Although cattle and sheep still graze parts of the island, the chief industry is tourism – a fairly recent phenomenon which developed with regular air services from mainland Chile and from Tahiti. It has had an overwhelming impact, as nearly everyone now makes a living, directly or indirectly, from the tourist trade.

In August 1985, General Pinochet approved a plan allowing the USA to expand Mataveri airport as an emergency landing site for the space shuttle, arousing opposition both locally and on the continent, but the Rapa Nui people had no say in the decision. In 1990, however, islanders protested against fare increases by LAN-Chile (the only air carrier) and successfully occupied Mataveri airport – even preventing the landing of a jetload of Carabineros by blocking the runway with cars and rubble. The global impulse toward self-determination has reached even this remote place, as some islanders argue vocally for the return of native lands and speak hopefully of independence or at least autonomy. Their aspirations are tempered by realism though; when asked if he would like to expel the Chileans, one islander responded, 'We can't – but we'd like them to leave'.

GEOGRAPHY

Just south of the Tropic of Capricorn, Rapa Nui is a small volcanic island formed where, in the distant past, lava from three separate cones of different ages coalesced in a single triangular land mass. Its total area is just 117 sq km, its maximum length 24 km and maximum width only 12 km.

All three major volcanos are now extinct. Terevaka, the largest, rises 600 metres above sea level in the island's north-east corner, while Pukatikei (about 400 metres); forms the eastern headland of the Poike peninsula; Rano Kau (about 410 metres) dominates the south-west corner. Smaller craters include Rano Raraku, from whose hard basalt islanders carved their giant moai, and Puna Pau, north-east of Hanga Roa, which provided the reddish scoria which forms the statues' topknots. At Orito, islanders quarried black obsidian for spearpoints and cutting tools. Rano Kau and Rano Raraku both contain freshwater lakes.

For the most part, Rapa Nui's volcanic slopes are gentle and grass-covered, except where wave erosion has produced nearly vertical cliffs. In contrast, rugged lava fields cover much of the island's interior, although several areas have soil adequate for cultivation – Hanga Roa and Mataveri on the west coast, Vaihu on the south coast, the plain south-west of Rano Raraku, and inland at Vaitea.

Vulcanism has left numerous caves, many in seaside cliffs. Some, consisting of larger and smaller chambers connected by tunnels through which a person can barely squeeze, extend for considerable distances into the lava. These could be permanent shelters, refuges in wartime, or secret storage or burial sites.

Rapa Nui rests on a geological platform some 50 or 60 metres below the surface of the sea, but from 15 to 30 km off the coast the platform ends and the ocean floor drops to between 1800 and 3600 metres. There are three tiny islands just off Rano Kau: Motu Nui, Motu Iti and Motu Kao Kao, of which Motu Nui is the largest. Motu Nui is (or was) a nesting ground for thousands of sooty terns. There are no coral reefs, although some coral occurs in shallow waters. In the absence of reefs, the ocean has battered the huge cliffs, some of which rise 300 metres. The cliffs composed of lava are usually lower but are also extremely rugged. There is no natural sheltered harbour on the island, and Anakena on the north coast has the only broad sandy beach, although there are a few shallow bays.

Rapa Nui's rainfall supports a permanent cover of coarse grasses, but its volcanic soil is so porous that water quickly drains underground. There are no permanent streams on the island and water for both humans and livestock comes either from the volcanic lakes or from wells. Vegetation was once much more luxuriant – including forests with palms, conifers and other species now extinct – but islanders cut the forests long ago. Most of today's trees, like the eucalypts, were planted only within the past century.

Like other remote islands, Rapa Nui lacks entire families of plants and is particularly poor in native fauna; even sea birds are relatively few. Some plants are endemic, most notably the tree species *Todomiro (Sophora toromiro)* and several genera of ferns. The original immigrants brought small animals like chickens and rats, while the Norway (or brown) rat escaped from European vessels; Europeans also brought horses and other grazing animals in the 19th century.

CLIMATE

Winds and ocean currents strongly influence Rapa Nui's subtropical climate. The hottest months are January and February, while the coolest are July and August. The average maximum summer temperature is 28°C and the average minimum 15°C, but these figures understate what can be a fierce sun and formidable heat. The average winter maximum is 22°C and the minimum 14°C, but it can seem much cooler when Antarctic winds lash the island with rain. Light showers, however, are the most frequent form of precipitation. May is the wettest month, but tropical downpours can occur during all seasons.

RAPA NUI STONEWORK

Although the giant moai are the most pervasive image of Rapa Nui, there are several other types of stonework. Some of the other important sites include the large ahu on which the moai were erected, burial cairns (large piles of rock under which bodies were entombed), and the stone foundations of the unusual *hare paenga* (boat-shaped houses). One of the most striking things about the island is the remarkable density of ruins, indicating there was once a much larger population than there is at present.

Although many structures were partially demolished or rebuilt by the original inhabitants and the moai fell during intertribal wars, CEDIP's regime was also responsible for major damage. Many ahu, burial cairns, house foundations, and other structures were dismantled and used to build the piers at Caleta Hanga Roa and Caleta Hanga Piko, as well as stone walls around grazing areas. Windmills were constructed over the original stone-lined wells to provide water for sheep, cattle and horses.

Collectors have pillaged other sites. Only a few moai were removed, but museums and private collections in Chile and elsewhere now feature wooden rongo-rongo tablets, painted wall tablets from houses at Orongo, small wood and stone moai, weapons, clothing, skulls and other artefacts. Islanders themselves were responsible for removing building materials from sites like Orongo.

On the other hand, archaeologists have restored a number of sites over the last 30 years. These include Ahu Tahai, Ahu Akivi, the Orongo ceremonial village, and Ahu Nau Nau. Others, such as Ahu Vinapu and Ahu Vaihu, lie in ruins but are nonetheless impressive.

Ahu

There are about 245 ahu, most forming an almost unbroken line along the coast, except for headlands around the Peninsula Poike and Rano Kau. They tend to be sited at sheltered coves and areas favourable for human habitation, but only a few were built inland.

Of several varieties of ahu, built at different times for different reasons, the most impressive are the *ahu moai* which support the massive statues. Each is a mass of loose stones held together by retaining walls and paved on the upper surface with more or less flat stones, with a vertical wall on the seaward side and usually at each end. The

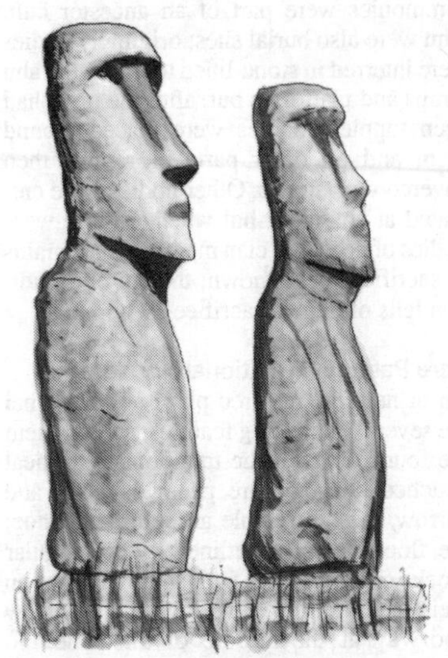

moai on these platforms range from two to almost 10 metres in height, although even larger moai were under construction in the quarry at Rano Raraku when work suddenly ceased, probably because of lack of timber to move and raise the moai.

Usually a gently sloping ramp, paved with rounded boulders or tightly placed slabs of irregular stones, comprises the landward side of the platform. Next to the ramp is a large, perhaps artificially levelled, plaza; in a few cases, these are outlined by earthworks which form rectangular or irregular enclosures. Sometimes there are small rectangular platforms which may be altars, and large circles paved with stones, while a bit farther inland there may be foundations of boat-shaped houses. Early islanders used one and two-person reed boats, and much larger reed boats were probably launched from *apapa* (stone ramps) leading into the sea by the side of the ahu.

Researchers have learned very little about the ceremonies connected with these ahu complexes. One theory is that the moai represented clan ancestors and that the ceremonies were part of an ancestor cult. Ahu were also burial sites: originally bodies were interred in stone-lined tombs in the ahu ramps and platforms but, after the moai had been toppled, bodies were placed around them and on other parts of ramps, then covered with stones. Other bodies were cremated at ahu sites, but whether these were bodies of deceased clan members or remains of sacrifices is unknown, though oral tradition tells of human sacrifice by burning.

Hare Paenga (Traditional Houses)

On or near the restored plaza at Ahu Tahai are several interesting features, among them the foundations of the traditional, elliptical thatched houses (hare paenga). Long and narrow, these resemble an upturned canoe; the floor shape is outlined by rectangular blocks or kerb stones with small hollows on their upper surfaces, with a single narrow doorway at the middle of one side. To support walls and roof, islanders inserted poles into these hollows, then arched them across the centre of the structure and, where they crossed, lashed them to a ridge pole.

As the space to be covered narrowed near the ends, the roofing poles decreased in length, lowering the roof level. A crescent-shaped stone pavement often covered the entry. These dwellings varied enormously in size; some could house more than 100 people, while others held but half a dozen.

Moai

Although all moai are similar, few are identical. The standard moai at Rano Raraku has its base at about hip level, with stiffly hanging arms and extended hands with long slender fingers, across a protruding abdomen. The heads are elongated and rectangular, with heavy brows and prominent noses, small mouths with thin lips, prominent chins and elongated earlobes, some of them carved for inserted ear ornaments. Hands, breasts, navels, and facial features are clear, while elaborately carved backs possibly represent tattoos.

It is interesting to speculate on the models for the moai, since their features – long straight noses, tight-lipped mouths, sunken eyes, and low foreheads – do not seem Polynesian. Large stone statues have also been found on the Marquesas, Raivavae, and other islands of eastern Polynesia, but also in western South America.

Since the moai at the quarry show all stages of carving, it's easy to visualise the process. Most were carved face up, in a horizontal or slightly reclining position. Workers excavated a channel, large enough for the carvers, around and under each moai, leaving it attached to the rock only along its back. Nearly all the carving, including the fine detail, occurred at this stage. The moai was then detached and somehow transported down the slope (sometimes a vertical wall), avoiding others below. At the base of the cliff, workers raised it into a standing position in trenches, where sculptors carved finer details on the back and decorated the waist with a belt surrounded by rings and symbols. When the carving was finished they were moved to their ahu on the coast.

Moai vary greatly in size; some are as short as two metres in length, whilst the

longest is just under 21 metres long. However, very few are shorter than three metres, and the usual length is from 5½ to seven metres. The 21-metre colossus is unique; the face alone is just over nine metres long, it measures just over four metres across the shoulders, and the body is about 1½ metres thick. Carvers completed the front and both sides, but never liberated it from the rock below.

Basalt *tokis*, thousands of which once littered the quarry site, were the carving tools. In *Aku-Aku: The Secret of Easter Island*, Heyerdahl recalls hiring a number of islanders to carve new moai at Rano Raraku; they quit after three days, but their efforts suggested that two teams working constantly in shifts would need perhaps 12 to 15 months to carve a medium-sized moai.

Many of the moai have distinctive features. One displays a three-masted sailing ship on its chest; from the bow, a line extends downward to a circular figure of what might be a head and four short legs, although the figure is so crude that it almost certainly has no connection with the carving of the moai itself. This may represent a European ship or a large *totora* reed vessel, while the figure below may be an anchor of some sort, although it could also be a turtle or tortoise held by a fishing line. Moai mostly depicted males, but a several specimens have carvings which clearly represent breasts and vulva.

A most unusual discovery at Rano Raraku was the kneeling Moai Tukuturi, which was almost totally buried. Slightly less than four metres high, it now sits on the south-eastern slope of the mountain, where placing it upright required a jeep, tackle, poles, ropes, chains, and 20 workers. It has a fairly natural rounded head, a goatee, short ears, and a full body squatting on its heels, with forearms and hands resting on its thighs. It has a low brow with curved eyebrows, hollow and slightly oval eyes, and pupils marked by small, round cavities. Both the nose and lips are considerably damaged, but the cheeks are round and natural.

Having carved a moai from hard basalt, it was removed from its cavity and lowered down the cliff face – which must have been difficult and dangerous, as broken moai suggest that ropes snapped or workers slipped. After standing it up at the base of the slope (probably by sliding it into a trench cut for the occasion) and completely carving the back, it was transported several km to the coast and stood upright on a raised platform.

Islanders placed 300 moai on ahu or left them along the old roads in various parts of the island. There are several explanations for this feat, but any valid one must account for the transport and erection of the biggest moai ever placed on an ahu – the 10-metre giant at Ahu Te Pito Te Kura.

Moving the Moai

Just moving the moai to the site must have been an even greater problem. Legend says that priests moved the moai by the power of *mana*, an ability to make the moai walk a short distance every day until eventually it reached its destination. After suggestions that islanders could have moved the moai with a Y-shaped sledge made from a forked tree trunk, pulled with ropes made from tree bark, Heyerdahl organised 180 islanders to pull a four-metre moai across the field at Anakena, and speculated that they could have moved a much larger one with wooden runners and more labour. Another explanation is that islanders inserted round stones under the moai, which were pushed, pulled and rolled to their destinations like a block on marbles, but this fails to explain how they were moved without harming the fine details carved at the quarry.

North American archaeologist William Mulloy proposed a different method of moving the moai which, though difficult, would have been physically possible with enough labour and is consistent with the shape and configuration of the moai. First, islanders would have fitted a wooden sledge to the moai (Figures 1 & 2, next page); the distribution of the statue's weight would have kept the relatively light and fragile head above ground when tipped over. They would then set up a bipod astride the statue's neck, at an angle to the vertical (Figures 3 & 4) and

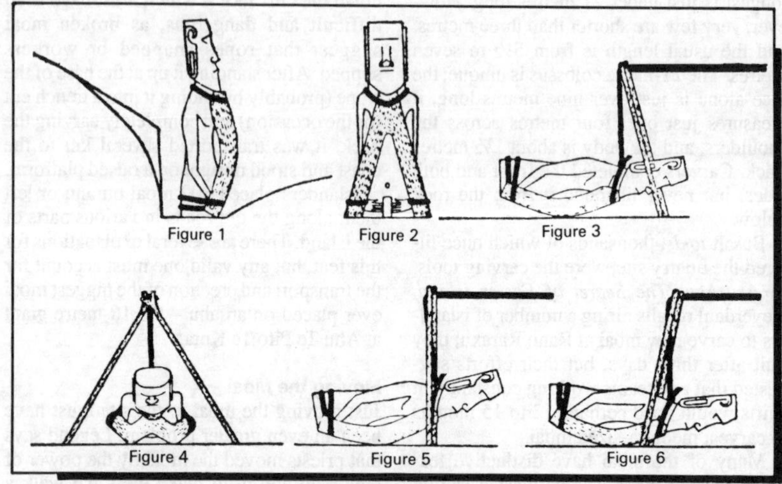

William Mulloy's statue-moving theory

tied a cable attached to the moai's neck to the bipod apex and pulled it forward. The head of the moai would then rise slightly (Figure 5) and the moai would be dragged forward. When the bipod passed vertical, the statue's own weight would carry it forward along its belly (Figure 6). By moving the legs of the bipod forward, the entire process could be repeated.

This repetitive series of upward and forward movements recalls the islanders' legend that the moai 'walked' to their ahu. It could also explain the broken moai along the old transport routes; the rope or bipod may have slipped or broken when the moai was raised, and the statue fallen to the ground. There are a few problems with Mulloy's method (for a start, it requires large trees to make the bipods) but it's theoretically possible and also a partial explanation for deforestation of the island.

Once at its ahu, the moai had to be raised onto an elevated platform. Restoration of seven moai in the 1960s by Mulloy and Gonzalo Figueroa (see the section on Aku Akivi, following) suggests that leverage and support with rocks may indeed have raised the moai.

Topknots

Some archaeologists thought the reddish cylindrical topknots on many moai were hats, baskets, or crowns, but there is now a consensus that these *pukao* reflect a common hairstyle of Rapa Nui males when Europeans first visited the island. Quarried from the small volcanic crater at Puna Pau, this stone is relatively soft and easily worked. Most pukao had a clearly marked knot on the top and a partly hollow underside which allowed them to be slotted onto the heads of the moai.

Since only about 60 moai had topknots, another 25 of which remain in or near the quarry, these appear to have been a late development. Carved like the moai, the topknots may have been simple embellishments, rolled to their final destination, and then, despite weighing about as much as two elephants, somehow placed on top of moai up to 10 metres in height. Early Europeans recorded that moai were still standing on their ahu with the topknots mounted.

Some believe that islanders carved the knot on top of the stone and its hollow underside only after transporting the stone to its ahu – probably to prevent its breaking in transport and to allow measurement of the head in order to carve a proper-sized hollow, but there are also hollow topknots within the crater itself. Oral tradition says that islanders built a ramp of stones to roll the topknot to the moai's head, but Mulloy thought the most likely method of attachment was to tie it to the moai and raise the two simultaneously. This would eliminate the clumsy, time-consuming method of building a ramp and rolling the topknot up it.

BOOKS

For general background on geography and environment, the most thorough source is Juan Carlos Castilla's edited collection, *Islas Oceánicas Chilenas* (Santiago, Ediciones Universidad Católica de Chile, 1987), which also deals with Chile's other insular possessions, including the Juan Fernández Islands.

Though dated, one of the most thorough works on Rapa Nui proper is *Reports of the Norwegian Archaeological Expedition to Easter Island & the East Pacific. Volume 1: Archaeology of Easter Island* (London, Allen & Unwin, 1962). Summarising the findings of the initial Heyerdahl expedition, it's fully illustrated, with detailed descriptions of all important sites (though none had been restored at the time). More readily accessible are Heyerdahl's popular account of his voyage in *Kon-Tiki* (Chicago, Rand McNally, 1952), and his *Aku-Aku: The Secret of Easter Island* (Allen & Unwin, 1958).

Englishwoman Katherine Routledge headed the first archaeological expedition, a private venture in 1914. The scientific notes of the expedition all disappeared, but she published *The Mystery of Easter Island: the Story of an Expedition* in 1919. Other pre-Heyerdahl accounts include J MacMillan Brown's *The Riddle of the Pacific* (1924) and anthropologist Alfred Metraux's *Ethnology of Easter Island* (1940, but reprinted by the Bishop Museum Press in Honolulu in 1971), based on field research during a French-Belgian expedition in the 1930s.

Bavarian priest Sebastián Englert spent 35 years on Rapa Nui until his death in 1970; his *Island at the Center of the World* (New York, Scribner's, 1970) retells the island's history through oral tradition. If you read Spanish, his *La Tierra de Hotu Matua* (Editorial Universitaria, Santiago, 3rd edition 1983, but first published in 1948) is a worthwhile acquisition. Englert also analysed indigenous speech in *Idioma Rapanui – Gramática y Diccionario del Antíguo Idioma de la Isla de Pascua* (Universidad de Chile, 1978). Both books are available in Santiago. Another German, Thomas Barthel, offered a unique perspective on local history via obscure indigenous manuscripts in *The Eighth Land: The Polynesian Discovery and Settlement of Easter Island* (Honolulu, University Press of Hawaii, 1978).

As the 'Navel of the World', Rapa Nui is also a focus of the debate over diffusion, independent invention, and trans-Pacific contacts. Heyerdahl's *American Indians in the Pacific: The Theory Behind the Kon-Tiki Expedition* (London, Allen & Unwin, 1952) compares American Indian and Pacific cultures, legends, religion, stonework, watercraft, physical characteristics and cultivated plants.

However, there is now consensus that the initial settlers were Polynesians who arrived by way of the Marquesas. For a review of trans-Pacific migration, see Peter Bellwood's 'The Peopling of the Pacific' in *Scientific American*, Vol 243, No 5, November 1980), or his *Man's Conquest of the Pacific* (New York, Oxford University Press, 1979), which also includes a lengthy section on Rapa Nui and the Polynesian-American argument.

A very valuable but diverse collection, dealing partly with pre-Columbian contacts across the Pacific is *Man Across the Sea* (University of Texas Press, 1971), edited by Carroll L Riley, J Charles Kelley, Campbell W Pennington and Robert L Rands. Based on meticulous research, it deals with a wide variety of related topics, particularly the diffusion of cultivated plants and domestic animals as indicators of human movement.

Some scientists have devised computer simulations of both drift and navigated voyages to try to resolve the matter of Polynesian peoples in the Pacific. One of these is *The Settlement of Polynesia: A Computer Simulation* (Canberra, ANU Press, 1973) by Michael Levison, R Gerard Ward and John Webb.

The Peruvian slave raid on Rapa Nui was no isolated incident; in the early 1860s, many Polynesian islands suffered such attacks, detailed in Henry Maude's *Slavers in Paradise: the Peruvian Labour Trade in Polynesia, 1862-1864* (published in Australia by ANU Press and in the USA by Stanford). For an account of the island from the mid-1800s almost to the present, see *The Modernization of Easter Island* (University of Victoria, British Columbia, Canada, 1981) by J Douglas Porteous. In a coffee-table format, try Michel Rougie's *Isla de Pascua*, published by Sernatur, whose superb photos record all the major sites, with text in Spanish, French, and English. German speakers especially will enjoy a collection of articles entitled *1500 Jahre Kultur der Osterinsel* (Mainz, Verlag Philipp von Zabern, 1989), but anyone can appreciate its lavish illustrations, not just of moai and archaeological sites, but of other indigenous artwork as well.

MAPS

Most maps of Easter Island are very poor, but *Isla de Pascua-Rapa Nui: Mapa Arqueológico-Turístico* (Santiago: Ediciones del Pacífico Sur), at a scale of 1:30,000, is outstanding. Available at the tourist office and in island shops for about US$10, it's a very worthwhile investment for any visitor.

GETTING THERE & AWAY

Unless you want to make a balsa raft like the *Kon- Tiki*, the only practical way to reach Easter Island is by air. LAN-Chile has two flights per week (three in summer) between Santiago and Tahiti, stopping at Easter Island. The standard fare is US$812 return.

Travellers from Australia or New Zealand can take a Melbourne/Sydney-Tahiti flight with Qantas or an Auckland-Tahiti flight with Air New Zealand and then transfer to LAN-Chile for the onward flight to Rapa Nui and Santiago. For details of fares, see the Getting There & Away chapter.

If you're coming from North America, it may be cheaper to take a LAN-Chile Circle Pacific fare (including Easter Island and Tahiti) than a return fare to Chile plus a Santiago-Easter Island return flight.

A LAN-Chile 21-day 'Visit Chile Pass' can include Easter Island for US$1080 – this is US$780 more than an air pass without the Easter Island option, so it's a minor saving (US$32) on the usual return fare. Because the air pass is only valid for a maximum of 21 days, using this option to visit Easter Island may not leave much time for the rest of Chile. (For more details about air passes, see the Getting Around chapter).

Flights to and from Rapa Nui can be very crowded, especially in the peak summer season, so be certain to reconfirm at both ends or you may arrive at the airport to find your reservation has been cancelled. The flight from Santiago takes 5½ hours, and LAN-Chile's service is excellent and attentive; the return flight from Rapa Nui is at least an hour faster because of the prevailing westerlies and the jet stream.

GETTING AROUND

There is no formal public transportation on Rapa Nui: rented horses, motorbikes and cars are your main options. It is possible to walk around the island in a few days, but the summer heat, lack of shade, and scattered water supply are good reasons not to do so. While distances appear small on the map, you may find visiting numerous archaeological sites tiring and time-consuming. With good transport, you can see all the major archaeological sites, at least superficially, in about three days, but many people take longer.

If you ride a horse or a motorbike around the island, carry a day-pack, a long-sleeved shirt, sunglasses, a large hat to shade the face and neck, plus a powerful sun-block for the sub-tropical rays. Carry extra food and a water bottle, since neither is easily available outside Hanga Roa.

Motorbikes & Cars

Established hotels rent Suzuki jeeps for US$70 per day, but locals will rent them for around US$40 or US$50 per 12-hour day – ask at the residenciales or at the tourist office. You can ask just about anywhere, but try Easter Island Rent-a-Car (☎ 328) on Policarpo Toro, Te Aiki (☎ 366) at the Residencial Tekena, or any of several other places which have signs in their windows. Outside high season, prices are very negotiable.

Locals will rent their own motorbikes for about US$30 to US$35 a day; motorbikes are also available from the Hotel Hanga Roa for US$40. Given occasional tropical downpours, a jeep is more convenient and can be more economical, especially for two or more people.

Petrol, subsidised by the Chilean government, costs about a third less than it does on the continent, so it is not a significant expense for the relatively short distances you will cover. Outside Hanga Roa, all the roads are unsurfaced, but most are in decent enough condition if you proceed with reasonable caution.

Horses

Horses can be hired for about US$15 per day, but see the beast before renting it – Rapa Nui has no glue factory and you won't want to risk being impaled by protruding ribs as your mount collapses under you. Most horse gear is very basic and potentially hazardous for inexperienced riders, but the Hotel Hotu Matua or Hotel Hanga Roa may organise riding excursions and locate a horse with proper stirrups and reins.

Horses are good for visiting sites near Hanga Roa like Ahu Tepeu, Vinapu, Ahu Akivi and Orongo, but for more distant places like Rano Raraku and Anakena motorised transport is superior.

Around the Archeological Sites

Approximate distances to important sites by road from Hanga Roa are:

Orito	2	km
Vinapu	5	km
Vaihu	9½	km
Akahanga	12½	km
Rano Raraku	18	km
Ahu Tongariki	20	km
Ahu Te Pito Te Kura	26	km
Ovahe	29	km
Anakena	30	km
Ahu Tahai	1½	km
Ahu Akivi	10	km
Puna Pau	15	km
Orongo	6	km

It's possible to take in all the major sites on three loops out of Hanga Roa – the South-West Route, the Northern Loop, and the Island Circle. These three routes involve a minimum of backtracking.

South-West Route From Hanga Roa take the road to the top of the Rano Kau crater and the Orongo ceremonial village. Backtrack to Hanga Roa, then follow the road along the northern edge of the airport to Orito, site of the old obsidian quarries. From here head southwards to Ahu Vinapu with its impressive, finely cut stonework.

Northern Loop Take the route from Hanga Roa to Puna Pau crater, source of the reddish volcanic scoria for the topknots of the moai. From here, continue inland to the restored Ahu Akivi, whose seven moai have been re-erected. From Ahu Akivi follow the track to Ahu Tepeu on the west coast, said to be the burial site of Tuu-ko-ihu, then head south to Hanga Roa, stopping off at Ahu Akapu, Ahu Tahai and Ahu Tautira, all of which have been restored and their moai re-erected. Because of the poorly marked trail/road between Ahu Akivi and the coast, it's probably easier to go from Hanga Roa to Ahu Akivi and then cut cross-country to Ahu Tepeu rather than the other way round.

Island Circle From Hanga Roa, follow the southern coast stopping off at the ruins at Vaihu and Akahanga, with their massive ahu and giant toppled moai. Continue west from Akahanga and detour inland to the Rano Raraku crater, source of the hard basalt for most of the island's moai, where statues in all stages of production still lie in place. Leaving Rano Raraku, follow the road west to Ahu Tongariki, a ruined ahu whose moai and masonry were hurled some distance inland by a massive tsunami after the Chilean earthquake of 1960.

From Tongariki, follow the road to the north coast to Ahu Te Pito Te Kura, which boasts the largest moai ever erected on an ahu. Continue east to the beach at Ovahe, and then to Anakena, the island's main beach and the site of two more restored ahu.

Tours

Several agencies organise tours around the island. Many have offices in Santiago as well as on the island; their Santiago addresses are given here: O Ta'i Agency (☎ 250, Santiago ☎ 690-2674); Kia Koe Tour (☎ 297, Santiago ☎ 632-1048), Moneda 772, Oficina 402-B; Aku Aku Tour (☎ 297, Santiago ☎ 211-6747), Badajóz 12, Oficina 301; Tiki Tour (☎ 327, Santiago ☎ 211-4412), Apoquindo 6415, Oficina 33; and Mahina Tour (☎ 220).

If you're only in transit en route to Tahiti or Santiago, Anakena Tours offers a whirlwind tour from Mataveri airport to Ahu Tahai and then back to the airport for your flight.

HANGA ROA

Only about 2000 people live on Rapa Nui, nearly all of them in Hanga Roa. About 70% are predominantly Polynesian, considering themselves Rapa Nui rather than Chileans, while most of the remainder are immigrants from the Chilean mainland. Nearly everyone depends directly or indirectly on the tourist trade, but there is some fishing, plus livestock (mostly cattle) rearing, as well as kitchen gardens growing fruit and vegetables on the outskirts of the village. Government agencies and small general stores are the only other source of employment.

Orientation

Hanga Roa, on the western shore of Rapa Nui, is a sprawling, decentralised tropical village with a highly irregular street plan. Although many of the streets bear formal names, in practice those names are rarely used, there are almost no street numbers, and most people would identify places with reference to landmarks such as the fishing harbour of Caleta Hanga Roa, the Gobernación, the market or the church. Although this section gives street directions whenever possible, it is easier to rely on the map than on street names.

Information

Tourist Office Sernatur (☎ 55) is on the corner of Tuu Maheere and Apina, near Caleta Hanga Roa. The staff usually speak Rapa Nui, Spanish, English and French. The airport office is open only when planes arrive or depart.

Money The Banco del Estado, adjacent to the tourist office, will change US dollars, but pays the less advantageous official rate and charges a hefty 10% commission on travellers' cheques, so bring as much Chilean currency as you think you may need. US cash can be changed readily with local people, but often at a disadvantageous exchange rate. Some businesses, such as hotels and car rentals, quote prices in US dollars and expect payment in that currency.

Post & Telecommunications The post office, Correos de Chile, is on Te Pito o Te Henua, half a block from Caleta Hanga Roa. ENTEL, easily located by its conspicuous satellite dish, is on a cul-de-sac opposite Sernatur and the Banco de Chile.

Medical Services Hanga Roa's hospital is one long block to the east of the church.

Film & Photography Take as much film as possible, since it's scarce and expensive on

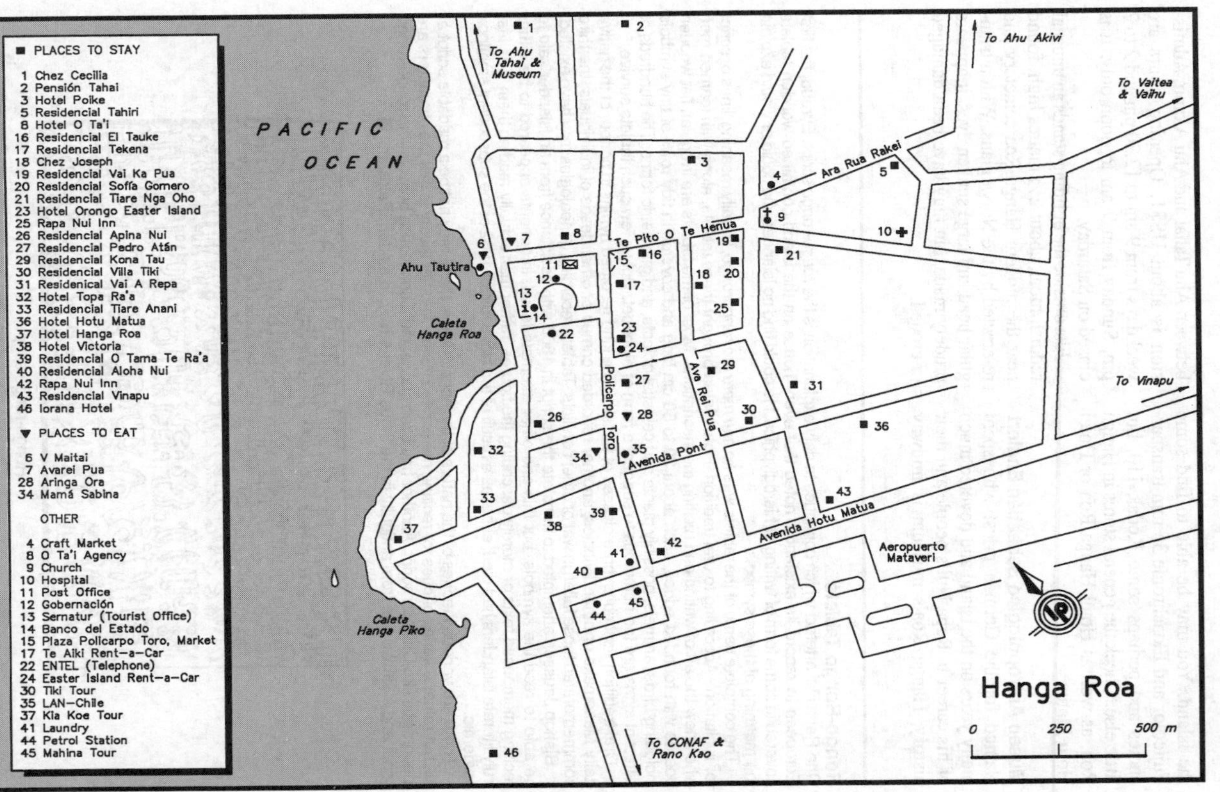
■ PLACES TO STAY
1 Chez Cecilia
2 Pensión Tahai
3 Hotel Poike
5 Residencial Tahiri
8 Hotel O Ta'i
16 Residencial El Tauke
17 Residencial Tekena
18 Chez Joseph
19 Residencial Vai Ka Pua
20 Residencial Sofía Gomero
21 Residencial Tiare Nga Oho
23 Hotel Orongo Easter Island
25 Rapa Nui Inn
26 Residencial Apina Nui
27 Residencial Pedro Atán
29 Residencial Kona Tau
30 Residencial Villa Tiki
31 Residenical Vai A Repa
32 Hotel Topa Ra'a
33 Residencial Tiare Anani
36 Hotel Hotu Matua
37 Hotel Hanga Roa
38 Hotel Victoria
39 Residencial O Tama Te Ra'a
40 Residencial Aloha Nui
42 Rapa Nui Inn
43 Residencial Vinapu
46 Iorana Hotel
▼ PLACES TO EAT
6 V Maitai
7 Avarei Pua
28 Aringa Ora
34 Mamá Sabina
OTHER
4 Craft Market
8 O Ta'i Agency
9 Church
10 Hospital
11 Post Office
12 Gobernación
13 Sernatur (Tourist Office)
14 Banco del Estado
15 Plaza Policarpo Toro, Market
17 Te Aiki Rent-a-Car
22 ENTEL (Telephone)
24 Easter Island Rent-a-Car
30 Tiki Tour
35 LAN-Chile
37 Kia Koe Tour
41 Laundry
44 Petrol Station
45 Mahina Tour
PACIFIC OCEAN
To Ahu Tahai & Museum
To Ahu Akivi
To Vaitea & Vaihu
To Vinapu
To CONAF & Rano Kao
Ara Rua Rakei
Te Pito O Te Henua
Policarpo Toro
Ava Rei Pua
Avenida Pont
Avenida Hotu Matua
Ahu Tautira
Caleta Hanga Roa
Caleta Hanga Piko
Aeropuerto Mataveri
Hanga Roa
0 250 500 m

the island. You may be able to find some Fujicolor and Ektachrome 35 mm transparencies and perhaps some Kodak 110, but little else. Check the general stores in Hanga Roa, as well as Hotel Hanga Roa or Hotel Hotu Matua.

Museo Antropológico Sebastián Englert
Named for the German priest who spent many years on the island and devoted much of his career to Rapa Nui's people and their history, Hanga Roa's museum is midway between Ahu Tahai and Ahu Akapu. Admission is about US$1. Opening hours are weekdays from 9 am to 12.30 pm and 2 to 7 pm, Sunday from 9 am to noon only. It is closed on Saturday.

Just outside the building stands an unusual reddish moai, about 2½ metres high, found near the modern Hanga Roa cemetery and re-erected by the Norwegians. With a triangular head and large sunken eyes, it appears crudely made, but may have been damaged or eroded.

Rongo-Rongo Tablets
One Rapa Nui artefact which continues to defy explanation is the *rongo-rongo* script. Eyraud, the first European to record its existence, noted that every house on the island contained wooden tablets covered in some form of writing or hieroglyphics. He could find no islander who could or would explain the meaning of these symbols.

The complete name of the tablets was *ko hau motu mo rongorongo*, literally meaning 'lines of script for recitation'. According to oral tradition, Hotu Matua brought these tablets, along with learned men who knew the art of writing and reciting the inscriptions. Most of the tablets are irregular, flat wooden boards with rounded edges, each about 30 to 50 cm long and covered in tidy rows of tiny symbols including birds, animals, possibly plants and celestial objects, and geometric forms. The hundreds of different signs are too numerous to suggest a form of alphabet. Only a few such tablets survive.

Oral tradition describes three classes of tablets. One kind recorded hymns in honour of the native deity Makemake or other divinities; another recorded crimes or other deeds of individuals; the third commemorated those fallen in war or other conflicts. Tablets recording genealogies may have existed.

Bishop Jaussen attempted to translate the script in 1866 with assistance from an islander said to be able to read the symbols, but this and other attempts failed; informants appeared to be either reciting memorised texts or merely describing the figures, rather than actually reading them. The last truly literate islanders had died, either as a result of the slave raid of 1862 or the subsequent smallpox epidemic.

There are various theories of the nature of the script. One is that it may not be a readable script at all, but rather a series of cues for reciting memorised verse. Another theory is that the characters are ideographs like Chinese script. Another has even suggested a connection between the rongo-rongo script and a similar one from antiquity in the Indus River valley, in modern Pakistan. ■

Rongo-rongo script

Top : Playa de Ovahe, Easter Island (WB)
Bottom : Ahu Akivi, Easter Island (AS)

Top : Anakena Beach, Easter Island (WB)
Bottom Left : Squatting statue, Rano Raraku quarry, Easter Island (AS)
Bottom Right : Ahu Nau Nau at Anakena, Easter Island (AS)

This is not the only unusual moai – a seated figure at Rano Raraku (see following) is another. Inside the museum there are also several oblong-shaped stone heads, known as 'potato heads', with eye-sockets and rudimentary features, including one with round ears. These are thought to be the oldest carvings on the island, pre-dating the Rano Raraku figures.

Rapa Nui is so renowned for its monuments that both researchers and visitors often fail to appreciate the islanders' traditional way of life, and their historic and modern experience, but the museum partly redresses this shortcoming. It clearly demonstrates, for instance, that the Rapa Nui are a Polynesian people whose subsistence depended on the cultivation of crops such as *kumara* (sweet potato), a staple which islanders still strongly prefer to wheat, which is consumed most by immigrant Chileans. Kumara, taro root, *maika* (banana), *toa* (sugar cane) and other crops grew in excavated household garden enclosures known as *manavai*, as well as on terraces on Rano Kau crater. Among the most interesting garden sites are the entrances to the volcanic caves on the north-west side of the island which provided sheltered, humid microclimates for plants which required a great deal of moisture. Garden tools, including the *okauve* and the *oka*, are also on display.

Copies of interesting historical photographs depict the encounter of Rapa Nui and European culture since the mid-19th century, although the prints are in unfortunately poor condition. Legal documents illustrate how, for instance, the Chilean civil register hispanicised the common Rapa Nui surname Te Ave into Chávez.

Other exhibits include: skulls from bodies originally entombed in ahu; basalt fishhooks and other implements; obsidian spearheads and other weapons; sketches of elliptical houses, circular beehive-shaped huts, and the ceremonial houses at Orongo; a moai head with reconstructed fragments of its eyes; *moai kavakava*; and replicas of rongo-rongo tablets.

Of all the carved wooden figures which islanders produce, the most common and at the same time the most exotic, are the moai kavakava, or the 'statues of ribs'. Each is a human figure with a large, thin and markedly aquiline nose; protruding cheekbones accentuating hollow cheeks; extended earlobes; and a goatee that curls back on the chin. Protruding ribs and a sunken abdomen imply starvation.

According to oral tradition, at Puna Pau King Tuu-ko-ihu chanced upon two *aku aku* (sleeping ghosts) with beards, long hooked noses, and pendulant earlobes reaching down to their necks. These figures were so thin that their ribs stood out. Tuu-ko-ihu returned home and carved their portrait in wood before he forgot their appearance, and since then islanders have always carved these statues.

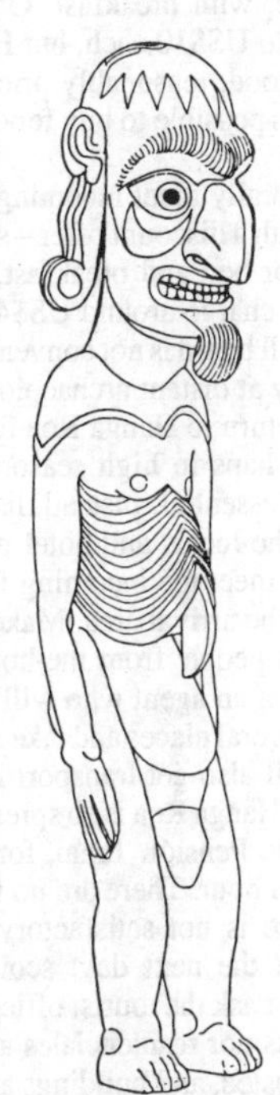

Moai kavakava - statue of ribs

Organised Tours
A number of agencies organise tours of the island. See the earlier Getting Around section for details.

Festivals
Every February islanders celebrate the Semana de Rapa Nui, a week-long celebration with music, dancing and other cultural events. Much of the impetus comes from Resguardo Cultural, an organisation of islanders committed to preserving local traditions.

Places to Stay
Rapa Nui is not inexpensive, but you can control costs by staying at one of the many residenciales or with a family. Most places expect US cash in payment. The least expensive rooms will be about US$15/25 a single/double, with breakfast. Other meals may cost up to US$10 each, but Hanga Roa has several good, reasonably priced restaurants, and it is possible to buy food and cook for yourself.

Hosts generally meet incoming flights at the airport with a discount offer – say US$10 per person for bed and breakfast, but most residenciales charge around US$45/75 with full board. Full board is not convenient if you spend the day at distant archaeological sites and cannot return to Hanga Roa for lunch.

Except perhaps in high season, reservations are not essential. Instead, listen to the offers from the locals and hotel proprietors who flock to meet the incoming flights and wait outside the arrival area. Make sure you are talking to people from the hotels themselves, and not an agent who will book you into any of several places and take a commission. You will also get transport into town, helpful since Hanga Roa is so spread out that walking to the Pensión Tahai, for instance, would take an hour. There are no taxis.

If the place is not satisfactory, you can always move the next day; scout out the competition or ask the tourist office for help. Neither streets nor residenciales are consistently sign-posted, and buildings and houses rarely have numbers, so it is easier to locate places by referring to the map of Hanga Roa. Phone ahead before walking across town in the midday heat.

Places to Stay – bottom end
Residenciales in Hanga Roa start at about US$15/25 with breakfast, including the popular and friendly *Residencial El Tauke* (☎ 253), *Residencial Tekena* (☎ 289), *Residencial Vai A Repa* (☎ 331), *Residencial Tiare Anani* (☎ 358), and *Residencial Tiare Nga Oho* (☎ 259).

Others cost around US$20. One perennial favourite is *Pensión Tahai* (☎ 395), charging US$20/35 a single/double with breakfast in a very clean bungalow set amidst a large, quiet and relaxing garden, a bit out of town on the road to Ahu Tahai. Additional meals are extra.

Another good place is the *Rapa Nui Inn* (☎ 228), near the airport at the corner of Policarpo Toro and the Avenida Hotu Motua. Rates are US$20/30 with breakfast, for a large, clean room with a double bed and private bath. *Residencial Apina Nui* (☎ 292) has identical rates, and also serves other meals, but one couple reported the kitchen was dirty. In the same general range, *Residencial Vinapu* (☎ 393) has been recommended, but try also *Residencial Taheta One One* (☎ 257), *Residencial Vai Ka Pua* (☎ 377), *Residencial Aloha Nui* (☎ 274), *Residencial Sofía Gomero* (☎ 313), *Residencial Tahiri* (☎ 263), *Chez Cecilia* (☎ 393), and *Residencial Kona Tau* (☎ 321).

Some residenciales offer camping in their gardens. Outside Hanga Roa, camping is officially permitted only at Anakena which, unfortunately, lacks any dependable supply of potable water – you must carry your own. By the time this book appears, CONAF may have improved the facilities and water supply at Anakena.

Places to Stay – middle
Most mid-range places call themselves hotels, but a few better residenciales are among them. Try *Residencial Manturara* (☎ 297) or *Residencial Pedro Atán* (☎ 329), both of which have rooms from US$25/45. *Residen-*

cial Villa Tiki (☎ 327) and *Hotel Orongo Easter Island* (☎ 294) are slightly dearer.

Another recommended place is *Hotel Victoria* (☎ 272), on a small hill to the south-east above Hanga Roa, midway between the airport and the settlement. Rates are US$40/70 with breakfast. In the same category are *Residencial O Tama Te Ra'a* (☎ 220), *Hotel Poike* (☎ 283), *Chez Joseph* (☎ 281), and the fine *Hotel Topa Ra'a*.

Places to Stay – top end

At the bottom of the top-end places is the very good *Hotel O Ta'i* (☎ 250), with rooms from US$50/80 with breakfast. Slightly up the scale is the *Hotel Hotu Matua* (☎ 242) at US$66/105. It's much closer to the airport than to town, so personal transport is a good idea. The *Iorana Hotel* (☎ 312) charges US$69/93 for rooms in a quiet area with outstanding views of the coastline.

Hotel Hanga Roa (☎ 299), on Avenida Pont near Caleta Hanga Piko, is a rather lengthy walk from the middle of town, but has a swimming pool, bar and restaurant, and several souvenir shops. Rooms cost US$121/151, considerably more with full board.

Places to Eat

Food at Hanga Roa's few restaurants is pleasantly surprising, especially the tasty seafood, and is fairly reasonably priced (except for lobster, which is very dear). Try *V Maitai* at Caleta Hanga Roa, *Avarei Pua* across the street, *Mamá Sabina* (with very well prepared and appetising food) across from LAN-Chile, or *Aringa Ora*.

Residenciales will rent a room with breakfast only, but there's no economic advantage in doing so unless you intend to eat at restaurants or feed yourself with produce from the market – you can import canned food from Santiago, but not fresh fruit and vegetables. Whether you arrive from Tahiti or from Chile, your bags may be checked for fresh produce at the airport.

If you intend to camp or cook your own food, there are provisions at general stores and bakeries on the main street where you can buy canned food, bottled drinks (soft drink, wine, beer) as well as fresh vegetables, fruit, and eggs. Fresh vegetables, fruit and fish are also available in the mornings at the open-air market on Policarpo Toro, across from the Gobernación.

Things to Buy

Hanga Roa has many souvenir shops, mostly on Policarpo Toro (where they tend to be dearer than elsewhere) and on the street leading up to the church. Look for small stone or carved wooden replicas of standard moai and moai kavakava, replicas of rongorongo tablets and cloth rubbings of them, and fragments of obsidian from Orito (sometimes made into earrings). The best selection and prices (open to haggling) are at the craft market across from the church. One reader suggests bartering with items of clothing in high demand, such as jeans and sneakers.

For transit passengers or desperate last-minute shoppers, airport shops have a selection of crafts and souvenirs, but prices are noticeably higher.

Getting There & Around

The airport, Aeropuerto Mataveri, is at the south end of Hanga Roa. LAN-Chile (☎ 78), the only airline which flies to Rapa Nui, has its office on Policarpo Toro near Avenida Pont.

The centre of Hanga Roa is only about a 20-minute walk from Mataveri airport. There is no public transport within the town, and it's very spread out, so you will probably be doing a bit of walking. To explore the rest of the island you really need independent transport – see the earlier Getting Around section.

PARQUE NACIONAL RAPA NUI

Since 1935, all the archaeological monuments of Rapa Nui have been part of the national park of the same name, administered by CONAF as an 'open-air museum'. There are admission charges to the Orongo ceremonial village and to Ahu Tahai which total about US$10 for non-Chileans, collected by rangers at each site. These fees are valid for the length of your stay.

Although the government, in cooperation with foreign and Chilean archaeologists as well as local people, has done a remarkable job in restoring monuments and attracting visitors, it is worth mentioning that some islanders view the national park as just another land grab on the part of invaders who, to them, differ little from Doutroux-Bornier or Williamson, Balfour & Company. A native-rights organisation which calls itself the Consejo de Ancianos (Council of Elders) wants the park, which constitutes more than a third of the island's surface, returned to its aboriginal owners. The Rapa Nui people control almost no land outside Hanga Roa proper, and have even taken their cause to the United Nations because of lack of faith in the Chilean judiciary. Many islanders, however, work for CONAF and other government agencies.

The West Coast

Lined up along the west coast of the island are four large ahu complexes. Ahu Tautira is next to Hanga Roa's small pier; from here a road/track leads north to the Ahu Tahai complex, connected to Ahu Akapu and Ahu Tepeu by another coastal track.

Ahu Tautira Ahu Tautira overlooks Caleta Hanga Roa, the fishing port at the foot of Calle Te Pito O Te Henua. The torsos of two broken moai have been re-erected on the ahu.

Ahu Tahai A short walk north of Hanga Roa, this site contains three restored ahu: Ahu Tahai proper, Ahu To Ko Te Riku, and Ahu Vai Uri. North American archaeologist William Mulloy directed the restoration work in 1968.

Ahu Tahai is the ahu in the middle, supporting a large, solitary moai with no topknot. To one side of Ahu Tahai is Ahu Ko Te Riku with a large, solitary moai with its topknot in place. Despite its size, it is a relative lightweight, only about one quarter the weight of the giant moai at Ahu Te Pito Te Kura on the north coast. On the other side is Ahu Vai Uri, which supports five moai of varying sizes.

Ahu Akapu Ahu Akapu, with its solitary moai, stands on the coast north of Ahu Tahai. North of here, the road is very rough but always passable if you drive slowly.

Ahu Tepeu Large Ahu Tepeu is on the north-west coast between Ahu Akapu and Cabo Norte. To the north-east rises Maunga Terevaka, the island's highest point, while to the south is a large grassy plain over a jagged lava sheet. To the west, the Pacific Ocean breaks against rugged cliffs up to 50 metres high.

The seaward side of the ahu is its most interesting feature, with a wall about three metres high near the centre, composed of large, vertically placed stone slabs. A number of moai once stood on the ahu but all have fallen. Immediately east is an extensive village site with foundations of several large boat-shaped houses and the walls of several round houses, consisting of loosely piled stones.

Ahu Vinapu

For Ahu Vinapu, follow the road from Mataveri airport to the end of the runway, then the road south between the airstrip and some large oil tanks to an opening in a stone wall. A sign points to nearby Ahu Vinapu, where there are two major ahu.

Both once supported moai which are now overturned, mostly broken and lying face-down. Accounts by 18th and early 19th-century visitors suggest that the moai were not overturned simultaneously, but were all tipped over by the mid-19th century. Some had their foundations undermined, while others may have been pulled down with ropes.

One interesting find is a long brick-red stone, shaped rather like a four-sided column, standing in front of one of the ahu. Closer inspection reveals a headless moai with short legs, unlike the mostly legless moai elsewhere, and resembling pre-Inca column statues in the Andes.

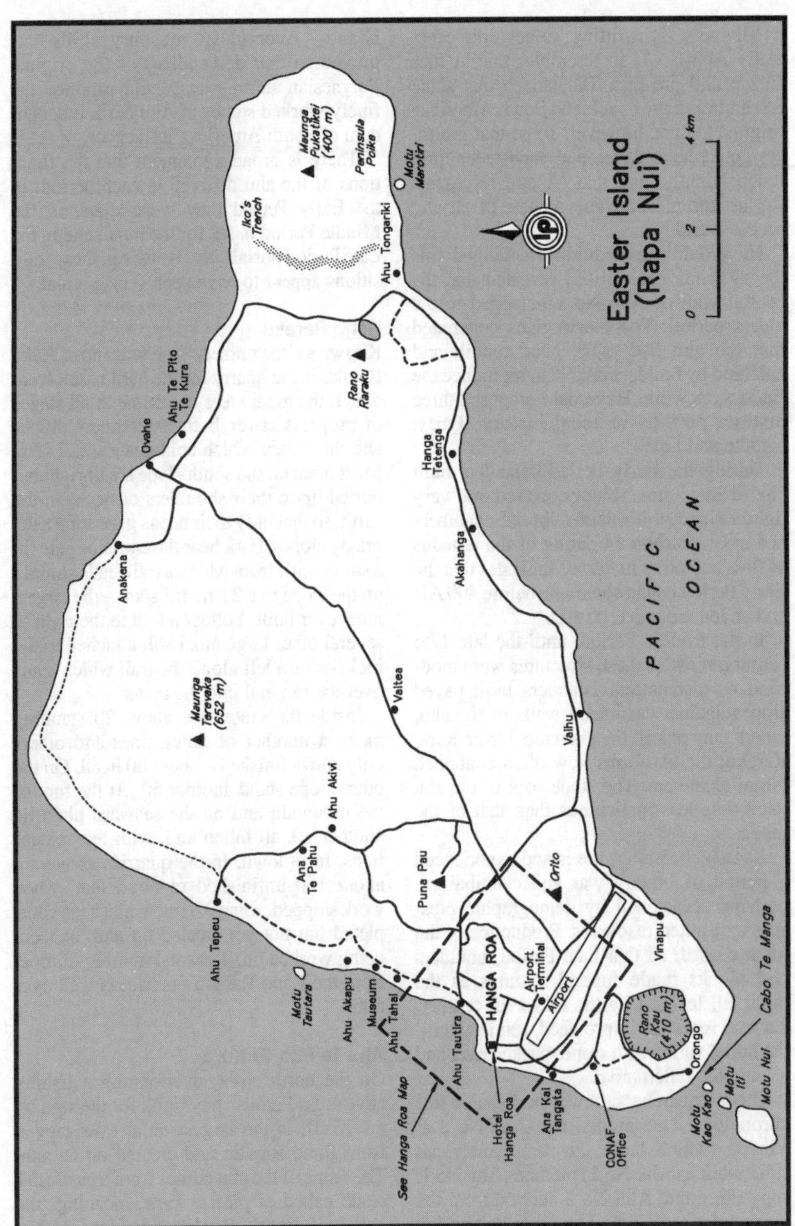
Easter Island
(Rapa Nui)
0
2
4 km
PACIFIC
OCEAN
Maunga
Pukatikei
(400 m)
Peninsula
Poike
Motu
Marotiri
Iko's
Trench
Ahu Tongariki
Rano
Raraku
Ahu Te Pito
Te Kura
Ovahe
Anakena
Hanga
Tetenga
Akahanga
Vaitea
Vaihu
Maunga
Terevaka
(652 m)
Ahu Akivi
Ana
Te Pahu
Puna Pau
Orito
Vinapu
Cabo Te Manga
Ahu Tepeu
Motu
Tautara
Ahu Akapu
Museum
Ahu Tahai
HANGA ROA
Airport
Terminal
Airport
Rano
Kau
(410 m)
Orongo
Motu
Kao Kao
Motu
Iti
Motu Nui
Ahu Tautira
Hotel
Hanga Roa
Ana Kai
Tangata
CONAF
Office
See Hanga Roa Map

Vinapu's tight-fitting stonework, especially Ahu No 1, so resembles that of Inca Cuzco and pre-Inca Tiahuanaco that some researchers have concluded South American origins. Others, however, argue that islanders could have developed such techniques independently, and that Vinapu represents the last and most advanced phase of carving on the island.

Heyerdahl's expedition challenged this theory when excavations revealed that the central wall of Ahu No 1 belonged to the oldest period. The Norwegians concluded that the ahu had twice been rebuilt and enlarged by builders unable to reproduce the finest stonework. Heyerdahl proposed three distinct periods in local history: Early, Middle and Late.

During the Early Period, islanders built ahu of large stone blocks, carved and very tightly fitted, with neither burial chambers nor moai. Carbon-14 dating of the remains of fires and other materials indicates that the Early Period began sometime before 400 AD and ended around 1100 AD.

In the Middle Period, until the late 17th century, most of these structures were modified or dismantled. Islanders built paved slopes against the inland walls of the ahu, where they placed the giant moai from Rano Raraku; the platforms now often contained burial chambers. The stonework of the ahu itself was less meticulous than that of the moai.

Shortly thereafter, the island experienced a period of bloody war and cannibalism, perhaps occasioned by demographic pressure on limited resources. Production of the moai ceased. In this Late Period, boulders and blocks made funeral mounds as the moai, all toppled by the mid-19th century, became roofs for improvised, semi-pyramidal burial vaults with stones packed over and around the fallen moai.

Other researchers, however, disputed this chronology. One argued that Ahu No 2 at Vinapu (which lacks the same finely cut stonework as Ahu No 1) predates Ahu No 1, suggesting that Ahu No 2 derived from the *marae* platforms found on other Polynesian islands. Eventually, masonry skills improved so that descendents of the original Polynesian immigrants could produce the finely-worked stones of Ahu No 1, independent of South American influence.

There is broad agreement that the functions of the ahu differed in each period. In the Early Period they were altars, in the Middle Period bases for the moai, and in the Late Period burial sites. However, these transitions appear to have been very gradual.

Rano Raraku

Known as 'the nursery', the volcano of Rano Raraku is the quarry for the hard basalt from which the moai were cut. Moai in all stages of progress cover both its southern slopes and the crater, which contains a small lake. Most moai on the south slope are upright but buried up to their shoulders or necks in the earth, so that only their heads gaze across the grassy slopes. Park near the entrance gate (in a stone wall) from which a trail leads straight up the slope to a 21-metre giant – the largest moai ever built. Follow a trail to the right to several other large moai still attached to the rock, or turn left along the trail which leads over the rim and into the crater.

Inside the crater are about 20 standing moai, a number of fallen ones and others only partly finished – about 80 in all. On the outer slope stand another 50. At the foot of the mountain and on the seaward plain lie another 30, all fallen and, with few exceptions, face-down. In the quarries above are about 160 unfinished moai so that, when work stopped, some 320 moai had been completed but not yet erected on ahu, or were being worked on. The total number of moai from the Rano Raraku quarries is well over 600.

Ahu Te Pito Te Kura

On the north coast, overlooking a fishing cove at La Perouse bay (look for the sign by the road), is the largest moai ever moved from Rano Raraku and erected on an ahu. The name of the ahu comes from a particular stone called *te pito te kura*, meaning 'the navel of light'. By legend, Hotu Matua himself brought this stone, symbolising the Navel of the World, to Rapa Nui.

According to oral history, a widow erected the moai to represent her dead husband; it was perhaps the last moai to fall, although the Norwegian expedition has made that claim for the moai re-erected at Anakena. In height, proportion and general appearance it resembles the tall moai still buried up to their necks at Rano Raraku. If those standing at the quarry site are the last to have been made, the Te Pito Te Kura moai was probably the last erected on an ahu.

Nearly 10 metres long, the moai lies face down on the inland slope of the platform. Its ears alone are more than two metres long. A topknot – oval rather than round as at Vinapu – lies nearby. The sheer density of remains at sites like nearby Hanga Hoonu is even more impressive.

Anakena

Playa Anakena Anakena beach is the legendary landing place of Hotu Matua. One of several caves is said to have been Hotu Matua's dwelling as he waited for completion of his boat-shaped house, but the Norwegian expedition found no traces of very early habitation. The nearby remains of an unusually large elliptical house, about 25 metres long, are said to have been that house, but the Norwegians failed to find anything of special interest. Of much greater interest are Ahu Ature Huki and Ahu Nau Nau.

This sheltered, white-sand beach is Rapa Nui's largest, very popular for swimming and sunbathing. Anakena is a pleasant place to spend the afternoon or overnight at the pleasant CONAF camping ground, but bring food and drinking water from Hanga Roa.

Ahu Ature Huki On the hillside above Anakena beach stands Ahu Ature Huki and its lone moai, re-erected by the Norwegians and islanders. In *Aku-Aku: the Secret of Easter Island*, Heyerdahl described raising the moai onto its ahu with wooden poles:

> ...the men got the tips of their poles in underneath it, and while three or four men hung and heaved at the farthest end of each pole, the mayor lay flat on his stomach and pushed small stones under the huge face...When evening came the giant's head had been lifted a good three feet from the ground, while the space beneath was packed tight with stones.

The process continued for nine days, the giant on an angle supported by stones, and the logs being levered with ropes when the men could no longer reach them. After another nine days and the efforts of a dozen people, the moai finally stood upright and unsupported.

Ahu Nau Nau In Rapa Nui, *Mata ki te rangi* means 'eyes that look to the sky'. Some Europeans interpreted this as a reference to the volcanic craters at the corners of the triangular island, but during the excavation and restoration of Anakena's Ahu Nau Nau in 1979 researchers learned that the moai were not 'blind' but actually had inlaid coral and rock eyes – the eyes that looked to the sky – some of which were reconstructed from fragments at the site.

Of the seven moai at Ahu Nau Nau, four have topknots, whilst only the torsos remain of two others. It's also thought the figures were painted and had inlaid earplugs. Fragments of torsos and heads lie in front of the ahu.

Playa de Ovahe

At Ovahe, between La Perouse and Anakena, is a small, attractive, and much less frequented beach with interesting caves. Beware of sharks.

Fundo Vaitea

Midway between Anakena and Hanga Roa, Vaitea was the centre of food and livestock production under Doutroux-Bornier and Williamson, Balfour & Company, who used the island as a gigantic sheep farm – the large building on the east side of the road is the former shearing shed, while the property on the west side belongs to CORFO, the state-controlled development corporation, which raises fruit and vegetables.

Ahu Akivi

This inland ahu, completely restored in 1960 by a group headed by Mulloy and Chilean archaeologist Gonzalo Figueroa, sports seven moai which, unlike most others, look out to sea. In raising the moai, they used methods similar to those used at Ahu Ature Huki and steadily improved their speed and technique. Mulloy later wrote that:

> Clearly the prehistoric islanders with their hundreds of years of repetition of the same task must have known many more tricks than modern imitators were able to learn.

Mulloy believed that the large number of stones in front of Ahu Akahanga on the south coast were leftovers of stones used to raise the moai, and that one moai appeared to have fallen sideways in the process. He also pointed to the tremendous numbers of stones near many ahu, including Ahu Te Pito Te Kura, as evidence that the moai may have been erected using stones for support.

Mulloy calculated that 30 men working eight hours a day for a year could have carved the moai and topknot at Ahu Te Pito Te Kura, while 90 could have transported it from the quarry over a previously prepared road in two months and could have raised it in about three months. Even if Mulloy was correct, there are complications with raising the topknots, carved from the reddish volcanic scoria of Puna Pau crater, to the heads of the moai.

Ana Te Pahu

After visiting Ahu Akivi, you can follow the faint, rough but passable track to Ahu Tepeu on the west coast. On the way, stop at Ana Te Pahu, a site of former cave dwellings whose entrance is via a garden planted with sweet potatoes, taro, bananas and other plants from the Polynesian horticultural complex.

Puna Pau

The small volcanic crater at Puna Pau has a reddish stone which is relatively soft and easily worked. It was from this stone that the pukao (topknots) were made. Some 60 of these were transported to sites round the island, and another 25 remain in or near the quarry.

Peninsula Poike

The eastern end of the island is a high plateau called the Peninsula Poike, crowned by the extinct volcano Maunga Pukatikei. Its western boundary is a narrow depression called Ko te Ava o Iko (Iko's Trench), running from the north side of the peninsula to the south.

According to legend, the Long Ears built this trench to defend themselves from the Short Ears. In one version, Long Ear rulers decided to clear loose rock from the peninsula for purposes of cultivation; the Short Ears tired of the work and rebelled, so the Long Ears – under command of chief Iko – gathered on the peninsula and dug a trench to separate Poike from the rest of the island. They then filled the trench with branches and tree trunks, ready to be set on fire should the Short Ears try to storm across.

One of the Long Ears, though, had a Short Ear wife who allowed the Short Ears to slip into Poike and surround them. When another Short Ear force marched towards the ditch the Long Ears lined up to face them and set the ditch on fire; the other Short Ears rushed them from behind and, in a bloody fight, the Long Ears fell and burned in their own ditch. Only three escaped: two were later killed, but the one who lived married a Short Ear and had children.

Although the ditch was once thought natural and the story a mere legend, excavations revealed thick layers of ash and charcoal, evidence of a great fire which produced very intense heat or else burnt for some time. The upper part of the trench was natural, but had been artificially enlarged to create a trench with a rectangular bottom, three to four metres deep, about five metres wide and running a couple of km across the hillside. Not continuous, it actually comprises a number of separate trenches. Carbon dating suggested that the great fire had burnt perhaps 300 to 350 years ago, while genealogical research suggested the onset of conflict around 1680.

Although the Long Ears, suddenly forced to retreat to the Poike peninsula, might have been able to fill the ditch with wood, they might not have had time to undertake the heavy and time-consuming labour of enlarging it. Dating of earlier fires indicates that the ditch was originally dug around 400 AD for other reasons, but was adapted for defensive purposes in the 17th century.

Orito

Weapons were made from hard black obsidian, quarried at Orito. The *mataa*, a common artefact, was a crudely shaped blade of obsidian used as a spearhead; embedded in the edges of flat wooden clubs, such blades made very deadly weapons. Non-lethal artefacts included obsidian files and drill bits which would have been attached to a wooden shaft and used to drill bone, wood or stone.

From the slopes of Rano Kau, the quarry resembles an enormous grey rectangle on Orito's southern slope, but quarrying actually took place around its whole circumference. Orito is not the only obsidian quarry – there are others on Motu Iti off Cabo Te Manga, and another on the north-eastern edge of Rano Kau crater.

The South Coast

On the south coast, east of Ahu Vinapu, enormous ruined ahu and their fallen moai testify to the impact of warfare on Rapa Nui. **Ahu Vaihu** has eight large moai which have been toppled and now lie face down, their topknots scattered nearby. **Akahanga** is a large ahu with large fallen moai, while across the bay is a second ahu with several more. On the hill slopes opposite are the remains of a village, including foundations of several boat-shaped houses and ruins of several round houses.

Also on the coast, the almost completely ruined **Ahu Hanga Tetenga** has two large moai, both toppled and broken into fragments. Just beyond Hanga Tetenga, a faint track off the main road branches inland towards the crater quarry of the previously mentioned Rano Raraku, which is readily visible.

Ahu Tongariki

East of Rano Raraku a Pacific tsunami, produced by an earthquake between Rapa Nui and the South American mainland, demolished several moai and scattered several topknots far inland. The ruined Ahu Tongariki was the largest ever built, supporting 15 massive moai. Several petroglyphs, cut into the flat stone outcrops among the strewn moai, include a turtle with a human face, a tuna fish, a birdman motif, and one which may represent a woman with her legs spread.

Orongo Ceremonial Village

Nearly covered in a bog of floating totora reeds, the crater lake of Rano Kau appears to be a giant witch's cauldron. Perched 400 metres above, on the edge of the crater wall, the ceremonial village of Orongo occupies one of the most dramatic sites on the island. Once the most important ceremonial site on the island, it is a much later construction than the great moai and ahu.

From the winding dirt road which climbs from Hanga Roa to Orongo, there are spectacular views of the entire island. Orongo, overlooking several small *motu* (offshore islands), was the centre of an island-wide bird cult linked to the gods Makemake and Haua in the 18th and 19th centuries.

Partly restored, the Orongo ceremonial village occupies a magnificent site overlooking the ocean. Built into the side of the slope, the houses had walls of horizontally overlapping stone slabs, with an earth-covered

Stone head in Orongo House

arched roof of similar materials, giving the appearance of being partly subterranean. Since walls were thick and had to support the roof's weight, the doorway is a low narrow tunnel, barely high enough to crawl through. At the edge of the crater is a cluster of boulders carved with numerous birdman petroglyphs, with a long beak and a hand clutching an egg.

A short distance before the village, a footpath descends into the crater, where the dense vegetation includes abandoned orange trees and grapevines whose fruit local people collect in autumn. It is possible to hike around the crater, but it is slow going – give yourself a full day and take plenty to drink, since the water in the crater lakes is muddy and brackish.

The Birdman Cult

Makemake, the supreme deity, is said to have created the earth, sun, moon, stars, and people, rewarding the good and punishing the evil, and expressing his anger in thunder. In times of trouble, he required the sacrifice of a child. Makemake is also credited with bringing the birds and presumably the bird cult to Rapa Nui, although Haua aided him in this venture.

No complete record of the cult's ceremonies exists and there are conflicting accounts with respect to schedules and duration. At a given time, worshippers would move up to Orongo where they lived in stone houses, recited prayers, made offerings, held rites to appease the gods and participated in fertility dances.

The climax of the ceremonies was a competition to obtain the first egg of the sooty tern *(Sterna fuscata)*, which bred on the tiny islets of Motu Nui, Motu Iti, and Motu Kao Kao, just off Cabo Te Manga. Each contestant or his *hopu* (stand-in) would descend the cliff face from Orongo and, with the aid of a small reed raft, or *pora*, swim out to the islands. He who found the first egg became 'birdman' for the ensuing year; if a hopu found it, he called out his master's name to a man in a cave in the cliffs below Orongo. The fortunate master's head, eyebrows and eyelashes were then shaved, his face was painted red and black, and he became birdman, sequestered in a special house. The reasons for the birdman's celebrity are vague, but it whoever found the first egg certainly won the favour of Makemake and great status in the community. The last ceremonies took place at Orongo in 1866 or 1867, a few years after the Peruvian slave raid.

Glossary

Note: RN indicates that a term is a Rapa Nui (Easter Island) usage

aerosilla – chairlift
afuerino – casual farm labourer
aguas – water, herbal teas
ahu (RN) – large stone platforms on which moai statues were erected
aku aku (RN) – sleeping ghosts
alameda – avenue or boulevard lined with trees, particularly poplars
albergue juveníl – youth hostel
alerce – *Fitzroya cupressoides*, large coniferous tree, resembling the California redwood; the Parque Nacional Alerce Andino is named after this tree
almuerzo – lunch
alpaca – *Lama pacos*, a type of domesticated llama
altiplano – high plains of northern Chile, Bolivia, southern Peru and north-eastern Argentina, generally above 4000 metres
apapa (RN) – stone ramp used to launch boats
apunamiento – altitude sickness
arrayán – reddish-barked tree of the myrtle family, common in the Valdivian forests of southern Chile
arroyo – watercourse
ascensore – funicular railway which climbs a steep slope or cliff, as in the hillside neighbourhoods of Valparaíso
Araucanians – major grouping of indigenous people, including the Mapuche and the Picunche Indians
Aymara – indigenous inhabitants of the Andean altiplano of Peru, Bolivia and northern Chile

bahía – bay
balneario – bathing resort or beach
barrio – neighbourhood
bencina – petrol
bencina blanca – white gas (Shellite) used for camping stoves; usually available in hardware stores or chemical supply shops
bodega – cellar or storage area for wine
bofedal – swampy alluvial pasture in the altiplano, used by the Aymara to graze alpacas
boleadoras – weapon of round stones joined by a leather strap, used by Patagonian Indians for hunting guanaco and rhea; also called *bolas*

cabildo – colonial town council
cacique – Indian chieftain; see also toqui
caleta – small cove
caliche – hardpan; a dry, hard layer of clay beneath the soil surface, from which mineral nitrates are extracted
callampas – 'mushrooms'; urban shantytowns which have emerged rapidly on the outskirts of Santiago
camanchaca – dense, thick fog in the hills of the coastal Atacama desert, usually occurring in the morning and the late afternoon
cama – bed; also a sleeper-class seat on a bus or train
camarote – sleeper class on a ship or ferry
caracoles – literally 'snails' or 'spirals'; a very winding road
carretera – highway
casa de cambio – money exchange house, which usually buys foreign cash and travellers' cheques at the 'parallel' exchange rate
casa de familia – modest family accommodation, usually in tourist centres
casco – the main house on a fundo or estancia
cerro – hill
cena – dinner
certificado – registered, as in mail
chachacoma – *Senecio graveolens*, a native Andean plant; Aymara Indians brew a tea from the leaves which helps to relieve altitude sickness
charqui – dried llama or alpaca meat
chifa – Chinese restaurant
Chilote – inhabitant of the island of Chiloé
ciervo – deer

ciudad – city
coa – lower class slang speech of Santiago
cobro revertido – reverse charge (collect) phone call
Codelco – Corporación del Cobre, the state-owned enterprise which oversees Chile's copper mining industry
colación – lunch
colectivo or **taxi colectivo** – shared taxi
comida corrida – a cheap set meal
comuna – local government administrative district
con gas – 'with gas'; carbonated, as in soft drinks
congregación – in colonial Latin America, the concentration Indians in settlements, usually for political control and/or religious instruction; see also reducción
congrio – conger eel, a popular and delicious Chilean seafood
cordillera – chain of mountains, mountain range
costanera – coastal road; any road along a sea coast, river side or lake shore
criollo – in the colonial period, a person of Spanish parentage born in the New World
curanto – Chilean seafood stew

desayuno – breakfast

elaboración artesanal – family production
encomendero – landholder exploiting labour under the encomienda system
encomienda – colonial labour system under which Indian communities were required to provide workers for Spanish land holders (encomenderos), in exchange for religious and language instruction; the system benefitted the Spanish far more than the Indians
estero – estuary
estancia – extensive cattle or sheep grazing establishment, with a dominant owner or manager and a dependent resident labour force

feria – artisans' market
ficha – public telephone token; also a token for use in a company store, paid to a worker instead of cash
fuerte – fort
fundo – small hacienda in central Chile, usually irrigated

garúa – coastal desert fog; see also camanchaca
gas-oil – diesel fuel
golfo – gulf
golpe de estado – coup d'etat, a sudden, illegal seizure of government
guanaco – *Lama guanicoe*, undomesticated camel-like animal native to the Andes; also a police water cannon, which 'spits' like a guanaco

hacendado – owner of an hacienda, often living in a city
hacienda – in colonial times, a large rural landholding with a dependent labour force; a Chilean hacienda was typically smaller, and usually called a fundo
hare paenga (RN) – a traditional, boat-shaped house
hospedaje – budget accommodation, usually a large family home with one or two extra bedroom for guests; the bathroom is shared
hostería – inn or guesthouse which serves meals, usually outside the main cities
huaso – horseman or cowboy, similar to the Argentine gaucho

ichu – bunch grass found on the altiplano
IGM – Instituto Geográfico Militar; organisation which produces maps for the military, many of which are available and useful to travellers
inquilino – tenant farmer on a fundo
intendencia – Spanish colonial administrative unit
invierno boliviano – 'Bolivian winter'; summer rainy season in the Chilean altiplano, so-called because of the direction from which the storms come
IVA – *impuesto de valor agregado*; the value added tax (VAT), often added to restaurant or hotel bills
isla – island
islote – small island, islet
istmo – isthmus

kumara (RN) – Polynesian word for sweet potato
kuchen – sweet, German-style pastries

La Frontera – region of pioneer settlement, between the Río Biobío and the Río Toltén, inhabitated by Araucanians until the late-19th century
lago – lake
laguna – lake
latifundio – large landholding; see also fundo, hacienda
lenga – a deciduous species of southern beech tree
lista de correos – poste restante
llano – plain, flat ground
llareta – *Laretia compacta*; a dense compact shrub in the Chilean altiplano; used by Aymara herders for fuel
lomas – coastal hills in the Atacama desert where condensation from fog supports the vegetation

machista – (normally used as an adjective) male chauvinist
manavai (RN) – excavated garden enclosures
maori (RN) – learned men; reportedly able to read rongo-rongo tablets
Mapuche – indigenous inhabitants of the area south of the Río Biobío
marae (RN) – platforms found on Polynesian islands which resemble the ahu of Easter Island
mataa (RN) – obsidian spearhead
matua (RN) – ancestor, father; associated with Hotu Matua, leader of the first Polynesian immigrants
mestizo – a person of mixed Indian and Spanish descent
micro – small bus, often travelling along the back roads
minifundio – small landholding, such as a peasant farm
minga – reciprocal Mapuche Indian labour system
mirador – look-out point, usually on a hill but often in a building
moai (RN) – large basalt statues of human figures
moai kavakava (RN) – wooden 'statues of ribs'
momios – 'mummies'; upper-class Chileans resistant to social and political change
motu (RN) – small offshore islet
municipalidad – city hall
museo – museum
música funcional – muzak

nalca – *Gunnera chilensis*, a plant resembling an enormous rhubarb, with large leaves and edible stalks; gathered for food on Isla Chiloé.
ñandú – large, flightless bird, similar to the ostrich
nevado – snow-capped mountain peak
Norte Chico – 'Little North'; the semi-arid region between the province of Chañaral and the Río Aconcagua
Norte Grande – 'Big North'; the very arid portion of the country north of Chañaral
Nueva Canción Chilena – the 'New Chilean Song' movement, which arose in the 1960s and combined traditional folk themes with contemporary political activism

oferta – 'offer'; a seasonal or promotional fare for air or bus travel
oficina – 'office'; a nitrate mining works in the 19th and early-20th century, in some cases almost a small city with a large dependent labour force
onces – literally 'elevenses', but actually afternoon tea

palafitos – on Chiloé, rows of houses built on stilts over the water where boats can anchor at the back at high tide
pampa – prairie, grassy plain
parada – bus stop
parque nacional – national park
parrilla – restaurant specialising in parrillada
parillada – Argentine-style grill of steak and other beef cuts
peatonal – pedestrian mall, usually in the centre of larger cities
pehuén – *Araucaria auracana*, the monkey-puzzle tree of southern Chile; its nuts are a staple of the Mapuche Indians' diet

peña – folk music and cultural club; many originated in Santiago in the 1960s as venues for the New Chilean Song movement, Nueva Canción Chilena
pensión – family home offering short-term budget accommodation, may also take permanent lodgers
pingüinera – penguin colony
playa – beach
pora (RN) – small reed raft used for paddling to offshore islets (motus)
porteño – a native or resident of Valparaíso
posta – clinic or first-aid station, often found in smaller towns which lack proper hospitals
postre – dessert
precordillera – the foothills of the Andes mountains
propina – a tip, at a restaurant or elsewhere
pukao (RN) – the topknot on the head of a moai; also a common hairstyle for Easter Island males
pucará – a pre-Columbian, hilltop fortressin the Andes
puente – bridge
puerto – port
pulpería – general store or food shop; the company store on a fundo, estancia or nitrate oficina
puna – Andean highlands, usually above 3000 metres
punta – point

quebrada – ravine; a brook or stream
quila – a solid bamboo found in southern Chilean rainforest, often forming impenetrable thickets; also known as *chusquea*
quinoa – native Andean grain, a dietary staple in the pre-Columbian era, still grown by Aymara farmers in the precordillera of the Norte Grande

Rapa Nui – the Polynesian name for Easter Island and its people, language and culture
reducción – the concentration of Indians in towns for purposes of political control or religious instruction, the term also refers to the settlement itself; see also congregación
refugio – a shelter, usually rustic, in a national park or other remote area
reserva nacional – national (military) reserve
residencial – budget accommodation, sometimes only seasonal, usually in a building designed as a short-term lodging house, not a domestic dwelling
restaurante – eating place of higher quality and service
rhea – large, flightless bird, similar to the ostrich
río – river
rodeo – annual roundup of cattle on an estancia or hacienda
rongo-rongo (RN) – an indeciphered script on wooden tablets, possibly a hieroglyphic script or an alphabet
rotos – 'ragged ones'; the dependent labourers on Chilean fundos
ruca – traditional thatched Mapuche Indian house
ruta – route; highway

SAG – Servicio Agrícola Ganadero, the Agriculture & Livestock Service; its officials inspect baggage and vehicles for prohibited fruit and meat imports at Chilean border crossings
salón cama – bus with reclining seats
salón de té – literally 'teahouse', but more like an upscale cafetería
salar – salt lake, salt marsh or salt pan
seno – sound, fjord
sierra – mountain range
siesta – afternoon nap during the extended midday break of traditional Chilean business hours
sin gas – 'without gas'; non-carbonated, as in soft drinks
s/n – 'sin número'; indicating a street address without a number
soroche – altitude sickness
Southern Cone – the area of South America comprising Argentina, Chile, Uruguay and parts of Brazil and Paraguay; a political and geographical term reflecting the shape of the area on a map

tajamares – dikes built to control flooding of the Río Mapocho in late colonial Santiago
tejuelas – the shingles of varying design

which distinguish the houses and churches of archipelagic Chile, especially on the island of Chiloé

telesférico or **teleférico** – gondola cable-car

tepú – *Tepualia stimulais*, type of tree with a contorted shape

todo terreno – 'all terrain'; a mountain bike

toki (RN) – carving tools made of basalt

toqui – Mapuche Indian chief; see also cacique

totora (RN) – type of reed used for making rafts

turismo aventura – non-traditional forms of tourism, such as trekking and river rafting

Unidad Popular – 'Popular Unity'; a coalition of leftist political groups which supported Salvador Allende in the 1970 presidential election

Valle Central – 'Central Valley'; the Chilean heartland which extends south from the Río Aconcagua to near the city of Concepción; this area contains most of Chile's population and its industrial and agricultural wealth

ventisquero – glacier

vicuña – *Vicugna vicugna*, wild relative of domestic llama and alpaca, found only at high altitudes in the Norte Grande

villa – village, small town

vizcacha – *Lagidium vizcacha*, a wild Andean relative of the domestic chinchilla

volcán – volcano

Yahgans – indigenous inhabitants of the Tierra del Fuego archipelago

zampoñas – pan pipes

zona – zone

zona franca – duty-free zone, as at Iquique and Punta Arenas, where imported goods such as cameras, clothing etc are available at very low prices

Index

ABBREVIATIONS

Arg - Argentina
Bol - Bolivia
EI - Easter Island
JF - Juan Fernández Islands

MAPS

TEXT

Map references are in **bold** type.

PLANET TALK

Lonely Planet's FREE quarterly newsletter

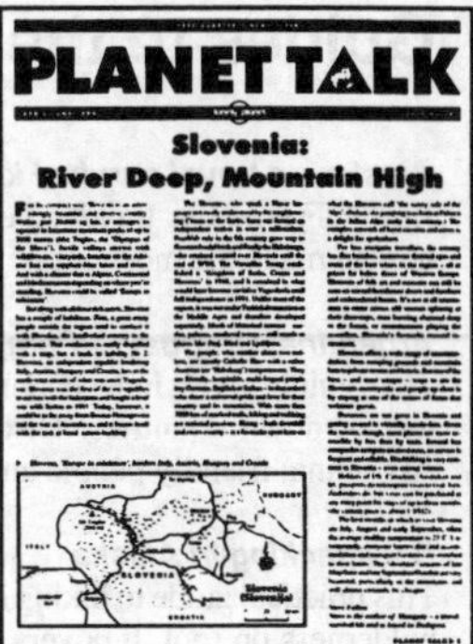

We love hearing from you and think you'd like to hear from us.

When...*is the right time to see reindeer in Finland?*
Where...*can you hear the best palm-wine music in Ghana?*
How...*do you get from Asunción to Areguá by steam train?*
What...*is the best way to see India?*

For the answer to these and many other questions read PLANET TALK.

Every issue is packed with up-to-date travel news and advice including:

- *a letter from Lonely Planet founders Tony and Maureen Wheeler*
- *travel diary from a Lonely Planet author - find out what it's really like out on the road*
- *feature article on an important and topical travel issue*
- *a selection of recent letters from our readers*
- *the latest travel news from all over the world*
- *details on Lonely Planet's new and forthcoming releases*

To join our mailing list contact any Lonely Planet office (address below).

LONELY PLANET PUBLICATIONS

Australia: PO Box 617, Hawthorn 3122, Victoria (tel: 03-9819 1877)
USA: Embarcadero West, 155 Filbert St, Suite 251, Oakland, CA 94607 (tel: 510-893 8555)
TOLL FREE: (800) 275-8555
UK: 10 Barley Mow Passage, Chiswick, London W4 4PH (tel: 0181-742 3161)
France: 71 bis rue du Cardinal Lemoine – 75005 Paris (tel: 1-46 34 00 58)

Also available: Lonely Planet T-shirts. 100% heavyweight cotton (S, M, L, XL)

Guides to the Americas

Alaska – a travel survival kit
Jim DuFresne has travelled extensively through Alaska by foot, road, rail, barge and kayak, and tells how to make the most of one of the world's great wilderness areas.

Argentina, Uruguay & Paraguay – a travel survival kit
This guide gives independent travellers all the essential information on three of South America's lesser-known countries. Discover some of South America's most spectacular natural attractions in Argentina; friendly people and beautiful handicrafts in Paraguay; and Uruguay's wonderful beaches.

Backpacking in Alaska
This practical guide to hiking in Alaska has everything you need to know to safely experience the Alaskan wilderness on foot. It covers the most outstanding trails from Ketchikan in the Southeast to Fairbanks near the Arctic Circle – including half-day hikes, and challenging week-long treks.

Baja California – a travel survival kit
For centuries, Mexico's Baja peninsula – with its beautiful coastline, raucous border towns and crumbling Spanish missions – has been a land of escapes and escapades. This book describes how and where to escape in Baja.

Bolivia – a travel survival kit
From lonely villages in the Andes to ancient ruined cities and the spectacular city of La Paz, Bolivia is a magnificent blend of everything that inspires travellers. Discover safe and intriguing travel options in this comprehensive guide.

Brazil – a travel survival kit
From the mad passion of Carnival to the Amazon – home of the richest ecosystem on earth – Brazil is a country of mythical proportions. This guide has all the essential travel information.

Canada – a travel survival kit
This comprehensive guidebook has all the facts on the USA's huge neighbour – the Rocky Mountains, Niagara Falls, ultramodern Toronto, remote villages in Nova Scotia, and much more.

Central America on a shoestring
Practical information on travel in Belize, Guatemala, Costa Rica, Honduras, El Salvador, Nicaragua and Panama. A team of experienced Lonely Planet authors reveals the secrets of this culturally rich, geographically diverse and breathtakingly beautiful region.

Colombia – a travel survival kit
Colombia is a land of myths – from the ancient legends of El Dorado to the modern tales of Gabriel Garcia Marquez. The reality is beauty and violence, wealth and poverty, tradition and change. This guide shows how to travel independently and safely in this exotic country.

Costa Rica – a travel survival kit
Sun-drenched beaches, steamy jungles, smoking volcanoes, rugged mountains and dazzling birds and animals – Costa Rica has it all.

Eastern Caribbean – a travel survival kit
Powdery white sands, clear turquoise waters, lush jungle rainforest, balmy weather and a laid back pace, make the islands of the Eastern Caibbean an ideal destination for divers, hikers and sun-lovers. This guide will help you to decide which islands to visit to suit your interests and includes details on inter-island travel.